# ESSAYS

IN

# LEGAL HISTORY

READ BEFORE THE INTERNATIONAL CONGRESS OF HISTORICAL STUDIES HELD IN LONDON IN 1913

EDITED BY

PAUL VINOGRADOFF, F.B.A.

CORPUS PROFESSOR OF JURISPRUDENCE IN THE UNIVERSITY OF OXFORD
ACTING-PRESIDENT OF THE SECTION OF LEGAL HISTORY OF THE CONGRESS

THE LAWBOOK EXCHANGE, LTD.
Clark, New Jersey
2004

ISBN 1-58477-351-0

*Printed in the United States of America on acid-free paper*

**THE LAWBOOK EXCHANGE, LTD.**
33 Terminal Avenue
Clark, New Jersey 07066-1321

*Please see our website for a selection of our other publications and fine facsimile reprints of classic works of legal history:*
www.lawbookexchange.com

**Library of Congress Cataloging-in-Publication Data**

International Congress of Historical Sciences (1913 : London)
Essays in legal history read before the International Congress of Historical Studies held in London in 1913 / edited by Paul Vinogradoff.
p. cm.
Originally published: London; New York: Oxford University Press, 1913.
Includes bibliographical references and index.
ISBN 1-58477-351-0 (cloth: alk. paper)
1. Law—History—Congresses. I. Title: Legal history. II. Vinogradoff, Paul, Sir, 1854-1925. III. Title.

K160.I58 2003
340'.09—dc21 2003047458

# ESSAYS
IN
# LEGAL HISTORY

READ BEFORE THE INTERNATIONAL CONGRESS OF HISTORICAL STUDIES HELD IN LONDON IN 1913

EDITED BY

PAUL VINOGRADOFF, F.B.A.

CORPUS PROFESSOR OF JURISPRUDENCE IN THE UNIVERSITY OF OXFORD
ACTING-PRESIDENT OF THE SECTION OF LEGAL HISTORY OF THE CONGRESS

OXFORD UNIVERSITY PRESS
LONDON, EDINBURGH, GLASGOW
NEW YORK, TORONTO, MELBOURNE, BOMBAY
1913

# INTRODUCTORY NOTE

THE collection of papers in this volume consists of the communications made to the Section of Legal History (VIa) of the International Congress of Historical Studies held in London in April 1913. All the papers read in the Section have been kindly contributed by their authors for this publication. In some cases, where the communications actually read were in the nature of extracts from longer treatises, the papers have been reproduced here *in extenso*. The papers of Geheimrath O. von Gierke and Dr. A. Lappo-Danilevskij were read at General Meetings of the Congress, but were written for the Section of Legal History, and naturally take a place in its transactions. The essays in the present volume are presented in a different order from that in which they followed each other at the Congress, as it was desirable to group them somewhat more systematically. On several occasions some discussion followed the reading of the papers, but it proved unnecessary to publish the minutes of such discussions, as most of the principal points were afterwards embodied in the revised texts of the communications.

The general course of the proceedings in the Section was as follows :—

*Thursday, April* 3.—The first meeting was held at 2 P.M. in the Old Hall of Lincoln's Inn, which was kindly lent by the Treasurer (Mr. Douglas Walker, K.C.) and the Masters of the Bench of Lincoln's Inn. Sir Frederick Pollock, on behalf of the President, Lord Alverstone, Lord Chief Justice of England, who was absent through ill health, welcomed the meeting. The Presidential Address was delivered by Professor Vinogradoff, Acting-President. Geheimrath O. von Gierke took the chair. Papers were read by Professor Wenger (No. III of this volume) and Professor Galante (No. XVIII).

*Friday, April* 4.—Professor Vinogradoff in the chair. Papers by Dr. W. Blake Odgers, K.C. (No. XII), discussed by Professor Galante, Mr. Bolland, Professor Vinogradoff; Dr. H. D. Hazeltine

(No. XIII), discussed by Professor Vinogradoff; Dr. W. S. Holdsworth (No. XV).

*Saturday, April* 5.—In the chair—Professor Vinogradoff in the morning, Professor Fockema-Andreae of Leyden in the afternoon. Papers by Geheimrath Lenel (No. V), discussed by Professor Ehrlich of Czernowitz, Professor Goudy, Professor Koschaher of Prague; Professor Riccobono (No. IV), discussed by Professor Ehrlich, Geheimrath Lenel, Professor Galante, Geheimrath von Gierke; Professor E. C. Clark (No. VI), discussed by Dr. Strachan-Davidson of Oxford and Geheimrath Lenel.

*Monday, April* 7.—In the chair—Sir Courtenay Ilbert in the morning, Geheimrath Lenel in the afternoon. Papers by Sir Frederick Pollock (No. XIV), discussed by Professor Vinogradoff; Professor Goudy (No. XI), discussed by Sir Frederick Pollock and Professor Astoul of Caen; the late Professor A. Esmein[1] (No. X), read in the absence of the writer by Professor Huvelin of Lyons; Professor Hübner (No. XX), discussed by Sir Courtenay Ilbert.

*Tuesday, April* 8.—Professor Galante in the chair. Papers by Professor Schreuer (No. VII), discussed by Professor Fockema-Andreae, Geheimrath von Gierke, Professor Hübner, Professor Huvelin; Professor Caillemer (No. IX), read in the absence of the writer by Professor Astoul; Professor Taranger (No. VIII); Dr. W. Konopczynski (No. XVII).

Professor Galante from the chair proposed a vote of thanks to the Acting-President, Professor Vinogradoff; to the Vice-Presidents, Sir Frederick Pollock and Sir Courtenay Ilbert; and to the Hon. Secretaries, Dr. W. S. Holdsworth and Mr. F. de Zulueta. Professors Schreuer, Huvelin, and Riccobono having spoken in the same sense, the vote was unanimously carried. Sir Frederick Pollock and Sir Courtenay Ilbert returned thanks.

The difficult enterprise of publishing a polyglot volume of this kind has only been rendered possible by the liberal support which the Delegates of the Oxford University Press have placed at the disposal of the Section of Legal History.

[1] While these sheets were in the press, the sad news arrived of the death of one of our most distinguished contributors, Professor A. Esmein. We are indebted to his son, Monsieur Paul Esmein, for the correction of the proofs which were forwarded to his late father.

# TABLE OF CONTENTS

# I

# WELCOME TO THE SECTION

DELIVERED BY

## SIR FREDERICK POLLOCK

BY the Lord Chief Justice of England's desire I have to inform you that to his great regret, a regret in which I am sure every one here fully concurs for our sake as well as his, ill health prevents him from carrying out his intention of welcoming the Section of Legal History and delivering the inaugural address. I am charged to bid you welcome in the Chief Justice's name and as his deputy; the inaugural address will be given by my friend Professor Vinogradoff, who is specially qualified for the task by his cosmopolitan learning and his mastery of historical and comparative jurisprudence.

As one of the delegates to this Congress of the Honourable Society of Lincoln's Inn, in whose Old Hall we now meet, I beg to add a hearty welcome on behalf of the Treasurer and my fellow Masters of the Bench.

This year 1913 is the year which some of our amateur alarmists, only a little while ago, had fixed upon as the time appointed for an invasion of this realm from lands beyond sea. We now see their prediction fulfilled after a sort, perhaps as near the letter as most amateur predictions are. The invaders are here, and the British Academy, we hope, was not altogether unprepared. For some months, at any rate, its heralds cried, like Hagen when he stands on the rock in the *Götterdämmerung*, 'Waffen durch's Land! Gute Waffen! Starke Waffen!' A multitude of more or less learned and academic persons, even more diversely equipped in their several Faculties than Gunther's vassals, answered the call, and when they came with like words in their mouth—'Was soll ihm das Heer nun noch helfen?'—the instructions they received, though not unexpected, were otherwise not unlike Hagen's. 'Starke Stiere sollt ihr schlachten': whatever else the invading host of historians were to find, there should be a festive meeting with the usual accompaniments. Committees and sub-committees have accordingly been engaged in preparations which may be called, in a general way, serving tables—I do not mean exclusively or chiefly dining tables. These preparations, useful and needful as they are, do not make it easier for those who are occupied with them to give adequate attention to making ready the feast of reason contemplated as the main object of our gathering. Nor can we expect, at this time of year, much reinforcement from our English-speaking brethren of the American schools.

But our spiritual feast is such that the guests do not come empty-handed, and the list of papers to be read gives ample warrant that any defects on the part of the British Academy and the British Faculties will be more than made good by contributions in which Continental seats of learning from Christiania to Palermo will be worthily represented.

I call on Professor Vinogradoff to take the chair.

# II

# PRESIDENTIAL ADDRESS

DELIVERED BY

## PROFESSOR P. VINOGRADOFF

IT is to be regretted that our proceedings should not be inaugurated by a distinguished member of the English Bench: in England more than in any other country one has to look to the considered decisions of learned judges for the historical development of legal doctrine. It is not mere chance that the two most influential expositors of English law—Bracton and Blackstone—were judges. As, however, the task of giving the inaugural address has been entrusted to me, I must approach it from what may be called the academic point of view. The duty of addressing an audience composed of representative jurists from the principal countries of Europe is not an easy one, but it would not be amiss, I think, if, before speakers take up the thread of their various subjects, I dwelt very briefly on some of the points which unite us all and supply the connecting links between the various researches in Roman and English, German and Slavonic, Civil, Canon, and Common Law. The attempt is not so presumptuous as it may seem at first sight, because certain guiding lines have been traced by generations of leading workers, and what is chiefly required on the present occasion is a summing-up of familiar inquiries. After all, every one of us, whether he treats expressly of general principles or not, is bound to make up his mind on this subject: investigations as to the legal systems of particular nations, states and periods, bear necessarily on the theory of law, and embody in concrete forms conceptions and methods of jurisprudence.

The fundamental unity of our study may be realized from two

main points of view. They are provided by continuity on the one hand and by similarity on the other. There are streams of doctrines and institutional facts which pass through the ages and cross national boundaries from one historical formation to another. These constitute what may be called the current of *cultural tradition*. Again, the solutions of legal problems on different occasions fall into groups according to similarities and contrasts, for which there is a common basis in the nature of the problems themselves. This gives rise to the application of the *comparative method*. The continuity of culture and comparative jurisprudence produce the atmosphere of what might have been called International Law, had not the term been appropriated to other uses.

It is not necessary to dwell at length on the progress which has been made in tracing cultural continuity in the history of legal systems. A classical example used to be drawn from the reception of Roman Law by mediaeval and modern Europe. In recent years we have witnessed another and hardly less remarkable movement of investigation in regard to the force of cultural traditions: the study of inscriptions and papyri has led to a rediscovery of Hellenism. In the hands of Mitteis, Dareste, Grenfell and Hunt, Rostowzew, Wenger, and many others, it has entirely changed the aspect of ancient history, connecting, as it does, the doctrines of the Digest and of the Code with Greek and Oriental antecedents. The other day Sir William Ramsay, one of the pioneers of this study, called attention to an interesting fact of this kind. In St. Luke's Gospel (ii. 1-5) it is stated that Joseph and Mary had to leave the town of Nazareth where they dwelt to go to Bethlehem, Joseph's birthplace, in order to be enrolled there for the census.

1. And it came to pass in those days, that there went out a decree from Caesar Augustus, that all the world should be enrolled (A.V. taxed). . . .

2. And all went to be enrolled, every one to his own city.

4. And Joseph also went up from Galilee, out of the city of Nazareth, into Judaea, unto the city of David, which is called Bethlehem; (because he was of the house and lineage of David:)

5. To be enrolled with Mary, his espoused wife, being great with child.

This idea, that a person's birthplace is a home to which he remains perpetually attached, is quite foreign to modern notions, but it played an important part in the legal arrangements of the ancient world. It appears as the *Origo* so rigidly kept up by the Emperors of the Lower Empire—Diocletian, Constantine, and their successors—and it has to be considered as one of the principal rules of the state of siege in which the Empire lived from the fourth century A.D. Yet the verses of St. Luke just quoted, and many other indications (e.g. a decree of a Roman governor of Egypt in 154 A.D.), connect it with another set of facts—viz. with the Eastern conception of populations firmly established in their homes—a notion expressed by the Hellenistic term ἰδία. We may add that it connects it also with Oriental forms of absolute rule tending to register and tax subject populations according to the requirements of fiscal utility.[1]

In this case the continuity of principle rests on the broad basis of social traditions. Sometimes similar results are produced by the development of what may be called juridical invention. When a technical method has been discovered which provides simple and adequate means for satisfying certain needs, it is not likely to disappear, even after vast changes have taken place in social conditions. For example, the law of jettison and salvage from shipwreck was settled by the naval customs of the Greeks. As Rhodian law,[2] it was received by the Romans and incorporated in the Digest (xiv. 2). It remained the basis of maritime law in the Byzantine Empire and took shape in the tract called Νόμος Ναυτικός. Thence it spread through the customs of Mediterranean and Adriatic cities, as exemplified, for instance, by the ordinances of Ragusa.[3] In substance, the rules formulated in this way still remain the basis of modern maritime law in European countries, including England.

The second method of connecting materials belonging to different spheres of national development arises from the comparison of analogous and contrasting formations of law. What I have particularly in view is not the accumulation of more or less similar facts which used to be the aim of writers like Post. The enthusiasm for comparison frequently led in this case to confusion: interesting

[1] See *The Expositor*, Dec. 1912. Cf. Rostowzew, *Studien zur Geschichte d. römischen Kolonats*; and de Zulueta, *De Patrociniis Vicorum*, in Vinogradoff's *Oxford Studies*, 1909.

[2] See Ashburner, *The Lex Rhodia.*

[3] See *Liber Statutorum Civitatis Ragusii*, ed. Bogišić and Jireček, 1904. Cf. Dareste, *Études d'Histoire du Droit*, iii. 93; and Vinogradoff, *Law Quarterly Review*, 1903.

data might be reduced to a mixture of commonplace statements and unproved assumptions which on closer inspection were often shown to be anything but homogeneous. The excesses of such uncritical accumulation have, indeed, thrown some discredit on the comparative method itself. Fortunately this method has found a better treatment at the hands of writers equally skilled in historical criticism and in juridical analysis. It is not the juxtaposition of resembling facts, but the dialectical examination of given principles in various surroundings, which yields fruitful and sometimes unexpected results. Let me take as an example the curious treatment of *obligation* in recent literature. Brinz, a leading authority on Roman Law, dissected the notion of the *obligatio* of the Digest. He observed that *obligatio* does not correspond to the German *Verpflichtung*: the latter points to duty, and any duty, including a legal one, resolves itself into a charge on the will of a person, whereas *obligatio* points at the same time to a state of subjection or liability (*Haftung*) which is derived from physical sway.[1] This led to a subtle analysis of the notions of legal duty and of liability as the two constituent elements of Roman obligation. Von Amira showed that the two elements were not only theoretically separable but actually distinct in Scandinavian law[2]; while Puntschart conducted a similar demonstration in regard to the mediaeval law of Saxon Germany.[3] Partsch applied the discovery in a brilliant manner to ancient Greek law, by showing that the process of enforcing an obligation was carried out by a recourse to a pledge over whom the obligee obtained physical sway.[4] A striking instance of this was drawn from the scene in the Odyssey in which Poseidon comes forward to release Ares and Aphrodite from the net thrown over them by the deceived husband, Hephaestus.[5] It is recognized that Ares owes the husband a customary compensation (αἴσιμα), and Poseidon offers himself as a security for the enforcement of the payment. The sea-god would be primarily liable in his own person as a hostage for Ares, but Hephaestus does not like the idea of binding so powerful a god, and prefers a promise from the pledge

1 Brinz, *Archiv für civilistische Praxis*, i. (1874) 15 ff.

2 Amira, *Nordgermanisches Obligationenrecht*, ii. 73.

3 Puntschart, *Schuldvertrag u. Treugelöbnis des sächsischen Rechts des Mittelalters* (1896).

4 Partsch, *Griechisches Burgschaftsrecht*, i. 10 ff.

5 *Od.* viii. 344 sqq.

to pay instead of Ares if the latter should take to flight. This suggestive interpretation of the scene serves as an appropriate introduction to the Greek law of pledge. Von Gierke investigated thoroughly the dualism of duty and liability (*Schuld* and *Haftung*) in German law.[1] He showed, among other things, how legal duty (*Schuld*) came to be treated as an object in itself, how it gave rise to real right, and was sometimes combined with possession of land. On the other hand, the development of securities for enforcement also assumed a peculiar bent, because the pledge was regarded not as a subsidiary help to the principal, but as a substitute for the direct fulfilment of the legal duty; while the wager was explained as a symbol of the surrender of property. It would lead us too far afield to consider the reaction of this historical analysis on the well-worn controversy as to the meaning and operation of the *nexum* in early Roman law.[2] I only mention the renewal of this famous dispute in order to recall to your minds that a discussion begun by a Romanist, carried on by eminent Germanists and by a student of Greek law, reverted, as it were, to the history of Roman law in its early stages.

The method of comparative investigation in such cases is characterized by the part assigned to the dialectics of principles. It starts from the definition of conceptions and traces their 'ramification' (*Abzweigung*), their conflicts and compromises. At the same time it opens the way for the study of the material conditions of development. It is not only from the point of view of logical distinctions that analogies and contrasts in law have to be considered. It is clear that there is a background of social conditions which account to a great extent for the stages of the doctrinal evolution. As regards this very dualism of legal duty and liability, for example, it was called forth historically by the characteristic attitude of early commonwealths to the question of the enforcement of law. We are so accustomed nowadays to the correspondence between legal rights and legal remedies that it is difficult for us to imagine a state of society in which such a direct correspondence did not exist. And yet it is with such states of society that we have to deal in early Germanic as well as in early Greek and Roman law. When self-help was the principal mode of enforcing right, when

[1] Von Gierke, *Schuld u. Haftung im alterer deutschen Recht.*

[2] See de Zulueta, *The Recent Controversy about Nexum*, Oxford, 1912.

juridical conflicts commonly resolved themselves into feuds, or had to be managed by arbitration, when even legal proceedings were initiated by ceremonial agreements, the practical enforcement of liability naturally took the shape of an appeal, not to public force, but to private execution. The two necessary elements of such an execution are recognition by the parties, and assured substitutes for the fulfilment of a recognized duty. The importance of *recognition* as a basis of law is as instructive in this case as it is in the formation of modern Constitutional and International Law. It is certainly important to realize that the formation of law proceeds in many, if not in all cases, not from the command of a sovereign, but from recognition by parties. The process of execution by the taking of pledges is quite as characteristic. The pledge is originally a hostage.[1] The treaties between contracting parties and litigants in Iceland, Norway, Saxon England, or Germany, had to be supplemented by the giving of pledge-hostages, and sometimes these pledges experienced the treatment of hostages in a literal sense: they might be imprisoned or coerced until the obligation had been fulfilled either by them or by the principal.[2] It is by comparing the evidence of Greek, Roman, and Germanic practice that we realize to what extent these features of technical law depended on the conditions of societies in the stage of what may be called primitive confederation.

This leads to a further step in the application of the comparative method. If juridical conceptions can serve as links in comparative analysis, it is natural to ask whether these links are themselves perennial or subject to transformation. How far have we to deal with certain constant attributes of legal thought which provided a frame for varying contents, and how far do vital and important legal doctrines take shape from historical conditions? Attempts to construct a science of law composed of constant and ever-recurring rules have been made again and again. Quite recently, an eminent representative of the Neo-Kantian school, Stammler, has brought together in a voluminous book the absolute requirements of juridical logic, and has inscribed on his work the significant motto—*Non est mortale quod opto.* Undoubtedly a certain amount

[1] Rintelen, *Schuldhaft u. Einlager im Vollstreckungsverfahren.*

[2] Esmein, *Mélanges de Rome*, viii. (1888) 426-436; cf. Glotz, *La Solidarité de la Famille.*

of logical doctrine arises in connection with law; it is necessary not only in order to explain the common phraseology of law, but to guide us in the process of juridical reasoning. But when too much insistence is laid on this department of jurisprudence, it is apt to degenerate into scholasticism, and to recall the famous strictures of Goethe's Mephistopheles on the teaching of logic:

> Then, the philosopher steps in
> And shows, no otherwise it could have been:
> The First was so, the Second so,
> Therefore the Third and Fourth are so;
> Were not the First and Second, then
> The Third and Fourth had never been.[1]

As in every other branch of knowledge, it is the contents of law that interest men rather than the formal framework; and the contents, even the most fundamental, are admittedly subject to variation. As Ihering has forcibly expressed it:

> Law is not less a product of history than handicraft, naval construction, technical skill: as Nature did not provide Adam's soul with a ready-made conception of a kettle, of a ship, or of a steamer, even so she has not presented him with property, marriage, binding contracts, the State. And the same may be said of all moral rules. . . . The whole moral order is a product of history, or, to put it more definitely, of the striving towards ends, of the untiring activity and work of human reason tending to satisfy wants and to provide against difficulties.[2]

The causes producing variations of legal principles are many: the influence of economic surroundings, of national character, of historical collisions, of cultural loans, the cross-currents of religious and philosophical thought, may be mentioned among the factors which lead to variations. It would be out of the question to make anything but a passing reference to these factors. One class of causes, however, deserves particular attention, because they not only differentiate theories and systems of law, but combine them

[1] Der Philosoph, der tritt herein
Und beweist euch, es müsst' so sein:
Das Erst' wär' so, das Zweite so,
Und drum das Dritt' und Vierte so;
Und wenn das Erst' und Zweit' nicht wär',
Das Dritt' und Viert' wär' nimmermehr.

[2] *Zweck im Recht*, ii. 112.

into groups. I mean the effect of the social type on the formation of definite sets of jurisprudential theory. There have not been so many fundamental types of social organization—at least in the Western world. Roughly speaking, we have to reckon with six great types. Human society has assumed the form of a tribe, that is, an association based mainly on real or supposed kinship; it has been concentrated in cities; it has adapted itself to the relations of a landed estate; it has expanded into churches; it has been made to serve the aims of free individuals under state control; lastly, it may be organized as an association for the purpose of controlling the production and distribution of goods.

According to the road selected by a community among these classes, certain points of view are created for the formulation and solution of juridical problems, as may be gathered from familiar examples. Property will be treated differently by individualistic and by socialistic communities, but it has also received a peculiar treatment at the hands of the Church and of the City-State, as well as in feudal and in tribal law. Again, the notions of crime and punishment have been differentiated according to the character of the social tie. In tribal society, crime was substantially 'contempt of court' or a direct offence against the tribe, while punishment appeared chiefly as revenge; the City was unsparing in its requirements from its children, the citizens, and relentless in its methods of educating and eventually suppressing them. The notion of breach of faith is as characteristic of feudal jurisprudence as the notion of sin is characteristic of the Church. The treatment of crime as an expression of perverse will and the psychology of deterrent punishment are natural to individualistic communities; whereas in societies with a socialistic bent crime comes to be considered from the pathological point of view, and punishment assumes the aspect of medical treatment. Even the fundamental conceptions of law itself are to a great extent dependent on submission to one or the other type of social order. In tribal societies, law is a declaration of custom; in city-states it is justice as conceived by the city—δόξα τῆς πόλεως; in feudal organizations it is based on express or tacit agreements; from the point of view of the Church, it is the recognition of Divine precepts in the government of the world; in individualistic societies it is the command of the sovereign will; from the socialistic point of view, it should be the means for carrying out social justice and expediency in the attribution of rights.

In laying stress on jurisprudential principles as realized by history, I do not wish to suggest for a moment that any one of these notions has reigned supreme in a particular commonwealth to the exclusion of all others. Juridical history, as well as history in general, shows to what extent political ideas slide and shade off one into the other, and how, on the other hand, every epoch presents contradictions and compromises between rival forces. Nevertheless, the study of juridical evolution discloses prevailing tendencies which change with the times—as has been brilliantly illustrated, for example, in reference to our own age, in Dicey's *Law and Opinion in England.*

This makes it both possible and desirable to group the facts supplied by history not only in their organic sequences of national development, but also according to the social types to which they correspond. Many partial attempts have been made in this direction. I may refer, for example, to Maine's and Leist's books on Aryan tribal law ; to statements of jurisprudence by Catholic writers like Cathrein, and by socialists like Wenger. But the method is worthy of a much wider application. For example, it would be an interesting task to treat from this point of view the theories of jurisprudence which correspond to modern systems of public and private law. It would be found, perhaps, that Hobbes' theory of the omnipotent state finds its opposite pole, and at the same time its necessary complement, in Bentham's theory of the summation of individual expediencies. Both elements are, as a matter of fact, blended in the rationalistic system of Austin. All these doctrines take root in the competition of the modern commercial world, and find a curious counterpart in the individualistic jurisprudence of the *Pax Romana* as encased in the political fabric of the Empire. It seems, in fact, as if, instead of seeking for the philosopher's stone in the shape of a single theory of law, we had better attend for the present to five or six theories of law derived from different social premisses.

However this may be, one thing seems clear. Jurists approach historical problems on their own lines, with their particular habits of mind. Whatever attention they may give to the careful study of evidence, to the proper sequence of events, and to exact knowledge of historical environment, they are sure to look out for doctrine in the end—that is, for statements of principles, of their consequences in theory and their application in practice. This being so, methods of analysis and of constructive reasoning which are exercised daily in pleading and deciding cases, in stating and interpreting rules, in formulating and safeguarding rights, are bound to reappear in the grouping and discussion of historical material by lawyers. Legal history as an exact reproduction of the past has, indeed, to be supplemented by historical jurisprudence in the sense of a reasoned account of the evolution of legal principles. Such a jurisprudence is free from the delimitations imposed on nations and periods: it derives its divisions and chapters from conceptional distinctions.

This feature is especially noticeable in those connecting studies with which I have been dealing in my address. The gravitation towards the home (or the traditions of maritime law) are not circumscribed by the boundaries of monarchies. The principles of legal duty and liability unfold their contents not only in theoretical discussion, but in the analogies and contrasts of various legal systems. The conceptions of property, of crime and punishment, of law itself, appear in correspondence to the social type in their environment. And, I should like to say in conclusion, it is perhaps this alliance between exact observation and dialectical reasoning which makes our mode of studying history, despite technical difficulties and the dryness of many details, so attractive to the mind. Thanks to the juridical method, masses of historical facts, accumulated as if by accident, are sifted and become capable of being treated as manifestations of a certain λόγος—of reason governing the moral world.

## III

# RÖMISCHE RECHTSGESCHICHTE

DIE Frage, welche ich vor Ihnen, wenn nicht zu beantworten, so doch zu erörtern versuchen will, veranlasst mich, obwohl vor einem internationalen Forum von Historikern und Rechtsgelehrten sprechend, doch einen nationalen Ausgangspunkt zu wählen. Wie Ihnen allen bekannt, hat Deutschland zur Jahrhundertswende sich ein neues nationales Privatrecht geschaffen und damit die früher weit verbreitete Geltung des altehrwürdigen *Corpus Juris Civilis* beseitigt. Der notwendige Rückschlag, den diese Neuregelung eines so wichtigen Gebietes der staatlichen Ordnung auf das Studium dieser Ordnung selbst ausüben musste, hat eine arge Unruhe in den Studienbetrieb an den juristischen Fakultäten hineingetragen. Die Zeiten, in denen das Pandektenstudium—im deutschen Sinne, d.h. also das Studium des durch Wissenschaft und Praxis ausgestalteten „gemeinen Rechts"—die vornehmste Aufgabe für Forschung und Lehre an den deutschen Universitäten war, sind dahin: Lehrer und in neuerer Zeit auch Schüler schlagen sich überstürzende Reformen vor: von Rückkehr zur alten Ordnung, Wiedereinführung des Pandektenstudiums erhoffen die einen Förderung, von Beseitigung des römischen Rechtsstudiums, insbesondere der sogenannten Rechtsgeschichte, aber nicht bloss der römischen, auch der deutschen, von rein praktischer Gegenwartsausbildung schwärmen die anderen. Ich brauche vor dieser Versammlung von Männern, die ihre Lebensarbeit in den Dienst historischer Forschung gestellt haben, die geschichtliche Methode des Rechtsunterrichts und der juristischen Forschung nicht zu verteidigen, nicht zu betonen, wie jene „Reformer" die Jurisprudenz in ihrem Lebensnerv bedrohen, die sie aus einer Wissenschaft zu einer positiven Kunde von Bestimmungen degradieren wollen, welche man im praktischen Leben unmittelbar brauchen könne. Es sind Banausen, die nicht nach der Idee der Publizität für den Immobiliarrechtsverkehr fragen, sondern nach der Art, wie ein Grundbuchsgesuch äusserlich aussehen muss, die nicht von den Gedanken gehandelt wissen wollen, die sich im Recht der Wertpapiere verkörpern, sondern verlangen, dass der Rechtsunterricht auf alle Einzelheiten der gegenwärtig geltenden Wechselordnung eingehend vorbereite!

Aber gerade dieser Ansturm gegen alles Geschichtliche zwingt die Vertreter einer historischen Rechtsforschung zur Anspannung aller Kräfte der Verteidigung. Es soll, um von der römischen Rechtsgeschichte zu sprechen, der Beweis erbracht werden, dass sie mehr ist, als was jene unkundigen Verächter von ihr behaupten, mehr als eine blosse Aufzählung von Leges und Senatsbeschlüssen, von Juristennamen und Juristenschriften, die heute niemanden mehr interessieren. Ich bin damit bei meinem Thema angelangt und werde in der Kürze der mir zu Gebote stehenden Zeit auf einiges von dem hinzuweisen versuchen, was meines Erachtens heute Aufgabe einer Darstellung der römischen Rechtsgeschichte ist.

Ich meine dabei eine Darstellung, welche dem Studierenden und dem Gebildeten geboten werden kann, welche die Resultate der Forschung zusammenfasst und die Zusammenhänge aufweist, die das Einst und Jetzt verbinden, aber auch die Gegensätze nicht verhüllt, die Vergangenheit und Gegenwart von einander scheiden. Und ich meine, dass es zur Zeit an einer über den Grundriss sich erhebenden Darstellung, die der Forschung auf allen Gebieten des öffentlichen und privaten Rechtslebens der Antike folgt, tatsächlich fehle. Es sei mir gestattet, wieder an einer deutschen Parallele zu exemplifizieren. Ein entsprechendes Werk wie etwa Schröders *Lehrbuch der deutschen Rechtsgeschichte*, oder auch nur Brunners *Grundzüge der deutschen Rechtsgeschichte* fehlt den Romanisten. Es existieren gute Arbeiten aus früherer Zeit: es liegt mir ferne, sie hier aufzuzählen oder gar zu kritisieren. Aber seit einem Vierteljahrhundert ist kein deutsches Lehrbuch der römischen Rechtsgeschichte mehr erschienen: auch keine Neuauflage eines älteren Buchs. Erst in allerjüngster Zeit (1912-13) macht Robert von Mayr in der bekannten Sammlung Goeschen den Versuch, die römische Rechtsgeschichte darzustellen—die Enge des verfügbaren

Raums, der Zweck der Sammlung bindet aber den Verfasser, der, wenn ich ihm nachempfinden darf, überall durch die ihm gezogenen Grenzen beengt ist. Man vergleiche etwa Schröders *Lehrbuch* mit Schröders eben erscheinender *Darstellung der deutschen Rechtsgeschichte* in Goeschens Sammlung! In gewisser Hinsicht gilt, wenn ich mir über eigene Arbeit ein Urteil erlauben darf, dasselbe auch von den Partien über *Verfassung und Verwaltung des europäischen Altertums* (1911) und von der eben im Druck befindlichen Abhandlung über das *Recht der Griechen und Römer* in Hinnebergs *Kultur der Gegenwart.* Ich habe in wiederholten Gesprächen mit Kollegen an deutschen und österreichischen Universitäten zu konstatieren Gelegenheit gehabt, dass dieser Mangel und die Wichtigkeit der Aufgabe einer Neudarstellung allgemeiner empfunden wird. Die römische Rechtsgeschichte ist ihrem umspannenden Namen untreu geworden, sie ist zur Geschichte der Quellen und Literatur zusammengeschrumpft, obwohl sie sich—wenigstens in den Universitätskatalogen—noch „römische Rechtsgeschichte" nennt. Ja, ich begegnete auch der Ansicht, dass eben nur das als „Rechtsgeschichte" in Betracht käme. Die gangbaren Lehrbücher des Privatrechts—ich nenne etwa als Vertreter Sohm, Czyhlarz, Girard, Costa—beschränken sich darauf, eine Quellengeschichte oder den Abriss einer solchen voranzustellen. Diese selbst erfreut sich eingehender Bearbeitung: P. Krüger ist (1913) in zweiter, Kipp (schon 1909) in dritter Auflage erschienen.

Eine Arbeit allerdings erfüllt in ihrer eben erschienenen Neuauflage eine auch weit gespannte Erwartung: Lenels Neudarstellung von Bruns' *Geschichte und Quellen des römischen Rechts.*[1] Hier finden wir in knappster Skizzierung grosse Partien einer modernen römischen Rechtsgeschichte, leider war der Verfasser durch Bruns' Stoffabgrenzung und die Anlage des ganzen enzyklopädischen Werkes gebunden.

Nicht unerwähnt soll endlich Pacchionis *Corso* (1905) bleiben, wenngleich auch er prinzipiell nur Staatsverfassung und Quellen bringen will.

Überall sind die wichtigen Probleme der — ich möchte zusammenfassend sagen — Staatsverwaltung in den Hintergrund gedrängt,

[1] Holtzendorff-Kohler, *Enzyklopädie der Rechtswissenschaft*, 7. Aufl. (1913), Bd. i. S. 303 ff.

höchstens gelegentlich gestreift, das interessante Gebiet des Strafrechts ist ganz vernachlässigt, nur das Privatprozessrecht erfreut sich im Anschluss an das dominierende Privatrecht eingehenderer Beachtung. Aber während die Darstellung des Privatprozessrechts meist kaum bis zum Kognitionsverfahren, jedenfalls nicht bis zum justinianischen Prozessrecht herabgeführt wird, liegt im Privatrecht alles Gewicht auf dem vom Rechtskaiser kodifizierten Recht.

Ich will hier die alte theoretisch natürlich unlösbare, praktisch-empirisch nach den Erfahrungen des einen so, des anderen anders zu beantwortende Frage nicht erörtern, ob die Darstellung geschichtliche Perioden der Entwickelung des Rechts fixieren und innerhalb dieser den ganzen Werdegang des Rechts darstellen, oder ein Rechtsinstitut von den grauesten Anfängen durch alle Zeit hindurch verfolgen soll. Beide Methoden haben ihre Vor- und Nachteile, beide lassen sich im mündlichen Unterricht verwerten, doch für buchmässige Darstellung ist meines Erachtens die Periodenteilung brauchbarer.

Die Frage, ob die herkömmliche Teilung der römischen Rechtsgeschichte in die bekannten vier Perioden beibehalten oder aufgegeben zu werden verdient, ist schwer zu entscheiden. Wenn man das Privatrecht oder den Prozess im Auge hat, da wird man an die Zwölftafeln, an die neu einsetzende Entwickelung des Rechts- und Wirtschaftslebens seit den siegreichen Kämpfen mit Karthago, oder im Privatprozessrecht an die Bedeutung der aebutischen Lex denken: aber die Verfassungsgeschichte heischt doch die altherkömmliche Teilung in Königsherrschaft, Republik, Prinzipatszeit und Despotie. Auch der Abschluss der Darstellung der Rechtsgeschichte ist von selbst mit Justinians Werk gegeben. Das öffentliche Recht ist von der Zeit der Gründung germanischer Reiche auf römischer Erde der Domäne der nationalen Rechtsgeschichte zugewiesen; naturgemäss ist auch die Darstellung des Privatrechts von da ab nationale Rechtsgeschichte, die ihrerseits freilich die Aufnahme der fremden Rechte in den Bereich der Darstellung ziehen muss. Ganz eigenartig und nur mit dem überragenden Einfluss der rezipierten römischen Rechtsmassen auf deutscher Erde erklärlich ist die Entstehung der deutschen Pandektenlehre und -Praxis, des im neuen bürgerlichen Gesetzbuch noch so lebhaft nachwirkenden „gemeinen Rechts."

Nach den zu behandelnden Gegenständen wird sich eine

Darstellung der „römischen Rechtsgeschichte" am besten in folgende Abschnitte gliedern können: Staatsverfassung und Quellengeschichte, Staatsverwaltung, Strafrecht und Strafprozessrecht, Privatrecht und Privatprozessrecht. Es sei gestattet, einige Fragen aus diesen Kapiteln für die einzelnen Perioden näher zu behandeln.

I. Die Königszeit.—Bei allen Zweifeln über die Anfänge Roms, bei aller Überwucherung der Königsgeschichte mit sagenhafter Ausschmückung, wird doch soviel behauptet werden dürfen, dass auch Rom beim Eintritt in die Geschichte von Königen beherrscht war—und dies selbst dann, wenn die Gründer der ewigen Stadt Etrusker gewesen sein sollten. So sehr schon hier die Hypothese anstelle sicherer Erkenntnis tritt, so müssen wir selbst den Versuch wagen, in die Zeit vor der „Gründung" der Stadt zurückzublicken. All die reizvollen Probleme der vorhistorischen Zeit tauchen da auch vor dem Auge des römischen Rechtshistorikers auf: wo sind die Vorväter der Römer her? wo sassen die Indogermanen? was weiss man über ihre Kultur? wo fängt die reine Hypothese an? Dann das gräkoitalische Problem. Ist etwas Wahres an der lange behaupteten engeren Verwandtschaft zwischen Griechen und Italikern? Gerade hier kann neben der Sprachvergleichung die Rechtsgeschichte der allgemeinen Geschichte durch Vergleichung der Rechtsinstitute einen Dienst erweisen. Endlich das italische Völkerproblem. Wo sind sie alle her, die in Italien sesshaft geworden, die Japygen, die Etrusker, die Latiner und die Samniten?

Und dann die Anfänge Roms: die Fragen nach der personalen Gliederung des Volks, nach Familie und Geschlecht und nach den Männerverbänden, den Phratrien und Kurien, aber auch nach der territorialen Gliederung der sesshaft Gewordenen, nach Dorf und Gau und der jüngeren Tribus.

Die Gründung der Stadt, die Bedeutung der Stadt und des Stadtbürgertums führen zur Frage nach dem Stadtstaat und seinem Gegensatz zum Territorialstaat. *Senatus populusque Romanus* ist Rom und *οἱ Ἀθηναῖοι* Athen, auch wenn der Feind die heimische Scholle erobert hat. Wir dürfen auch an diesem Punkte Halt machen und der griechischen Staatsphilosophie gedenken, die politische und wirtschaftliche Autarkie der Polis noch zu der Zeit forderte, als Alexander das Erbe der orientalischen Weltmonarchie, des grossartigsten Territorialstaates, angetreten hatte.

Die Gründung der Stadt und die Königsgeschichte rührt aber wiederholt auch an das etruskische Rätsel. Dann überhaupt: wie ist das Königtum gekommen, wie hat es gewirkt, wie ist es beseitigt worden? Welch böse Schuld hat es auf sich geladen, dass selbst Caesar noch für den Zuruf Rex mit dem Tode büssen musste? Welcher historische Kern liegt der „servianischen Reform" zugrunde und ist etwa die Episode der Tarquinier absolutistische Restauration?[1]

Dann die Stände des Volks: Patrizier und Plebejer. Worin lag der Gegensatz begründet? Ist er zuerst nur wirtschaftlicher, sekundär politischer Natur? Wie stellen sich die Plebejer zu den Klienten?

Die in dem Abschnitt über Staatsverwaltung zu erörternden Fragen nach Gross- und Kleinbesitz treten schon in der Königszeit entgegen: dann muss auch der primitivste Organismus — der übrigens das königliche Rom gewiss nicht mehr gewesen ist — die Heeres- und Finanzverwaltung regeln.

Ebenso schwierige als interessante Probleme stellen die in dieser ältesten Zeit der römischen Rechtsgeschichte wurzelnden Institute des Privat- und des damit innig zusammenhängenden Privatprozessrechts dar. Eher noch können wir über Familien- und Erbrecht Genaueres wenn nicht behaupten, so doch vermuten. Freilich auch da ist Raum für Zweifel genug: schon die Erklärung der verschiedenen Eheschliessungsformen mit dem gleichen Ergebnis legitimer Vollgewalt des Mannes über die Frau ist nur in hypothetischer Form möglich. Adoption und Testament, die wir recht früh ansetzen dürfen, erinnern an Parallelen aus der griechischen Entwickelung. Natürlich ist gerade bei dieser Rechtsvergleichung äusserste Vorsicht am Platze. Noch unsicherer sind die Anfänge des Vermögensrechts. Da stehen zunächst die Anschauungen in einem Punkte einander ganz entgegen: ist das Eigentum Gemeineigentum oder Individualeigentum? Hier kann wohl nur weitausgreifende Rechtsvergleichung, wie sie ja gerade auf diesem Gebiete schon angewendet ist, zu einem Resultate führen,

[1] Wieviel hier unsichere Überlieferung ist, wie wenig wir hier und in der Folgezeit bis auf die Zeit der Gracchen Sicheres wissen, ist so recht wieder bei einer Besprechung dieser Fragen im Freundeskreise der „Münchener Philologischen Gesellschaft" zum Ausdruck gekommen. Es ist richtig: auch die neueste juristische Literatur ist recht konservativ.

das Anspruch auf Wahrscheinlichkeit erheben darf. Hier hat sich auch Mommsen zur Konstruktion einer kommunistischen Agrargenossenschaft verleiten lassen, von der, wie Pöhlmanns scharfe Kritik[1] dartut, nichts übrig bleibt, als die blosse Möglichkeit gemeinwirtschaftlicher Elemente in der ältesten Agrarverfassung. Da gilt es, manche landläufige Theorie zu revidieren und manche Behauptung zu überprüfen, die sich wie ein Axiom von Lehrbuch zu Lehrbuch vererbt. Auf dem Gebiete des Vertragsrechts haben sich wohl auch im ältesten Rom die Prinzipien der Barleistung und der Entgeltlichkeit geltend gemacht, während das später so überall vorbildliche römische Obligationenrecht von der scharfen begrifflichen Scheidung von Schuld und Haftung, dem Leistensollen des Schuldners und dem Einstehen des Bürgen oder selbstbürgenden Schuldners, nicht minder beherrscht gewesen sein wird, als das Recht der Germanen und das der Griechen, ja auch das der Babylonier und der Assyrer. Gerade diese Fragen müssen für die römische Rechtsgeschichte noch der Antwort näher gebracht werden, als dies bisher der Fall ist. Und hier hilft, wie die neuen Arbeiten von Partsch und Koschaker gezeigt haben, die Rechtsvergleichung weiter. Dass auch wichtige Fragen des Prozessrechts mit der Schuld-Haftungslehre zusammenhängen, ist nach neueren Vermutungen recht wahrscheinlich.

Noch ist der Anfänge des staatlichen Strafrechts zu gedenken, dabei aber die Vorstufe nicht zu übersehen, die das Straf- oder richtiger Racheverfahren der Familie und der Sippe bildet. Schon in diese Zeit ist aber gewiss die Scheidung der *delicta privata* von den *crimina publica* zu verlegen, und die bewusste oder unbewusste Erweiterung des Kreises der letztgenannten auf Kosten der Delikte zu beachten, die der privaten Ahndung—wenn auch nicht mehr immer der Selbsthilfe—überlassen sind.

Schon ins „königliche“ Rom müssen endlich die Anfänge des Verkehrs mit dem Auslande fallen: die verschiedenartigen Verträge mit anderen Städten über Rechtshilfe und gegenseitigen Rechtsschutz der Bürger und über das *hospitium*, das dem staatlichen Recht auch hier vorangeht. Es ist von grossem Interesse, diese

[1] *Geschichte der sozialen Frage und des Sozialismus in der antiken Welt*, 2. Aufl. (1912), ii. 415-433. Vgl. auch Bruns-Lenel, a. a. O. 311. Vgl. für Hellas Pöhlmann Bd. i. Vgl. auch allgemein und insbesondere für die Germanen R. Hildebrand, *Recht und Sitte*, 2. Aufl. (1907).

Wurzeln des „Völkerrechts" blosszulegen und bedeutende Arbeiten gerade englischer Herkunft [1] haben diese Probleme wesentlich gefördert. Neben diesen losen Beziehungen zum Auslande steht aber der eigenartige latinische Bund, dessen Bedeutung für den später so fruchtbaren Gedanken, dass es über der Poliszusammengehörigkeit noch grössere Zusammenhänge geben könne, nicht gering eingeschätzt werden darf.[2] Überall und nicht zuletzt auf dem Gebiete der internationalen Beziehungen werden aber mit Vorteil die griechischen Parallelen heranzuziehen sein.

II. Die Zeit der Republik.—In helleres Licht scheint die Geschichte Roms nach dem Sturz seiner Könige zu treten. Die von der römischen Überlieferung geschilderten Verfassungskämpfe sind uns in grossen Zügen schon von der Schule her bekannt: wir sehen die nicht immer parallel verlaufenden, sondern sich wiederholt auch kreuzenden wirtschaftlichen und politischen Gegensätze. Darin wird bei allen sonstigen Zweifeln gewiss Wahres stecken. Wir verstehen die Bedeutung der Zwölftafelgesetzgebung, deren Authentizität freilich in neuerer Zeit hart angefochten, aber dank Girards, Lenels und anderer Gegenkritik nun als fester erhärtet gelten mag, als vor Pais' und dem viel weiter gehenden Angriff Lamberts. Dabei haben freilich auch die Angreifer manches Richtige beobachtet und namentlich Pais' besonnene Stellungnahme auf unserem letzten Kongress in Berlin sei noch in Erinnerung gebracht.[3] Auch weiten Juristenkreisen Frankreichs und Deutschlands ist aber die Beachtung der historischen Tatsache recht eindringlich nahezulegen, dass „freies Recht" kein Freiheitspostulat ist, und dass das antike Richterkönigtum überall der Herrschaft des Gesetzes wich, unter dessen Tyrannis sich auch der Grieche willig beugte.

Die römischen Verfassungskämpfe führen nach der Überlieferung wenigstens formell zu einer Demokratie, wie sie selbst Athen nie gekannt hat: ich meine den für verschiedene Jahrhunderte bezeugten, und freilich schon darum bedenklichen Satz *ut quod tributim plebes iussisset populum teneret*. Die Gesetze der

[1] Coleman Phillipson, *The International Law and Custom of Ancient Greece and Rome*. 2 Bde. 1911.

[2] Für die Königszeit freilich mit allen nötigen Vorbehalten und Fragezeichen.

[3] Literaturübersicht neuestens bei Bruns-Lenel, a. a. O. 325 A. 2 und 3.

Plebejerversammlung, zu welcher der Patrizier nicht einmal Zutritt hat, sollten auch ihn binden. Die Geschichte der Verfassungskämpfe bietet auch sonst noch genug des Dunklen: manches Licht ist in jüngster Zeit erst angesteckt worden. Sicher erscheint aber im Widerspruch zur Theorie der Überlieferung die Tatsache, dass Rom praktisch eine vollendete Demokratie doch nie geworden ist. Wir dürfen ja bei all den Schilderungen der inneren Kämpfe, die schliesslich angeblich das Übergewicht der Plebejer endgiltig festlegen, nicht vergessen, dass die äussere Geschichte Roms von dieser Demokratisierung der Verfassung, wenn sie wirklich so oder ähnlich, wie uns erzählt wird, vor sich gegangen ist, wenig spüren lässt. Während die Regierung der Imperienträger führt, der Inhaber von Gewalten, deren Vereinigung ihm eine ganz besondere Stellung verlieh, liegt die äussere Politik — auch damals die ungemein wichtigere Äusserung des Staatslebens — in den Händen des Senats.

Was ist aber „Rom" in der republikanischen Zeit geworden? Drei Bestandteile hat es: die herrschende Stadt, die dienenden Provinzen und die verbündeten oder sonstwie angegliederten Städte. Hier muss eindringlich auf die merkwürdige Verleihung des Bürgerrechts an Leute hingewiesen werden, die politisch mangels einer Repräsentativverfassung damit nichts anzufangen wissen: denn wer wollte nach Rom reisen, um dort in die Volksversammlung zu gehen, wenn er in Spanien seine Heimat hatte? Rom hat den Fehler vermieden, der Athens Herrlichkeit zu Fall gebracht hat: es hat den Bundesgenossen in weitestem Ausmass das Danaergeschenk seines Bürgerrechts gemacht. Da der römische Zivität erwerbende Bürger einer Landstadt die Eigenschaft eines Bürgers dieser Stadt nicht verliert, so ist damit der Gegensatz zwischen dem Staatsbürgerrecht und dem Stadtbürgerrecht tatsächlich gegeben.

In aller Stille vollzieht sich auch die Latinisierung erst Italiens, dann des ganzen Westens, soweit der Römer Herrschaft reicht. Das ist eine Erscheinung, die mir wenigstens immer zu den merkwürdigsten der ganzen römischen Geschichte zählte. Die Stadt, die von sich aus eine solche Entnationalisierung weiter Gebiete durchführt, wie wir sie doch annehmen müssen, muss eine ganz gewaltige Lebenskraft besessen haben. Freilich sind wir im ganzen Westen über das Fortleben des nationalen Elements und seine

Äusserung in der Volkssprache und dem Volksrecht viel schlechter orientiert, als im Osten — aber es muss doch wohl ein bedeutender Unterschied zwischen den Beziehungen Roms zu dem kulturell so viel tiefer stehenden Westen und zu den politisch unterworfenen, kulturell aber stets als Lehrer verehrten Griechen bestanden haben.

Wir kommen damit auf ein besonders wichtiges Gebiet der römischen Rechtsgeschichte, auf die Frage des griechischen Einflusses. Sie ist oft und viel erörtert worden, aber sie ist noch keineswegs erledigt. In der republikanischen Periode begegnet sie, Antwort verlangend, in der Zwölftafelgesetzgebung; sie begegnet allgemein bei den Beziehungen Roms zu Grossgriechenland und weiter zum griechischen Mutterlande und allen Gebieten des hellenistischen Ostens. Wir dürfen aber, wenn wir das Mass griechischen Einflusses auf der Römer Recht zu ergründen suchen, auch nicht vergessen, die Frage zu überprüfen, inwieferne etwa unsere Quellen tatsächlich griechisches Recht bringen, wenn sie lateinisches zu geben scheinen: ich denke natürlich in erster Linie an Plautus und Terenz.

In der Darstellung der Staatsverwaltung dieser Zeit wird neben der voranstehenden Erörterung des Staatsgebietes und der Verwaltungskörper, worauf schon die Sprache kam, die des Heer- und Finanzwesens, dann aber der Agrargeschichte und der Entwickelung des Handels einen breiten Raum einnehmen. „Recht und Wirtschaft" ist kein bloss modernes Schlagwort: kein Rechtshistoriker darf die Wirtschaftsgeschichte beiseiteschieben.

Das führt zu Partien, die mit mehr oder weniger Grund herkömmlich im Privatrecht verhandelt werden: Ständegliederung, steigende Bedeutung der Sklaverei, damit wohl zusammenhängend der privatrechtliche Grundsatz von der Unzulässigkeit freier Stellvertretung, Zwischenbildungen verschiedener Arten von Halbfreiheit, dann aber auch die Bildung des neuen Adels, der Nobiles[1] und der Ritter.

Für das Privatrecht der republikanischen und der Prinzipatszeit ist jetzt Mitteis' *Römisches Privatrecht bis auf die Zeit Diokletians* richtunggebend. Zwar behandelt der bisher vorliegende erste Band (1908) nur die Grundbegriffe und die Lehre von den juristischen Personen, aber diese Gebiete eingehend

[1] Dazu jetzt M. Gelzer, *Die Nobilität der römischen Republik* (1912)

und grossenteils ganz in neue Bahnen weisend. In seiner Stellungnahme zu grundlegenden Fragen, die bereits gestreift wurden, ist das Werk vorbildlich: so zum Problem des arischen Rechts, zum Verhältnis des Römerrechts zu dem der Umbro-Samniten, endlich zum griechischen Recht.

Ungeschrieben ist noch eine Geschichte des römischen Privatprozessrechts, die Wlassaks peinlich sorgfältige Forschungen verwertet hätte, von den „Prozessgesetzen" an bis zu den neuesten Arbeiten über Exzeptionen und Präskriptionen. Lenels Ediktsrekonstruktion, Girards Studien und so manche andere Arbeit muss erst erworben werden, damit wir sie auch voll besitzen. Kellers vorzügliches Zivilprozessbüchlein ist seit 1883 nicht wieder erschienen und seither auch kein anderes. Wie viel Arbeit steckt aber in einzelnen Artikeln von Pauly-Wissowas Realenzyklopädie!

III. Die Zeit des Prinzipats.—Bewundernswert ist Augustus' kluges Werk, mit dem die Revolutionsepoche abschliesst. Die Republik ist scheinbar wiederhergestellt: *eadem magistratuum vocabula*, und doch: *quotus quisque reliquus qui rempublicam vidisset?* Wie viel besagt diese taziteische Charakteristik des Reichs beim Regierungsantritt des Tiberius (Annal. i. 3)! Die staatsrechtliche Umgestaltung ist unschwer zu schildern, aber der im modernen Staatsrecht zum Kampfe zweier Richtungen gewordene Gegensatz zwischen juristischer und politischer Betrachtung des Staatslebens tritt hier klar entgegen. Politisch ist die Republik tot und die Monarchie auf dem Wege, und in dieser Hinsicht darf man jetzt schon sagen, dass der Schwerpunkt des Reichs in den hellenistischen Osten verlegt ist. Sind doch dort die Kaiser Götter, ein Gedanke, der dem Römer, auch seit die alte Virtus nur selten mehr auf Erden wandelte, doch hart in den Kopf ging. Die Verfassungsgeschichte dieser Zeit muss zeigen, wie aus der Republik die Monarchie wird, wie erst die Volksversammlung depossediert wird und wie dann in energischem Ringen die beiden übrig bleibenden Gewalten, Senat und Prinzeps, nach der Beseitigung des Rivalen streben, bis endlich der Reorganisator Diokletian den Staat als orientalische Despotie neu aufrichtet.

In der Staatsverwaltung spielen die Provinzen eine immer mehr hervortretende Rolle. Und da ist aus Inschriften und neuerdings aus den Papyri ein Erkenntnismaterial geboten, wie es lange den antiken Rechtshistorikern vorenthalten geblieben war. Wir haben aus den Papyri Einzelheiten einer römischen Provinzialverwaltung kennen gelernt, nach denen früher kein Einsichtiger zu fragen gewagt hätte. Wir lernten dabei aber auch das Mass dessen richtiger einschätzen, was die Römer neu eingeführt, und dessen, was sie von ihren Vorgängern in der Macht übernommen hatten. Und das war auf verwaltungsrechtlichem Gebiete gewiss nicht wenig. Freilich Ägypten, wo wir diese Dinge an den Papyri am besten studieren können, ist nicht der Typus einer normalen Provinz. In diesem richtiger als kaiserliche Domäne bezeichneten Erbe der Ptolemäer ist der Prinzeps von je das gewesen, was er erst nach und nach in den anderen Reichsgebieten wurde: der göttliche König oder auch der königliche Gott. Aber je mehr eben die Gewalt des Prinzeps steigt, umsomehr darf Ägypten als Typus des römischen Provinziallands genommen werden. In Ägypten lernen wir, wie die Regierung Gesetze und Verordnungen durch eingehende Publikationshandlungen zur allgemeinen Kenntnis brachte, wie Beamte und deren Stellvertreter amtierten, wie sie mit den Parteien, wie mit den vor- und nachgeordneten Behörden verkehrten, wie und welche Steuern und Abgaben erhoben wurden, aber auch wie der grosse und der kleine Grundbesitz verwaltet wurde.

Aber die Papyri zeigen noch mehr. Aus ihnen lernen wir das Leben des kleinen Mannes mit all seinen Freuden und Leiden, mit seinen hässlichen und schönen Zügen kennen: wir lernen ihn als Gläubiger und Schuldner, als Hausherrn und Mieter kennen, als Übeltäter und Beleidigten, als Kläger und Verklagten, wir sehen ihn in der Familie als Eheherrn und Hausvater, wir finden ihn als Arbeiter und Arbeitgeber, als Gutsherrn und Verwalter, als Schiffer und Soldaten. Schubarts eben erschienene Sammlung verdeutschter Briefe aus dem Altertum[1] sagt auch dem Rechtshistoriker sehr viel. „Antike Seelen, die für immer verschollen schienen, werden wieder lebendig“: ein Wort, das ich Deissmann[2] nachspreche. Die Prosopographie der ersten drei Jahrhunderte der Kaiserzeit hat nur die der antiken aristokratischen Geschichtsbetrachtung bedeutsam erscheinende Oberschicht berücksichtigt,

[1] *Ein Jahrtausend am Nil* (1912).

[2] *Licht vom Osten*, 2. u. 3. Aufl. (1909), S. 217. Vgl. zum Folgenden Deissman 217 f.

*sed hominum plebeiorum infinita illa turba qua scripta ecclesiastica et auctorum iuris referta sunt procul semota est.*[1] Für Verwaltungs-, Prozess- und Privatrecht sind aber diese die in Betracht kommenden Personen.

Aber noch für etwas anderes: unter diesen Kleinen, unter den Armen und Demütigen ist die Saat des Christentums aufgegangen, unter der „grossen Schar, die niemand zählen konnte, aus allen Völkern und Stämmen, und Nationen und Sprachen" (Offenb. Joh. vii. 9). Wie das grosse Problem des Verhältnisses des Staats zu seinen Nationen, tritt jetzt auch das weltbewegende Problem „Staat und Kirche" in die Rechtsgeschichte ein. Der heidnische Staat kennt das Problem nicht, er kann es nicht kennen, da der Götterkult ein durchaus nationaler ist, und als solcher der staatlichen, nicht irgendwelcher vom Staate unabhängigen Macht, eigen ist. Die Stellung des Staats zum Christentum verdient eine eingehende Betrachtung. Auch hiezu, insbesondere zu den Christenverfolgungen unter Decius haben die Papyri viel Material beigesteuert.[2] Um sich vom Verdachte mangelnder Götterverehrung zu reinigen, reichen die in diesen Verdacht gekommenen *libelli* ein, dass sie mit Weib und Kind immer und so auch jetzt vor der Opferkommission geopfert und vom Opferfleisch genossen haben, und die Kommission bestätigt diese *libelli* durch einen Bescheinigungsvermerk.

Für Privatrecht und Prozess möchte ich auch nur dessen in wenigen Worten Erwähnung tun, was wir aus den Papyri zulernen können und müssen. Nach antiker Auffassung lebt jeder nach seinem Personalrecht. So natürlich vor allem der Grieche in der griechischen Reichshälfte. Als nun Caracalla das Bürgerrecht in weitem Ausmasse austeilte, waren demgemäss alle damit Beglückten zur römischen Rechtsordnung verpflichtet. Das Volksrecht aber lebte nichtsdestoweniger fort: das hat L. Mitteis[3] schon vor mehr als zwei Dezennien festgestellt und das hat die rechtshistorische Papyrusforschung seither durchaus bestätigt. Nicht anders als in Ägypten war es aber in den anderen Diadochenstaaten: eine Tat-

[1] Klebs, *Praefatio zur Pros.* i. p. viii.

[2] P. M. Meyer, *Die Libelli aus der decianischen Christenverfolgung* (1910).

[3] *Reichsrecht und Volksrecht in den östlichen Provinzen des römischen Kaiserreichs* (1891).

sache, die uns am besten im syrisch-römischen Rechtsbuche entgegentritt. Jetzt erst können wir eine Reihe kaiserlicher Konstitutionen bewerten, die anscheinend—für den Kenner bloss des römischen Rechts—Selbstverständliches mit Emphase einschärfen: es ist da stets die Annahme berechtigt, dass irgend ein volksrechtlicher Brauch sich der römischen Ordnung zum Trotz hartnäckig erhielt. Doch ich darf bei diesen Dingen, über die sich sovieles sagen liesse, nicht länger verweilen, so schwer es hier wird, auch nur Schlagworte darüber zurückzudrängen, wie uns diese wunderbaren Quellen die römische Rechtsgeschichte der Wirklichkeit, nicht der, wenn auch antiken, Theorie, näher gebracht haben.

IV. Der absolute Staat.—Ἐν ὀνόματι τοῦ κυρίου καὶ δεσπότου Ἰησοῦ Χριστοῦ τοῦ θεοῦ καὶ σωτῆρος ἡμῶν βασιλείας τοῦ θειοτάτου καὶ εὐσεβεστάτου ἡμῶν δεσπότου Φλαυίου Μαυρικίου Τιβερίου τοῦ αἰωνίου Αὐγούστου Αὐτοκράτορος ἔτους δωδεκάτου καὶ ὑπατείας τῆς αὐτῶν γαληνότητος ἔτους ἑνδεκάτου † Μεχεὶρ κα τῆς ιβ ἰνδικτίονος ἐν Συήνῃ †. So beginnt eine Dialysisurkunde, die am 15. Februar 594 n. Chr. zwischen Schwägern abgeschlossen wird, nachdem ein Presbyter den Frieden vermittelt hat. Die Urkunde, der Münchener Papyrus Inv. Nr. 102,[1] ist typisch für das Ende der Entwickelung des Absolutismus.

Wohl ist der Staat christlich, aber das hindert nicht, Christus δεσπότης zu nennen und in einem Atem damit auch dem Kaiser dasselbe Beiwort zu geben; bei Gott dem Allmächtigen, bei der hl. und wesensgleichen Dreieinigkeit zu schwören und zugleich νίκην καὶ διαμονήν, ja selbst τὴν θείαν καὶ οὐράνιον τύχην des Kaiserpaars im Eide anzurufen,[2] der Herrscher der Welt, der ewigen Erlauchten und Selbstherrscher. Nirgends, in keiner offiziellen Rechtsquelle, in keinem Schriftstellertext spiegelt sich der Wandel der Zeiten so sehr wieder, wie in unseren Papyrusurkunden. Ihre Formalien sind keine Zufälligkeit, sie zeigen den Wandel der Zeiten und den Wandel der Menschen. Was den Orientalen gewohnt sein mochte, ist jetzt auch den Römern geläufig geworden, denn unter den Parteien und Zeugen der Grenzgarnison in Syene, die uns in den genannten Münchenerurkunden begegnen, zu denen die ergänzenden

[1] Nr. 14 in der im Druck befindlichen, von Heisenberg und mir herausgegebenen *Sammlung byzantinischer Papyri* in der K. Hof- und Staatsbibliothek zu München.

[2] So P. Mon. Inv. Nr. 104 Z. 46-48; Nr. 12 der Ausgabe.

Paralleltexte das British Museum birgt,[1] finden wir Kopten, Griechen und Römer in buntem Gemisch, alle aber dem Staatsbürgerrecht nach römische Bürger.

Die Theorie der Staatsverfassung ist die einfachste der Welt: alles ist der Kaiser, Gesetzgeber, Regent und Richter; alles, was geschieht, geschieht in seinem Namen. Die Juristen, die in der früheren Epoche selbständig redend aufgetreten sind und das grossartige römische Privatrecht geschaffen haben, sie sprechen jetzt nur mehr im geheimen kaiserlichen Konsistorium und das Ergebnis ihrer Arbeit ist formell ein Wort aus des Kaisers Munde. Sie sind aufgegangen in der namenlosen Schar der Untertanen, deren höchstes Glück es sein muss, dem kaiserlichen Herren zu dienen.

Aber auch der *θειότατος αὐτοκράτωρ* kann die Welt nicht ohne Organe verwalten. Wiederum zeigen uns die Papyri die Staatsverwaltung dieser neuen Epoche. Jetzt gibt das ägyptische Bild noch getreuer die Lage im ganzen Reiche wieder. Denn die Römer selbst sind überall Untertanen geworden und die Zeiten, da der Kaiser nur *princeps civium* gewesen, sind längst dahin.

Die Verkleinerung der Provinzen, die Zerschlagung historisch gewordener Individualitäten und all die sonstigen Mittel zentralistischer Verwaltungsversuche können doch nicht den Zerfall des Reiches in das Westreich und Ostreich verhindern, und sie können im Innern des Reichs den Feudalisierungsprozess, das unverkennbare Zeichen schwacher Zentralgewalt, nicht aufhalten. Die dunkle Zeit des vierten und fünften Jahrhunderts ist auch durch die Papyri noch nicht genügend erhellt worden. Aber die Grundzüge der Entwickelung können wir sehen. Von entscheidender Bedeutung sind die Agrarverhältnisse. Dem Kolonat muss in einer römischen Rechtsgeschichte ein besonders eingehendes Kapitel gewidmet werden. Wir sind jetzt dank Rostowzews Studien[2] über die weit in die hellenistische Zeit hineinragenden Wurzeln dieses Instituts und über seine Entwickelung, insbesondere in Afrika, aufgeklärt. Wir sehen eine auch sonst wiederkehrende Erscheinung. Der Latifundienbesitz müsste brach liegen, gelänge es nicht, Bauern in halber, stets wachsender Abhängigkeit zur Bewirtschaftung heranzuziehen. Neben der Ausnützung wirtschaft-

[1] Vgl. Bell, *Klio* xiii. 160-174.

[2] *Studien zur Geschichte des römischen Kolonates* (1910).

licher Abhängigkeit kam es dabei wohl auch oft genug zu brutaler Gewaltanwendung, die den freien Nachbarn in den Gutsleibeigenen verwandelte. Die Bindung an die Scholle lässt sich deutlich verfolgen, bis sie zur Rechtsinstitution wird und nur mehr als natürliche Folge der Erblichkeit der Berufe erscheint. Aber der staatliche Steuerzwang hat nicht minder der Feudalisierung indirekt Vorschub geleistet. Um der Steuererpressung zu entgehen, verkauft manch ein Freier sein bischen Freiheit und wird Klient eines Patrons. Diese Patroziniumsbewegung, die, unter schliesslicher staatlicher Sanktion, eine Reihe von Freien zu Halbfreien und zu Hörigen macht, haben in neuester Zeit Gelzer [1] und de Zulueta [2] genau untersucht.[3]

Von den traurigen Verwaltungszuständen des 6. Jahrhunderts geben uns jetzt die Papyri aus dem Museum zu Cairo, die Jean Maspero in dankenswert rascher Folge publiziert,[4] Auskunft. Sie haben bei den Historikern und Juristen berechtigtes Aufsehen erregt, sie zeigen uns Dinge, welche die Rechtsbücher verbieten, in vielfach praktischer Anwendung, zeigen uns die Gewaltigen, die das Recht wohl prinzipiell als Macht werten, und die Kleinen, die um Haus und Hof kommen, die im Schuldturm sitzen und Peinigungen aller Art erdulden müssen, deren Leben nicht sicher ist, wenn nicht ein Patronus den Schutz bietet, den der Staat nicht mehr bieten kann, und den seine pflichtvergessenen und geldgierigen Beamten nicht bieten wollen. Auch die Münchener Papyri werden dazu einen Beitrag bringen, den ich für so unwahrscheinlich hielt, dass ich lange nach anderer Erklärung suchte. In einem Prozesse Inv. Nr. 103 [5] kommt zum Vorschein, dass der mit seiner Mutter in einen Erbstreit verwickelte Sohn dem einen Richter eine Nachlassquote angeboten hat, wenn dieser der Mutter die strittigen Objekte durch

[1] M. Gelzer, *Studien zur byzantin. Verwaltung Ägyptens* (1909).

[2] F. de Zulueta, *De patrociniis vicorum*, in Vinogradoff, *Oxford Studies in Social and Legal History*, vol. i. (1909).

[3] Vgl. zur ganzen Frage die Ausführungen Wilckens, *Grundzüge d. Papyruskunde*, 314-326.

[4] *Catalogue général des antiquités égyptiennes du Musée du Caire*, i. (1910–11), ii. (1911–13).

[5] P. Mon. 6 der Ausgabe. Ein Stück der Urkunde befindet sich als Lond. Inv. Nr. 1807 im British Museum. Danach ist die Datierung auf das Jahr 583 möglich. Ich darf schon hier den Herren Kenyon und Bell für freundliche Mitteilungen und Gestattung der Einsichtnahme in die Londoner Gruppe der Syene-Papyri herzlichst danken.

einen Exekutor kurzerhand wegnehmen lasse, der Richter aber ist dazu bereit gewesen; und der andere Richter, vor den die Frage zur neuerlichen Entscheidung kommt, hat das mit dem milden Tadel zugegeben, die Richter sollten nicht χύδην vorgehen.

Auch die Militärverwaltung wird erst durch diese Papyri in rechtes Licht gestellt. Eine vor Kurzem erschienene Arbeit Masperos [1] hat denn auch ausser den Kairenern schon die Münchenertexte ausführlich herangezogen.

Für die Heeresverwaltung ist entsprechend dem Streben nach zentralistischer Einheit die starke Verwendung lateinischer *termini* nur natürlich. Eine Auslese aus den Münchenertexten bringt den ἀδιούτωρ, ἀκτουάριος, αὐγουστάλιος, βικάριος, βικαριανός, δοῦξ, δρακονάριος, καβαλλάριος, κεντυρίων, ὀρδινάριος, πραίφεκτος, πριμικέριος, die πριόρες, den τείρων und τριβοῦνος. Neben dem φρούριον steht das κάστρον, neben dem ἀριθμός die λεγεών. Auf Grund der προβατωρία wird der Rekrut (νεόστρατος, τείρων) in die μάτριξ eingetragen und am Ende schreibt man ihm auf die Bescheinigung in wohl griechischen Lettern βενε βαλεας. In der Prozesssprache begegnen die θεία ἀδνουτατιών, die *divina adnotatio*, und die θεῖα βέρβα des Kaisers.[2]

Neben dem Verwaltungsrecht haben die byzantinischen Papyri aber auch das Privat- und Prozessrecht ungemein bereichert. Hier ist die herkömmliche Darstellung noch durchaus rückständig. Das hat schon bald nach dem Erscheinen des ersten Heftes der Kairo-Papyri Mitteis konstatiert und eine zusammenfassende Betrachtung des justinianischen Rechts nicht als Endpunkt von Untersuchungen über frühere Zeiten, sondern als eines selbständigen Erkenntnisgegenstandes als dringendes Bedürfnis bezeichnet.[3] Partsch [4] hat aus diesen Urkunden wertvolle neue Resultate zum justinianischen Reskriptenprozess gewonnen, und Collinet [5] hat kürzlich einem beginnenden Werke über das justinianische Recht den Untertitel gegeben: *Le caractère oriental de l'œuvre législative de Justinien et les destinées des institutions classiques en occident.* In der Betrachtung der justinianischen Gesetzgebung droht über der Inter-

[1] *Organisation militaire de l'Égypte Byzantine* (1912).

[2] Zu alledem verweise ich auf die alsbald erscheinende Ausgabe der Münchener Papyri und einstweilen auf meinen Vorbericht in den *Sitz. Ber. Bayer. Akad.* (1911), 8. Abh.

[3] *Zeitschr. Savigny Stift. f. Rechtsgesch.*, Rom, Abt. xxxi. S. 393.

[4] *Gött. Nachrichten*, phil.-hist. Kl. (1911), 201 ff.

[5] *Études historiques sur le Droit de Justinien*, i. (1912).

polationenjagd die Wertung der interpolierten Texte, das eigentlich Justinianische am ganzen Werk, zu kurz zu kommen.

Diese justinianische Gesetzgebung darf aber nicht bloss nicht als Endpunkt vorhergehender Rechtsentwickelung, sondern auch nicht bloss als Anfangspunkt der späteren nationalen Privatrechtsgeschichte in den Ländern der Rezeption aufgefasst werden. Für sich, als selbständige Grösse gehört sie in die Darstellung der vierten Periode der römischen Rechtsgeschichte.

Ich habe endlich des Strafrechts nur ganz zu Anfang Erwähnung getan. Es muss natürlich in seiner Entwickelung durch alle Perioden verfolgt werden. Mommsens *Römisches Strafrecht* erleichtert uns diese Aufgabe ganz besonders. Auch dieses Werk des Meisters darf nicht ungenützt verstauben. Und wenn jüngst, von der Kritik Mommsens ausgehend, James Leigh Strachan-Davidson[1] einzelne Fragen des römischen Kriminalrechts in ausführlicher Behandlung gesammelt hat, so hat er gewiss in Mommsens Sinne gehandelt, der nichts weniger wollte, als dass auch mit seiner Arbeit ein Arbeitsgebiet als ausgeschöpft verlassen werde.

Kaum irgendwo sehen wir so wie im Strafrechte eine Wellenbewegung in der römischen Kulturentwickelung: die Frage nach dem, was Straftat sein könne und die Frage nach dem Übel, nach der Strafe, welche die Tat vergelten oder den Täter bessern oder andere von gleicher Tat abschrecken soll, und was an Strafrechtstheorien es sonst noch geben mag, all diese Fragen beantworten die Jahrhunderte auch der römischen Geschichte verschieden. Wie hat sich, um nur eines zu nennen, Begriff und Ahndung des Staatsverbrechens und des *crimen laesae maiestatis* im Laufe der Zeiten gewandelt! Hier auch zeigen uns jetzt die Urkunden Menschen, die fehlen und büssen, Richter, die verurteilen und strafen. Ich erinnere etwa nur an den Papyruskodex, *Berliner Griechische Urkunden* IV. Nr. 1024, worin uns Prozesse vor dem Statthalter aus dem 4. Jhd. n. Chr. überliefert sind. Immer resümiert der Statthalter den Tatbestand und schliesst daran das Urteil: einmal handelt es sich um Ermordung der mit dem Ehebrecher ertappten Frau durch den beleidigten Gatten, hier ist das Urteil verloren; in einem anderen Falle hat der Täter sich Grabschändung zu Schulden kommen lassen: da sagt der Richter in rhetorisch gehobener Sprache:

[1] *Problems of the Roman Criminal Law*, 2 Bde., 1912.

„Du hast den Toten ausgegraben, den die Stadt auf Volksbeschluss beerdigt und betrauert hat. Du scheinst mir das Herz eines Tieres zu haben und nicht eines Menschen, oder eigentlich auch nicht einmal das eines Tieres. Denn auch die Tiere greifen zwar die Menschen an, sie schonen aber die Toten. Du aber hast dich an einem Leichnam vergriffen, der schon ausgeschieden war aus dem Geschlechte der Menschen. Wo nahmst du den Mut her, den schon zur Ruhe Gelegten auch noch der letzten Hoffnung zu berauben? Fürwahr beim Zeus es war der letzte Schmuck, den die Gesetze gewähren, es waren Geschenke der Stadt an den Toten, es waren Sühngaben. So wirst du denn für deine Tat mit deinem Haupte büssen."

Nicht weniger wirken schon rein menschlich die folgenden Fälle, die in der genannten Urkunde beisammen stehen.[1]

Doch ich muss mit Einzelheiten abbrechen.

Wie im Strafrecht, so in der Geschichte der Latifundien, wie in der Schutzvorschrift für den Schuldner gegen den wuchernden Gläubiger, so in der Norm der freien Beweiswürdigung und der entgegenstehenden Festlegung bestimmter Beweisregeln, wie in der Regelung des Erbrechts, so in der Frage, wer im Heere dienen soll, jeder Bürger oder der fremde Söldling, wie in den Problemen der Steuergesetzgebung, so in denen des Verhältnisses des Staats zu seinen Nationen und Konfessionen, und wie die Fragen alle heissen mögen, die der Rechtshistoriker stellt und beantwortet zu sehen wünschte—überall sind es nicht bloss Probleme, die den Juristen interessieren, sondern Probleme der Geschichte der Menschheitskultur.

Das alles aber — wir dürfen mit einem Schlagwort sagen: Mommsens Lebensarbeit—soll in einer römischen Rechtsgeschichte verarbeitet sein. Sie wird dann allerdings an Umfang zunehmen müssen, aber es lässt sich vielleicht auch hier ein Mass finden, das dem Studierenden und Gebildeten doch mehr bietet, als eine Aufzählung von Leges und Senatuskonsulten, als eine trockene Aneinanderreihung der Namen der Juristen, die das römische Recht geschaffen haben, und der Titel ihrer Werke. Nie darf der Ausblick auf die antike Rechtsgeschichte überhaupt versäumt werden. Nie sollte aber auch der Rechtshistoriker an dem vor-

[1] Besprochen von Wenger in Gross' *Archiv für Kriminal-Anthropologie*, xvi. 304-323.

übergehen, was auf anderen Gebieten der antiken Geschichtsforschung und der Philologie zu Tage kommt. Die Zeit der *splendid isolation* der römischen Rechtswissenschaft ist auch für Deutschland vorüber und soll, so wollen wir hoffen, nicht wieder kommen.

Mag es unerfüllbarer Optimismus sein, dass ein einzelner, dessen eigene Arbeit nur auf kleinem Gebiete sich bewegt, das weite Arbeitsfeld auch nur ganz zu übersehen vermöchte, dass es ihm, auch wo er bescheiden nur sichten und sammeln wollte, gelänge, überall die Spreu vom Weizen zu sondern—aber welche Arbeit ist je ohne frischen Optimismus begonnen worden? Freilich, mehr denn bisher bedarf das neu zuströmende Quellenmaterial der Bearbeitung in entsagender Einzelforschung und hier darf vielleicht der Jurist an die Universalhistoriker die Bitte richten, mehr noch als bisher den juristischen Quellen, den Rechtsurkunden vor allem, ihr Augenmerk zuzuwenden. Viel gemeinsame Arbeit ist noch zu tun, um auch auf dem Gebiete der Rechtserkenntnis vorwärtszukommen, um auch hier aus der Geschichte die Lehre fürs Leben zu ziehen, zu sehen, welche kulturellen Voraussetzungen diese oder jene Folgen zeitigen, das Ideal zu verwirklichen, soweit Menschenkraft es vermag, das, wie jedem Geschichtsforscher, so auch dem Rechtshistoriker vorschwebt:

*Rerum cognoscere causas.*

L. WENGER.

# IV

# DALLA *COMMUNIO* DEL DIRITTO QUIRITARIO ALLA COMPROPRIETÀ MODERNA

1. La comproprietà osservata negli scritti dei giureconsulti romani ha la proporzione di una figura geometrica, in cui l' insieme dei punti e delle linee concorrono a formare una superficie compassata con precisione e che perciò costituisce ancora la base di tutte le trattazioni moderne; cioè a partire dal sec. xvi fino ai nostri giorni. Ma nondimeno è vero che nel *Corpus Juris Civilis*, lungo quelle linee regolari, tratto tratto appariscono delle curve che sono delle incognite nella scienza; e siccome esse premono sui punti fondamentali dell' istituto, ne turbano d' un tratto l' armonia e conducono gli scrittori a formule indecise, complicate e tortuose.

La presente trattazione è dedicata a svelare la natura di quelle deviazioni ed il loro valore, che è veramente altissimo; perchè quelle linee divergenti nella figura della *communio* romana costituiscono in realtà i fondamenti della comproprietà moderna.

Ma è imprescindibile che anche qui l' impostatura dello istituto classico sia designata come quella che costituisce il punto di partenza da cui si muove la formazione dell' opera futura.

## CAP. I

### DIRITTO CLASSICO

2. La comproprietà romana vive e si esplica in tutto secondo i principii fondamentali del dominio quiritario, che è essenzialmente esclusivo ed abbraccia la cosa intera in tutti i suoi rapporti.

Di conseguenza è impossibile che il dominio su di una cosa possa appartenere *in solidum* a più persone. È possibile invece che diritti molteplici di dominio coesistano sulla cosa medesima in maniera da limitarsi a vicenda. La limitazione è di natura meccanica; nel senso che il diritto di ciascuno dei titolari incontra un ostacolo nel concorrente diritto di altri; e perciò esso deve di necessità arrestarsi entro un limite insuperabile. E la limitazione è di natura meccanica ancora nel senso che essa non porta tra i diritti molteplici alcun coordinamento; e quindi nessuna distribuzione delle facoltà di dominio e nessuna dipendenza tra i titolari del medesimo. I quali sono tutti *domini*,[1] ed hanno tutti rispetto alla cosa una posizione pari. Tale posizione si manifesta in tutta la sua efficienza nelle conseguenze.

(*a*) Ciascuno dei titolari esercita il suo potere di dominio colla massima indipendenza dagli altri; può disporre del suo diritto come e quando vuole, presupposto che con ciò non offenda il diritto pari degli altri. Tale carattere hanno, di regola, tutti gli atti di disposizione giuridica della cosa. E pertanto guardata da questo punto di vista la comproprietà romana ha nulla di particolare; essa si esplica in tutto nel modo consueto, secondo i principii e le norme che valgono per il dominio solitario.

(*b*) All' opposto qualsiasi disposizione che si realizza con atti materiali sulla cosa, ovvero quella disposizione giuridica che per sua natura investe la cosa intera, non sono consentite ad uno dei condomini singolarmente; infatti l' agire in quel modo di un socio verrebbe a costituire una menomazione del diritto, una invadenza della sfera giuridica degli altri:

> quodammodo sibi alienum quoque ius praeripit, si quasi solus dominus ad suum arbitrium uti *iure* commune velit.[2]

Atti di questa sorta possono effettuarsi sulla cosa comune soltanto col consenso di tutti i titolari, nessuno eccettuato. Se la volontà di un solo manca, abbia pur questi nella comunione una parte minima, l' atto è illegittimo. E perciò, quando le volontà dei singoli condomini sono in disaccordo rispetto a quella data categoria di disposizioni della cosa ne deriva un conflitto di diritti, e l' effetto che segue deve di necessità essere negativo: colui che nega è poziore. Ciò è inevitabile.

Onde il principio *potior est causa prohibentis* forma precisa-

[1] *D.* x. 1, 4, 5, Paul. xxiii. ad ed. *plures dominos*; *D.* viii. 2, 26; 10; 3, 28, *nemo dominorum*.

[2] *D.* viii. 5, 11.

mente l' asse dell' istituto della *communio*; in quanto l' istituto assurge, per aspetti determinati, ad una figura particolare di diritto.

Ed il principio entra in azione, come s' è detto, tutte le volte che i titolari dei dominii non si accordano circa l' uso, il godimento, la conservazione, la destinazione della cosa, o rispetto ad atti di disposizione giuridica che colpiscono necessariamente la cosa intera. È appena necessario poi notare che quel principio stesso rappresenta pure la manifestazione più vivace ed estrema della indipendenza assoluta dei singoli condomini. Ed invero, nel disaccordo il potere dei singoli si paralizza e l' azione deve arrestarsi, perchè la risultante di più forze eguali applicate in senso contrario sullo stesso corpo non può essere che negativa : l'immobilità.

3. Tale effetto fu constatato dai giuristi più antichi. Labeone lo applica come di evidenza intuitiva ; perciò nega tra condomini la denuncia di nuova opera : *et putat Labeo non posse nuntiare, quia possum eum alia ratione prohibere aedificare.*[1]

E Proculo, citato da Paolo, asseriva già *non posse prohiberi vicinum, quo minus balineum habeat secundum parietem communem.*[2] Il giurista contemplava in questo luogo casi in cui uno dei condomini del muro avesse operato qualcosa entro i confini della sua proprietà attigua *in suo*, in maniera da non invadere la cosa comune. Per contrario si deduce che *posse prohiberi* quando l' opera o qualsiasi disposizione materiale si realizzino sulla cosa medesima.

4. Ma la dottrina dello *ius prohibendi* va particolarmente sotto il nome di Sabino, il quale la formulò in una massima celeberrima, che costituisce appunto il cardine dello istituto della comproprietà.

fr. 28 *D*. x. 3, Pap. vii. qu. Sabinus ait *in re communi neminem dominorum iure facere quicquam invito altero posse. Unde manifestum est prohibendi ius esse ; in re enim pari potiorem causam esse prohibentis constat.*

La massima propria di Sabino è riferita da Papiniano integralmente, e si contiene nel primo periodo : *Sabinus . . . posse*, come è palese per la costruzione indiretta e dai confronti che vedremo subito.

Nei periodi che seguono Papiniano enuncia : dapprima la conseguenza immediata che scaturisce da quel principio di diritto, cioè

[1] *D*. xxxix. 1, 3, 2. [2] *D*. viii. 2, 19 pr.

lo *ius prohibendi*; ingiunge poi la ragione intrinseca di tal diritto in modo positivo, vale a dire: «perchè essendo pari la condizione dei titolari dei *dominii* il diritto di veto è necessariamente poziore.» Il testo contiene così tutta la dottrina della *communio* romana: il principio di fondo, la conseguenza più diretta ed operativa, ed infine la ragione dommatica che rivela la intima essenza di tutte le norme e degli effetti specifici del condominio, e li coordina.

Il testo merita per ciò di essere annoverato tra i più cospicui usciti dalla penna del grande giurista. Papiniano vi è tutto presente, con la visione completa dell' istituto, con la sua logica temprata, che sa concatenare in modo rapido e saldo i fatti, i principii di diritto ed insieme gli effetti.[1]

5. Ora sappiamo dunque che lo *ius prohibendi* aveva costituito già il punto di partenza nella formazione della dottrina della comproprietà, e che è veramente il cardine su cui l' istituto si muove. Per ciò si riscontra in applicazioni varie negli scritti dei giureconsulti, che vanno qui considerate.

fr. 11 *D.* viii. 5, Marcell. vi. dig. . . . prohibendi potius quam faciendi esse ius socio, quia magis ille, qui facere conatur, ut dixi, quodammodo sibi alienum quoque ius praeripit, si quasi solus dominus ad suum arbitrium uti iure[2] communi velit.

Il fondamento che Marcello attribuisce qui allo *ius prohibendi* ha una direzione particolare, che verrà posta in luce più oltre; per ora dico solo che quell' elemento approssimativo espresso dal *quodammodo* non diminuisce, in confronto, la *ratio iuris* espressa da Papiniano; ma anzi la esalta, perchè Marcello giunge a considerare, in certo modo, il socio che opera senza il consenso dell' altro sulla cosa comune, come un estraneo che affronti il diritto di proprietà altrui. L' analogia è di grande rilievo, come l' effetto che ne deriva, che vedremo ben tosto.

fr. 27 *D.* viii. 2, Pomp. xxxiii. ad Sab. . . . *socius prohibendi ius habet . . . quia invito socio in iure*[3] *communi* non habeas ius aedificandi.

Qui la massima di Sabino serve di base alla decisione, ed ha la forza di una regola di diritto da cui quella conseguenza promana.

[1] Si noti per altro che la parità della posizione giuridica dei condomini è messa in evidenza da Giuliano: fr. 27 *D.* viii. 3 . . . quia par utriusque domini ius in utroque fundo esse incipit.

[2] re *Mo.*

[3] re *leg.*

Ed infine Paolo ne fa un' applicazione particolarissima in materia di servitù:

fr. 26 *D.* viii. 2, Paul. xv. ad Sab. In re communi nemo dominorum [*iure servitutis*] neque facere quicquam invito altero potest neque prohibere quo minus alter faciat; nulli enim res sua servit.

Nella prima parte la formula di Paolo combacia perfettamente con quella di Papiniano; essa è dunque tratta alla lettera dall' opera di Sabino. Ma vi è tuttavia una differenza rimarchevole che si manifesta subitamente per la parola *servitutis* incuneata nella formulazione di Sabino, e che viene a limitare inaspettatamente ed in maniera essenziale la forza e la estensione della regola medesima.

Secondo Sabino il socio può nulla fare sulla cosa comune senza il consenso degli altri; e ciò *iure* = per diritto, e non già *iure servitutis.*

Tra l' una cosa e l' altra, come ognun vede, la distanza è enorme. Non si tratta di semplice proporzione, come di cose che stanno fra loro nel rapporto del generale al particolare, ma di enunciazioni sostanzialmente diverse. Quella che si legge nel testo di Paolo è falsa; perchè il socio può mai operare sul fondo comune *iure servitutis*, nemmeno col consenso dell' altro. Infatti l' ostacolo alla servitù è nel potere di dominio che egli ha sulla cosa comune, e non già nel divieto del socio.

Questo principio, che peraltro discende dalla struttura del condominio romano, è messo in evidenza da Giavoleno, il quale nega tra socii la possibilità dell' *actio negatoria*, appunto perchè quel che è comune appartiene a ciascuno dei compartecipi di pieno diritto: *nam quod communiter socius habet et in iure*[1] *eum habere constitit.*

Per la stessa ragione non è possibile la costituzione di servitù tra due fondi, dei quali uno sia comune e l' altro di proprietà esclusiva di uno dei socii.[2]

[1] fr. 4 *D.* xxxiii. 3, Jav. ix. ep. La preposizione *in* è nel brano riferito sicuramente inopportuna; Mommsen corregge: *item iure me habere*, ma l' emendazione è arbitraria e nel risultato banale; io proporrei: *pleno iure* [*domini iure?*] *eum habere*; cfr. *D.* x. 1, 4, 7; xi. 3, 14, 2 . . . *perinde atque si proprius meus servus cet*; *D.* xlvii. 10, 15, 36 . . . *cum iure domini id fecerit.*

[2] Cfr. 32 *D.* viii. 3, Afric. vi. quaest.

E nelle stesse condizioni di fatto è esclusa l' *actio finium regundorum* perchè *ego et socius meus . . . unius loco habemur.*[1]

E perciò la frase *invito socio,* che è essenziale nella formula di Sabino, respinge con fermezza qualsiasi riferimento alla *servitus.* E tuttavia non bisogna supporre una grave alterazione del testo, dacchè io credo si possa rimettere in ordine con un semplice spostamento della parola *servitutis,* che deve avere piuttosto la sua collocazione nel secondo membro del periodo, come segue:

*In re communi nemo dominorum neque facere* [*iure*] *quicquam invito altero potest neque prohibere* [*iure servitutis*] *quo minus alter faciat: nulli enim res sua servit.*

Paolo, dunque, metteva in relazione la massima di Sabino con la dottrina delle servitù, e ciò in modo veramente opportuno, perchè egli trattava in quel luogo *de servitutibus,*[2] ed intendeva precipuamente far notare che il socio nemmeno ha facoltà di proibire *iure servitutis quo minus alter faciat.*

La ragione è manifesta; chè avendo ciascuno dei condomini un pieno diritto sulla cosa, tra i medesimi non vi è possibilità di esercizio o pretesa di servitù, e di conseguenza è preclusa la via allo esperimento dell' *actio negatoria*: *nulli res sua servit.* Questo punto di diritto, per altro, ci è noto dal passo di Giavoleno sopra riferito, e da altri testi classici che verranno subito in esame; esso fu posto in grande evidenza da Cuiacio, che interpretò rettamente il fr. in esame, senza proporne l' emendamento.[3]

I moderni hanno avvertito le difficoltà del passo, ma non le hanno superate. Se poi la dislocazione della frase *iure servitutis* debba attribuirsi a svista di amanuensi ovvero all' opera dei compilatori è cosa che non posso giudicare.

Certo molti argomenti rendono più verisimile la seconda ipotesi; infatti il lettore troverà più oltre prove sufficienti per convincersi che Giustiniano si adoprò deliberatamente a stremare in tutti i modi la regola di Sabino, che affermava nella maniera più recisa la indipendenza dei singoli condomini rispetto alla cosa comune, e che inoltre egli trasformò lo ius prohibendi in un' azione giudiziaria.

6. E lo *ius prohibendi* si determina ora con precisione. Esso

[1] *D.* x. 1, 4, 7.

[2] Cfr. Lenel, *Pal.* i. c. 1289.

[3] Cfr. *Opp.* vol. vii. p. 676 ad l. 27 (8-2); ibid. p. 674 ad l. 26 eod.; ibid. p. 737 ad l. 11 (8-5); ibid. p. 945 e, p. 2223 ad l. 4, *D.* xxxiii. 3.

scaturisce, come conseguenza ineluttabile, dalla posizione pari dei condomini. È un effetto naturale del dominio posto in quella particolare situazione; e perciò è enunciato come un diritto fondamentale e caratteristico, che entra in azione tutte le volte che l' accordo tra i condomini si rompe.

*Prohibere* non s' intende nel senso che al socio competa l' *actio negatoria* o *prohibitoria* contro l' altro. Ma significa, invece, che ciascuno dei socii può direttamente impedire con la forza, di sua autorità, l' opera o qualsiasi azione sulla cosa intrapresa dall' altro. Tale significato è fuori dubbio. Marcello contrappone *prohibere* a *facere*, ed i due termini si rapportano sicuramente all' ingerenza materiale, che è positivamente (*facere*) inibita a ciascuno dei socii ove manchi il consenso degli altri; ed è invece negativamente (*prohibere*) permessa a ciascuno per impedire qualsiasi uso della cosa contro la sua volontà. Ma il passo di Marcello subì una grave mutilazione ed è nei *Digesti* del seguente tenore:

fr. 11 *D.* viii. 5, Marc. vi. dig. An unus ex sociis in communi loco invitis ceteris iure aedificare possit, id est an, si prohibeatur a sociis, possit cum his ita experiri ius sibi esse aedificare, et an socii cum eo ita agere possint ius sibi prohibendi esse vel illi ius aedificandi non esse: et si aedificatum iam sit, num possint[1] cum eo ita experiri ius tibi non esse ita aedificatum habere, quaeritur [*et magis dici potest*][2] prohibendi potius quam faciendi esse ius socio, quia magis ille, qui facere conatur, ut dixi, quodammodo sibi alienum quoque

---

[1] *num possint* Hal.; *non possit* F.

[2] La frase *et magis dici potest* è interpolatizia, inserita dai compilatori per sopprimere la più estesa dimostrazione di Marcello. Sospetta è la frase per sè stessa, che ritorna in molti testi rimaneggiati da Triboniano (*magis* infinite volte; *potest dici* qualche volta; cfr. *D.* xlvii. 2, 9, 1; *D.* ix. 4, 19 pr.) inoltre, a breve distanza, s' incontra di nuovo *magis* che era nel testo genuino, e l' espressione *ut dixi* non ha più riscontro nel passo dei *Digesti*, mentre Marcello ricollegava così la decisione alla argomentazione più ampia (*quaeritur*) che precedeva.

Anche il Lenel (*ZSS.* vol. xii. p. 12) osservò con il solito acume la diminuzione del testo operata dai compilatori, ma non la precisa, e perciò nell' interpretazione tien conto degli elementi che vi si leggono, concludendo che Marcello ammetteva l' *actio prohibitoria* e non la *negatoria*. Di ciò più oltre.

Non ha invece fondamento il sospetto da Beseler (*Beiträge*, i. p. 79, 1) manifestato sul periodo: *id est . . . habere*; perchè, in verità, il giurista aveva posto quesiti fondamentali che si presentavano naturalmente in una trattazione larga della dottrina.

Ed è ovvio che tutte quelle formule rassegnate da Marcello rappresentavano ius praeripit, si quasi solus dominus ad suum arbitrium uti iure[1] communi velit.

Marcello aveva dovuto negare recisamente la possibilità di qualsiasi azione tra i socii a titolo di servitù, come l' aveva negato Giavoleno; ed aveva dovuto invece ammettere il diritto del socio ad impedire l' opera comechesia, nel senso che ho dichiarato di sopra. La motivazione di Marcello, sopravvissuta nel testo, acquista così il suo giusto valore e perfetta proporzione; perchè essa è indirizzata a giustificare la violenza privata contro il socio che disponendo della cosa a suo arbitrio: *sibi alienum quoque ius praeripit.* Nè può sorprendere in questo luogo la legittimazione della privata difesa; avvegnachè il diritto di ciascuno dei socii d' impedire con la forza qualsiasi ingerenza o di distruggere l' opera eseguita sulla cosa comune, senza preventivo accordo, deriva dal potere essenziale di dominio che ciascuno ha sulla medesima. Il proprietario non è tenuto a tollerare che altri faccia *in suo* alcunchè contro il suo volere; piuttosto egli può distruggere l' opera di sua autorità: *iure suo posse eum intercidere, et merito, . . . quod hic in suo protexit.*[2]

Questo principio non soffre restrizione nel condominio; precisamente per il motivo che i condomini sono tutti *in pari causa* ed indipendenti l' uno dall' altro. E siffatta conseguenza era probabilmente affermata da Pomponio nel fr. 27 *D.* viii. 2, con la frase *rem perdere*, ove le si attribuisca il valore che le diedero gl' interpreti fin dalla Glossa, cioè che il socio possa *opus sua auctoritate destruere* quando il condomino agisca senza il suo consenso; la quale frase perciò deve essere genuina, nel testo rifatto largamente dai compilatori.[3]

7. Onde i Romani, considerando lo stato di anarchia in cui i socii si trovavano rispetto all' uso ed al godimento della cosa, poterono dire che la *communio* è *mater rixarum*, e constatare, di

---

varii attegiamenti dell' *a. negatoria* secondo le diverse ipotesi. Nè la parola *prohibere* inclusa in quelle formule ha un valore speciale:

cfr. *D.* viii. 5, 8, 5: *prohiberi posse fumum immittere . . . agique sic posse . . . ius ei non esse fumum immittere.*

[1] re *scr.*

[2] fr. 29 § 1 *D.* ix. 2.

[3] Per l' esame di questo passo v. cap. ii. n. 29, p. 61.

conseguenza, ogni giorno che *propter immensas contentiones plerumque res ad divisionem pervenit.*[1]

E questa affermazione è vera nella sua interezza, per la stessa struttura del condominio e per le attestazioni concordi degli antichi;[2] comunque, per altro, il periodo che la contiene possa essere stato rimosso o ricollegato dai compilatori.

8. Affermato così il punto centrale della dottrina del condominio è agevole ora procedere all' esame di tutte le conseguenze giuridiche che ne derivano, che debbono per ciò stesso manifestarsi chiare ed incontestabili.

La posizione dei socii nella comunione è, come s' è visto, determinata sempre dai principii fondamentali del dominio, senza attenuazione o modificazione di sorta. Nei particolari ciò si dimostra mirabilmente con un rapido esame degli effetti giuridici che scaturiscono dallo stato di comproprietà, sotto l' aspetto positivo e negativo; e cioè:

(*a*) in ordine alla disposizione giuridica della cosa comune, che compete a ciascuno dei socii.

(*b*) in ordine agli atti di disposizione materiale della cosa, che non possono attuarsi senza il concorso di tutti i compartecipi. In questa categoria va pure annoverata qualsiasi disposizione giuridica che investe di necessità la cosa intera, come avviene per le servitù attive o passive.

9. Rispetto al primo punto è certo che ognuno dei comproprietarii può esercitare tutte le facoltà di disposizione giuridica del dominio con la massima indipendenza. Ciascuno quindi può vendere,[3] donare, sottoporre ad ipoteca,[4] costituire usufrutto, dare in dote,[5] disporre per testamento o altrimenti alienare la cosa, in proporzione della parte che gli spetta, senza attendere il consenso dei socii, e senza che una qualsiasi ingerenza di essi sia ammessa.[6] L' atto dispositivo dell' alienante ha naturalmente efficacia reale solo nel limite del diritto che effettivamente gli compete sulla cosa comune.

[1] fr. 26 *D.* viii. 2.

[2] fr. 77 § 20 *D.* xxxi. . . . *cum discordiis propinquorum sedandis prospexerit, quas materia communionis solet excitare.*

[3] *Cod.* iv. 52, 3 (*Diocl. et Max.*); c. 4 e 5 eod.; *D.* x. 2, 44, 2.

[4] *D.* x. 3, 6, 9; xx. 4, 3, 2; xx. 6, 7, 4.

[5] *Cod.* v. 12, 16 (*Diocl. et Max.*).

[6] *D.* l. 17, 26; cfr. Lenel, *Pal.* Ulp. n. 2748; *Cod.* iv. 52, 3.

Tale conseguenza è affermata da Papiniano per la vendita come per l' ipoteca disposta dal condomino.

Il passo che si riferisce alla vendita è alquanto oscuro rispetto agli elementi di fatto, che furono certamente ridotti dai compilatori; ma per quel che concerne il punto in esame il testo è sicuro e di grande significazione.

Nei *Digesti* è così riferito :

fr. 64 § 4 *D.* xxi. 2, Pap. vii. 9. Qui unum iugerum pro indiviso solum habuit, tradidit : *secundum omnium sententias non totum dominium transtulit, sed partem dimidiam iugeri, quemadmodum si locum certum aut fundum similiter tradidisset.*[1]

L' alienazione per ciò ha efficacia solo per la parte che il socio ha nella comunione.[2] E lo stesso vale per l' ipoteca ; onde Papiniano con una fine argomentazione ne deduce che si possono avere su di una parte d' un fondo ipoteche non concorrenti ; cioè l' una costituita durante la comunione, che graverà, dopo la divisione, sulle parti *pro diviso*, in ragione di metà : e l' altra costituita per garanzia in favore del socio, nell' atto divisorio, che investe l' altra metà : *sed priorem*

[1] Nel passo la *traditio* fu sostituita alla *mancipatio* (Lenel, *Pal.* ad h. l.); ma i compilatori soppressero inoltre molti elementi nella relazione del fatto, che era certamente più complicato. Così il *solum*, aggettivo o avverbio che sia, restò nel passo senza alcun significato ; ed invero che importa ciò nel trasferimento per *manc.* di cosa determinata ? Ma il *similiter tradid.*, poi, rivela che il giureconsulto aveva riferito avanti una speciale clausola della mancipatio.

Io suppongo che in un fondo di Tizio era stato legato un solo iugero a due conliberti senza designazione della regione, e che uno dei legatarii mancipò l' intero ingero che era *pro indiviso* nel fondo di Tizio.

Papin. potè scrivere :

*Qui unum iugerum pro indiviso solum [in fundo Titii commune cum Simplici conliberto habuit mancipio dedit Seio hac formula : unum iugerum quod est in praedio Titii pro indiviso] cet.*

Si spiegherebbe allora l' avv. *similiter* che presuppone un' analogia di specie che Papiniano usa altre volte, ed inoltre il confronto con il *locus certus* o *fundus*. Nel caso esaminato da Papiniano si doveva trattare di *locus* indeterminato :

cfr. *D.* l. 16, 60 : *locus est . . . portio aliqua fundi . . .* § 2 . . . *locus vero latere potest quatenus determinetur et definiatur.* La *mancipatio* di *pars pro indiviso* doveva del resto essere frequente nella comunicazione di fondi *societatis causa*, cfr. Riccobono, *Traditio ficta*, c. iii.

E quindi errava Cuiacio (*Opp.* iv. p. 795 ad h. l.) supponendo che la *traditio* fosse avvenuta nel testo in esame mediante la semplice consegna dei titoli di proprietà, in base all' erroneo concetto che non fosse possibile tradizione corporale di *pars pro indiviso*.

[2] fr. 68 *D.* xvii. 2.

*secundo non esse potiorem, quoniam secundum pignus ad eam partem directum videbatur, quam ultra partem suam frater non consentiente socio non potuit obligare.*[1]

E parimenti i frutti del fondo spettano a ciascuno dei soci *iure soli*, in proporzione della parte di dominio che risulta dalla concorrenza dei diritti degli altri: *ita qui communem fundum possidet, non faciet suos fructus pro ea parte, qua fundus ad socium eius pertinebit.*[2] La stessa attribuzione vien fatta per gli incrementi del fondo.[3]

Il quale principio assume poi una grande importanza nella comunione di schiavi, dacchè conduce alla regola generale che gli acquisti dello schiavo comune, anche se fatti *ex re alterius dominorum*, vanno attribuiti, per lo meno quanto alla forma, a tutti i socii *pro parte dominii.*[4] Effetti cotesti ben congrui e proporzionati alla struttura del condominio, e per ciò sotto ogni riguardo necessarii ed inderogabili; avvegnachè, se, come si esprime Papiniano,[5] i condomini hanno sulla cosa una posizione pari, ne deriva per necessità imprescindibile che ciascuno dei titolari non può avere una facoltà di disposizione al di là della sua parte, e ciascuno non può far suoi i frutti, o pretendere dagli acquisti a mezzo di schiavi, che una parte corrispondente a quella *ex qua dominus est.* Nè vi è ragione per ciò di concepire il condominio romano come un concorso di proprietà parziali sulla cosa medesima; perchè cotali effetti si coordinano con perfetta misura al concetto della comproprietà integrale; in cui ciascuno dei titolari incontra un limite insuperabile nel diritto concorrente degli altri. Onde necessariamente tutte le facoltà del dominio si riducono entro quel limite in cui esso è in realtà ristretto, a causa del concorso degli altri diritti.

Il che vuol dire, che la posizione pari dei condomini rispetto al diritto sulla cosa, è poi immanente in tutti gli effetti giuridici proprii del dominio. E così deve essere. Un' affermazione

[1] fr. 3 § 2 *D.* xx. 4, Pap. xi. resp.; cfr. Gai in *D.* xx. 6, 7, 4: . . . *divisione facta cum socio non utique eam partem creditori obligatam esse, quae ei optingit, qui pignori dedit, sed utriusque pars pro indiviso pro parte dimidia manebit obligata.*

[2] fr. 25 pr. *D.* xxii. 1 Jul. vii. dig.

[3] fr. 4 § 5 *D.* x. 1 *unusquisque portionem habebit quam in fundo habet et pro indiviso.*

[4] *D.* xli. 1, 45, Gai vii. ad ed. pr.; *D.* x. 3, 24, pr. Jul. viii. dig.

[5] *D.* x. 3, 28.

diversa non avrebbe che un valore metafisico, contrario alla natura ed alla forza del diritto.

10. E per altro se la struttura del condominio si manifesta così limpida, osservata dal lato positivo, cioè rispetto alle facoltà che ciascuno dei titolari può esercitare in modo indipendente dagli altri, e che dai giureconsulti romani sono ammesse con tutta naturalezza; essa deve poi mostrarsi in maggior rilievo, esplorata nelle sue manifestazioni negative, che rivelano appunto la impossibilità di qualsiasi regolamento obbiettivo della comunione, in ordine agli atti dispositivi sulla cosa. I quali, come la natura della proprietà esige, in qualsiasi contingenza, dipendono unicamente dalla volontà unanime dei compartecipi. In contrapposto agli atti di disposizione giuridica compiuti dal condomino, che mai possono ledere il diritto degli altri, sotto il secondo aspetto si contemplano, in primo luogo, gli atti materiali sulla cosa comune, i quali per la loro natura, necessariamente, invadono in una volta il diritto dei socii. Per ciò essi sono inibiti ai singoli compartecipi in modo assoluto. Onde qui entra in azione e spiega la sua forza la regola di Sabino: *in re communi neminem dominorum iure facere quicquam invito altero posse.*[1] Il verbo *facere* si riferisce appunto a tutti gli atti materiali. E da ciò segue, che nessuno dei socii può di propria iniziativa usare la cosa, coltivare il fondo o eseguirvi miglioramenti, costruzioni o in generale opere nuove, nemmeno semplicemente conservative, senza il consenso di tutti i condomini.

Nè giova distinguere qui tra gli atti che sono rivolti ad un uso normale della cosa, conforme alla sua destinazione, e gli atti che esorbitano da questo limite e che importano un utilizzamento difforme o contrario alla destinazione della medesima.

La distinzione non può aver luogo; perchè il divieto del *facere*, qualunque esso sia, deriva dalla forza del diritto degli altri, e per ciò è assoluto, ed ha nulla che vedere con la natura dell' uso e la specie degli atti.

E pertanto, come la volontà unanime dei socii è necessaria per abbattere o riedificare un muro o parte di un edificio, così pure le riparazioni necessarie ai muri ed agli edificii comuni esigono il volere concorde di tutti.[2] A nessuno quindi è consentito fare uso del muro comune o utilizzarlo in qualsiasi modo, come appoggiandovi fabbriche o scale o tubi per la condotta delle acque.

[1] fr. 26 *D.* viii. 2; fr. 28 *D.* x. 3.

[2] *D.* viii. 2, 8, Gai vii. ad ed.

11. Su questo punto però è bene fermarsi; perchè fin dalla Glossa si asserisce il contrario, particolarmente rispetto a determinati utilizzamenti della parete comune, non che per le opere riparative degli edificii. La quale affermazione è esatta ove si abbia riguardo al diritto giustinianeo, come vedremo più oltre; ma per il diritto classico, invece, è sicuramente falsa.

Infatti se in frammenti notissimi dei giuristi romani si permette al condomino di tenere il bagno dappresso la parete comune, o di costruire una camera o una scala addossata alla stessa, in tutte quelle decisioni è presupposto che egli deve eseguire le opere entro i limiti della sua proprietà esclusiva; e non solo che il bagno, la camera o la scala non debbono recar danno al muro, ma che debbono inoltre stare del tutto indipendenti da esso. I testi cui alludevo sono lucidissimi in questo senso, e si esprimono nel modo seguente:

fr. 19 *D.* viii. 2, Paul. vii. ad Sab. Fistulam iunctam parieti communi, quae aut ex castello aut ex coelo aquam capit, non iure haberi Proculus ait; sed non posse prohiberi vicinum, quo minus balineum habeat secundum parietem communem, quamvis humorem capiat paries; non magis quam si vel in triclinio suo vel in cubiculo aquam effunderet. Sed Neratius ait, si talis sit usus tepidarii ut assiduum humorem habeat, et id noceat vicino, posse prohiberi eum.

§ 1. Iuxta communem parietem cameram ex figlino opere factam, si ita retineatur, ut etiam sublato pariete maneat [*si modo non impediat refectionem communis parietis*], iure habere licet.

§ 2. Scalas posse me ad parietem communem habere, Sabinus recte scribit, quia removeri hae possunt.

Tutti i giuristi, come si vede, sono concordi nell' enunciare condizioni di fatto tali che escludono l' uso del muro comune a sostegno di quelle opere o impianti; che son fatti bensì *iuxta*, *secundum parietem*, cioè addossati al muro ma non sostenuti da esso. Il muro comune è dunque fuori quistione; tanto è vero che si esige pure che la costruzione *etiam sublato pariete maneat*.[1]

Nello stesso senso è diretta la argomentazione di Proculo rispetto al bagno: egli dice, giustamente, che non è sufficiente motivo

[1] E per ciò l' inciso '*si modo non impediat refectionem communis parietis*' è evidentemente interpolatizio; perchè la condizione enunciata dal giurista è già assorbente. Indizii della interpolazione: *si modo* — la superflua ripetizione del sostantivo: *communis parietis*, che precede immediatamente. La ragione dell' inciso verrà in evidenza nel c. ii. n. 47.

d' impedire al socio di tenere il bagno addossato alla parete il fatto che vi si comunica l' umidità ; perchè ciò avviene pure nel lavare il pavimento del triclinio o del cubiculo versandovi l' acqua a getto.

Da ciò si desume che in tutti quei casi presi in esame la parete comune non è adibita a sostegno delle opere. Il presupposto essenziale è questo appunto. Se ciò non è, in fatto, interviene il divieto. Così nel caso di tubi infissi al muro per lo scarico delle acque piovane o dal castello, o di appoggio di una fabbrica.[1]

Ma il divieto poi di tenere un forno applicato alla parete comune[2] o caloriferi ha un' altra ragione più generale, il danno cioè che ne viene alla fabbrica dal continuo calore o dalla fiamma. E Proculo fa notare precisamente la distinzione tra i due casi, con le parole : *de tubulis eo amplius hoc iuris est, quod per eos flamma torretur paries.*[3]

È evidente, dunque, che il richiamo di quei passi è erroneo ; e che in essi non può trovar appoggio quell' antica dottrina che consente al socio l' uso normale della cosa comune, secondo la sua destinazione.[4] E soggiungo che tale dottrina nemmeno si giustifica, per quanto attiene al diritto classico, invocando la facoltà che ha il condomino di abbellire con pitture o stucchi la parete comune ; perchè se è lo stesso Proculo[5] che ammette ciò, egli non poteva contradirsi ; mentre a togliere qualsiasi valore alla decisione per la dottrina in esame della destinazione, basta osservare che le pareti non si costruiscono per le pitture o per gli stucchi, nè quando vi si eseguano può dirsi che si faccia un uso normale della cosa. La permissione deve avere perciò altri motivi ; e cioè in primo luogo quello che le pitture e gli stucchi non toccano e non ledono la sostanza della cosa comune ; ed inoltre poi la considerazione che le esigenze del diritto non vengono mai a porsi in contrasto col buon senso, come verrebbero a trovarsi vietando al condomino di tenere la parete decorosa o di spazzar via i ragnateli dalla medesima, senza il consenso degli altri.[6]

12. Dopo tutto resta la sola quistione delle riparazioni agli

[1] *D.* viii. 2, 13 pr.
[2] *D.* ix. 2, 27, 10.
[3] *D.* viii. 2, 13 pr.
[4] Cfr. p. es. Ferrini, *Pand.* p. 450.
[5] *D.* viii. 2, 13, 1.
[6] Ma pur troppo il diritto è trascinato spesso non solo in contrasto col buon senso ma pure in situazioni ridicole, come avviene oggi presso di noi con la ormai famosa iscrizione d' ufficio del Re nelle liste elettorali politiche.

edificii e muri comuni, che è in realtà assai intricata. Ma l' esame più largo di essa deve essere rimandato al c. ii., appunto perchè le interpolazioni giustinianee sono in questa materia emergenti nel *Corpus Iuris.*

Or per quel che concerne il diritto classico abbiamo due dati certi per ritenere anche in questo punto di diritto il vigore della regola di Sabino.

In primo luogo il passo di Gaio, più volte richiamato, che attesta nella maniera più esplicita per il muro comune *alterutri . . . reficiendi ius non esse.*[1] E poi il Senato consulto provocato da M. Aurelio, che concedette ai singoli condomini, che avessero eseguite le riparazioni necessarie agli edificii, il diritto di esigere in proporzione la spesa erogata entro 4 mesi con gl' interessi, e, nel caso di mora dei socii al pagamento o di rifiuto, l' acquisto della proprietà delle parti dell' edificio loro spettanti. Soltanto queste disposizioni attribuiscono le fonti[2] alla *Oratio* di M. Aurelio; ma essa doveva contenere certamente, come premessa, l' obbligo rivolto ai singoli condomini di tenere in ordine gli edificii, ai fini principalmente della loro stabilità.

L' occasione a tali provvedimenti potè essere apprestata dalla inondazione del Tevere, che, giusto in quel tempo, fu spaventevole e che a dire di Capitolino[3] *multa urbis aedificia vexavit et plurimum animalium interemit et famem gravissimam peperit.*

Del resto è nota la cura somma degli Imperatori e del Senato[4] per il decoro edilizio della Città, che diede luogo a disposizioni gravissime limitatrici della proprietà, che furono estese pure alle Provincie[5] e severamente custodite. E pertanto il provvedimento legislativo di carattere eccezionale conferma, come a me sembra, la regola dello *ius civile*, quale è riferita da Gaio; nel senso che ai

[1] *D.* viii. 2, 8.

[2] *D.* xvii. 2, 52, 10 (Ulp.-Papin.); *Cod.* viii. 10, 4 (Philipp. a. 245); Harmenopulo, *Exab.* x. 3, 27.—Male Cuiacio, *Opp.* iv. p. 785 ad l. 28 *D.* x. 3 spiega pure con la *Oratio divi Marci* la l. 32 *D.* xxxix. 2. Cf. c. ii. n. Nelle *Leges saeculares* (L. 98 ed. Ferrini) le disposizioni del SC. sono applicate pure ai proprietarii dei diversi piani di una casa, essendo, come ora sappiamo, nelle provincie orientali ammessa la proprietà divisa dei piani di un edificio; cfr. Wenger, *ZSS.* v. 32, p. 334; ma v. Partsch, *Archiv Pap.* v. p. 496.

[3] *Hist. M. Ant. Philoph.* 8.

[4] Cfr. Riccobono, *Fontes*, p. 233.

[5] Cfr. *Epistula Hadriani ad Stratonicenses Hadrianopolitas* (Riccobono, *Fontes*, p. 325 ed ivi citati).

singoli condomini non è data facoltà di provvedere alle riparazioni necessarie agli edificii, senza il concorso della volontà degli altri. Mentre, d' altro lato, può ben dirsi che la disposizione del Senato non venne qui ad alterare nessun principio fondamentale dell' istituto della comproprietà; avvegnachè il singolo condomino, se può e deve ora eseguire le riparazioni agli edificii cadenti, ciò facendo non esercita una facoltà di dominio, ma adempie piuttosto un precetto d' indole amministrativa, munito perciò di speciale sanzione.

13. Onde per quel che riguarda il *facere* possiamo conchiudere che le applicazioni della regola di Sabino sono tutte concordanti nello stesso senso, come dovevano essere; perchè la materia non poteva qui offrire occasione a dubbii e controversie, trattandosi di deduzioni semplici ed incontrovertibili dei principii fondamentali del dominio.[1]

Infatti, se la condizione dei singoli compartecipi è pari in diritto, qualsiasi atto compiuto nella cosa da uno o dai più contro la volontà di altri costituisce certamente una menomazione del diritto di questi ultimi, un' invadenza della loro sfera giuridica. Ma, d' altro lato, non vi è ragione nè posto per ammettere la prevalenza della volontà di uno sull' altro, o anche dei più contro uno. Perchè, essendo tutti *domini*, ciascuno può disporre della cosa come vuole; e qualunque cosa voglia non può essere soggetta a contraddizione.

E perciò l' effetto deve essere negativo; colui che nega è poziore, nel senso che qualsiasi disposizione materiale della cosa comune viene ad essere impedita. E così è vero, negativamente, che nessuno può disporre di fatto della cosa a suo talento, per l' energia del diritto pari degli altri; come è pur vero, in senso positivo, che ciascuno ha il potere d' impedire con la forza il tentativo del socio che voglia far prevalere la sua volontà operando sulla cosa; perchè questi allora *quodammodo sibi alienum quoque ius praeripit, si quasi solus dominus ad suum arbitrium uti* [*re*] *communi velit*.

[1] Nella presente trattazione non sono considerati i casi di comunione di sepolcri e le facoltà di seppellire nel luogo puro comune; perchè in questa materia le innovazioni di Giustiniano sono ancora più profonde e determinate da l' idea prettamente religiosa. Onde mi parve necessario dedicare all' argomento un lavoro speciale. E per altro, per quel che qui interessa, è fuori dubbio che nel diritto classico il condomino non ha facoltà di far religioso il luogo puro introducendovi il cadavere; cfr. *D.* xi. 7, 41, che del resto è interpolato nella seconda parte: *cum extranei* . . *sepeliretur*; e *D.* x. 3, 6, 6.

14. E la posizione è identica e quindi identico lo effetto, quando per via di atti giuridici la disposizione di uno dei socii investe di necessità la cosa intera; perchè anche in questo caso si determina un conflitto tra i molteplici dominii come in seguito al *facere*; e perciò il potere del singolo socio deve arrestarsi.

Nessuno dei socii può quindi acquistare al fondo una servitù, per quanto ne sia evidente il vantaggio o la necessità;[1] e nessuno può singolarmente gravare il fondo di servitù.[2]

Nell' uno e nell' altro caso si richiede il *consensus omnium*, o, per meglio dire, quell' atto dispositivo congruo a costituire la servitù, che può essere simultaneo ovvero successivo da parte dei singoli.[3]

La denunzia di nuova opera rispetto al fondo comune può essere attiva o passiva; e cioè da parte dei condomini a causa di opera eseguita in alieno e che invade il fondo o ne minaccia in modo qualsiasi la libertà o la consistenza fisica; ovvero, dal lato passivo, contro i condomini per opera che s' inizia sul fondo comune.

Ma in ambo i casi gli effetti giuridici si riflettono su tutti i condomini solo quando vi sia il consenso di tutti.[4] Ove tale consenso non vi sia per la denunzia, o nel caso inverso per l' opera, la responsabilità incombe solo all' autore della denunzia; nel secondo caso a chi iniziò l' opera sul fondo.[5] E pari è la decisione intorno alla *cautio damni infecti*, nei casi in cui ha luogo.[6]

Abbiamo qui dunque esempii perspicui per dimostrare che il principio della indipendenza dei socii è inalterabile nella comunione, e che il diritto romano in nessun caso pervenne a riconoscere la facoltà di un socio di rappresentare gli altri, per garentire l' interesse comune o per la responsabilità di fronte ai terzi. Nè questa affermazione resta infirmata dal fatto che ciascuno dei condomini ha potere di rivendicare *in solidum* la servitù dovuta al fondo[7] o di assicurare con l' esercizio l' esistenza della medesima,[8] perchè cotali effetti,

[1] *D.* viii. 3, 19.

[2] *D.* xxxix. 3, 10 pr. *omnium voluntatem esse sequendam*; *D.* viii. 1, 2; *D.* xxi. 2, 10.

[3] *D.* viii. 3, 11, per altro interpolato.

[4] *D.* xxxix. 1, 18, Pap. 3 qu. *si . . . ex voluntate omnium opus fiat.* 5 § 6 *D.* eod.

[5] fr. 18 *D.* xxxix. 1 *in solidum obligabitur.*

[6] *D.* x. 3, 6, 7 *necesse tibi non fuerit in solidum cavere, sed sufficere pro parte tua.*

[7] *D.* viii. 5, 4, 3 [*itaque . . . possit*]. *Trib.* conf. Eisele, *ZSS.* xxx. p. 120.

[8] *D.* viii. 6, 16.

come è ovvio, dipendono unicamente dalla natura della servitù, che è per sè stessa indivisibile, e quindi non si può nè acquistare nè rivendicare nè perdere *pro parte*.[1]

15. Sono disegnati così i lineamenti essenziali, cioè quelli che appariscono i soli necessarii a rappresentare la struttura più rilevata e caratteristica dell' istituto del condominio, secondo i classici. Essi ci hanno rivelato che i singoli hanno sulla cosa comune un vero e pieno diritto di proprietà, e che questo diritto si comporta del tutto con la stessa forza e la stessa energia come nella proprietà unica, secondo i principii del diritto quiritario; per cui il domino ovvero i condomini hanno sulla cosa un potere assoluto che esercitano con la massima indipendenza in qualsiasi momento e situazione. Le conseguenze di questa posizione sono evidenti e note. Le facoltà di disposizione giuridica restano illimitate nei singoli condomini. Ma l' uso ed il godimento della cosa non può aver luogo che mediante l' accordo di tutti, per ogni singolo atto ed in ogni momento.

Quando quest' accordo non si raggiunga la comunione si paralizza subitamente. Si tratta pertanto di un rapporto senza disciplina e senza regolamento di sorta, ed in questo senso addirittura anarchico; in cui il sistema individualistico romano si manifesta in tutta la sua potenza.

Il risultato è sicuramente antieconomico ed antisociale, ma non in modo diverso che tutto l' ordinamento della proprietà. E perciò non è a pensare che i Romani abbiano avvertito le durezze del loro sistema di comproprietà; di certo non tentarono mai di apportarvi alcuna mitigazione, chè, come s' è visto, applicarono sempre il principio di fondo con tutte le conseguenze sopra rilevate, con la logica più perfetta ed inesorabile.

16. Quando il disaccordo si manifesta tra i socii, in ordine all' esercizio delle facoltà di dominio sulla cosa, vuoi per la maniera o la distribuzione del godimento, vuoi per la condotta di uno pregiudizievole agli interessi degli altri o semplicemente alla volontà degli altri, non vi ha nessun mezzo e nessuna azione che intervenga a comporre il dissidio, che rimetta l' ordine, che costringa l' uno o gli altri a consentire od agire in modo ragionevole e vantaggioso per l' interesse comune; ovvero che possa impedire l' abuso o il danneggiamento della cosa. Preminente, sempre, resta il principio:

[1] *D.* viii. 1, 11.

*potior est condicio prohibentis*, lo stato cioè d' inazione, di paralisi. E *potior* s' intende *iure*; per ciò in qualsiasi evenienza, al di sopra di qualsiasi interesse, vantaggio o danno dei singoli cointeressati.

17. E la paralisi può risolversi soltanto con un mezzo energico e definitivo, cioè con lo scioglimento della comunione.

Per ciò ciascuno dei socii può chiedere la divisione mediante l' *actio communi dividundo* in qualsiasi momento.[1] Ed a questo diritto non si ammette rinunzia. Ma di più i giureconsulti con esitanza, come pare, riconobbero la validità del pactum *ne intra certum tempus dividatur*.[2] Il motivo ne era evidente. Dacchè il patto di non dividere, anche limitato nel tempo, non poteva avere efficacia reale, e se in un modo qualsiasi si fosse potuto consentire siffatto valore, esso avrebbe arrecato una limitazione essenziale al diritto assoluto ed alla indipendenza dei condomini.

Giustiniano, s' intende, superò la barriera facilmente accordando alla convenzione efficacia reale.[3]

In questo punto però, giova rilevarlo, anche la giurisprudenza classica aveva ammesso un' eccezione al principio dell' assoluta libertà dello scioglimento della comunione in qualsiasi momento e per volontà di un solo; cioè rispetto al vestibolo comune, che non può essere dedotto nel giudizio divisorio invito altero:

fr. 19 § 1 *D*. x. 3, Paul. vi. ad Sab. De vestibulo communi binarum aedium arbiter communi dividundo invito utrolibet dari non debet, quia qui de vestibulo liceri cogatur, necesse habeat interdum totarum aedium pretium facere, si alias aditum non habeat.

Come si vede il motivo è di quelli che rompono qualsiasi teoria, sia pure costruita su basi di granito, quale era quella romana della comproprietà.[4]

18. Raccogliamo ora i fili sparsi in questo breve saggio. E la prima constatazione che emerge spontanea dall' insieme ci mostra l' istituto del condominio rigorosamente costruito sui principii della proprietà solitaria, senza alcuna attenuazione. Così gli effetti giuridici di sopra descritti sono tutti normali, e dipendenti dalla

[1] *D*. x. 3, 8 pr.; x. 2, 43; viii. 2, 26, nella parte genuina.

[2] *D*. xvii. 2, 14, pr., vedi la nota appresso.

[3] *D*. xvii. 2, 16, 1, fortemente interpolato; 17 pr. eod. *aut c. div. Trib.*; x. 3, 14, 2: *Trib.*; § 3 eod. rimaneggiato da Triboniano: *quare emptor* [*quoque*] *communi dividundo agendo eadem exceptione* [*non* Paul] *summovebitur, qua actor eius summoveretur*.

[4] Cfr. Harmenopuli *Exab*. III. x. 30; *Bas*. xii. 2, 19 e scolii.

teoria del dominio quiritario, che esiste illeso in ciascuno dei compartecipi. Per ciò è manifesto che quelle dottrine che vedono nella *communio* una proprietà unica, attribuita ad una molteplicità di subbietti ovvero all' insieme dei titolari considerato come un gruppo collettivo, con o senza personalità giuridica, sono certamente erronee e lontane dall' ordinamento della comproprietà classica. È vero, per altro, che esse hanno nelle fonti un qualche fondamento, ma lo hanno precisamente in passi interpolati da Giustiniano, e perciò saranno a suo luogo prese in considerazione.[1]

19. La comproprietà classica, invece, quale ci si è manifestata nelle trattazioni dei giureconsulti si determina nettamente come una pluralità di dominii su di una cosa medesima, coesistenti in maniera che il singolo diritto rimane compresso dalla forza dell' altro; e per ciò ciascuno dei titolari ha, per effetto del concorso di diritti molteplici di pari forza, un dominio sulla cosa intera *pro indiviso pro parte.* È questa appunto la designazione molto precisa che Celso attribuisce al condominio in *D.* xiii. 6, 5, 15—*sed totius corporis pro indiviso pro parte dominium habere*; dove i due caratteri salienti della figura del condominio sono perfettamente messi in evidenza; e cioè in primo luogo la proprietà integrale di ciascuno, e poi la forzata riduzione di essa quanto agli effetti dinamici entro un limite insuperabile, a causa del concorso degli altri dominii.

Nello stesso senso si esprime Ulpiano, di cui il pensiero come di solito assume una forma più trasparente:

*D.* xxxix. 2, 15, 18: equaliter omnes quasi in totum missi concursu partes habebunt.

Il testo si riferisce alla *missio in possessionem damni infecti nomine, ex primo decreto*, che non attribuisce invero il dominio.

Ma alla *missio* può seguire in un secondo momento la proprietà, e non si vede davvero ragione per sospettare che la posizione giuridica dei *missi* debba, per questo rispetto, vale a dire quanto alla struttura dei rapporti tra i concorrenti, mutarsi col sopravvenire del dominio. Si può dire anzi il contrario; che cioè il giureconsulto si sforza di attribuire ai *missi* non proprietarii quella tale relazione giuridica che è nota dal condominio.

Nella comproprietà quindi il rapporto tra i condomini è per-

[1] Cfr. c. iv.

fettamente identico a quello dei coeredi nella *hereditas*. I coeredi sono tutti chiamati alla eredità intera, e solo per effetto del concorso ciascuno consegue una parte proporzionale al numero dei concorrenti, o quella parte che la legge o il testatore gli conferisce. Anche qui il diritto di ciascuno sull' asse ereditario si determina precisamente *pro indiviso pro parte*. Di conseguenza, se uno dei chiamati rinuncia o non può acquistare la parte che gli era designata, essa si accresce, di regola, agli altri coeredi, in proporzione della quota di ciascuno.

20. Cosi avviene nella *communio*. Se uno dei condomini, in un modo qualsiasi, rinuncia al suo dominio, per manomissione del servo o per derelizione etcc., la parte si accresce *ipso iure* agli altri socii. Ciò è attestato rispetto allo schiavo.[1]

Ma sicuramente non vi è ragione di negare lo stesso effetto per la derelizione di altri oggetti della proprietà, come si suol fare.[2] Perchè in nessun caso il diritto romano ammise una differenza qualsiasi tra il *dominium* su schiavi e quello su altre *res mancipi*, nè per il contenuto nè per l' intensità nè per le forme di trasferimento. Una differenza si nota bensi, ma solo riguardo al possesso, perchè è *res facti*; e quindi il possesso si configura diversamente secondo la natura dell' obbietto.[3] In materia di diritto, all' opposto, tale distinzione non ha senso.

E per altro l' applicazione dello *ius adcrescendi* tra condomini si evince in generale da un testo di Modestino, annoverato sempre tra i *loci conclamati*, e che realmente è oscuro, per il fatto che la conclusione vi fu soppressa. Il testo dice:

fr. 3 *D.* xli. 7, Mod. vi. differ. An pars pro derelicto haberi possit, quaeri solet et quidem si in re communi socius partem suam reliquerit, eius esse desinit, ut hoc sit in parte, quod in toto: at quin totius rei dominus efficere non potest, ut partem retineat, partem pro derelicto habeat [verius est partem pro derelicto haberi non posse, nam socius rei communis, si alter partem suam reliquerit, totius rei solus dominus efficitur].

[1] Dosithei, fr. 10; Ulp. Reg. i. 18; Paul. S. iv. 12, 1; cfr. *I.* ii. 7, 4.

[2] V. Pernice, *ZSS.* xix. p. 177 n. 1. Lo *ius adcrescendi* rispetto allo schiavo sarebbe per il P. un effetto della *potestas*; e non si accorge che la sua opinione s' infrange dinanzi alla dottrina di Proculo [testi cit.] che ammetteva appunto lo *ius adcrescendi* anche in seguito a man. *inter amicos*, per ciò, necessariamente, sul fondamente della derelizione, compiuta da uno dei condomini.

[3] Cfr. *D.* xli. 2, 3, 13; fr. 47 eod.

Il completamento del passo, così come io l' ho tentato ai fini della dimostrazione, mi sembra necessario, perchè la incompiutezza ne è evidente.

Il testo ha un indirizzo teorico, conforme all' indole dell' opera da cui fu ricavato,[1] e vuol risolvere una quistione sorta tra i giuristi intorno alla possibilità della *derelictio partis*. La conclusione manca. Ma se noi indaghiamo la ragione dei dubbii elevati dai giuristi, è certo che non può rinvenirsi dal lato soggettivo, cioè rispetto alla perdita della proprietà di colui che non vuole esser domino della parte, dacchè negarlo sarebbe assurdo: *ut hoc sit in parte quod in toto.* Ma il contrasto poteva bensi pronunziarsi dal lato obbiettivo, cioè se la parte ora relitta dal socio poteva considerarsi come derelitta in senso giuridico, e quindi acquistarsi dall' altro socio o da qualunque terzo come *res nullius*; ovvero, data la natura del condominio, in cui ciascuno: *totius rei pro indiviso pro parte dominium habet*, non si dovesse piuttosto ritenere la cosa comune soggetta interamente al dominio di ciascuno, e quindi in nessun momento priva in parte di domino, per effetto dell' abbandono di uno dei titolari. L' argomentazione di Modestino si appunta verso quest' ultima conclusione, che è ben fondata. E pertanto lo *ius adcrescendi* tra condomini appare sicuramente discusso tra i giuristi, ed ammesso in generale, con argomenti tratti dalla struttura stessa dell' istituto.

21. Ed il riconoscimento di tale effetto è d' una importanza decisiva; chè esso rivela nella maniera più sfolgorante l' intima essenza della comproprietà, quando la si valuti, come si deve, alla stregua di quella regola enunciata da Celso che suona: *totiens ius adcrescendi esse, quotiens in duobus, qui solidum habuerunt, concursu divisus est.*[2]

Il principio invero è applicato qui al concorso nell' usufrutto; ma esso è del pari efficace ed incontrovertibile in tutti i casi in cui un diritto è attribuito per intero a più persone; quindi ha vigore nella *hereditas*, nel legato, come nel condominio, qualunque sia la causa che lo determina.

22. Ed accertato questo punto, quella dottrina che vede nel condominio romano una comproprietà plurima parziale diviene

[1] Cfr. fr. 11 *D.* viii. 1: estratto dallo stesso libro e che concerne l' acquisto o la perdita della servitù *pro parte* [Lenel, *Pal.* i. c. 704].

[2] V. F. 79.

esanime. Perchè un diritto parziale, in sè, non può aver forza in nessun caso di espandersi al di là del suo limite, come non ha forza di dilatarsi l' obbligazione parziaria, che in realtà cade su più oggetti varii, unificati casualmente in un oggetto complessivo. E l' errore per altro nella dottrina del condominio è visibile, determinato dall' osservazione che tutti gli atti dispositivi del socio hanno valore, e gli emolumenti che provengono dalla cosa comune si dividono, sempre *pro parte*.[1] Ma tali effetti, fu già avvertito, dipendono dalla resistenza opposta dagli altri diritti di pari forza, che per ciò formano un limite insuperabile.

23. Ed ora che da un nucleo centrale compatto e forte abbiamo visto irradiarsi in linee ben precise, quanto in direzioni necessariamente varie, tutti gli effetti del condominio romano, fatti ormai chiari nella loro essenza, possiamo e dobbiamo intendere che tra il condominio del diritto privato e la collegialità dei magistrati non vi è nessun punto di contatto. Tra l' esercizio della *potestas*, infatti, dei magistrati e l' esercizio del potere dei condomini la differenza è essenziale. Perchè l' attribuzione della *potestas* ai colleghi nella magistratura è intera ed indipendente, nel senso che ciascuno di essi può esercitarla in ogni momento senza la cooperazione ed il concorso della volontà dell' altro. Nel condominio invece qualsiasi atto esecutivo sulla cosa deve essere necessariamente consentito da tutti, in modo positivo, come affermò già splendidamente il più grande interprete del diritto classico, Cuiacio,[2] il quale scrisse: *invitum . . . accipere debemus non eum qui contradicit, sed eum qui non consentit.*

Il dubbio in questo punto non è lecito.[3]

E se nell' un ordine e nell' altro può intervenire lo *ius prohibendi*, si tratta di una coincidenza del tutto esteriore, diversa nel fondamento, nella forma e nell' efficacia e che non può farci smarrire la esatta nozione delle cose. Vero è per altro che lo *ius prohibendi*, che ricorre nei due casi, se potè impressionare la mente del

[1] Cfr. avanti al n. 9.

[2] *Opp.* vol. iv. p. 944: ma s' intende che Cuiacio attribuisce pure alla parola un altro significato secondo i testi che comentava. Così nel v. iv. p. 783 ad l. 28 *D.* x. 3 scrive: *invitus est proprie qui prohibet alteri . . . invitus est etiam ius qui abest et per absentiam prohibere non potest.* Ma il Cuiacio si trovava qui di fronte ad un testo interpolato, come vedremo più oltre. Varii significati ammette Fadda, *Studii Brugi*, p. 145.

[3] Cfr. Perozzi, *Mél. Girard*, ii. p. 371.

Mommsen e di cultori insigni del diritto privato, quali il Fadda,[1] il Bonfante ed il Pacchioni, ciò si deve, in buona parte, alla deformazione dello *ius prohibendi* tra condomini operata da Giustiniano, e che sarà tosto messa in chiaro.

24. Dalla struttura del condominio classico derivano altre conseguenze di maggior rilievo, di cui fu fatto cenno, e che si coordinano convenientemente al concetto fondamentale qui svolto.

Tra condomini sono ammissibili ben poche azioni ; e cioè solo quelle che mirano a fare ottenere ad uno dei titolari il riconoscimento del suo diritto o la partecipazione al possesso e godimento della cosa ; e perciò è possibile la *reivindicatio*, la *publiciana* o la *condictio furtiva*. L' esperimento di queste azioni non può trovare ostacolo di sorta in qualsiasi contingenza ; ciò è intuitivo, perchè si tratta in definitivo dell' attivazione del diritto di proprietà, che è essenzialmente leso per la perdita del possesso.

Ma le altre azioni, che di solito competono al domino, non sono ammesse tra socii. Così se uno di essi abusa della cosa comune o la danneggia o tenta di stabilire uno stato di cose che agguagli l' onere di una servitù o delle opere, di suo arbitrio, non vi è un mezzo giudiziario per reprimere l' abuso, ottenere il risarcimento del danno o una penale, ovvero per impedire o far rimuovere le opere.

Quindi tra socii non si può esperire l' *actio legis Aquiliae*,[2] non la *negatoria*,[3] non l' *a. finium regundorum*,[4] nemmeno l' *a. de servo corrupto*[5] o *iniuriarum*,[6] o l' *actio noxalis* per delitto del servo comune.[7]

Anche il rimedio della *cautio damni infecti* fu oggetto di discussione tra le scuole dei giuristi.[8] E tutto ciò è ben intelligibile.

[1] *Studii Brugi*, p. 142 ed ivi citati.

[2] *D.* ix. 2, 27, 1 : [*ne sit in potestate servi ut tibi soli serviat*] *Trib.*; § 10 eod. [*et ideo aequius puto . . . cautionem*] *Trib.*; cfr. 26 *D.* x. 3, Alfen.

[3] *D.* xxxiii. 3, 4 ; cfr. avanti n. 5.

[4] *D.* x. 1, 4, 6, 7, Paul. xxiii. ad ed. : *quia ego et socius meus* (*in hac actione?* glossa) *adversarii esse non possumus, sed unius loco habemur.*

[5] *D.* xi. 3, 14, 2, Paul. xix. ad ed.: *Sabinus non posse agi cum socio, perinde atque si proprius meus servus corrupisset conservum.* Il fr. 9 pr. eod. è interpolato.

[6] *D.* xlvii. 10, 15, 36, Ulp. 77 ad ed. : *cum iure domini id fecerit.* Cfr. 17 § 9 eod.

[7] *D.* ix. 4, 8, Ulp. 37 ad ed.: *dominus enim pro parte factus non potest cum socio noxali experiri* ; quel che segue contiene elementi giustinianei.

[8] Cfr. *D.* xxxix. 2, 32, Gai xxviii. ad ed. pr. ; *D.* viii. 2, 13, 1 ; *D.* ix. 2, 27, 10.

L' ostacolo insuperabile per tutte quelle azioni sta nella posizione giuridica che hanno i socii tra loro. Se ciascuno è *dominus*, ed ha un diritto sulla cosa pari a quello dell' altro, ne deriva che qualunque sia l' agire del socio e qualunque cosa faccia, egli opera *in suo* e non *in alieno*. E quindi nessuna delle formule di quelle azioni potrebbe dirigersi contro di lui, chè esse competono al proprietario avverso chi tale diritto non può vantare sulla cosa. Manca quindi la condizione precipua per la legittimità e l' efficacia di quelle azioni, come è dichiarato espressamente dai giureconsulti nei passi rimasti illesi nella Compilazione di Giustiniano.[1]

Nè da ciò deriva che l' agire inconsulto, arbitrario o pregiudizievole di un socio sia, in tutti quei casi, senza alcun rimedio; chè ciascuno ha contro l' altro lo *ius prohibendi*; di propria autorità, *suis manibus*, in forza del suo diritto che è pari a quello dell' altro, che tenta di sopraffare il suo. *Prohibere*, come sappiamo, significa vietare, *impedire* in qualsiasi modo.

Ed in ultima analisi se la cooperazione e l' accordo si rendono impossibili, chi desidera la pace può chiedere lo scioglimento della comunione con l' *actio c. dividundo*; nella quale inoltre vengono dedotte tutte le ragioni personali per danni, spese ed utili, suscitate dalla comunione.

## CAP. II

### DIRITTO GIUSTINIANEO

25. Tutta la struttura della *communio* appare profondamente alterata nella compilazione di Giustiniano, dove i passi relativi alla materia sono folti di interpolazioni, sparse nei diversi volumi a guisa di temperamenti e correzioni, nella forma consueta, come per smorzare la durezza delle decisioni classiche. E la critica moderna ha potuto facilmente scovrire molte delle aggiunte inserte dal legislatore del VI sec. nei testi classici, ma nessuna attenzione ha rivolto ai passi mutilati, e sopratutto poi non si è curata di abbrac-

[1] Non è possibile affrontare in questo luogo tutto il problema delle azioni che competono tra condomini, perchè esso richiede un esame analitico di un numero considerevole di passi, che di regola furono alterati da Giustiniano nelle forme più varie. La dimostrazione per ciò sarà data a parte. Ma per quel che urge qui credo si debbano ritenere sufficienti i motivi resi dai giurist per escludere tra condomini l' ammissibilità delle azioni più gravi; motivi che ho riportati nelle note che precedono.

ciare in una sintesi complessiva l' insieme di quelle riforme, onde non ha potuto giudicare se effettivamente l' istituto classico sia uscito dalle mani di Giustiniano solo attenuato o non piuttosto svelto dalle sue basi.

In realtà il nucleo centrale, e quindi le linee più rilevate dell' istituto, ne furono spezzati, come mi accingo a dimostrare.

### I. *IUS PROHIBENDI*

#### (*a*) *La* prohibitio *tra condomini*

26. La regola di Sabino è ancora riportata nei *Digesti*, come sappiamo : ma effettivamente essa ha ora un campo di applicazione più ristretto e quindi un valore diverso. La conseguenza più immediata ed energica di essa, a dire di Papiniano, si manifestava nello *ius prohibendi* ; per cui ciascuno dei socii poteva proibire con tutti i mezzi, di propria autorità, qualsiasi azione iniziata dagli altri sulla cosa e distruggere l' opera compiuta senza il suo consenso. Questo diritto essenziale aveva fondamento nel potere di dominio assoluto ed indipendente che ciascuno dei titolari conserva nella comproprietà.

Nel diritto giustinianeo, invece, lo *ius prohibendi* ha un contenuto diverso ed una nuova direzione ; fu trasformato in un mezzo giudiziario, che si può sperimentare per via di *actiones* varie ed *interdicta*. La riforma legislativa determinò in primo luogo la mutilazione del fr. 11 *D*. viii. 5 di Marcello, esaminato di sopra,[1] e che pertanto assunse altro significato. È questo, dunque, un caso insigne in cui ha luogo la *duplex interpretatio*.

Soppressa[2] dai compilatori, come fu notato, la dimostrazione di Marcello, diretta ad escludere nella specie l' applicabilità della *negatoria*, la frase [*et magis dici potest*] *prohibendi potius esse ius* si riallaccia nel nuovo testo, immediatamente, alle varie formule di azioni proposte nella introduzione della quaestio, delle quali una per lo meno figura ammessa.

Dubbia può essere solo la scelta. E la designazione di essa è stata per più di mezzo secolo oggetto di sapienti discussioni. Gli antichi si attennero di preferenza all' *actio c. div.*, per evitare la

[1] Cfr. n. 5.

[2] Anche il Lenel, *ZSS*. xii. p. 12, sospettò nel testo, come dissi, una mutilazione ; cfr. ora Segrè, *Mél. Girard*, ii. p. 528.

contraddizione con altri testi; ma si affermò pure l' applicabilità della *negatoria*[1] o, più recentemente, della *prohibitoria*, rivelata giusto dallo Zacharia,[2] o dell' una e dell' altra insieme.[3] Nè in contrario c' è nulla da dire; perchè come affermò il Lenel, cui dobbiamo l' analisi più profonda del passo, da quel che di esso sopravanza si desume con certezza che il socio può impedire l' opera iniziata dall' altro sulla cosa comune per via di una azione. Se però questa norma, come io dico, è di Giustiniano, la quistione della specie dell' *actio* svanisce; diviene cosa di secondaria importanza. I compilatori infatti poterono bene riferirsi alla *negatoria* o alla *prohibitoria* od al *iudicium c. d.*, come vedremo più oltre.

27. Per ora urge radunare i testi nei quali si tratta dello *ius prohibendi*, onde vedere come si esplica nel diritto di Giustiniano. E sul proposito è ovvio pensare che la ricerca deve dirigersi su quei passi che nelle trattazioni dei giureconsulti riportavano giusto i fondamenti dell' istituto della comproprietà; perchè se la trasformazione dello *ius prohibendi* è vera, come io la suppongo, quei passi dovevano tutti esser rifatti da Triboniano, per togliere per sempre dalla vista degli interpreti il significato classico del prohibere in questo luogo.

E così è di fatto.

La riforma fu applicata immediatamente nei due frammenti più cospicui della materia che tramandavano la dottrina di Sabino, cioè in quello di Paolo: *D.* viii. 2, 26 ed in quello di Papiniano: *D.* x. 3, 28.

Nel passo di Paolo la massima di Sabino era ricondotta alla materia della servitù, e vi si affermava, convenientemente, che il socio nulla può *facere* sulla cosa comune *invito altero*, nè *prohibere iure servitutis*. Così il giureconsulto escludeva direttamente la possibilità della *negatoria* tra socii; e doveva nel seguito, come

[1] Per gli antichi v. Zachariä, *Zeit. f. g. RW.* vol. xii. p. 277 (a. 1845).

[2] *L. c.* p. 259 seg.

[3] Così Ferrini, *Per l' viii cent. dell' Università di Bologna*, p. 96, che riporta p. 99 n. 5 l' opinione posteriore dello Zacharia, che avrebbe in seguito riconosciuto le due formule egualmente applicabili, mentre sagacemente nell' art. cit. aveva escluso la negatoria, come fa tuttora il Lenel, *ZSS.* vol. xii. *l. c.*; Segrè, *l. c.* p. 525 segue il Ferrini. Secondo una opinione particolare di Beseler, *Beiträge*, i. p. 79, « Marcellus meint in Wirklichkeit die a° pro socio »; uno svarione certamente, generato dalla critica « a turbina »; che s' indulge volentieri, per altro, per il prezioso contributo di nuove osservazioni che l' illustre scrittore ha saputo portare allo studio del Digesto.

io ritengo, far menzione della proibizione privata che il socio dissenziente poteva adoperare. Il tratto però fu dai compilatori eliminato e sostituito dal seguente periodo:

[Sed per communi dividundo actionem consequitur socius, quo minus opus fiat aut ut id opus quod fecit tollat, si modo toti societati prodest opus tolli.]

L' *a. c. d.* serve, dunque, ora a regolare i rapporti tra i socii durante la comunione, e serve qui particolarmente ad impedire l' opera che uno dei socii voglia eseguire sulla cosa *invito altero*, ovvero quando sia compiuta a farla rimuovere. E pertanto la interpolazione di questo passo combacia perfettamente, quanto al risultato sostanziale, con quella osservata di sopra nel testo di Marcello.

E la sovrapposizione è più visibile nell' altro di Papiniano, già noto, e che così continua:

[fr. 28 *D.* x. 3. Sed etsi in communi prohiberi socius a socio ne quid faciat potest, ut tamen factum opus tollat, cogi non potest, si cum prohibere poterat, hoc praetermisit: et ideo per communi dividundo actionem damnum sarciri poterit; sin autem facienti consensit, nec pro damno habet actionem, quod si quid absente socio ad laesionem eius fecit, tunc etiam tollere cogitur.]

Lo *ius prohibendi*, nel senso a noi chiaro, che Papiniano riportava all' uguaglianza dei diritti dei socii, subì qui un' illustrazione sovversiva, da parte di Triboniano, mediante varie distinzioni di cui ci occuperemo in luogo opportuno, ma che son dirette pure a render palese che il mezzo con cui esso si esplica è appunto l' *a. c. d.*, resa ora necessaria per chiedere risarcimento del danno o per far rimuovere l' opera, e quindi anche per ostacolarne l' inizio.

Anche questo testo, così, si riannoda a quelli di Marcello e di Paolo, in quanto concerne la forma giudiziaria del *prohibere*.

28. In altri due testi accanto al *iudicium c. d.* si fa pure menzione del pretore che può essere adito per attuare l' impedimento all' opera iniziata da uno dei socii. I passi sono consecutivi e del seguente tenore:

fr. 3, § 1, *D.* xxxix. 1, Ulp. 52 ad ed. Si in loco communi quid fiat, nuntiatio locum habebit adversus vicinum, plane si unus nostrum in communi loco faciat, non possum ego socius opus novum ei nuntiare, sed eum prohibebo [*communi dividundo iudicio vel per praetorem*].

§ 2. Quod si socius meus in communi insula opus novum faciat et ego propriam habeam, cui nocetur, an opus novum nuntiare ei possim? et putat Labeo non posse nuntiare, quia possum eum alia ratione prohibere aedificare, [*hoc est vel per praetorem vel per arbitrum communi dividundo:*] *quae sententia vera est.*

Le aggiunte tribonianee sono evidentissime:[1] e mirano appunto a dare all' *iudicium c. d.* quella funzione a noi nota di regolare i rapporti dei socii, in qualsiasi evenienza.

I giureconsulti negavano l' applicabilità tra socii della *o. n. n.*, per la natura stessa del condominio, perchè, essendo ciascuno di essi domino, poteva, secondo la frase di Labeone: *alia ratione prohibere*, cioè di propria mano. È possibile anzi che Ulpiano avesse in questo luogo dichiarata la forma della proibizione, cui poteva ricorrere il socio, ma i compilatori si affrettarono a sostituirvi quella legale; o per mezzo del *iudicium c. d.* ovvero *per praetorem.* In quest' ultimo caso con quale formula? Non certamente con l' *Uti possidetis*, come si ritiene, perchè tra due possessori l' interdetto resterebbe inefficace.[2] E se la domanda ed il dubbio restano qui senza una congrua risposta, noi vedremo che in questa materia il caso si ripeterà assai di frequente. Tenga pertanto il lettore memoria, per ora, della frase *per praetorem* ripetuta nei due testi, e che incontreremo in altri passi.

29. Anche Pomponio, che escludeva, come sappiamo,[3] tra condomini il *iudicium finium regundorum*, appare in altro luogo fermo nell' ammettere tra essi un' azione *per impedire immissioni* da parte di uno nell' edificio comune:

27 *D.* viii. 2 Pomp. xxxiii. ad Sab. Sed si inter te et me communes sunt Titianae aedes, et ex his aliquid non iure in alias aedes meas proprias immissum sit, nempe tecum mihi agere licet aut rem perdere. Idem fiet si ex tuis propriis aedibus in communes meas et tuas aedes quid similiter esset proiectum: mihi enim soli tecum est actio.

L' azione accordata con una certa baldanza non è poi determinata, nemmeno qui. Intanto la *negatoria* non può essere, chè Giavoleno l' esclude recisamente,[4] tanto meno il *iudicium c. d.* che non aveva siffatta funzione.

[1] Cfr. Berger, *Teilungskl.* p. 235; ivi per la letteratura.
[2] *D.* xliii. 17, 3 pr.
[3] Cfr. *D.* x. 1, 4, 7, e sopra n. 24.
[4] *D.* xxxiii. 3, 4.

Dunque è un mezzo nuovo introdotto dai compilatori, e che si ricongiunge al fr. 26 di Paolo, che precede nel titolo, dove la proibizione del socio si esplica mediante il *iudicium c. d.*; o che si può riconnettere al fr. 11 *D.* viii. 5 di Marcello, vale a dire ad una di quelle formule della *negatoria* o della così detta *prohibitoria*, che già conosciamo. E di fatto le due interpretazioni sono rappresentate.[1]

Ma per il diritto classico la cosa è ben diversa. Pomponio doveva ivi contemplare la *negatoria*, escludendola appunto, come l' aveva esclusa Paolo, nella maniera che sappiamo, nel luogo corrispondente dell' *opera ad Sabinum*; e Pomponio doveva pure ricordare in quel tratto che il socio ha sovratutto lo *ius prohibendi*, in forza del quale può distruggere di sua autorità l' opera fatta nell' edificio comune: *aut rem perdere.*

Se questa frase, come è stato sempre ritenuto,[2] ha un tal significato, noi abbiamo qui una traccia ben marcata dell' indirizzo che aveva il passo di Pomponio, e delle alterazioni compiutevi dai compilatori.[3] Tentarne la restituzione non è possibile, perchè gli elementi sono scarsi; ma la dimostrazione esauriente che ne ho data, e sopratutto la confluenza di tutte le interpolazioni verso lo stesso punto non possono lasciare dubbio di sorta.[4]

E così è provato che l' attuazione dello *ius prohibendi* a mezzo del magistrato, con una formula qualsiasi spesso neppure designata, è un' innovazione di Giustiniano.

[1] Ferrini (*Per l' viii centenario della Univ. di Bologna*, pp. 97, 99; *Pand.* p. 449 n. 1) riferisce la decisione alla *negatoria*, e vi si richiama per spiegare altri passi; così ora Segrè, *Mél. Girard*, ii. p. 525 nota.

[2] Cf. Glossa e Gotofredo ad h. l., che danno della frase una doppia spiegazione; (*a*) *perdam ius prohibendi*; (*b*) *id est destruere opus.* Cuiacio accolse la prima (*Opp.* v. p. 550): *si non egero rem perdidero*; ed in altro luogo spiega: *libertatem praedii amittere.* Ma la maggioranza degli interpreti e Glück stesso che ne riferisce (*Erläut.* v. x. p. 76) abbracciò la seconda spiegazione, cioè: *opus factum propria auctoritate destruere*, con richiamo al fr. 29 § 1 *D.* ix. 2.

[3] Un altro passo di Pomponio alterato nello stesso senso si ha in *D.* viii. 5, 14, pr. . . [*imo etiam agere tecum potero, ut ea, quae nova immiseris tollas*] mentre il giurista ammetteva sola la proibizione: *prohiberi a me potes.* E così nel § 1, . . . *potero tecum agere*: Pomp. avrà scritto: *non potero t. a.* L' interpolazione è visibile nel pr. del testo, dacchè la *prohibitio* vi appare in contrasto (*immo*) con l' *agere.*

[4] Come semplice chiarimento della dimostrazione fatta, si può supporre che Pomp. avesse scritto nella parte centrale così: *nempe tecum mihi agere* [*non*] *licet*; [*ius tibi non esse ita immissum habere*; *sed possum*] *rem perdere.* [*Quod si*] . . .

(*b*) *Formula prohibitoria*

30. E dalla dimostrazione che precede fluisce un' altra conseguenza di singolare rilievo, che riflette la *formula prohibitoria* messa in luce dallo Zachariä [1] da uno scolio di Stefano al fr. 5, § 1, *D.* vii. 6, e che ha avuto un' esistenza travagliata.[2] Ma in ultimo essa ebbe posto onorevole nell' Editto, per l' adesione manifestata dal Lenel, che ne era stato l' avversario più formidabile ed autorevole.[3] Tra i casi di applicazione della *prohibitoria* quello offerto dal fr. 11 *D.* viii. 5 di Marcello era certamente il più insigne, sovratutto il più verisimile, perchè già lo Zachariä e poi il Lenel avevano notato la inamissibilità della *negatoria* tra condomini. Si disse, per ciò, che lo *ius prohibendi* consentito da Marcello doveva riportarsi alla *formula prohibitoria.*

Il risultato qui raggiunto intorno al significato del *prohibere* tra condomini, ed in particolare nel passo genuino di Marcello, toglie ogni base a quelle interpretazioni, e di conseguenza a questa applicazione precipua della *formula prohibitoria.*

E così è chiusa la breve storia della nuova formula rivelata da Stefano; avvegnachè tolto di mezzo il testo di Marcello, quell' altro concernente l' usufrutto, cui il maestro bizantino direttamente si riferisce nella sua parafrasi, è meno che mai idoneo a giustificare l' esistenza nell' editto d' una speciale azione proibitoria. Nè per ciò abbiamo noi bisogno di svalutare le notizie dei giuristi bizantini e delle fonti greche in generale. Perchè esse hanno importanza di prim' ordine sotto un doppio aspetto: (*a*) per il diritto classico, e quindi per ricostruire i testi antichi, quando lo scoliaste trae i suoi materiali dai lavori compiuti dagli ἥρωες sulle fonti romane;[4] (*b*) per il diritto giustinianeo, negli altri casi in cui l' interprete greco lavora direttamente *sui libri* di Giustiniano.

Nel caso nostro non è dubbio che Stefano in quel punto interpretava e commentava il passo dei *Digesti*, senza l' aiuto di esemplari

[1] *Zeitschrift f. g. RW.* v. xii. (1844), p. 259 seg. Bas. Suppl. p. 112, scol. 6.

[2] Contro specialmente, Lenel, *ZSS.* ii. p. 72 seg.; in favore Ferrini, *Per l' viii centenario della Univ. di Bologna*, p. 92 seg.

[3] *ZSS.* v. 12, p. 1 seg.; Ed. Perp. 2ª ed. p. 186. Per la letteratura cfr. Audibert, *Studii per Fadda*, v. 5, p. 363 seg.; Segrè, *Mél. Girard*, ii. p. 525 seg.

[4] Molti esempii nei miei scritti: cfr. *ZSS.* v. 33, p. 288, e citazioni ivi, n. 1.

antichi. La parafrasi in discorso è sotto molti aspetti miserabile, tra i prodotti più scadenti del maestro coevo di Giustiniano. Ma della notizia che egli dà non si può nè si deve dubitare.[1] La *formula prohibitoria* è riportata dal comentatore, particolareggiata, in contrapposto alla *negatoria*: ἄλλον τύπον προυιβιτόριον; ed è poi confermata da altre testimonianze;[2] ed è applicata ad un testo sicuramente[3] rimaneggiato dai compilatori, come io credo con l' aggiunta delle parole *vel sibi ius esse prohibendi*; e per ciò non abbiamo motivo per negar fede a Stefano, che riferisce appunto lo stato del diritto e della pratica del suo tempo. Se la formula in discussione sia poi da considerare come un mero prodotto della Compilazione, o piuttosto della pratica bizantina avanti Giustiniano, è un problema su cui d' ora innanzi potrà l' indagine indirizzarsi. Per ora è accertato questo: che nei *Digesti* è visibile la distinzione tra una *formula negatoria* e altra *prohibitoria*, come Stefano insegna; e poi, che i compilatori diedero sicuramente significato e valore processuale al *prohibere*, che era inteso dai classici in altro senso.[4]

### (*c*) *La difesa privata*

31. L' affermazione ultima fatta nella chiusa del paragrafo che precede deve essere posta qui al sicuro da ogni dubbio, ed approfondita per via di una rapida indagine sul diritto alla difesa privata, che era ammesso in molti casi nell' ordinamento giuridico del periodo classico; ed appare, invece, con singolare perseveranza, soppresso da Giustiniano, surrogato dovunque con un mezzo processuale qualsiasi.

32. I casi sono di vario ordine:

(*a*) Il proprietario poteva impedire di propria autorità, anche

[1] Per Beseler, *Beiträge*, i. p. 79, è una «leggenda».

[2] Cfr. Zachariä, *l. c.*; Lenel, *Ed.* p. 186, n. 1.

[3] Così già Zachariä, *Z.* cit. p. 263, n. 4, che vi suppone «etwas ausgefallen e poi Ferrini, *l. c.* p. 96, e Lenel, *Z.* cit. 12, p. 12; Beseler, *Beiträge*, i. 78, dichiara interpolata tutta la parte centrale; Segrè, *Mél. Girard*, ii. p. 527, la frase *vel . . . prohibendi*.

[4] Per ciò riprendono ora tutta la loro forza i relievi del Lenel fatti in *ZSS.* ii. *loc. cit.*, e principalmente la constatazione che nei comentarii all' Ed. non vi è traccia di una tale formula. Il Ferrini (*l. c.* p. 95), nel fervore per l' *actio prohibitoria*, giunse a dire che essa dovette essere oscurata dai compilatori, che intendevano fonderla con la *negatoria*; asserzione questa del tutto gratuita.

con la forza, qualsiasi costruzione o immissione nel fondo, senza ricorrere alla denuncia di nuova opera. Giustiniano ne ha fatto divieto, come si può dimostrare con l' esame del passo che segue:

| | |
|---|---|
| 5 § 10 *D.* xxxix. 1, Ulp. 52 ad ed. Meminisse autem oportebit, quotiens quis in nostro aedificare vel in nostrum immittere vel proicere vult [*melius esse eum per praetorem vel per manum id est lapilli ictum*] prohibere, quam operis novi nuntiatione. Ceterum operis novi nuntiatione possessorem eum faciemus, cui nuntiaverimus. At si in suo quid faciat, quod nobis noceat, tunc operis novi denuntiatio erit necessaria. [*Et si forte in nostro aliquid facere quis perseverat, aequissimum erit interdicto adversus eum quod vi aut clam aut uti possidetis uti.*] | Ulpianus. Meminisse autem oportebit, quotiens quis in nostro aedificare vel in nostrum immittere vel proicere vult [posse nos eum per manum] prohibere, quam operis novi nuntiatione *cet.* |

La ragione per cui Ulpiano sconsigliava il mezzo della denuncia è rimarchevole; e qui va notata particolarmente, perchè non se n' è fatto il conto che merita. Infatti è ovvio che il proprietario non deve esser messo nella condizione più sfavorevole processualmente, come lo sarebbe con la denuncia; la quale costituisce l' avversario possessore[1] e riversa gli oneri della prova, ed un pericolo maggiore per l' esito della lite, a chi è già nel possesso del fondo. Questi pertanto ha facoltà momentaneamente di respingere il tentativo fatto dal terzo, che menoma il suo diritto; e lo può respingere con la forza, *per manum*, come si esprimeva Ulpiano in maniera significativa ed appropriata. Ma Giustiniano reprime il consiglio turbolento e, sconvolgendo il testo, addita la via migliore cioè *per praetorem*, ovvero mediante l' innocuo getto del lapillo, che qui diventa ridicolo.[2] Il rinvio al pretore, con l' identica frase e nella medesima situazione occorre, come sappiamo, due volte nel fr. 3 dello stesso titolo; ed in tutti cotesti casi solo la credenza

[1] *D.* xxxix. 1, 1, 6.

[2] E perciò la frase si è ritenuta una glossa: cfr. Windscheid, *Pand.* § 465, n. 18; Lenel, *Pal.* ii. c. 745 n. 2; Audibert, *l. c.* p. 360, n. 2.

radicata nell' incontaminata riproduzione dei passi dei giuristi ha potuto intendervi l' *Uti possidetis*, cosi designato da uno scrittore classico. Certo nella compilazione tale significato non solo è possibile ma è piano; come lo dimostra già la chiusa dello stesso frammento, che è pure evidentemente interpolatizia.[1]

33. (*b*) Colui che si trova nel godimento pacifico di una servitù può impedire prontamente, di sua autorità, qualsiasi innovazione sul fondo servente, che verrebbe a ledere l' esercizio del suo diritto.

fr. 6 § 1 *D.* viii. 5, Ulp. 17 ad ed.
Sciendum tamen in his servitutibus possessorem esse eum [*iuris et petitorem*]; et si forte non habeam aedificatum altius in meo adversarius meus possessor est: nam cum nihil sit innovatum, ille possidet et aedificantem me prohibere potest [*et civili actione et interdicto Quod vi aut clam: idem et si lapilli iactu impedierit.*] sed et si patiente eo aedificavero ego possessor ero effectus.

Questo passo si agguaglia in tutto al precedente. Sullo stesso fondamento il giureconsulto insegnava che colui il quale gode il possesso della servitù non deve perdere tale vantaggio per l' opera o il fatto arbitrario di chi l' appresta; nè deve egli per ciò assumere le parti di attore; chè piuttosto può *prohibere* con qualsiasi mezzo, l' inizio delle opere che modificherebbero lo stato delle cose. Ma se poi egli non si oppone alla edificazione e tollera le opere intraprese dall' avversario, allora perde la qualità di possessore e deve assumere, quando voglia, le parti di attore.

Il testo di Ulpiano era, dunque, lucidissimo e cospicuo; ma fu rovinato da Giustiniano per bandire ogni traccia della difesa privata. E pertanto egli ingiunge, che il possessore di siffatte servitù deve di necessità essere pure *petitorem*, quando l' avversario per via di opere o altrimenti menoma il suo diritto; ed in luogo della *prohibitio* privata regala al possessore i mezzi più varii: una *civilis actio*, un interdetto e, dopo tutto questo, con atroce ironia, il diritto del «lapillo».

S' intende che nessuno di cotali mezzi s' è potuto finora giustificare o soltanto spiegare; come ha mostrato di recente l' Audibert[2] in una speciale dissertazione, persuasiva e stringente nella parte

[1] Osserva: *si forte . . . aequissimum erit . . . uti.* Ma perchè molto equo? È vero per altro che quando la proibizione privata resta inefficace vi hanno tutte le condizioni per esperire l' Int. *Quod vi aut clam.*

[2] *Studii per Fadda*, vol. v. p. 341 seg.

critica o negativa che si voglia dire, ma che per il resto risuscita più vivo lo sconforto per la soluzione del problema.

Infatti l' Audibert ha voluto vedere nella *civilis actio* indicata nel testo nientemeno che la *o. n. nuntiatio*; cioè giusto quel mezzo che Ulpiano escludeva nel fr. 5 § 10 *D.* xxxix. 1, onde il possessore non avesse a perdere il vantaggio della sua posizione ed esser costretto a iniziare la lite da attore. Ed è questo rilievo e le ulteriori coincidenze tra i due passi che debbono attirare la nostra attenzione, senza per altro indugiare sulla strana terminologia che si attribuisce ad Ulpiano per designare la *nuntiatio*. Io affermo per ciò che i due testi coincidevano anche rispetto al mezzo di difesa additato da Ulpiano.

34. Ma si dirà che tra i due passi v' è un punto di differenza che non si può colmare; perchè il fr. 5 § 10 *D.* xxxix. 1, riguarda il proprietario, che al postutto può essere autorizzato a distruggere le opere o impedire l' invasione del proprio fondo, perchè agisce *in suo*; mentre nel caso del fr. in esame ammettere la proibizione privata contro colui che inizia le costruzioni entro i confini della sua proprietà sarebbe cosa gravissima ed inaudita.

La osservazione è impressionante a prima vista; ma non nella sostanza. Perchè giusto l' elemento del possesso attuale, nell' uno e nell' altro testo, è messo in rilievo dal giureconsulto ai fini processuali; e su quell' elemento è fondata la decisione, eguale nei due casi, perchè pari è la posizione. Chi è nel godimento di una servitù, che presuppone uno stato di cose permanente, è considerato possessore, ed ha diritto di fronte all' avversario di veder mantenuto quello stato, fino a tanto che non intervenga un pronunziato del giudice che dichiari la libertà del fondo servente. E perciò il tentativo di alterare, arbitrariamente, la faccia dei luoghi, in modo lesivo per l' esercizio della servitù, può essere represso con la forza; nella stessa misura che il proprietario può respingere con la forza l' invasione di altri nel proprio fondo. La differenza tra chi opera *in alieno* ovvero *in suo* esiste certamente ai fini della liceità o meno della difesa privata; ma essa viene in considerazione solo quando colui che opera *in suo* non lede uno stato di diritto che altri gode.[1] Quando ciò avvenga, invece, anche colui che opera *in suo* secondo la felice espressione di Marcello: *quodammodo*

[1] È il caso del fr. 29 § 1 *D.* ix. 2: *nullo iure habebam.*

*sibi alienum quoque ius praeripit.* E per ciò la proibizione immediata è legittima.[1]

35. E del resto nelle fonti vi hanno tracce evidenti di tale diritto, in materia di servitù precipuamente. Così Africano in *D.* xxxix. 1, 15 dice: che quando il possessore della *servitus altius non tollendi*—ed è proprio il caso del fr. 6 § 1 in esame—non si difende, vien punito *ut iure suo probare necesse haberet*; e per ciò deve prestar cauzione *nec opus novum se nuntiaturum nec aedificanti vim facturum.* Or io chiedo, perchè deve egli garentire che non opporrà violenza all' opera che sarà per fare il proprietario del fondo servente? La risposta è semplice: perchè ha il diritto di servitù ed il godimento attuale.[2] E pertanto solo ai fini processuali, per pena, gli è inibito di proibire con la forza l' alterazione dello stato dei luoghi che il proprietario del fondo servente potrà con nuove opere arrecare. Se ha ragioni da far valere: *iure suo probare necesse habet.* Nel fr. 15 *D.* viii. 2, Ulpiano, *a proposito* di opere fatte che impediscono la *servitus luminis* pone, in primo luogo, il diritto del titolare della medesima a *prohibere* e così si esprime: *quodcunque igitur faciat ad luminis impedimentum, prohiberi potest, si servitus debeatur; [opusque ei novum nuntiari potest,*

[1] La riforma di Giustiniano in questo punto di diritto ha per ciò una grande importanza, chè essa venne a stabilire una eccezione gravissima al principio che spetta all' attore, cioè a colui che non hà il possesso della cosa o il godimento del diritto, l' onere della prova. Qui per reprimere la difesa privata si rovesciò quella massima, e si disse: *possessorem eum esse iuris et petitorem.* Io ritengo ora fermamente che sia questo appunto l' *unus casus* famoso delle *Inst.* iv. 6, 2. Infatti la riforma così grave attuata dai compilatori doveva bene aderire alla loro mente, e poteve inoltre essere accennata di sfuggita nel libro di scuola, come quella che nei *latioribus digestorum libris* era indicata *apertis verbis.* Cfr. per altro, da ultimo, Segrè, *Studii Brugi*, p. 411 e seg.

[2] Che questo elemento sia decisivo emerge sotto altro aspetto dal fr. 7 § 2 *D.* xliii. 24: *Iulianus ait . . . licere enim debet aedificare ei, qui satisdederit, cum possessor hoc ipso constituatur cet.* Dunque, chi è in possesso può edificare senza temere proibizione di sorta; mentre la quistione di diritto rimane impregiudicata. Ma quando il possesso è dalla parte del titolare della servitù, questi può impedire con la forza qualsiasi opera che muti lo stato dei luoghi. Si noti ancora nel testo di Giuliano la frase *possessor . . . constituatur* usata rispetto all' esercizio o meno di una servitù, nella specie per la libertà del fondo, e quindi ai fini unicamente processuali; dal che emerge che Ulpiano nel fr. 6 § 1 *D.* viii. 5, non poteva scrivere *possessorem esse eum iuris*? La determinazione *iuris* fu aggiunta dai Compilatori certamente; perchè per l' attribuzione delle parti di attore o convenuto in processo è decisivo solo *possessorem esse* cioè che sia nel godimento di un certo stato, di una posizione di fatto.

*si modo sic faciat, ut lumini noceat*]. La *prohibitio* ha luogo dunque se la *servitus* è dovuta. La *nuntiatio* forma nel passo un' appendice tribonianea, che si manifesta tale per la ripetizione del verbo (*potest*) e del presupposto dell' impedimento alla servitù (*si modo . . . noceat*).

Per ciò anche nel fr. 6 § 7 *D.* viii. 5. Ulpiano doveva ammettere in primo luogo la proibizione privata contro il proprietario dell' edificio che deteriora il muro gravato dalla *servitus oneris*, mentre Giustiniano vi sostituisce delle azioni: *deteriorem si facit* [*aut per hanc actionem aut per operis novi nuntiationem*] *prohibetur.*

36. E la proibizione privata la sorprendiamo viva in molti testi, nel momento della sua attuazione e del conflitto.

1 § 11 *D.* xliii. 24: si te volentem ad prohibendum venire deterruerit aliquis.

20 § 1 eod.: Prohibitus autem intellegitur quolibet prohibentis actu, id est vel dicentis se prohibere vel manum opponentis lapillumve iactantis prohibendi gratia.

5 § 1 eod.: ut intra diem occurrere ad prohibendum non possit.

4 § 7 *D.* viii. 5: adversus dominum Seianarum volo experiri altius me tollere prohibentem.

111 *D.* xlv. 1: si me non prohibeas, uxorem autem meam prohiberes, vel contra uxore mea stipulata me prohiberes, an committatur stipulatio?

14 fr. *D.* viii. 5: prohiberi a me potes.

Ed in tutti questi casi il divieto si esplica in difesa della proprietà o della cosa comune, o del possesso di una servitù, per opere fatte in privato o in pubblico e con tutti i mezzi, fino alla distruzione dell' opera eseguita in alieno, come si vede dagli esempi che seguono.

(*c*) fr. 7 § 3 *D.* xliii. 24, Ulp. 72 ad ed. Bellissime apud Iulianum quaeritur, an haec exceptio noceat in hoc interdicto, 'quod non tu vi aut clam feceris'? ut puta utor adversus te interdicto quod vi aut clam, an possis obicere mihi eandem exceptionem quod non tu vi aut clam fecisti?

et ait Iulianus aequissimum esse hanc exceptionem dare: nam si tu, inquit, aedificaveris vi aut clam, ego idem demolitus fuero vi aut clam et utaris adversus me interdicto, hanc exceptionem profuturam [*quod non aliter procedere debet, nisi ex magna et satis necessaria causa: alioquin haec omnia officio iudicis celebrari oportet*].

L' eccezione giova a colui che usò violenza e che distrusse l' opera fatta *in alieno*, soltanto perchè egli proteggeva in tal modo il possesso di un diritto, che l' avversario, malgrado la proibizione, aveva leso con le nuove costruzioni. Da che si deduce, che se è ammissibile la difesa privata quando l' opera è compiuta, a maggior ragione la si può esplicare in tutti i modi per impedire l' inizio della stessa.

L' interpolazione dell' ultimo brano fu avvertita dal Fabro. E di fatto Giustiniano non poteva lasciar correre senza protesta un esempio così improbo.

37. (*d*) fr. 2 § 33 *D.* xliii. 8: Scio tractatum, an permittendum sit specus et pontem per viam publicam facere: [*et plerique probant interdicto eum teneri*:] non enim oportere eum deteriorem viam facere.

Il passo è stato di recente discusso [1] e denunziato per le mende formali evidentissime. Che il brano dovette essere compresso dai compilatori è rilevato dal Mitteis, che suppone sagacemente, al posto di *plerique.* Ulpiano avesse riportati nomi dei *veteres.* Certo il giureconsulto inizia con certa solennità la trattazione, che è poi ridotta a nulla. Ed io suppongo che anche qui Ulpiano faceva menzione della privata difesa,[2] come si legge, a proposito di un caso che ha una certa analogia con il presente, nel

fr. 50 *D.* xli. 1 Pomp. vi.: ex Plautio: Quamvis quod in litore publico vel in mare exstruxerimus nostrum fiat, tamen decretum praetoris adhibendum est, ut id facere liceat: immo etiam manu prohibendus est, si cum incommodo ceterorum id faciat; nam civilem eum actionem de faciendo nullam habere non dubito.

È questo l' unico esempio, per quanto è a mia conoscenza, in cui è ammessa la legittimità della difesa privata, ed è veramente prezioso, come una sopravvivenza storica.

Ma nella compilazione il testo genuino fu indubbiamente annullato in *D.* xxxix. 1, cioè nel titolo in cui Triboniano usò più vigilanza nell' eliminare lo *ius prohibendi* nel senso classico, e perciò noi leggiamo ora nel fr. 1 § 18—[*si quis igitur velit ibi aedificantem prohibere, nullo iure prohibet; neque opus novum nuntiare; nisi ex una causa potest si forte damni infecti velit sibi*

[1] Cfr. Beseler, *Beiträge*, ii. p. 16; Mitteis, *ZSS.* vol. xxxiii. p. 193.

[2] Non affronto qui la quistione se l' *ed. de damno infecto* avesse contenuto una clausola relativa a *opus quod in via publica fiet*, ciò che io negherei. Ma v. Lenel, *Ed.* p. 360, n. 1, che ha già ben valutato le ragioni del dubbio.

*caveri*]. I contorcimenti del periodo e le forme bizantine consuete rivelano l' alterazione del testo.

38. (*e*) Nel caso di rilascio del possesso da parte dei *missi in possessionem.*

fr. 1 § 2 *D.* xxv. 5, Ulp. 34 ad ed. Necessario praetor adiecit, ut, qui per dolum venit in possessionem, cogatur decedere: coget autem eum decedere [non] praetoria potestate vel manu ministrorum [*sed melius et civilius faciet si eum per interdictum ad ius ordinarium remiserit*].

Qui sembra che il giurista dia al pretore il consiglio di agire con più correttezza e più civilmente, costringendo il possessore doloso ad abbandonare il possesso per mezzo di un interdetto. Quale non si scorge nè si rinviene.[1] Ed è vero, invece, che la costrizione aveva luogo in simili casi *praetoria potestate,* ed occorrendo *manu ministrorum.* Ciò vieta Giustiniano.

(*f*) fr. 5 § 2 *D.* xlii. 4, Ulp. 59 ad ed. Ait praetor: si is pupillus in suam tutelam venerit eave pupilla viripotens fuerit et recte defendetur: eos, qui bona possident, de possessione decedere iubebo.

§ 3. . . . ergo oblata defensione deici poterit [*interdicto reddito*].

Finita la causa che diede luogo alla *missio in possessionem,* e nel caso in esame quando il pupillo è già in grado di difendersi o è difeso da altri, il pretore ordina ai *missi* il rilascio del possesso. E venuta meno la *iusta causa possidendi* autorizzata dal magistrato, ove il detentore non ubbidisca all' ordine di abbandonarlo, può esserne impunemente deietto per mano degli interessati. Infatti ora il suo possesso è vizioso.

C' è bisogno per ciò di un interdetto? Ma dove mai si rinviene un interdetto che permetta la *deiectio*? Non lo ritrova appunto il Lenel che noi veneriamo come il più insigne conoscitore dell' Editto, dopo Salvio Giuliano.

La interpolazione per altro è lampante;[2] oltre il mistero dell' interdetto, due ablativi assoluti riferiti a diversi agenti, nessuna

[1] Cfr. Lenel, *Mélang. Girard,* ii. p. 82.

[2] Identica interpolazione in *D.* xxxvi. 3, 11, Gai xiii. ad ed. . . . [*mihi praetor accommodat interdictum quo*]; quel che resta corrisponde al procedimento effetivo in tutti i casi di *missio*; cf. *D.* xlii. 5, 33, 1—*satisdatione interposita iudicium accipiatur et a possessione discedatur.* Quindi, senz' altro rimedio processuale.

traccia di soggetto del *verbo poterit.*[1] Identica interpolazione si riscontra nel fr. 40 *D.* xlvi. 3 Marc. 3 Inst. . . . [*alioquin nascitur heredi interdictum, ut eos deicere possit*].[2] Qui la mano di Triboniano si manifesta nel *nascitur* che non mi sembra possa adoperarsi per un rimedio che presuppone ogni volta speciale formulazione.[3]

E finalmente nella chiusa del

fr. 1 § 9 *D.* xliii. 3 : . . . [*Tutius tamen erit dicendum hoc interdictum competere, maxime si satisdatum sit iam legatorum nomine nec recedat, tunc enim etiam possidere videtur*].

Il rimedio che Ulpiano indicava in questo luogo è già visibile nel *Digesto* dal fr. 5 § 2 *D.* xlii. 4, sopra richiamato, da cui risulta che l' Editto provvedeva particolarmente perchè i *missi in possessionem* si ritraessero dal possesso quando la causa della immissione era cessata. All' ordine del pretore poteva seguire la *deiectio*, come rilevai or ora.

Direi anzi che ciò è attestato direttamente da Ulpiano, a proposito della *missio d. inf. nomine*, in

*D.* xxxix. 2, 4, 4 ; si forte duretur non caveri ut possideri liceat, quod causa cognita fieri solet, non duumviros sed Praetorem vel Praesidem permissuros, item ut ex causa decedatur de possessione.

Che questo brano possa essere stato compresso dai compilatori, come dimostra la forma infelice, non importa ; l' ultimo periodo, che qui interessa, è sicuramente genuino ; e vi si attesta che il pretore provvede, senz' altro, con decreti alle ulteriori fasi della *missio* ; cioè :

(*a*) *ut possidere liceat* (cfr. Lenel, *Ed.* p. 53).

(*b*) *ut decedatur de possessione.*

E pertanto si manifesta in tutta la sua evidenza in tutti quei passi avanti esaminati il motivo delle interpolazioni, foggiate tutte su di uno stampo, con le frasi consuete : *melius*, *civilius*, *tutius* e che introducono un mezzo processuale qualsiasi, sostituito alla difesa privata. Nel brano ultimo, riferito i caratteri dello stile bizantino vi sono impressi.[4]

[1] Il Lenel (*l. c.* p. 83) pensa a interdetti formulati per i singoli casi *in factum*.

[2] Lotmar (*ZSS.* vol. xxxi. p. 100) intende l' Int. *Quod legatorum* ; contro Lenel, *l. c.* p. 81.

[3] Cfr. Lotmar, *l. c.* p. 101 ; ma vedi Lenel, *l. c.* p. 83, n. 1.

[4] Per altri argomenti sostanziali v. Lenel, *l. c.* p. 84 ; ma essi hanno per me un valore ancora più assoluto, da escludere nel caso fatto da Ulpiano l' Int. *Quod legatorum*, o altro mezzo giudiziario. Diversamente Lotmar, *l. c.* p. 103.

39. (*g*) Una costituzione dell' a. 205 attesta, anche per il diritto dell' Impero, l' uso e l' efficacia del patto in forza di cui il creditore ipotecario era autorizzato ad immettersi di propria autorità nel possesso dell' ipoteca, quando al termine stabilito il suo credito non fosse sodisfatto. Se tale convenzione era pure inclusa nella *lex commissoria* non possiamo giudicare.[1] Ma dal diritto dei papiri greco-egizii è documentata ora a dovizia l' efficacia del titolo esecutivo munito della clausola καθάπερ ἐκ δίκης[2] in forza della quale, sembra,[3] che il creditore avesse diritto di pervenire senza alcun procedimento nel possesso e nel dominio del fondo. Ma nel diritto di Giustiniano, a parte il divieto della *lex commissoria* stabilito da Costantino, è inibito al creditore d' immettersi nel possesso senza l' autorizzazione del magistrato, come risulta dalla c. seguente:

3 *C.* viii. 14 (Impp. Sev. et Ant.): Creditores qui non reddita sibi pecunia conventionis legem, ingressi possessionem exercent, vim [*quidem*] facere non videntur [*attamen auctoritate praesidis possessionem adipisci debent*].

L' interpolazione delle parole segnate in corsivo è nota,[4] ed essa, come fu pure avvertito dal Naber determinò inoltre la soppressione del *non* avanti al verbo *potest* nella c. 5 *Cod.* ix. 12, dell' a. 294.[5]

40. E Giustiniano a ricacciare da ogni angolo della sua opera qualsiasi vestigio di privata difesa attacca pure le massime più venerande, che secondo i Romani erano fondate sulla *naturalis ratio.* E cosi la legge decemvirale: *Si nox furtum faxsit, si im occisit, iure caesus esto*, fu ridotta nei *Digesti* nei termini seguenti:[6]

4 § 1 *D.* ix. 2, Gai vii. ad ed. Lex XII. tab. furem noctu deprehensum occidere permittit [*ut tamen id ipsum cum clamore testificetur*]: interdiu autem deprehensum ita permittit occidere, si is se telo defendat, [*ut tamen aeque cum clamore testificetur*].

[1] Papin. *V. F.* 9.

[2] Per la letteratura v. Bertalan Schwarz, *Hypothek und Hypallagma*, p. 71 n. 2; cfr. Mitteis, *Grundzüge*, ii. 1, p. 94.

[3] Cfr. Bertalan, *o. c.* p. 94.

[4] Cfr. Naber, *Mnemos.* vol. xxiv. p. 171; Gradenwitz, *ZSS.* vol. xxvi. p. 348 n. 1.

[5] Un altro caso di *vis legittima* punita da Giustiniano è in *D.* xlvii. 8, 2, 18: *quidem . . . sed aliter multabitur.* Ma sul proposito della violenza nell' esercizio del diritto abbiamo la nota legge di Valentiniano dell' a. 389 riportata nel Cod. Just. viii. 4, 7, che commina la grave pena della perdita del dominio.

[6] Cfr. Riccobono, *Fontes*, p. 47 n. B.

Il clamore deve qui togliere il dubbio che l' uccisore non abbia agito in stato di necessità, per la difesa della persona.[1] I vicini accorrenti ne potranno fare la verificazione.

Ed il vivo senso di repulsione per qualsiasi atto di privata difesa manifesta con forza il legislatore in una delle solite motivazioni aggressive, che egli aggiunge alle decisioni pratiche: *Cur enim, inquit Iulianus, ad arma et rixam procedere patiatur praetor, quos potest iurisdictione sua componere?*[2] L' interrogazione è tutto un programma legislativo; da cui scaturisce poi quella massima di diritto, una tra le più cospicue e realmente universali nel sistema nuovo, cioè:

fr. 176 pr. *D.* L. xvii. Paul. 13 ad Plaut. Non est singulis concedendum, quod per magistratum publice possit fieri: ne occasio sit maioris tumultus faciendi.

La quale pel diritto elaborato dai giureconsulti non è vera. Se essa fu scritta effettivamente da Paolo, doveva avere una struttura più limitata, e riferimento particolarissimo.[3]

41. Ed ora possiamo conchiudere ed affermare che la riforma di Giustiniano rispetto allo *ius prohibendi* trascende di molto i confini e l' importanza del tema in esame. Poichè essa ci ha rivelato un nuovo atteggiamento della legislazione di Giustiniano, rispetto al diritto classico, che appare per ciò diffuso in tutta l' opera ed attuato con fermezza, mediante amputazioni profonde di decisioni e motivi e principi classici, tanto da sconvolgere tutta la fine orditura delle *actiones* e dei mezzi di difesa giudiziaria del diritto antico. E l' importanza della riforma non va ricercata alla superficie, ma nell' intimo pensiero e nella forza da cui fu prodotta. Perchè essa non è vicenda esteriore, quanto nuova luce, che rivela nel contrasto aspetti profondi delle due più grandi civiltà della storia.

In quel nucleo di norme, infatti, che è venuto alla luce, rimettendo a posto nel libro immortale ogni parola della sapienza antica, vi è un grande movimento di vita e di forza, che si esplica con l' affermazione energica della volontà individuale, e quindi con la

[1] Cfr. per altro fr. 5 pr. *D.* ix. 2 = Collatio vii. ii. iii. 3: *sin autem . . . tenebitur*; che contiene certe limitazioni in proposito, che non possono derivare dai giuristi classici.

[2] fr. 13 § 3 *D.* vii. 1. Cfr. Beseler, *Beiträge*, ii. p. 88.

[3] Ma il nesso non è dato scorgerlo: cfr. Lenel, *Pal.* i. c. 1167 n. 5: *haec ad interdicta multa posse referri palam est.* Ed il campo ora è davvero ristretto.

potenza del diritto dei singoli, che non soffre menomazione alcuna, neanche momentanea. E di sopra a questo punto centrale è incardinato e si muove tutto il sistema del diritto privato, elaborato con saggezza profonda.

Ma quella base si corrodeva ogni giorno, e la forza del diritto individuale si svigoriva nell' ultima fase dell' Impero fino a Giustiniano; in quel periodo in cui i più grandi rivolgimenti sociali e politici e spirituali si maturarono. Ora la prepotenza[1] più facilmente usurpava il posto del diritto, e nell' esquilibrio delle forze sociali lo Stato doveva assumere a sè un potere maggiore, che si estrinseca nella organizzazione amministrativa dioclezianea, salda, ordinata nei più minuti particolari, e preveggente.

Lo Stato ne esce rinvigorito, ed allarga ogni giorno più le sue funzioni, assumendo un carattere pacificatore; e per ciò per ottenere l' ordine, la disciplina, il vantaggio generale Esso esige qualsiasi restrizione della libertà dei singoli, ed in primo luogo dello assoluto diritto individuale.

Questa evoluzione si compie nella legislazione del VI secolo; essa ebbe nel suo cammino la cooperazione di una grande forza, quale era quella della dottrina cristiana,[2] che deprime e annulla i sentimenti egoistici ed inculca, come primi doveri, la pace e l' amore fra tutti gli uomini, anche per conseguire i fini della vita terrena; sentimenti che ebbero in realtà una potente penetrazione in tutti gli atti della vita.[3]

[1] Cfr. Mitteis, *Mélang. Girard*, ii. p. 226.

[2] In questo senso Leonhard, *Inst.* p. 531 n. 2 ed. ivi cit.; cfr. ora anche Lenel, *Holtzendorff's Enc.* 7 ed. p. 375 § 63. Quanto poi al problema generale dell' influenza cristiana sul diritto privato potremo volutarla via via con la conoscenza dei principî direttivi della Compilazione del sec. VI, che, come si vede, sono per noi tutti ancora un mistero; cfr. più oltre, nota ultima del presente cap.

[3] E perciò il motivo della tolleranza, della pace, della considerazione del prossimo s' insinua pure nella legislazione, come si osserva in una decisione cospicua che si ricollega alla difesa privata e quindi all' argomento in esame. Nessun dubbio, come diceva Q. Mucio, che il proprietario può cacciar via dal fondo gli animali penetrativi, con tutti i mezzi idonei allo scopo, e che non può rispondere con la *lex Aquilia* qualora un danno ne derivi alle bestie; fr. 39 *D.* ix. 2, Pomp. 7 ad Q. M. Ma Giustiniano soggiunge subito; Pomponius: *quamvis alienum pecus in agro suo quis deprehendit, sic illud expellere debet quomodo si suum deprehendisset, quoniam si quid ex ea re damnum cepit, habet proprias actiones. itaque qui pecus alienum in agro suo deprehenderit, non iure id includit, nec agere illud aliter debet, quam ut supra diximus*

Nel diritto giustinianeo si manifesta per ciò un mondo tutto nuovo, in cui la difesa privata del diritto era inconcepibile. Ed essa è surrogata dal più svariato campionario di *actiones*, *interdicta*, provvedimenti e mezzi giudiziari; perchè ciascuno deve in ogni evenienza invocare l' aiuto del magistrato, che è il solo tutore dei diritti dei singoli.

Tra i nuovi mezzi escogitati dal legislatore o dalla pratica bizantina si annovera la προυιβιτορία ἀγωγή.

## II. *IUDICIUM COMMUNI DIVIDUNDO*

42. Ma l' azione che può dirsi propria e generale per il regolamento dei rapporti tra condomini è l' *a. c. div.*, che da Giustiniano fu adibita insieme agli altri mezzi processuali nei casi più svariati. E per ciò può affermarsi che all' azione divisoria venne conferita nella Compilazione una nuova funzione, cioè quella di dirimere tutti i conflitti tra i socii e regolare la vita della comunione, senza per altro condurre allo scioglimento della medesima. Nei passi dianzi esaminati si hanno le testimonianze più cospicue del nuovo carattere assunto dal *iudicium c. d.*

E ci è noto pure che in tal modo Giustiniano ne alterò in

---

*quasi suum: sed vel abigere debet sine damno vel admonere dominum ut suum recipiat.* E qui, come si vede, la mansuetudire evangelica si scioglie in precetti e consigli che suonano duri anzi sovrumani al fiero agricoltore: *quod tibi non vis alteri ne feceris.* E perciò il proprietario deve trattare gli animali altrui come i proprii, non deve loro far male, non deve includerli, perchè del resto ha per il danno ricevuto *proprias actiones.* Deve piuttosto avvertire l' interessato (!). Indizii della mano di Triboniano: *quamvis . . . deprehendit*, *in agro*, *proprias actiones*, *quasi*, *ut suum recipiat*, e poi la ripetizione del concetto fondamentale e sovratutto lo spirito. Sospetti già in Di Marzo, *Libri ad Q. Mucium*, p. 89.

E lo stesso motivo opera nella chiusa del celebre frammento di Alfeno II. dig. che tratta del bettoliere che rincorre *in semita noctu* colui che gli aveva rapita la lucerna: fr. 52 § 1 *D.* ix. 2. . . . [*sed si ab eo non prior vapulasset*, *sed cum ei lucernam eripere vellet*, *rixatus esset*, *tabernarii culpa factum videri*]. Giustiniano, dunque, ammonisce, che chi esercita la difesa del proprio diritto e rincorre il rapitore delle cose proprie, deve usare moderazione e pacatezza; cercherà di strappare al malvivente le cose sottratte, ma non deve attaccare la persona; deve prima lasciarsi battere, e poi magari non avrà colpa del danno che nella reazione apporterà all' altro. Per la critica del brano, vedi le osservazioni finissime di Huvelin, *Mél. Girard*, i. p. 259 seg., il quale per altro non attribuisce le addizioni ai Compilatori. Io ritengo decisivo il confronto con le aggiunte al testo di Q. Mucio, avanti riportato.

maniera essenziale la natura; poichè nel diritto classico ogni azione *divisoria* mirava in via principale ad effettuare lo scioglimento della comunione, con l' attribuzione della parte spettante a ciascuno dei socii; ed in secondo luogo poi a definire in una volta tutti i rapporti personali sorti per causa della comunione.

Così si spiega che un profondo conoscitore delle fonti romane quale era Cuiacio[1] potè vigorosamente negare l' ammissibilità del *iudicium c. d.* durante la comunione; perchè in realtà la Compilazione di Giustiniano contiene tutti gli elementi proprii dell' uno e dell' altro sistema, in linee rilevate; ma al grande interprete si manifestava solo quello arcaico, perchè egli accostava il *Corpus Iuris* con spirito d' umanista, che gl' impediva di scorgere e comprendere l' opera di Giustiniano. E l' influenza del Cuiacio fu somma, come si sa, ed anche qui perniciosa; e valse a velare la verità per lungo tempo, tanto che il Windscheid[2] giustamente lamentava, che l' *actio c. d.* era stata trascurata nella dottrina rispetto alla sua funzione regolatrice dei rapporti tra socii, e riporta pure decisioni giudiziarie che fino agli ultimi tempi si ostinavano a negarla.

Ma i Greci e la Glossa avevano ben conosciuto l' indole dell' *a. c. div.* giustinianea, senza ombra di dubbio. E la critica più recente ha definitivamente[3] stabilito i confini tra il vecchio ed il nuovo in questa materia, come è tramandato alla rinfusa nel *Corpus Iuris*.

43. E pertanto in questo luogo non interessa prendere in esame tutti i singoli testi che provano la nuova funzione dell' *a. c. d.*, quanto piuttosto adunare i precipui tra essi, o quelli che offrono maggiori difficoltà d' interpretazione, e presentarli ordinati in V categorie, alle quali si aggregano i passi adibiti:

(*a*) per attuare lo *ius prohibendi*, nei casi e nei limiti in cui esso ha luogo nella Compilazione;

(*b*) per la partizione ed il conseguimento delle spese fatte da uno dei socii;

(*c*) per il danneggiamento apportato dal socio alla cosa comune;

(*d*) per la esecuzione di opere conservative sulla cosa, ed in particolare per le opere relative ad edificî e muri comuni;

[1] *Opp.* vol. vii. p. 575 ad l. 3 *D.* Com. div.

[2] *Pand.* § 449 n. 4, ed ivi citati.

[3] Accenni già in Pernice, *ZSS.* vol. xix. p. 173 n. 4; ma ora in modo esauriente Berger, *Teilungsklagen*, p. 221 seg., che tuttavia lascia insoluti molti punti, del resto secondari.

(*e*) per applicazioni varie del *iud. c. d.* e *fam. erc.*, anche per conferire efficacia giuridica a rapporti che non l' avevano nel diritto classico.

44. (*a*) *Prohibitio.*

E per quanto concerne il primo gruppo non occorre indugiare oltre sul tema dello *ius prohibendi*, che è stato discusso sotto ogni aspetto nelle pagine che precedono; onde è sufficiente qui referirci all' esame compiuto sui fr. 26 *D.* viii. 2; 28 *D.* x. 3; 3 §§ 2, 3 *D.* xxxix. 1.

45. (*b*) *Impensae.*

Il *iudicium c. d.* adibito, durante la comunione, per il conseguimento di spese fatte da uno dei socii è più direttamente attestato dai seguenti passi.

fr. 14 § 1 *D.* x. 3, Paul. 3 ad Plaut.—quae cum ita sint, rectissime dicitur etiam impendiorum nomine utile iudicium dari debere mihi in socium [*etiam manente rei communione*] . . . igitur et si abalienavero praedium quia in ea causa fuit, ut mihi actio dari deberet, danda mihi erit, ut Iulianus quoque scribit [*negotiorum gestorum actio*].

Questo frammento collocato *in sede materiae* contiene delle riforme gravissime, ed è interpolato in varî luoghi. Ma qui non è il caso di prendere in esame il testo intero, tanto più che la ricostruzione di esso, fatta già or sono parecchi anni nel mio Seminario, sarà pubblicata fra breve.[1]

Ma i due punti che qui occorre rilevare possono ora dirsi lievi. Nel passo si accorda il *iud. c. d.* utile per le spese fatte da un socio sulla cosa comune, che deve pur aver luogo *etiam manente rei communione.* In secondo luogo si dà l' *actio negotiorum gestorum* al socio che abbia alienato il fondo. E sono appunto coteste azioni che furono in ogni tempo causa di dubbii e discussioni.

Infatti l' ammissibilità di quelle azioni nei termini presupposti perturba nel modo più strano tutte le nostre conoscenze. E per ciò, rispetto al primo punto, si volle ristabilire una concordanza artificiale con l' inserzione[2] di un *non* dopo la parola *etiam*

[1] V. per ora Berger, *o. c.* p. 210 e seg. ed ivi citati; per altro i punti essenziali in cui dissento dal Berger e dagli altri scrittori, circa l' interpretazione del passo giustinianeo, si mostreranno da sè stessi.

[2] Cuiacio, *Opp.* vol. v. p. 907, e così ancora l' opinione dominante.

della prima frase sopra trascritta ; e si attribuì facilmente poi ad una glossa maldestra la menzione dell' *actio negotiorum gestorum*.[1]

Rimedii vani ed arbitrarî, consueti per altro e suggeriti soltanto dalla imperfetta conoscenza che si è avuta del dritto giustinianeo, che è restato fin dal sec. xvi, in grazia degli studî più profondi, come offuscato dallo splendore dei passi classici, serrati, tersi e coordinati sempre in una suprema armonia.

Ma oggi quei dibattiti hanno termine. Si sa che il *iudicium c. d.* fu ammesso dai Compilatori in realtà *etiam manente rei communione*, e si dirige appunto per costringere il socio a non impedire un' opera sulla cosa comune, ovvero a pagare gli oneri che gli incombono, o la parte delle spese, e così via. E parimenti dovrebbe esser noto che Giustiniano accordò pure al socio, accanto all' *actio c. d.*, anche la *negot. gest.* per rendergli possibile il conseguimento delle spese fatte. E l' *actio neg. gest.* ritorna, precisamente congiunta ai *iudicia divisoria*, nelle costituzioni, 18 *C.* iii. 36 ; 20 *C.* eod., inserita nei rescritti con le parole *vel negotiorum gestorum*.

La stessa interpolazione che abbiamo riscontrata nel fr. 14 § 1 in esame si riaffaccia poi, in una forma più larvata, nel fr. 29 *D.* x. 3, Paul. 2 quaest. e che tratta una delle ipotesi contenute in quel testo ; cioè di spese fatte da un socio sulla cosa comune nella credenza che il compartecipe fosse Tizio invece di Caio. Ebbene nel fr. 29 si legge :

*recte dicitur etiam communi dividundo iudicium ei sufficere.*

Paolo aveva scritto assai probabilmente *recte dicitur in communi dividundo iudicium ea quae impendisset venire.*

Nel testo rifatto da Giustiniano e la congiunzione *etiam* ed il verbo *sufficere*[2] stanno ad indicare che il socio a conseguire dall' altro la parte delle spese può adoperare varî mezzi, *anche* l' *actio c. d.* laddove il giureconsulto non poteva ammettere qui che il giudizio divisorio, e mai altra azione personale. Infatti la spesa sulla cosa comune, non essendo eseguita in considerazione della

[1] Così già Cuiacio, *l. c.*; Scialoja ad h. l. nella nostra edizione del *Digesto* ; Berger, *Teilungskl.* p. 217, ma v. Krüger ad h. l. (ed. 12[a]).

[2] Verbo frequente nei brani interpolati : *D.* vi. 2, 7, 17 : *Nec quisquam putet hoc nos existimare, sufficere* ;—*D.* xv. 1, 19, 2 : *Idem etiam contra eveniet quamvis in duobus dominis sufficiat pro socio vel communi dividundo actio* : Ulp. aveva scritto presso a poco : *contra eveniet in duobus dominis, nam inter eos est c. d. iudicium.*

persona, non può mai dar luogo all' *actio negot. gest.* La quale è esclusa dal giureconsulto nella stessa dimostrazione, esplicitamente: *neque enim negotia socii gero, sed propriam rem tueor, et magis ex re, in quam impenditur quam ex persona socii actio nascitur.*[1] Ho ragione per ciò di ritenere che il *sufficere* fu inserto dai Compilatori al posto della proposizione in cui Paolo escludeva nel caso in esame l' *a. negot. gest.*

46. (*c*) *damnum.*

Il danno arrecato da uno dei socii alla cosa comune può ora immediatamente essere perseguito in giudizio per mezzo del c. d.

Il principio è appunto codificato nel celebre passo di Papiniano, che giova qui riportare per intero:

fr. 28 *D.* x. 3—Sabinus ait in re communi neminem dominorum iure facere quicquam invito altero posse. unde manifestum esse prohibendi ius esse: in re enim pari potiorem causam esse prohibentis constat [*sed etsi in communi prohiberi socius a socio ne quid faciat potest, ut tamen factum opus tollat, cogi non potest si cum prohibere poterat, hoc praetermisit: et ideo per communi dividundo actionem damnum sarciri poterit sin autem facienti consensit, nec pro damno habet actionem. quod si quid absenti socio ad laesionem eius fecit, tunc etiam tollere cogitur*].

L' interpolazione è variamente indicata.[2] Ma io ritengo che in realtà essa comprenda tutta la seconda parte dello squarcio.[3] Nel periodo *sed etsi . . . praetermisit*, si dispone che il socio non ha diritto di ottenere la rimozione dell' opera fatta dall' altro, qualora egli abbia omesso, potendolo, di opporre il suo divieto. Questo è sicuramente un concetto nuovo, che è in vivo contrasto, come sappiamo, con la natura del condominio classico, in cui ciascuno dei socii conserva una signoria piena ed indipendente, *pro indiviso*, sulla cosa comune; e che perciò non può soffrire menomazione

[1] Si sa che l' *a. negot. gest.* può aver luogo tra condomini, ma solo quando si verifichino le condizioni espresse appunto da Paolo nel testo; cfr. *D.* iii. 5, 39, Paul. x. ad Sab.—*quia potui partem meam ita defendere, ut socii partem defendere non cogerer.* *D.* x. 3, 6, 2 Ulp. 19 ad ed.—*ceterum non alias c. d. iudicio, locus erit, ut et Papinianus scribit, nisi id demum gessit, sine quo partem suam recte administrare non potuit: alioquin si potuit, habet negotiorum gestorum actionem eaque tenetur.*

[2] Cfr. Lenel, *ZSS.* xii. p. 14 n. 3 [*si cum prohibere . . . praetermisit*]; Fadda in *Studii Brugi*, p. 144 n. 2 [*sin autem . . . cogitur*].

[3] Così già Segrè, *Rivista it. per le scienze giur.* vol. viii. p. 373; Berger, *Teilungskl.* p. 233; Paozzi, *Mélanges Girard*, ii. *l. c.*

per un semplice atto di negligenza. Ma di più la forma del tratto ha varî indizii rivelatori della mano di Triboniano; e cioè il mutamento del soggetto a cominciare dalla proposizione *cum prohibere poterat*; l' imperfetto indicativo *poterat*; la frase *ut tamen* = *dummodo*, adoperata con vera prodigalità dai compilatori, per introdurre limitazioni e nuovi presupposti alle massime riferite dai classici.[1]

Nella continuazione poi l' aggiunta interpolatizia è manifesta per i riscontri ormai noti: e qui appunto si rinviene l' *actio c. d.* diretta unicamente al risarcimento del danno. Ed inoltre, nella chiusa, emerge quel concetto tutto giustinianeo: che l' opera fatta nell' assenza del socio deve esser rimossa, *si . . . ad laesionem eius fecit*. Significa questo che l' elemento della lesione dell' interesse del socio è essenziale, onde sia autorizzata dalla legge la rimozione della opera? Ma se così è, si deve certamente riconoscere che il socio in assenza dell' altro, o quando questi non contraddica, può fare sulla medesima tutte le opere che siano di vantaggio, senza timore nè dello *ius prohibendi*,[2] nè dello *ius tollendi* e nemmeno del risarcimento del danno.[3] La questione è molto grave, e sarà esaminata più oltre. Qui interessava solo accertare, che per il danno dato da uno dei socii si può provocare il *iud. c. div.*, senza chiedere lo scioglimento della comunione, e che questo principio è d' origine giustinianea.

47. (*d*) *refectiones aedificiorum*.

Il condomino secondo il diritto classico non poteva fare nemmeno le riparazioni necessarie all' edificio o muro comune senza il consenso degli altri. E non è dubbio che questa norma è schietta applicazione di un principio fondamentale. Ma tosto essa è abbandonata da Giustiniano:

fr. 12 *D.* x. 3, Ulp. 71 ad ed. *Si aedes communes sint aut* paries communis et eum reficere vel demolire [*vel in eum immittere quid opus sit, communi dividundo iudicio erit agendum, aut interdicto uti possidetis experimur*].

Il significato di questo passo è molto piano, e la interpretazione ferma fin dalla Glossa. Vi si dice che ciascuno dei condomini di

[1] Cfr. *D.* vi. 1, 21 (due volte); *D.* ix. 2, 4 (due volte); *D.* xli. 1, 54, 2-3 (due volte); *D.* xlvii. 8, 1.

[2] Cfr. fr. 26 *D.* viii. 2.

[3] In questo senso giustamente il Fadda, *Studii Brugi*, p. 144; e così gli antichi, cfr. Baldo ad h. l.

un edificio o di un muro può costringere gli altri socii a riparare o demolire l' edificio, ed anche a consentire una immissione nel muro. La coazione cui il testo si riferisce è giudiziaria. Il socio ha a sua disposizione vari mezzi, e cioè l' *actio c. d.* o l' int. *Uti possidetis*, coi quali può costringere l' altro a non impedire la riparazione o demolizione dell' edificio, ovvero qualsiasi opera necessaria.

E l' int. *Uti possidetis* serviva in realtà al possessore solitario allo scopo indicato, cioè per respingere la violenza dei terzi :

fr. 3 § 2 *D.* xliii. 17, Ulp. 69 ad ed. Hoc interdictum sufficit ei, qui aedificare in suo prohibetur : etenim videris mihi possessionis controversiam facere, qui prohibes me uti mea possessione.

Ma nuova è l' applicazione che Giustiniano volle fare di questo mezzo nei rapporti fra i condomini ; perchè nel dritto classico l' interdetto non poteva avere effetto alcuno tra due possessori. Lo stesso Ulpiano nel fr. 3 pr. eod. scrive : *neuter nostrum vincetur nam et tu possides et ego.* E se vi è caso in cui si deve applicare questa massima, quello qui considerato della comproprietà è il più sicuro.

Non occorre quindi di cercare altre spiegazioni del testo in esame, perchè certamente Giustiniano volle concedere anche l' interdetto possessorio tra comproprietari. E l' *actio c. d.* è pur qui rivolta al fine di comprimere il divieto del socio, che impedisce le riparazioni, o le nuove opere sull' edificio comune, la quale funzione del *iudicium c. d.* sappiamo che è giustinianea.

L' interpolazione del testo è nota, per altro ;[1] ma io ritengo che salvo le parole *paries communis et eum reficere vel demolire* tutto il resto è opera di Triboniano. E credo che il testo dicesse semplicemente che mediante l' *actio c. d.* il socio può ottenere nel caso di disaccordo la divisione del muro comune. I compilatori lo ampliarono, come di solito, con altri esempii, perchè in esso avevano consacrato un nuovo ordinamento che giovava mettere in evidenza.

48. Più fine e perciò difficile a dimostrare è l' alterazione introdotta in un altro passo di Gaio, che ha un significato di grande rilievo :

fr. 32 *D.* xxxix. 2, Gai. 28 ad ed. prov. Si aedibus meis proximae sint aedes meae et tuae, quaeritur, an, si hae vitium mihi faciant, cavere mihi debeas pro damno propriarum mearum aedium, scilicet

[1] Pernice, *ZSS.* xix. p. 173 n. 3 ; ed ora più pienamente Berger, *Teilungskl.* p. 237.

pro qua parte dominus existes. et hoc plerisque[1] placet: sed movet me, quod ipse meas[2] aedes reficere possim et impensas pro socio aut communi dividundo iudicio pro parte consequi. nam et si unas aedes communes tecum habui eaeque vitium faciant et circa refectionem earum cessare videaris, nostri praeceptores negant cavère te debere [*quia ipse reficere possim recepturus pro parte, quod impenderim iudicio societatis aut*] communi dividundo: ideo et interpositam cautionem minus utilem futuram, quia alia ratione damnum mihi posset sarciri. [*et est plane nostrorum praeceptorum haec sententia, ut credamus inutilem esse damni infecti stipulationem, quo casu damnum alia actione sarciri possit: quod et in superiore casu intelligendum est.*]

Il passo di Gaio a prima giunta appare perfetto nella struttura ed illibato nella forma; perciò è bene qui procedere con ogni circospezione.

Quello che si enuncia nei punti segnati in corsivo è sicuramente prodotto di alterazioni giustinianee. Di più il caso esaminato nell' inizio del passo fu male compreso dal Mommsen, che, seguendo la Glossa, propose la correzione *meas* in *eas*, per significare che il socio ha facoltà di riparare liberamente la cosa comune. Questo senso del passo è arbitrario, e svisa i presupposti di fatto e turba la limpidezza delle norme giuridiche vigenti in questa materia. Infatti Gaio suppone il caso di chi abbia comune un edificio con altri, e contiguo allo stesso uno di sua esclusiva proprietà. L' edificio comune ha cagionato danno a quello proprio del socio, e si cerca il mezzo per il risarcimento. La maggioranza degli autori, dice il testo, accordavano tra socii la *cautio damni infecti*;[3] Gaio invece oppone: che nella specie il proprietario danneggiato può riparare il suo edificio, *meas aedes*, e chiedere poi dal socio la quota delle spese coll' *actio c. d.* ovvero con l' *actio pro socio.*[4] Gaio rafforza la decisione supponendo un altro caso più tipico, in cui il danno sia avvenuto nell' unico edificio comune ai due condomini; nel qual caso, se il socio indugia o vien meno a provvedere alle riparazioni necessarie all' edificio, secondo la sentenza dei Sabiniani, non si può ricorrere alla *cautio damni infecti*. Quale la ragione? Qui appunto

[1] Cassio? cfr. apud Ulp. fr. 28 *D.* xxxix. 2.

[2] *Eas* Mo., e certamente male.

[3] Cfr. fr. 35, 37 *D.* xxxix. 2; *D.* ix. 2, 27, 10 = Collatio xii. 7, 8; *D.* xxxix. 2, 39, Pomp. 21 ad Sab.

[4] Cfr. *D.* xxxix. 2, 28, Ulp. 81 ad ed.: *propter vitium communis parietis . . . aedificia sua fulsit.*

si nasconde il vizio del testo, poichè vi si dice cosa del tutto contraria alla essenza della *communio*, affermandosi che il socio diligente possa, malgrado la negligenza o il diniego dell' altro, eseguire le riparazioni ed ottenere poi coll' *actio c. d.* la quota di spese dal socio. Ma noi sappiamo, e per fortuna da Gaio stesso e dalla medesima opera, che il socio non può senza il consenso degli altri riparare il muro comune:

fr. 8 *D.* 8, 2, Gaio 7 ad ed. prov. Parietem qui naturali ratione communis est, alterutri vicinorum demoliendi eum et reficiendi ius non est, quia non solus dominus est.[1]

E questa decisione ha un fondamento certissimo nella essenza della comunione classica, e nell' insegnamento di Sabino, maestro ed autore del nostro Gaio. Il quale non poteva non applicare in proposito la celebre massima: *Sabinus, in re communi neminem dominorum iure facere quicquam invito altero posse.*

La contraddizione quindi è patente. E come tale non poteva sfuggire alla Glossa, perchè il testo in esame di Gaio [fr. 32] dice: *ipse reficere possim*, cioè in ogni caso, senza alcuna considerazione del consenso degli altri. E perciò la Glossa usò qui il consueto espediente, distinguendo: le riparazioni dalle opere nuove; Glossa *possim; sed hic de reficiendo, ibi de novo opere faciendo.*[2]

Ma per sostenere siffatta distinzione la Glossa richiamava in confronto il fr. 12 *D.* x. 3; giusto quello in cui l' alterazione giustinianea è oggi accertata. Non resta pertanto alcuna via di scampo per mantenere il testo di Gaio come ci è tramandato, e per ciò deve ritenersi dimostrata l' origine emblematica del periodo: *quia ipse reficere possim recepturus pro parte quod impenderim.* E l' interpolazione consente, in modo ben preciso, che ciascuno dei socii possa, in ogni caso, eseguire nell' edificio comune le opere necessarie, e costringere poi gli altri a contribuire la loro quota mediante il *iudicium c. d.*

Ed a chiarire l' interpolazione, altri argomenti balzano ora fuori; invero il bel periodo di stile gaiano, uscito dalle mani dei compilatori, non è in realtà che una riproduzione di quello redatto da Gaio nel caso esposto avanti, e che si riferiva, come sappiamo, ad una specie ben diversa: *quod ipse meas aedes reficere possim et impensas pro socio aut communi dividundo iudicio pro parte consequi.*

[1] Cfr. *D.* viii. 2, 40: *nullo iure fenestras immisisse.*

[2] Vedremo nel c. iv. che questa opinione è ancora dominante.

I due brani coincidono appieno nella sostanza, e parzialmente anche nelle parole. Per i compilatori una decisione unica per i due casi, che ritennero assai vicini nei presupposti di fatto, esercitava sempre una grande attrattiva. La semplificazione del diritto, e particolarmente dei mezzi di attuazione, era obbiettivo precipuo che Giustiniano si propose e con tutte le forze si sforzò di conseguire. Sappiamo altresì che l' abuso dei mezzi generò equivoci, contraddizioni e quindi dibattiti senza fine.

L' interpolazione inoltre risulta dalla designazione giustinianea dell' *actio pro socio* comunemente indicata: *iud. societatis*, e poi dal confronto con la motivazione classica che segue nel testo: *ideo et interpositam cautionem minus utilem futuram, quia alia ratione damnum mihi posset sarciri.*

Dove è facile notare come Gaio nella seconda ipotesi contemplava unicamente il mezzo per il risarcimento del *damnum*, e non per il compenso delle *impensae*. Può mai il termine *damnum* includere anche le *impensae* fatte appunto per evitarlo? Non credo che ciò sia conforme alle consuetudini dei giuristi, che possedevano un linguaggio tecnico meraviglioso, per cui potevano sempre esprimere i loro concetti con grande rilievo, precisione e simmetria.

Anche la chiusa del testo è sospetta; avvegnachè essa non contiene nulla di nuovo, ma riassume parafrasandola la motivazione che precede: inoltre *alia actione* è troppo determinato in una formula di carattere generale, e Gaio poco avanti aveva bene scritto *alia ratione*; e così Labeone in una specie analoga riferita da Ulpiano in *D.* xxxix. 1, 3, 2.

Il *plane* è ora segnalato come indizio per scorgere la mano di Triboniano.[1] E nel riepilogo del testo vi è per altro un pensiero legislativo ben intellegibile; chè avendo Giustiniano ammesso tra socii il *iud. c. d.* per regolamento di tutti i rapporti, la *cautio d. infecti* perdeva qualsiasi funzione.[2]

[1] Cfr. Peters, *ZSS.* vol. xxxii. p. 254.

[2] E il disfavore per la *cautio d. inf.* si manifesta in altri passi interpolati, così in *D.* xxxix. 2, 39, Pomp. 21 ad Sab.: *Inter quos paries communis est, aedificiorum nomine, quae quisque propria habet stipulari d. inf.* [*solet. sed tunc ea cautio necessaria est, cum aut alter solus aedificat et vitium ex opere futurum est, aut alter pretiosiora aedificia habet et plus damni sensurus sit decidente pariete; alioquin si aequale periculum est, quantum quis vicino praestat tantum ab eo consequitur.*]

Distinzioni tutte balorde queste, che provano soltanto la inutilità della *cautio*. Per l' interpolazione del verbo *solet* vedi più oltre p. 101, n. 1.

Dunque, in conclusione, abbiamo qui un testo fondamentale, che fu alterato dai compilatori,[1] e che rende una precisa testimonianza del mutamento del diritto in questa materia. Poichè i Sabiniani reputavano inutile la *cautio damni infecti* tra socii, adducendo che ciascuno potesse far valere le proprie ragioni nell' *iudicium c. d.*, nel momento della divisione; Giustiniano invece dispone che ciascuno dei socii può riparare la casa senza attendere il consenso e la cooperazione degli altri, e che mediante l' *actio c. d.* egli può ottenere, in qualsiasi momento, da ciascuno la parte di spese che gli spetta. A togliere ogni dubbiezza in questa materia o ragione di equivoco, è bene ricordare che nelle fonti è frequentissimo il caso di ripetizione di spese fatte sulla cosa comune da uno dei socii nel giudizio divisorio. Ma appunto nei testi genuini si intende sempre che il giudizio è ordinato per la divisione, ed inoltre che le spese furono fatte o da chi aveva la amministrazione della cosa comune, e quindi col consenso dei socii, ovvero in casi in cui il condomino è ignoto; mai però in seguito ad un dissenso come può intendersi il testo di Gaio che abbiamo esaminato; in cui il contrasto tra i condomini è per lo meno possibile, e la decisione è formulata in un modo assoluto. La cosa dunque è ben diversa. I passi più notevoli, nei quali si accenna alla valutazione di spese fatte in re communi nell' *iudicium c. d.*, sono riportati in nota.[2]

La opinione infine di Cuiacio,[3] che spiegava la decisione gaiana con l' *Oratio divi Marci* non ha bisogno di confutazione, perchè l' opera ad ed. da cui il fr. deriva fu compiuta avanti di Marco Aurelio;[4] ma poi, e questo è decisivo, la coazione dei socii a pagare le spese di riparazioni agli edificii non si attuava secondo il SC. mediante il *iud. c. d.*, sibbene con la minaccia della perdita della proprietà.[5]

---

Probabilmente Pomponio riferiva la dottrina contraria di Sabino, i compilatori, per ciò, soppressero tutta la trattazione.

[1] Diversamente Berger, *Teilungsklagen*, p. 230.

[2] fr. 4 § 4 e 5 *D.* x. 3 (vi si discute dell' actio, non dei presupposti); 6 § 12 *D.* x. 3 (pena); 6 pr. *D.* x. 3 (socio ignoto); 11 pr. *D.* x. 3 (presupposto accordo); 38 § 1 *D.* xvii. 2 (accordo); 65 § 13 *D.* xvii. 2 (si discute solo dell' actio); 15 § 19 *D.* xxxix. 2 (come il precedente); 46 *D.* xliv. 7 (cosa comune col pupillo amministrata dal socio?).

[3] *Opp.* v. iv. p. 785; cfr. c. i. n. 12, p. 47.

[4] Cfr. Fitting, *Alter und Folge*, p. 54; Lenel, *Pal.* i. p. 189 n. 1.

[5] I compilatori non fecero ricorso mai nei *Dig.* all' *Oratio divi Marci*, perchè le riforme da loro introdotte in questa materia erano più profonde.

49. Ed ora possiano valutare un passo di Paolo riferito dai Visigoti e che è sorprendente:

Paul. Sent. v. 10, 2: *De communi pariete utilitatis causa hoc coepit observari, ut aedificet quidem cuius aedificare interest, cogatur vero socius portionis suae impensas agnoscere*

Il testo è veramente strano, e non ha riscontro alcuno nemmeno nei libri di Giustiniano. Ma è davvero un' inezia, quando si consideri che la credibilità di quest' altra fonte scade ogni giorno sempre più.

Il senso della sentenza è piano. Vi si afferma che il condomino del muro comune può edificare senza il consenso del socio, e che questi può esser costretto a pagare la sua quota di spese. E qui non è dubbio che vi si supponga un socio dissenziente, come lo prova la coazione cui si ricorre per obbligarlo al contributo. Di più, la frase *utilitatis causa* indica già che vi si enuncia una norma eccezionale; e l' altra *cuius aedificare interest* presuppone e designa un interesse particolare o più immediato di uno dei socii. Ma è ciò possibile? Come poteva affermarlo un giureconsulto, quando tutti i testi classici negano ad uno dei socii anche la semplice facoltà di reficere il muro comune, anche nell' interesse di tutti? Il nostro testo invece ammette pure la *aedificatio*. Ma l' origine spuria del testo si mostra per varî indizî: non è indicata l' azione con la quale il socio può costringere l' altro a contribuire per l' opera fatta; manca il soggetto di *aedificet*, e la frase *coepit observari* è indeterminata ed insolita ai giuristi. Tutto ciò induce a ritenere che i compilatori visigoti ebbero a mutare profondamente il passo di Paolo, riferendosi alla pratica del loro tempo. Certo ad una pratica male appresa; perchè in nessun diritto e tanto meno nella vita pratica, può esser mai consentito ad uno dei socii, che ha un interesse esclusivo (*sic*) ad innalzare il muro comune, che egli possa costringere il male avventurato condomino a pagare una parte della spesa. La norma di diritto in tali casi è ben diversa, come appare dalle legislazioni moderne.[1]

Ed è rimarchevole che la interpretatio visigota riconduce quella

Ma i Compilatori del *Codice* accolsero un rescritto di Filippo: c. 4 *Cod.* viii. 10, che vi si riferiva, e, come sembra, lo ampliarono pure; infatti il brano: *etenim . . . constiterit* è fortemente sospetto [*aedificaveris* ?] e certamente spuria la frase *vindicare vel.*

[1] *Cod. civ. italiano*, art. 555.

sentenza così sbalestrata alla sua giusta misura, e così spiega: *sed si ab uno ex his communis paries propter metum ruinae fuerit reparatus expensas fabricae socius illi pro portione sua praestare cogendus est.*

Così per lo meno si ritorna all' ipotesi delle riparazioni. E la interpretatio inoltre premette al periodo ora riferito una nozione esatta della *cautio damni infecti*, che sicuramente è tratta da buone fonti.

50. E così tutta questa materia del *paries communis*, giustamente malfamata in ogni tempo per le sfrontate contraddizioni con cui fu presentata nei *Digesti*,[1] riprende la sua figura semplice e dignitosa; separando precisamente le norme del diritto classico dal nuovo assetto che Giustiniano le diede. Onde non solo essa ebbe un' impronta che 'può servire di modello al diritto moderno' come già osservò il Brugi,[2] ma costituisce nelle sue linee essenziali il diritto moderno.

51. (*e*) *Applicazioni varie.*

In questo gruppo ho raccolti casi varii che dimostrano l' applicazione costante del *c. d. iudicium* per definire subito, in tutte le evenienze, i rapporti obbligatorî sorti per causa della *res communis.*

fr. 15 *D.* x. 3, Paul. 5 ad Plaut. Si socius servi communis nomine conventus et condemnatus sit [*aget c. d. et antequam praestet*]; nam et si noxali iudicio cum uno actum sit [*statim aget cum socio ut ei pars traderetur, cautionibus interpositis, ut, si non dederit, reddat*].

Che il *c. d.* serve qui al socio per ottenere immediatamente la prestazione dall' altro è detto nel testo: *statim . . . ut*; perciò il testo è giustinianeo; come inoltre si dimostra dalla forma *aget*, che nel secondo periodo manca poi del soggetto, invece di *agere potest.* Ed invero il verbo *agere* al futuro o al congiuntivo concessivo *agas* è indizio certo d' interpolazioni.[3]

[1] Cfr. Zachariä, *Zeitschr. f. g. RW.* vol. xii. p. 271 in nota, che la designa come una delle materie più aggrovigliate; Berger, *Teilungskl.* p. 238 ed ivi cit.

[2] *Rivista ital. per le s. giur.* vol. iv. p. 405.

[3] Cotali forme sono soltanto giustificate nelle *Epistulae* o nei brani da esse derivati, così p. es. in *D.* xii. 5, 15; d' ordinario hanno impronta legislativa in quanto esprimono la facoltà concessa dal legislatore, e non quella che viene all' individuo dal proprio diritto. Esempii: 30 § 1 *D.* xxxiii. 2 (Riccobono, in *BIDR.* vi. p. 139); fr. 20 *D.* xliii. 16 (forse un sunto dell' originale); fr. 60 § 2 *D.* xix. 2 (cfr. Gradenwitz, *Interpol.* p. 29; ma l' interpolazione s' inizia con la parola *agis*; fr. 18 § 2 *D.* x. 3 (cfr. più oltre in questo lavoro); fr. 21 *D.* xvii. 2 (il brano è indicato da Eisele e Krüger come glossa; certamente male).

La trattazione di questa materia nelle opere dei giuristi era ben più complicata, come è ancora visibile dal fr. 8 *D.* ix. 4 di Ulpiano, che peraltro è fortemente interpolato. Ma l' argomento potrà essere esaminato nel capitolo relativo alle azioni tra condomini.[1]

52. fr. 23 *D.* x. 3, Ulp. 32 ad Ed. Si convenerit inter te et socium tuum, ut alternis annis fructum perciperetis, et non patiatur te socius tui anni fructum percipere, videndum, utrum ex conducto sit actio an vero communi dividundo. Eadem quaestio est et si socius, qui convenerat ut alternis annis frueretur, pecus immisit et effecit, ut futuri anni fructus quos socius percipere oportuit, corrumperentur. [*et puto magis communi dividundo iudicium quam ex conducto locum habere* (*quae enim locatio est cum merces non intercesserit ?*) *aut certe actionem incerti civilem reddendam.*]

La frase *locum habere* si riporta al *iud. c. d.* nella sua nuova funzione regolatrice della comunione, ed è perciò giustinianea. La soluzione è sostanzialmente di Ulpiano ; il *puto magis* avverte però che i compilatori hanno eliminato la trattazione più ampia del giurista, condensandone il risultato e aggiungendovi la famosa *civilis incerti a.*[2]

fr. 17 *D.* xvii. 2, Paul. 6 ad Sab. Sed et si socius alienaverit contra pactionem accipit committit et tenetur [*societatis aut communi dividundo*] iudicio.[3]

Paolo aveva scritto : *iudicio pro socio.*

fr. 19 § 2 *D.* xv. 1 ; cfr. supra, p. 79, n. 2.

fr. 4 *D.* xxxiii. 3. Iavol. 9 rp. [*itaque de ea re arbiter communi div. sumendus est.*[4]]

53. E la riforma attuata con perfetta vigilanza si propaga quasi naturalmente al *iudicium familiae erciscundae*, in cui fu applicata pure per munire di coazione rapporti che nel diritto classico non avevano sanzione giuridica. Un esempio insigne si rinviene appunto nel

fr. 18 § 2 *D.* x. 2, Ulp. 19 ad ed. Idem quaerit, si quis testamento caverit, ut servus exportandus veneat, officio familiae erc. iudicis contineri, ut voluntas defuncti non intercidat. sed et cum

[1] Diversamente Berger, *Teilungskl.* p. 227.

[2] Cfr. Pernice, *ZSS.* xix. p. 174 nota.

[3] La denominazione *iudicium societatis* deve considerarsi sospetta.

[4] Pernice, *ZSS.* xix. p. 174, considera qui il *iud.* come « ein letztes Auskunftsmittel » e così Berger, *Teilungskl.* p. 239. Ma Giavoleno discuteva solo il diritto o meno del socio di fare immissioni nel *paries communis*, è perciò la quistione della divisione non gli si poteva presentare alla mente.

monumentum iussit testator fieri, familiae erciscundae [*agent, ut fiat*]. idem tamen temptat, quia heredum interest, quos ius monumenti sequitur, praescriptis verbis posse eos experiri, ut monumentum fiat.

Nel § che precede Pomponio negava, ed Ulpiano plaudiva vivamente (*rectissime*), che si potessero dedurre nel *iudicium f. erc.* indagini circa la morte del testatore ecc., poichè: *haec ad divisionem rerum hereditariarum non pertinere.* L' introduzione del § sopra trascritto: *idem quaerit* è dell' amanuense ($F^1$), ma nel ms. si legge pure l' emendazione del correttore ($F^2$): *idemque erit*, che rappresentava la dizione originaria del testo. Infatti i casi che seguono dovevano avere entrambi [1] la stessa soluzione negativa, approvata avanti da Ulpiano. L' interpolazione è evidentissima nella frase: *agent, ut fiat*; di cui invano si cercherebbe il soggetto. Anche il seguito è mal connesso col precedente, perchè i Compilatori, nel mutare e condensare la trattazione, vi eliminarono i nuovi presupposti considerati dal giurista (cfr. *quia heredum interest, quos ius m. sequitur*).

L' alterazione del testo è dunque, anche in questo luogo, di grande rilievo; perchè il *iud. f. erc.* è adoperato come il *c. div.* (26 *D.* viii. 2) per costringere il coerede a fare qualche cosa, e quindi per regolare singoli rapporti dei coeredi.[2]

54. Il motivo per altro dell' interpolazione è dichiarato, per il caso concernente il monumento, dal legislatore in altro luogo ed in una formula generale, che si legge a guisa di riepilogo nel testo che segue:

fr. 7 *D.* xxxiii. 1, Pomp. 8 ad Q.M.—Pomponius. In testamentis quaedam scribuntur, quae ad auctoritatem dumtaxat scribentis referuntur nec obligationem pariunt. haec tamen talia sunt. si te heredem solum instituam et scribam, uti monumentum mihi certa pecunia facias: [*nullam enim obligationem ea scriptura recipit, sed*] ad auctoritatem meam conservandam poteris, si velis, facere [*aliter atque*][3] si coherede tibi dato idem scripsero: nam sive te solum

[1] Il primo esempio relativo all' ordine dato dal testatore: vendita del servo con la condizione che sia esportato, è contemplato dalla c. 5 *Cod.* iii. 36 di Aless. Severo, e la decisione è conforme a quella che si legge ora nei *Digesti.* Ma la struttura del rescritto è quanto mai strana, perchè nella decisione, contenuta nella seconda parte: *proinde . . . sequetur* spunta una folla di nuovi presupposti del tutto inaspettati. Per ciò dovette pure essere modificata l' introduzione: *in ipsius . . . mutare.*

[2] V. in senso contrario: Ulp. in *D.* x. 2, 2 pr.

[3] item. Pomp.

damnavero, uti monumentum facias, coheres tuus[1] agere tecum poterit familiae herciscundae, uti facias, quoniam[2] interest illius: qui etiam si utrique iussi estis hoc facere, invicem actionem[3] habebitis. ad auctoritatem scribentis hoc quoque pertinet, cum quis iussit in municipio imagines poni: 'nam si non honoris municipii gratia id fecisset, sed sua, actio eo nomine nulli competit.' itaque haec Quinti Mucii scriptura: 'liberi mei ibi sunto, ubi eos mater sua esse volet' nullam obligationem parit, sed ad auctoritatem defuncti conservandam id pertinebit, ut ubi iusserit ibi sint. nec tamen semper voluntas eius aut iussum conservari debet, veluti si praetor doctus sit non expedire pupillum eo morari ubi pater iusserit 'propter vitium, quod pater forte ignoravit in eis personis esse, apud quas morari iussit.' si autem pro cibariis eorum in annos singulos aurei decem relicti sint, sive hoc sermone significantur, apud quos morari mater pupillos voluerit, sive ita acceperinus hunc sermonem, ut ipsis filiis id legatum debeatur, utile erit: et magis enim est, ut providentia filiorum suorum hoc fecisse videatur. [*et in omnibus ubi auctoritas sola testatoris est, neque omnimodo spernenda neque omnimodo observanda est. sed interventu iudicis haec omnia debent, si non ad turpem causam feruntur, ad effectum perduci.*]

La trattazione di Pomponio riprende il suo carattere perspicuo e quindi la sua forza riponendo a posto, come ho fatto nelle note, le negazioni eliminate dai Compilatori, per ridurre la decisione di alcuni casi nel senso affermativo. E malgrado le inversioni giustinianee il ragionamento di Pomponio è ancora trasparente. Vi hanno disposizioni del testatore, egli dice, che non sono coercibili, ma riescono tuttavia efficaci, perchè la loro effettuazione è assicurata dalla sua autorità morale, come avviene nel caso che egli imponga all' erede di fargli un monumento; nè il valore giuridico dell' ordine si muta se gli eredi sono due o più; perchè in ogni caso per la disposizione concernente la statua o il monumento, se mira ad onorare la memoria del testatore: *actio eo nomine nulli competit.*

E quel che Pomponio insegnava è accertato per ogni rispetto. Sappiamo che i Romani custodivano religiosamente la volontà espressa del testatore, anche se non munita di efficacia giuridica; gli scrittori, a cominciare da Cicerone, attestano con orgoglio ed esaltano questo tratto del costume romano. Così Plinio[4] scrive ad un coerede: *Confido accessurum te sententiae meae, cum religiosissime soleas custodire defunctorum voluntatem, quam bonis heredibus*

[1] non. Pomp. [2] non. Pomp. [3] non. Pomp. [4] *Epist.* iv. 10.

*intellexisse pro iure est. Neque enim minus apud nos honestas quam apud alios necessitas valet.* Nella specie contemplata da Plinio si trattava di una manomissione e d' un legato allo stesso servo inefficaci.

Ma sovratutto poi si deve considerare che il coerede non può avere un' azione contro l' altro se non ha un interesse; e nel caso della statua in memoria del testatore la posizione dei coeredi è pari, nel senso che nè l' uno nè l' altro vi ha interesse. Onde a conseguire tali fini il legato con un *modus* era di consueto ordinato in favore d' un terzo ovvero d' un Ente, ed in particolare di Municipî.[1]

La riforma di Giustiniano, pertanto, in questa materia mirava a dar forza giuridica, per lo meno nel caso che vi fossero più eredi, alle disposizioni testamentarie che avevano lo scopo di onorare la memoria del defunto; ed allora il legislatore attribuì un' azione all' uno degli eredi contro l' altro. Nella chiusa del testo anzi la formulazione è più larga; perchè vi si dice che in tutti i casi, la volontà del testatore che sia onesta e meritevole di protezione, deve essere osservata mercè l' opera del giudice. Ma qui evidentemente intervenne Triboniano,[2] che con due tratti di penna condensò nella chiusa tutto il pensiero legislativo.

55. Ed un altra applicazione immediata e cospicua della stessa norma si rinviene appunto *in sede materiae*, cioè nel

> fr. 44 § 8 *D.* x. 2, Paul. 6 ad Sab. Si duo coheredes damnati sint statuam ponere et altero cessante alter eam fecerit, non [*esse iniquum*] Iulianus ait familiae erciscundae iudicium [*dare*], ut pars impendiorum boni viri arbitratu praestetur.

Il termine *damnati* era pure di frequente usato nei testamenti con riferimento a disposizioni incoercibili;[3] come nella specie in esame. Ma la decisione affermativa ora non sorprende; e si rivela come opera di Giustiniano per il nudo richiamo all' equità; laddove, come sappiamo, l' elemento decisivo era l' esistenza dell' interesse giuridico di uno degli eredi a fare, che solo poteva generare l' azione.[4] E l' alterazione del testo si manifesta poi nella forma

[1] Cfr. *D.* xxxiii. 1, 21, 3, Scaev. 22 digest.; *Testamentum Postumii Iuliani* in Bruns-Gradenwitz, *Fontes*, n. 121 p. 316.

[2] Cfr. Pernice, *Labeo*, iii. p. 39 ed ivi cit. Di Marzo: *Libri di Pomp. ad Q. M.* p. 67.

[3] Pernice, *l. c.* p. 32.

[4] Cfr. *D.* x. 2, 18, 2—*quia heredum interest, quos ius monumenti sequitur.* Cfr. avanti al n. 53.

impersonale della seconda parte (*praestetur*) in disaccordo con i presupposti riferiti; ed inoltre nella frase: *iud. dare*, che mette in evidenza la nuova funzione dei *iud. divisoria.* Forse il testo diceva:[1] *non posse eum Iulianus ait, familiae erciscundae iudicio consequi, ut pars impendiorum sibi praestetur.*[2]

Ma qui bisogna interrompere la revisione critica dei testi che provano il nuovo ufficio delle azioni divisorie nel diritto di Giustiniano, perchè gli esempii recati dimostrano a dovizia come i compilatori, con sovrapposizioni pazienti e continue, tendevano a coprire i tratti che ricordavano la funzione determinata dei *iudicia divisoria*, e che invece seppero rivolgere agli scopi più varî, per disciplinare la vita dell' istituto della comunione.

### III. LA UTILITÀ SOCIALE

56. Azioni, interdetti e mezzi varî, per lo più innominati ed a volte maldestri ed anche contradditorî, accordati da Giustiniano ai condomini sono tutti convergenti verso un segno ben determinato. E lo scopo, come ho avuto occasione di rilevare più fiate, era quello di regolare la vita della comunione, disciplinarla, onde potesse durare ed esplicarsi in perfetta pace, con la cooperazione di tutti per il vantaggio comune. Per conseguire un tale effetto il legislatore doveva in primo luogo annullare il principio della indipendenza assoluta dei singoli condomini, che costituiva il punto centrale della comunione classica. E quel principio fu annullato. Infatti ciascuno socio ha ora potere e mezzi di costringere gli altri ad eseguire riparazioni sulla cosa comune, a consentire una particolare opera o qualsiasi altra cosa; e viceversa ciascuno può impedire il socio dal fare un' opera o immissioni ecc., sempre mediante *prohibitio* giudiziaria. Tutto ciò è stato dimostrato nelle pagine che precedono.

Ora, per ciò, bisogna vedere il risultato del nuovo ordinamento stabilito da Giustiniano. Dacchè è evidente che tutte quelle azioni concesse ai condomini presuppongono una serie di diritti e facoltà, che ciascuno di essi ha ormai sulla cosa comune, e che può eserci-

[1] Il modello per la restituzione del passo si ha in *D.* x. 3, 4, § 4: *scribit Iulianus . . . sumptum istum c. d. iudicio consequi me non posse.*

[2] Cfr. c. 5, *Cod.* iii. 44 dell' a. 224, dove appunto la incoercibilità di tale disposizione anche nel testamento militare è presupposta. E per ciò erroneamente il Pernice, *ZSS.* xix. p. 173 n. 4, attribuisce quelle decisioni ad un progresso della giurisprudenza, per opera di Giuliano.

tare mediante opere e disposizioni, anche senza il consenso degli altri. Nel caso di opposizione ha mezzi coercitivi legali. Ed allora è certo, in primo luogo, che se ciascuno dei condomini ha ora, positivamente, facoltà di agire sulla cosa in contraddizione agli altri: La regola di Sabino fu sostanzialmente abolita; perchè essa negava che il socio *quicquam facere posse invito altero.*

Ma fino a qual punto fu quel principio messo da parte? E nella ricerca della risposta a questa domanda, si deve pure necessariamente porre in evidenza il principio che fu collocato al posto di quello classico; perchè senza un nuovo regolamento, senza una vera organizzazione dei compartecipi, le facoltà dei singoli avrebbero condotto ora ad un' anarchia ancora più grave di quella che avevano sperimentato i giureconsulti classici. Tutto questo sarà messo in luce nella trattazione che segue.

57. Cominciamo dall' osservare il

fr. 6 § 12 *D.* x. 3, Ulp. 19 ad ed. Urseius ait, cum in communi aedificio vicinus nuntiavit, ne quid operis fieret, si unus ex sociis ex hac causa damnatus fuisset, posse eam poenam a socio pro parte servare. Iulianus autem recte notat ita demum hoc verum esse, si [interfuit aedium hoc fieri].

Il testo è piano. Vi si dice che uno dei condomini che aveva fatta una nuova opera nell' edificio comune fu condannato in seguito alla denuncia del vicino. Debbono i socii contribuire al pagamento della pena? Urseio lo affermava. Giuliano appose al responso una delle solite note esplicative, che però fu modificata dai compilatori. La frase finale *si interfuit aedium hoc fieri* è sicuramente interpolata; lo si desume dalla personificazione delle *aedes*, che è di stile bizantino, in luogo della *utilitas rei*; e poi, perchè *aedium* e non *aedificiorum*, cioè il termine più generico che era nell' ipotesi proposta? Di più *hoc* si riferisce a *damnatus fuisset*, mentre evidentemente l' interpolatore voleva significare *hoc = opus fieri.*

E per altro la nota di Giuliano si ricostruisce sicuramente col sussidio di un passo di Papiniano che tratta lo stesso caso:

fr. 18 *D.* xxxix. 1, Pap. 3 quaest. Aedibus communibus, si ob opus novum nuntiatio uni fiat, si quidem ex voluntate omnium opus fiat, omnes nuntiatio tenebit, si vero quidem ignorent, in solidum obligabitur, qui contra edictum praetoris fecerit.

La decisione qui è correttissima e proporzionata in ogni sua parte ai principii fondamentali della comunione.

E perciò la nota di Giuliano doveva dire:

Iulianus autem recte notat: ita demum hoc verum esse si ex voluntate omnium opus fieret, quod si quidam ignorent in solidum obligabitur qui contra edictum praetoris fecerit.

La ragione, che indusse i compilatori a sopprimere una distinzione così equilibrata, non può essere ora occulta; quel che dispiacque appunto fu il consenso *omnium*, come fondamento e norma dei rapporti tra condomini; cui si sostituì un elemento obbiettivo, il vantaggio della cosa comune, che pertanto è indipendente dall' arbitrio dei singoli e dal concorso della volontà di tutti.

Lo spostamento dei concetti è qui essenziale, dunque. E perciò l' interpolazione in questo punto ha investito il principio centrale dell' istituto del condominio.

58. Ed ora si scorge tutto il significato di una frase adoperata da Giustiniano dove egli ammette tra condomini l' efficacia del patto *ne intra certum tempus dividatur.* Perchè il legislatore pone ivi in risalto questo nuovo elemento del vantaggio collettivo, dichiarando valido il patto: *quod etiam ipsius rei qualitati prodest*[1], così non la volontà unanime dei socii ne determina la validità, ma bensì l' utilità per sè stessa, il vantaggio della cosa comune.

59. Or, se un siffatto principio, che aveva in sè la potenza di travolgere d' un tratto tutta la struttura della *communio*, era in realtà nella mente del legislatore, egli doveva di necessità metterlo in evidenza immediata là dove i giureconsulti avean posti i fondamenti incrollabili del nostro istituto, e doveva precisamente sovrapporlo all' altro di Sabino, che esigeva essenzialmente, in ogni momento e per qualsiasi disposizione materiale della cosa, il concorso di tutti i socii. E ciò era imprescindibile, perchè la comunione classica, come sappiamo, era tutta improntata come in un conio nella formulazione di Sabino, in cui lo schema di mirabile perfezione, dai tratti vigorosi ed indelebili, si mostrava tutto. Per ciò la regola di Sabino precludeva la via a qualsiasi riforma o deviazione nella materia della comunione. Anche la semplice vicinanza era fatale. E Giustiniano quindi sentì la necessità di stremarla là sul posto, con sovrapposizioni ponderose, che dovevano opprimerla.

[1] *D.* x. 3, 14, 2.

I passi che riportavano la massima di Sabino erano due, e furono entrambi, come sappiamo, transfigurati.

60. Al fr. di Paolo fu aggiunto il periodo che segue:

26 *D.* viii. 2—*sed per communi dividundo actionem consequitur socius, quo minus opus fiat aut ut id opus quod fecit tollat, si modo toti societati prodest opus tolli.*

Quest' interpolazione si determina soltanto ora nei suoi particolari, ed illumina l' istituto giustinianeo. Essa rende tutta la nuova struttura della comproprietà. Lo *ius prohibendi* vi è rinnovellato; e l' *actio c. d.* serve ormai a regolare tutti gl' interessi dei socii. Mediante essa si impedisce l' opera che uno voglia eseguire sulla cosa; ovvero quando l' opera sia compiuta se ne ottiene la rimozione. La quale non deve aver luogo in ogni caso, bensì quando giovi alla comunione, o meglio alla società, come Giustiniano vuole si dica: *si modo toti societati prodest opus tolli.*

La volontà dei singoli socii anche qui è interclusa, di fronte al vantaggio della collettività. Nè occorre avvertire che tra le due cose non v' è coincidenza. La *voluntas omnium* da una parte ed il *prodesse societati* dall' altra sono quantità eterogenee. Anzi nella formula sovrapposta da Giustiniano, è prospettato un caso in cui si giunge alla distruzione dell' opera eseguita da uno dei socii, perchè torna di vantaggio alla collettività. E quindi il proposito di uno è frustrato. Naturalmente; perchè il criterio della *utilitas rei* è obbiettivo, quello della *voluntas* è soggettivo; e per ciò l' uno è indipendente dall' altro.

E così siamo ritornati allo stesso principio che ci si rivelò avanti, in altri testi, quasi di soppiatto. Vale a dire, mentre nel diritto classico solo la volontà di tutti i socii ha efficacia rispetto al *facere* sulla cosa comune, e la volontà di un solo, per conseguenza, può impedire qualsiasi atto od opera sulla medesima, in forza della *prohibitio*; al contrario, nella compilazione, alla volontà dei singoli si surroga la *utilitas rei*, la quale ora determina e regola i poteri dei socii sulla cosa. Lo *ius prohibendi* è non solo trasformato, ma in molti casi pure escluso. Fino a qual punto?

61. La risposta la ricaviamo dal celebre testo di Papiniano, là dove egli enunciava precisamente la massima di Sabino, ed in cui la violenza usata da Giustiniano all' antica dottrina si manifesta nella maniera più aperta.

Il testo ben noto continua così:

fr. 28 *D.* x. 3 . . . *sed etsi in communi prohiberi socius a socio ne quid faciat potest, ut tamen factum opus tollat, cogi non potest, si, cum prohibere poterat, hoc praetermisit: et ideo per communi dividundo actionem damnum sarciri poterit, sin autem facienti consensit, nec pro damno habet actionem. quod si quid absente socio ad laesionem eius fecit, tunc etiam tollere cogitur.*

Dunque, lo *ius prohibendi* c' è ancora, ma solo per impedire l' inizio dell' opera. Che se questa fu compiuta senza proibizione di alcuno, allora, chi omise di intervenire a tempo non può altro pretendere che il risarcimento del danno, mediante l' *actio c. d.* E se poi, per un motivo giustificato, egli non potè interporre divieto in tempo opportuno, allora l' opera dev' essere rimossa da chi la eseguì, solo quando risulti che ridonda a danno del socio; anzi, il testo dice: quando risulti che fu fatta a danno del socio: *si . . . ad laesionem eius fecit.*

Ed anche qui l' aggiunta, con le molteplici distinzioni, rivela in tutta la sua comprensione il nuovo principio regolatore della *communio.*

Lasciamo da parte la questione che è secondaria, se nella frase *ad laesionem eius fecit* non si rifletta pure un raggio della nota dottrina giustinianea del divieto di atti emulativi, ma qui preme sopratutto trarre da quest' ultimo inciso le conseguenze più certe ed immediate. E cioè, che secondo quel dettato, l' opera fatta da uno dei condomini senza la volontà dell' altro non si può rimuovere, per disposto di legge, quando non leda l' interesse del socio che nega. È il lato positivo della nuova formula. E perciò quando la disposizione di uno dei socii, o l' opera eseguita, tornano di vantaggio alla comunione, e non ledono gli interessi dell' altro, allora la volontà di colui che ha ordinato l' opera prevale; o meglio, in realtà, prevale l' interesse sociale.

Coincidenza dunque perfetta di parole, di concetti e di norme in tutte le correzioni ed aggiunte fatte da Giustiniano nella materia in esame.

62. Nè l' attività di Giustiniano s' arresta a paralizzare solo la forza dei principî astratti; chè le riforme in quella nuova direzione investono, di necessità, tutti i punti della teoria della *communio*, e tutte le conseguenze; e dimostrano che il nuovo regolamento di essa ebbe nella compilazione pieno e decisivo sviluppo.

Così circa la costituzione di servitù sul fondo comune leggiamo nel

fr. 10 *D.* xxxix. 3, Ulp. 53 ad ed. Si autem plures sint eiusdem loci domini, unde aqua ducitur, omnium voluntatem esse sequendam non ambigitur: [*iniquum enim visum est voluntatem unius ex modica forte portiuncula domini praeiudicium sociis facere*[1]]. An tamen subsequi voluntas possit, videamus. [*et placet nihil interesse utrum praecedat voluntas aquae ductionem an subsequatur, quia et posteriorem voluntatem praetor tueri debet.*]

Ulpiano esigeva la *voluntas omnium.* E non si poteva dubitarne: *non ambigitur.* Ma Giustiniano nota «essere iniquo che la volontà di uno che abbia nella comunione una piccola porziuncola possa pregiudicare gli altri».

Sarebbe errore intendere quell' inciso che è nel pr. del testo, come giustificazione o comento alla parola *omnium*; perchè se si esige la volontà unanime dei socii il *plus* o il *minus* delle quote non conta. Per ciò la Glossa con semplicità spontanea disse: *idem et si maximam partem habet.* E ciò è vero. Ma allora, nemmeno è giusto attribuire ai compilatori un comento così stupido. Ed in verità il periodo aggiunto ha valore per sè stesso, per quel che dice. Esso ha non il valore di una chiosa alla decisione che precede, ma quello piuttosto di una limitazione, e cioè per significare che in ogni caso la volontà di uno che ha nella comunione un interesse minimo non deve pregiudicare agli altri.

Ecco di nuovo l' interesse collettivo posto in risalto da Giustiniano, in confronto della volontà dei singoli. E per ciò è sicuro che anche il testo in esame rappresenta un punto di vista che si coordina perfettamente al nuovo principio qui posto in evidenza, e fatto palese dai frammenti più cospicui della materia. Se poi la decisione del comune vantaggio spetti alla maggioranza numerica dei socii, ovvero a coloro che hanno la prevalenza degli interessi, è cosa che vedremo più oltre.

L' applicazione del nuovo principio in materia di servitù sul fondo comune deve valere, *a fortiori*, per l' acquisto, precisamente il contrario di quello che insegnavano i classici.[2]

Ma ritornando al testo in esame osservo che la interpolazione contenuta nel § 1 ha un significato ancora più sovversivo; perchè essa ammette la validità di concessione di servitù fatta da un gruppo

[1] Eisele, *ZSS.* vol. xxx. pp. 133, 135. [2] *D.* viii. 3, 19, *si omnes stipulentur.*

di socii, cui più tardi potranno accedere gli altri quando sia costituita. Il senso del periodo non può essere equivoco. Non si vuol dire certamente che la servitù viene ad esistere coll' atto di concessione fatto dall' ultimo, perchè invece vi si suppone, espressamente, che altri possano accedere alla concessione della servitù costituita: *et placet nihil interesse, utrum praecedat voluntas aquae ductionem an subsequatur.* Ed allora se non si vuole attribuire a Giustiniano, oltre che un' eresia giuridica pure un' incongruenza, è d' uopo sottintendere anche qui ripetuta la condizione posta avanti, nel principio del testo; cioè che la concessione deve aver luogo con l' effettivo vantaggio della collettività, e che non può esser posta nel nulla da coloro che hanno nella comunione un minimo interesse.

Ed allo stesso risultato, per quanto concerne la possibilità della cessione della servitù da una parte dei socii, conduce il

fr. 11 *D.* viii. 3, Celsus 27 dig. Per fundum, qui plurium est, ius mihi esse eundi agendi potest separatim cedi. ergo [*subtili ratione*] non aliter meum fiet ius, quam si omnes cedant et novissima demum cessione superiores omnes confirmabuntur: [*benignius tamen dicetur, et antequam novissimus cesserit, eos, qui antea cesserunt, vetari uti cesso iure non posse*].

Le superstrutture giustinianee sono qui evidenti e notissime.[1] Il legislatore dispone la efficacia giuridica della cessione fatta da una parte dei condomini, che è irrevocabile, e per ciò produttiva degli effetti proprî ad essa, anche prima che avvenga la disposizione dell' ultimo. Proprio il contrario di quel che insegnava Celso nel testo originale, e che era inevitabile per la natura del dritto che compete ai singoli titolari della cosa comune, che dava a ciascuno una posizione pari ed indipendente sulla cosa, per cui: *non aliter meum fiet ius, quam si omnes cedant, et novissima demum cessione superiores omnes confirmabuntur.*[2]

Così sono anche questi testi coordinati attorno al nuovo principio, e lo determinano e lo confermano in tutte le conseguenze.

63. Ma un altro punto, che riguarda lo scioglimento della comunione di cose, inita per contratto, dev' essere qui considerato; non solo per il motivo che gl' interpreti antichi lo collegarono al fr. 26 *D.* viii. 2, ma perchè in realtà il nuovo ordinamento di Giustiniano vi si manifesta con grande rilievo. Il passo cui alludo è il

[1] Krüger ad h. l.

[2] Cfr. *D.* viii. 4, 6, 2.

fr. 65 § 5 *D.* xvii. 2, Ulp. 32 ad ed. Labeo autem posteriorum libris scripsit, si renuntiaverit societati unus ex sociis eo tempore, quo interfuit socii non dirimi societatem, committere eum in pro socio actione: nam si emimus mancipia inita societate, deinde renunties mihi eo tempore, quo vendere mancipia non expedit, hoc casu, quia deteriorem causam meam facis, teneri te pro socio iudicio. Proculus hoc ita verum esse ait, [*si societatis non intersit dirimi societatem: semper enim non id, quod privatim interest unius ex sociis, servari solet, sed quod societati expedit. haec ita accipienda sunt,*] si nihil de hoc in coeunda societate convenit.

La decisione di Labeone era indubbiamente per ogni rispetto giusta, come quella che discendeva dai principî più fermi, che regolano la società. La quale al pari della comunione non era riguardata dai giureconsulti classici come un ente organizzato, con interessi distinti da quelli dei singoli, bensi come una semplice aggregazione d' individui per conseguire determinati scopi; e per ciò, quando la società fosse convenuta senza termine, ciascun socio poteva rinunziarvi, in qualsiasi momento, salvo la responsabilità che gli incombeva per la rinunzia fatta in tempo inopportuno pregiudizievole ai singoli come tali: *interfuit socii non dirimi societatem.* Il che vuol dire che il fondamento dell' *actio pro socio* si deve ricercare nella lesione dell' interesse dei singoli, e non già nel pregiudizio che uno possa arrecare all' interesse collettivo.

Proculo consentiva certamente in ciò: *verum esse.* Ma a rimuovere qualsiasi ragione di equivoco notava: *Proculus hoc ita verum esse* [...] *si nihil de hoc in coeunda societate convenit*;[1] perchè allora il socio è legato dal contratto, che limita la sua libertà di rinunzia. Tutto il resto che si legge nel passo è opera dei compilatori. Nella F manca la frase *ait si* e cotali omissioni sono di frequente una conseguenza delle saldature delle interpolazioni.[2] Nella frase *servari solet* si manifesta la incertezza di un principio direttivo, la quale non può essere nemmeno tolta di mezzo dal *semper* che precede. E *solet* è verbo frequentissimo nelle correzioni

[1] L' identica chiusa in *I.* iii. 25, 5.

[2] Non sappiamo ancora il procedimento pratico adottato dai compilatori nel correggere i passi; ma indizii di vario ordine fanno ritenere che le modificazioni erano apposte sui mss., tra le righe o nel margine con richiami. Nel punto in esame sono visibili direi come due note sovrapposte: *hoc ita verum esse . . . haec ita accipienda sunt* che non possono derivare dalla stessa mano. E perchè il plurale: *accipienda sunt* in luogo del singolare *accipiendum*? L' uso del plurale in questi casi è indizio d' interpolazione; cfr. *D.* xli. 3, xliv. 3; Riccobono, *ZSS.* vol. xxxi. p. 359.

giustinianee ai testi classici, adoperato sia nelle aggiunte che portano una modificazione ai principii fondamentali, sia per attenuare le decisioni ferme della giurisprudenza classica, ovvero per limitare una sentenza avulsa dai suoi presupposti.[1] Nel nostro caso il verbo in parola è incongruo ed impressionante; poichè tra l' interesse della *societas* considerata come unità e quello dei singoli socii come tali la distanza è enorme. Se Proculo mirava veramente a contraddire il maestro, in un punto così essenziale, avrebbe scritto con fermezza *servatur*. Di più se Proculo, contrastando, riusciva a colpire così in pieno la decisione di Labeone, egli non avrebbe potuto iniziare la nota con la frase: *hoc ita verum esse*. Il dissenso su di un principio fondamentale non ammette concessioni. Or alla stregua della dottrina esposta nella nota la decisione di Labeone cade tutta, irremissibilmente, perchè non è più vero che contro il socio rinunziante possa accordarsi un' azione, *si interfuit socii non dirimi societatem*. Questo motivo non ha più valore; e per conseguenza nulla conta che a causa della rinunzia intempestiva, come si esprimeva Labeone, *deteriorem causam meam facis*.

Ecco pertanto come la nota di Proculo investe a fondo la decisione che precede; appunto perchè quella muove da un principio diverso, secondo cui è l' interesse sociale non quello dei singoli che va tenuto in considerazione.[2]

E se guardiamo i termini del dissenso tra Labeone e Proculo da un altro punto di vista la contraddizione diviene ancora più stridente; avvegnachè Labeone ammetteva l' *actio pro socio* in seguito alla rinunzia intempestiva fatta da uno dei coobbligati, e ciò in quanto derivasse una lesione all' interesse dell' attore: *interfuit socii non dirimi societatem;* Proculo invece avrebbe detta questa decisione vera, ma solo nel caso *si societatis non intersit dirimi societatem;* cioè giusto enunciando un presupposto di fatto contrario a quello indicato da Labeone, e che induce per sè la inammissibilità dell' *actio*, e di conseguenza la decisione contraria a quella data dal suo maestro.

[1] Cfr. *Cod.* viii. 53, 7; Riccobono, *ZSS.* vol. xxxiii. p. 292; *D.* iv. 4, 7 § 2; *D.* xxvii. 10, 1 pr.; *D.* l. 17, 111, in confronto col fr. 23 § 8 *D.* ix. 2; e specialmente nel titolo de R. I. ha una funzione limitatrice come *fere*, *praesertim*, *maxime*, *plerumque*, *saepe*, onde contenere entro certi limiti la massima che avulsa dai suoi presupposti assumeva una portata generale: cfr. fr. 19, 58, 86, 94, 114 *D.* l. 17. Pel fr. 39 pr. *D.* xxxix. 2 di Pomponio cfr. p. 85, sotto il n. 48.

[2] Cfr. *B.* xii. 1, 62 scol. 8 (Heimb. 1, p. 774).

Si può immaginare incongruenza più manifesta tra due termini, così discordanti sia nei presupposti, nel fondamento, nella decisione e tuttavia congiunti l' uno all' altro con la frase: *ita verum esse*? Si sarebbe dovuto perlomeno aspettare nella nota: *si societatis intersit non dirimi societatem*, come corresse Aloandro, e già il glossatore Giovanni, ed ora i moderni contro la F.[1]

Il lettore ha ora tutti gli elementi per decidere. E dirà che la correzione del testo è necessaria; ma che insieme il brano esaminato è tutto dei compilatori; il quale giudizio, a mio modo di vedere, s' impone in questo luogo per le considerazioni di vario ordine esposte avanti, ma sopratutto poi per il riflesso che la nota attribuita a Proculo s' inquadra perfettamente nell' ordine di idee di Giustiniano.

64. Fu infatti Giustiniano che, come sappiamo, sostitui ogni volta nella comunione alla volontà dei singoli l' interesse sociale; e così Egli giunse pure a considerare la società come un gruppo collettivo, che ha volontà ed interessi distinti da quelli dei singoli socii. E perciò i compilatori ritoccando i testi, con tutta spontaneità, rappresentavano la *societas* come una unità, e scrivevano:

fr. 49 *D.* xvii. 2, Ulp. 31 ad ed. [*Si hoc facto societatem laesit*,] si verbi gratia negotiatorem servum vulneraverit vel occiderit.

In questo passo il primo periodo è emblematico; i giuristi esprimono il concetto con le frasi *damnum in re communi socius dedit* fr. 47 § 1 eod.; *rei communi socius nocuit* fr. 52 § 2 eod.

Nello stesso ordine di confronti è caratteristico il

fr. 58 § 1 *D.* xvii. 2, Ulp. 31 ad ed.

Item Celsus tractat, si pecuniam contulissemus ad mercem emendam et mea pecunia perisset, cui perierit ea. et ait, si post collationem evenit, ut pecunia periret, quod non fieret, nisi societas coita esset, utrique perire, ut puta si pecunia, cum peregre portaretur ad mercem emendam, periit; [*si vero ante collationem, posteaquam eam destinasses, tunc perierit, nihil eo nomine consequeris, inquit, quia non societati periit*].

L' interpolazione della parte riprodotta in corsivo è manifesta

[1] La correzione è già nella Glossa (Giovanni), seguita da Aloandro, dagli edd. italiani, ed ha un appoggio nei *B.* xii. 1, 62 (Heimb. v. 1, p. 775), dove Stefano nella paragrafe (scol. 10) scrive: εἰ μὴ τῇ κοινωνίᾳ διαφέρει τὸ μὴ ταύτην λυθῆναι.

principalmente per la inversione dei soggetti[1]; poichè l' ipotesi fondamentale, esaminata dal giurista era: *et mea pecunia periisset*, la quale si capovolge nel seguito del testo: *si vero . . . destinasses . . . quia non societati periit.*[2] E pertanto nella parte prima si dice *utrique perire*, nella seconda invece *non societati periit*. È vero che qui la frase è senza conseguenze.

Tutta la dottrina della *societas* merita per ciò una revisione da questo punto di vista; perchè come s' è constatato il fr. 65 § 5, nella parte interpolata coincide precisamente con quelle riforme introdotte da Giustiniano nella comunione. In questo luogo interessava porre in relievo il confronto, che dà forza alla nostra dimostrazione.

## IV. LA VOLONTÀ DELLA MAGGIORANZA

65. L' autonomia dei singoli nella comunione e nella società fu certamente soppressa nella Compilazione di Giustiniano, in cui, come s' è visto, la considerazione dell' interesse collettivo prende il posto del vantaggio e del volere dei singoli compartecipi. Ed in rispondenza perfetta con questo nuovo principio si rinviene pure surrogata alla unanimità del consenso di tutti, per qualsiasi disposizione materiale della cosa, la volontà della maggioranza, la

[1] Essa aveva soltanto lo scopo di completare l' esame del caso, invertendo i presupposti enunciati avanti. Indizii: *si vero . . . tunc perierit . . . periit.* Cfr. Harmenopuli *Exab.* iii. 10, 21.

[2] Nei fr. genuini dei giureconsulti è costante la terminologia *conferre in societatem*, *imputare societati*, *omnibus*, *ceteris*, le quali frasi sono perfettamente equivalenti, e si riferiscono sempre all' interesse dei singoli socii considerato in complesso solo per il lato economico, ma non giuridicamente. Infatti per quel che concerne le conseguenze giuridiche soltanto l' interesse e la persona dei singoli vengono posti in azione; così in *D.* xvii. 2, fr. 60 Pomp. 13 ad Lab. . . . *usuras quoque eum praestare debere Labeo ait . . . sed quod socii intersit moram eum non adhibuisse.*—fr. 73 eod. Ulp. 1 resp. . . . *ea quoque, quae in honorem alterius liberorum erogata sunt, utrisque imputanda.*—2-3 pr. eod. . . . *sociis praestet.*

E più rimarchevole ancora è vedere che nello stesso fr. 65 *D.* xvii. 2, richiamato sopra, Cassio e Paolo usano gli stessi termini adoperati da Labeone nel decidere i singoli casi: § 3 (Cassius) . . . *se autem ab illis non liberare.* § 4 . . . *teneberis quanti interest mea.* § 5 (Labeo) . . . *interfuit socii non dirimi societatem . . . deteriorem causam meam facis.* § 6. (Paulus) . . . *socium a se, non se a socio liberat*; cfr. 21 *D.* eod. (Ulpianus) . . . *nos cum eo non communicabimus.* Cfr. Cuq, *Inst.* ii. p. 442. È vero, per altro, che le alterazioni tribonianee sono continue nel senso inverso accennato in questo scritto.

quale ora ha il potere di deliberare intorno al godimento, alla conservazione o destinazione della cosa comune.

Come di solito le interpolazioni giustinianee sono anche in questo proposito saltuarie, e non rendono a prima giunta una norma ben precisa e determinata; ma la cosa tuttavia è certissima, come si scorge dalla dimostrazione che precede, e come deve emergere con evidenza osservando i testi fondamentali che si riferiscono alla comunione, e che riunisco qui per coordinarli in una sintesi:

fr. 11 *D.* viii. 3 . . . benignius tamen dicetur et antequam novissimus cesserit, eos, qui antea cesserunt, vetare uti cesso iure non posse.

fr. 10 *D.* xxxix. 3. . . . iniquum enim visum est voluntatem unius ex modica forte portiuncula dominii praeiudicium sociis facere.

fr. 26 *D.* viii. 2. . . . si modo toti societati prodest opus tolli.

fr. 65 § 5 *D.* xvii. 2. si societatis intersit non dirimi societatem.

Nei quali passi al consenso unanime dei socii è costantemente sostituita la volontà o la disposizione di una parte di essi, che, a volte espressamente, è autorizzata ad agire in opposizione ad uno dei socii, che ha nella *communio* un interesse minore.

Ed allo stesso risultato si giunge quando si tenga conto di quelle altre frasi in cui Giustiniano non si riporta alla volontà dei socii, ma sì bene all' interesse della cosa medesima; perchè, come s' è detto, l' interesse obbiettivo non coincide per sè stesso con la volontà dei singoli socii:

fr. 6 § 12 *D.* x. 3. si interfuit aedium hoc fieri.

fr. 14 § 2 *D.* x. 3. quod etiam ipsius rei qualitati prodest.

fr. 28 *D.* x. 3. ut tamen factum opus tollat cogi non potest [in confronto con 26 *D.* viii. 2].

66. E del resto su questo proposito vi è un passo di grande importanza che può essere ora esaminato con ben altra perspicacia:

fr. 14 *D.* xvi. 3, Gai. ix. ad ed. Si plures heredes exstiterint ei qui deposuerit, [*dicitur, si maior pars adierit, restituendam rem praesentibus: maiorem autem partem non ex numero utique personarum, sed ex magnitudine portionum hereditariarum intelligendam: cautela idonea reddenda*].

Questa decisione è nuova,[1] ed ha un' importanza di prim' ordine nell' argomento in esame.

[1] L' interpolazione si manifesta per varii indizii: l' ablativo assoluto finale fu rilevato dagli antichi, dal Brissonio e dal Fabro: *Coniect.* xii. 16, 6; il quale

E dico avanti tutto che non c' è modo di aggregare una siffatta decisione ai principii più certi seguiti dai giureconsulti. Infatti, ove si supponga che i coeredi siano condomini della cosa depositata e che vogliano agire con la *rei vindicatio* non è dubbio che ciascuno deve *agire pro parte*; e parimenti se esperiscono l' *actio depositi* deve ciascuno *agire pro parte*, sul fondamento del titolo di eredità. Tutto ciò è sicuro. Il dubbio ha ragion d' essere solo nella compilazione di Giustiniano, e particolarmente rispetto al deposito di cose indivisibili; perchè anche questa materia fu profondamente rimescolata da Giustiniano. Ma secondo il diritto classico nè uno degli eredi nè la maggioranza di essi hanno diritto a richiedere la restituzione dell' intero, che li esporrebbe alla *plus petitio*. Ciascuno deve invece chiedere sempre la parte che gli spetta per il titolo di erede. Soltanto questo è vero, che il depositario può evitare la condanna dichiarandosi pronto a *restituere rem* anche ad un solo, quando gli si offra cauzione per le possibili molestie da parte degli altri coeredi. Tale procedimento è attestato dallo stesso Giustiniano, che lo accolse in passi interpolati (cfr. fr. 1 § 36 *D.* xvi. 3) in confronto con quello in esame, ed è per altro il rimedio consueto in qualsiasi evenienza.

Esso è applicato da Giuliano nella specie che segue:

fr. 1 § 37 *D.* xvi. 3 Ulp. 30 ad ed. Apud Julianum libro tertio decimo digestorum talis species relata est: ait enim, si depositor decesserit et duo existant, qui inter se contendant unusquisque solum se heredem dicens, ei tradendam rem, qui paratus est adversus alterum

---

raccolse altre identiche aggiunte di Triboniano; cfr. De Ruggiero, *Studii Fadda*, ii. p. 217 nota; appare inoltre dalle molteplici ellissi che si riscontrano nello squarcio; e cioè dopo *deposuerit* si richiederebbe *rem*, il genitivo *eorum* dopo *maior pars*; ed infine vanno notati i due gerundii: *restituendam*, *intellegendam* privi del verbo ausiliare. Ma più di tutti cotesti indizii ha peso quel disgraziato *adierit* non determinato nell' oggetto, e che perciò ha fatto difficoltà di interpretazione. L' opinione dominante presso gli antichi volle intendere: *adierit hereditatem* [cfr. Glück, *Erläut.* vol. xv. p. 231], ed essa ha il conforto dei *B.* xiii. 2, 14, scolio 1 di Stefano (Heimb. v. ii. p. 47). La Glossa più accorta spiegò: *ad repetundum depositum*. A. Fabro, *l. c.*, corresse il testo in modo arbitrario; ma la sua argomentazione nella parte negativa è ineccepibile. Egli scriveva: *legendumque aderit, nam priora illa 'si plures heredes exstiterint' ostendunt ab omnibus heredibus aditam fuisse hereditatem, quia nec testamentarii nec legitimi heredes nec alii denique quam sui prius exstiterunt heredes quam adierint. sequentia vero 'restituendam rem praesentibus' demonstrant eum casum tractari quo pars tantum heredum adsit petatque depositum.*

reum defendere, [hoc est eum qui depositum suscepit]:[1] quod si neuter hoc onus suscipiat commodissime dici ait non esse cogendum a praetore iudicium suscipere: [*oportere igitur rem deponi in aede aliqua, donec de hereditate iudicetur*].[2]

E per altro l' azione di deposito si dà *pro parte* quando due o più sono i deponenti:

fr. 17 pr. *D.* xvi. 3 . . . quod aliter est [*scilicet* non in solidum], cum rem communem plures deponunt;—fr. 1 § 31 *D.* eod. . . . unicuique dominorum in partem competit depositi.

Dunque la soluzione del quesito proposto da Gaio nel fr. in esame era pronta; perchè i coeredi debbono esperire l' *actio depositi pro parte.* E se la cosa è indivisibile l' attore deve offrire cauzione al convenuto per la parte degli altri coeredi, dai quali il depositario deve essere garentito e protetto da ogni possibile molestia. La *cautio* mette in evidenza che ciascuno dei coeredi ha diritto di esercitare le azioni del defunto solo per la quota di eredità a lui pervenuta; non potendo il dritto degli altri essere in modo alcuno leso o solo menomato dall' azione di uno o di una maggioranza qualsiasi degli eredi.

E perciò possiamo ritenere sicura in questo punto la innovazione legislativa di Giustiniano, il quale all' accordo di tutti i coeredi all' azione dei singoli *pro parte* sostituì l' azione concessa ad un gruppo, costituito da coloro che nell' eredità rappresentano la maggioranza degli interessi. Si noti che nel passo non è fatta distinzione di obbietto divisibile o indivisibile; quale rilievo è gravissimo, perchè induce un' evidente contraddizione tra il passo in esame e gli altri citati più sopra. Giustiniano per altro trattò con vera predilezione e cura la materia del deposito, e volle particolarmente porre riparo a quel sistema dell' *actio pro parte*, specie in seguito ad eredità, che a suo modo d' intendere era complicata; e che poteva dar luogo a tergiversazioni da parte di uno o dei pochi, che avendo nella eredità una *modica portiuncula*, potevano facilmente assumere un atteggiamento astioso, pregiudizievole agli altri.[3]

[1] Glossa, cf. Lenel, *Pal.* ii. c.

[2] Triboniano. Infatti la conseguenza (*igitur*) non si ricava dalle premesse contenute nel testo e riguarda per nulla la lite tra i pretendenti della eredità. La *depositio in aede*, del resto, è rimedio consueto adoperato da Giustiniano, come si vedrà subito.

[3] Le riforme di Giustiniano in questa materia indicate sommariamente furono le seguenti:

(*a*) Egli stabilì che ove la cosa depositata sia indivisibile la restituzione deve essere *in solidum* a ciascuno dei titolari;

La riforma, dunque, anche in questo luogo è determinata da

---

fr. 22 *D.* xvi. 3 : [—*et nisi pro solido res non potest restitui. nec tamen absurde sentiet, qui hoc putaverit, plane nisi integrae rei restitutione eum, cum quo actum fuerit, liberari non posse, condemnandum tamen, si res non restituetur, pro qua parte heres extitit.*] Il giureconsulto trattava solo della responsabilità solidale dei coeredi per la contrettazione dolosa del deposito, e Giustiniano rivolge la decisione alla restituzione della *res*. Per la interpolazione del brano : *Nec tamen* . . . *extitit* cfr. Eisele, *ZSS*. xxx. p. 120.

Altra interpolazione, che in alcuni punti coincide con quella or indicata, nel fr. 1 § 44 eod. Sed si duo deposuerint et ambo agant, [*si quidem sic deposuerunt; ut vel unus tollat totum, poterit in solidum agere; sin vero pro parte, pro quae eorum interest, tunc dicendum est in partem condemnationem faciendam*]. La conclusione è banale, e la forma del testo pessima, d' impronta bizantina.

(*b*) Ammise l' intervento del magistrato per la consegna ai coeredi della loro parte ; ed ove la cosa fosse indivisibile anche il deposito *in aede* : cfr. 1 § 36 *D.* eod. interamente interpolato, come vide già Fabro, *Con.* xii. 16, 8. Il rimedio del deposito si riscontra pure nel fr. 5 in f. eod. *nisi* . . . *deponi.* E così in materia di pagamenti da fare al minore nel fr. 7 § 2 *D.* iv. 4. . . . [*Sed hodie solet pecunia in aedem deponi*], ut Pomponius l. xxviii scribit, ne vel debitor ultra usuris oneretur, vel creditor minor perdat pecuniam, [*aut curatoribus solvi, si sunt*]. La citazione di Pomp. si riferiva appunto alla necessità di nominare un *curator* al minore, di cui si tratta nel seguito del testo.

(*c*) In armonia col fr. 14 *D.* xvi. 3, esaminato sopra, ammise che la cosa depositata indivisibile si restituisse alla *pars heredum* ma in seguito a *iussus praetoris* ; fr. 81 § 1 *D.* xlvi. 3 : Si lancem deposuerit apud me Titius et pluribus heredibus relictis decesserit : [*si pars heredum me interpellet optimum quidem esse, si praetor aditus iussisset me parti heredum eam lancem tradere, quo casu depositi me reliquis coheredibus non teneri. sed et si sine praetore sine dolo malo hoc fecero liberabor aut* (*quod verius est*) *non incidam in obligationem. optimum autem est id per magistratum facere*].

La struttura del passo, a cominciare dalla frase : *si pars heredum me interpellet* dà luogo a gravi sospetti per le ripetizioni : *si lancem* . . . *eam lancem* . . . *pars heredum* . . . *parti heredum* . . . *reliquis* . . . Per i tempi dei verbi etcc. cfr. anche Di Marzo, *Libri di Pomp. ad Q. M.* p. 52 ; l' interpolazione del periodo finale *sed etsi* . . . *facere* fu notata dal Pernice (*Berliner Sitzungsber.* a. 1886 p. 1180 n. 5); ed ora sappiamo meglio che tutti questi espedienti per effettuare la restituzione del deposito a parte degli eredi sono giustinianei. Solo che qui, richiedendosi l' intervento del magistrato, non si esige la consegna ne sia fatta alla *maior pars heredum.* E per ciò tutta la materia è folta d' interpolazioni che suscitarono in ogni tempo controversie ; Accursio dà come opinione dominante fra i glossatori quella che ammetteva sempre l' *actio pro parte,* salvo patto in contrario : fr. 1 § 44 *D.* xvi. 3 ; altri però distinguevano l' oggetto divisibile da quello indivisibile, accordando in quest' ultimo caso la petizione in solido : così Baldo ad l. 14 *D.* xvi. 3 ; Duareno, *Opp.* iii. p. 500 ; e già gl' interpreti greci : Stefano : *B.* xiii. 2, 14 (Heimbach, ii. p. 47).

quello stesso ordine di idee e da quel medesimo spirito, che indussero un così profondo mutamento in tutto il diritto di comproprietà.

67. Ma qui conviene indugiare un momento per gettare uno sguardo su altri rapporti regolati *ex novo* nella compilazione, e dai quali potremo apprendere, che in realtà il diritto di disposizione della cosa comune, conferito da Giustiniano alla maggioranza dei socii, risponde ad un principio generale applicato dal legislatore tutte le volte che più persone si trovano in una medesima situazione, collegate da un comune interesse. Lo rinveniamo, pertanto, adottato tra coeredi e condomini, nella cessione dei beni come nel concorso dei creditori, sempre negli stessi termini, cioè con la prevalenza accordata, in primo luogo, a coloro che hanno la parte o l' interesse maggiore.

In ordine alla cessione dei beni la innovazione è annunziata da Giustiniano direttamente nella c. 8 *Cod.* vii. 71, diretta a Giovanni, emanata durante la formazione dei *Digesti*.

Il legislatore dice: *Et sancimus ut vel ex cumulo debiti vel ex numero creditorum causa iudicetur.* I creditori che hanno il maggiore interesse, sia uno o più, hanno il diritto di decidere: *ipsius sententia optineat—amplior debiti cumulus minori summae praeferatur—Pari autem quantitate debiti inventa . . . tunc amplior pars creditorum optineat, ut quod pluribus placeat statuatur. Sin vero undique aequalitas emergat—tunc eos anteponi qui ad humaniorem declinant sententiam, non cessionem exigentes sed inducias.*

Le stesse statuizioni si riscontrano applicate nei *Digesti* con grande coerenza, quantunque saltuariamente.

In primo luogo nel

fr. 7 § 19 *D.* ii. 14 Ulp. 4 ad ed. *Hodie tamen ita demum pactio huiusmodi creditoribus obest, si convenerint in unum et communi consensu declaraverint quota parte debiti contenti sint: si vero dissentiant, tunc praetoris partes necessariae sunt, qui decreto suo sequetur maioris partis voluntatem.*

L' interpolazione in questo punto[1] fu inserita per dare ai creditori, che siano d' accordo, un potere dispositivo, nel senso che la loro deliberazione è munita per sè stessa d' efficacia giuridica. L' intervento del pretore si esige soltanto nel disaccordo degli stessi, e solo in questa ipotesi il magistrato con decreto darà esecuzione alla volontà della maggioranza. Tale ordinamento è

[1] Beseler, *Beiträge*, ii. 97.

nuovo. Perchè nel diritto classico ove è fatta menzione dell' assemblea dei creditori e della maggioranza di essi, per la creazione del *magister*,[1] per la nomina del *curator bonorum*,[2] per la *lex bonorum vendundorum*[3] si richiede sempre la proposta o il consenso degli interessati, della maggioranza di essi, essendo per altro la creazione del *magister* o la nomina del *curator* o le condizioni della vendita poste in essere da un decreto del pretore. La differenza dunque risalta: nel diritto classico i creditori cooperano col magistrato e sono adunati per far proposte; nel diritto di Giustiniano hanno entro certi limiti facoltà di disporre direttamente.

Il passo che segue nei *Digesti* contiene applicazioni di altre norme sancite nella c. 8 cit., ed è così riportato:

fr. 8 eod. Pap. 10 resp. Maiorem esse partem pro modo debiti, non pro numero personarum placuit [*quod si aequales sint in cumulo debiti, tunc plurium numerus creditorum praeferendus est; in numero autem pari creditorum auctoritatem eius sequetur praetor, qui dignitate inter eos praecellit. sin autem omnia undique in unam aequalitatem concurrant, humanior sententia a praetore eligenda est*] hoc enim ex divi Marci rescripto colligi potest.

L' interpolazione della parte centrale del testo fu accertata dal Gradenwitz;[4] il quale, con la consueta perspicacia, rinvenne pure di recente, nella così detta legge delle citazioni di Teodosio e Valentiniano il modello di cui si servirono i compilatori.[5]

Lo schema di quella celebre legge è davvero interessante e val la pena di riprodurlo qui per un altro riscontro che ci occorrerà subito.

c. 3 Th. i. 4: Ubi autem diversae sententiae proferuntur, potior numerus vincat auctorum, vel si numerus aequalis sit eius partis praecedat auctoritas, in qua excellentis ingenii vir Papinianus emineat. . . . Ubi autem pares eorum sententiae recitantur, quorum par censetur auctoritas, quod sequi debeat eligat moderatio iudicantis.

68. Or è degno di nota che cotesto criterio della maggioranza e

[1] Gai iii. 79 (creari); Theoph. iii. 12 (προβάλλεσθαι); su questi passi v. Kniep (*Mél. Girard*, i. p. 630 e seg.; Cic. *ad Att.* vi. 1, 15).

[2] fr. 2 pr. § 1 *D.* xlii. 7; Lenel Ed. p. 419.

[3] fr. 58 § 1 *D.* xvii. 1; Paul. 4 quaest.—*maiore parte creditorum consentiente a praetore decretum est.*

[4] *Interpolationen*, pp. 62, 63; Lenel, *Pal. Pap.* 650.

[5] *ZSS.* vol. xxxii. p. 383.

della parità di voti si rinviene adottato, negli stessi termini come nei passi avanti riferiti, pure in un' opera occidentale contemporanea, cioè in un passo di Paolo Visigoto a proposito del servo comune:

Paul. *S.* iv. 12, 5. Communem servum unus ex sociis vinciendo futurae libertati non nocebit. [*Inter pares enim sententia clementior severiori praefertur: et certe humanae rationis est favere miserioribus, prope et innocentes dicere quos absolute nocentes pronuntiare non possunt.*]

Nella parità dei voti dei compartecipi si dice anche qui che deve prevalere *sententia clementior*; come nella c. 8 *Cod.* si antepongono: *qui ad humaniorem declinant sententiam*, e nel fr. 8 *D.* ii. 14, *humanior sententia . . . eligenda est.* Ma in qual momento potè introdursi tale principio per il diritto privato? Io dico che il passo or riferito non può essere di Paolo. La frase *inter pares* priva di un sostantivo ha fatto difficoltà. Huschke ridusse all' accusativo la parola *sententia* che segue, senza accorgersi che allora il comparativo *clementior* resta in aria. Ma tutto ciò importa poco. Il senso del passo è chiaro e si determina nella continuazione, dove si dice certamente che nella parità dei voti deve prevalere la disposizione più clemente in favore della libertà; e dove la massima si costruisce pure con un argomento che è proprio per i corpi deliberanti di diritto pubblico, cioè che nella parità non vi può essere condanna, perchè il giudizio sfavorevole è annullato dai voti contrarii: *quos absolute nocentes pronuntiare non possunt.* Il lettore vede già che il verbo *possunt* spunta come un fungo, e attesta in maniera irrefutabile che tutto il brano è d' origine postclassica. Genuino è solo il primo periodo: *communem . . . non nocebit*, che contiene precisamente l' applicazione del principio classico del condominio, per cui uno dei socii non può menomamente pregiudicare la facoltà di disposizione dell' altro rispetto alla cosa comune;[1] e non può, pertanto, nè dare la libertà al servo nè impedirla in modo assoluto. Più tardi, è vero, anche nel periodo della giurisprudenza classica, furono adottate disposizioni di favore per la libertà dei servi, svolte poi largamente da Giustiniano.[2]

69. Tutti cotesti elementi, dunque, raccolti da fonti tarde[3] e

[1] Cfr. Paul. *S.* iv. 12, 1.

[2] Const. un. Cod. 7, 7; Riccobono, *BIDR.* vol. vii. p. 244; Mitteis, *Archiv f. Pap.* iii. p. 252 seg.

[3] Per quel che concerne il diritto privato si trova menzione della facoltà di disposizione della *maior pars in una lex mancipio dicta*, aggiunta alla

varie rendono più chiara la visione del nostro problema; perchè in realtà noi rinveniamo applicati nella Compilazione di Giustiniano gli stessi principii al condominio; in primo luogo il diritto della maggioranza di disporre della cosa comune.

E per ciò la posizione indipendente che i singoli avevano nella comproprietà, secondo la struttura classica dell' istituto, resta, nel nuovo sistema inaugurato da Giustiniano, essenzialmente annullata. Ora, invece, la comunione può dirsi organizzata in una certa forma; ha una volontà complessiva, la quale custodisce, regola ed esplica l' interesse collettivo sotto tutti gli aspetti. Di conseguenza, al consenso di tutti i socii, che era necessario per qualsiasi disposizione materiale della cosa comune, si sostituì la facoltà di disposizione della maggioranza.

70. E pertanto le aggiunte giustinianee ai passi dei giuristi classici acquistano ora un significato preciso e grande rilievo, chè esse si aggregano tutte perfettamente attorno al nuovo ordinamento, che ha un deciso carattere sociale. Si può negare forse un tale significato a quella norma legislativa che permette la rimozione dell' opera fatta da un socio solo nel caso che giovi alla collettività?: *si toti societati prodest opus tolli*, 26 *D.* viii. 2. E la stessa formula, come sappiamo, ritorna nel fr. 65 § 5 *D.* xvii. 2: *si intersit societati non dirimi societatem.* E più vivamente ancora quel concetto è accentuato nel fr. 10 pr. *D.* xxxix. 3: *iniquum enim visum est voluntatem unius ex modica forte portiuncula dominii praeiudicium sociis facere.* Che eresia giuridica è mai questa? Colui che ha parte nella comunione, e sia una minima parte, ha diritto di far valere la sua volontà come gli altri, perchè la sua posizione giuridica è pari a quella degli altri. Così ragionava la giurisprudenza aurea. Ma nell' inciso giustinianeo si dà un gran rilievo

*donatio Flavii Syntrophi* del II o III sec. p. C. (Bruns-Gradenwitz, n. 139, p. 337): *et si quis ibi inhabitare voluerit ex communi omnium consensu maiorisve partis eorum qui vivent, id ei liceat.* Naturalmente il potere conferito alla maggioranza non ha qui un valore speciale, perchè si tratta di una condizione espressa dal disponente, e nulla si oppone, inoltre, alla validità di una tale convenzione tra condomini che sia diretta a regolare il godimento o l' amministrazione della cosa comune. Nel documento citato si tratta in realtà di condominio; perchè se la *mancipatio* degli orti fu fatta ad un liberto, egli deve comunicarli a tutti i conliberti, e tutti insieme devono godere del reddito dei beni, che sarà impiegato per il culto della tomba del disponente, nei giorni designati.

alla utilità ed alla considerazione dei maggiori interessati, e quindi la prevalenza a coloro che rappresentano la parte maggiore; il quale interesse non deve essere paralizzato, si dice, da colui che ha nella comunione una modica porzioncella. Nella frase stessa usata dal legislatore, l' interesse del singolo, e per giunta minore al confronto, scade fino al dispregio. Naturalmente. Perchè nella Compilazione di Giustiniano l' idea dell' interesse sociale, del vantaggio dei più, considerato sempre in modo obbiettivo, irrompe su ogni angolo, e si diffonde come un getto di sole vivo. E per ciò nella comunione e nella società alla volontà ed agli interessi dei singoli debbono sempre prevalere la volontà della maggioranza, e l' utilità sociale. Così nell' eredità: la *maior pars* degli eredi ha diritto di chiedere il deposito fatto dal loro autore, qualunque esso sia; e la maggioranza si determina *ex magnitudine portionum hereditariarum.*[1]

È la maggioranza che in caso di conflitto sceglie, per votazione, il depositario delle *cautiones hereditariae*: fr. 5 *D.* x. 2 [*vel suffragio*].[2] E, cosa veramente sorprendente, alla maggioranza dei coeredi si attribuisce la facoltà di alienare validamente l' intera cosa ereditaria:

fr. 44 § 2 *D.* x. 2. Si coheredes absente uno coherede rem vendiderunt et in ea re dolo malo fecerunt, quo plus ad eos perveniret [vel familiae erciscundae iudicio praestabunt ei qui abfuit vel hereditatis petitione].

L' interpolazione si manifesta nel *praestare* senza oggetto; dacchè la correzione del Mo. è arbitraria. Or se l' assente, come dice il testo, ha soltanto le azioni contro i coeredi, ciò significa che l' alienazione è considerata efficace per la cosa intera. Vedi contro fr. 64 § 4 *D.* xxi. 2, esaminato più sopra a p. 42, e principalmente poi il fr. 54 *D.* x. 2 di Nerazio, che esclude il *iud. fam. erc.* rispetto al fondo venduto da parte di alcuni eredi.

## V. LA STRUTTURA DELLA *COMMUNIO* NEL DIRITTO GIUSTINIANEO

71. La ricostruzione dommatica di un istituto di dritto presuppone ferma conoscenza dei principii di fondo del medesimo e

[1] fr. 14 pr. *D.* xvi. 3.

[2] L' interpolazione nel testo è forse più estesa.

delle norme particolari; e quindi la determinazione precisa del loro valore.

Nella legislazione di Giustiniano esistono, come si è visto, due ordini di principii riguardo alla comunione; e di conseguenza molte disposizioni particolari sono in perfetta opposizione tra loro.

Qui dunque bisogna intendersi preliminarmente sui criterii che l' interprete deve seguire nella ricostruzione dello istituto. Ed io suppongo che per questo rispetto l' accordo non dovrebbe incontrare ostacolo di sorta; avvegnachè tutti debbono consentire in ciò: che ove la compilazione di Giustiniano si voglia considerare come un Codice, per ricavarne i principii fondamentali dei singoli istituti, per l' applicazione pratica o per la trattazione scientifica, è sempre necessario procedere ad un confronto tra i testi contraddittorii, dar la prevalenza ai concetti affermati dal legislatore nella sua opera, lasciando cadere poi quegl' altri che nel corpo della Compilazione figurano come una sopravvivenza storica, e perciò come punti morti nell' organismo del nuovo diritto.

Siffatto metodo è imposto dalla natura stessa dell' opera legislativa, formata in una maniera così singolare.

La Glossa adoperò, se guardiamo i risultati, un processo identico. Essa, come è noto, mise alla luce tutto il contenuto del *Corpus Iuris*, e lo dotò di nuova forza, ma secondo l' indole dei tempi giunse a quel risultato mediante distinzioni, conciliazioni ed artifici molti, considerati nei singoli casi come idonei a superare le difficoltà dei testi contraddittori. Oggi noi arriviamo più direttamente e con maggior sicurezza alla meta, mercè la critica storica.

Il metodo è quindi diverso, ma i risultamenti debbono pareggiarsi, come vedremo tosto nel c. iii. della presente trattazione.

72. Or applicando cotali criterii nello studio della *communio*, noi siamo costretti a tagliar fuori avanti tutto il principio di fondo, quale era rappresentato dai giuristi classici, e che appare in tutta la sua energia nella formulazione di Sabino, che è stata già largamente discussa.

Secondo i giuristi ciascuno dei socii ha pieno il diritto di proprietà sulla cosa comune. E perciò i singoli hanno una posizione di dritto perfettamente uguale; sono liberi ed indipendenti; e per consequenza la volontà di ciascuno deve valere quanto la volontà degli altri. Da ciò deriva necessariamente la regola: che colui che vieta è poziore; effetto inevitabile per il concorso di dritti che hanno forza pari. La comunione pertanto è un istituto senza disciplina, che non sopporta norme regolatrici, le quali sarebbero in contrasto col dritto assoluto dei titolari della proprietà. Quando il disaccordo si manifesta non v' è altro rimedio che la divisione.

Or è certo che tutta questa struttura della *communio* fu distrutta da Giustiniano, perchè i testi che contenevano appunto i principii e le conseguenze or esposti furono annullati direttamente dalle nuove aggiunte legislative, applicate giusto in tutti i passi fondamentali dei diversi titoli del Digesto. E sono queste aggiunte e quelle riforme che debbono apprestare all' interprete gli elementi precipui per la ricostruzione del nuovo istituto; perchè, come bene osservò il Lenel,[1] una interpolazione, ed a maggior ragione una serie di interpolazioni, costituiscono sempre un «deliberato atto legislativo» ed il risultato *als bewusster Gesetzgebungsakt* lega l' interprete con la forza di un ordine.

Ed abbracciando per ciò in una volta, in una sintesi generale, tutte quelle riforme dianzi discusse, la struttura della *communio* risulta nella legislazione di Giustiniano come segue.

73. La comunione del diritto giustinianeo è disciplinata da norme generali, le quali elisero in primo luogo quella indipendenza che i socii avevano in virtù della loro posizione pari, secondo il diritto quiritario del dominio.

Ed accertata questa nozione fondamentale e generalissima, il nuovo schema dell' istituto si disegna come appresso.

(1) La regola centrale di tutto l' istituto classico formulata da Sabino, che vietava a ciascun socio qualsiasi disposizione materiale della cosa, fu essenzialmente abolita.

(2) Ogni condomino può ora, positivamente, compiere atti dispositivi che si esplicano sulla cosa, anche contro la volontà degli altri; esigendosi soltanto che gli atti di disposizione o le opere siano di vantaggio alla collettività.

(3) Di conseguenza, lo *ius prohibendi*, rinnegato come privata difesa, fu ammesso in via giudiziaria entro certi limiti soltanto; e cioè prima dell' inizio delle opere o per rimuovere quelle che fossero riconosciute pregiudizievoli all' interesse della comunione.

(4) I condomini hanno rispetto alla cosa una posizione pari, come prima; ma essi non sono più indipendenti e sciolti, sibbene collegati tra loro ed organizzati in un gruppo collettivo.

[1] *Archiv f. civ. Praxis*, vol. lxxviii. p. 362.

(5) L' organizzazione dei socii si manifesta nel diritto che spetta alla maggioranza di essi di decidere intorno al godimento, alla conservazione ed alla destinazione della cosa. La maggioranza si determina anche qui mediante il computo del maggior valore delle quote rappresentate dai singoli socii.

(6) A tutelare le facoltà attribuite ai singoli compartecipi servono ora tutte le azioni che di norma competono al domino solitario, e che possono esperirsi tra socii vicendevolmente; e ciò sia per costringere gli altri a prestare il loro consenso per l' esecuzione di un' opera o l' attuazione di qualsiasi atto dispositivo, sia per impedire nuove opere ovvero ottenere la rimozione di quelle fatte, sia per conseguire indennizzo per il danno arrecato da uno alla cosa comune; ed infine per la partizione di spese e utili.

(7) Il *iud. communi dividundo* può esperirsi durante la comunione, per far valere tutte le ragioni di sopra indicate. Come tale il *iudicium c. d.* può designarsi quale un mezzo generale e proprio a tutela dei diritti dei condomini; l' azione per antonomasia che regola la vita ed il buon andamento della comunione in qualsiasi evenienza. Ma tutte le altre azioni speciali, di cui si disse (6), concorrono, a scelta dell' interessato, per ovviare o reprimere abusi, danni, immissioni, etcc. a seconda i particolari presupposti richiesti per l' esercizio delle medesime.

Tutte queste proposizioni nel loro insieme costituiscono la nuova struttura della *communio* del diritto giustinianeo; esse non esigono alcuna illustrazione e nemmeno citazioni di testi; perchè si appoggiano, in tutti i particolari, sulla dimostrazione che precede.

74. Ma se le aggiunte e gl' incisi giustinianei più sbalestrati e finora deserti acquistano nella presente trattazione un carattere di unità così saldo, io chiedo, mi siano consentite, nel chiudere questo capitolo, alcune riflessioni d' indole più generale.

La dimostrazione fornita ha accertato nel modo più sicuro che la comunione ebbe nel diritto giustinianeo una disciplina, nel senso più particolare che i socii sono ormai reciprocamente legati da un ordinamento che viene dalla legge, e che deve in ogni caso attuarsi, anche contro la volontà dei compartecipi. Ma caratteristico e nel contempo insigne è il pensiero centrale che anima tutta quella nuova disciplina, e che è costituito dalla utilità collettiva che deve attuarsi in ogni caso, senza considerazione degli interessi dei singoli.

E questo pensiero, inciso fortemente in tutte le norme, ebbe la potenza di soppiantare tutte le regole del diritto classico in materia di comunione: colpì anzitutto la concezione stessa del dominio nella sua radice più vigorosa, ed annientò così la indipendenza dei singoli socii; e per conseguenza l' arbitrio, la onnipotenza della volontà, e lo *ius prohibendi*, affermazione virile sempre pronta del diritto individuale. Ora, invece, l' interesse sociale deve in ogni caso prevalere. La volontà della maggioranza annulla quella dei singoli socii. In caso di dissenso o di opposizione materiale ha luogo la coazione giudiziaria; qualunque ne sia la causa; si manifesti cioè per il godimento della cosa, per le opere conservative ovvero per innovazioni sulla cosa comune. In proposito non vi ha limite alcuno nei testi, come pretese la Glossa,[1] e non occorre per ciò distinguere tra atti dispositivi riguardanti l' uso normale della cosa e altri che importerebbero innovazioni.

E così, io dico, nel diritto giustinianeo la comunione dei beni, comunque derivata, ebbe un assetto del tutto nuovo e diametralmente opposto a quello che aveva nelle opere dei giureconsulti. E pertanto su questo punto abbiamo elementi nuovi che ci inducono a modificare le idee e le conoscenze ritenute finora come verità infallibili. E ciò va bene.

75. Ma lo scopo più essenziale di questo risultato andrebbe perduto, in gran parte, se noi si tralasciasse una ulteriore indagine, onde porre in evidenza le forze che hanno determinato trasformazioni così essenziali, che appaiono d' un tratto nell' opera legislativa, travolgendo tutto un sistema di diritto, che aveva radici profonde e, sovratutto, una grande perfezione e proporzione in tutti i particolari, e lo splendore e la dignità che i giureconsulti avevano saputo conferirgli nella trattazione. Quelle forze dissolventi di un' opera cotanto insigne dovevano per ciò essere irresistibili; energie vive e possenti nel tempo in cui la legislazione fu compiuta.

76. E l' indagine si rende più attraente ed ansiosa quando subito ci accorgiamo che un ricollegamento delle riforme giustinianee al diritto greco, considerato pure nella sua ultima fase del periodo bizantino, non è possibile in questo punto. Infatti il condominio, quale ci si rivela nei documenti greco-egizii, ha la struttura ferma di una proprietà divisa tra i titolari,[2] che si manifesta in ogni

[1] Cfr. c. iii.

[2] Cfr. Weiss, *Archiv f. Papyr.* iv. p. 353 e seg.

direzione ; e cioè nell' assenza del *ius adcrescendi* tra condomini,[1] nella facoltà di disposizione giuridica che compete ad ognuno senza il concorso degli altri[2]; nelle singole denunzie catastali e nei libri catastali, dove ciascun comproprietario figura iscritto per la sua parte anche infinitesimale; nella obbligazione parziale e non solidale di ognuno per l' imposta.[3]

Un condominio che ha tutte queste linee diritte e semplici si raffigura, perciò, come una comproprietà parziale su di una stessa cosa, che non ammette legami di sorta e reciproca dipendenza.

E se nessuna traccia si rinviene nel diritto greco degli ordinamenti giustinianei in questa materia ; e nessun possibile nesso può esistere tra quelle riforme ed i diritti provinciali che avevano subita influenza ellenica, bisogna rivolgersi altrove. Dal nulla, nulla può divenire.

77. Ma è sufficiente il semplice confronto dei due sistemi, il classico ed il giustinianeo, per stabilire nella maniera più semplice il nesso storico, ed insieme la energia che apportò un così profondo mutamento in questa materia.

L' istituto romano, come sappiamo, traeva la sua struttura dall' ordinamento prettamente individualistico della proprietà. Per ciò l' autonomia individuale nel sistema del diritto privato non si piega e non si arresta nè davanti alla posizione pari o alla libertà degli altri, nè davanti agli interessi collettivi ; perchè il principio fondamentale è l' individuo, l' affermazione della propria volontà, della propria indipendenza, che contiene in sè l' anarchia. In contrasto l' istituto giustinianeo è regolato in conformità della più viva considerazione degli interessi sociali ; è tutto compenetrato dal principio etico, che ove gli uomini s' incontrino in un comune interesse, là non vi è ragione di lotta, ma ragione permanente di cooperazione.[4] Le conseguenze sono immediate : l' interesse individuale, l' arbitrio, la indipendenza dei singoli sono annullati, irremissibilmente.

E questo principio di socialità rinvigorito e diffuso soltanto dalla dottrina cristiana, divenne coscienza popolare e si tradusse in norme giuridiche nella prima codificazione dell' epoca cristiana.

1 Cfr. Mitteis, *Archiv f. Papyr.* iii. p. 253 ; e *Reichsrecht*, p. 386.
2 Cfr. Wenger, *Gött. g. Anz.* 1907, p. 291 ; e Weiss, *l. c.* p. 358.
3 Weiss, *l. c.* p. 356.
4 Riccobono, *Rivista di diritto civile*, vol. iii. p. 52.

78. Così il divenire del diritto si rende visibile ed appare naturale, come il prodotto di quella specie d' atmosfera in cui la legislazione fu compiuta, e si ricollega a tutte quelle forze vive del tempo. Nè le riforme poste qui in luce possono essere isolate. Perchè, in realtà, la penetrazione di quell' idea fondamentale della solidarietà umana si manifesta in tutto il campo del diritto privato, e più energicamente nell' istituto della proprietà, che ne esce svigorito nella sua complessione, per via di limitazioni infinite, d' ogni ordine, dirette sempre a soddisfare esigenze sociali, ad attuare il principio che la proprietà deve per quanto è possibile essere utile ai più, e contribuire nella maggiore misura al benessere sociale.[1] Nel condominio l' applicazione di questi nuovi ideali era soltanto più ovvia ed immediata. E nel condominio, come fu ordinato da Giustiniano, si mostra gagliardo quel vivo e comune sentimento di cooperazione e di fratellanza, che doveva prontamente trasformare l' istituto nella sua struttura e nelle norme particolari. Alla volontà libera ed indipendente dei singoli fu, per ciò, sostituita l' utilità sociale che è ora il centro attivo che dà vita a questa figura di diritto e la disciplina in ogni sua parte.

La spiegazione ed il nesso sono quindi semplici, più che si possa richiedere; non potendosi mettere in dubbio che quel principio della utilità generale, quei sentimenti di solidarietà umana furono diffusi e resi attivi nel mondo dalla dottrina cristiana; e che soltanto essi poterono via via travolgere tutto il sistema individualistico romano, e fin da principio comprimerlo nell' opera legislativa, quanto alle sue manifestazioni più spietate.

Chi non sa vedere tale ricollegamento nella materia che ci occupa, dovrebbe mostrare, positivamente, che sul cadere del mondo antico altre forze operarono un rivolgimento, così essenziale nella concezione della vita e negli ordinamenti giuridici.

Certo le difficoltà più gravi si riscontrano quando noi ci facciamo a valutare i fattori morali della civiltà, perchè non si possono misurare nè pesare, non hanno corpo, sono niente; e pur sono tutto. Fattori prodigiosi, invisibili che giorno per giorno creano situazioni nuove, portano argomentazioni definitive, insinuano negli uomini sentimenti che divengono forze vive nel campo dell' azione, per cui visibilmente ne appare spostato il corso della civiltà.[2]

[1] Riccobono, *Rivista di dir. civ.* iii. p. 54.

[2] Per ciò non posso consentire nella spiegazione che in deffinitivo dà il

Ed ora potremo meglio valutare e stabilire in quale misura la legislazione di Giustiniano influì sulla formazione del diritto comune, ed in particolare dell' istituto della comunione, che è argomento della trattazione.[1]

S. RICCOBONO.

Lenel (Holtzendorff's *Enc.* p. 375) di quelle tendenze filantropiche che si mostrano nella legislazione da Costantino in poi, e particolarmente in quella di Giustiniano. Il Maestro è disposto ad ammettere l' influenza cristiana, particolarmente rispetto alla protezione dei deboli, in largo senso, al divieto della difesa privata, al favore per la beneficenza. E tutto ciò non sarebbe poco; perchè se si ammette l' influsso di quelle idee così generali nell' opera legislativa, esse dovevano agire come un fermento in tutta la materia del diritto privato. Ma qui non importa discutere i limiti; dacchè il Lenel poi inclina a ricondurre tutte le manifestazioni accennate «a quella tendenza propria al despotismo di mostrarsi generoso con la borsa di altri». Or questa spiegazione, dico, mi sembra esteriore. Perchè in verità nel corso del diritto possono in dati momenti manifestarsi direzioni o deviazioni speciali, determinate da forze e tendenze precarie; ma che necessariamente si irrigidiscono e si annullano col cessare della causa. Se gli effetti, invece, sono permanenti, e sempre più rigogliosi, come è nel nostro caso, tutte quelle riforme debbono aver radici più profonde e vive, nel sentimento comune degli uomini. E si sa che quell' idea cristiana della fratellanza, che viene qui particolarmente in considerazione, costituì appunto il fulcro di tutta la civiltà nuova, in contrasto aperto per questo riguardo, con quella del mondo antico.

[1] La trattazione ha preso uno sviluppo così esteso quale io non supponevo da principio, e che non può essere oltre tollerato in questo luogo. Mi riserbo perciò di pubblicare a parte la continuazione (c. iii. Dalla Glossa alle legislazioni moderne e c. iv. La dottrina dal sec. xvi al sec. xx) che sarà esposta oralmente al Congresso.

V

# ZUR GESCHICHTE DER HEREDIS INSTITUTIO

ÜBER das Wesen der römischen Erbfolge und folgeweise auch der römischen Erbeinsetzung herrscht bekanntlich Streit. Der rein vermögensrechtlichen Auffassung beider steht eine familienrechtliche gegenüber, die in dem *heres* der Urzeit einen Nachfolger in der Hausherrschaft erblickt [1] und sich in Bezug auf die *heredis institutio* bei manchen Schriftstellern zu der bestimmten Hypothese verdichtet, dass diese aus einer ursprünglichen Adoption hervorgegangen sei,[2] ja in ihrer ältesten Gestalt noch selbst als eine — von der Arrogation verschiedene — *adoptio in hereditatem* gedacht werden müsse.[3] Dabei besteht wieder Meinungsverschiedenheit darüber, ob die Loslösung der Erbeinsetzung von der Adoption im Recht der zwölf Tafeln bereits vollzogen sei oder nicht.[4]

In diesem Widerstreit der Meinungen ist eine Vorfrage nicht genügend erwogen worden, die m. E. der Erörterung recht sehr bedarf: die Frage nach dem Alter der testamentarischen Erbeinsetzung überhaupt. Man hält es eben sehr allgemein für selbstverständlich, dass die *heredis institutio* bereits dem Rechte

[1] Scialoja, *Bullett.* iii. 176 f.; Bonfante, *Bullett.* iv. 97 f., *Istit.*[4] 511 f.; Costa, *Storia del dir. rom. priv.* 462 f. Auch Mitteis, *röm. Privatr.* i. 93 f., und v. Mayr, *röm. R. Gesch.* i.[2] 91 f., betonen die familienrechtliche Grundlage der römischen Universalsukzession.

[2] Gans, *das Erbrecht in weltgeschichtl. Entwicklung* (1825) ii. 49 f., Schulin, *d. griech. Testament vergl. mit dem röm.* (1882) 50 f., *Lehrb. d. Gesch. d. r. R.* 458; Lambert, *La Tradition rom. sur la succession des formes du testament* (1901); Appleton, *Le Test. rom.* (1903) 61 f.; Sohm, *Institut.*[14] 721; Perozzi, *Istit.* ii. 359 f.

[3] So bestimmt Lambert, a. a. O.

[4] In ersterem Sinn Appleton, in letzterem Lambert, a. a. O.

der zwölf Tafeln angehöre, dass der Satz *heredis institutio est caput et fundamentum testamenti* so alt sei wie das römische Testament selber.[1] Ganz unbestritten ist freilich diese Meinung schon bisher nicht geblieben. In einer 1886 veröffentlichten Abhandlung spricht Cuq dem altrömischen Testament die Erbeinsetzung zwar nicht geradezu ab, aber er lehrt doch, dass der *heres extraneus* „ne différait alors du légataire que par l'étendue de ses droits."[2] Weiter ging Ehrlich in einem 1903 vor dem historischen Kongress in Rom gehaltenen Vortrag.[3] Das älteste Testament war nach ihm ein reines Legatentestament. Allerdings nimmt er an, dass es „in Rom schon in sehr früher Zeit bei der testamentarischen Erbfolge neben Legataren auch *heredes* gegeben habe"; diese *heredes* waren aber nach ihm die gesetzlichen Erben, nicht beliebige *heredes instituti*.[4] Ebenso findet sich bei Binder (*die Plebs*, 1909, S. 353) die Äusserung, dass „erst das jüngere Manzipationstestament ein letztwilliges Erbeinsetzungsgeschäft im Sinne des klassischen römischen Rechts gewesen sein kann." Im folgenden soll die Frage nach dem Inhalt des altrömischen Testaments einer erneuten Prüfung unterzogen werden: hat das Recht der zwölf Tafeln eine *heredis institutio* gekannt? war nicht der einzige Weg, auf dem sich damals ein Erblasser künstlich einen Universalsukzessor zu schaffen vermochte, der allbekannte der Arrogation?

Bei dieser Untersuchung nehme ich zwei Thesen als feststehend an, die, obwohl bestritten, doch immer noch der herrschenden Meinung entsprechen. Erstens: dass die Zwölftafelgesetzgebung im 5. Jahrhundert v. Chr. entstanden ist, — meine Gründe dafür

[1] Dieser herrschenden Meinung gibt Appleton, a. a. O. 86, scharfen Ausdruck, wenn er die *heredis institutio* für „l'essence même du testament à Rome" erklärt.

[2] *NRH.* x. 542. Wendungen, die Cuq 537 f. gebraucht („en présence de *sui* le testament . . . ne devait contenir que des dispositions particulières, comme un legs," „en l'absence d'héritiers siens, on pouvait *léguer* tous ses biens à une personne étrangère à la famille"), legen den Gedanken nahe, dass er für das alte Testament die Erbeinsetzung auch formell leugne; doch ist dies nach dem obigen Zitat wohl nicht seine Meinung gewesen. Ganz ausdrücklich spricht er sich für das Vorhandensein der Erbeinsetzung schon vor den zwölf Tafeln in seinen *Instit. jurid.*[2] i. 124 aus; nur beschränkt er ihre *Möglichkeit* auch hier auf den Fall, dass keine *sui* vorhanden sind.

[3] *Z. f. vgl. Rechtswiss.* xvii. 99 f.

[4] a. a. O. 101 f.

habe ich anderwärts ausgeführt.[1] Zweitens: dass das Testament der zwölf Tafeln noch das Komitialtestament war;[2] dafür ist mir schon entscheidend der Umstand, dass den Römern schwerlich eine Erinnerung an das Komitialtestament geblieben sein würde, wenn es bereits in so grauer Vorzeit aus der Anwendung verschwunden wäre. Ein näheres Eingehen auf diese Thesen ist im Zusammenhang dieses Vortrags nicht möglich, wohl auch nicht nötig.

Wer eine Frage, wie die vorliegende, zu beantworten versucht, wird gut tun, nicht von den Erörterungen der klassischen Juristen auszugehen, die durch eine vielhundertjährige Entwicklung von den zwölf Tafeln geschieden sind, sondern — ohne auf der anderen Seite diese Erörterungen zu ignorieren — von dem überlieferten Texte des Gesetzes selbst. Jedem aufmerksamen Leser dieses Textes muss es auffallen, dass das Gesetz das Wort *heres* nur in Bezug auf den *suus heres* verwendet zu haben scheint, und dass in eben dem Satze, wo dies geschieht, der *proximus adgnatus* nicht durch ein *heres esto*, sondern mit den Worten *familiam habeto* berufen wird. Man hat daraus schliessen wollen, dass der Name *heres* damals nur für den *suus heres* gebraucht und auf den sukzedierenden Agnaten nicht angewendet worden sei.[3] Es wird eine Zeit gegeben haben, für die dies zutrifft; für die zwölf Tafeln ist mir der Schluss bedenklich. Umgekehrt: wenn es keine anderen *heredes* gab, als die *sui heredes*, wozu dann die Wendung *cui suus heres nec escit*? Mir scheint die Beifügung des Wortes *suus* an dieser Stelle kaum anders zu erklären, als durch die Annahme, dass es eben schon damals auch *extranei heredes* gab. Aber allerdings verlangt die berührte Terminologie eine Erklärung. Sollte man befürchtet haben, durch ein gesetzliches *heres esto* den Agnaten zum Zwangserben gleich dem *suus* zu machen? Aber dem wäre ja durch Hinzufügen eines *si volet*, wie es die zwölf Tafeln anderwärts zu ähnlichem Zwecke verwenden, leicht vorzubeugen gewesen. Die richtige Erklärung liegt anderswo. Uns Modernen ist der Ausspruch Papinians in D. v. 3, 50 pr. *hereditas etiam sine ullo corpore iuris intellectum habet* in

[1] *ZRG.* xxxix. 498 f., Holtzendorff-Kohlers *Enzyclop.*[7] i. 324 f.

[2] Vgl. dazu noch Mitteis, *röm. Privatr.* i. 82 n. 24, und die dort Angeff.

[3] Perozzi, *Istit.* ii. 362 (vgl. 356) „il nome di *heres* esprimeva non il solo fatto della successione, ma anche la qualità di figlio." S. auch Cuq *Instit. jurid.*[2] i. 123.

Fleisch und Blut übergegangen. Aber dürfen wir eine solche Abstraction schon dem fünften Jahrhundert v. Chr. zutrauen? Ich meine, für die naiv-sinnliche Vorstellungsweise, die wir in dieser frühen Zeit voraussetzen müssen, konnte die *hereditas* kein blosses Gedankending sein; den Römern der zwölf Tafeln war sie etwas körperlich greifbares:[1] Haus und Hof, Sklaven und Vieh. So darf man denn auch die klassischen Begriffe von Delation und Acquisition der Erbschaft nicht in das Zwölftafelrecht versetzen. Diese Begriffe beruhen auf der Vorstellung, dass die *hereditas* eine blosse Rechtsstellung sei, die dem *extraneus* vom Gesetz angeboten und dann von ihm durch einfachen Willensakt erworben werde. Ist aber die *hereditas* etwas körperliches, so kann sie, so wenig wie sonst eine herrenlose Sache, durch eine blosse Willenserklärung erworben werden. Wer vielmehr nicht schon wie der *suus* als Hausherr im Hause sitzt, wird *heres* nur dadurch, dass er sich der *familia* tatsächlich bemächtigt, und eben darum erblickt das Gesetz seine Aufgabe lediglich darin, denjenigen zu bezeichnen, der sich in Ermangelung eines *suus heres* der *familia* bemächtigen dürfe, —*familiam habeto; heres* wird er dann durch die wirkliche Inbesitznahme.[2] Dass dies in der Tat die alte Auffassung war, lässt sich, wie ich glaube, mit grosser Sicherheit erweisen. Der Beweis liegt in dem Mangel einer zivilen Form für den Antritt der Intestaterbschaft. Erwägt man, eine wie ausnahmslose Herrschaft die Form sonst im alten Zivilrecht übt, so erscheint es unbegreiflich, dass sich für ein so ungemein wichtiges Geschäft wie den Erbschaftsantritt keine Form ausgebildet hätte, wenn man darin überhaupt ein Geschäft erblickt hätte. Nun glaubt ja freilich eine heute weitverbreitete Ansicht eine solche Form wirklich entdeckt zu haben, — in der *cretio* nämlich.[3] Aber diese Ansicht

[1] Das empfand schon ganz richtig Kuntze in seinem Programm *Über die Erbeinsetzung auf bestimmte Nachlassstücke* (1875) 9 f., nur dass die Art, wie er dieser Empfindung Ausdruck gibt, durch die Hereinziehung der Begriffe Tauschwert und Gebrauchswert Anstoss erregen muss. Ganz im Sinne des Texts Cuq, *NRH.* x. 542 f.

[2] Wie aber, wenn er — vielleicht von einem anderen Prätendenten — an dieser Inbesitznahme gehindert wird? Man beachte, dass die *legis actio* der *hereditatis petitio* immer mit einem symbolischen Besitzakt, dem *vindicare*, verbunden ist, und dass der Gegner gezwungen wird, die Vornahme dieses Besitzaktes zu dulden.

[3] Vgl. u. a. Karlowa, *RG.* ii. 896 und die dort Angeff.; Girard, *Manuel*[5] 871 n. 7; Sohm, *Institut.*[14] 698 n. 7; Czyhlarz, *Institut.* § 124; Bonfante,

steht nicht nur mit der klassischen Überlieferung im Widerspruch, die nur von testamentarischer Festsetzung, nichts von gesetzlicher Geltung der *cretio* weiss, sondern sie unterstellt auch eine sachlich unmögliche Entwicklung. Wenn man in Testamenten die *cretio* festzusetzen pflegte — *solet cretio dari*, wie Gaius ii. 164 sagt —, so kann das doch nur geschehen sein, weil man eine solche Form für den Erbschaftsantritt zweckmässig fand. Wie verträgt sich damit die Annahme, dass man diese selbe zweckmässig befundene Form da, wo sie kraft rechtens gefordert war, soll haben fallen lassen? Nein: dies Formalgeschäft ist dem alten Rechte fremd; es ist für die testamentarische Erbfolge, einerlei einstweilen wann, erfunden worden; der Erwerb der Intestaterbschaft aber fand von jeher nicht durch *cretio*, sondern durch körperliche Inbesitznahme statt.[1] Das *adire* ist in seinem ursprünglichen Sinn ganz wörtlich zu nehmen als ein Betreten der Erbschaftsgrundstücke, wie das griechische ἐμβατεύειν εἰς τὴν οὐσίαν und das germanische „zu dem Erbe gehen."[2] Und das *familiam habeto* der zwölf Tafeln hat genau den gleichen Sinn, wie ursprünglich das *do lego* des Vindikationslegats, dem ja in der Tat späterhin ein *sumito* oder *sibi habeto* oder *capito* gleichgeachtet wurde:[3] es will eben jene Inbesitznahme gestatten.

Habe ich in obigem das *familiam habeto* des Gesetzes richtig gedeutet, so ergeben sich daraus wichtige Folgerungen für das altrömische Testament. Denn wenn das Gesetz die Wendung *heres esto* deshalb nicht gebrauchte, weil man Herr der körperlich gedachten Erbschaft nicht durch ein blosses Wort des Gesetzes werden kann, sondern nur durch die Tat, so scheint es undenkbar, dass im Testament gerade jene Wendung auch nur üblich, geschweige denn, dass sie für die Giltigkeit des Testaments geradezu vorgeschrieben gewesen sein sollte. Auch der Testator verfügte nicht über das Gedankending der Erbschaft, sondern über

---

*Istit.*[4] 488 n. 1; Costa, *Storia del dir. pr. rom.* 520. Anders Perozzi, *Istit.* ii. 505.

[1] Damit dürfte auch zusammenhängen, dass die *usucapio p. h.* nach Gai. ii. 52 nur zugelassen war in Bezug auf eine *res hereditaria, cuius possessionem heres nondum nactus est.* Die Inbesitznahme war der Erwerbsakt. In dieser Beziehung übereinstimmend: Perozzi, *Istit.* ii. 505.

[2] Grimm, *Rechtsaltertümer*,[4] i. 659.

[3] Man beachte, dass es auch für den Erwerb des Vindikationslegats keine Form gab.

sein Haus, seinen Hof, seine Sachen überhaupt, indem er den Bedachten ermächtigte, sie nach seinem Tode an sich zu nehmen. Dafür aber war die gegebene Form nicht die Erbeinsetzung, sondern die älteste [1] Form des Legats, das Vindikationslegat: das Komitialtestament war ein reines Legatentestament. Dafür, dass dem so war, haben wir sichere Anhaltspunkte. Vor allem: die einzige Bestimmung, die die zwölf Tafeln über Testamente enthielten, handelt nur vom Legat, unter welchen Begriff nach dem alten Sprachgebrauch allerdings auch die *tutoris datio* gefallen sein muss: [2] *uti legassit* (*super pecunia tutelave*) [3] *suae rei, ita ius esto.* Pomponius in einer allbekannten Stelle [4] findet in diesem Satze freilich auch die Ermächtigung zur Erbeinsetzung ausgesprochen: *latissima potestas tributa videtur et heredis instituendi* u.s.w. Die Stelle, mag sie nun lediglich Äusserung des Pomponius sein oder auf den von ihm kommentierten Q. Mucius zurückgehen, ist als historisches Zeugnis wichtig, nicht um ihres positiven Inhalts willen, — sie belehrt uns nicht über den ursprünglichen Sinn des Satzes, sondern über den Sinn, den eine weit spätere *interpretatio* ihm beilegte —, wohl aber deshalb, weil sie beweist, dass die zwölf Tafeln eine die *heredis institutio* zulassende Bestimmung nicht enthielten. Ausgeschlossen scheint mir, dass das Gesetz, wenn ihm neben dem Legat auch die Erbeinsetzung bekannt war, das für ersteres formelmässig technische Wort auch für die letztere verwendet hätte.[5] Ausgeschlossen aber nicht minder auch der schon mehrfach laut gewordene Gedanke, jener Satz habe für Legate, nur für Legate (oder auch nur für Legate von *res nec mancipi*) die von der Zustimmung der Komitien unabhängige Autonomie des Erblassers proklamieren wollen, während für Erbeinsetzungen (oder wenigstens für die von Nichtintestaterben) jene Zustimmung noch immer erforderlich sein sollte.[6] Ich untersuche hier nicht, ob das Testament überhaupt jemals eine der

[1] Vgl. hierzu die überzeugenden Ausführungen Wlassaks, *ZRG.* xliv. 198 f.

[2] Hölder, *ZRG.* xliii. 72.

[3] Die Authentizität der eingeklammerten Worte kann hier dahin gestellt bleiben. Vgl. dazu und dagegen besonders Appleton, *Le Test. rom.* 59 n. 1.

[4] D. l. 16, 120; vgl. auch Gai. ii. 224.

[5] Vgl. Mitteis, *röm. Privatr.* i. 82 n. 24; Wlassak, *ZRG.* xli. 70 n. 1, auch Hölder, *Beiträge*, 65.

[6] Sohm, *Instit.*[14] 722, Cuq, *Instit.* i.[2] 130 f., und in anderer Formulierung Mitteis, a. a. O., Wlassak, *ZRG.* xliv. 218.

Zustimmung des Volkes bedürftige *lex* gewesen ist; undenkbar scheint mir, dass, wenn es dies war, die Zustimmung zu irgend einer Zeit für etwas anderes gefordert gewesen sein kann, als für die Totalität des letzten Willens. Es ist ja doch klar, dass es für die Genehmigung der Erbeinsetzung, wenn eine solche erforderlich war, nicht hätte gleichgiltig sein können, ob und welche Legate der Erblasser z. B. enterbten oder übergangenen Verwandten hinterliess; dass es eine Farce gewesen wäre, wenn man für die Erbeinsetzung Zustimmung der Komitien verlangt, den Erblassern aber gestattet hätte, die *institutio* durch Legate mehr oder weniger ihres Inhalts zu berauben.[1] Der ganze Testamentsinhalt bildet vielmehr eine untrennbare Einheit, die nur in ihrer Gesamtheit einer Genehmigung des Volkes hätte unterliegen können.

Für die Auffassung des Komitialtestaments als Legatentestament spricht nun aber noch eine zweite ganz sichere historische Tatsache, die Fassung der Nunkupationsformel des *testamentum per aes et libram*, die allein auf Legate und zwar Vindikationslegate[2] zugeschnitten war, *ita do ita lego ita testor itaque vos Quirites testimonium mihi perhibetote*. Dass diese Formel zu einem Erbeinsetzungstestament nicht passt, wird heute sehr allgemein anerkannt.[3] Man erklärt aber den Mangel einer Bezugnahme auf die *heredis institutio* daraus, dass im älteren *testamentum per aes et libram* der *familiae emptor* selbst *heredis loco* gewesen sei, sodass sich die Beschränkung der Formel auf die Bestätigung von Legaten von selbst ergeben habe. Gewiss! Nur bleibt dabei unerklärt, warum man, als auch die *heredis institutio* im Manzipationstestament Unterkommen fand, nicht jetzt zurückgriff auf die umfassendere Formel, die die herrschende Meinung notwendig dem Komitialtestament zuschreiben muss. War die Erbeinsetzung selbst trotz Aufkommens des älteren Manzipationstestaments nicht in Vergessenheit geraten, dann, so müsste man annehmen, kann man auch den auf sie bezüglichen Teil der alten Bestätigungsformel nicht vergessen haben. Die Erbeinsetzung, wenn sie dem Komitialtestament eigen war, hätte aber niemals in Vergessenheit geraten

[1] Dies gilt, wenn gleich in gemindertem Masse, auch dann, wenn man für die zwölf Tafeln nicht volle Legierfreiheit, sondern, was ich freilich für unbegründet halte, solche nur hinsichtlich der *res nec mancipi* annimmt. Auch diese konnten ein recht beträchtlicher Bestandteil des Vermögens sein.

[2] Wlassak, a. a. O. 206.

[3] Vgl. etwa Sohm, *Instit.*[14] 725, Wlassak, a. a. O.

können, aus dem einfachen Grunde nicht, weil das Komitialtestament als Testament mit Erbeinsetzung vor dem blossen Legatentestament die wesentlichsten Vorzüge besessen und sich daher ohne Zweifel so lange erhalten haben würde, bis die Erbeinsetzung in das Manzipationstestament Aufnahme fand.[1] Als dieser letzte bedeutsame Schritt geschah, wäre also die umfassendere Formel nicht nur noch bekannt, sondern in häufigem praktischem Gebrauch gewesen; alles hätte darauf hingewiesen, sie nunmehr auch für das Manzipationstestament zu verwerten, und gleichwohl hätte man dies unbegreiflicherweise unterlassen! Glatt und einfach erklärt sich dagegen das überlieferte *ita do ita lego*, wenn man mit der hier vertretenen Anschauung annimmt, dass auch das Komitialtestament selbst ein blosses Legatentestament war und gerade in der überlieferten Formel seine zutreffende Bestätigung fand. Dann hat eben hier wie so oft eine uralte Formel trotz Wechsels des durch sie zu deckenden Inhalts sich unverändert durch die Jahrhunderte erhalten, ein redendes Zeugnis des älteren Rechtszustands.

Wer mit uns glaubt, das Komitialtestament sei ein reines Legatentestament gewesen, steht nun freilich vor gewissen Fragen, die der Antwort harren.

Wir sind vom klassischen Testament her gewohnt, uns als unentbehrliche Basis für die Legate eine *heredis institutio* zu denken. Wenn nun das alte Testament keine solche enthielt, wer figurierte dann als *heres*? wer haftete für die Erbschaftsschulden? etwa der *heres legitimus*? Der Wortlaut der zwölf Tafeln führt zur Verneinung der letzteren Frage. Der *heres legitimus* ist nur berufen, *si intestato moritur*, d. h. in Ermangelung eines Testaments; der Satz, dass niemand *ex parte testatus*, *ex parte intestatus* sterben könne, ist allem Anschein nach schon Bestandteil des ältesten Rechts.[2] Dieser Satz nun gilt immer noch als das grosse Rätsel des römischen Erbrechts, und man macht immer neue Versuche, ihm eine oft mehr oder weniger mystische Erklärung zu geben. Gerade für ein Legatentestament aber war jener Grundsatz das natürlichste von der Welt. Man muss sich hier folgendes klar machen. Ein Testament, zu dem man die Komitien bemühte, war sicherlich nicht gedacht als ein Mittel, dem oder

[1] Vgl. hierzu auch Wlassak, a. a. O. 214.

[2] A. M. Ehrlich, *Z. f. vgl. Rswiss.* xvii. 102. Vgl. für das *testamentum per aes et libram* auch Schulin, *Lehrb. d. Gesch. d. r. R.* 460.

jenem ein kleines Andenken zu hinterlassen; dazu hätten sich die Komitien sicher auch als Zeuge nicht gebrauchen lassen. Es muss vielmehr gedacht und auch geübt gewesen sein als planmässige Verteilung des ganzen Vermögens, als *divisio bonorum*, bei der normalerweise nur durch ein Versehen irgend ein Stück unverteilt bleiben konnte.[1] Wenn nun der Testator bei Aufstellung eines solchen Verteilungsplanes den Intestaterben, der ohne das Testament alles erhalten hätte, übergangen oder mit irgend einem einzelnen Stück bedacht hatte, so war damit auf das klarste zu erkennen gegeben, dass er ihn von der Erbschaft sei es ganz und gar sei es im übrigen habe ausschliessen wollen, und alles musste daher den alten Juristen näher liegen, als dennoch gerade dem Intestaterben auf die etwa versehentlich unverteilt gebliebenen Sachen ein Vorrecht zuzugestehen.[2] Jeder beliebige stand für sie diesen Sachen mindestens ebenso nahe oder näher als der Intestaterbe. Diese Sachen waren vakant, und ihr rechtliches Schicksal wird bestimmt worden sein durch jenes Rechtsinstitut, das als ein Rudiment uralten Rechtes noch bis in die klassische Zeit hereinragt: die *usucapio pro herede*. Tatsächlich wird diese wohl in der Regel hauptsächlich den Legataren von Haus und Hof zugute

[1] Ähnlich schon Jhering, *Geist des r. R.* iv. 147, der aber ein Erbeinsetzungstestament annimmt, wo die Sache minder klar liegt. Aus jenem Charakter des alten Testaments erklärt sich auch, dass ein neues Testament notwendig das alte aufhebt. Man kann nicht zwei Verteilungspläne für dieselbe Erbschaft aufstellen.

[2] Es scheint mir nicht überflüssig, darauf hinzuweisen, dass auch unser modernes Recht die Intestaterben neben einem Testament im Grunde nur beruft, weil wir annehmen, dass dies dem vermutlichen Willen des Erblassers entspreche, und von ihrer Berufung absieht, wo diese Vermutung offenbar nicht zutrifft. Wenn z. B. ein Vater von seinen drei Kindern das älteste auf die Hälfte einsetzt, so wird es niemandem einfallen, auf die andere unvergebene Hälfte die Intestaterbfolge zu eröffnen, wo das älteste wieder zu 1/3 partizipieren würde, sondern diese Hälfte erhalten die beiden jüngeren allein. Hat ferner jemand in einem Testament unter Übergehung der Intestaterben den A. zum Alleinerben und dann in einem zweiten den B. auf die Hälfte eingesetzt, so wird man die in dem zweiten Testament nicht vergebene Hälfte dem A. und nicht etwa den Intestaterben überweisen. Man könnte mit gutem Fug behaupten, auch das moderne Recht kenne keine wirkliche Konkurrenz von Testaments- und Intestaterbfolge; der Unterschied vom altrömischen liege vielmehr allein darin, dass es — was in dem vom Formalismus beherrschten altrömischen Recht freilich unmöglich war — neben dem erklärten Willen auch den unausgesprochenen, aber aus den Umständen erkennbaren Willen des Testators berücksichtige, möge dieser nun auf Berufung der Intestaterben oder anderer Personen gehen.

gekommen sein, die meist am ehesten in der Lage sein mussten, sich auch der unvergebenen Sachen zu bemächtigen.

Die Erwähnung der *usucapio pro herede* führt uns sofort zu der anderen oben aufgeworfenen Frage: wer haftet auf Grund des Legatentestaments für die Erbschaftsschulden? Wir müssen uns hüten, die Ideen, nach denen sich in klassischer Zeit die Haftung für die Erbschaftsschulden regelte, in die Zeit der zwölf Tafeln zu übertragen; über die Anschauung der alten Zeit gibt uns, wie ich glaube, die *usucapio pro herede*, deren rohe Struktur höchstes Alter verrät, ganz sicheren Aufschluss, vorausgesetzt nur, dass man sich an das hält, was über dieses Institut authentisch überliefert ist, und darauf verzichtet, eine durch nichts beglaubigte Urgeschichte desselben zu erfinden.[1] Jeder Beliebige, so berichtet uns Gaius ii. 52 f., konnte sich der Sachen einer nicht in Besitz genommenen (und so sicher auch der einer völlig vakanten) Erbschaft bemächtigen und sie durch einjährigen Besitz usukapieren. Dadurch aber erwarb er nach der alten (*olim*) Anschauung nicht etwa bloss diese Sachen, sondern *ipsam hereditatem* und wurde für die Erbschaftsschulden haftbar. Dieser Bericht lässt freilich mancherlei Zweifel übrig. Zunächst: was bedeutet das *velut ipsae hereditates usucapi credebantur* bei Gaius? Soll das etwa heissen, dass jeder Usukapient einer beliebigen Erbschaftssache nach vollendeter Usukapion als *successor in universum ius defuncti* behandelt wurde? Man braucht sich diese Frage nur vorzulegen, um zu sehen, dass man auf diesem Wege zu Unmöglichkeiten gelangt.[2] Dann würde ja die Vollendung der ersten Usukapion sei es auch an dem geringwertigsten Gegenstand, da nunmehr die Erbschaft einen Herrn gehabt hätte, jede weitere Usukapion ausgeschlossen haben, und der Usukapient etwa eines Schafes

[1] Dahin gehört insbesondere die Hypothese, die *usucapio p. h.* sei ihrer ursprünglichen Idee nach dazu bestimmt gewesen, den Mangel der zum Erbschaftserwerb eigentlich erforderlich gewesenen *cretio* zu decken. So Karlowa, *RG.* ii. 897 f., ihm folgend Sohm, *Instit.*[14] 694. Wir haben gesehen, dass das alte Recht die *cretio* noch gar nicht kennt. Ebenso willkürlich scheint mir die Annahme Perozzis, die *usucapio p. h.* sei ursprünglich nur z. G. des *familiae emptor* zugelassen worden und habe lediglich die Unwirksamkeit der *familiae mancipatio* gedeckt (*Istit.* ii. 383 f.).

[2] Dagegen auch Hölder, *Beiträge* 129 f. und Karlowa, *RG.* ii. 899, der aber (so auch Scheurl, *Krit. Vjschr.* xxiv. 219) willkürlich annimmt, in alter Zeit habe der Besitz der *maior pars pecuniae* genügt, um zur Ersitzung der ganzen Erbschaft zu führen.

würde dem von Haus und Hof, wenn dieser vielleicht einen Tag später als er den Besitz ergriffen hatte, Haus und Hof haben abfordern können. Oder, wenn man dies nicht annehmen will, nach welchem Massstab sollten die verschiedenen Usukapienten die Gesamterbschaft untereinander teilen? Vielmehr scheint mir klar und sicher, dass der Usukapient *pro herede* an Aktiven niemals mehr erwarb als er sich angeeignet hatte,[1] und mit der bei Gaius überlieferten Wendung wird nicht auf eine Gesamtnachfolge in die Aktiva, sondern nur auf die mit dem Erwerb verbundene Schuldenhaftung hingedeutet. Wer nun diese Schuldenhaftung jemandes, der nicht Universalsukzessor ist, von dem Vorstellungskreis des klassischen Rechts aus betrachtet, dem muss sie freilich als unbegreifliche Anomalie erscheinen. Ganz anders aber, wenn man sie unter das Licht stellt, das von der Rechtsvergleichung ausgeht. Dann erscheint die Haftung des Usukapienten nur als eine allerdings eigentümliche Anwendung eines Prinzips, das auch das germanische und, wie kaum zu bezweifeln, auch das griechische Recht beherrscht:[2] die Schuldenhaftung ruht auf der Erbschaft. Ein Recht aber, das, wie das römische, in Ermangelung von *heredes* die Usukapion der Erbschaftssachen gestattete, musste notwendig dazu kommen, die Erbenhaftung an jede einzelne Erbschaftssache zu knüpfen und also jeden haften zu lassen, der etwas aus der Erbschaft sich aneignete. Galt aber dies Prinzip bei der *usucapio pro herede*, so ist es sehr unwahrscheinlich, dass seine Geltung sich auf diesen einen Fall beschränkt habe, und wer mit uns überzeugt ist, dass das Komitialtestament ein reines Legatentestament war, darf nicht zögern, neben die Schuldenhaftung des Usukapienten die des Legatars zu stellen, der sich der ihm legierten Sache bemächtigt hat. Vielleicht erscheint manchen eine solche Annahme als unerhörte Ketzerei. Aber man beachte wohl: die Schuldenhaftung der Legatare war im alten Recht praktisch gar nicht zu entbehren, selbst dann nicht zu

[1] Dass dem z. Zt. des Q. Mucius so war, dürfte daraus hervorgehen, dass er die Haftung für die *sacra* in Ermangelung von *heredes* demjenigen auferlegte, *qui de bonis . . . usu ceperit plurimum possidendo* (Cic. *de leg.* ii. 48). Aber auch schon in der älteren Ordnung (Cic. *eod.* ii. 49) war bei dem *si maiorem partem pecuniae capiat* der Usukapient gewiss mitverstanden und nicht als Universalsukzessor gedacht. A. M. Karlowa, *RG.* ii. 901.

[2] Wegen des germanischen Rechts bedarf es wohl keiner Nachweisungen; wegen des griechischen vgl. Partsch, *Bürgschaftsrecht*, i. 232 f.

entbehren, wenn die *heredis institutio* entgegen unserer Ansicht ein Urbestandteil des römischen Testaments gewesen wäre. Man setze den Fall, ein mittelloser oder überschuldeter Erbe habe die Erbschaft angetreten. Im klassischen Recht gewährt hier das *beneficium separationis* den Erbschaftsgläubigern die Möglichkeit, im Weg des Separatkonkurses die ganze Erbschaft zu ihrer Befriedigung heranzuziehen und sich so vor Schaden zu schützen. In die Zeit der zwölf Tafeln wird niemand dies Benefiz zurückrücken wollen. Sollten damals die Gläubiger kein Mittel gehabt haben, auf die *per vindicationem* legierten Sachen zu greifen? Sollten sie darauf beschränkt gewesen sein, sich an den *heres institutus* zu halten, und leer ausgegangen sein, indes die lachenden Legatare die Erbschaftssachen okkupierten?[1] Und zu diesem Argument tritt eine sichere historische Tatsache, die beweist, dass den alten Römern eine Schuldenhaftung der Legatare durchaus nicht so fremdartig vorgekommen sein kann, wie man glaubt. Ich denke an die bekannte Ordnung der Haftung für die *sacra hereditaria*, wie sie uns bei Cicero (*de legib.* ii. 48 ff.) überliefert ist. Zu Ciceros Zeit hafteten für die *sacra* in Ermangelung von *heredes* freilich nicht mehr alle Legatare, sondern nur der Partitionslegatar qui *tantundem capit quantum omnes heredes*. Aber Cicero selbst berichtet von einer älteren Ordnung, wonach die Haftung auf drei Weisen begründet werden konnte: *hereditate aut si maiorem partem pecuniae capiat aut* [*si maior pars pecuniae legata est*] *si inde quidpiam ceperit*. Die beiden letzten Haftungsgründe beziehen sich selbstverständlich nicht bloss auf Usukapienten,[2] sondern auch auf Legatare, und streicht man, wie man m. E. muss, die eingeklammerten Worte als in den Text geratenes Glossem,[3] so ist hier für die *sacra* sogar die Haftung jedes einzelnen Legatars bezeugt, die wir auch für die Schulden behaupten. Der Gedanke

[1] Keinen Gegenbeweis kann C. iv. 16, 7 liefern. Der Schluss von der in den zwölf Tafeln sanktionierten Haftung der Erben, worunter im Sinne des Gesetzes m. E. nur die Intestaterben zu verstehen waren, auf die Nichthaftung der Legatare ist keineswegs zwingend.

[2] Andere (z. B. Scheurl, *Krit. Vjschr.* xxiv. 220) nehmen an, dass der Usukapient schon von dem Haftungsgrund *hereditate* mitgetroffen wurde.

[3] Das Glossem sollte den zweiten Haftungsgrund erläutern. Es verrät sich schon durch den Indikativ *est* statt des in der indirekten Rede zu erwartenden *sit*. Sachlich erscheint es mir unverständlich, warum haftbar erwartden Erwerb irgend eines Stücks nur der werden soll, dem die *maior* durch *ecuniae* vermacht ist. A. M. freilich Hölder, *Beiträge*, 140 f.,

liegt nahe, dass der zwischen der Haftung des Erben und des einzelnen Legatars eingeschobene zweite Haftungsgrund — *qui maiorem partem pecuniae capiat* — bereits eine Abwandlung des noch älteren nur zweigliedrigen Haftungssystems enthalte. Sei dem wie ihm wolle, der Schluss von der Sacrahaftung der Legatare auf die Schuldenhaftung drängt sich geradezu zwingend auf: warum sollte man den Gläubigern verweigert haben, was den Göttern recht war? Aller Wahrscheinlichkeit nach handelt es sich hier um eine Erscheinung, die wir auch sonst sowohl im griechischen wie im römischen Recht beobachten können: dass nämlich eine ursprünglich allgemeine Haftungsform im Laufe der Zeiten auf solche Ansprüche beschränkt wird, bei denen ein öffentliches oder religiöses Interesse obwaltet.[1]

Die Haftung der Legatare — wir dürfen dieser Frage nicht ausweichen — kann nur als beschränkte gedacht werden. Niemand wird annehmen wollen, dass die Aneignung des geringfügigsten Legats unbeschränkte Schuldenhaftung mit sich brachte. Wir sind vom klassischen Rechte her so sehr daran gewöhnt, in der unbeschränkten Schuldenhaftung des Erben ein Grundprinzip des römischen Rechts zu erblicken, dass es fast verwegen aussieht, dem altrömischen Recht eine beschränkte Schuldenhaftung zuzuschreiben. In der Tat glaube auch ich, dass die unbeschränkte Schuldenhaftung schon dem ältesten römischen Rechte bekannt war, nämlich als Haftung des *suus heres*. In alter Zeit wird sich das Zugriffsrecht der Gläubiger auch auf die Gewaltunterworfenen des Schuldners erstreckt haben, und diese persönliche Haftung erlosch sehr natürlich nicht mit dem Tode des Schuldners.[2] Dem *suus heres* mag dann aus Gründen praktischer Zweckmässigkeit,

Karlowa, a. a. O. 902. Von den Editoren streichen den Passus Christ und Baiter, während Vahlen ihn beibehält, mit der unzureichenden Begründung, dass sonst das folgende *si inde quidpiam* in der Luft schwebe. *Inde*, d. h. *ex ea pecunia*.

[1] Ich erinnere aus dem römischen Recht an die Beschränkung der ursprünglich gewiss allgemein zulässigen Privatpfändung auf die wenigen bei Gaius erwähnten Fälle der *legis actio per pignoris capionem*. Ganz anders freilich Mitteis, *röm. Privatr.* i. 98 n. 12: das die *sacra* betreffende Pontifikaledikt habe mit der Schuldenhaftung nichts zu tun. Diese Behauptung erklärt sich nur daraus, dass Mitteis Vorstellungen, die aus dem Gedankenkreis des klassischen Rechtes stammen, ohne weiteres in das älteste Recht versetzt.

[2] Lenel, *krit. Vjschr.* xxviii. 175. So auch Cuq, *NRH.* x. 547, freilich mit Beschränkung auf das problematische *nexum*.

auf die ich noch komme, im Laufe der Zeit der *proximus adgnatus* angeglichen worden sein; die Legatare aber werden für die *sacra* wie für die Schulden persönlich nur dann gehaftet haben, wenn sie die Sache, an der die Haftung hing, dem Gläubiger nicht überliessen.[1] Ebenso kann ich mir auch die Haftung des Usukapienten *pro herede* nur als beschränkte vorstellen. Das Gegenteil ist ja herrschende Meinung, die besonders drastisch in der bekannten scherzhaften Darstellung Jherings[2] hervortritt, wo die *usucapio pro herede* als „die Mausefalle des alten Erbrechts" figuriert. Ich halte diese Auffassung für kaum möglich. Man könnte sie sich allenfalls zurechtlegen, wenn die alte Zeit in der *usucapio pro herede* ein Delikt erblickt hätte, das durch die Schuldenhaftung hätte gewissermassen bestraft werden sollen. Aber von diesem Standpunkt aus bliebe die Zulassung dieser Art Usukapion ein Rätsel, und die Schuldenhaftung hätte man dann wohl nicht an die vollendete Usukapion, sondern an die blosse Aneignung geknüpft. Der alten Zeit war die *usucapio p. h.* m. E. nichts als eine Ergänzung des engbegrenzten Intestaterbrechts, die wohl meist den Nächststehenden zugute gekommen sein wird. Und gab es nicht eine auch im modernen Sinn durchaus redliche *usucapio p. h.*, seitens dessen nämlich, der sich bona fide für den Erben hielt? Ist es glaublich, dass man diesen, der alles, was er nicht bereits usukapiert hatte, dem wahren Erben herausgeben musste, unbeschränkt für die Schulden haften liess? Dass wir bei Gaius von der Beschränkung der Haftung[3] nichts mehr erfahren, darf nicht wundernehmen. Für ihn war ja die ganze Haftung des Usukapienten eine verschollene Antiquität, auf deren Details einzugehen er keinerlei Veranlassung hatte, vorausgesetzt, dass er davon überhaupt noch etwas wusste.

[1] Wie aber, wenn ein Legatar aus Besorgnis vor dem Angriff von Erbschaftsgläubigern den Erwerb seines Legates ganz unterliess? Dann muss es den Erbschaftsgläubigern freigestanden haben, sich zu ihrer Befriedigung der so freigewordenen Erbschaftssachen zu bemächtigen, und dies wird nicht als *usucapio p. h.* gegolten haben.

[2] *Scherz und Ernst in der Jurisprudenz*,[4] 127 f., 384 f.

[3] Dagegen wird die Haftung dessen *qui usu ceperit plurimum possidendo* für die sacra (Cic. *l.c.*) allerdings als unbeschränkte zu denken sein. Den Göttern soll ihre Befriedigung erleichtert werden; darum können sie sich für ihre ganze Forderung an jenen einen halten. Solange aber jeder einzelne Usukapient haftete, scheint mir die unbeschränkte Haftung kaum denkbar.

Ich habe im bisherigen versucht, ein Bild des Rechtszustandes zur Zeit des alten Legatentestaments zu geben. Je weiter nun dies Bild von verbreiteten Vorstellungen abweicht, um so unerlässlicher ist es, darzulegen, wie sich von hier aus der ganz andere Rechtszustand entwickeln konnte, der uns im klassischen Recht vor Augen steht. Wie ist die *heredis institutio* aufgekommen? Es versteht sich, dass wir, bei dem Mangel jeder zuverlässigen Überlieferung über die auf die zwölf Tafeln folgenden Jahrhunderte, auf Hypothesen angewiesen sind; aber diese Hypothesen dürften sich zu einem hohen Grade der Wahrscheinlichkeit führen lassen. Es war, wie ich glaube, die Sach- und Rechtslage beim älteren Manzipationstestamente, was die römischen Juristen auf den Gedanken der *heredis institutio* brachte. Gaius berichtet bekanntlich, der *familiae emptor* bei diesem Testament sei *heredis loco* gewesen (*heredis locum optinebat*). Was Gaius sich bei dieser Charakterisierung dachte, ob er damit eine vollkommene Gleichheit oder nur eine weitgehende Ähnlichkeit mit der Erbenstellung ausdrücken wollte, kann hier dahingestellt bleiben. Denn auch im zweiten Fall bleibt die von mir vermutete Entwicklung verständlich, und dass eine solche Ähnlichkeit vorlag, kann auch der nicht bezweifeln, der, wie auch ich es für richtig halte, in dem *familiae emptor* wesentlich nur einen Treuhänder oder Testamentsvollstrecker sieht.[1] Zunächst war die Giltigkeit aller von dem Erblasser getroffenen Verfügungen, wie späterhin von der der *heredis institutio*, so in alter Zeit von der der *familiae mancipatio* abhängig. Der *familiae emptor* muss ferner in der Lage gewesen sein, seine Rechtsstellung, mit der das Testament stand und fiel, gegen den drohenden Angriff der Intestaterben zu verteidigen, es muss ihm eine *legis actio* nach Art der *hereditatis petitio* zugestanden haben; die Gefahr eines solchen Angriffs mag bei dem im Angesicht des ganzen Volks errichteten Komitialtestament gering gewesen sein, musste sich aber notwendig einstellen, als man den Versuch machte, die alte Form durch den Kunstbau des Manzipationstestaments zu ersetzen, und wer hätte sonst die Verteidigung des Testaments übernehmen sollen? Der *familiae emptor* wird weiter—wahrscheinlich beschränkt und neben den Legataren—für die Erbschaftsschulden gehaftet haben. Eine solche Haftung des

[1] Vgl. u. a. Sohm, *Institut.* 722 f.; Cuq, *Instit. jurid.* i. 128, und besonders Lambert, a. a. O. 52 f.

Treuhänders oder Testamentsvollstreckers findet sich bekanntlich auch in anderen Rechten;[1] bei der Sachlage, wie sie sich aus der *familiae mancipatio* ergab, war sie kaum zu entbehren. Nimmt man, was ich für sehr wahrscheinlich halte, an, dass das uns überlieferte Formular der *familiae mancipatio* nicht das ursprüngliche ist, dass ursprünglich der *familiae emptor* nicht bloss die *custodela*, sondern das Vermögen des Erblassers selbst erwarb und zur Ausführung der Anordnungen des Erblassers damals gar nicht juristisch, sondern nur moralisch verpflichtet war,[2] so zwang sich seine Haftung geradezu auf. Aber auch in der Zeit, wo der *familiae emptor* nunmehr die *custodela* am Vermögen für sich in Anspruch nahm, und man das Eigentum an den vermachten Sachen vermöge der *nuncupatio* unmittelbar den Vindikationslegataren zufallen liess, war nichts natürlicher, als dass man die Erbschaftsgläubiger gleichwohl nicht bloss auf letztere, sondern auch auf den *familiae emptor* verwies; blieb doch immer die Möglichkeit, dass Legatare vor dem Erblasser starben oder das ihnen Hinterlassene nicht an sich nehmen wollten, oder die Annahme sich verzögerte, oder dass nach Entrichtung sämtlicher Legate noch ein unvergebener Rest der Erbschaft sich herausstellte, der doch ebenfalls den Gläubigern haften musste. Ein solcher Rest dürfte, solange die *familiae mancipatio* in irgend einem Sinne ernst genommen wurde, dem *familiae emptor* verblieben sein und so seine Haftung begründet haben. Ja, es darf angenommen werden, dass die Testatoren in der Regel die Erbschaft durch Legate nicht erschöpft, sondern mindestens soviel davon freigelassen haben werden, als zur Befriedigung der (irdischen und himmlischen) Erbschaftsgläubiger erforderlich war; musste ihnen doch daran gelegen sein, dass die Legatare das ihnen Hinterlassene unverkürzt und ohne Besorgnis vor dem Angriff durch Gläubiger erhalten konnten. In alledem also war die Stellung des *familiae emptor* der des Erben verwandt. Aber daneben bestanden er-

[1] Für die germanische Treuhand vgl. A. Schultze, *die langobardische Treuhand*, 50 n. 15, 112 n. 24, 178; ferner Caillemer, *Orig. et dével. de l'exéc. test.* 74 f., 429 f., 431 f.

[2] So Cuq, *NRH.* x. 755; Lambert, a. a. O. 79. Auf Gaius, ii. 103, möchte ich mich freilich hiefür nicht berufen. Gaius hat von dieser Stufe der Entwicklung des Testaments schwerlich mehr irgend eine Kenntnis, und mit den ungenauen Worten *ob id ei mandabat* wird er nicht auf formlose Aufträge, sondern auf die *nuncupatio* haben hinweisen wollen.

hebliche Verschiedenheiten, und gerade in diesen werden wir die Motive zu suchen haben, die die Juristen dahin führten, die *familiae emptio* zu einem blossen Scheinakt zu degradieren und an Stelle des *familiae emptor* einen künstlichen im Testamente selbst zu ernennenden *heres* zu setzen. Vor allem war, solange die *familiae mancipatio* ernst genommen wurde, ein Widerruf des Testaments nur mittels *remancipatio familiae* möglich, die die Mitwirkung des *familiae emptor* erforderte, so dass der Testator von dessen gutem Willen abhängig war. Weiter: der *familiae emptor* konnte vor dem Testator sterben; dann konnte schwerlich das Testament bestehen bleiben,—eine Substitution in die Rolle des *familiae emptor* war ausgeschlossen. Endlich: die Schuldenhaftung des *familiae emptor* ist kaum anders denn als beschränkte zu denken; diese beschränkte Haftung aber, neben der die der Legatare unentbehrlich blieb, musste zu grossen Schwierigkeiten führen. Denn haftete den Erbschaftsgläubigern in seiner Hand nur das, was nach Befriedigung sämtlicher Legatare übrig blieb, so wird dessen Belauf, in Ermangelung der Vorsorgemassregeln, die das moderne Recht trifft, unendlich oft sehr schwer festzustellen gewesen sein; hafteten aber, was ich für viel wahrscheinlicher halte, solange die Legatare die vermachten Sachen nicht an sich genommen hatten, diese den Gläubigern auch in der Hand des *familiae emptor*, so litten die Interessen der Legatare not. Sollten diese Übelstände die Juristen nicht beschäftigt haben? Suchten sie aber nach Mitteln der Abhilfe, so wurden sie notwendig auf den Weg gewiesen, den sie auch eingeschlagen haben: nämlich einerseits die *familiae emptio*, in der die Wurzel jener Übelstände lag, der ernstlichen Bedeutung zu entkleiden, andererseits dem im Testament zum Vorschein kommenden letzten Willen einen breiteren Spielraum zu gewähren. Für letzteres gab der Zwölftafelsatz *cum nexum faciet* jederzeit den formalen Anhalt; frei interpretiert, bot dieser Satz die Möglichkeit, die Wirksamkeit der *nuncupatio* soweit zu erstrecken, als man irgend zweckmässig fand. Wie sollte man aber vorgehen? Es kam darauf an, die *familiae mancipatio* durch eine Form der Bedenkung zu ersetzen, die dem Bedachten den ganzen Nachlass überwies, soweit nicht durch Legate darüber verfügt war, Substitution zuliess und zugleich die Schwierigkeiten beseitigte, die die beschränkte Haftung mit sich brachte. Durch ein Legat, wie man es auch formulieren mochte, konnte man dies letztere niemals bewirken; einen Legatar hinsichtlich der Schuldenhaftung anderen Grundsätzen zu unterwerfen als die sonstigen Legatare, dazu würde es an jeder Handhabe gefehlt haben. Ein *legatum familiae* ferner — worauf man durch die Erwägung hätte kommen können, dass es sich um einen Ersatz für den *familiae emptor* handelte — würde ja die ganze *familia* umfasst haben, also auch die einzeln vermachten Sachen, und würde daher, der Absicht zuwider, die Einzellegatare eingeschränkt haben, indem sie sämtlich dem Legatar der *familia* gegenüber blosse *collegatarii re coniuncti* gewesen wären. Es galt also, eine neue Art letztwilliger Verfügung zu erfinden, und dies wird auf den kühnen Gedanken geführt haben, den *heres*, der bis dahin nur im Intestaterbrecht eine Rolle gespielt hatte, in das Testament einzuführen und mit den Legataren zu kombinieren. Ich vermute, dass man den *heres scriptus* nach dem Vorbild des *suus heres*, dem der *heres legitimus* wohl längst gleichgestellt worden war, von allem Anfang an unbeschränkt für die Schulden haften liess.[1] Wie sehr man aber die ganze Neuerung der *heredis institutio* als künstliche empfand, auf wie unsicherem Boden man sich fühlte, das können wir noch heute erkennen an der merkwürdigen, gewiss sehr alten Formel der *cretio cum exheredatione*, die ursprünglich jede *heredis institutio* begleitet haben wird. *Quodni ita creveris, exheres esto!* Wie kam man dazu, jemanden, der doch — nach der klassischen Auffassung — noch gar nicht Erbe ist, ausdrücklich zu exheredieren, wie den *suus heres*? Wer diese Formel verfasste, der wusste sicher noch nichts von *hereditas delata* und *hereditas adquisita.* Er stand vielmehr, wie mir scheint, unter der Vorstellung, das *heres esto* des Testaments, in Verbindung mit dem *uti lingua nuncupassit*, *ita ius esto* der zwölf Tafeln würde den Ernannten, gleich einem *suus heres*, auch ohne und wider seinen Willen zum Erben machen, wenn ihm das Testament nicht selber die Möglichkeit eröffne, sich der Erbeneigenschaft zu entledigen; darum wird ihm, für den Fall, dass er die Erbschaft haben will, die

[1] Daneben wird man die beschränkte Sachhaftung der Legatare gewiss nicht alsbald aufgegeben haben; sie war, wie gezeigt, bis zur Einführung des *beneficium separationis* gar nicht zu entbehren. Aber sie wird subsidiär geworden und damit praktisch in den Hintergrund getreten sein, sodass ihre spätere Beseitigung, als man sie nicht mehr brauchte, nicht als grundstürzende Reform erschien.

Beobachtung einer Form auferlegt, und wird er, wenn er diese Form nicht beobachtet, ausdrücklich exherediert.

Den Satz *heredis institutio est caput et fundamentum testamenti* hält die herrschende Meinung für einen Urbestandteil des römischen Testamentsrechts.[1] Wie wäre dies möglich, da doch jedenfalls das ältere Manzipationstestament die Erbeinsetzung gar nicht kannte! M. E. gehört er erst der Zeit an, da sich die Umwandlung des Manzipationstestaments vollzog. Mehreres mag da zusammengewirkt haben. Man hatte in dem *familiae emptor* einen Verteidiger und Vollstrecker des Testaments besessen und war der Vorteile einer solchen Einrichtung inne geworden: man wird diese Vorteile nicht haben aufgeben wollen, als man ihn durch den *heres scriptus* ersetzte. Vor allem aber: die Juristen müssen die Gefahren der beschränkten Schuldenhaftung, die sich notwendig einstellen, wo nicht, wie im justinianischen und den neueren Rechten besondere Schutzmassregeln getroffen werden, durch vielfältige Erfahrung kennen gelernt haben. War es da nicht ganz natürlich, dass man die Giltigkeit des Testaments von dem Vorhandensein des unbeschränkt haftenden *heres scriptus* abhängig machte, der den Gläubigern die Notwendigkeit ersparte, ein Dutzend verschiedener Legatare angehen zu müssen? Für den Fall, dass der Eingesetzte nicht Erbe wurde, konnte der Testator durch Substitution Vorsorge treffen. Äusserlich wird die Abhängigkeit des Testaments von der Erbeinsetzung kaum sehr aufgefallen sein; war man doch daran gewöhnt, dass der Universalerwerb — des *familiae emptor* — die sämtlichen Singularerwerbe bedingte. Uns ist die Regel nur deshalb ein Stein des Anstosses, weil wir es als das natürliche ansehen, dass, was die letztwilligen Verfügungen übrig lassen, den Intestaterben zufalle. Den Römern aber, die von altersher sowohl (wie ich oben zu zeigen versuchte) beim Komitialtestament wie beim Manzipationstestament daran gewöhnt waren, das Testament als Verfügung über das ganze Vermögen anzusehen, wird das Gegenteil natürlich erschienen sein; sie werden von demjenigen, der seinen Intestaterben bedenken wollte, erwartet haben, dass er dies ausdrücklich tue.

Dass die republikanische Jurisprudenz eine Neuerung von solcher Tragweite durchzusetzen vermochte, darf nicht wunder-

[1] Anders Cuq, *NRH.* x. 550, 568.

nehmen. Man erinnere sich, dass dieselbe Jurisprudenz Rechtsinstitute wie die Emanzipation und Adoption geschaffen, das gesetzliche Intestaterbrecht der Frauen eingeschränkt,[1] das Frauentestament ermöglicht, das Pflichtteilsrecht erfunden hat u. ä. m. Das waren Neuerungen von nicht geringerer Kühnheit. Man kann die produktive Kraft und die Macht jener Jurisprudenz gar nicht hoch genug einschätzen. Was Pomponius von P. Mucius, Brutus und Manilius berichtet — *qui fundaverunt ius civile* —, darf nicht als leere Redensart angesehen werden ; an dieser Fundierungsarbeit aber hatten sicherlich auch zahlreiche literarisch nicht hervorgetretene Vorgänger ihren Anteil, und zu ihrem Werk gehört auch die Schöpfung der *heredis institutio.*

Das Datum der Neuerung entzieht sich, wie so vieles in den auf die zwölf Tafeln folgenden Jahrhunderten der Rechtsentwicklung, unserer Kenntnis. Bei Plautus lässt sich, wie schon Lambert[2] gezeigt hat, die Erbeinsetzung nicht nachweisen. Wir begegnen allerdings wiederholt bei ihm der Wendung *heredem facere*, bald in Verbindung mit einer vorgängigen Adoption[3] bald ohne solche.[4] Man muss sich aber wohl hüten, in diesen Worten einen sicheren Beweis der damaligen Existenz der Erbeinsetzung zu sehen. In den erstgenannten Stellen heisst es übereinstimmend :

> adoptat (puerum) . . .
> eumque heredem fecit, quum ipse obiit diem.

In diesem Zusammenhang aber dürfte *heredem fecit* nicht auf einen besonderen Einsetzungsakt hinweisen, sondern einfach als die rechtliche Folge des Adoptionsakt gedacht sein : der Erblasser adoptiert und macht demgemäss den Adoptierten durch seinen Tod (*quum ipse obiit diem*) zum Erben.[5] Darum heisst es auch *Poen*. iv. 2, 82 von dem gleichen Falle schlechthin :

[1] Die Überlieferung darüber wird bekanntlich von manchen angezweifelt und die obige Beschränkung schon dem altrömischen Rechte zugeschrieben, — wie mir scheint, ohne Grund. Solange die Frauentutel in voller Kraft bestand, waren die Frauen in der Hand ihrer Agnaten, und ebendeshalb eine Einschränkung ihres Intestaterbrechts überflüssig.

[2] a. a. O. 98 n. 1.

[3] *Menaechm*. prol. 60-62, *Poen*. prol. 76, 77.

[4] *Poen*. prol. 68-70, v. 2, 109, 10. Vgl. auch iv. 2, 17.

[5] Im griechischen Vorbild mag κληρονόμον ποιεῖσθαι im Sinn von „ sich einen Erben schaffen " gestanden haben.

is in divitias homo adoptavit hunc, quum diem obiit suum.[1]

Damit verlieren aber auch die Stellen ihre Beweiskraft, wo das *heredem facere* ohne Adoption vorkommt. Es handelt sich da (*Poen.* prol. 68-70, v. 2, 109, 110) um das Erbewerden eines *frater patruelis* des Verstorbenen, und wenn es davon heisst *et is me heredem fecit, quum suum obiit diem*, so dürfte es auch hier viel näher liegen, diese Worte davon zu verstehen, dass der Verstorbene durch seinen Tod den anderen als nächsten Verwandten zum Erben „machte", als von einer dem Tod vorausgehenden Erbeinsetzung. So bleibt nur die eine Stelle übrig, in der über einen Sklaven gesagt wird:

omnia edepol mira sunt, nisi erus hunc heredem facit

(*Poen.* iv. 2, 17). Gewiss geht daraus die Möglichkeit hervor, einen Sklaven künstlich zum Erben zu machen. Den Weg aber, auf dem dies geschah, lässt die Stelle im Dunkeln, und nichts zwingt dazu, hier eher an eine eigentliche *heredis institutio* als an eine Adoption wie in den ersterwähnten Fällen zu denken.[2] Ist hienach das Rechtsinstitut der Erbeinsetzung in den Komödien des Plautus nicht nachzuweisen, so folgt freilich daraus keineswegs, dass es nicht damals schon bestand. Die folgende Erwägung aber macht es wahrscheinlich, dass es doch nicht sehr viel älter ist. Sobald das Erbeinsetzungstestament aufkam, brachte es die Gefahr mit sich, dass der *heres scriptus* infolge von Überlastung mit Legaten die *cretio* unterliess und so das ganze Testament zum Scheitern brachte. Dieser Gefahr entgegenzutreten hatte man Ursache sowohl deshalb, weil man damals wohl bereits die Ordnung der Sukzession durch letzten Willen gegenüber der Intestaterbfolge begünstigte, als auch deshalb, weil bei der Enge des Kreises der *heredes legitimi* die Intestaterbfolge gewiss sehr oft versagte, ein insbesondere für die Erbschaftsgläubiger sehr unerwünschter Fall. Die ältesten Gesetze nun, die nach der Überlieferung[3] jener

[1] Zu Grunde liegt natürlich eine εἰσποίησις im griechischen Vorbild.

[2] S. auch Lambert, a. a. O.

[3] Gaius ii. 225 f. Diese Überlieferung scheint mir aus den im Text angeführten Gründen durchaus glaublich, und ich kann mich den Schriftstellern, die dem überlieferten Zweck einen anderen substituieren wollen (vgl. besonders Lambert, a. a. O. 100, Ehrlich, *Z. f. vgl. Rwiss.* xvii. 104 f.), nicht anschliessen. Auch an eine Verwandtschaft der Tendenz der *lex Furia* mit der der *lex Cincia* glaube ich nicht. Die Gefahr, der diese entgegenwirken sollte, bestand bei den stets widerruflichen letztwilligen Verfügungen nicht.

Gefahr zu begegnen bestimmt waren, die *leges Furia* und *Voconia*, liegen schwerlich sehr weit auseinander, und die *lex Voconia* datiert erst vom Jahre 169 v. Chr. Die Tatsache ist vom Standpunkt der herrschenden Meinung, die von uraltersher Erbeinsetzung und Legate nebeneinander stehen lässt, auffallend genug. Sie lässt sich nicht durch die Annahme erklären, dass in älterer Zeit Überlastungen des *heres* nicht oder nur selten vorgekommen seien. Bewusst wird freilich nicht leicht jemand die Erben überlasten, wenn er weiss, dass von ihrem Antritt die Giltigkeit des ganzen Testamentes abhängt; aber unabsichtliche Überlastungen—infolge von Überschätzung des Vermögensbestands, nachträglich eingetretener Vermögensverluste, neu erwachsener Schulden—sind bei dem Erbeinsetzungstestament immer eine sich leicht verwirklichende Möglichkeit. Sehr einfach löst sich das Rätsel, wenn man unserer Vermutung folgt, dass die Erbeinsetzung selber die *lex Furia* gar nicht so sehr an Alter überragt.[1]

Wenn der Entwicklungsgang des testamentarischen Erbrechts im obigen richtig gezeichnet sein sollte, so tritt das altrömische Erbrecht aus der isolierten Stellung heraus, die es nach der herrschenden Ansicht gegenüber allen anderen Rechten ähnlicher Entwicklungsstufe einnehmen würde. Eine Universalsukzession, die unabhängig wäre von jeder sei es leiblichen sei es künstlichen Verwandtschaft, hat das altrömische Recht ebensowenig gekannt wie das altgriechische und altdeutsche. Das altrömische Legatentestament stellt sich neben die Arrogation, wie das altgriechische neben die εἰσποίησις, wie die altdeutsche *donatio post obitum* neben die *affatomie* und die *thingatio*. Sicherlich bestehen zwischen diesen Rechtsinstituten sehr erhebliche Unterschiede; aber das

[1] Ähnliche Folgerungen, freilich anders motiviert, zieht auch Lambert, nur nicht für das Alter der Erbeinsetzung überhaupt, sondern für den Zeitpunkt ihres Auftretens im Manzipationstestament.

Wie kommt es, dass die *lex Furia* die Legate so mechanisch durch Festsetzung eines absoluten Maximums einschränkte? Wenn die Römer von jeher daran gewöhnt waren, über ihr ganzes Vermögen in Form von Legaten zu verfügen, so begreift sich, dass infolge dieser Gewohnheit die Einführung der Erbeinsetzung in die Praxis auf Schwierigkeiten stiess, und die Tendenz der *lex Furia* wird gewesen sein, die Testatoren im Interesse der Erbschaftsgläubiger zu nötigen, die Hauptbedenkungen in die Form der Erbeinsetzung zu kleiden. Dass man mit dem absoluten Maximum zu weit gegangen war, wird man später eingesehen haben, und so trat dann an seine Stelle das relative der *lex Voconia*.

ist den drei Rechten gemeinsam, dass der Ausgangspunkt des testamentarischen Erbrechts die Einzelvergabung, nicht die Erbeinsetzung ist. Die Einführung und Ausgestaltung dieser erscheint als eine Grosstat der römischen Jurisprudenz, ist aber auch nur als solche verständlich, und nicht als Produkt primitiven Gewohnheitsrechts.

O. Lenel.

# VI

# NUMISMATIC ILLUSTRATIONS OF ROMAN LAW

I FEAR the title of my subject is somewhat misleading. Starting with a much wider plan, I find myself narrowed, by shortness of time for the making and the reading of my paper, to archaeological illustration by *coins* only, and that extending over a comparatively limited period.

I do not propose to enter on the obscure early history of the subject, but will accept without remark what I think is still the general view,[1] that the beginning of any *regular coinage* at Rome cannot be admitted before that codification of customary law by the Decemviri, in which I still believe, and which is dated about 450 B.C. I need not give specimens of its well-known devices. I incline to believe the head of Janus borrowed from Greek art.[2] The ship's prow was persistently connected by the Romans themselves with victories over the maritime power of *Antium*, by some referred to a time just before the Decemviri (468 B.C.),[3] by some to a considerably later date (338) at which C. Maenius is represented as carrying the *rostra* of the Antiates to Rome.[4] We have an obvious reference to this family legend in a *triens* of P. Maenius *Antiaticus*, a moneyer of 110 B.C.[5]

Of the political changes effected at this time, or later, by members of the Maenian *gens* I have no note to show you.

1 Babelon, *Monnaies de la république romaine*, Introd. p. vi.
2 Babelon, *ib.* x.
3 Livy ii. 65; Babelon, *ib.* vii.
4 Pliny xxxiv. 5. 11; Livy viii. 14.
5 No. 1 on p. 145; Babelon ii. 164 (see, however, Introd. p. vii.).

A silver coinage was, according to Pliny, introduced for the first time at Rome in 269 B.C., a date when the defeat of Pyrrhus and the conquest of Southern Italy had brought a supply of the more precious and portable metal into the Treasury.[1] Shortly afterwards the officers charged with the administration of the mint began to insert[2] on their coins both of bronze and silver symbols of high office held by some member of their family, or of canting heraldry on its name, or abbreviations of the name itself, with which I will not trouble you. But in the last two centuries B.C. the silver coinage came to bear artistic representations of family history or legend. It is in these so-called Consular coins that I have sought to find some record of the political movements or of the stages of development of which we read in Roman Law. I am afraid I must confess to having drawn almost a blank.

With but few exceptions these beautiful *denarii* refer to successes in war or treaty claimed for the moneyer's family, to its divine or heroic lineage, furnished probably by some Greek Burke or Debrett; but very little to such ordinary human matters as the peaceful growth of law.

The well-known reverse of the Dioscuri is now most frequently traced to a prevalent cult in maritime Magna Graecia, where a coasting commerce thoroughly appreciated a clear sky with the two great stars—*lucida sidera*—in the stormy nights of March. But their symbol was appropriated, in another light no doubt, by many an ancient family whose ancestors fought at the battle of the Regillus, as some of our own were at Hastings or at least came over with the Conqueror. There are, however, rather special presentations of Castor and Pollux washing or watering their horses 'at the well that springs by Vesta's fane' on coins struck by members of the *gens* boasting among its ancestors the *dictator* of that day.[3] This reverse of the *gens Postumia* dates actually from 89 B.C. It is interesting to note that among the families which were, if we can place any reliance upon the *Fasti*, of comparatively later 'arrival,' we find, as is perhaps not unusual in modern times, claims of the highest descent. A *denarius*, for

1 Ridgeway, *Origin of Currency and Weight-Standards*, p. 383.

2 Babelon, Introd. p. xxxiv.

3 No. 2 on p. 145; Babelon ii. 379.

1. Coh. p. lviii. Marcia 2.

2. Coh. p. xxxv. Postumia 4.

3. Coh. p. xxvi. Marcia 8.

4. Coh. p. xxxiv. Pomponia 2.

5. Coh. p. xxiii. Junia 12.

6. Coh. xl. Valeria 5.

instance, of the *Marcian gens*,[1] of actual date about 60 B.C., besides indicating real achievements of alliance or conflict with the last kings of Macedonia, or of bringing the first great aqueduct, the *Aqua Marcia*, to Rome, will find a founder of the family in Ancus, the august doublet of Numa, fourth among the many questionable predecessors of the probably historical Tarquinii. Beyond this fabulous ancestry there is no indication of patrician rank in the Marcian *gens*, except the beautiful story, which one scarce has the heart to touch, about Caius of Corioli. Neither is there among the Pomponii, whose heraldic history goes back to Numa himself.[2]

To return, however, to quasi-historical times of the early Republic, I have sometimes hazarded the suggestion that a Junius in the first reported pair of Republican Consuls may possibly indicate some tradition of a brief union against a common tyranny, and some idea of representing *both orders* in the famous dual magistracy, which was not permanently realized till the Licinian Rogations. Anyhow the coin which was struck by the murderer of Caesar about 43 B.C. represents his supposed ancestor, Brutus the Ancient, simply in a dignified procession *as Consul.*[3] It has nothing to do with the story of his sons' execution which Vergil skates over so dexterously in the 6th *Aeneid* (820–824).

With regard to another hero of the same revolution, if there is in the coins of the historical Valerii any reference to the ancient Publicola, it is not to a limitation of the new magistracy by an alleged *lex de provocatione*, but solely to the overthrow of the old Royalty.[4] Of the convenient charge of conspiring for the restoration (*regni affectandi*) of kingly power we have a memorial in another Junian *denarius* of 43 B.C. Here we see, coupled with the Brutus of the early Republic,[5] that Servilius Ahala who is so warmly eulogized in Livy (iv. 14) for the butchery of Sp. Maelius 439 B.C. And to the alleged informer against Maelius, on this occasion, I find an undoubted reference in a *denarius* of an old plebeian family. This informer was, we are told, one Lucius

1 No. 3 on p. 145; Babelon ii. 187, 197.
2 *Ib.* No. 4.
3 *Ib.* No. 5; see Cohen, *Texte*, 174.
4 *Ib.* No. 6.
5 No. 7 on p. 147.

7. Coh. p. xxiii. Junia 11.

8. Coh. p. xxviii. Minucia 4.

9. Coh. p. xviii. Flaminia 2.

10. Coh. p. xli. Veturia.

11. Coh. p. xxxiv. Porcia 3.

Minucius, who gained a temporary popularity, and had a statue erected to him (Livy iv. 13, 16) for distributing at a low price the confiscated corn stores of the unfortunate Maelius. Here[1] we have the corn and the statue on the coin of a moneyer, Ti. Minucius, of whose *cognomen* I shall speak presently. Besides this Act of Attainder, if I may dignify it with that name, there is scarcely any numismatic notice, during the whole time occupied by the struggle between the two Orders, of aught but achievements in the field.

Ap. Claudius, obviously the main author of the XII Tables, and probably the victim of an aristocratic reaction, has been so successfully blackened by family spite or sensational romancing that we are not surprised to find little record but lies of his legislation. When we pass on, however, to the influential and wealthy *gens Licinia*, in which the family of *Stolones* were still of high rank and importance under Augustus, we look naturally for some reference to the famous Rogations of 367 B.C. or their result. But we look in vain.

Of the Q. Publilius Philo who comes in so abruptly in Livy's 8th Book, 339 B.C., with his convenient dictatorship and his Junius Brutus for a *magister equitum*, and his laws anticipating the Hortensian settlement of fifty years later—of all this the only numismatic record that I can find is on a Greek coin of Naples (of which I do not give a drawing, as it is not Roman), apparently referring to the dubious success gained by Publilius about this time, with the help of a traitor, over Palaepolis, henceforth Neapolis (Naples).[2]

To take up once again the strange story of the Claudian reformers, on whom Mommsen has shed the first true light. Claudii occur, as we know, still bearing the ancient name of Appius, quite to the close of the Republic. But there is no record on their *denarii* of the famous Censorship of Ap. Claudius Caecus in 312—no Censorinus to follow, though that achievement is common in at least two other *gentes*. One trace only can I find of the many consequences of Appius's reform, and that indirectly as a result of the *lex Ogulnia*, which law, by the way, is entirely ignored in the *denarii* of the *gens Ogulnia* itself.

The *lex Ogulnia* of 300 B.C., as we learn from Livy,[3] threw

[1] No. 8 on p. 147.

[2] Livy viii. 26; see Babelon i. 15.

[3] Livy x. 6. 9.

12. Coh. p. xxxviii. Silia.

13. Coh. p. x. Calpurnia 24.

14. Coh. p. xviii. Fufia.

All the drawings, except the last, are from H. Cohen's *Médailles Consulaires*, 1857 (Planches).

open the Pontificate and Augurate to the Plebeians, one of those elected to the latter office being a Minucius. It is clearly to the first attainment of this honour by one of the family that the *cognomen* Augurinus refers on the coin last cited.[1] The whole matter may seem unimportant, but students of Roman Private Law know how much of its development results from this primarily religious career becoming *ouverte aux talents.*

Of the dictatorship of Quintus Hortensius or his law, which fills so important a place in our legal records, I can find no illustration, nor to my knowledge does a *gens Hortensia* appear at all on any known Republican coin.

The introduction of a silver coinage in 269, of which I spoke just now, is by many good authorities connected with a reduction of the original heavy bronze (*as libralis*) to what was practically a token.[2] It is perhaps more probable that this was a depreciation of the coinage due to the troubles of the First Punic War, which was followed by a more serious one during those of the Second.[3] This last reduction is generally attributed to a *lex Flaminia* connected with the name of the unfortunate general who fell in the disastrous battle of Thrasimenus in 217, of which Livy and Polybius make him the scapegoat.[4] The history of this C. Flaminius is important, but obscure to a degree. He is undoubtedly the champion of the later *plebs* as against the senatorial party, and in the demoralization of the assemblies, attributed to him, we clearly recognize a principal turning-point in the history of Rome. Of all this we have no numismatic record. I hardly dare to suggest that in the much contested legend of a Flaminian *denarius* we may possibly recognize an exceptional attainment of the rigidly guarded office of Flamen by some ancestor of low birth, and even the formation of a quasi-gentile name. I refer to the Pri. Fla. of a Flaminian moneyer, struck 44 B.C., which has been interpreted *Primus Flamen*,[5] though Mommsen, more in accordance, no doubt, with the rest of the legend, reads *Primus Flavit.*

I wish briefly to mention here a reference not indeed directly to law, but to an early *treaty* between Rome and some Campanian or other Greek nationality, on a coin of the Veturii, the idea of which

[1] No. 8 on p. 147.
[2] Babelon, Introd. p. xiii.
[3] Pliny xxiii. 44, 46.
[4] Livy xxii. 4-6; Polybius iii. 82, 83.
[5] No. 9 on p. 147; Babelon i. 494, 496.

is supposed to have been furnished by the reduction of Capua in 211 B.C.[1] A Roman and a Greek lay their hands jointly on a pig held ready for sacrifice by a *sacerdos fecialis*. This is interesting as illustrating Livy's picturesque account (in i. 24) of the ancient ceremony *foedus ferire*.

The obscurity surrounding the institution of a second Praetor, and the reform in Private Law which we vaguely describe as the *lex Aebutia*, derive no light from numismatics.

The first undoubted *direct* reference to a historical enactment on a coin is to be found in the *provoco* of Publius Laeca, a moneyer of about 110 B.C.[2] It symbolizes that final narrowing of the *imperium* which was effected in the *leges Porciae*. This *appeal* against sentence of flogging was carried or first brought forward in 199 B.C.

A *denarius* of about the same minting date (110 B.C.) by P. Licinius Nerva, gives an interesting representation of the ballot-voting introduced by his ancestor C. Licinius Crassus in 145 B.C.[3] The voter, you see, steps up to the *rogator*, receives his ballot, and passes singly over the *pons* to deposit it in the urn.

What was practically a beginning of the largesses of the later Republic and the Empire may be recognized in a coinage expressly issued to meet a scarcity of corn under the *lex frumentaria* of Saturninus, 100 B.C.[4] Note the quaestors *ad fru*[*mentum*] *emu*[*ndum*] (Piso, Caepio, Q.) and the head of Saturn with his *falx*, for the Treasury, and probably a reference to the name Saturninus.

The end of the formidable Social War, and the incorporation of the Italian allies with the Roman people, is indicated in a *denarius* of the *genus Fufia*.[5] This striking coin of the moneyer Q. Fufius Calenus is dated by Babelon 82 B.C., when the pacification of Italy was completed.

In the stormy close of the Republic there are not wanting occasional coins of legal or political significance, nor in the Julian and Augustan or in the first centuries of the Empire generally. These I am obliged to omit for lack of time. In one coin only I

[1] No. 10 on p. 147; Babelon ii. 534.
[2] *Ib.* No. 11; Babelon ii. 370.
[3] No. 12 on p. 149; Babelon ii. 129; see Varro, *De re rustica*, ii. 2.
[4] *Ib.* No. 13; Babelon i. 288.
[5] *Ib.* No. 14; Babelon i. 512.

should like to bring to your notice what has been regarded as the numismatic record of a wider gift of Roman citizenship than that last mentioned, in fact throughout the Roman world, *in orbe Romano*, as Ulpian says.[1] This gift is attributed by Justinian [2] to the Emperor Antoninus Pius, erroneously, as is usually held by modern writers on the strength of a passage in Dio Cassius,[3] which gives the credit, though not on any very high ground, to Caracalla, who amongst several other later Emperors debased that honoured name. There is, however, in the Cabinet de France a bronze medallion of Pius[4] bearing the striking legend *Ampliatori civium* within a wreath of oak-leaves. That this really refers to a vast extension of citizenship by that great and humane Emperor has been strongly maintained by authorities who were quite aware of the passage in Dio.[5] The difficulties arising in subsequent law are about the same in both cases. This medallion is placed by Cohen between A.D. 140 and 143. The disputed question as to its meaning I leave to you.[6]

E. C. CLARK.

[1] *Dig.* l. 5. 17.

[2] Nov. 78. 5.

[3] Dio Cassius, lxxvii. 9.

[4] Cohen, *Monnaies de l'Empire*, ii. 347, no. 789; see last drawing on p. 149.

[5] E.g. Hommel.

[6] The discovery of the papyrus published as P. Giess. 40 seems, as has been pointed out to me by Professor Lenel, to confirm the conclusion that the universal grant of Roman citizenship is to be attributed to Caracalla. I still think that the medallion of Pius may refer to some less advanced or less effective measure in the same direction, of which we otherwise know nothing.

# VII

# GÖTTER UND TOTE ALS RECHTS-SUBJEKTE BEI DEN ALTEN GERMANEN

UNTER Rechtssubjekt verstehen wir ein Wesen, das Rechte (und allenfalls auch Pflichten) haben kann. Wir nennen ein solches Wesen auch Person im Rechtssinne. Die Gottheit in unserem modernen Sinne ist sicherlich auch Person. Wir legen ihr Vernunft, Willen, Handlungsfähigkeit bei. Wir glauben an einen persönlichen Gott. Aber unser Gott ist Person nur im moralischen, im ethischen Sinne. Nicht im Rechtssinn. Unser Gott ist nicht Eigentümer im Rechtssinn.

Anders schon das Mittelalter. Das Mittelalter spricht Gott und den Heiligen Rechtspersönlichkeit zu. Sie haben Eigentum an Grundstücken und Fahrnis. Sie haben Vasallen, Dienstmannen und Hörige. Die Heiligen gehen Verträge ein und werden daraus berechtigt und verpflichtet. Sie haben öffentliche Rechte. Die Rolle des heiligen Petrus in der Entwicklung der staats- und kirchenrechtlichen Verhältnisse ist bekannt. Gott als Grundherr und Eigentümer der Welt hat Anspruch auf Zehent. Raub von Kirchengut ist Beraubung Gottes und seiner Heiligen. Das hat bereits vor rund 50 Jahren Otto Gierke festgestellt und voll eindringend erörtert.

Ich meine, man kann eine solche überaus lebendige, sinnliche Auffassung auch schon im vorchristlichen Germanentum nachweisen. Die anthropomorphistisch theokratische Anschauung des Mittelalters findet sich bereits im germanischen Altertum vorgebildet. Nicht nur im Keim, sondern womöglich noch viel sinnlicher.

Es scheint mir reizvoll, diesem Problem nachzugehen, umsomehr, als sich dabei tiefere Einblicke in die Rechtsinstitutionen des menschlichen Verkehrs ergeben. In einer in Kürze erscheinenden Publikation [1] biete ich eingehende Erörterungen. Hier möchte ich eine gedrängte Übersicht der Hauptresultate vorführen, die sich mir ergeben haben.

## I. Das Wesen der germanischen Götter

Es ist notwendig, zuerst das Wesen der germanischen Götter einigermassen herauszuarbeiten. Die germanischen Götter, soweit wir ihrer habhaft werden können, sind von Haus aus reale Mächte, die sich handgreiflich bemerkbar machen. Caesar B. G. vi. 21 nennt *Sol, Vulcanus, Luna*; *reliquos ne fama quidem acceperunt.* Das wären also zunächst Naturkräfte, die uns als gegebene, aussermenschliche und übermenschliche Mächte von ungeheurer Wirksamkeit entgegentreten, die man zu spüren bekommt. Das wäre das Reale. Die Naturvölker lieben es aber, Kräfte, denen sie begegnen, als Äusserungen menschenähnlicher Subjekte sich vorzustellen. Hinter den Naturerscheinungen von Sonne, Mond und Blitz (Feuer) sieht der Germane Wesen, die der menschlichen Seele verwandt sind. Die—wirklichen oder auch eingebildeten—Funkzionen von Sonne, Blitz und Mond sind ihm Tätigkeiten psychischer Wesen. Der Schade, den sie verursachen, erscheint ihm als Feindseligkeit, der Nutzen als Wohlwollen (Animatismus, Animismus). Die Ohnmacht des Menschen gegenüber den Naturgewalten wird so zur Unterordnung unter die Herrschaft übermächtiger Götter. Es ist kein Wunder, dass man diesen überlegenen Geistern auch höheres Wissen beilegt.

So schon nach den Angaben Caesars. Dies beweist unter Anderem der Gebrauch von Orakel und Opfer. *Vulcanus* ist der germanische *Thonaraz*, *Sol* ist *Tiwaz.* Es kann auch gar kein Zweifel sein, dass diese Götter männlich gedacht sind. Ihnen gegenüber steht eine weibliche Gottheit, *Luna*, wie ich meine die weibliche Gottheit κατ᾽ ἐξοχήν. Das ist schon eine sehr weitgehende Vermenschlichung.

Noch weiter geht die Vermenschlichung der Götter nach den Angaben des Tacitus. Die Götter stehen da zu einander in menschlichen Familienverhältnissen, ja die germanischen Völker leiten ihre Herkunft von den Göttern ab, vor allem von dem uralten

[1] *ZSS*, 1913.

Haupt- und Obergott *Tiu*. Ich glaube nicht zu viel zu sagen, wenn ich den Germanen auch eine göttliche Stammesmutter, etwa kurz gesagt, die Mutter Erde, zuschreibe. Nicht mit allen physiologischen Einzelheiten, aber doch unter Festhaltung der Familienrechtsbegriffe: Vater und Mutter.

Diese Auffassung hat sich mir als gemeingermanisch, urgermanisch ergeben. Die Germanen sind von Haus aus Tiu-Söhne gewesen, wie es noch zur Zeit des Tacitus ganz besonders die Herminonen (Sueben), speziell die Semnonen sind. Ja ich bin sehr geneigt, diese Vorstellungen als arisches Urerbe anzusehen.

Diese Versippung der Götterwelt mit dem Menschengeschlechte ist für das religiöse aber auch für das Rechtsleben von tiefstgreifender Bedeutung.

Götter und Menschen sind durch den Friedens- und Rechtsverband der Sippe organisch zusammengeschlossen. In religiöser Beziehung tritt zur Macht die Liebe, die Innigkeit. In juristischer Beziehung erscheint die sakrale Götterherrschaft ahnenkultlich konstruiert. Die religiöse Vorstellung der Götterherrschaft wird durch das ahnenkultliche Element der menschlichen Rechtsordnung eingegliedert.

## II. Rechtsstellung des Toten

Die Verschmelzung der Götter mit den Ahnen führt auf die Rechtsstellung des Toten. Die Lehre von der Fortdauer der Rechtspersönlichkeit nach dem Tode ist in letzter Zeit namentlich durch Heinrich Brunner belebt und vertieft worden. Einiges kann ich aus eigenen Untersuchungen, die nun neun Jahre zurückliegen, hinzufügen.

Nach altgermanischer Anschauung erlischt die Persönlichkeit des Menschen mit dem Tode nicht. Im Gegenteil bewirkt der Tod eher eine Steigerung der Persönlichkeit an Wissen und Können. Für das Rechtsgebiet kann man geradezu den Grundsatz aufstellen, dass prinzipiell die Rechtsfähigkeit und die Handlungsfähigkeit, dass die Rechtsverhältnisse, soweit nicht besondere Gründe eintreten, auch nach dem Tode fortbestehen. Als Sitte und Pietät ragen ja diese Vorstellungen noch in unsere Tage hinein. Nach altgermanischem Rechte dauert das Personenrecht des Toten fort. Schon am Körper kann eine Ehrung, Beschimpfung, Bestrafung des Toten vollzogen werden. Die eheliche Treue und die Gefolgschaft währen über das Grab hinaus. Ebenso das Vermögensrecht. Der Tote hat Eigentum an seinem Grabe (als an seiner Behausung) und an Allem, was er mitbekommt.

Mit eherner Logik und in schärfster Ausprägung haben die Römer das Recht des Toten festgehalten. Der *pater familias* bleibt Rechtssubjekt seines Vermögens. So erklärt sich m. E. die eigentümliche Anschauung, dass der Erbe, der *heres*, die Persönlichkeit des Toten in sich aufnimmt, dass er sie fortsetzt. Daher auch die ungeheuer frühzeitige Testirfreiheit der Römer. Weil eben dem Toten wie bei Lebzeiten das Gut gehört, und zwar das ganze Gut, darum kann der Lebende ohne weiteres über den Tod hinaus darüber verfügen. Noch tiefer fassend und in fernste Zeiten zurückgreifend wird man wohl sagen dürfen, dass auch die *patria potestas* den Söhnen, den *sui heredes*, durch Absorpzion der Seele des Vaters überkommen sei. Die römischen Begräbnis- und Totengebräuche zeigen die zu Grunde liegende Anschauung in grosser Lebhaftigkeit. Der Tote lebt in dem Erben fort.

Auch bei den Germanen stirbt der Tote nicht. Der Tote, der Ahn, bleibt insbesondere Eigentümer seines Hauses, er bleibt Hausherr. Noch im Mittelalter ist im deutschen Handgemal, im englischen *frumstol, eðel*, im nordischen *oðal*—kurz im Erbgut der Gedanke von Eigentum und Herrschaft des Toten lebendig. Noch in später, geschichtlicher Zeit okkupiert ein toter Norweger (*Kvelldulfr*) Land auf Island. Und ausdrücklich erklären die Hochsitzpfeiler des nordischen Bauernhauses, die *ondvegissulur*, dass an dem Hochsitz die Seele des Ahnen hause. Auch für das deutsche Institut des sog. „Dreissigsten" und dessen Parallele, das nordische Erbbier, muss ich — entgegen Homeyer — als den einen Grundgedanken das Recht des Toten in Anspruch nehmen.

Selbst die familienrechtliche Gewalt des Hausvaters bleibt bestehen. Nicht nur folgt ihm freiwillig die Treue über das Grab. Der Tote erscheint auch selbst und stellt Forderungen. Bei wichtigen Anlässen wird er beschworen und um Weisungen ersucht.

Andererseits zeigen die germanischen Anschauungen gegenüber dem römischen Recht eine Abschwächung der Rechte des Toten. Der Tote ist da nicht Eigentümer seines ganzen Nachlasses, wie in Rom. Er erhält blos bestimmte Vermögensstücke oder eine Quote, kurz den Totenteil. Das entspricht aber dem Verhältnis schon bei Lebzeiten. Schon bei Lebzeiten steht das Vermögen in gemeinschaftlichem Eigentum der Familienglieder, allerdings unter voller Gewere des Vaters. Ich will ganz davon absehen, in wiefern die Bestattung ausserhalb des Hauses, der Gedanke von Walhall und christlichem Jenseits nach germanischer Anschauung lösend wirken musste. In dem deutschen „Dreissigsten" sehe ich als zweiten Grundgedanken die Abfindung, Abschichtung des auswandernden Toten. Aber schon für die Urzeit tritt der Gesichtspunkt in Kraft, dass die laufende Ausübung der Rechte dem Toten genomnen war. Die Gewere hat der Erbe. (Dieser Vorstellung mag auch der spätere Satz entsprechen: *Le mort saisit le vif.*) So ergibt sich ein Nebeneinander, Miteinander in der Herrschaft, in dem Haus- und Familienregiment des Ahnen und des Erben. Der Erbe hat eine unmittelbare Gewere, die in historischer Entwicklung leicht zu Nutzungseigentum und schliesslich Ablösung, Abstossung des Obereigentums führt.

### III. Das Recht der Götter und Menschenrecht

Zieht man nun das ahnenkultliche Element der altgermanischen Religion heran, so werden nicht nur diese erbrechtlichen Grundsätze bekräftigt. Durch das Totenrecht tritt auch das Sakralrecht mit juristischer Plastik hervor — sowohl das sakrale Vermögensrecht, wie das sakrale Personenrecht. Zweifellos ist die Gottheit Eigentümerin ihres Haines, ihres Tempels, ihrer Schätze, der Tiere in ihrem Gehege. Auch die bekannten nordischen Privattempel sind Eigentum der Gottheit. Der *Gode* ist von Haus aus nur Priester, wie die *Gydja* Priesterin. Als solcher ist er allerdings Organ der Gottheit; er führt deren Handlungen aus; er übt Amtsgewere, die dann freilich weitgehender Säkularisierung, Allodialisierung fähig ist. Ja selbst der einfache Hausvater ist in seiner Stellung als Haus- und Grundherr transzendental, götter- und ahnenkultlich verankert. Der Hausfriede ist nicht sein Friede sondern sakral. Die zwangsweisen Grundanweisungen durch die Fürsten Caesars können nur durch das sakrale Eigentum resp. Obereigentum der in der Volksversammlung anwesenden Gottheit erklärt werden. Und noch in spätgeschichtlicher Zeit weisen Heiligkeit der Grenzzeichen, feierliche Umgänge, das nordische *fara eldi um landit*, der Hammerwurf u. A. auf die sakrale Wurzel des Grundeigentums. Auch im

Personenrecht regiert die Gottheit, die vom Könige, Landespriester oder Hausvater um ihre Weisung befragt wird.

Die Heiligkeit der Eltern aber auch die Banngewalt der Obrigkeit, die *iubendi potestas* hat eine götter- und ahnenkultliche Wurzel. Das *cogere* der *principes* Caesars, dessen *magistratus, qui vitae necisque habent potestatem*, all das ist bei dem charakteristischen Unabhängigkeitssinn der Germanen nur auf sakraler Grundlage möglich.

## IV. Der Rechtsverkehr

Es erübrigen noch einige Worte zu der Frage, wie sich diese transzendenten Rechtssubjekte im Rechtsverkehr dieser Welt geltend machen. Sie bringen sich selbständig oder befragt, beschworen durch sinnlich wahrnehmbare Äusserungen zur Geltung. Es sind reale Geschehnisse, die als Äusserungen der göttlichen Ahnen, Freunde oder Feinde, gedeutet werden. Die Personen, an welche und durch welche sich die Gottheit an die anderen wendet, erscheinen da in priesterlicher Funkzion. Von besonderer Wichtigkeit sind dabei gewisse Attribute der Gottheit. Über die Vorstellungen, welche hier durchgreifen, gibt vor Allen Tacitus Auskunft: *Deum adesse bellantibus credunt. Effigiesque et signa quaedam detracta lucis in proelium ferunt.* Diese Wahrzeichen des Gottes sind Wahrzeichen seiner Anwesenheit. Der Gott ist da, sichtbar durch sein Wahrzeichen. Derjenige, der das Wahrzeichen handhabt, ist ein Werkzeug in der Hand des Gottes. Er bringt den göttlichen Willen zur sichtbaren, vernehmbaren Äusserung. Daher umgekehrt: wer das Wahrzeichen des Gottes hat, ist dessen Priester, Bote, Stellvertreter. Daher soll der isländische *Gode*, wenn er in Funkzion tritt, den Opferring an der Hand tragen. Dann ist es der Gott, der aus ihm spricht. So wird mit dem Feuer das Land geheiligt, ebenso mit dem Hammer Thors das Land ausgemessen. Das ist die tiefere Bedeutung des germanischen Königsspeers, der Königsfahne, des Schwertes und wohl auch des Gerichtsstabes. Noch die späteren Krönungsformeln lassen den Stab als Zauberstab erkennen. Auch hier tritt der Gedanke der Amtsgewere und Allodialisierung ein: Der Bote wird zum Stellvertreter, dieser zum Eigenberechtigten von Gottes Gnaden.

H. Schreuer.

# VIII

# THE MEANING OF THE WORDS *ÔÐAL* AND *SKEYTING* IN THE OLD LAWS OF NORWAY

## I. The Legal Terminology

*Ôðal.*—If we consider the terms used in contrast to the word *óðal*, we shall best understand its original meaning.

The first term of this kind is *aurar* (moveables). This distinction is observed throughout in the oldest of our legal sources, the *Gulathingslaw.* A deceased person's property is either *oðal* or *aurar*: *tertium non datur.*[1] In the *Frostathingslaw*, dated 100 years earlier, we find the same distinction indicated by the words *jǫrð* and *aurar.*[2]

Another term used in contradistinction to *óðal* is *fǫng* (acquired land)[3] or *kaupijǫrð* (purchased land).[4] The last distinction also reappears in the *Frostathingslaw*, where we find *kauplendingr* (the owner of *kaupland* or *kaupijǫrð*) distinguished from *óðalsmaðr* (the odaller).[5] In the *Landslaw* of Magnus Lagabøtir (the Lawmender), 1274, *fǫng* and *kaupijǫrð* are comprised in the term *ûtjǫrð* (outland).[6]

*Skeyting.*—The *skeyting* (Lat. *scotatio*) is the very ancient Scandinavian form for 'transfer of property in land.' This at least is the *communis opinio doctorum.*[7] But in my opinion the correct definition of the legal act of *skeyting* is this: the *skeyting* is originally the legal form for 'transfer of *óðal*-right in *óðal*-land.' 'To buy land

[1] *G.* 103, 104; cpr. 270, 275. [2] *F.* v. 13; cpr. *G.* 53.
[3] *G.* 285. [4] *G.* 223. [5] *F.* xiii. 25. [6] *L.* v. 7.
[7] See Ebbe Hertzberg, *Glossary to the Old Laws of Norway*, s.v. 'Skeyting.'

for skeyting' (*at kaupa jǫrð til skeytingar*)[1] is the same as 'to buy land for *óðal*' (*at kaupa jǫrð ser til óðals*).[2] The old provincial laws for Gulathing[3] and Frostathing[4] only use the terms *skeyta* and *skeyting* in connexion with transfer of *óðal*-land, and the same is the case in *Landslaw*.[5]

## II. The Original Meaning of *Óðal* and *Skeyting*

In 1907 Professor Vinogradoff published in the *Harvard Law Review* a paper on 'Transfer of Land in Old English Law.' It is this paper which has prompted me to make the following remarks about the original meaning of the words *óðal* and *skeyting* in the old laws of Norway.

As to the general meaning of the word *óðal*: it signifies the family-ownership of land, and also land as the object of such ownership. Mr. Hertzberg in his Glossary of our old laws, however, has put this conception of the word as a secondary one, and has made it evident, or at least tried to make it evident, that the original legal meaning of *óðal* was simply ownership in land and land as an object of such ownership. The word concerns only property in land or soil.

My own investigations have led me to the same conclusion. But what does 'property in land' indicate? What kind of 'land' is owned?

Everywhere in the Teutonic world we observe that the oldest valuation of land only comprises the arable land. And I believe it to be just as certain that only the arable land originally was the object of ownership. The real basis of land-ownership is the tilling of the soil.[6]

Having studied our old laws, particularly the oldest one, the *Gulathingslaw*, I found that the real *óðal*-land was the arable land,

[1] *G.* 278, 279. [2] *F.* xii. 4. [3] *G.* 278, 279, 292.

[4] *F.* xii. 1, 2, 4; ix. 4 (*jǫrð*). I do not think that *F.* xii. 1 is against my opinion, that the common intention of the *skeyting* originally is transfer of *óðal*-right in *óðal*-land; but, as I will show later on (p. 170), the *skeyting* in *F.* has more the character of transferring the *gewere* than that of transfer of a 'right.' This was formerly my view of the *skeyting*; see my paper 'Den norske besiddelsesret' in *Tidsskrift for Retsvidenskab*, x. 105 *sqq.*

[5] *L.* vi. 8, 10.

[6] Adolf Åström, *Svensk jordäganderätt* (Stockholm, 1897), has treated this subject at large and in a very convincing way.

the tilled ground, the 'fenced-in' fields, meadows and pastures, in fact the *homestead.* This is the original *óðal,* both in the vulgar and the legal meaning of the word.[1] We have two convincing evidences of this fact. The one is the act of *óðalsskipti,* the other is the act of *skeyting.*

The act of *óðalsskipti* (division of the *óðal*) is, according to the *Gulathingslaw,* 87, only a division of houses or tilled ground (*hus æða jǫrð*), or of *bøar* (townships). The division of mountain-pastures (*sætr*) or forest (*mǫrk*) is regulated in quite a different way in *G.* 86.

The act of *skeyting* is once described in the *Gulathingslaw* before its revision by King Olaf the Saint (ob. A.D. 1030) or King Magnus Erlingsson (A.D. 1163). Of this description we still have a notice in *G.* 292, which gives us a clear idea of its peculiarities.

The most essential act of the *skeyting* was the 'mould-taking' (*moldtaka*), generally performed by the seller; but if the seller refused to perform this duty, the purchaser himself might do so. In the latter case *G.* 292 provides: 'He shall take the mould according to the order of the law: Take some mould from the four corners of the hearth, from the seat of honour (the *ǫndvegissæti,* the 'high seat'), from where the field and meadow meet, from where the fenced-in pastureland and grove meet.'[2] From other sources we know that the mould thus taken was cast into the lap (*skaut*) of the purchaser, and hence the whole ceremony was named *skeyting,* which verbally would correspond to an English word 'lapping' (from 'lap').

This old ceremony of *skeyting* takes us back to the very primitive days of Norwegian peasant life. We find ourselves in the ancient peasant house with its hearth in the middle of the

[1] According to Falk u. Torp, *Etym. WB.*, *óðal* means "'eigentum, heimat, vaterland, grundbesitz, vorkaufrecht' = ags. ôþel, êþel 'heimatland,' afries. ôthol, êthel, as. ôthil 'erbgut,' oht. uodal in ders. bedeut.; vgl. got. haimôþli 'heimatliches gut.' Eine ursprünglichere bedeutung liegt vor in poet. anord. ôðal 'gemüt, natur, wesen' = aðal, eðli. Daraus entwickelte sich die bedeutung 'geschlecht, herkunft' (so bei anord. eðli und bei adel) und daraus wieder 'heimat' usw. Die älteste bedeutung der wortgruppe wäre 'eingeweide,' falls as. inôthri, ahd. inuodili und inâdiri 'eingeweide,' Gr. ἦτορ, 'hertz' verwandt sind."

[2] 'Hann á mold at taca sem i logum er mælt: Taca at arenshornom fiorum oc i ondveges sæte. oc þar sem acr oc eng møtezt. oc þar sem holt oc hage møtezt.'

earthen floor, and the seat of honour, belonging to the master, placed in direct contact with the same earthen floor. The hearth and the high seat were the chief things within the old *óðal*-house of Norway. The ancient Norwegian peasant, looking at his *óðal*-homestead, would, I believe, consider himself as much a lord as the English landowner when he declares, 'My house is my castle.'[1] Nobody could enter against the will of the *óðal*-householder. If anybody wished to summon him before the *Thing*, or tribunal, he had first to summon him 'home'; because the summoning to the courts of law was not lawful when the defendant was not sitting 'in his *ǫndvegi*.'[2] When the heir took the seisin of the ancestral property the act was symbolized by the heirs taking their place in the high seat.[3] Thus the *ǫndvegi* may be named the 'throne' in the *óðal*-householder's realm, which comprised the house and the fenced-in land, the fields, meadows, grove, and home-pasture. When transferring this 'realm' to another householder, he had to make it over to his successor in this dramatic way of 'mould-taking' and 'mould-*skeyting*.'

I presume we are not very far from the truth in asserting that the above-mentioned formula of *skeyting* dates from a time when every Norwegian free peasant was an *óðal*-man, that is, the owner and the farmer of his own *óðal*-homestead. Leaseholders (*leigulendingar*) of *óðal*-land had not yet made their appearance in the agrarian history of Norway, in which they were afterwards to play so prominent a part. The *óðal*-householder farmed his land himself with the assistance of his family and his serfs.

How far back in our history have we to go in order to find such conditions? The answer to that question was given as long ago as 1889 by Konrad Maurer in his paper on *Die norwegischen höldar*. He has proved that the word *hauldr* (*höldr ags. hold*) originally was synonymous with the word *bondi* (husband, free peasant), and we still find these words used as synonyms in the laws of Eastern Norway in the twelfth century. But in the laws of Western Norway (the *Gulathingslǫg* and the *Frostathingslǫg*)

[1] Note the answer of a defendant in the procedure of redeeming *óðal*-land: 'thou shall never get this land from me, without taking it from my corpse' (*þu fær þá iord eigi af mér. nema þu af mér dauðum drager*, *G.* 268, cpr. 265).

[2] See *G.* 35, 266; *F.* x. 2.

[3] *G.* 115: 'Nu er maðr dauðr, arve skal i ondvegi setjazt.'

*hauldr* is synonymous with *óðalborinn maðr* or *óðalsmaðr*, while *bondi* here means an inferior class of free peasants, who are not *óðal*-born or *óðal*-men. This division of the peasant community may have taken place before the beginning of the ninth century, when we meet the Norwegian *hold* in the Anglo-Saxon Chronicles and in the *Northleôda laga* as a man standing in the middle rank between the *ealdorman* and the *þegn*,[1] just as the Norwegian *hauldr* ranks between the *lendrmaðr* and the *bondi*.

This division of the peasants living round the Western fjords is no doubt one of the many evolutionary factors which the raids of the Vikings introduced into Norway. During this period the sons of the ancient *óðal*-families developed more and more into a class of warriors and merchants, to whom farming seemed degrading and inadequate for the economic needs of their new households, which were greater and more costly than under the old standard of living on a single *óðal*-estate. They developed from *óðal*-peasants into landlords. The story of Hárek in Tjotta (first half of the eleventh century) is very significant in this respect.[2] His father, Eyvind Skaldaspiller, had not been *storaudigr* (very rich), and in his time there lived in Tjotta many small peasants. His son Hárek at first bought only one farm, and that not very large; but in a few years he bought out all the small *bøndr*, who had lived there before, so that he himself alone owned the whole island and built a big 'manse' upon it.

Under such circumstances the small *óðal*-peasants were transformed into leaseholders of *óðal*-land belonging to others, or they founded new *óðal*-estates by clearing away the forests and tilling uncultivated soil. About a thousand years after the advent of Christianity this development got a new impulse in that Christianity did away with serfdom. Olaf and his Anglo-Saxon court bishop, Grimkell, had very effectively advocated the abolition of serfdom. They ordered in their new Christian law that every year at every

1 Maurer, *Die höldar*, pp. 198-99.

2 'I þjóttu bjoggu þá smáir bøndr ok eigi allfáir. Hárekr keypti þar einn bø fyrst ok eigi allmikinn ok fór þar buðum til; en á fám misserum hafði hann rutt i brot ǫllum bóndum, þeim er þar bjoggu áðr, svá at hann átti þá einn alla eyna ok gerði þar þá hǫfudbø mikinn' (*Heimskringla*, ed. Finnur Jónsson, ii. 215).

*Lawthing* and *Fylkisthing* in the land a serf should be set free;[1] the inhabitants of the *thinglǫg* should every year give the sum of money which was needed to pay the *freedgeld* to the owner of the serf, and the solemn act of free-giving was performed on the first Sunday in the session. K. Maurer has expressed the opinion that the object of this act of free-giving was to establish a contrast to the heathen sacrifices of serfs at the commencement of the earlier *things*. It was truly an effective way of preaching the Gospel, and one which commended itself to the understanding of the people. Its consequences were that 150 years after the death of King Olaf (1030) there existed no more serfs in Norway, this being 100 years earlier than their disappearance in Denmark and about 200 years before their disappearance in Sweden.

## III. The Evolution of the *Ôðal*-Conception (11th to 13th Centuries)

From the unfree population there now grew up a stock of free labourers, who naturally found their way into the class of small leaseholders and new settlers.[2] The cultivation of the land was extended. During the first Christian centuries the woods and valleys of Norway are cleared, and the inhabited land gets the shape and extension it has kept up to recent times. The place-names composed with *ruð*—about 3000 in number—spread over all the inland districts, show us the value of the cultivation carried on by these petty strugglers for life.

There was created a great deal of fresh *óðal*, in the ancient meaning of the word, i.e. cultivated land. But who were the '*óðal*-men' to this *óðal*? Were they the tillers and settlers themselves, or were they the old *óðal*-families whose domains were extended in this way, or were they the King and Crown, whose 'commons' (*almenningar*) were transformed into *bygðir* (inhabited districts)?

Of course both these things happened, and the principal result of the *ruðningr* (reclaiming of land) is an immense increase of the leaseholders. An undated statute of King Magnus Lagabøtir (1263-80) assumes that every inhabitant of a *ruðstaðr*

[1] *G.* 4: 'Þat er nu þvi nest, at ver skolom geva manne frælsi ár hvert her i Gula.'—5: 'Þat er nu þvi nest at ver scolom manne frælsi geva i fylki hveriu i Gulaþings logum.'

[2] In the sense of persons reclaiming land for cultivation (*ryðningsmænd*).

is a leaseholder; but it assumes, too, that many of these settlers do not know who is their landlord. It is therefore their duty to go to the *heraðsthing* and 'call for a landlord (*bondi*)'; and if they do not find one, the King is the owner of the *ruðstaðr*.[1]

But, after all, we must presume that in these early Christian centuries there also grew up a new class of independent owners—in other words, new *óðal*-men and *óðal*-families. In Eastern Norway such *parvenus*, when free-born, seem to have been regarded as *bøndr* and *hauldar* in the eye of the law. Perhaps this view was not taken as early as the first generation; but when their homestead had passed from father to son, it became *óðal* in Norway as it became *arvejord* (*terra hereditaria*) in Sweden.[2]

In Western Norway also this rule originally prevailed. In *G.* 270 are mentioned 'the land (*þær jarðir*) which shall follow the *óðals*: it is that which the forefather has left to his successor (*sú er ein er ave hever ava leift*).' The use of the word *ave* for both of them indicates that the land for many generations has been in the same family.[3] But when we remember that *óðal* simply means tilled ground, we are bound to assume that originally it was enough to make it *óðal*, in the sense of *terra hereditaria*, that it had at some time or other passed to an heir.

Now we meet in the *Gulathingslaw*, 266, another provision for the *óðalsbrigð* (the redemption of *óðal*-land). The person redeeming the land must 'tell off (count) his 5 ancestors, who have owned (the land), and the 6th, who held both in ownership and in *óðal*.'[4] And the *Frostathingslaw*, xii. 4, provides: 'The land of no man shall become *óðal* before 3 ancestors have owned it and it has come into the possession of the 4th without interruption.'[5] These regulations, I think, are consequences of the above-mentioned aristocratic tendencies in West Norway to distinguish between the *óðal*-born men and the common peasants (*bøndr*). I do not think it was the original rule that a homestead

[1] *Norges gamle Love*, ii. 485.

[2] Nordström, *Svenska Samhälls författningens historia*, ii. 140 *sqq*.

[3] See Hertzberg, *Glossarium* s.v. 'afi'; Fritzner, *Ordbog*, s.v. 'afi' 2. *DN*. iv. No. 848: 'þat hefir fylgt afi eptir afa.'

[4] 'Þeir scolo telia til langfeðra sinna v. er átt hava, en sá hinn sette er bæðe átte at eign oc at ôðrle.'

[5] 'Engum manni verðr iǫrð at ôðali fyrr en iij. langfeðr hafa átt oc kemr undir hinn iiij. samfleytt.'

first got the quality of *ôðal* after six or four generations of successive possession in the same family. In ancient times it becomes *ôðal* as soon as it is established as a homestead for a free-born *bondi.* In my opinion it was the extensive and common 'free-giving' of serfs which was the chief cause of the provision as to the six or four generations. Then it was an old rule that the family of a freedman could not enter the class of the *bøndr* till after at least four generations.[1]

The natural effect of the above-mentioned regulation was to diminish both the *ôðal*-land and the *ôðal*-families. Magnus Lagabøtir accepted in his *Landslaw* (vi. 2) the rule of the *Frostathingslaw* relating to the four generations. But the common rule amongst the people was that an *ôðal*-witness should make clear the pedigree of the ancestors 'as far back as the *haugr* (burial mounds) of heathen times.'[2]

A perfect *ôðal*-estate possessed a burial-mound (*haugr*) of the heathen ancestor. In the pedigrees of the ancient ruling families in Söndmör we find the following characteristic remarks:

Herbjörn ligger i hougen i Drifftvig. Aatte til eigu och odel Helgabostad och Holm och Starrin.

Barder Nessiakonung ligger i hougen paa Bardarstad; hand aatte all Roma och alla Strandarvig och Gudöy och Hundeidavig.

Eilifr jarl ligger i Eilifshoug i Gudö.
Tosten Bláfotr ligger indeni Hundeid.
Rafn som ligger i Hval i Heimdal.
Grimr ligger i hougen paa Hjordal paa Sundmör.[3]

It cannot be wondered at that under such conditions the class of *haulds* was decreasing. Both the *Frostathingslaw* (xiv. 7) and the *Landslaw* (vii. 61) reckon with the possibility that in a *fylke* (county) there may not be found as many as twelve *haulds.* Indeed, the exact meaning of the term *hauldr* is no longer familiar to the common mind; therefore the *Landslaw* (vii. 64) must

[1] See Konrad Maurer, *Die Freigelassenen nach altnorwegischem Rechte* (1878). Seebohm, *Tribal Custom in Anglo-Saxon Law*, p. 319. Paul Vinogradoff, 'Geschlecht und Verwandtschaft im altnorwegischem Rechte' (*Zeitschrift für Social und Wirtschaftsgeschichte*, vii. 1 sqq.).

[2] 'Greinande skilvislega langfæðgatal til haugs ok til heiðni,' *Norges gamle Love*, iii. 121 (1316). In the *Landslaw* vi. 16 this *ôðal* is named *haugs* or *haugaôðal.* It is opposed to *útjarðir* in DN. ii. No. 694 (A.D. 1427).

[3] Gustav Storm, 'Indskuddene i Fagrskinna' (*Kristiania Videnskabsselskabs Forhandlinger*, 1875, pp. 100-106).

define it: 'But he is *hauldr* who has *ôðals* by inheritance both from his father and his mother, which his forefathers have owned before them and which have not been the *ôðals* of other men, who have got it by purchase or by collateral inheritance.'[1] This definition makes it evident that the genuine *ôðal* is the *ôðal* inherited from lineal ancestors, not from collaterals. The *ôðal* is *terra hereditaria* κατ' ἐξοχήν.

## IV. Transfer and Prescription of *Ôđal*-Right

The ordinary way of acquiring *ôðal*-right in *ôðal*-land was that of inheritance. In *G.* 270 inheritance is mentioned as the first method of acquiring *ôðal*-right to land. The second is forfeiture of land as *gjold* for a manslaughter. The third is *branderfð*; that is, when a man takes into his household another man with all his property in order 'to maintain him until he is carried to the funeral-pyre' (*til brannz oc til báls*).[2] The fourth is the 'gift of honour' (*heiðlaun*) from a king or prince. The fifth is the 'gift for drink' (*drekkulaun*),[3] if it is given by the king. The sixth the 'gift for child-fostering' (*barnfostrlaun*). The seventh is the *ôðalsskipti*.

Although it is not stated in the law, we must presume that the form of *skeyting* originally was in use for all these 'gifts,' and also for the *gjold* (forfeiture), where it was performed by the *thing* with *wapentak*, unless the *manslaier* performed it himself on the *ôðal*-estate.

But it is to be observed that 'sale' is not mentioned in *G.* 270 as a title creating *ôðal*-right. Our old laws knew different kinds of 'sale,' as *sal til stefnu* (for 15 years) or *sal til mála* (pawn), all of which were conditional and possessed a form of pledging the land. But in *G.* 278 and 279 we hear of a *sal til skeytingar*, and, as I have said before (p. 160), that must have been a sale of the *ôðal*-right, and *skeyting* is the form of transferring that right. If the seller refuse to perform it, the *thing* shall perform

1 'En sá er hauldr er hann hefir ôðaul at erfðum tekit bæðe eptir faður oc moðor þau er hans forellrar hafa átt áðr firir þeim oc eigi annara manna ôðaul i at telia, þau er með kaupi eru at komin eða úterfðum.'

2 'Su er hin xvi. (erfð) er heitir branderfð. ef maðr tecr mann á hond sér at liufu oc at leiðu. oc føðer hann til brannz oc til báls, kveðr at fernomále' (*G.* 108).

3 Cp. *drikkelaun* in the *North. preosta lagu*, i. 67 § 1. See Vinogradoff, *Transfer of Land*, pp. 537 sqq.

it by *wapentak*, if the purchaser can prove that he has lawfully 'taken mould' (*G.* 279, 292). In selling *óðal*-land, the vendor had first of all to offer it publicly in the *thing* to his *óðal*-fellows, who had the right of 'first refusal.' If none of them would buy it at the price which he might be expected to get from outsiders, he could sell it out of the *óðal*-group. But if he sold it 'unoffered,' the *óðal*-men could redeem it in twelve months. Such is the provision in *G.* 278 by *sal til skeytingar.*[1]

If the land was sold with a right of redemption by the seller, he had to keep this right alive by 'publication' (*lysing*) in the *thing*. If *lysing* was neglected for twenty years the contractual right of redemption was deemed to be extinct by prescription; the seller, however, still had his *óðal*-right of redemption, if the land was his *óðal*; but he had now to pay full value for the land, not merely the sum he had got by the conditional sale.[2] In this case the *Gulathingslaw* says that 'the land has become *óðal*,' viz. for the purchaser; 'then he (the purchaser) may deny the *óðal* (of the seller) and assert it for himself.'[3] Here we have clear evidence that *óðal* means simple ownership, not family ownership; but it is assumed that the latter is still retained by the seller, who can redeem it by *óðalsbrigð*.

We have seen that the *óðal*-group lost their right of redemption in regard to 'offered' *óðal*-land after a very short period of prescription, viz. twelve months. I think this provision dates from a time which regarded *óðal*-right mainly as simple ownership. But whether it is old or not, it is a valuable concession to the right of free disposition by the actual owner of the land. Then, of course, the family right of redemption was a hampering restriction on the free trade in *óðal*-land, which as early as the first centuries after the introduction of Christianity had become more and more extensive.

It is, however, quite another question whether the sold *óðal*-land became the family-*óðal* of the purchaser and his kinsmen at once

[1] 'Nu kaupir maðr iorð til skeytingar. oc tecr skeyting á þá scolo þeir oðalnautar hans ef their ero innan fylkis. oc vilia brigt hava. þá scolo þeir brigt hava á fyrstum xii. mánaðom. ellar scal sá hava er keypt hafðe' (*G.* 278, cp. 289).

[2] *G.* 272 and 276 in fine.

[3] 'Nu liggr iorð um stefnu. oc liggr xx. vetr. oc hava þeir enga lysing þar á. þá er hon at ôðrle orðen. þá má hann (*purchaser*) dula *óðals* oc kenna ser' (*G.* 276).

or in a twelvemonth. Personally I am convinced that the *skeyting*-act was intended to transfer the *ôðal*-right, not merely the ownership, from the seller and his offspring to the buyer and his offspring. None of the seller's offspring had any right of redeeming sold *ôðal*-land, if it had been lawfully 'offered.' On the contrary, he had to 'offer' it even to his own son.[1] Only, if he would sell *til stefnu* and not *til ôðals*, he was not required to 'offer' to his son.[2] That this is the intention of the *skeyting* is stated expressly in many *skeyting*-deeds. I will quote as an instance one of the oldest that has come down to us, viz. a donation-deed of 1281. The donor says: 'This land, which hitherto has been my *ôðal*, shall henceforth be considered by everybody as the *ôðal* of the said monastery.'[3] The common phrase runs that the land is sold or given *til alda ôðals*, or *til æfiligrar eignar ok alda ôðals*, or *til alda ôðals ok ubrigðiligrar eignar*.[4] Here redemption by the seller or donor and his offspring is certainly excluded.

But in regard to the acquisition of family *ôðal*-right by prescription, the old provincial laws have only the above-mentioned (p. 165) rules relating to possession for five (*G.*) or three (*F.*) generations. The last rule is the later in date and was first, I think, introduced in favour of the King and the Church. As an exception it is in *G.* 271 applied to the King, who acquires *ôðal*-right by prescription in 'three kings' time.' According to *F.* xiv. 7 the possessor of land, cultivated in the King's Commons, gets ownership if the land was cultivated 'before three kings' time, of whom none was in the land for a shorter space than 10 years.' The shortest time of prescription is thus thirty years, or just the term within which the Church may obtain prescriptive ownership of *ôðal*-right.[5] Of course the *ôðal*-right of 'offering' and 'redemption' was not favourable to the greatest landlords, the King and the Church; but in the old Gulathingslaw (271) the King is bound to

[1] *G.* 276.

[2] *G.* 288. I do not agree with the conjecture of Boden, 'Das altnorwegische Stammgüterrecht' (*ZSS*, xxii. 109), that the phrase in *G.* 288 in fine, 'ef hann vill,' means 'if the son will.'

[3] *DN.* xii. No. 5: 'scal þessi eigh[n] er mit hefuir værith odhal her til, uerdha hædhan af odhal firir sagdz stadhar firir huariom manne.'

[4] See Fritzner, *Ordbog* s.v. 'ôðal,' 1.

[5] *F.* xiv. 3: 'En þat verðr kirkiu at ôðali ef hon hefir at xxx. vetra. en þat vitni beri henni kirkiusócnar menn.'

allow the *bøndr* to make use of them both against him. In the *Frostathingslaw*, however, none of them may be used against the King; and if the King *skeytir* land to a man, the possessor may not offer it to anybody if the King was before the lawful owner.[1] This provision shows that the *skeyting* in the *Frostathingslaw* was not always intended to transfer *óðal*-right; indeed, the *skeyting* is used even in 'conditional' sales, where the seller has reserved a right of redemption.[2] The *skeyting* in *F.* is rather a form for transfer of *gewere* than of a right of ownership. In fact, there are in this law of the twelfth century many 'modern' tendencies which obscure the more archaic features of Norwegian land-law in the provincial law as shown in the *Gulathingslǫg*.

The Norwegian Justinian, King Magnus Lagabøtir, had a sharp eye for these 'modern' tendencies, which threatened to weaken the bond which the *óðal*-right had set between the land and the people. And before he published his new Norwegian *Code*, he issued a statute about acquisition of *óðal*-right. Here he laid down the new provision that *óðal*-right should be acquired by sixty years' prescription. This new rule he put in the first paragraph in his *Code* which relates to this matter. In the second paragraph he put the old rule from the *Gulathingslaw*, 270, that land given by the King is *óðal*, 'if he has not given it subject to other conditions.' In the third place, he took the rule from the *Frostathingslaw* concerning possession for three generations; and in the fourth the *óðalsskipti*.[3]

Next, he laid down new provisions for the 'offer' and the 'redemption.' I shall not go into details; but the alterations are essential and go very far in favour of the person redeeming the land. His redemption-right is not lost by prescription in a twelvemonth as in the *Gulathingslaw*, but in ten years. And if he has lawful exceptions (*nauðsyn*), he may publish them every tenth year, and thus keep his *óðal*-right alive for sixty years. The first exception is very favourable to a poor man using the right of redemption: he can publish his 'lack of money,' and that suffices. Another provision, quite as favourable to him, is that the sum of

[1] *F.* xii. 4: 'En ef konungr sceytir manni iörð, þá scal þá iörð engum manni bióða þó at hann vili selia hvergi er átti áðr, ef konungr átti siðan heimila. En engi maðr scal bióða konungi iörð. oc eigi konungr öðrum manni.'

[2] See *F.* xii. 1.

[3] *L.* vi. 2.

redemption-money should not be the price the owner could get in free trade, but the sum assessed by a body of six men.[1]

It is evident that the new *óðal*-law was intended to secure the *óðal*-right for the common peasantry. But the popular King did not achieve his object. In every decade before the great disaster of the Black Death (1349–50) both the nobility and the clergy grew richer by land which for centuries had been got out of the *óðal* possessions of the *bøndr*. It is the common view that the Church obtained most of her landed property by gifts or testaments. In some degree this view is right in regard to the parish churches and chapels; but it is not so in regard to the greater ecclesiastical institutions—the episcopal sees, the cathedrals, the chapters, and the monasteries. The only instance in which we can verify the truth of this assertion is that of the monastery of Munkelif to Bergen. Between 1223 and 1349 this institution acquired 64½ *mánaðsmatabol* by gifts, 157½ by purchase of *provent* ("board" in the cloister), 181 by purchase, and 232 by conditional sale with right of redemption reserved by the seller. But none of these sellers were economically in a strong enough position to make use of their redemption-right, and the land became the property and the *óðal* of the monastery. Thus the great ecclesiastical institution played the same part in the economic life of the Norwegian peasant in the Middle Ages as the 'Hypothecary Banks' to-day, furnishing them with ready money and getting their land in mortgage. The best and most favourable *óðal*-right could not prevent this economic evolution, or rather degradation, of the peasantry. Against the want of money nothing is of avail but money; and for ready money the Norwegian peasants sold not only their land, but also their *óðal*-right. If the buyer was willing to pay the *skeytingsaurar*[2] or *óðalskaup*[3] or *óðalslausn*,[4] he got the *óðal*-rights of the seller at once.

It is, however, a significant fact that from the time of Magnus Lagabøtir the terms *skeyta* and *skeyting* disappear in the title-deeds of land. We have thousands of such deeds published in *Diplo-*

1 *L.* vi. 4.

2 *DN.* iv. No. 147 (1321), 899 (1447); cp. von Amira, *OR.* ii. 687, who has a different view.

3 *Dipl. Orcad.* i. No. 48 (1575).

4 *DN.* ix. No. 577 (1526), 793 (1565).

*matarium Norwegicum*, but as far as my knowledge goes we shall scarcely find the terms *skeyta* and *skeyting* in fifty of them. According to von Amira[1] they were changed into *afhenda* and *afhending*. I am not convinced that the last-named terms really took the places of *skeyta* and *skeyting*. In the title-deeds prevail the terms *selja* (sell) and *sal* (sale), or *kaupa* (buy) and *kaup* (purchase). The fact is, in my opinion, that *skeyta* and *skeyting* disappear, because the transfer of *óðal*-right became more and more infrequent. As we learn from the title-deed book of Munkelif the 'conditional' sales are in an absolute majority.

## V. The Expansion of the *Óðal*-Conception

Finally, I shall in a few words, and without collecting the evidence, try to point out another change which the Middle Ages brought into the old *óðal*-conception. This was, as already mentioned, originally meant to include only the tilled field and the fenced-in pastureland. Outside this lay the commons (*almenningar*), and the commons were not an object of ownership (*eiga*, *eign*) but of possession (*hafa*). In the *Gulathingslaw*, however, a part of the common is already attached to the *óðal*, viz. the *mǫrk* (forest) and the *sætr* (summer pastures in the mountains). Of this the odaller can get ownership by twenty years' use (prescription). Nevertheless it is not yet *óðal* and not included in the *óðalsskipti*.[2] In the later *skeyting* formulas the chief object of the transfer is the *óðal*, or more commonly the *jǫrð* (the tilled ground) and the 'appurtenances' (*lunnendi*) belonging to the same. 'Appurtenances' include *hafn* (pasture), *hogg* (wood), *vatn* (water), *veiðistaðir* (fishing or hunting places), and various other uses. All these 'appurtenances' are included in the term *eign* (owned land), but not in the term *óðal*. We see that the right of ownership in untilled land surrounding the *óðal* grew up out of these many 'uses' in it. Originally only the *óðal* is owned, and *óðal* is obviously synonymous with *eign*, and was perhaps the most common term for *eign*. Afterwards the *eign* was expanded to the regularly 'used' woods and pastures outside the *óðal* in the commons. And lastly, the *óðal*-conception comprises the whole *eign*. Such is its meaning in the *óðalsskipti* of Magnus Lagabøtir's *Landslaw* (vi. 3), which, as opposed to its

[1] *OR*. ii. § 64

[2] *G*. 86 compared with 87.

source, *G.* 87, includes the whole *eign*, inside and outside the fence, and not merely the fenced-in *óðal.* But the tilled ground, as being the more valuable, has to be divided by stick (*skapt*) or string (*alburðr*); for the land outside the fence the 'eye-measure' (*augnaskot*) is sufficient.

*Takmǫrk* and *heimrǫst* are the terms which are used in Magnus Lagabøtir's *Code* to indicate the *eign* as a whole, or most commonly the land outside the fences. *Takmǫrk*,[1] according to Hertzberg's *Glossary*, means 'boundary,' but the common term for 'boundary' is *takmark.* I am inclined to believe that the *takmǫrk* is the *taken mǫrk* (wood, forest), which also is a feminine word; but it is impossible for me to establish this view with philological precision.

The term *heimrǫst* may be verbally translated by 'home-mile.' In the *Landslaw* it evidently means 'homeway,' viz. 'the way from the highway to the *bœr*,'[2] or 'the way from the home to the out-pastures.'[3] In a document from Gudbrandsdalen (1432) we learn that the *heimrǫst* reaches from the storehouse to the commons,[4] a distance of 6-7 kilometres.[5] This document gives us an idea of an *óðal*-peasant's claims in regard to wood and pasture-land. Under such circumstances it is not surprising that the commons soon became private property; and the fixing of the boundaries between *eign* and common was placed in the hands of the *haulds* or 'best peasants.' The *thing* was to elect twelve of them, and two of the twelve were to 'swear to the limit.'[6] As a contrasting fact I will mention that a settler in the common had no power of disposition over a greater distance from his fence than he could throw his *snidl*, a knife for cutting twigs. But in later times the *lagretsmen* (a kind of jury), who had to fix the boundaries of the reclaimed plots, were more generous, and considerable portions of the commons were often attached to them. There was land enough to draw from, and the poor eremites sometimes obtained forests which are now sold for fortunes.

A. TARANGER.

[1] *L.* vii. 60. [2] *L.* vii. 46. [3] *L.* vii. 41, 58. [4] *DN.* iii. No. 717.

[5] In Shetland *hemrost* is synonymous with *hemhoga*, the nearest pasture-land outside the hedges. In the Pharoes *heimrustir* means the ground around the houses = Icel. and Norw. *tun.* See Jakobsen, *Etymologisk ordbog over det norröne sprog paa Shetland*, s.v. 'hemrost,' and *Tillæg til Forslag og Betænkninger afgivne af den færöiske Landbokommission*, p. 426.

[6] *F.* xiv. 7; *L.* vii. 61.

# IX

# LES IDÉES COUTUMIÈRES ET LA RENAISSANCE DU DROIT ROMAIN DANS LE SUD-EST DE LA FRANCE

LES régions du Sud-Est de la France, qui ont constitué au moyen âge la partie méridionale du royaume d'Arles,[1] vallée du Rhône et versant occidental des Alpes, Lyonnais, Bresse, Savoie, Dauphiné et Provence, ont été comprises dans les « pays de droit écrit ». Mais on oublie trop que, pendant le haut moyen âge, ces régions ont pratiqué un droit coutumier original, très nettement distinct du droit romain, très voisin du droit des « pays coutumiers » de la France du Nord. Ces idées coutumières n'ont pas brusquement disparu, au XII^e^ siècle et au XIII^e^, au contact des idées romaines. La renaissance de l'étude et de l'enseignement du droit romain n'a pas changé soudainement le droit antérieur. Les survivances des vieilles idées coutumières, au XIII^e^ siècle et au XIV^e^, sont nombreuses et frappantes ; elles montrent que le triomphe des idées romaines fut, sur beaucoup de points, lent, difficile et incomplet.

Cette lenteur de la pénétration des idées romaines est d'autant plus remarquable que, de très bonne heure, ce pays a été touché par la renaissance du droit romain savant, plus tôt que le reste de la Gaule. Il n'est pas certain que les *Exceptiones Petri* aient été

[1] Ces régions, politiquement séparées du reste de la Gaule lors du démembrement de l'Empire carolingien, ont vécu d'une vie indépendante durant une grande partie du moyen âge. Même lorsque, en 1032, elles furent rattachées au Saint Empire, l'action des Empereurs ne fut que très intermittente, leur influence resta presque nulle, et l'autonomie politique de la région a duré jusqu'au jour où les Capétiens s'en emparèrent.

composées à Valence. Par contre, au milieu du XII^e siècle, un livre remarquable, le *Codi*, a été composé à Arles; puis, au XIII^e siècle, des jurisconsultes tels que *Johannes Blancus* en Provence, *Johannes de Blanosco* en Mâconnais, ont apporté dans notre région les idées qu'ils avaient apprises dans les écoles d'Italie. Il ne faut pas oublier aussi que Henri de Suze a composé, alors qu'il était archevêque d'Embrun, au moins une partie de sa Somme des Décrétales. Il ne semble pas qu'aucune influence politique ou religieuse se soit exercée dans nos régions, comme la chose a pu se produire ailleurs, contre l'enseignement du droit romain. Le terrain paraissait donc admirablement préparé pour la réception pratique des idées romaines. La résistance des anciennes idées coutumières n'en est que plus caractéristique.

C'est à dessein que nous employons ce mot: «droit coutumier». Ce droit est, comme le droit coutumier de la France du Nord, un droit d'origine assez hybride, où se sont fondus des éléments germaniques et des éléments pris au droit romain vulgaire, mais qui contient surtout des éléments nés spontanément, destinés à satisfaire des besoins nouveaux, ceux de la société du moyen âge, qui ne ressemble ni à la société romaine, ni à la société des Germains avant les Invasions. Dans la vallée de la Saône et du Rhône, des races très diverses se coudoient; les *professiones juris* mentionnent la loi salique, la loi romaine, la loi burgonde, la loi lombarde. En réalité, le droit que l'on y pratique est un droit très unifié, et qui n'est ni franc, ni burgonde, ni romain.

Cependant la thèse de la survie de l'ancien droit burgonde a été parfois soutenue, et, récemment, Julius Ficker s'en est fait le défenseur. Étudiant l'extension de l'augment de dot dans les coutumes de la fin du moyen âge, il a cru trouver une coïncidence entre cette extension et la sphère d'action des Burgondes; il a attribué à l'augment de dot une origine très ancienne, et l'a rattaché au vieux droit burgonde; puis il a entrepris une démonstration du même genre pour quelques autres particularités du droit de la Bourgogne et de l'Auvergne.[1] Mais sa thèse, que nous ne pouvons discuter ici en détail, nous semble inadmissible. Nous verrons plus loin que l'augment de dot date tout au plus du XIII^e

[1] Ficker, *Untersuchungen zur Erbenfolge der ostgermanischen Rechte*; v. surtout Nos. 1300 et suiv. R. Caillemer, *La Formation du droit français médiéval et les travaux de Julius Ficker*, p. 34 et s.

siècle et n'a jamais été une institution générale dans nos régions : jusqu'au XIII^e siècle, les coutumes de la région que nous étudions ont connu un droit de survie tout différent.[1]

Comme exemple de ces idées coutumières, très différentes des idées romaines, nous avons déjà pu, dans des travaux antérieurs, signaler la conception de la propriété foncière et des droits réels sur les immeubles. Loin d'opposer la propriété proprement dite et les *jura in re aliena*, les textes de notre région, au haut moyen âge, considèrent les divers droits de jouissance, se traduisant par la possession d'un immeuble, comme des modalités d'un même droit réel fondamental. Le droit de l'usufruitier (p. ex. du donateur avec réserve d'usufruit ou de *beneficium*) est un droit de propriété viagère ; le droit du créancier gagiste est un droit de propriété limitée, et les textes lyonnais appellent toujours l'engagiste *emptor*.[2] Un acte lyonnais prévoit, le cas échéant, l'aliénation de la terre soumise à l'usufruit par l'usufruitier.[3] Le

[1] Dans cette étude, nous nous servirons surtout des nombreux recueils de documents lyonnais et dauphinois publiés : M.-C. Guigue, *Cartulaire lyonnais*, 2 vol. in-4°, Lyon, 1885-1893 ; Aug. Bernard, *Cartulaire de l'abbaye de Savigny*, suivi du *Petit Cartulaire de l'abbaye d'Ainay*, 2 vol., Paris, 1853 ; De Charpin-Feugerolles et M.-C. Guigue, *Grand Cartulaire de l'abbaye d'Ainay*, 2 vol. in-4°, Lyon, 1885 ; De Charpin-Feugerolles et M.-C. Guigue, *Cartulaire du prieuré de Saint-Sauveur en Rue*, 1 vol. in-4°, Lyon, 1881 ; De Charpin-Feugerolles, *Cartulaire des Francs-fiefs du Forez*, Lyon, 1 vol. in-4°, 1882 ; Valentin Smith et M.-C. Guigue, *Bibliotheca Dumbensis*, 2 vol. in-4°, Trévoux, 1884-1885 ; M.-C. et G. Guigue, *Bibliothèque historique du Lyonnais*, I, Lyon, 1886, in-8° ; M.-C. Guigue, *Petit Cartulaire de l'abbaye de Saint-Sulpice en Bugey*, Lyon, 1884, in-8° ; Aug. Bernard et Aug. Bruel, *Recueil des chartes de l'abbaye de Cluny*, 6 vol. in-4°, Paris, 1876-1903 ; Valbonnais, *Histoire de Dauphiné*, Genève, 2 vol. in-f°, 1722 ; M. Fornier, *Histoire générale des Alpes*, publiée par l'abbé Guillaume, 3 vol. in-8°, Paris et Gap, 1890-1892 ; Ul. Chevalier, *Collection de cartulaires dauphinois*, notamment le t. 1^er, *Cartulaire de Saint-André le Bas*, Vienne et Lyon, 1869, in-8° ; le t. vii, *Choix de documents historiques inédits sur le Dauphiné*, Montbéliard et Lyon, 1874, in-8° ; et le t. ix, 1^e livr., *Codex diplomaticus ordinis Sancti Rufi Valentiae*, Valence, 1891, in-8° ; P. Guillaume, *Chartes de Durbon*, Paris, 1893, in-8° ; Auvergne, *Cartulaire de Saint-Robert et Cartulaire des Écouges*, Grenoble, 1865, in-8°. Pour les régions plus méridionales, nous avons utilisé surtout le *Cartulaire de l'abbaye de Saint-Victor de Marseille*, publié par Guérard, Paris, 2 vol. in-4°, 1857 ; et le *Cartulaire de la commanderie de Richerenches*, publié par M. de Ripert-Monclar, Avignon et Paris, 1907, in-8°.

[2] V. notre étude sur l'engagement, *Festschrift Heinrich Brunner*, p. 294 et s.

[3] *Cart. de S.-André le Bas*, app., N° 114 : usufruitier qui a le droit de vendre, de donner, d'échanger, etc.

droit de l'usufruitier ou du créancier gagiste n'est pas un simple *jus in re aliena*: c'est une propriété temporaire, un *estate in use*, comme dirait le droit anglais, qui a admirablement conservé sur ce point la vieille idée médiévale ; saisine actuelle, que vient limiter un *estate* futur, en *reversion* ou en *remainder*.

Nous pourrions encore signaler une autre idée coutumière, tout à fait étrangère au droit romain, et que l'on relève dans les actes du Sud-Est de la France, comme dans les actes d'autres régions : l'idée que les seuls actes stables et définitifs sont les actes à titre onéreux, assurant à chacune des parties un avantage en échange du sacrifice qu'elle consent ; idée commune aux diverses races germaniques, et qui se manifeste si nettement dans le *launegild* des coutumes lombardes. Elle revit, en plein moyen âge, dans divers documents, et notamment dans les chartes du cartulaire de Richerenches. Les donataires remettent aux donateurs une *caritas* ou une *securitas*, en argent ou en nature ; et cette petite contre-prestation a pour but d'assurer la stabilité de la donation : les chartes le disent expressément. Dans un autre document, nous trouvons une donation, accompagnée de cette contre-partie, que l'on pense rendre plus stable en lui donnant l'aspect d'un acte à titre onéreux, et en la qualifiant de *emptio* et de *venditio*.[1]

On a quelquefois soutenu que l'emphytéose avait persisté dans

[1] *C. de Richerenches*, N° 43 (1148) : transaction : « Et, ut sic observem et sic faciam, *seccuritatis* nomine ab Ugone de Bolbotone de helemosinis Templi xii$^{cim}$ sextarios accipio boni frumenti, et iiii$^{or}$ ordei, et unum equum, id est caballum, precio l sol. Val. » N° 49 (1149) : autre *dimissio* : « Ut autem ista nostra dimissio et libera desemparatio semper seccura et firma remaneat . . . x$^{cem}$ solidos bone monete Val. et unam saumatam de frumento accipimus, *caritatis* nomine. » N° 50 (1149) : « Ut autem ista mea donacio firma et stabilis perpetuo remaneat, de bonis de Templo habui xi$^{cim}$ sol. et dim. Val., et unum palafridum cum sella et freno. » N° 51 (1150) : « Facta est hec donacio et guirpicio . . . in manu . . . militum Templi, a quibus *caritative* helemosinis Templi accepimus ccc sol. Val. monete. » N° 54 (1147) : « Ut autem hec nostra donatio stabilitatem et securam semper habeat firmitatem, . . . accepimus septuaginta solidos vet. den. Melg. » On peut rapprocher de ce dernier acte le N° 58, qui est qualifié de *vendicio-empcio*, sans indication de prix de vente, dans le corps de l'acte. Mais, après la signature, vient la note suivante : « Propter hanc empcionem fratres milicie Templi his supradictis venditoribus septuaginta solidos vet. Melg. dederunt. » L'acte se présente plutôt comme une donation, suivie d'une *caritas* de 70 sous, comme dans le N° 54. Cf. Schröder, *Deutsche Rechtsgeschichte*, 3$^{e}$ éd., p. 294 et s.

le Sud-Est de la France pendant tout le moyen âge ; mais aucun texte n'en parle avant le XIII^e^ siècle ; les nombreux contrats que nous avons conservés, relatifs à la culture de la terre, sont, soit des contrats de *prestaria* (on ne dit guère : *precaria* dans notre région), soit des concessions *ad medium plantum*, soit, dans la suite, des albergements. Ce n'est que plus tard, après la renaissance du droit romain, que le nom d'emphytéose a été donné à l'albergement.[1]

Nous pourrions encore noter, dans le domaine du droit des obligations, la persistance des anciennes formes de garantie réelle (*impignoratio*[2]) et de garantie personnelle (*hostagium*). L'*hostagium*, même décoré du nom romain de *fidejussio*, n'a rien de commun avec le cautionnement romain.[3]

Mais nous voudrions surtout parler du droit de famille, et montrer que, sur ce point, le triomphe du droit romain a été incomplet, tardif et péniblement acheté.

## § 1er *LAUDATIO* DES HÉRITIERS

Nous noterons d'abord, à ce point de vue, la force des liens familiaux, se traduisant par la nécessité du concours des plus proches héritiers de l'aliénateur aux aliénations immobilières. Aux XIe et XIIe siècles, les transferts d'immeubles sont faits avec la *laudatio* des hoirs ; s'il n'y a pas eu de *laudatio*, à la mort de

[1] Dans les actes lyonnais, l'emphytéose apparaît en 1255 (*C. lyonnais*, ii. N° 518) : « Donant . . . in emphiteosim nomine albergamenti im perpetuum, pro xl solidis nomine intragii jam solutis, et pro xviii denariis . . . annuatim de supra servicio persolvendis. . . . Renunciant . . . exceptioni intragii non soluti. » Dans le recueil des chartes de Durbon, le mot *emphytéose* n'apparaît qu'en 1327 (N° 687).

[2] V. notre étude sur l'engagement, citée plus haut.

[3] *C. lyonnais*, i. N° 219 (1226) : « Dederunt *fidejussores* . . . qui . . . juraverunt quod si . . . prefata Michola vel filii vel filie sue ea que supra dicta sunt non observarent vel in aliquo contravenirent, ipsi . . . *ostagium* tenerent inl oco sibi . . . designato. » N° 235 (1228) : « Dederunt *fidejussores* . . . qui similiter juraverunt se tenere *ostagia* Lugduni si premissi Hugo et frater suus non observarent premissa. » N° 389 (1244) : « Dedit ecclesie *fidejussores pacis* juratos de dicta vendicione in perpetuum tenenda in pace . . . qui ad ammonicionem dicte ecclesie infra xv dies postquam fuerint moniti, juraverunt tenere tamdiu *ostagium* Lugduni, donec a dicta ecclesia licentiam habuerint recedendi. » N° 402 (1245), acte très curieux, où des tuteurs, vendant des biens de mineur, se portent *fidéjusseurs* et promettent de tenir *ostagium*.

l'aliénateur ses héritiers s'efforcent de reprendre les biens aliénés, et se font souvent payer très cher par l'acquéreur leur ratification.[1]

Cet usage de la *laudatio* persiste après la renaissance du droit romain, et il n'est pas rare, même dans la seconde moitié du XIII^e^ siècle, de voir l'aliénateur, donateur ou vendeur, promettre d'obtenir la *laudatio* de ses fils ou de ses frères, alors absents ou empêchés.[2] Dans toute donation importante, le donateur tient à s'entourer du concours de ses parents et de ses amis, à obtenir leur consentement, qui parfois ne sera donné que moyennant des sacrifices pécuniaires, plus ou moins considérables, consentis par l'acquéreur.[3] Ces pratiques ont leur utilité, et ces précautions ne sont pas superflues. Au XIII^e^ siècle comme précédemment, il n'est pas rare de voir, après la mort de l'aliénateur, ses héritiers

[1] Exemples de réclamations d'héritiers, au XII^e^ siècle: Valbonnais, i. p. 39, S (1132): à la suite d'une transaction, les deux fils de l'une des parties attaquent l'acte, disant: «absque consilio et assensu eorum fuisse factum, ideo minime tenendum.» Selon la vieille conception médiévale, les témoins de l'acte viennent prendre sa défense, et obtiennent une renonciation des enfants. Giraud, *C. de S.-Barnard de Romans*, ii. preuves, p. 20: «. . . Imposueramus calumpniam super unam terram . . ., quam terram ecclesia Romanensis S^ti^ Bernardi ab antiquo tempore acquisierat de nostro genere.» Les réclamants cèdent, moyennant 13 sous, et la concession à l'un d'entre eux de la jouissance viagère du bien litigieux. *C. lyonnais*, i. N° 163 (1190 env.): «Moricinus vendidit domum suam. . . . Postea vero tres filii ejus calumniaverunt . . . vendicionem»; on leur donne 22 sous.

[2] Aliénateurs promettant d'obtenir la *laudatio* de leurs fils: *C. lyonnais*, i. N° 465 (1251): «Promitto nichilominus sub virtute prestiti juramenti, quod omnia premissa et singula faciam in perpetuum a filiis meis Bosone, Symboudo et Alberto rata habere et firma, et servare illesa, prout superius sunt expressa.» ii. N° 552 (1259): acte de vente: «Promittit insuper sepedictus Berlio venditor, sub prestito juramento et sub obligatione omnium bonorum suorum, quod ipse procurabit, faciet et efficiet quod dominus Jacobus de Spina miles, Guillelmus de Spina domicellus, Albertus de Gorgi frater ipsius Berlionis, Quarta uxor, Jaquemetus et Guionetus filii ejusdem Alberti, ad requisitionem dicte domine Brune . . . dictam venditionem . . . laudabunt, approbabunt, gratificabunt et acceptabunt per juramentum et sub testimonio litterarum»: ainsi le frère, l'épouse, deux neveux du vendeur, et deux *milites*, sans doute deux vassaux (parmi les biens vendus figurent les «taschiae illorum de Spina»). N° 589 (1261): transaction; consentement d'un frère présent, et promesse de *laudatio* de deux frères absents.

[3] *C. de S.-Sulpice en Bugey*, N° 29 (1239), p. 83: don fait par Étienne de Luyrieux avant de partir pour la Terre Sainte, «de voluntate et consilio amicorum meorum et parentum sive consanguineorum, assensuque G. domini de Luyrieux nepotis mei et Hu., fratris ejus, super hoc accedente.» Le donateur reçoit 300 florins «nomine placiti», l'un des neveux 20 florins, et l'autre 10.

revendiquer les biens aliénés, sous ce prétexte qu'ils n'ont pas donné leur *laudatio*, et ne renoncer à leurs prétentions que moyennant un dédommagement pécuniaire.[1]

La nécessité de ce consentement des plus proches héritiers prend même, à ce moment, une netteté plus grande. Les conditions de la *laudatio* se précisent. Lorsque l'héritier dont la *laudatio* est requise a moins de 14 ans, on assure, au moyen de promesses spéciales, garanties par des fidéjusseurs, sa *laudatio* ultérieure, lorsqu'il aura atteint ses *anni legitimi*.[2] Les enfants de plus de 14

[1] *C. lyonnais*, i. N° 409 (1246): « Asserebat . . . Stephanus (Étienne de Chandieu) duas vercherias . . ., quas . . . prior de Plateria nomine dicte ecclesie detinebat, ad se jure hereditario pertinere, et ideo eas sibi restitui postulabat, nonobstante quadam venditione, quam *eo inscio* et *minime requisito*, Berlio frater suus . . . fecerat. » Sentence arbitrale: le réclamant devra céder tous ses droits, moyennant 7 livres et 20 sous. V. encore N° 251 (1229); N° 444 (1250). *C. des Écouges*, N° 20 (1232): Lantelme de Saint-Quentin a donné divers biens aux religieux des Écouges, mais, après sa mort, ses fils veulent reprendre les biens donnés. A la fin, grâce à l'intervention du Doyen de l'église de Grenoble, l'un des fils, Guillaume de Saint-Quentin, renonce à sa réclamation, et promet même de défendre le monastère contre toute attaque, toute « calumnia » nouvelle. Il se fera le défenseur de la donation même vis-à-vis de ses frères; toutefois, il ne s'engage pas à leur faire la guerre ni à dépenser sa fortune à ce sujet: « excepto quod bellum contra fratres facere vel sua expendere non tenetur »!

[2] Sur cette question de la *laudatio* de l'enfant, il y a, au haut moyen âge, des systèmes divergents: tantôt on fait intervenir l'enfant lui-même, tantôt on assure, par des fidéjusseurs ou par des serments, qu'il donnera plus tard sa *laudatio*. Ce dernier système triomphe dans les actes lyonnais du XIII^e^ siècle. On n'admet plus la *laudatio* émanée des enfants eux-mêmes. V. *C. lyonnais*, i. N° 167 (1220); *laudatio* des fils, « qui talis erant etatis quod ad eos laudare pertinebat. » N° 188 (1222): les fils ne donnent pas de *laudatio*: « nullus adhuc erat talis etatis, quod ad eum laudare pertineret. » N° 216 (1225): « laudaverunt omnes filii mei, qui tales erant etatis, quod ad ipsos laudare pertinebat. » Dès lors, si l'enfant est trop jeune, on promet sa *laudatio* pour le jour où il arrivera à ses *anni legitimi*, *ad plenam etatem*. N° 219 (1226): « et quum minor filius Odo nondum videbatur *ad annos legitimos* pervenisse. » N° 221 (1226): « Ut hec venditio rata et firma habeatur, dederunt fidejussorem Vincencium de Poimia, donec eorum infantuli pervenerint *ad plenam etatem* et concesserint plenarie dictam venditionem. » V. encore t. ii. N° 508 (1255): *ad etatem congruam*. Quelques textes parlent de *minor* et de *major aetas*: i. N° 287 (1234): « Promisit etiam sub eodem juramento quod, cum Jaquemeta filia ipsius, qui tunc temporis *minoris etatis* erat, *ad annos legitimos* pervenerit, faciat eam laudare et jurare pacem de hac venditione. » N° 269 (1231): « Et obligamus nos eodem juramento quod heredes nostri, qui tempore donationis erant *in minori etate*, quando essent *in majori*, eamdem donationem laudarent et confirmarent. » Mais ces expressions: *minor aetas*, *major aetas* ne doivent pas être interprétées comme des allusions

ans, mais mineurs de 25 ans, fournissent eux-mêmes leur *laudatio*, sur le *mandat* de leur père, en renonçant aux exceptions de minorité et de puissance paternelle.[1] L'importance de la *laudatio* paraît telle, que cette *laudatio* est souvent consignée dans une charte spéciale, attestée par des témoins particuliers.[2] Et enfin, pour entourer cette institution, si complètement étrangère au droit romain, de formes romaines, on voit apparaître à la fin des actes une renonciation nouvelle : à l'*exceptio concessionis et laudationis non facte*.[3]

Cet ancien usage de la *laudatio* des héritiers a laissé, en Provence et en Dauphiné, des traces curieuses. En 1456, Louis II, le futur Louis XI, alors Dauphin de Viennois, promulgua un statut exigeant, pour la validité d'une donation, la présence du bailli, du juge ou du châtelain du domicile du donateur, et, de plus, le concours de trois de ses plus proches parents habitant la même

---

à la majorité de 25 ans. Il s'agit en réalité de la puberté, que nos coutumes fixent à 14 ans. N° 445 (1250) : « Dictus siquidem Stephanus promisit per stipulationem et sub prestito juramento quod, quam cito Hugo, Uldricus et Placencia liberi ipsius *ad annos pubertatis* pervenerint, ipse faciat et efficiet, quod ipsi liberi . . . dictam venditionem laudabunt et approbabunt. » ii. N° 511 (1255) : « Hanc autem venditionem Zacharias filius dicti Guidonis, *major quatuordecim annis*, prout ipsi pater et filius per juramentum asserunt, sponte sciens et prudens laudat, approbat, gratificat et acceptat. » V. aussi N° 522 (1255) : « facti puberes, prout ipsi per juramentum asserunt. »

[1] *C. lyonnais*, ii. N° 536 (1256) : reprise de fief : « Hanc autem receptionem feudi . . . Petrus, filius dicti Aemari, coram nobis constitutus, sciens, prudens et spontaneus, de *mandato* ipsius Aemari, laudat, approbat, gratificat et acceptat. . . . Renuntiant . . ., et dictus Petrus exceptioni quod metus causa, minoris etatis, beneficio patrie potestatis. » V. aussi N° 509 (1255), où les trois fils du donateur, accordant leur *laudatio*, renoncent « minoris etatis auxilio et beneficio, et patrie potestati. »

[2] *Cart. de S.-Ruf*, N° 93 (1205) : « Quando Guntardus et Eicburgis, amita Raimundi, hoc laudaverunt, presentes erant. . . . Quando Ymbertus Runini (frère du donateur Raimond) hoc laudavit in claustro Sancti Jacobi, et etiam super iiii^or evangelia juravit, presentes erant. . . . » De même N° 96 (1207).

[3] *C. lyonnais*, ii. N° 757 (1279) : confirmation par 4 frères : « Johannes, Guillermetus, majores viginti et quinque annis, Bartholomeus et Jaquetus, minores viginti quinque annis, majores tamen decem et septem annis » ; et renonciation : « exceptioni . . . concessionis et confessionis . . . legitime non factarum. » N° 813 (1287) : *laudatio* d'un neveu : « renuncians exceptioni ratificationis, acceptationis, confessionis, concessionis, remissionis et promissionis . . . non factarum vel sine justa causa factarum. » N° 827 (1290) : confirmation par les deux fils du donateur (donation d'une rente d'un fromage) : ils renoncent « exceptioni dictarum quittationis, laudationis et concessionis non factarum. »

paroisse.[1] Et c'était seulement si l'on ne pouvait trouver ces trois parents, ou s'ils refusaient d'intervenir à l'acte, que le magistrat pouvait appeller comme témoins d'autres *probi viri*.

Du Dauphiné, la règle est passée en Provence. En 1472, un statut du roi René est venu exiger, pour la validité des donations, la présence de deux parents du donateur ; et ici ce ne sont plus de simples témoins ; ils viennent éclairer le donateur sur la portée de la donation. Le statut exige, non seulement leur présence, mais leur *conscientia*.[2] Visiblement, le but de ces deux statuts est moins de protéger la famille du donateur, que de garantir le donateur lui-même contre ses propres entraînements. Mais, dans le procédé qu'ils emploient pour atteindre ce but, en faisant intervenir les parents du donateur, ces statuts nous présentent une curieuse survie des anciennes idées médiévales.

D'autre part, le retrait lignager s'est développé, à la fin du moyen âge, dans un assez grand nombre de coutumes locales de la région. Il est né d'un désir de concilier les intérêts de la famille de l'aliénateur avec la nécessité des aliénations immobilières. Dans quelques documents, nous voyons des disposants instituer une sorte de retrait lignager conventionnel. Aliénant un de leurs biens, ils prévoient la possibilité d'un rachat de ce bien par leurs héritiers ;[3] ou encore, réglant le sort de l'ensemble de leur fortune

[1] Ce statut a été souvent imprimé ; il figure, avec le commentaire de Joannes a Cruce, à la suite de certaines éditions des *Decisiones* de Guy Pape. V., p. ex., l'éd. de Genève, 1653, 2e pagin., p. 69 et s. : « . . . Decernimus donationes praedictas (inter vivos) de caetero fiendas non esse aliter valituras, quam si in baillivi, judicis aut castellani loci sive parochiae domicilii donatoris, vel locatenentis eorumdem, et trium ex proximioribus consanguineis sive parentibus ipsius donatoris in dicta parochia existentibus, vel, ubi non reperirentur in dicta parochia, aut vocati adesse nollent in donatione praedicta, aliorum virorum proborum dictae parochiae non suspectorum, per alterum ex dictis officiariis, pro numero parentum non repertorum, aut adesse ut supra nolentium, surrogandorum, praesentia factae fuerint, recitatae et publicatae. »

[2] V. notre étude sur *le Retrait lignager dans le droit provençal* (*Studi in onore di Carlo Fadda*), p. 11 et s. (Naples, 1906).

[3] On trouve, dès le XIe siècle, des actes de ce genre dans les *Ch. de Cluny*, iv. N° 2525 (1000 env.) : « Facio autem hanc donationem eo tenore, ut, dum aliquis ex filiis meis ad perfectam etatem venerit, si redimere voluerit, redimat xl[ta] solidis. » N° 2972 (1048–1049) : « Dono . . . unum mansum . . . ea ratione ut filius meus Wichardus, si voluerit eum redimere, det pro ipso manso habitatoribus supranominati loci (monasterii Cluniacensis) xx solidos ; sin alias, ipsi monachi teneant et possideant. » V. aussi le N° 2973 (même date), acte mutilé : « Dono . . . si legalem heredem de uxore

par un partage d'ascendant, ils stipulent que, si l'un des biens de la succession est vendu par un de leurs héritiers, les autres héritiers auront à son égard un droit de préemption. Ainsi, dans un acte lyonnais de 1243, une veuve, répartissant sa fortune entre ses enfants, décide que, si l'un des enfants veut vendre ou obliger les biens compris dans son lot, il devra d'abord les offrir à ses frères, ou même à d'autres parents.[1]

Cette institution du retrait lignager ne s'est pas développée partout dans la région qui nous occupe. On ne la rencontre ni en Savoie, ni en Bresse, ni en Lyonnais ; mais, au XIII<sup>e</sup> siècle et au XIV<sup>e</sup>, elle a été consacrée par d'assez nombreuses coutumes locales du Dauphiné et de la Provence ; et elle a été enfin étendue à tout le comté de Provence par un statut de 1469.[2]

## § 2. Régime matrimonial

L'étude du régime des gens mariés est aussi caractéristique, qu'il s'agisse des apports de la femme, ou des donations que son mari lui fait au moment du mariage.

### *A. Apports de la femme.—Inaliénabilité de la dot.*

Pendant tout le haut moyen âge, nous trouvons dans nos régions, comme dans la France coutumière, une association étroite des deux époux dans tous les actes qui se rapportent à la gestion des biens du ménage. Qu'il s'agisse des biens du mari, ou qu'il

---

habuero, si tenere voluerit, ducentos solidos . . . redimi. . . . » Cf. *Festschrift Brunner*, p. 294, note 1. *C. lyonnais*, ii. N° 570 (1260) : testament d'un bourgeois de Beaujeu, léguant, pour son anniversaire et celui de sa femme, une vigne à l'église Notre-Dame de Beaujeu : « Si autem dilecti filii mei Johannes et Bernardus vel alter ipsorum potuerit assignare dictis presbiteris quindecim solidos Viennensium debitales vel solvere quindecim libras Viennensium ad emendos redditus pro dicto anniversario faciendo, volo quod dicta vinea, hoc facto, ad ipsos redeat pleno jure. » Acte de 1272, cité dans notre étude sur *le Retrait lignager dans le droit provençal*, p. 16. Dans d'autres actes, le droit de rachat est limité à certains cas déterminés, p. ex., au cas où le donataire ne respecterait pas les clauses de la donation, où les biens donnés ne seraient pas laissés à l'usage collectif des moines.

[1] *C. lyonnais*, i. N° 378 : « . . . Item voluit et ordinavit dicta A., quod, si predicti filii sui vel alter eorum de rebus supradictis . . . vellent aliquid vendere, obligare seu alio modo alienare, primo presentarent sive presentaret fratribus suis aliis predictis vel eorum propinquis. » V. aussi *Bibl. Dumbensis*, i. p. 331 (1402).

[2] V. notre étude sur *le Retrait lignager*, *l. cit.*, p. 16 et s., 25 et s.

s'agisse des apports de la femme (désignés, non pas du terme de *dos*, mais des noms de *maritagium*, *matrimonium*, *maritamentum*,[1] *vercheria* en Provence[2]), les deux époux agissent ensemble et disposent ensemble de leurs biens. Aucune trace de l'inaliénabilité dotale ne peut être relevée. Encore au milieu du XIII^e^ siècle nous trouvons çà et là des femmes aliénant leurs immeubles dotaux avec le concours de leur mari, sans qu'aucun doute s'élève sur la validité de ces actes.[3] Pendant tout le haut moyen âge, la nécessité de la *laudatio* des plus proches héritiers de la femme pour l'aliénation des immeubles de celle-ci rendait superflu tout autre système de protection. Certains documents sont, à cet égard, très caractéristiques. En Bugey, en 1234, Pierre de Noiret donne aux Chartreux de Meyriat, du consentement de sa femme, des biens faisant partie de la *dos* de celle-ci. Plus tard, il attaque cette aliénation ; or, il n'invoque nullement le caractère dotal des biens aliénés ; il allègue des raisons toutes différentes : ces biens sont occupés par des tiers, qui les détiennent en vertu d'un albergement ; et ces tenanciers, n'ayant pas consenti à l'aliénation, déclarent qu'elle ne leur est pas opposable. L'arbitre choisi, l'évêque de Belley, oblige Pierre de Noiret à faire *laudatio* de sa propre donation, en obtenant cette fois la *laudatio* de ses fils et des tenanciers récalcitrants. Il ne semble pas mettre en doute, au point de vue du régime matrimonial, la pleine validité de cet acte.[4]

[1] *Maritagium : Bibl. Hist. du Lyonnais*, p. 29 (1229) ; *C. lyonnais*, i. N° 256 (1229) ; 236 (1228). *Maritamentum : C. de S.-André le Bas*, N° 193. *Matrimonium : C. lyonnais*, i. N° 163 (1219). Cf. *C. de S.-Vincent de Mâcon*, N° 477 : « Nepti sue donavit in *maritatu*. . . . »

[2] *Vercheria* : hommage d'Amauri de Montfort à l'archevêque d'Embrun, en 1222, à raison des biens de sa femme en Embrunais, Fornier, iii. p. 226. Le mot est resté dans la langue provençale. V. Mistral, *Lou Tresor dou felibrige*, v° *verquiero* :

*Fiho poulido porto sa verquiero au front.*

[3] P. ex., en 1247 (*C. lyonnais*, i. N° 417), une femme vend une maison avec le consentement de son mari, sans que l'acte contienne la moindre allusion aux obstacles tenant au régime dotal ; v. encore N^os^ 221 (1226) ; 287 (1234). *C. de S.-Sauveur en Rue*, N° cxxxviii. (1253) : « Ego Pictavina, . . . consentiente et volente praedicto viro meo, . . . dono et concedo . . . terram meam *dotalem* . . . cum censibus et usagiis et pleno dominio dictae terrae. » Peu importe le mode d'aliénation, vente ou donation, et l'on pourrait multiplier les exemples de ce genre.

[4] *C. de S.-Sulpice en Bugey*, N° 27 (1234). Cette question de la nécessité du consentement des tenanciers dans les aliénations a été, jusqu'ici, assez peu

L'idée de la communauté entre époux, qui triomphera plus tard dans la France coutumière, mais que le régime dotal romain chassera de la région que nous étudions, se manifeste dans diverses chartes, et notamment dans certains documents lyonnais du haut moyen âge. Il arrive souvent que deux époux, faisant une donation avec réserve d'usufruit, stipulent que, au décès du prémourant, l'usufruit s'éteindra pour une moitié, que cette moitié ira au couvent et servira de donation *pro sepultura* pour ce prémourant; tandis que l'usufruit se continuera pour moitié au profit du conjoint survivant.[1] Et ce partage par moitié est particulièrement remarquable quand le bien donné par les époux est un bien qu'ils ont acquis au cours du mariage, p. ex., par suite d'un contrat de concession foncière *ad medium plantum*.[2]

---

étudiée dans les actes français. Cette question se rattache à celle de la nécessité de la saisine pour une aliénation valable, principe qui s'affirme dès l'époque franque, et qui a subsisté dans certaines coutumes (p. ex. dans les coutumes anglaises) avec une grande netteté.

[1] *C. de Savigny*, N° 83 (env. 970): «Tali convenientia ut, quandiu vixerimus, teneamus, . . . et qualiscumque de nobis duobus primus obierit, *medietas* ipsius mansi in dominicatum veniat.» N° 170 (env. 980): «Eo videlicet tenore ut quamdiu vixero fructum percipiam; post mortem vero meam *ex medietate ejus sepulturam habeam*; aliam autem medietatem Adalendis uxor mea, quamdiu vixerit, possideat; et, qualiscumque ex nobis prius obierit, absque ulla contradictione, ad cultores ipsius ecclesiae medietas de ipsa haereditate perveniat; post decessum vero utrorumque omnia vobis cedo.» *C. d'Ainay* (Bernard), N° 72 (av. 993): deux époux donnent «aliquid ex rebus nostris, hoc est curtilem unum,» avec réserve d'usufruit; «et, quisquis ex nobis duobus primus obierit, unam medietatem predicti monachi ex suprascriptis rebus recipiant. Post amborum quoque discessu . . . totum ad integrum teneant et possideant.» N° 105 (989): mêmes formules. N° 111 (env. 1000): «Ita ut quicumque de nobis duobus prius mortuus fuerit, statim monachi prescripti loci *suam medietatem* accipiant, subsequens vero *suam medietatem* teneat dum vixerit; post mortem autem illius, medietatem illam monachi prefati in suo jure ponant.»

[2] V. notamment *C. de Savigny*, N° 266 (970 env.). Deux époux donnent des terres qu'ils ont acquises par un partage avec les moines de l'Ile-Barbe: «quicquid cum monachis Insulae Barbarae partiendo visi sumus habere; . . . ita tamen ut medietas de ipsis rebus ad ipsam ecclesiam pro *sepultura* corporis mei a die praesenti perveniat; aliam vero medietatem, quamdiu Dulcisina uxor mea vixerit, possideat, et post suum decessum *sepulturae* locum exinde accipiat.» La terre acquise se partage donc également entre les deux époux, et chacun d'eux dispose de sa part *pro sepultura*. V., sur ces tendances des coutumes de la France méridionale, avant la renaissance du droit romain, les très justes observations de M. Lefebvre, *Nouv. Rev. hist. de Droit*, 1911, p. 369 et s., notamment p. 390, où l'auteur cite encore d'autres actes des cartulaires d'Ainay et de Grenoble.

Tel était le droit de nos régions avant la renaissance du droit romain, et il ressemblait en somme singulièrement à celui de la France coutumière. La romanisation s'est faite peu à peu ; elle ne se traduit d'abord que dans les mots et dans les formules, et elle ne modifie pas au début le fond du droit.

Le mot *dos* reparaît avec son sens romain, et il remplace peu à peu, pour désigner le patrimoine de la femme, les autres termes rappelés plus haut.[1] Puis, dans les renonciations qui terminent les actes, on voit apparaître des clauses se rapportant à la *lex Julia* (avec le sens que les romanistes du moyen âge donnent à ces mots), au Sénatus-consulte Velléien, au privilège de dot, à l'hypothèque de la femme sur les biens du mari.[2] Quand une femme reprend en fief une de ses terres, elle renonce *juri prohibenti ne super re*

[1] Parmi les actes des Dauphins, le premier qui parle de *dos* au sens romain est l'acte de 1202 par lequel Guillaume, comte de Forcalquier, donne à sa fille Béatrix, qui doit épouser André Dauphin, ses possessions de Gap et d'Embrun. Fornier, iii. p. 222. Vers la même époque, dans un acte lyonnais de 1206 (*C. lyonnais*, i. N° 99), *dos* désigne sans doute aussi la dot romaine. Pour l'époque antérieure, on ne peut relever que quelques très rares documents où *dos* désigne l'apport de la femme : *Ch. de Cluny*, N° 2528 (acte mâconnais non daté, des environs de l'an 1000 ?). Partout ailleurs, jusqu'à la fin du XII^e^ siècle, le mot désigne la donation du mari (*Ch. de Cluny*, N^os^ 1777, 2628, etc.).

[2] Dans le *C. de S.-Victor de Marseille*, les premières renonciations de ce genre remontent aux années 1202 (N° 977), 1212 (N° 930), 1229 (N° 909) ; ces documents ont été déjà signalés par M. Meynial, *Nouv. Rev. hist. de Droit*, 1901, p. 275, n. 2, et p. 689, n. 2. Dans les actes lyonnais, on trouve vers 1215, sous une forme encore rudimentaire, les premières renonciations relatives au régime matrimonial. *C. lyonnais*, i. N° 140 (1216) : « Renuncians omni juri sibi in his rebus competenti vel in futurum ratione dotis vel propter nuptias donationis vel alicujus melioramenti competituro, juramento ab ea interposito. » N° 164 (1219) : « Preterea predicte Dideria et Rollenz promiserunt sub eodem juramento, quod ratione dotis vel alia qualibet ratione contra hanc venditionem non venirent, nec eundem Stephanum super re vendita presumerent aliquatenus molestare. » N° 233 (1228) : « abrenuntiantes . . . exceptioni dotis. » N° 236 (1228) : « Abrenunciavit omni juri quod habebat in eisdem mansis ratione maritagii vel aliqua alia ratione. » N° 261 (1230) : « Expresse renuncians omni exceptioni et omni benefitio et auxilio juris canonici et civilis, que ipsam contingerent in hac parte. » Au N° 256 (1229), la femme renonce simplement au *privilegium dotis*. Les renonciations détaillées n'apparaissent que plus tard : *Bibl. Dumbensis*, ii. Suppl. N° 111 (1253). V., sur l'histoire des renonciations en général, l'étude précitée de M. Meynial. On rencontre des renonciations en Dauphiné et en Lyonnais depuis le début du XIII^e^ siècle seulement. Au XII^e^ siècle, elles sont exceptionnelles : *C. des Écouges*, N° 5 (1139) ; mais cette charte ne nous est parvenue que par un vidimus du XIV^e^ siècle.

*dotali aliqua servitus imponatur.*[1] Ces clauses sont insérées régulièrement et sans discernement dans tous les actes où des femmes interviennent, même s'il s'agit de femmes non mariées ou veuves.[2]

Peu à peu, cependant, l'idée d'une véritable protection de la dot se dégage ; et cette protection deviendra de plus en plus nécessaire, au fur et à mesure que s'atténuera l'ancienne garantie résultant de la *laudatio* des proches parents. Et il est même très remarquable que cette idée nouvelle va pénétrer en dépit des renonciations et des cautèles. Même dans les actes où les femmes déclareront renoncer au bénéfice de la loi Julia, l'idée d'inaliénabilité dotale triomphera ; en dépit de leur renonciation, les femmes se préoccuperont de garantir leur dot. Tant il est vrai qu'il y a deux romanisations distinctes : celle des formes, la plus connue et la plus facile à étudier ; celle du fond du droit, plus lente, parfois moins complète, mais dont les résultats, une fois acquis, seront infiniment plus solides.[3]

Mais, au XIII^e siècle, au moins dans la région lyonnaise,[4] ce n'est point l'inaliénabilité absolue du droit romain qui s'introduit. La dot reste aliénable, à condition que le mari fournisse à sa femme

[1] *C. lyonnais*, ii. N° 546 (1258) : « I. R. miles et domina A. uxor ejus . . . recipiunt in francum feudum . . . quicquid juris dictus miles nomine dicte domine uxoris sue et ipsa habent. . . . Renunciantes . . . exceptioni . . : dotis et Velleiani privilegio, et juri prohibenti ne super re dotali aliqua servitus imponatur. »

[2] *C. lyonnais*, ii. N° 535 (1256) : Jaquette de Vaux, non mariée, reprenant des biens en fief du chapitre de Saint-Paul, renonce au « privilegium dotis et ypothece ».

[3] Peut-être trouvons-nous, dans un litige survenu en 1229, l'une des premières manifestations de l'inaliénabilité dotale (*C. lyonnais*, i. N° 257). Aymon d'Escullon, avec le concours de son fils, vend à l'église Saint-Just de Lyon un bien appartenant à sa femme. Puis il veut reprendre le bien vendu, et son beau-frère soutient cette réclamation : « Duranz Gaudemars, cujus sororem idem Aymo habuerat in uxorem, de cujus *dote* idem Duranz dicebat res predictas fuisse. . . . » Les réclamants renoncent cependant à leurs prétentions, moyennant 12 livres viennoises. Toutefois l'acte n'indique nullement que la base de ces réclamations soit le caractère dotal du bien vendu ; et, dans les renonciations qui terminent cette transaction, il n'est fait aucune allusion à la dotalité.

[4] Les documents imprimés relatifs aux autres régions que nous étudions, et en particulier à la Provence, sont trop peu nombreux pour nous permettre de connaître l'extension territoriale du système que nous présentent les textes lyonnais.

une *recompensatio*, un *excambium*, en lui cédant des immeubles ou des droits immobiliers ; au besoin, il devra acheter des immeubles pour les donner à sa femme en échange du bien dotal aliéné. Le principe est posé très nettement dans un acte lyonnais de 1236 : *Res dotales vendi vel distrahi a maritis non possunt, sine recompensatione sufficienti facta uxoribus.*[1]

Dans les premières années du XIII^e^ siècle, ce système nouveau n'est pas encore constitué, et la dot semble encore pleinement aliénable.[2] Vers 1200, B. d'Andilly, faisant son testament, lègue à sa femme divers immeubles, pour lui tenir lieu des biens dotaux vendus ou engagés.[3] Mais il semble bien qu'il n'y ait encore là qu'un scrupule du mari, et non pas une obligation stricte ; peut-être aussi la femme n'avait-elle pas consenti à l'aliénation.

Mais, à partir de l'an 1220, la doctrine se fait plus précise et plus exigeante. Désormais le remploi doit être déjà effectué et accepté par la femme, au moment où l'aliénation du bien dotal devient définitive. Dans quelques documents, la femme se contente de déclarer qu'elle a reçu une *recompensatio* suffisante ;[4] mais d'ordinaire, dans l'acte d'aliénation du bien dotal, les biens fournis en remploi par le mari sont indiqués avec précision. Peu importe d'ailleurs le mode d'aliénation du bien dotal, qu'il s'agisse d'une vente,[5]

[1] *C. lyonnais*, i. N° 305.

[2] V. les actes cités plus haut.

[3] *C. lyonnais*, i. N° 80 : « Uxori sue, pro terra sua quam vendiderat, et pro quadem curte sua quod invadiaverat, dimisit, pro velle suo facere, curtem . . . et vineam . . . et terram . . . et gageriam. »

[4] *Bibl. Dumbensis*, ii. Suppl. N° 74 (1228) : « Confessa est insuper comitissa se pro predicto castro, quod ad ipsam ratione successionis et jure hereditario pertinebat, a domino et marito suo Johanne prefato comite *permutacionem* sufficientem et ydoneam recepisse ; et supradicta omnia rata habuit et sponte in manu nostra concessit. » *Gr. Cart. d'Ainay*, ii. p. 181 (1263) : « Et quoniam dicte res vendite erant de dote dicte Guigone, ut ipsa asserit, ipsa confitetur se habuisse et recepisse a dicto marito bonum et legitimum *escambium* pro ipsis rebus de dote sua, ut asserit, existentibus, de quo ipsa se tenet integre pro pagata. »

[5] *C. lyonnais*, i. N° 256 (1229) : « Cum autem hec essent de maritagio predicte Guicharde, facta sibi *recompensatione* ab Umberto marito suo de eo quod apud Chal habebat, ambo laudaverunt predictum curtile. » N° 261 (1230) : vente de 3 *solidi debitales* aux Templiers de Laumusse : « Et cum dicti tres solidi debitales nominate Dannon fuissent a matre sua legati, propter quod ad dotem suam videbantur pertinere vel dotis privilegio fungi, *ne super hoc dicti fratres vel alius pro ipsis possent in posterum molestari*, prenominatus Willelmus, uxori sue *recompensationem* faciens, tres solidos debitales eidem assignavit in appendiciis . . ., propter quod eadem dictis tribus solidis renunciavit. »

d'une donation, ou encore d'une transaction.[1] A en croire

N° 305 (1236), acte cité plus haut : « Quum igitur res dotales vendi vel distrahi a maritis non possunt sine *recompensatione* sufficienti facta uxoribus, dictus G. in sufficientem *recompensationem* dedit in perpetuum dicte Agneti uxori sue et heredibus ejus clausum. . . . » Entre autres éléments de la *recompensatio* figure la renonciation du mari et de son frère à une obligation de 100 livres grevant à leur profit les biens dotaux. V. encore le N° 437 (1249) : « In *concambium* vero et *permutationem* rerum venditarum dotalium dicte Petronille, assignat et concedit dictus Jarento miles prefate Petronille uxori ejusdem . . ., de quibus rebus sibi nomine dicte *concambii* et *permutationis* assignatis dicta Petronilla se tenet et tenuit coram nobis integre pro pagata. » T. ii. N° 522 (1255): vente de bien dotal par le père du mari : « que res vendite ad Beatricem, filiam quondam dicti Hugonis, nunc uxorem Thomassini filii dicte Thome militis jure hereditario pertinebant. » Les jeunes époux, *facti puberes*, approuvent. « Dictus vero Thomas in *recompensationem* et *escambium* dictarum rerum venditarum reddit, tradit et assignat et concedit dicte Beatrici curtile. . . . De qua *recompensatione* et *escambio* dicta Beatrix et dictus Thomassinus de mandato dicti Thome se tenent pro pagatis ; asserentes per juramentum quod propter hoc eorum condicio non est in aliquo pejorata, immo quod melior est effecta. » N° 555 (1259) : « Et quoniam dicte res erant . . . de *dote* dicte Ysabelle, dictus Stephanus (le vendeur) maritus suus reddidit ei . . . in *escambium* et *recompensationem* ipsarum rerum quicquid idem Stephanus habet in parrochiis . . . ; de quo *escambio* et *recompensatione* dicta Ysabella se tenet per juramentum pro pagata ; asserens per idem juramentum quod propter hoc dotis sue conditio melior est effecta. »

On pourrait relever encore, dans les autres recueils lyonnais, au XIII^e siècle, de nombreux exemples de ces aliénations de biens dotaux, moyennant remploi en biens du mari. *Gr. C. d'Ainay*, ii. N° xi (1279) : « Et cum dicte res vendite essent de dote dicte domine Margarite, idem miles in *recompensationem* et *escambium* . . . reddit et assignat eidem domine res que secuntur. . . . » *C. des francs-fiefs du Forez*, N° 41 (1257): vente de 5 sous de rente et du haut domaine d'une vigne : « Et quia predicti quinque solidi forcium novorum et dominium ad dictam Aalis pertinent racione dotis, dictus Petrus eidem volenti et ex certa scientia recipienti reddit et assignat in *recompensacionem* predictorum tres jornalatas vinee . . . ; et de istis rebus habitis et receptis dicta Aalis, cerciorata de jure et de facto, pro supradictis venditis dicto capellano, se tenet integre, ut asserit, pro pagata. »

Il arrive que le mari, au lieu de donner à sa femme la propriété même de ses immeubles, en remploi, lui assigne une rente sur ses immeubles. *C. lyonnais*, i. N° 173 (1221): vente d'un courtil et de vignes : « Et ob *reconpensacionem* rei vendite, Johannes Dumbeis dedit et concessit uxori sue Proetan x libras et x solidos super domum quam habet apud Ansam, et inde pacem ipse et filii sui eidem Proetan in perpetuum juraverunt. » Ce texte est l'un des plus anciens où l'on voie fonctionner le système de la *recompensatio.*

[1] La plupart des documents que nous venons de citer concernent la *vente* d'un bien dotal. Mais le même système d'aliénabilité moyennant remploi se rencontre aussi dans des donations, ou dans des transactions portant sur la dot.

certains documents, il faut même que le bien donné en *recompensatio* ait une valeur nettement supérieure à celle du bien dotal aliéné. On exige, par exemple, que les biens donnés en remploi rapportent 60 sous de rente, si les biens dotaux aliénés valaient 50 livres, ce qui fait un revenu de 6 %.[1] Ajoutons enfin que cet usage de l'aliénation moyennant remploi a sa répercussion sur la liste des renonciations : l'on voit apparaître, à côté de la renonciation à la loi Julia ou au Velléien, la renonciation *exceptioni legitime remunerationis non habite.*[2]

D'ordinaire, les deux opérations, vente du bien dotal et *recompensatio*, sont réunies dans le même acte, mais logiquement elles restent distinctes, et la *recompensatio*, l'*excambium* doit même théoriquement précéder l'aliénation. Un document lyonnais de 1244 est particulièrement curieux à cet égard. Au lieu de vendre directement le bien dotal à l'acquéreur, sauf à assigner à sa femme une *recompensatio*, le mari commence par conclure avec sa femme un échange. Le mari et son frère cèdent à la femme un immeuble qui leur appartient, en échange de l'immeuble dotal ; ce premier acte est fait avec le consentement des enfants d'un premier lit de cette femme, et celle-ci déclare que l'échange est avantageux pour elle. Puis le mari et son frère, ayant ainsi acquis la libre disposition du bien dotal, le vendent à une Maison de l'Ordre de Malte.[3]

---

*Gr. C. d'Ainay*, ii. N° xlix. p. 89 (1227) : procès relatif à un moulin, « que ad se pertinere dicebat (Radulphus) ratione Aalis uxoris sue. » Une transaction intervient ; les époux renoncent à leurs droits sur le moulin, moyennant 12 livres viennoises : « Quia vero jus prefate querele ad uxorem dicti Radulphi militis pertinebat, ut ipsi dicebant, reddidit ei maritus ejus ex causa *permutationis* quicquid habebat apud . . ., quam *permutationem* ipsa domina gratam habuit et recepit. »

[1] *C. des francs-fiefs du Forez*, N° 27 (1246), p. 121 : Guigues de Montagny et sa femme vendent, pour 50 livres, des droits immobiliers à Feurs : « Et qum res superius nominate erant de dote vel de patrimonio dicte Agnetis, dictus Guigo dedit et tradidit ei, in recompensationem earumdem, quicquid habebat. . . . Et, si hec non valerent sexaginta solidos fortium censuales, dictus Guigo debet eos dicte Agneti perficere de redditibus suis quos habet in mandamento de Fontaneis ; ut de eis faciat quicquid facere poterat de rebus que erant de dote vel de patrimonio ejus. »

[2] *Gr. C. d'Ainay*, ii. N° vii. (1268) : « exceptioni legitime remunerationis non habite » ; N° xi. (1279) : « exceptioni legitimi escambii non habiti. » *C. lyonnais*, ii. N° 522 (1255) : « exceptioni legitime remunerationis non habite. »

[3] *C. lyonnais*, i. N° 393 (1244) : « . . . Uxor domini Willermi de Pavenens,

Ainsi, au XIII^e siècle, dans la région lyonnaise, la dot échappe encore à l'application rigoureuse des règles romaines relatives à l'inaliénabilité dotale, et est soumise à un régime en somme assez différent du système romain. La règle romaine d'inaliénabilité absolue ne triomphera que plus tard.[1]

Cette inaliénabilité relative ne s'est appliquée tout d'abord, semble-t-il, qu'aux immeubles dotaux de la femme. Mais, dans le courant du XIII^e siècle, un système de protection analogue, quoique moins net et moins énergique, a été étendu aux immeubles du mari, dans la mesure où la dot mobilière de la femme était *assignée* sur ces immeubles, et où ils en garantissaient la restitution.

Au début du XIII^e siècle, aucune protection spéciale de la dot mobilière de la femme n'apparaît encore. Quand le mari vend un de ses biens propres, la femme renonce purement et simplement à tous les droits qu'elle peut exercer sur ce bien à raison de sa dot.[2] L'hypothèque que le droit romain lui accordait sur les immeubles de son mari ne semble guère avoir eu d'application pratique : on la mentionne rarement, et seulement pour y renoncer.[3] Il arrive

dicta Boicharda, laudantibus et consentientibus . . . liberis dicte domine Boicharde, quos ab alio marito suscepit, permutavit dicto W. de Pavenens marito suo et Jocerando de Pavenens militi, fratribus . . . mansum . . ., quem dederat dicto Willermo in dotem cum eam accepit in uxorem, cum manso . . . et cum his que habebant vel possidebant dicti milites apud Granges . . . ; et juravit dicta domina super sancta Dei evangelia dictam permutationem sibi utilem esse, et se imperpetuum per se vel per alium contra non venturam.—Deinde dicti W. et Jocerandus . . . dictum mansum . . ., quem ex dicta permutatione habuerunt, vendiderunt . . . »

[1] Guy Pape ne semble plus connaître l'aliénabilité de la dot moyennant un remploi. La seule question qu'il se pose est la fameuse question de savoir si un serment de la femme peut valider l'aliénation de la dot.—Qu. 190 ; cf. Expilly, *Arrêts*, ch. 123.—On sait que plus tard, le 20 avril 1664, une ordonnance royale, rendue à la requête du prévôt des marchands et des échevins de Lyon, est venue abroger l'inaliénabilité de la dot dans le Lyonnais, le Mâconnais, le Forez et le Beaujolais. Cf. Lefebvre, article précité, p. 428 et s.

[2] V. *C. lyonnais*, i. N° 236 (1228), cité plus haut, et un grand nombre d'actes du même recueil.

[3] V., p. ex., *Bibl. Dumb.* ii. Suppl. N° 73 (1228), à la suite d'une obligation d'immeubles : « Blancha quoque, dicti domicelli uxor, dictam obligationem expresse laudavit, . . . renuncians cum juramento ypothece dotis generali vel speciali, tacite vel expresse, in rebus supradictis, et omni juri et auxilio legum vel canonum sibi competenti vel competituro. » N° 111 (1253), à la suite d'une *receptio feudi* faite par un mari avec la *laudatio* de sa femme : « Renunciantes . . . exceptioni . . . dotis et ypothece tacite et expresse privilegio, et Velleiani privilegio, legi Julie de fundo dotali non alienando. »

même que la femme du vendeur cède expressément à l'acheteur les sommes dotales que l'immeuble vendu garantissait.[1]

Cependant son désintéressement n'est pas toujours aussi complet. Il arrive que la femme, apportant ainsi sa *laudatio* à l'aliénation de l'immeuble du mari, se fasse payer par l'acquéreur cette *laudatio* et cette renonciation à ses droits éventuels[2]; ou bien encore elle se fait donner par l'acquéreur les «drouilles», les prestations accessoires qu'il est d'usage de joindre au prix de vente.[3] Quelquefois enfin, la femme reçoit, lors de l'aliénation, une somme d'argent plus considérable encore: elle se fait remettre par son mari, à concurrence du montant de sa dot, le prix du bien vendu.[4] Mais ces procédés,

[1] *C. lyonnais*, i. N° 99 (1206): «Supradicta vero domina in omnibus possessionibus supradictis habet l libras de dote, quas predicte domui Templi dedit et concessit.» N° 163: même acte refait en 1219.

[2] *C. lyonnais*, ii. N° 557 (1259): transaction entre Albert de La Tour et l'abbé d'Ambronay au sujet de leurs droits à Lagnieu; l'abbé remet, *pro bono pacis*, 11 l. vienn. à Albert et 30 sous à son épouse: «Nos vero Alasia, domina de Turre, receptis dictis xxx solidis *pro laudibus*, laudamus et approbamus compositionem predictam.»

[3] *C. lyonnais*, ii. N° 573 (1261): vente par Bertrand de Tassin à l'église de Lyon: «Hanc autem venditionem et precii solutionem domina Elyoz, uxor dicti militis . . . sponte sua laudat, approbat, ratificat et acceptat, et omne jus et ypothecam . . . quitat. . . . Confitetur etiam ipsa domina se habuisse a dictis emptoribus sex solidos Viennensium pro *druelliis*.» V. Du Cange, v^is^ *druaylia*, *drueleria*, *droillia*, *drolia* et *draulia*; Collet, *Explication . . . des statuts . . . de Bresse*, art. 83. *Chartes de Cluny*, vi. N° 4711 (1237): «pro laudationibus seu drueleriis,» acte déjà signalé par Du Cange.

[4] *Cart. lyonnais*, i. N° 193 (1223): vente par Guillaume Bernard à l'église de Lyon: «De precio quoque supradicto confessus est coram nobis predictus Willelmus sibi plene satisfactum fuisse, et illud totum Willelme uxori sue pro dote sua solvit; unde propter hoc tam dictus Willelmus quam Willelma uxor ejus omni juri sibi in prefatis rebus aliquando competenti vel competituro cum juramento renuntiarunt.» N° 271 (1231): Bérard de Pizay et sa femme Guillelmine, ne pouvant payer leurs dettes, vendent à Amédée de Miribel, frère de Bérard, tous leurs immeubles situés à Soucieu, moyennant 25 livres payées immédiatement et un complément à percevoir sur les revenus d'Amédée à Ornacieu, jusqu'à ce que les vendeurs aient reçu en tout 7500 sous: «Dictum autem rerum venditarum precium et dictos redditus . . . pro precio assignatos dictus Berardus assignavit dicte Willelme uxori sue pro dote sua; quam assignationem ipsa gratam habuit et acceptam, confitens et recognoscens dictas res sibi assignatas plus valere quam res que in dotem fuerant sibi date. Preterea domina Willelma . . . renuntians . . . juri ypothecarum quod habebat generaliter vel specialiter in rebus et possessionibus omnibus supranominatis. . . . Sub eodem quoque juramento renuntiavit sepedicta Willelma litteris, si quas habebat, quod dicte res sibi essent pro dote specialiter assignate; et promisit se eis decetero non usuram.» N° 274 (1232): Étienne

aboutissant à remettre entre les mains de la femme, au cours du mariage, des sommes d'argent plus ou moins importantes, sont évidemment très imparfaits. Une telle restitution anticipée de la dot n'est guère admissible.

Aussi, depuis 1240 environ, apparaît un autre système, plus conforme aux règles normales du régime matrimonial, plus voisin des règles qui protègent la dot immobilière. L'aliénation de l'immeuble garantissant la dot n'est valable que si la femme déclare formellement, au besoin sous la foi du serment, que la restitution de sa dot est assurée au moyen d'autres biens du mari, que de nouveaux immeubles ont été affectés à la garantie de la dot, en *recompensatio* des immeubles aliénés,[1] ou du moins que son mari possède d'autres biens « apparents », suffisants à assurer la restitution de sa dot.[2] Toutefois il convient de noter que l'acte n'indique

Charreton et son épouse vendent une maison pour 28 livres. « Et ipsa Petronilla expresse renunciavit sub eodem juramento omni juri ypothecarum et omni alii juri quod ratione maritagii vel qualibet alia ratione posset ei competere in domo supradicta vel prodesse quoquomodo. Confessa fuit etiam quod de pecunia memorata satisfactum ei fuit in XXIIII libris forcium, quas maritus ipsius confessus fuerat ab eadem se in dotem recepisse. »

[1] *Bibl. Dumbensis*, ii. Suppl., N° 91 (1236) : « Recognoscens dicta Maria sibi satisfactum de dote sua, et sibi fuisse cautum alibi de eadem » : ces derniers mots semblent indiquer que la dot n'a pas été restituée, mais a été assignée sur de nouveaux biens.—*C. de Saint-Sauveur en Rue*, N° civ. (1242) : « Hec omnia facta sunt praesente et consentiente Luca uxore mea, et renuntiante per juramentum privilegio in hoc sibi competenti ratione rei dotalis, recognoscente et confitente cautum sibi a me alibi de dote sua. »—*Grand Cart. d'Ainay*, i. N° 49 (1256) : « Hanc autem venditionem . . . domina Sibilla mater dicti Petri et Eliouz uxor sua . . . laudant . . ., et, si forte eis vel alteri ipsarum predicta fuerunt pro dote vel dotalicio aut alia causa obligata tacite vel expresse, obligationem et omne jus, quod in predictis habent, quittant dicto priori . . ., asserentes se recepisse a dicto P. alias possessiones in *recompensationem* plus valentes, in quibus condicio sua melioratur, et non modicum aumentatur ; et hoc ita esse . . . juraverunt. »—V. aussi *C. de Saint-Sauveur en Rue*, N° cxii. (1251) : engagement réalisé par Hugue Falco, sa femme, son fils et sa belle-fille : « Et nos praedictae Aalis et Beatrix renuntiamus praestitis juramentis . . . omni juri et privilegiis dotis et donationis propter nuptias, et tacitis sive expressis hipothecis pro dotibus nostris, confitentes alibi in terra dicti militis et filii sui de dotibus nostris sufficienter cautum esse. »

[2] *C. lyonnais*, N° 386 (1244) : à la suite d'une vente de rentes : « confessa est etiam dicta nobilis (femme du vendeur) sub prestito sacramento, quod alias de bonis dicti B. mariti sui de dote sua potest sibi consuli competenter. » —N° 426 (1247) : « Hanc autem venditionem et precii solutionem laudavit et approbavit et ratam habuit domina Guibors, uxor dicti Hugonis, promittens

jamais avec précision quels sont les nouveaux biens du mari ainsi affectés à la garantie de la dot; et, dès lors, ce système de *recompensatio* ne fonctionne pas ici avec la même netteté et la même rigueur que lorsqu'il s'applique aux aliénations de la dot immobilière.

Ainsi, soit en ce qui concerne l'inaliénabilité de la dot immobilière, soit en ce qui touche la garantie de la dot mobilière, nous voyons apparaître au XIII^e siècle, non pas les pures idées romaines, mais des systèmes originaux de protection des intérêts de la femme: ni l'inaliénabilité absolue, ni la garantie résultant de l'hypothèque de la femme sur les biens du mari n'ont pénétré à cette époque dans la pratique.

Quant aux paraphernaux, la pratique les a longtemps ignorés. Les chartes parlent bien des *bona dotalia et parafernalia*, mais sans que les contractants sachent ce que ce dernier mot signifie. Une charte provençale, au début du XIII^e siècle, englobe même les paraphernaux dans l'inaliénabilité dotale.[1] L'idée de biens réservés à la femme, laissés à son administration et à sa jouissance, était trop contraire aux anciennes conceptions médiévales pour pouvoir pénétrer dans la pratique.[2]

---

per sacramentum se contra aliquatenus non venturam de jure vel de facto, . . . confitens et asserens sub eodem *juramento* quod ob hanc alienationem seu venditionem sue *dotis* conditio deterior non fiebat, cum vir suus plura alia bona habeat, ob quorum existentiam, prout ipsa asserebat, *dos* sua sibi large potest salva consistere et manere.»

*Grand Cart. d'Ainay*, ii. p. 191, Suppl., N° 20 (1272): «predicta Amfelisia, uxore dicti domini Guichardi, *per juramentum* asserente sibi posse satis consuli alibi de dote sua super certis rebus et possessionibus apparentibus mariti supradicti.»

[1] *C. de S. Victor de Marseille*, ii. N° 909 (1229): Barrale des Baux, faisant avec le consentement de son mari et de ses enfants une donation immobilière à Saint-Victor, renonce: «specialiter juribus que decernunt res dotales seu *parafernales* alienari non posse.»

[2] La jurisprudence de la France du Midi déclarera que, s'il n'y a pas constitution de dot préfixe, ou s'il n'y a pas du tout de contrat de mariage, tous les biens de la femme sont tenus pour dotaux: Roussilhe, *Traité de la Dot*, i. p. 165 et s. Les paraphernaux sont une anomalie, une institution étrangère et que l'on tend à restreindre. De plus, cette même jurisprudence tend à donner au mari l'administration et la jouissance des paraphernaux. V. Guy Pape, qu. 468: il distingue trois espèces de biens de la femme, 1°, la dot; 2°, les paraphernaux, dont il donne la définition suivante: «Bona paraphernalia sunt illa quae ipsa uxor, tempore quo inducitur in domum mariti, secum defert, *et in quibus administrationem concedit marito tacite vel expresse*»;

B. *Gains de survie*

Comme dans les régions plus septentrionales, nous rencontrons dans nos pays, au haut moyen âge, le *douaire*. Tantôt le mari, au moment du mariage, attribue à la femme certains biens déterminés (*sponsalicium*), tantôt il lui donne une quote-part de tous ses biens (*dotalicium* ; mais cette terminologie n'est pas très ferme) : souvent, dans un même acte, ces deux genres de libéralité sont réunis.[1] Ce douaire appartient en propriété à la femme, mais on relève nettement dans nos régions, comme dans beaucoup d'autres, des tendances à réserver le douaire aux enfants à naître du mariage, et aussi, à défaut d'enfants, à stipuler le retour du douaire aux parents du mari : tendances qui, dans d'autres pays, conduiront au *douaire des enfants* et au *douaire en usufruit*.[2]

A partir du XIII^e^ siècle, il se fait un changement dans les termes, et dans le fond du droit.

L'idée coutumière et germanique du calcul du douaire sur la fortune du mari va faire place à l'idée d'un gain de survie proportionné à la dot : ce sera l'*augment de dot* des pays méridionaux, largement inspiré des règles romaines relatives à la *donatio propter nuptias*. Toutefois l'égalité entre la dot et la *donatio propter nuptias*, qui a triomphé dans quelques coutumes locales du Midi, semble n'avoir jamais pénétré dans la région qui nous occupe. D'ailleurs l'augment de dot n'a pas remplacé dès la fin du moyen âge tous les autres gains de survie. La transformation a été plus complexe. Encore aux XIV^e^ et XV^e^ siècles, on retrouve le mot *dotalicium*. Ce mot a pris, il est vrai, des sens variés. Tantôt il s'agit, comme dans les siècles précédents, d'un douaire véritable, calculé sur la

---

enfin 3°, les biens qui ne sont ni dotaux, ni paraphernaux, « quae mulier habet omnino separata a viro et in suo regimine ac dominio reservata. »

[1] V., comme exemple très caractéristique de cette institution, le douaire (*in sponsalitio sive in dotalitio*) constitué par Guigue le Gras, comte d'Albon, en 1070, au profit de sa fiancée, Agnès (*Bull. de l'Acad. delphinale*, 3^e^ Série, t. XX. p. 369 et s.) : ce douaire comprend une série de *castra* déterminés, avec leurs mandements, et le tiers des *placita*. V. aussi Marion, *C. de l'église de Grenoble*, A, N° 21 (1023) ; *Ch. de Cluny*, N^os^ 7, 88, 105, 229, 439, 659, 686, 687, etc. ; *C. de S. Victor de Marseille*, N^os^ 65, 189, 704, 705. Le mot *sponsalicium* se retrouve encore, en 1257, dans le *C. de Saint-Sauveur en Rue*, N° CVIII. Cf. Gavet, *Sponsalitium et Dotalitium dans les chartes de l'abbaye de Cluny* (*Mélanges F. Ciccaglione*, I.).

[2] V. notre étude sur les origines du douaire des enfants (*Studi in onore di Vittorio Scialoja*, Prato, 1904).

fortune du mari ou fixé à une somme déterminée. En 1273, le contrat de mariage entre Anne, héritière des Dauphins de la seconde race, et Humbert de La Tour, contient un *dotalicium et doarium* « selon les usages de la Bourgogne » : le fiancé attribue à sa future épouse, outre certains biens déterminés, l'usufruit de la moitié de tous ses biens.[1] De même, en 1347, dans un projet de mariage entre Humbert II et Blanche, sœur du comte de Savoie Amédée, Humbert promet à sa fiancée, en *dotalicium*, une rente annuelle de 10,000 florins. Mais ce *dotalicium* doit cesser lorsque la dot aura été restituée, et, pour ce cas, on stipule un augment de dot, si la femme survit et s'il n'y a pas d'enfants du mariage : la rente annuelle fera place alors à un capital une fois payé.[2]

Au XV^e^ siècle encore, Guy Pape connaît et étudie le douaire, *dotalicium* ou *doarium*, constitué par le mari au profit de sa femme pour le cas de survie de celle-ci ; et, suivant sur ce point la vieille conception médiévale, il déclare que la femme, bien que n'ayant sur ce douaire qu'une jouissance viagère, en est cependant vraiment propriétaire, et qu'elle doit supporter toutes les charges qui pèsent sur la propriété foncière, impôts, cens, etc.[3]

Dans d'autres textes cependant, le mot *dotalicium* prend des

[1] Valbonnais, *Hist. de Dauphiné*, ii. p. 11 et s.

[2] *Ibid.* ii. p. 569 et s., N° ccli. : « Item actum est quod dictus dominus Dalphinus teneatur dare et assignare dictae dominae Blanchae ratione *dotalitii* 10,000 flor. annuales, assignandos in castris Visiliae, etc. . . . et quod dicta castra sibi tradantur. » Et plus loin : « Item, in casu ubi restitutio praedictae dotis fuerit plenarie facta, quod tunc cesset totaliter dotalitium supradictum. » Si Blanche, devenue veuve, se remarie, le douaire s'éteindra aussitôt, ou bien il faudra imputer les produits de ce douaire sur le chiffre de la dot à restituer. Si Blanche ne se remarie pas, et reprend cependant sa dot par fractions, à chacun des termes de restitution de la dot, le douaire sera réduit de 1200 florins. V. encore, en 1369, le *dotalicium* de Béatrix de Châlon, mentionné dans le testament de son mari Humbert de Villars, et qui comprend un certain nombre de *castra*, avec leurs mandements. *Bibl. Dumbensis*, i. p. 305.

[3] Guy Pape, *Decisiones*, qu. 524-525 : « Si dotalitium seu doarium constituatur sponsae futurae in casu quo vir praedecederet, utrum valeat ? Dic quod sic . . . Et ita in judicando servatur . . . — Sed . . . pone quod maritus assignat uxori *doarium in vitam*, vel aliquam rem ad alimenta aut pro statu suo tenendo sibi donat vel legat, nunquid istis casibus censebitur uxor proprietaria ? . . . Et per hoc dico quod mulier, vita sua durante, tenetur pro talibus rebus solvere collectas quae pro ipsis rebus imponentur, census et alia onera ex ipsis bonis debita, cum etiam in mulierem talium rerum transeat dominium . . . Et ita de consuetudine etiam servatur in hac patria, in locis in quibus collectae et subsidia Delphinalia solvuntur. »

significations nouvelles, inconnues pendant le haut moyen âge. Tantôt le mot désigne une assignation d'immeubles du mari, destinée à garantir à la femme la restitution de sa dot en deniers : *assignatio facta mulieri causa dotis assequrande.*[1] Tantôt enfin le mot *dotalicium* désigne un « contre - douaire », un droit d'usufruit constitué par la femme ou par les parents de la femme au profit du mari, pour le cas de sa survie.[2]

Puis apparaît un gain de survie appelé *supravita*, qui est mentionné dans les textes lyonnais depuis le XIIIe siècle,[3] et qui, plus tard, usité en Mâconnais, en Bresse,[4] en Dauphiné,[5] en Provence,[6] consiste en une donation réciproque d'une somme d'argent, que le survivant prendra dans la fortune du prédécédé. Ordinairement, la « survie » de la femme est double de celle du mari.

[1] Telle est la définition du *dotalicium* donnée au cours d'une contestation entre l'avocat fiscal et le procureur général du Dauphin et le seigneur de Sassenage, en 1420, au sujet de la terre de Pont en Royans. Cette terre avait été constituée en *dotalicium* par le seigneur de Sassenage au profit de son épouse, Alice de Châlon, pour garantir, à concurrence de 10,000 florins, la restitution de la dot de celle-ci. Les gens du Dauphin réclament, sur cette constitution de *dotalicium*, le paiement des lods et ventes dûs en cas d'aliénation immobilière. Le seigneur de Sassenage « dixit se non teneri, quia tale dotalicium, sive assignacio facta mulieri causa dotis assequrande, non transfert dominium. » Il ajoute que la coutume dauphinoise n'impose pas en pareil cas le paiement des lods et ventes, puisque la terre doit lui revenir dès que la dot aura été restituée. U. Chevalier, *Choix de documents inédits*, p. 254 et s.

[2] Guigue, *Bibl. Hist. du Lyonnais*, p. 29 (1229) : Humbert de Beaujeu, après avoir constitué un *maritagium* à sa sœur, Sibille, fiancée à Renaud de Bagé, ajoute : « Ego siquidem H., de voluntate et mandato expresso S. sororis mee, dicto R. contuli in *dotalicium* medietatem omnium rerum supradictarum, si forte, quod absit, eam absque libero mori contingeret, quoad vixerit possidendam, et post mortem ipsius ad me et ad meos pleno jure revertetur. »

[3] *C. Lyonnais*, i. N° 464 (1251) : « Hanc autem venditionem. . . . Aalys, uxor dicti Guigonis, sponte sua laudat, . . . et omnem ypotecam . . . et omnes actiones, si quas habet in dictis rebus venditis . . . pro dote sua aut *supravita* . . . quitat. »

[4] V., sur les donations de survie, Ch. Revel, *L'Usage des pays de Bresse*, n. éd., Bourg, 1729, p. 253 : « Item, lesdits Époux et Épouses futurs se sont faits les donations de survie suivantes : Sçavoir, que le dit Époux venant à mourir avant ladite Épouse, ayant enfans ou non, ce Mariage consommé ou non, il lui donne de survie 100. Et au même cas de prédécès, ladite épouse donne audit époux 50. »

[5] Guy Pape, qu. 565.

[6] De Cormis, *Consult.* i. col. 1363. — En Provence, cette donation réciproque est le seul gain de survie pratiqué.

Quant aux mots : *augmentum dotis*, *melioratio*, *melioramentum*, ils ont désigné tout d'abord un accroissement quelconque de la dot, qu'il vînt du mari, ou des parents du mari, ou même des parents de la femme.[1] Puis le mot *augment de dot* a pris un sens plus étroit, et a désigné un gain de survie calculé sur la dot. Cet augment de dot n'a jamais eu, dans le Sud-Est de la France, une grande extension. Il a pris le caractère d'un gain de survie *légal* dans quelques pays (Suisse romande, Savoie, Lyonnais, et aussi Franche-Comté, où les roturiers le pratiquent sous le nom de *douaire*).[2] En Dauphiné, il n'a jamais existé qu'en vertu d'une clause formelle.[3]

[1] *Bibl. hist. du Lyonnais*, p. 29 (1229) : *melioramentum* constitué par le frère de la femme au profit du mari. Valb. ii. p. 61 : *augmentum dotis* constitué par le père de la femme. *C. Lyonnais*, i. N° 140 (1216) : « Renuncians omni juri . . . ratione . . . alicujus *melioramenti* competituro » ; N° 220 (1226) : *melioratio dotis* constituée par le père du marié : « Cum Johannes filius meus contraxisset matrimonium cum filia Boni Johannis, dedi ei et concessi in *melioratione* quicquid idem Johannes acquisierat vel acquirere poterat cum vinea mea de Poimie. » De même pour un autre fils.

[2] V., pour la Suisse Romande, von Wyss, *Eh. Güterrechte*, p. 177, 178 et s., 194 et s., 197 et s. ; pour la Savoie, le Bugey, le Valromey, le pays de Gex, Ant. Favre, *Codex Fabrianus*, v. 1, *De don. ante nupt.* 3 et s. : pour la Franche-Comté, cout. de 1459, art. 26. Au contraire « le douaire » des nobles francs-comtois est un véritable douaire, calculé sur les immeubles du mari.

[3] On peut voir un exemple d'augment (sans le nom) en 1309, dans Valbonnais, i. p. 199, HHH ; la fiancée apportant une dot de 20,000 l., son fiancé lui fait une donation entre-vifs de 10,000 l. La donation du mari est ainsi égale à la moitié de la dot.

L'*augmentum dotis* figure dans le projet de mariage, cité plus haut, entre Humbert II et Blanche de Savoie, en 1347, Valbonnais, ii. p. 370 ; cet augment ne doit prendre naissance que si la dot est restituée à la veuve, et s'il n'y a pas d'enfants nés du mariage : « Item memorandum quod, si dotis restitutio locum haberet, domino Dalphino praemoriente, non superstitibus liberis ab eisdem communibus, dat sibi dominus in *augmentum dotis* decem millia flor. » En cas de prédécès de Blanche, le Dauphin doit garder de même 10,000 florins sur la dot : on nommera ce droit, plus tard, le contre-augment.

Guy Pape parle à plusieurs reprises de l'augment : qu. 274, 363, 430, en se préoccupant surtout d'écarter l'application à l'augment des règles romaines sur la *donatio propter nuptias*. Il cherche à établir que l'augment sera dû à la femme, même si la dot n'a pas été payée au mari : « et ita in judicando servatur in hac curia Parlamenti » (qu. 274). Il montre que l'augment de dot peut fort bien ne pas être égal à la dot : « Licet in pactis de dote et dotis augmento lucrandis aequalitas debeat servari . . ., tamen inaequalitas dotis et augmenti quandoque toleratur . . . , primo videlicet, si usus et consuetudo patriae habeat oppositum . . . : sicut est in patria Delph., quia videmus quotidie quod ex pacto maritus de dote lucratur pro *supervita* centum vel

Il est resté à peu près inconnu en Bresse[1] et en Provence.[2] Né tardivement, après la renaissance du droit romain, l'augment ne saurait évidemment être rattaché, comme le voulait Ficker, au vieux droit burgonde.

En somme, malgré la renaissance du droit romain, les coutumes du Sud-Est de la France n'ont pas adopté le système romain de la *donatio propter nuptias*. Ici encore, en matière de gains de survie comme en matière de protection de la dot, ces coutumes ont élaboré une série d'institutions originales, et ici la résistance aux idées romaines a été plus durable, car, tandis que l'inaliénabilité dotale a fini par triompher, cette organisation spontanée des gains de survie a persisté jusqu'à la Révolution.

Nous pourrions faire, en ce qui concerne les actes à cause de mort, des observations analogues. Jusqu'au XII^e^ siècle, le Sud-Est de la France a complètement ignoré le testament proprement dit, unilatéral et révocable. Les actes appelés « testaments » sont des donations ou des ventes. On ne connaît que la donation avec réserve de jouissance viagère. Le *gadium* dauphinois et provençal, difficilement révocable, n'est qu'une donation *post obitum*. Lorsque, au XII^e^ et surtout au XIII^e^ siècle, le testament reparaît, il se débarrasse péniblement de ces anciens caractères des actes à cause de mort. L'institution d'héritier n'apparaît qu'avec des formes hésitantes (institution de Dieu ou des Saints; très nombreuses institutions *ex re certa*). Le contenu du testament continue de s'inspirer d'idées étrangères au droit romain. — Mais cette étude est faite ou va être faite ailleurs, et elle nous entraînerait trop loin.

---

ducentos florenos, et uxor duplum. » Il est curieux de voir Guy Pape, voulant donner un exemple de l'augment dauphinois, choisir un cas de *supravita*.

1 V., pour la Bresse, Ch. Revel, *L'Usage des pays de Bresse*, nouv. éd., Bourg, 1729, p. 254 et s.: « L'augment est une complaisance éféminée et une mauvaise drogue qui nous est venue de de-là les Monts ou de la Savoye: le droit romain ne l'a jamais aperçû; nos Coûtumes n'en parlent point. . . . Cet augment est descendu jusqu'en Bugey, mais il n'a pas passé la rivière d'Ain . . . » En Bresse, il n'existe que s'il est expressément stipulé, « et on le peut apeller l'oprobre et l'infâmie de nôtre siècle. » Dans la seconde partie de cet ouvrage, p. 119 et s., Revel étudie l'augment tel qu'il fonctionne dans le Bugey, le Valromey et le pays de Gex.

2 V., sur cette extension de l'augment à la fin de notre ancien droit, Boucher d'Argis, *Traité des gains nuptiaux*, éd. de 1787, p. 37.

Pour terminer, nous indiquerons encore que les idées romaines sur la tutelle, la curatelle, la puissance paternelle, l'émancipation sont absentes du droit du haut moyen âge. Les premiers actes d'émancipation révélateurs d'une puissance paternelle perpétuelle, sont du XIII^e^ siècle. En 1204, André Dauphin, donnant des franchises à St- Vallier, date l'acte: *anno mee milicie primo*; il a environ 20 ans; jusqu'alors, sa mère administrait le comté d'Albon : c'est encore la majorité féodale, marquée par l'adoubement.[1] Au contraire, en 1237, dans son testament, il distingue, pour son jeune fils Guigue, la période de la tutelle (jusqu'à 14 ans) et celle de la curatelle:[2] les idées romaines ont donc, en cette matière, pénétré dans le premier tiers du XIII^e^ siècle dans la Maison des comtes d'Albon.

Ces quelques indications, que l'on pourrait encore allonger, nous paraissent caractéristiques : ces « pays de droit écrit » ont été, au haut moyen âge, profondément pénétrés d'idées coutumières, qui ont sur quelques points opposé, à la réception du droit romain, une vive résistance.

R. CAILLEMER.

[1] Franchises de Saint-Vallier, dans la *Petite Revue des bibliophiles dauphinois*, Grenoble, 1869-1874, p. 59.

[2] Valbonnais, i. p. 60 : « Item dedit eidem Guigoni tutricem Beatricem. . . . Item post expirationem tutelae dedit eandem Beatricem curatricem filio suo supradicto. »

# X

# LA MAXIME *PRINCEPS LEGIBUS SOLUTUS EST* DANS L'ANCIEN DROIT PUBLIC FRANÇAIS

## I

LE Digeste, au titre *de legibus senatusconsultis et longa consuetudine* (i. 3), contient un fragment d'Ulpien (L. 31) qui commence ainsi : *Princeps legibus solutus est.* Peu de textes ont exercé une influence plus profond sur le développement du droit public dans certains pays d'Europe et surtout en France. Seul peut revendiquer le même prestige et même l'emporter à cet égard un autre fragment du même jurisconsulte Ulpien qui forme la loi du titre suivant, *de Constitutionibus principum* et qui commence par cette assertion célèbre et menaçante : *Quod principi placuit legis habet vigorem.*

La première règle formulée par Ulpien et sur laquelle porte notre étude, avait dans le droit romain du IIIe siècle une portée précise et limitée. L'Empereur n'était point affranchi des lois ; il leur était au contraire soumis en principe. Mais il arrivait que telle ou telle loi nouvelle exemptait le prince régnant de certaines des règles qu'elle édictait, et la *Lex de imperio Vespasiani* montre que l'habitude était de maintenir ces exemptions à ses successeurs.[1] En dehors de ces franchises spéciales et légalement édictées, l'Empereur pouvait obtenir du Sénat, compétent à cet égard, la *dispense* de certaines règles légales. Puis, et c'est là un nouvel état du droit romain déjà établi au temps d'Ulpien, on admit que l'Empereur pouvait lui-même accorder des dispenses de cette

[1] *Lex de imperio Vespasiani*, dans P. F. Girard, *Textes de droit romain publiés et annotés*, 4ème édition, p. 108 : « Utique quibus legibus plebisve scitis scriptum fuit ne divus Aug(ustus), Tiberiusve Julius Caesar Aug(ustus), Tiberiusque Claudius Caesar Aug(ustus) Germanicus tenerentur, iis legibus plebisque scitis imp(erator) Caesar Vespasianus solutus sit. »

espèce et, comme il pouvait le cas échéant se les accorder à lui-même, on admit qu'une telle dispense pour lui-même allait de soi : pour plus de simplicité il fut considéré comme affranchi des règles légales dont il pouvait accorder la dispense. Tel est le sens vrai et la portée originelle de cette petite phrase écrite par Ulpien : *Princeps legibus solutus est.*[1] Mais cette faculté ne s'appliquait qu'aux lois concernant le droit privé[2] et, ajoute Mommsen, aux lois de police.[3] L'Empereur restait tenu des lois concernant le droit public[4] et même des lois criminelles, bien qu'en vertu des principes généraux aucune poursuite ne fut possible contre lui pendant son principat.[5]

Mais lorsque, lors de la première renaissance des études de droit romain, le texte d'Ulpien sortit de la poussière et fut remis

[1] Voyez le magistral exposé de Theodor Mommsen sur cette question, *Römischer Staatsrecht*, zweiter Band, II. Abtheilung, zweite Auflage, p. 728 et s.—traduction française par P. F. Girard.

[2] Mommsen fait justement remarquer que le texte d'Ulpien est tiré de son commentaire *ad legem Juliam et Papiam*, c'est-à-dire, sur une matière essentiellement de droit privé, et que cela est confirmé par ce qui y est dit de l'*Augusta*, laquelle n'avait aucune part au gouvernement et pour laquelle il ne pouvait s'agir que de privilèges se rapportant au droit privé : « Augusta tamen licet legibus soluta non est, principes tamen eadem illi privilegia tribuunt quae ipsi habent. » Dans ce dernier cas il y a manifestement une dispense accordée par l'Empereur. D'après une constitution de l'empereur Alexandre il semblerait même que les princes sur certains points aient de parti pris restreint leur exemption, *Cod. Just.* vi. 23, 3 : « Ex imperfecto testamento nec imperatorem hereditatem vindicare saepe constitutum est. *Licet enim lex imperii solemnibus juris imperatorem solverit*, nihil tamen tam proprium imperii est quam legibus vivere. » Mais la vraie raison de la décision donnée là est qu'il s'agissait de la validité d'un acte accompli non par le Prince, mais par un tiers. Voyez une constitution de Justinien (*Cod.* v. 16, 26) qui déclare absolument et immédiatement valables les donations entre époux faites par l'Empereur à l'*Augusta* ou par l'*Augusta* à l'Empereur.

[3] Mommsen, *op. cit.* p. 728 : « Nicht mit Unrecht wurde darum späterhin, wenn ein vom Kaiser vollzogener Rechtsakt einer privatrechtlicher *oder nur polizeilichen* Prohibitivvorschrift zuwiderlief, derselbe aufrecht erhalten als die Dispensation derselben in sich tragend. »

[4] Un passage de Suétone me paraît montrer que, dans l'Administration de la justice qu'il rendait en personne, Auguste se croyait obligé de se conformer aux lois, *Divus Augustus*, c. 33 : « Dixit autem jus non diligentia modo summa sed et lenitate, siquidem manifesti parricidii reum, ne culleo insueretur, quod nonnisi confessi adficiuntur hac poena, ita fertur interrogasse : *Certe patrem tuum non occidisti?* » Si, par sa seule volonté Auguste avait pu écarter la peine du *culleus*, il n'aurait pas eu besoin d'arrêter l'aveu sur les lèvres du coupable.

[5] Mommsen, *op. cit.* p. 729.

au jour avec les autres, on lui donna une portée nouvelle et absolue. On lui fit dire que le monarque n'était pas tenu des lois, qu'il en était affranchi d'une manière générale. Les Glossateurs, qui avaient fait un dépouillement intégral des textes compris dans la Compilation de Justinien, en trouvaient bien qui leur paraissaient contraires à cette règle ; mais ils les écartaient par cet argument principal que le Prince, quoique non tenu des lois, pouvait s'y soumettre de sa libre volonté.[1]

On regardait donc comme une règle incontesté et absolue du droit romain que le Prince était affranchi de l'observation des lois et cette règle, comme tant d'autres appartenant au même fonds, se fit recevoir en France. Elle s'y fit recevoir dans le cours du XIII^e^ siècle, car, comme on le verra plus loin, elle est visée comme certaine dans la *Practica aurea libellorum* de Petrus Jacobi qui fut terminée en 1311.[2] Dans le dernier tiers du XIV^e^ siècle elle est invoquée dans un texte officiel, dans l'ordonnance de Charles V de 1374, qui fixe à quatorze ans la majorité des rois.[3]

[1] Le texte principal qui semblait contraire était une constitution des empereurs Théodose et Valentinien (*Cod.* i. 14, 4) ainsi conçue : « Digna vox majestate regnantis legibus alligatum se principem profiteri : adeo de auctoritate juris nostra pendet auctoritas. Et re vera majus imperio est submittere legibus principatum. Et oraculo praesentis edicti quod nobis licere non patimur indicamus. » C'est sur ce texte que la glose produit les diverses conciliations qu'avait trouvées l'école. L'une consistait à dire qu'il était noble et digne de déclarer que l'empereur était soumis aux lois, bien que cela fût faux ; glose, v^is^ *Digna vox* : « Sed quomodo est digna vox, cum sit falsum ? *ff. L. Princeps et ff. de leg.* III *ex imperfecto et in authent. de consulibus* § *fin*(*ali*) *cap.* III, *et I*(*nfra*) *l. ex imperfecto ?* Responde : digna est si dicat se velle quod non sit, *Inst. quibus modis infir*(*mantur testamenta*) § *finali et in praeallegata l*(*ege*) *ex imperfecto.* »—Une autre opinion soutenait qu'en pareil cas il était permis de mentir ; la glose citée continue ainsi : « Alii dicunt quod hic permittitur mentiri ut *Inst. de act*(*ionibus*) § *alia*, quod non placet. » Enfin on soutenait que cela s'appliquait parce que c'était en vertu de la loi même que le Prince était affranchi des lois, par l'effet de la *lex regia de imperio* ; glose sur la loi *Digna vox*, v^is^ *de auctoritate* : « hoc est ratio primi dicti et quod dicit *juris*, s(cilicet) regis regiae quae est de imperio transferendo de populo in imperatorem. »

[2] Savigny, *Geschichte des römischen Rechts im Mittelalter*, zweite Ausgabe, sechster Band, § 12, p. 37.

[3] (Dupuy), *Traité de la majorité des rois et des régences du royaume*, 1722, t. i. p. 237 : « Super adoptione et administratione regni non reperiatur certa aetas constituta vel praefinita a jure in Rege, *qui solutus est legibus*, cum jura dicentia aetatem exigi in minoribus loquantur (de) jurium ditioni subjectis. » Le texte repousse ici l'application des règles du droit romain sur les mineurs de vingt cinq ans parce que le roi *legibus solutus est*, et constate d'autre part que ce droit n'a pas de règles spéciales sur la majorité des rois.

D'autres pays avaient eu le bonheur d'échapper à cette influence. Telle l'Angleterre. Dès le XIII^e^ siècle Bracton y proclamait l'empire absolu de la loi ; le roi lui-même lui était soumis car «c'était la loi qui faisait le roi».[1] Au XV^e^ siècle Fortescue expose magistralement la même thèse. Il montre que l'Angleterre de son temps vit sous le *regimen politicum* et non simplement sous le *regimen regale* ; c'est une monarchie limitée, tandis que la France lui apparaît comme une monarchie absolue, bien qu'en réalité elle ne le fût pas encore à cette époque. Fortescue établit clairement la souveraineté des lois anglaises. Non seulement il déclare que toutes les lois humaines sont sacrées aussi bien que celles du Deutéronome,[2] mais il rappelle qu'à son couronnement le roi d'Angleterre promet par serment d'observer ses propres lois.[3] Fortescue s'attaque d'ailleurs, non proprement à la règle *Princeps legibus solutus est*, mais à la règle *Quod principi placuit legis habet vigorem.* Il reconnaît encore au roi, du moins dans un de ses ouvrages, le droit de *dispenser* des lois, lequel ne sera définitivement aboli que par le *Bill of Rights.*[4]

[1] *Henrici de Bracton de legibus et consuetudinibus Angliae libri quinque*, Londini, 1640, L. i. c. 8, § 5, p. 5 : « Ipse tamen rex non debet esse sub homine sed sub Deo et sub lege, quia lex facit regem. Attribuat igitur rex legi quod lex ei attribuit, videlicet dominationem et potestatem ; non est enim rex ubi dominatur voluntas et non lex. Et quod sub lege esse debeat, cum sit Dei vicarius, evidenter apparet ex similitudine Jesu Christi. »—Cf. Pollock and Maitland, *The History of English Law before the Time of Edward I*, tome i. pp. 160-1.

[2] Fortescue, *De laudibus legum Angliae* . . ., Londini, 1775, c. 3, p. 3 : « Scire igitur te volo quod non solum Deuter. leges sed et omnes leges humanae sacrae sunt, quia lex his verbis definitur : lex est sanctio sancta, jubens honesta, prohibens contraria. »

[3] *De laudibus legum Angliae*, c. 34, p. 28 : « Audisti namque superius quod inter leges civiles praecipua sententia est maxima sive regula illa quae cavit *quod principi placuit legis habet vigorem* : qualiter non sanciunt leges Angliae, dum nedum *regulariter* sed *politice* rex ejusdem dominatur in populum suum, *quo ipse in coronatione sua ad legis suae observantiam astringitur sacramento.* »

[4] *The Governance of England: otherwise called The Difference between an Absolute and a Limited Monarchy*, by Sir John Fortescue, a revised text edited with introduction, notes, and appendices by Charles Plummer, M.A., Oxford, Clarendon Press, 1885, p. 83 : « There is, however, in the *De Natura* a passage (c. 24 sq. *Works*, pp. 85-87) not found in his other works. Et à la note 3 M. Plummer ajoute : « As this passage is rather important as bearing on the question of the dispensing power, I give Fortescue's exact words : « Ad libitum « etiam tuum tu semper regis omnia criminalia et poenas cunctas moderaris vel « remittis : omnimodo sic facere poteris sine subditorum iactura et offensa « consuetudinum et statutorum regni tui. » On this dispensing power of the

## II

En France, nous l'avons dit, la maxime *Princeps legibus solutus est* fut reçue dans le cours du XIII^e siècle et elle se maintint dans la suite ; elle faisait vraiment partie du droit public de l'ancienne monarchie. Elle y avait une grande portée et l'on en tirait deux séries de conséquences.

Les premières concernaient le droit privé. Si le roi accomplissait un acte rentrant dans le droit privé, un acte qu'aurait pu faire un particulier, s'il faisait son testament, une donation, un contrat, il les faisait valablement sans tenir compte des règles établies par les lois ou par les coutumes, en violant ces règles et en les écartant. C'était, somme toute, ce qu'avait permis jadis aux empereurs romains la règle *Princeps legibus solutus est.* Bodin en cite des applications topiques, notamment le testament de Philippe de Valois « portant la clause dérogatoire aux coutumes et loix civiles, comme n'étant pas obligé à icelles ».[1] Il cite aussi une donation du même roi à sa femme, de l'an 1330, qui était ferme et valable, bien que les donations entre époux fussent prohibées par la plupart des coutumes de France. Les contrats de mariage des rois fournissent de notables exemples. Celui de Louis XIII et de « l'infante Anne » portait : « que leurs dites Majestés très-chrétiennes et catholiques approuveront et ratifieront ladite capitulation et tout le contenu en icelle, s'obligeant et promettant par leurs foy et paroles royales de le garder et accomplir inviolablement et seront dépêchées toutes lettres en la forme et manière accoutumée, avec les dérogations à quelconques loix, coutumes et dispositions qui sont au contraire. »

Mais la seconde série de conséquences était autrement grave et importante, visant le droit public. On tenait que lorsque le roi intervenait en personne, pour décider lui-même un acte d'administration ou de juridiction, il pouvait le faire valablement sans tenir compte des lois, que ses officiers, au contraire, étaient tenus d'observer et de respecter. Cela était surtout remarquable quand il s'agissait

---

Crown during the Middle Ages see *S.C.H.* iii. 579, 582. The exercise of this power was more frequent in the Middle Ages than we should consider consistent with Constitutional Government, but it was often rendered necessary by the unwise minuteness of many mediaeval statutes. »

[1] Bodin, *Les Six Livres de la République*, édit. Genève, 1629, L. i. ch. 8, p. 154.

de l'administration de la justice, que le roi, s'il le voulait, pouvait rendre lui-même à ses sujets. Cette intervention directe et personnelle du monarque justicier était d'ailleurs conforme à la tradition ancienne ; et Bodin discute encore une opinion, d'après laquelle ce serait là la meilleure forme de l'administration de la justice. Il note en même temps que le roi jugeant en personne pouvait, en toute liberté, ne juger que d'après sa conscience : « Si le Prince jugeoit, lui qui est la loi vive et par-dessus toutes les lois civiles, accompagné de son Conseil, il feroit bonne et briève justice, ayant esgard au fond sans beaucoup s'attacher aux formalités. »[1] C'est par la même conception qu'il interprète un privilège obtenu par les nobles polonais : « La noblesse de Pologne obtint de Louis roy de Hongrie et de Pologne un privilège que les nobles ne pourroient être jugés que par le roy quand il y va de la vie et de l'honneur, croyant qu'ils pouvoient aisément échapper le jugement du roy et non pas des juges qui sont obligez aux loix. »[2]

Il résultait de là que le Conseil du roi, quand il jugeait au fond les causes des particuliers, pouvait toujours décider en ne consultant que le sentiment de l'équité ; car le Conseil du roi, c'était le roi lui-même, celui-ci étant toujours censé présent dans son Conseil ; c'était lui que faisaient parler les arrêts du Conseil.[3] Nos anciens auteurs insistaient sur ce pouvoir général de juger en simple équité ;[4] ils relevaient que, dans les

[1] *Les Six Livres de la République*, L. iv. ch. 6, p. 612.

[2] *Ibid.* p. 623.

[3] *Histoire du Conseil du roy*, par Guillard, avocat au Conseil du roy, Paris 1717, p. 68 : « Mais si les Cours ont cette liberté (d'évoquer les causes) dans quelques occasions, celui qui la leur a donnée conserve toujours en sa personne la plénitude de puissance dont il peut user selon son bon plaisir et son Conseil étant inséparable de sa majesté, dont il n'est que l'organe, personne ne peut dire que le Conseil ne puisse pas dans certaines occasions connoistre des affaires des particuliers, les évoquer à soy, les décider diffinitivement, sans les renvoyer à des juges ordinaires comme il les renvoie le plus souvent parce qu'il s'occupe d'affaires plus importantes. »

[4] Guillard, *Histoire du Conseil du roy*, p. 72 : « Il faut convenir que l'équité naturelle, qui est l'âme des lois et des ordonnances, mérite beaucoup d'attention au Conseil du roy pour peu qu'il soit besoin d'entrer dans l'interprétation de quelques ordonnances, Edits ou Déclarations ; et quand on découvre une iniquité évidente dans quelque jugement des Cours, le Conseil du Prince est d'autant plus obligé de soutenir la partie opprimée que l'on ne doit pas souffrir que pour quelque formalité mal observée ou obmise les plaideurs de mauvaise foi profitent du dol et des surprises qu'ils ont mis en usage pour tromper leurs juges et leurs parties. »

serments du sacre le roi promettait de rendre la justice *en équité*.[1]

Là il n'y avait encore que demi mal, bien que le respect du droit technique soit le meilleur garant des intérêts légitimes ; mais le principe entraînait, dans d'autres applications, de terribles dangers. Il en résultait en effet que le roi, statuant en personne, pouvait infliger les peines les plus graves sans qu'elles fussent prononcées par aucune loi et sans forme de procès. Logiquement il aurait pu le faire en siègeant comme juge.[2] Mais dans les audiences privées que les rois tinrent pendant longtemps,[3] ils ne tranchaient que des causes civiles de peu d'importance. D'autre part le Conseil du roi cessa de bonne heure de revendiquer aucune compétence en matière criminelle.

Mais les *Lettres de cachet* étaient sûrement une application du principe. Elles pouvaient contenir un ordre quelconque du monarque. Mais en fait, employées comme moyen de répression, elles ne contenaient jamais qu'un ordre d'emprisonnement sans jugement dans une prison d'État, ou un ordre d'exil. Il est vrai que les rois anciennement ont parfois fait mettre à mort sans jugement, par ordre verbal, des personnes qu'ils considéraient comme

[1] Guillard, *op. cit.* p. 72 : « Nos rois s'engagent même à leur sacre par un serment solennel à suivre en tout les règles de *l'équité* et de condamner *l'iniquité* en toutes occasions. » C'était là une interprétation forcée ; dans les serments du sacre le mot *équité* (*aequitas*) était pris dans un autre sens ; il voulait dire que le roi statuerait avec impartialité. On se rappelle que, d'après Fortescue, le roi d'Angleterre jurait d'observer, non l'équité, mais les lois, ses propres lois ; voyez ci-dessus, note 3, p. 204.

[2] Fortescue, *De laudibus*, c. 35, p. 30, paraît bien dire qu'il en était ainsi : « Nobilis tamen non sic exactionibus opprimitur. Sed si eorum aliquis calumniatus fuerit de crimine, licet per inimicos suos, non semper coram judice ordinario ipse convocari solet, sed quam saepe in Regis Camera et alibi in privato loco, quandoque vero solum per internuncios ipse inde alloqui visus est et mox ut criminosum eum Principis conscientia, reatu aliorum, judicaverit, . . . qualiter et mori audivisti numerum multo majorem hominum quam qui legitimo processu juris convicti extiterunt. » Ce passage de Fortescue qui paraît reposer sur des bruits non fondés, ne serait point inexact s'il se rapportait aux lettres de cachet ; mais les lettres de cachet ne contenaient jamais l'ordre de mettre à mort une personne quelconque. Ce passage ne peut pas non plus se rapporter aux *Jugements par Commissaires*, dans lesquels était suivie une procédure extraordinaire mais complète.

[3] L'ordonnance de Blois de 1579 contient encore une disposition sur cette administration de la justice intime et familière.

coupables.[1] Nos anciens auteurs appelaient cela *procéder par des voies de fait*; mais ils estimaient que le monarque ne devait procéder que par des *voies de droit*, c'est-à-dire par les procédures régulières.[2]

## III

Il ne faudrait pas croire cependant que la maxime *Princeps legibus solutus est* n'ait pas rencontré en France de contradicteurs.

Dès le premier tiers du XIVe siècle, dans sa *Practica aurea libellorum*,[3] Petrus Jacobi s'efforce d'en écarter l'application. Il ne conteste point directement que le roi soit exempt des lois; il l'admet au contraire en droit. Mais il tient qu'il est digne d'un monarque, que c'est même son devoir de vouloir ce que veulent les lois et ne pas écouter les flatteurs, les courtisans qui tâchent de lui inspirer une volonté différente.[4] Cette influence néfaste des courtisans reviendra dans des textes postérieurs.

Mais c'est là une note isolée et timide. Il faut attendre la

[1] Il semble que Louis XI ait agi assez souvent ainsi à l'égard de petites gens. La Roche-Flavin, *Treize Livres des Parlements de France*, Bourdeaux, 1617, L. xiii. ch. 13, N° 5: « Le roi Louis XI sur la fin de ses jours trouva sa conscience grandement oppressée du mépris de la justice et, entre autres, d'avoir poussé jusqu'à l'excès le pouvoir absolu allant faire prendre par le Prévost les prisonniers de la Conciergerie du Palais qui les faisoit noyer à l'endroit de la Grange aux Merciers. » Dans le passage de Fortescue (*De laudibus*, c. 35) cité p. 207 n. 2, il est fait allusion aux mêmes faits qui, sans que le nom de Louis XI soit prononcé, sont rapportés comme une pratique ordinaire des monarques français: « In sacco positus absque figura judicii per Propositi marischallorum ministros noctanter in flumine projectus submergitur. » La source à laquelle ont puisé Fortescue et La Roche-Flavin doit être la même. Ce mode d'exécution était sûrement familier au XVe siècle; qu'on songe aux vers de Villon:

> Semblablement où est la royne
> Qui commanda que Buridan
> Fût jeté en un sac en Seine?

[2] La Roche-Flavin, *Treize Livres des Parlements de France*, L. xiii. ch. 12.

[3] Édition Venetiis, 1502.

[4] *Practica aurea libellorum rubrica*, XXV. *de condictione ex lege*, *Institution. de actione* § *quadrupli*, N° 19: « Princeps debet sibi cavere ne alias laedat sub coloribus quaesitis et per curiales suos adinventis. Quia, licet princeps sit solutus legibus, ut ff. *de leg. l. Princeps*, tamen dignum est sibi profiteri secundum leges vivere velle, ut *C. de leg. l. digna vox*, et idem dicitur de Papa, 12, *qu.* 2, *c. non liceat papae.* »

seconde moitié du XVI^e^ siècle pour trouver une répudiation énergique de la maxime, une contestation formulée en vertu de principes bien arrêtés. Elle émane des écrivains qui, dans la période des guerres de religion, s'efforcèrent de développer en France les principes de liberté politique. Elle est particulièrement nette dans les *Vindiciae contra tyrannos* et dans le *De jure magistratuum in subditos et officio subditorum erga magistratus.*[1] L'auteur, pour respecter la grande autorité du droit romain, conserve pourtant à la maxime la première série d'effets qu'on lui attribuait, celle qui se rapportait aux règles du droit privé dont le Prince était exempt, mais il l'écarte, avec preuves à l'appui, en ce qui concerne le droit public et le gouvernement de l'État. Il affirme aussi en termes saisissants que le roi est tenu par le droit naturel et par le droit divin ; mais cela alors personne ne le contestait. L'auteur des *Vindiciae contra tyrannos* paraît contester même que le roi soit exempt des règles du droit privé.[2] Il s'élève spécialement contre l'idée que le roi peut juger sans respecter les lois et les formes de la justice,[3] et qu'il ait sur ses sujets le droit de vie et de mort.[4]

[1] Édition *Ursellis apud Cornelium Sutorium*, 1600, à la suite des *Vindiciae contra tyrannos*, p. 253, *Repetitio quaest.* vi. : « Quod excipere solent *Regem legibus non astringi* in genere nec potest nec debet accipi, ut dicunt regum assentatores regnorumque eversores. Nam ut taceam tot omnium fere nationum exempla, quae supra allata sunt, quot sunt graves veterum juris consultorum sententiae e jure naturae excerptae ? Cujusmodi sunt : *eos qui leges ferunt legibus quoque obtemperare.* Et *quod quisque juris in alium statuit erit, ipse ut eodem jure utatur.* Et *nihil imperio magis conducere quam ut rex legibus utatur* ; dignam denique vocem esse *Principem se legibus subditum profiteri.* Itaque quod alibi a juris consultis dici videtur *Principem esse supra leges* aut *Principem legibus esse solutum* nonnisi de legibus civilibus deque particulari privatorum jure est intelligendum, verbi gratia de testamentis, de detractione Trebellianae vel Falcidianae : non autem de jure publico et ad statum, ut dici solet, pertinente, multoque minus de jure naturali et divino, cui cum omnes singuli homines subiciantur, quatenus homines nati sunt, omnino efficitur aut reges homines non esse aut illos hoc jure teneri. »

[2] En effet (quaest. iii. p. 91) il montre que des Princes, pour pouvoir faire ce que la loi défendait, ont changé celle-ci à l'égard de tous : « Valentinianus, imperator bonus alioquin, quia duas uxores simul habere voluit, singulis lege permisit. Cambyses, Cyri filius, nuptias cum germana sorore, quia sororem appetebat, licitas esse voluit. Chabades, Persarum rex, adulteriorum poenam sustulit. »

[3] *Vindiciae*, quaest. iii. p. 89 : « An autem rex, quia juri dicendo praeest, ex arbitrio jus dicet ? Rexne, inquam, a lege an lex a rege pendebit ? »

[4] *Vindiciae*, quaest. iii. p. 98 : « Adulatorum aulicorum axioma percelebre est *Principes in subditos eam quam domini olim in servos potestatem vitae,*

Ce ne sont pas seulement au XVI^e^ siècle des écrivains politiques, dont les ouvrages d'ailleurs sont profondément imprégnés de droit technique, qui déclarent le roi soumis aux lois, ce sont aussi de purs juristes. En voici un, qui n'est pas à proprement parler un homme supérieur, mais qui a joué un rôle notable de son temps, éditant ou rééditant de vieux textes qu'il commente, tels que la *Somme rural* de Boutillier, composant des livres dont les titres sont presque romains mais qui se rapportent au droit français. C'est Charondas le Caron, dont les deux principaux ouvrages sont *Les Réponses du droit français* et les *Pandectes du droit français.* C'est dans ce dernier écrit qu'il a traité notre question.[1] Il l'aborde avec une grande netteté, car il se demande si les rois sont exempts des lois qui concernent le droit public et le gouvernement de l'État.[2] Il admet que les rois peuvent facilement se dispenser d'observer les dispositions de droit privé et sont exempts des peines portées par les lois.[3] Ce n'est pas qu'il passe sous silence le texte d'Ulpien ; il en exagère même la portée.[4] Mais il a pour soutenir sa thèse des raisons meilleures que des

---

inquam, *et necis habere.* Adeo vero istis nugis principibus imposuerunt ut plerique ea saevitia non utantur non minus tamen sibi licere putent sed de suo jure quodammodo cedere videantur. Dicimus vero nos contra *Principem tanquam legis ministrum et executorem in eos tantum quos lex jusserit gladium stringere posse. Sin fecerit, non regem amplius sed tyrannum, non judicem sed praedonem, non legis custodem sed violatorem esse.* »

[1] *Pandectes ou Digestes du droit français*, par Charondas le Caron, docteur ès droits, conseiller du roy et son lieutenant général au bailliage et Comté de Clermont en Beauvoisis, Lyon, 1596, ch. iii. *Des loix et ordonnances et quelles doivent estre et si le souverain est exempt d'icelles*, p. 29 *sq.*

[2] *Pandectes du droit français, loc. cit.* p. 41 : « On demande s'il est subject aux loix establies pour l'estat public, honnestes et politiques. »

[3] *Pandectes, loc. cit.* p. 43 : « Je n'ignore qu'il y ait des Édits et Ordonnances qui ne concernent l'estat public dont les roys se peuvent facilement dispenser, d'autant que la transgression n'est de grande conséquence et ne préjudicie à l'utilité commune ; aussi les rois sont exempts des peines portées par les loix, parce que leurs personnes ne sont subjectes à aucuns juges, ne recognoissans que Dieu pour souverain et seul juge de leurs actions. »

[4] *Pandectes, loc. cit.* p. 42 : « Je sçay bien que le jurisconsulte Ulpian dit que le Prince est exempt et absous des loix, ce qu'aucuns ont voulu restraindre aux loix pénales, c'est à dire à celles qui sont ordonnées contre ceux qui délinquent, puisque le Prince n'y est subject : mais il semble que les Romains ont entendu plus largement ceste exemption et absolution des loix, comme déclare Dion au livre cinquante-troisiesme de son histoire, parlant de l'empereur Auguste auquel fut donnée ceste prérogative, et l'interprète n'estre tenu à aucune nécessité de loy, ains estre exempt de tout droit escrit. »

textes, des plus belles et des plus fortes, et il expose courageusement son opinion, malgré les discours des courtisans, dont la mention revient constamment en cette matière.[1] Pour Charondas la loi est la règle normale de tous les êtres raisonnables, et il rappelle que le roi doit gouverner par raison ;[2] d'autres disaient qu'il devait gouverner conformément à la loi naturelle. Devançant sur ce point Montesquieu, il dit, dans le langage de son temps, que Dieu même a des lois.[3] Comme le disaient les *Monarchomaques*, ses contemporains, en parlant surtout des lois fondamentales, il affirme que la loi est une convention entre le Prince et ses sujets, qui lie les deux parties. Comme Bracton, il proclame que le Prince doit respecter la loi, parce qu'il ne règne que par elle.[4] Il considère d'ailleurs que le monarque est un officier public et remplit une charge,[5] et il doit à ses sujets l'exemple nécessaire du respect des lois.

Dans un pareil milieu l'autorité de la règle *Princeps legibus solutus est* devait décroître progressivement. On tendait à y voir

[1] *Pandectes*, *loc. cit.* p. 41 : « La question qui se présente est très espineuse et ne se peut qu'avec difficulté traicter en une monarchie à cause des flatteurs courtisans qui tirent souvent en mauvaise part ce qu'on allègue de la bonté et modération du Prince. Toutesfoys j'en diray mon opinion conformément à ce que nos Roys, vrais et excellens princes, ont tousjours observé.» P. 42 : « Si quelques courtisans veulent dire qu'il ne faut donner frein ni bride au souverain, je leur respondray que la Loy n'est une bride forcée, ains un doux lien qui le retient en son devoir et rend plus fort son estat. »

[2] *Pandectes*, *loc. cit.* p. 41 : « Mais le Prince, qui est homme et commande aux hommes libres qui sont participans d'une mesme nature et sçavent que c'est de gouverner par raison, ne se peut plus seurement maintenir avec eux que par commun lien et accord de la loy. »

[3] *Pandectes*, *loc. cit.* p. 41 : « S'il faut plus avant philosopher, il semble combien que Dieu par sa puissance souveraine et absolue puisse remuer tout l'ordre de l'Univers et n'y soit aucunement astraint, toutesfoys que pour le conserver il s'y rende aucunement subject, c'est à dire qu'il y accommode sa volonté et puissance qu'on appelle ordinaire.»

[4] *Pandectes*, *loc. cit.* p. 41 : « La loy qui est (à bien dire en peu de paroles) une mutuelle convention entre le souverain et le peuple de bien commander et bien obéir, pourquoy donc le souverain n'y sera subject ? Tous les roys, empereurs et monarques qui ont mérité le tiltre de bons princes, ont tousjours dict que le Prince devoit obéir aux loix, d'autant qu'il régnoit par l'auctorité d'icelles. »

[5] *Pandectes*, *loc. cit.* p. 42 : « Car si le Prince doit obeyir à la loi divine et naturelle, il peut apprendre par icelle qu'il faut que par son exemple il incite ses subjects à bien vivre, ce qu'il ne peut faire s'il ne se rend subject aux loix de son royaume, parce que la personne publique ne doit seulement bien vivre en son particulier, ains aussi selon le droit que requiert sa charge. »

une ressource, fondée en droit, mais qui normalement restait dormante par la volonté même du monarque, celui-ci préférant le règne des lois.[1] Nos anciens auteurs signalaient en particulier et avec raison sa jurisprudence reçue en France, qui rendait le roi justiciable de ses propres cours, et permettaient à ses sujets d'agir contre lui, pour faire valoir le droit résultant de la propriété ou des contrats. Il est vrai qu'alors le procureur du roi figurait seul en nom au procès ; c'était contre lui que le jugement était rendu, mais c'était le roi qui en subissait les conséquences. Tout cela d'ailleurs n'empêchait point que la pratique des lettres de cachet n'entrât dans son plein ; mais elle prenait l'aspect d'une institution particulière, ayant sa valeur propre.

Dans la seconde moitié du XVII^e siècle, les grands esprits qui construisaient la théorie de la monarchie absolue, alors réalisée, s'efforcaient de réduire, autant qu'il était possible, la portée de la maxime ; ils en avaient vraiment honte. Écoutons Bossuet, dans sa *Politique tirée des propres paroles de l'Écriture Sainte* : « Les rois ne sont pas pour cela affranchis des lois. C'est ce que les Princes ont peine à entendre. . . . De là cette belle loi d'un empereur romain : c'est une parole digne de la Majesté du Prince que de se reconnaître soumis aux lois. »[2] Et, continuant, voici en quels termes il expose sa théorie : « Les rois sont donc soumis comme les autres à l'équité des lois, et parce qu'ils doivent être justes et parce qu'ils doivent aux sujets l'exemple de garder la justice ; mais ils ne sont pas soumis aux peines des lois, ou, comme parle la théologie, ils sont soumis aux lois, non quant à la puissance coactive, mais quant à la puissance directive. » Dans la *proposition* précédente, intitulée *qu'il n'y a point de puissance coactive contre le Prince*, il avait écrit : « On entend par force coactive une puissance pour contraindre à exécuter ce qui est ordonné légalement. Au Prince seul appartient le commandement légitime, à lui seul appartient la force coactive. » Cela revenait à dire que moralement et même juridiquement le Prince était tenu de se conformer aux lois, mais qu'il pouvait s'en écarter *impunément*, n'étant pas soumis aux peines des lois, et aucune sanction n'étant possible contre lui.

[1] La Roche-Flavin, *Treize Livres des Parlements*, L. xiii. ch. 13, N° 6 : « Chose digne de la majesté d'un Prince que nos rois, à qui Dieu a donné puissance absolue, aient d'ancienne institution voulu réduire leurs volontés à la civilité des lois. »

[2] Livre iv. article 1, quatrième proposition.

La doctrine du grand jurisconsulte Domat, dans son *Droit public*, est à peu près la même : « On peut ajouter pour dernier devoir du souverain et qui renferme aussi tous les autres, qu'encore que sa puissance semble le mettre au-dessus des lois, personne n'ayant droit de lui faire rendre compte de sa conduite, il doit observer celles qui peuvent le regarder et y est obligé, non seulement pour donner l'exemple aux sujets et leur rendre leur devoir aimable, mais encore parce qu'il n'est pas dispensé du sien par cette puissance de souverain et qu'au contraire ce rang l'oblige même à préférer à ses intérêts particuliers le bien commun de l'État et qu'il est de sa gloire de regarder comme le sien propre. »[1]

Cependant jusqu'à la fin de l'ancien régime la règle resta dans le droit public, comme subsistèrent les lettres de cachet, qui ne furent abolies que par l'Assemblée Constituante. Les esprits libéraux qui restaient attachés aux principes traditionnels de l'ancienne monarchie n'osaient pas répudier ce droit anormal du roi. Voici ce qu'on lit encore dans un livre publié quelques années avant la Révolution et qui eut plusieurs éditions : « De quelque utilité que soient les formes légales pour intimider le coupable par la certitude de la peine que la loi prononce et pour tranquilliser l'innocence contre les efforts de la calomnie, pour mettre le monarque à l'abri des surprises, elles lui laissent cependant l'administration libre, forcées de céder elles-mêmes à l'intérêt public dont le monarque est le seul juge. »[2] L'auteur, qui est un esprit éclairé cependant, considère cette faculté laissée au roi comme une loi fondamentale de l'État, et il y rattache les lettres de cachet, qu'il approuve dans leurs principales applications. Moreau, dans son livre intitulé *Les Devoirs du Prince ramenés à un seul principe ou Discours sur la justice dédié au roi*,[3] qui avait été composé pour l'éducation de Louis XVI et de ses frères, soutient une thèse semblable. Voici comment il défend les lettres de cachet contenant un ordre d'emprisonnement ; il est vrai que suivant lui ce doit être là simplement une mesure provisoire et le prisonnier doit être dans un court délai renvoyé devant ses juges naturels : « Les formes qui accompagnent essentiellement la marche de celle-ci (la justice) sont lentes et

1 Domat, *Droit public*, L. i. tit. 2, sect. 3, N° 14.

2 *Les Vrais Principes du gouvernement français*, *démontrés par la raison et par les faits*, par un François, Genève 1782, p. 66.

3 A Versailles de l'imprimerie du roi, Départ. des aff. étr. 1775, p. 160.

tardives. Elles furent inventées pour être le rempart de l'innocence. Doit-on souffrir qu'elles facilitent l'évasion du crime et lui servent en quelque façon de barrière? Non. Les ordres rapides de l'administration dans ce moment vont au secours de la juridiction elle-même. Le coupable que désigne la voix publique est alors arrêté par le commandement du Prince. Ce n'est point un jugement qu'il prononce. C'est une précaution par laquelle il empêche que ce jugement soit un jour inutile. Mais cette même autorité qui a ôté au malfaiteur le pouvoir de fuir, le doit livrer aussitôt à la justice, dont elle n'a fait que prévenir et faciliter les démarches.»

Mais la philosophie du XVIII^e^ siècle, reprenant avec une force nouvelle la doctrine exposée par les *Monarchomaques* du XVI^e^ siècle, proclamait, comme une règle essentielle de l'État, l'empire absolu et inévitable de la loi. Je ne citerai qu'un passage de Voltaire, qui dans un de ses Dialogues fait ainsi parler un Anglais: «Ce que je trouve de plus juste c'est *liberté* et *propriété*. . . . Je veux que chacun ait sa prérogative. Je ne connais de lois que celles qui me protègent, et je trouve notre gouvernement le meilleur de la terre parce que chacun y sait ce qu'il a, ce qu'il doit et ce qu'il peut. Tout est soumis à la loi, à commencer par la royauté et par la religion.»[1] C'était une cause gagnée devant l'opinion publique, et la Constitution française de 1791 enregistrait la règle nouvelle dans ces termes, d'une précision et d'une élévation admirables: «Il n'y a point en France d'autorité supérieure à celle de la loi. Le roi ne règne que par elle, et ce n'est qu'au nom de la loi qu'il peut exiger l'obéissance.»[2]

A. ESMEIN.

[1] *L'A, B, C ou Dialogues entre A, B, C*, traduit de l'anglais de M. Huet, troisième dialogue.

[2] Constitution du 3 septembre 1791, tit. ii. ch. 2, sect. 1, art. 3.

# XI

## TWO ANCIENT BROCARDS

THE object of this paper is to explain the import and trace the history, so far as possible, of two ancient brocards familiar to modern lawyers and in daily use in British Courts. The term brocard (low Latin *brocarda*, also *brocardica* and other forms[1]) is mediaeval. Calvin, in his *Lexicon*, says contemptuously: *Vocabulum est barbarum in nostro eleganti Jure Civili; relinquendum igitur barbaris.* It means a legal maxim or axiom or rule—a *regula juris.* Brocards are rather apt to be dangerous weapons in the armoury of lawyers. They are apt to represent conclusions based on slender premisses, or generalizations from an inadequate number of particulars, the exceptions to the rule being often more or less disregarded or left out of view in formulating the rule. Sometimes they have acted as Will-o'-the-wisps to lead the Courts astray in their decisions. In his preface to the second edition of Barbosa's *Axiomata*, J. O. Tabor discusses the utility of collections of so-called *loci communes* and mentions several noted jurisconsults (including Duarenus and Cujacius) who wholly discountenanced them. *Plaustra ista brocardicorum*, said one old jurist, *obscurare sacrosanctam veritatem et cognoscendi religionem.*[2]

Nevertheless brocards and maxims have a certain utility in concentrating ideas, stimulating the memory, and otherwise, and they have been much employed both by the classical jurists of Rome and the great lawyers of the Middle Ages.

1 See Calvin, *Lexicon jurid.* and Du Cange, s.v.

2 Herman Lather, *de Cens.* 1618, lib. 2, c. 3, Num. 9, § 60; see Cujac. *Epist. consult. praefat.*

## I. Actio Personalis Moritur cum Persona

(*a*) *Its Import.—General Observations on the Meaning of Personal Action in English Law.*

Though this is one of the most familiar maxims of English Law, the veil of obscurity covers not only its origin but its true import and significance. It is certainly an ancient maxim; the late Lord Justice Bowen claimed for it (though erroneously, I think) an antiquity as great as that of the English Common Law itself.[1] It was not taken from the Roman Law nor from any mediaeval civilian; indeed to a Roman lawyer or to a civilian it would have sounded nonsensical; yet it has, as we shall see, an indirect connexion with the Roman Law. Many cases in our English Courts have been decided on the strength of it, and it has been the source of not a little injustice. Though sometimes a lance has been raised on its behalf, it has, in my opinion, been rightly denounced by one of our best English lawyers as 'a barbarous rule.'[2]

We may translate the maxim thus—'a personal right of action comes to an end by the death of either of the parties.' Now, first, we must see what is meant here by personal action. The familiar division of Roman Law into actions *in rem* and *in personam*—the former being vindications of property and real rights, the latter arising out of obligations—was never received into English Law. On the other hand, old English Common Law divided actions into *real* and *personal* in a special and peculiar sense: the former, the real actions, being those by which rights to heritable property (realty) were enforced; the latter, the personal actions, being those by which rights to moveable chattels, choses in action, etc., were enforced.[3] This division, old apparently as the Conquest, was due to the Feudal Law, which, unlike the Roman, made a fundamental distinction between rights in lands and other immoveables and

[1] *Phillips* v. *Homfray*, 1883, L.R. 24 Ch. Div. 439: In *Finlay* v. *Chirney*, 1887, 20 Q.B. Div. p. 494, Bowen and Fry, L.JJ., say of the maxim that its origin is 'obscure and post-classical.'

[2] Pollock, *Torts*, p. 64.

[3] Mixed actions (partly real and partly personal) need not be referred to. The term *realis actio* is purely mediaeval. The term *personalis actio*, in the sense of *actio in personam*, appears occasionally in the *Digest* (e.g. *Dig.* x. 4, 3 § 3), but it may be due to interpolation of the compilers.

rights in moveable or personal property. Real actions, however, in the above sense gradually became obsolete and were ultimately abolished by statute, their effects being obtained indirectly by personal actions. There is no such thing as *rei vindicatio* in modern English Law.

Personal actions in English Law are, in the words of Blackstone, 'Such whereby a man claims a debt or personal duty or damages in lieu thereof; and likewise whereby a man claims a satisfaction in damages for some injury done to his person or property. The former are said to be founded on contracts, the latter upon torts or wrongs.'[1] Now it is in this wide sense that *actio personalis* in our brocard should be *prima facie* understood, but, as we shall see, it was never, from the time it was first formulated, extended so far in practice. Had the maxim been taken literally the result would have been that every right of action, whether arising out of contract or of tort or other obligation, would have come to an end by the death of either party. A covenant, for instance, would have ceased to be actionable by the death of either covenantor or covenantee or a contract of bailment by the death of bailor or bailee. But an examination of the Reports from early times shows that the Common Law never went so far. Apart from torts, the utmost that can be said is that the old English Law, for a brief period, refused to recognize the transmission passively of actions on *contract*, and even this can only be admitted subject to exceptions, e.g. actions on covenant under seal. But it clearly ceased to be the rule once a definite theory of contract was developed and the action of assumpsit established. When this stage was reached we find that, apart from one or two special contractual claims such as the old actions of Debt and Account,[2] and (later) the action of breach of promise of marriage, actions on contract survived *ab utraque parte*, and non-transmissibility on death became restricted in practice to actions based on tort or on facts analogous to tort. In other words, non-transmissibility applied as a rule only to actions for reparation of damages for injuries and penalties for wrongful acts. As is said in Dyer's Reports, 'actio personalis

[1] Bl. *Com.* iii. p. 117.

[2] I.e. as regards passive liability of executors. The action of account seems not to have transmitted against executors. See Bacon, *Abridgment*, ii. p. 444; Holdsworth, *Hist. of English Law*, iii. p. 455.

quae oritur cx contractu dieth not, yet quae oritur ex delicto moritur cum persona, as all trespasses.'[1] This suggests that our maxim was originally deduced from a misunderstanding of the Roman Law and, before going further, it may be useful to state here very briefly what the rules of that Law were on transmissibility of actions on death.

(*b*) *Transmissibility of Actions on Death by Roman Law.*

As is well known, a material difference existed from a pretty early period in Roman Law between contracts on the one hand and delicts on the other as regards transmission of actions to and against the heirs of the parties. In contracts the right of action almost invariably transmitted both to the heirs of the creditor and against the heirs of the debtor; in delicts transmission depended largely upon whether the action was of a penal nature or not. If it were *poenalis* the general rule was that it transmitted to the heirs of the injured party (i.e. actively) but not against the heirs of the wrongdoer (i.e. passively). The maxim was *actio poenalis transit heredibus sed non transit in heredes.*[2] The *actio furti*, for example, could be brought by the heirs of the injured party against the thief but not by the injured party against the heirs of the thief. Where, on the other hand, a delictal action was not strictly penal—e.g. the *actio doli*—it transmitted both actively and passively, except that as a rule passive transmission was only allowed so far as the deceased's heir had received benefit from the wrong.[3]

But to the rule *actio poenalis transit heredi sed non in heredem* there were several well-known exceptions of much importance. To the first part of the maxim—viz. *transit heredi*—I remind you of the two following:—

1st.—Injury to a freeman which caused his death gave no right of action to his heirs for damages either *in factum* under the *lex Aquilia* or otherwise. The reason for this usually given by the jurists was that no money-value can be put on the life of a freeman: *liberum corpus nullam recipit aestimationem.*[4] To this harsh rule the Roman Law steadily adhered down to Justinian; the jurists were apparently obsessed by the idea that the person of a

[1] Dyer's Rep. 271, 14a.

[2] *Dig.* xlvii. 1, 1; Gaius, *Com.* iv. 112.

[3] On the extent of this exception the Roman texts are not altogether consistent.

[4] *Dig.* ix. 3, 3; ix. 3, 1 § 5; cf. *Dig.* ix. 2, 13 pr.

freeman had no money-value and that there could be no patrimonial loss to a man's family where the injury to himself could not be estimated. This has also always been the rule of English Common Law, based on our brocard, though, as we shall see in a moment, it has been considerably modified by modern statutes.

2nd Exception.—Injury to a man's person or reputation done wilfully, as by assault, slander, etc., gave no right of action to his heirs. In short, the *actio injuriarum* and a few similar actions did not transmit at all. The principal reason given by the jurists for this exception was that the object of such actions was more one of revenge than of reparation—far from a satisfactory reason once pecuniary compensation had taken the place of self-revenge. It and the other actively intransmissible actions of a similar character in the classical law were called actions *vindictam spirantes*.[1]

On the other hand, to the second part of the maxim—viz. *non transit in heredem*—an important exception occurred in penal actions for injuries to *property*, in which it could be shown that the estate of the deceased tort-feasor had received benefit from the delict committed. The injured party was allowed in such case (just as I have said in the case of non-penal actions based on delict) to sue the heirs of the tort-feasor *in quantum lucrati sunt*.[2] The *actio legis Aquiliae* is a well-known example.[2]

Finally—all actions *ex delicto*, whether penal or not, transmitted both to and against heirs, if the suit had already begun in the lifetime of the principal parties. This was on the theory of litis contestation having created a judicial contract between the parties: *Litis contestatione poenales actiones transmittuntur ab utraque parte*.[3]

Such, then, broadly stated, were the rules of the Roman Law as regards transmissibility of actions *ex delicto*.

(*c*) *Transmissibility of Actions on Death by English Law.*

The English Common Law from early times proceeded to a large extent on different lines from these doctrines of the Roman jurists. I have already broadly indicated how far it held actions to enforce simple contracts to be extinguished by death of either party; and for the moment I leave contracts aside. Apart from

[1] E.g. 'querela inofficiosi testamenti.' See Gaius iv. 112; *Dig.* iii. 6, 4.
[2] *Dig.* l. 17, 38; ix. 23 § 8.
[3] *Dig.* xxvii. 7, 8 § 1.

contracts, English Common Law has, as a rule, treated death of either party as sufficient to bar all action on tort both by and against executors. And whether the plaintiff was seeking damages by way of penalty or as simple reparation or otherwise, and whether the action had been already begun during the lifetime of the principal parties or not, made no difference. To this latter point I will recur in a moment. The only Common Law exception to the rule was that property positively appropriated by a deceased tort-feasor to his benefit, or its value, could be recovered from his executors by an action which was substantially one for recovery of property. In other words, passive liability of executors was recognized where the deceased's estate had been enriched by the wrong.[1] This Common-Law bar to right of action on tort by death of either party often proved very inequitable, especially in cases of damage to property, and certain remedies were gradually, though tardily, supplied by statute. The first remedial step was indeed taken pretty early, viz. by 4 Edward III cap. 7, which enacted that for trespass done to a man's goods and chattels during his lifetime his executors might sue. This statute, though liberally construed, did not go far, being limited to active transmissibility and to *personal* property. But nearly five centuries had to elapse before a wider step in the same direction was taken, viz. by 3 and 4 William IV cap. 42. This Act, in the first place, made actions for wrongful damage to *real* property transmissible to personal representatives of the injured party, just as the Act of Edward had done for personal property, but subject to the condition that the damage had been done within six months prior to the death and that the action was begun within twelve months after the death. In the second place it sanctioned *passive* transmissibility by providing that the personal representatives of one who had caused wrongful damage to property, whether real or personal, of another should be liable by action of trespass or trespass on the case to the extent of his assets, but subject always to similar limitations as to time of injury and of raising action.

The practical effect of these statutes of Edward and William was to put the English Law (as regards transmission on death of actions for damage to *property*) on pretty nearly the same footing

[1] See *Phillips* v. *Homfray*, *supra*, per Bowen, L.J.; Holdsworth, *Hist. E. L.* iii. 455.

as the Roman Law on the subject, apart from the just-mentioned limitations of time.[1] One great difference was left unaltered, viz. the effect of action begun *ante mortem.* While by Roman Law, as we have seen, litis contestation ensured transmissibility of the action to the heirs in every case, English Common Law gave no effect to it. If, after an action on tort has been competently brought, one of the parties dies, the action abates by English Law *in accordance with our brocard*, and does not pass to or against his personal representatives. Despite some slight attenuations introduced into modern practice,[2] the rule remains as stated. This is strongly illustrated by the case of *Bowker* v. *Evans*, in 1885, where an action on tort having been referred by the judge to arbitration, in accordance with previous agreement of parties, and one of the parties having died while the arbitration was pending, his executor was not allowed to take his place, although it had been expressly stipulated by the parties that the award should take effect though either party died before it was issued.[3] It seems impossible to justify this in equity or good sense.[4]

The statutes of Edward and William just mentioned relate, it will be noticed, solely to injuries to property.[5] For injuries to person, on the other hand, little change was made by legislation. One or two recent statutes, however, have caused English Law in one respect to make a step in advance of the Roman, viz. by allowing actions of damages to be brought under certain circumstances by the personal representatives of persons killed by fault (actual or constructive) of others. This was first done in 1846 by the Fatal Accidents Act (commonly called, after its author, Lord

1 Equity in this matter follows the law. See *Peek* v. *Gurney*, 1873, 6 H.L. App. 393.

2 See *Twycross* v. *Grant*, 1878, 4 C.P.D. 40. But see note 4 *infra.*

3 15 Q.B.D. 565. The agreement for reference to arbitration was held to be mere matter of procedure, which could not affect the rights of parties under the action.

4 Oddly enough, in a marginal note to some MSS. of Bracton, fol. 114b (which cannot be well attributed to B. himself), it is said: 'Notandum quod poenalis actio non datur in heredes nec transit in eos nisi lis fuerit contestata cum defuncto.' See Maitland, *Bracton and Azo* (Selden Series), p. 213.

5 It should be noticed that while the Roman Law only allowed damages to be claimed from *heredes*, so far as they were *lucrati* by the wrongful act, English Law under 3 and 4 Wm. IV allows action for injury to property, if timeously brought, to have effect so far as the deceased left assets. This is in accordance with Canon Law and mediaeval practice. See *infra*, p. 228 n. 1.

Campbell's Act),[1] which enabled children and certain other near relatives of persons killed to recover through the executors (under certain conditions as to time of raising action, etc.) damages for pecuniary loss thereby sustained by them. Subsequently the Employers Liability Act enabled executors of certain employees to sue where death was caused by injuries specified in the Act.[2] This is a more enlightened view than is contained in the Roman maxim *liberum corpus nullam recipit aestimationem.*

But these several statutory reforms, important though they are, do not after all go very far. The Common Law still remains in force as regards ordinary actions on tort, and so far *actio personalis moritur cum persona* retains its force as a binding maxim.

(*d*) *Traces of Origin of Brocard.*

I shall now endeavour to trace the origin of our brocard. We have seen that it is not Roman; neither is it traceable to any of the post-Justinian civilians or to the *Corpus Juris Canonici.* We must, I think, turn in the first place to Bracton. The maxim indeed is not to be found in his pages, but he may be none the less its *fons et origo.* Bracton, who wrote his *De Legibus et Consuetudinibus Angliae* in the middle of the thirteenth century, borrowed, as is well known, a large amount of his matter (not purely feudal) from the Roman Law. He did so in part (but only in small part) from the texts of the *Corpus Juris* directly, but to a large extent, as Dr. Carl Güterbock pointed out long ago, from the Summa of the *Code* and *Institutes* of the famous glossarist Azo. Now, in dealing with obligations, which he does under the general head of actions, he says this about the modes of their extinction (fol. 101): *Item tollitur* [*obligatio*] *morte alterius contrahentium, vel utriusque, maxime si sit poenalis, vel simplex—si autem duplex, scilicet poenalis et rei persecutoriae, in hoc quod poenalis est tollitur, et non extenditur contra heredes, nec datur heredibus, quia poena tenet suos auctores et extinguitur cum persona,* i.e. an obligation is 'also got rid of by the death of either of the contracting parties or of both, especially if it is a penal obligation or a simple one; but if it be a double one, namely penal and for recovery, it is got rid of as far as it is penal and it does not extend to the heirs, nor is it

[1] 9 and 10 Vict. c. 93, ss. 1, 2.

[2] 43 and 44 Vict. c. 42, s. 1. See also Workmen's Compensation Act (1906), s. 13.

allowed to the heirs, because a penalty binds the original parties and is extinguished with the person.'[1] This is wholly confused. It is evident that in seeking to apply the Roman doctrine on this matter to English Law (and he is plainly not stating existing English rules) he has failed to distinguish between *obligatio* and *actio.* As I have said, he treats the doctrine of obligations under the head of actions (which in itself is not without justification, as we know from Theophilus); but he mixes them up in a strange way. The whole section about the dissolution of obligations has been taken, as Maitland points out,[2] in part from Azo's *Commentary on Inst.* iii. 29 (*Quibus modis obligatio dissolvitur*) and in part from the *Institutes* directly. But the passage I have just cited is not in Azo, nor anything like it, much less in the *Institutes*, and is, I need hardly say, very far from representing Roman Law. Whether it is Bracton's own or was taken by him from some other source, I am unable to say. It looks like his own.[3] What Bracton may perhaps have had before his mind in composing it was contracts of a penal character, i.e. contracts in which non-performance was treated as delictal and punished by a penalty or amercement (e.g. the action of debt). Nearly all contracts seem to have been of this character in his age; they were, with few exceptions (as where made in writing by solemn form, or perhaps where there was *res data*), enforceable only by actions of a delictal character. Contracts and torts were, in short, hardly distinguished. The fact is—one cannot dispute it—that, great as were Bracton's merits in other respects, his knowledge of Roman Law was utterly defective. In appropriating passages from the *Corpus Juris* and from Azo, he over and over again fails to understand them, makes the most bewildering statements, and is not seldom self-contradictory. This must be said even in view of Professor Maitland's warning about possible defects in the manuscripts.[4] As glaring illustrations of such blunders, I may be permitted to refer to one or two other passages in addition to the one cited. Thus in the same section as

[1] Edition of Twiss, ii. p. 123. Cited by Bowen, L.J., in *Finlay* v. *Chirney*, *supra*, p. 216 n.

[2] *Bracton and Azo* (Selden Series), p. 162.

[3] 'Culpa tenet suos auctores' is in Code *De Poenis*, l. 24. That Bracton borrowed from some other civilian than Azo is very probable; who this was remains to be discovered.

[4] *Bracton and Azo* (Selden Series), p. xvii.

the above he explains the dissolution of obligations *confusione* in this way: *Item per confusionem [obligatio tollitur] ut si massa confusa fuerit cum alia, ita quod non appareat*, here understanding *confusio* in the sense it has in the doctrine of property—mixture of different materials. Again, on folio 99b, he applies a sentence in Justinian's *Institutes*, iii. 14, which relates to *mutuum* to the contract of *commodatum*, so as to make the *commodo accipiens* liable for injury to the thing by *casus*, though a little farther on he negatives such liability. Attempts have been made to rectify this passage as a MS. error, but to me it appears an evident blunder due to want of knowledge. Again, on folio 102, he treats actions *rei persequendae causa* as equivalent to actions *in rem* and says: *Omnes fere personales actiones sunt ex contractu, sicut mutui commodati*, etc., obviously misunderstanding the passage in the *Institutes*, iv. 6, § 17, which runs: *Earum vero actionum quae in personam sunt, hae quidem quae ex contractu nascuntur fere omnes rei persequendae causa videntur.* But it is needless to multiply examples; they abound.[1] In view of what I have just said, it is impossible to be sure of what Bracton intended in the passage above cited, asserting that contracts perished by the death of either of the contracting parties. I think he probably meant no more than that contracts were so dissolved in which non-performance was treated as delictal and amercement or fine followed judgment (e.g. Action of Debt), because he says later, fol. 102: *Personales vero actiones . . . locum habent adversus eum qui contraxit et heredem suum, nisi sint poenales.*[2] But, whatever he meant, his statement was copied by Fleta,[3] and to some extent influenced

[1] These and other instances have been noted by Maitland in *Bracton and Azo, supra.* A specially glaring case is iii. 3, § 9, fol. 103b, which Maitland describes as a 'marvellous mess.'

Where Azo (or his MS.) is wrong Bracton follows him—e.g. compare Azo in *Inst.* ii. 1, f. 244, No. 7 with Bracton ii. 1, § 2, where both use *apprehensionem* apparently for *aucupium* and misunderstand *Dig.* xli. 1, 55. Did Bracton in his constant slight changes in the phraseology of Azo (e.g. substituting Sempronius for Seius and Maenius for Maevius) intend to compound with his conscience for plagiarizing him?

[2] See also folio 101b, where, dealing specially with delictual actions, he says: 'In iis autem delictis sive maleficiis obligatur ille qui delinquit ei contra quem delinquitur, nec dissolvitur obligatio *quoad poenam* nisi morte utriusque vel alterius.'

[3] ii. 60, § 9. The extent of the influence of Bracton on the Common Law

the Courts, so that for a time apparently nearly all personal actions (whether on contract or delict) were held to be intransmissible (either actively or passively) on death of one of the parties, though, as already indicated, this soon became restricted to actions on tort. But however this be, in the Year Books after Edward I there is little evidence that an action purely on contract was intransmissible either to or against executors, apart from the passive intransmissibility of actions of Debt and Account already mentioned. The law, however, was anything but settled. The Report in *Y.B.* 15, Ed. IV *Term. Hill.* 16, 3, bears that in certain cases an action for *debt* did not lie against an executor of a testator, for the reason that the testator might have waged his law, which executors could not do.[1] Most, if not all, other cases in the Year Books in which transmission was not allowed (so far at least as text-writers have noticed them) were in form actions for damages to person and property (e.g. actions of waste and trespass). In *Y.B.* 19 Hen. VI 66, pl. 10 (A.D. 1440) (an action by churchwardens for things carried off from a church), Chief Justice Newton said, 'If one doeth a *trespass* to me and dieth, the action is dead also, because it should be inconvenient to recover against one who was not a party to the wrong.' It is curious, however, that we do not find our maxim, *actio personalis moritur*, cited in the Year Books anywhere. It is said indeed by Reeves to have been employed in *Y.B.* 12 Hen. VIII.[2] This Report is interesting. It was an action on the case brought by executors to enforce a personal promise of guarantee, and the Court was unanimous in holding the action competent. Fineux, Chief Justice, said—and his words deserve attention—'This is not a case where *actio moritur cum persona*, for that only applied where the hurt or damage is corporal; as if one beats me, and dies, my action is gone; or if I die, my executors will not have an action, for the party cannot be punished when he is dead.' This means, I take it, that in the opinion of the Chief Justice it was only penal actions that were terminated by death of party. But Reeves[3] apparently makes a mistake in attributing to the Chief Justice the words *actio personalis moritur*; the words of the Report in the black-letter

is much disputed. It may be perhaps compared to that of Craig (*Jus Feudale*) in Scots Law.

[1] See also Bacon, Abr. s.v. *Executors*, ii. p. 444.

[2] Fol. 11, pl. 3.

[3] *History of English Law*, iii. p. 403.

edition of the Year Books are simply *actio moritur cum persona*, and there seems no reason for supplying the word *personalis* rather than *poenalis*.

The decision in this case of 12 Henry VIII is subsequently denounced by Fitzherbert in an opinion delivered by him in the year 1536 and reported in the Year Book 27 Henry VIII, fol. 23. Though this eminent judge does not cite our maxim, he expressly declares that the last-mentioned decision was bad law, telling us at the same time that he himself had been counsel for one of the parties in it. It is difficult to avoid the conclusion that Fitzherbert took the view that personal actions generally (whether on contract or on tort) did not transmit at Common Law either to or against executors. No reason is reported to have been given by him; and, though his opinion may have governed the practice of the Courts for a time,[1] the question was soon after settled by the case of *Norwood* v. *Reid*[2] and that of Pinchon, *tempore* James I (1609), reported by Coke.[3] The latter of these was an action on Contract (*assumpsit*); and here for the first time, so far as I have been able to discover, the phrase *actio personalis moritur cum persona* was judicially used. Perhaps Coke himself invented it. In Pinchon's case the Court disregarded the opinion of Fitzherbert and in effect followed the earlier judgment in 12 Henry VIII, above cited. After this, our maxim seems to have become common in practice, but, save in the old action of Debt and the modern action for breach of promise of marriage, it never received any effect in actions on contract or quasi-contract. Its currency in the Law Courts after Elizabeth is undoubted. It appears in Noy's *Grounds and Maxims of the English Laws*,[4] first published in 1640. Noy, who was Attorney-General under Charles I, seems to have understood the maxim in its literal sense as applicable to contractual as well as delictual obligations. As a legal writer, however, he is of little authority. What is rather interesting is that in the fifth edition of this book, published with notes and additions in 1757, Bacon is referred to as authority for the maxim. Now Lord Bacon did write a small work on legal maxims. It is styled *Rules and Maximes of the Common Lawes of England*, and was dedicated to Queen Elizabeth. It was not

[1] Reeves, *ut supra*.
[2] Plowd. p. 180.
[3] 9 Rep. 86b.
[4] Noy, 6th ed. 1794, Maxim 14.

published, however, till 1630. When we turn to this work we find that Bacon does not include *actio personalis moritur* among his collected maxims, nor does he make the mistake of using that expression at all. But, oddly enough, he does give incidentally a maxim which differs by only one word from Noy's, viz. *actio injuriarum moritur cum persona*, and it is to this presumably that Noy's editor refers. Now, this maxim of Bacon, if taken in its literal sense, would, as I have shown, quite accurately represent the Roman Law. But unfortunately Bacon misunderstands, on his part, the meaning of *actio injuriarum*—showing that his knowledge of Roman Law must have been very slight. He applies it to damage to property—viz. waste by a tenant for years, thus failing to distinguish between *injuria* as a personal wrong and injury to property or *damnum injuria datum*.

Such, then, is the early history of our maxim. If I am right in my reading of the authorities, I think it came into our law owing to the misunderstanding by Bracton of the Roman Law, his inaccurate use of its language, and the consequently erroneous doctrine adopted by Fitzherbert and others. We can see from the older cases cited in Bacon's *Abridgment* how fluctuating and diverse were the applications of the maxim in practice. It has been suggested that the expression *actio personalis* is merely a mistake for *actio poenalis*, due originally to some careless manuscript copyist.[1] But in view of the language of Bracton and Fitzherbert this conjecture may be discarded. Nor of course, as we have seen, would *actio poenalis moritur cum persona* be at all correct for Roman Law.

(*e*) *Its Application in Scots Law.*

Till quite recent times our brocard was unknown to Scots Law. It is nowhere referred to by the great Scotch institutional writers, such as Stair and Erskine, nor does it appear in any of the Reports of Cases prior to the nineteenth century. It has indeed crept into the terminology of the Courts in some recent decisions, but without being, in my opinion, properly appreciated—an exotic borrowed from English Law. Speaking generally, both as regards active and passive transmission of penal actions (i.e. actions for damages in excess of bare reparation), Scots Law has for the most part followed the Roman, but in part the Canon Law. Thus for passive survival

[1] See B. *Abridg.* ii. pp. 444-5.

the rule of the Canon Law is applied, and personal representatives are liable only so far as deceased left assets.[1] On the other hand, as regards the effect of litis contestation or pendency of suit at death of either the wrongdoer or the injured party, Scots Law follows the rule of the *Corpus Juris*.[2] Nevertheless in one or two respects, and particularly as regards transmission to representatives of the injured party, Scots Law has varied from the Roman rather remarkably. It has done so, in my opinion, on grounds of logic and good sense. Thus actions for personal injury, corresponding to the *actio injuriarum*, seem not to have been in older Scots Law barred as *vindictam spirantes* or on other grounds, but were held transmissible actively to the executors of the injured party. Such at least was decided in 1874 in an action of slander raised by an executrix of the person alleged to be slandered, in which the early authorities were all carefully considered.[3] The executrix averred that patrimonial damage had been caused to the deceased by the slander, and the action was held to be competent. It must, however, be admitted that in one or two recent cases of a similar nature the trend of judicial decision has been unfortunately to depart from this doctrine and accept, as regards personal injuries, our English brocard to a considerable extent. The doctrine on this point seems hardly settled.[4]

Further the law of Scotland, by long and well-established custom, allows the near relatives of persons who have been killed wilfully or negligently to sue the wrongdoer for damages—such damages including not only patrimonial loss but also solatium for mental distress. Only near relatives, however, who are in the

[1] *Davidson* v. *Tulloch*, 1860, 3 Macq. 783. Canon Law allowed transmission against executors, but only so far as the deceased's estate was available. This was a consequence doubtless of the limited representation by personal representatives in that system, but was based on religious grounds. See Savigny, *System*, v. § 211 ; and *infra*, p. 229 n. 3.

[2] *Neilson* v. *Rodger*, 16 D. 325 ; *Wood* v. *Gray*, 19 Ret. (H.L.) 31.

[3] *Auld* v. *Shairp*, 1874, 2 Ret. pp. 199, 940. In this case Moncrieff, J.C., seems to speak of 'actio personalis moritur' as a Roman maxim, and fails to distinguish between *personalis* and *poenalis*.

[4] See *General Bill Posting Co.* v. *Yonde*, 1910, S.C. 934, and cases there cited. The case of Bern's Executor, 1893, 20 Ret. 859, where the Court refused an action to the executor of a deceased lunatic for injuries done to the lunatic, causing patrimonial damage, was, in my opinion, a retrograde step. See criticism by Mr. R. M. Williamson in *L.Q.R.* x. p. 182, with which I agree.

position of dependents on the deceased, can sue, at least where death has been instantaneous. They sue in their own right and not in any representative capacity.[1] So far, then, Scots Law has disregarded the Roman maxim, *liberum corpus nullam recipit aestimationem.* The doctrine is one peculiar to Scotland, and was judicially admitted many centuries ago in the action of so-called assythment or kinbuit by which the near relatives of a murdered man could recover under certain conditions pecuniary damages from his murderer.[2] This action of assythment is now in desuetude, but an ordinary action for damages for fatal injury due to fault can always be brought. Lord Campbell's Act had no application to Scotland, and was never needed there.

In my judgment these variations of Scots Law from both the Roman and English Law are based on sound principles of equity. There is no sufficient reason why the representatives of a deceased person to whom personal wrong has been done should not have a right to damages which such person would have been able to enforce had he lived. It is a civil debt which should transmit like other debts. In short, there is no good reason why a deceased's estate, if he leaves assets, should not be held liable for every kind of injury done by him causing damage to another, and that whether the estate was positively enriched by the wrongful act or not.[3]

## II. Cujus est Solum ejus est usque ad Coelum

This brocard may be translated, 'He who owns land owns also that which is above it,' or, more literally, 'He who owns land owns everything above it up to the sky.'[4] It appears also in the

[1] In *McEvaney* v. *Caledonian Railway Co.*, *Scot. Law Times*, April 1913, the right of executors and other personal representatives of a person killed by negligence of another to sue for damages was held to depend on the deceased having made a claim for damages antecedent to his death. See also Erskine, *Principles*, 20th ed. p. 100.

[2] See Balfour, *Practicks*, p. 516—case of *Bairnis of James Steuart* v. *Robert Steuart*, 1539—for the grounds on which the rule is based.

[3] On the want of equity in the Roman Law as regards the limited transmission of delictal actions against heirs, see Savigny, *System*, v. § 211 (p. 50 sq.). Compare Bethmann-Hollweg, *Civil Progress*, ii. p. 298, n. 19, who takes a different view.

[4] See Broom, *Maxims*, pp. 300, 371, 376.

form *Cujus est solum ejus est a coelo usque ad centrum* (or *usque ad inferos*), i.e. 'He who owns land does so from the sky above it to the centre of the earth (or to Hades) below it.'[1] It is cited in Croke's Reports, in an action for stopping lights, as *Cujus est solum ejus est summitas usque ad coelum*, and a reference is there[2] made to its use in the time of Edward I. It is as old as the glossarists, though whether due to Irnerius or another I am unable to say. It appears in the Accursian gloss in the form *Cujus solum ejus esse debet usque ad coelum*.[3] On the other hand, I do not find that it was much used by the commentators or other Continental civilians after Accursius. Cujacius gives a somewhat different locution, viz. *Quo jure est coelum eodem jure esse debet solum et contra.* Barbosa does not give our maxim at all.

Unlike *actio personalis moritur cum persona*, our present brocard, though it appears nowhere in the Roman texts, is consistent with the Roman Law, and would not have sounded strange to the classical jurisconsults. The text that comes nearest to illustrating it is *Dig.* xliii. 24 fr. 22 § 4. It is from Venuleius, and he tells us there that the interdict *Quod vi aut clam* could be raised against anyone who caused anything to project over another's burial-place, for the reason that a burial-place includes not only the *solum* but the air-space (*coelum*) above it: *Si quis projectum aut stillicidium in sepulcrum immiserit, etiamsi ipsum monumentum non tangeret, recte cum eo agi quod in sepulcro vi aut clam factum sit, quia sepulcri sit non solum is locus qui recipiat humationem sed omne etiam supra ad coelum.*

The case figured is—Some one has placed a *projectum* which interferes with the free air-space above the burial-ground of a neighbour (*sepulcrum*). If no right of servitude exists the owner can have the interdict *Quod vi aut clam* just as much as if the *solum* itself had been encroached upon by an *opus manufactum.*

Another text is *Dig.* viii. 2, 1 pr., where it is stated that no servitude projiciendi or stillicidii could exist where a public place, such as a public road, intervened between the dominant and servient tenement, because *coelum liberum esse debet*, which means, I take

[1] See Lord Mackenzie, *Roman Law*, p. 170; Dart, *Vendors and Purchasers*, p. 129.

[2] Croke, *Eliz.* p. 118.

[3] Gloss to *Dig.* viii. 2, 1 pr.

it, that the air-space above the road should be free to all, like the road itself.[1] It was only from the point of view of vicinage and servitude that the Romans had occasion to consider the *coelum* in this sense. And it was the same with the mediaevalists. By our older British lawyers the maxim was usually cited in the following connexions: (1) in describing the nature and extent of property generally;[2] (2) in affirming the acquisition *ipso jure* by the owner of the soil of what is built or planted on it;[3] (3) in asserting the legal right not to have one's uses of one's own land prevented or restricted by one's neighbour using his for building, etc. (Baten's Case, *tempore* James I);[4] (4) in connexion with restrictions by servitudes of light, air, prospect, etc.

The maxim also, in its form *Cujus est solum ejus est a coelo usque ad centrum*, has been used in relation to mining claims and the like, in support of the doctrine that ownership of land extends beneath the surface in a direct line to the centre of the earth.[5]

Neither the Romans nor the mediaevalists had to consider the important questions of overhead rights that we moderns have to consider. Balloons and aeroplanes and other air-craft were beyond their ken. How the Romans would have dealt with such questions as interference with privacy, disturbance from noise, etc., arising from air-craft must, of course, be left to conjecture. But I venture to think that the right of property in the *coelum* would have sufficed to prevent air-transit over a man's ground and interdicts to prevent it would have been granted had damage been caused or threatened. The assertion of some recent writers that because the air, like the sea, is *res communis* and free to all, the circulation of air-craft would not have been prevented by Roman Law, is, to my mind, based on an erroneous assumption. It is assumed that *aër* and *coelum* mean the same thing. But though no formal distinction was made between them by the Roman jurists, and though the terms are sometimes used as equivalents, a distinction none the less existed. It was the *aër*—the omnipresent medium, never at rest and incapable of appropriation—that was *res communis*. It was

[1] See also *Dig.* xliii. 24, 21 § 2.

[2] Coke on Littleton, 4a.

[3] Stair, *Inst.* i. p. 296.

[4] 8 Jac. I, 9 Co. 54. This case is similar to *Dig.* xliii. 24, 22 § 4.

[5] Broom, *Legal Maxims*, p. 302.

so because necessary for the life and health of all. But in contrast with it the *coelum* was *res soli* and capable more or less of appropriation by the owner of the soil. In this sense it was not so much *aër* as *spatium* (or *regio*) *aëris*, and it is only in this sense that it can be understood in the two passages above cited. The common user of *aër* is indeed asserted by many passages in the Digest, but private ownership of the *coelum* is also asserted. There is no inconsistency.

Whether and how far actions of trespass, nuisance, or the like are by English Law competent to prevent transit by aeroplanes, etc., over private ground, are questions on which I do not enter. They have been abundantly discussed by recent writers, and the balance of authority seems greatly in favour of such actions being competent.[1] But whatever view may be taken, it is plain that our maxim will have much play in the judicial discussions that are likely to arise on the subject in the near future, and the matter is one that calls for regulation by statute. On the other hand, for International Law—resting partly on the same principles as the private law and partly on other considerations—we must hold that every State has the right of sovereignty over the air-space above its territory, and the consequent right to exclude foreigners from it, and rules for transit will have to be provided by international treaties. From the point of view of international rights air cannot be treated like the high seas, and we do not need a second Grotius to write an *aër liber*.

H. GOUDY.

[1] See the interesting French case, *Brinquant and others* v. *Farman and others*, July 1912, discussed by Valentine in *Juridical Review*, vol. xxiv. p. 321.

# XII

# A SKETCH OF THE HISTORY OF THE FOUR INNS OF COURT

## THE LAND ACROSS THE FLEET

THERE was no town or village on the site of the present City of London when Julius Caesar landed in Britain in 55 B.C. At that time, indeed, the estuary of the Thames was probably eight or ten times as wide as it is now; there was a considerable ebb and flow of the tide; and most of the land to the south of our present Holborn and Cheapside was then mere marsh or fen. Nor was there any London when the Romans occupied Britain for the second time in A.D. 43. This is shown by the fact that those who originally constructed the Watling Street—probably on the track of an earlier British road—ignored our metropolis and made their road pass half a mile or so on the western side of Westminster where it could more safely cross the Thames.

But there was a London of some kind before Agricola left England; Tacitus in his *Annals* (xiv. 33) mentions a Londinium as existing in A.D. 61. At first it was nothing more than a fortified barrack posted on a rocky hillock that rose out of the marshes of the Thames, on or near what we now call Ludgate Hill, and occupied only by soldiers and camp-followers. As trade developed merchants and hucksters and other non-combatants came to reside under its shelter, and London grew to be a colony. About A.D. 340, in all probability, it became a municipality, and at some date between A.D. 350 and 370 the famous Roman wall was built. It enclosed not only buildings but nearly a square mile of open country as well, in order to secure a supply of water and grazing for horses and cattle. This wall played a most important part in the subsequent history of London. It was wonderfully well and strongly built, and portions of it still exist.

We are not concerned to-day with the history of the City of London, most interesting though it is. I have to deal only with a small portion of the land which lay to the immediate west of the old Roman wall. This locality has for many centuries been largely frequented by lawyers, and it has therefore been sometimes styled the 'legal quarter of London.' In Norman times the monks called it the 'territory *ultra Fletam*.'

The Holeburn, or the stream in the hollow, rose in the Highgate ponds beneath Ken woods, and soon met another brook, which had its source in the Hampstead ponds that lie to the east of Haverstock Hill. The united stream ran down by Battle Bridge, round the north of Holborn Hill, and discharged itself into the estuary known as the Fleet. This was a tidal creek of the Thames flanked on each side by high banks where Holborn Viaduct now stands, but opening out more widely at the foot of Fleet Hill, which we now call Ludgate Hill, and then running into the Thames close under the Roman wall. At high tide it was wider than Farringdon Street is now. Poor little Fleet brook! After helping for centuries to guard the City of London on its western side, it came to be called the 'Fleet ditch,' and is now shut up in a sewer under Bridge Street. You may see it at low tide pouring its contents into the Thames through a round opening in the wall which supports St. Paul's railway station.

The land bordering on the Thames to the immediate west of the Fleet brook was in Roman and Saxon times full of creeks and runnels, though meadows were gradually emerging from the marsh. This is shown by the names which we still find there—such as Bridewell, Water Lane, Milford Lane, etc. There was a nameless stream which was once the chief tributary of the Thames between the Fleet and the Tyburn. Its source was near the Church of St. Giles-in-the-Fields, whence it ran across the meadows in a south-easterly direction towards the site of the future Church of St. Clement Danes. Before it reached what we till lately knew as Wych Street, it fell into the creek which was called the Old Wych; and close to this spot there was subsequently a water mill and a ford, at the top of what we now call Milford Lane. The Old Wych then curled round and fell into the Thames 'just at the bottom' of Essex Street, where the barges lay in the days of Sir George Rose! Then a little farther on, between what we now call Catherine Street and Wellington Street, there was a bridge called Strand Bridge; so there must have been another stream running into the Thames just there. This all tends to show that the southern portion of the territory *ultra Fletam* was originally more or less a marsh. It was indeed sometimes called 'London Fen.'

A little farther inland from the Thames there soon came to be fair meadows, sloping up towards Holborn Hill. But in Roman and in Saxon times there were practically no houses to the west of the Fleet brook—no Fleet Street and no Strand existed before the Conquest. There was no road or lane at this time south of Holborn, and there was no gate in the Roman wall at the foot of Fleet Hill. There was indeed no use or need for such a gate, as the Fleet brook was there too wide to jump and too deep to ford, and there was no bridge. For 800 years after the Romans left Britain the only gate in the Roman wall on the west side of the City was the one afterwards called New Gate. An abbey was founded at Westminster a little more than a century before the Norman Conquest; and shortly after that event the King had a palace at Westminster. But if either Abbot or King desired to journey from Westminster to the City of London, he had either to go by water—for the Thames was the great highway between the two cities—or else he had to go by road through the village of Charing and farther northwards till he joined the road from Oxford, then along Holborn and enter the City at the New Gate. That was then the only way by road from Westminster to London.

Very few people before the accession of Henry I ventured to live outside the Roman wall; and indeed there was no reason why they should do so, as there was plenty of room within its protection. Those who were bold enough to reside outside it naturally clustered round the existing highway and the neighbourhood of the City gate. There were houses on both sides of Holborn almost to the top of the hill for at least a hundred years before there was anything like a street nearer the Thames. But all the flat ground on the crest of the hill was devoid of any buildings. In the Manor of Portpool—that is where now stands Gray's Inn—there were no houses at the time of which I am speaking, but merely a windmill and a chantry. The priest who served this chantry came from St. Bartholomew the Great in Smithfield. He did not dare to sleep in the wild unknown country of Portpool; he returned every night to St. Bartholomew's.

But in the eleventh and twelfth centuries attempts were successfully made to embank a portion of the Thames and the mouth of the Fleet brook. Thus much of the marshy ground came to be meadows which attracted a few bold persons to come and live outside the City walls. At first these were chiefly ecclesiastics, as monasteries and churches were less likely to be attacked by robbers and housebreakers than private dwelling-houses, and priests could rely both on their sanctity and their poverty. The churches of St. Bride and St. Dunstan were built on the west side of the Fleet, and in 1115 we know that the Dean and Chapter of St. Paul's owned four tenements *ultra Fletam*, one of which was occupied by a loriner. There must have been some road or lane by which folk could go to these churches and to this loriner's. This is the beginning of Fleet Street. Then about 1150 or a little later the Lud Gate was opened, and a bridge of some kind was no doubt made across the Fleet. King Lud never had anything to do with this gate; it was not even named after him. The word 'ludgate' simply means the back gate, the postern gate.

For centuries there had been wrangling between the City of London and the Abbot of Westminster as to how much of the marshy ground south of the Holborn Road belonged to each of them. At last in the reign of Henry II—about the year 1183—this dispute was settled, and a clear line was drawn separating the two dominions, which to the present day is still the boundary between the City of London and the City of Westminster. This line started from the New Gate, crossed the Hole-burn, and came up Holborn Hill to where still stand Holborn Bars. A little further on, it turned sharply to the left and ran southwards to where Temple Bar afterwards stood. At first there were only two posts and a chain there to guard the new entrance to the City; this was known as the *Barra Novi Templi* as early as 1301. Later a gate of stone was built there, but not the Temple Bar which we older men so well remember—that was built by Sir Christopher Wren in 1672, and removed in 1879. The boundary line between the two cities then passes due south through the corner of Messrs. Twinings' tea warehouse at the top of New Court, then by Ruth Pinch's fountain and through Garden Court. It cuts off a portion of the Middle Temple library, and emerges on the Thames Embankment just where there is a monument to Queen Victoria on the railing of the Middle Temple Garden.

The area between this boundary and the old Roman wall was at once treated as a suburb of the City and placed under civic rule, although it was not till 1223 that it was expressly declared to be a City ward. It was called at first the ward of Holborn and Fleet Street, and later the ward of Farringdon. Half of our Inns of Court and of Chancery lay within this new ward, and half without it. Thus it contained both the Inner and the Middle Temple, Staple Inn, Barnard's Inn, Thavie's Inn, Clifford's Inn, and both the Serjeants Inns; while Lincoln's Inn, Gray's Inn, Clement's Inn, and New Inn never were within the City of London.

We will now briefly trace the history of each separate Inn of Court.

## The Knights Templars

It was in the year 1118 that the Knights of the Holy Sepulchre at Jerusalem first came to England. They were bound by the strictest vows to poverty, chastity, obedience, to succour the Holy Land, and especially to 'save the Holy Sepulchre from thrall.' But they did not always devote the whole of their time to compliance with these vows. Being both soldiers and ecclesiastics, they did not fear to live outside the Roman wall, so they settled on a vacant piece of land on the south side of Holborn between the future Staple Inn and the top of the future Chancery Lane. There they built a hall and a round chapel; all the churches dedicated to the Holy Sepulchre were round. They remained for over forty years on this site, which was long afterwards known as the 'Old Temple.'

When the Templars came to England it was natural, no doubt, for them to settle near Holborn, for that was then the only road out of London on the western side. But towards the close of the twelfth century, as we have seen, Ludgate had been opened and a road carried over the lower Fleet and along what we now call Fleet Street. And eventually the Templars, wanting more room than they could get in Holborn, where houses were springing up all around them, obtained from Robert de Beaumont, second Earl of Leicester and Lord High Steward of England, the grant of a fine open meadow sloping down to the Thames on the southern side of the new road, and there built a great house and a second round church. They also acquired a field on the north side of the new road; it was called Fickett's Field, and extended from the Church of St. Clement Danes almost to the future Chancery Lane. This field they used for tilting; and doubtless the forge in the south-east corner of it, for which the City still pays, I believe, a rent to the Crown, was the place where the armour of the Templars was fitted and riveted, and their horses shod.

The exact date when the Knights Templars left the Old Temple and settled in their new habitation, cannot be now definitely fixed, but it was probably about the year 1162. At first they had no chapel of their own; they held their services in the Church of St. Clement Danes, over which King Henry II gave them certain rights, but they were busy building the circular portion of our present Temple Church. And on February 10, 1185 this was consecrated by Heraclius, Patriarch of the Church of the Holy Resurrection, Jerusalem, in the presence of King Henry II, his consort, and his Court. King James I in his Charter of 1608 still described this matchless specimen of pure Norman architecture as 'the Church of the New Temple of London.' There are only two other examples of the true Norman work above ground in London—the Chapel of St. John at the Tower of London, and the Church of St. Bartholomew the Great at Smithfield—though there are two or three Norman crypts in the City under ground.

Later, in 1220, was built St. Ann's Chapel, the crypt of which is still to be seen. The Templars also erected a noble refectory of stone, which stood upon the site of the present Inner Temple Hall; indeed two arched crypts which belonged to the refectory are still standing there. And here the Templars lived in pride and pomp. They associated only with the nobles. King John himself came and lodged with them for a week at a time. They looked down upon the knights of all other religious orders, and at last their arrogance was their ruin. At the beginning of the fourteenth century grave charges were brought against them, most of which, I believe, were unfounded. They were accused, among other things, of conducting in secret unholy Rosicrucian ceremonies and other mystic rites, which they were said to have brought from Palestine. An inquiry was held in St. Dunstan's Church in 1312, and the charges were declared to be proved. Under rigorous cross-examination, and probably under torture, some of the weaker brethren confessed to crimes which they had never committed, and, what was worse, to heresies, which they possibly may have held. All the property of the Knights Templars was confiscated, and they were expelled from the kingdom in the year 1313.

There were many reasons for their expulsion. First and foremost they were reputed to be very wealthy. Then they had done nothing for many years in performance of their vows. The Knights Hospitallers of St. John of Jerusalem were jealous of them. Lastly, the Pope turned against them, and then their doom was sealed.

But the King obtained little or no booty from his cruel and unjust treatment of the Knights Templars. The Pope intervened on the ground that their property was consecrated, and by a decree made at Vienne in 1312 gave their possessions in England to the rival Knights of St. John, who continued to hold them till the dissolution of the monastic orders under Henry VIII. This property included what was afterwards known as the Inner and Middle Temple.

But the Knights of St. John found their new acquisition rather a white elephant. They preferred the open country at Clerkenwell in which they had been for several years comfortably established. They had, moreover, a struggle with the King before they could obtain possession of the Templars' Hall and its precincts, for that monarch had put into possession of it, first Aymer de Valence, Earl of Pembroke, and then his own cousin Thomas, Earl of Lancaster. But the latter nobleman was executed in 1322, and in 1324 the Pope again insisted that all the property of the Templars must be handed over to the Knights of St. John, lest, as the decree ran, 'the same should be put to profane uses.' And so, some years later, in the early part of the reign of Edward III, the Knights of St. John leased it to the lawyers!

### THE INNER AND THE MIDDLE TEMPLE

The exact date of this letting (or, more technically, subinfeudation) is unknown; Master Worsley is content to say that it took place in 'some part of the reign of Edward III.'[1] Still less do we know to what lawyers the land was leased. Was it to an accidental group of persons who had never previously been associated? Was it to a Society of lawyers, who till then occupied some neighbouring hospice? We know that there were already many little communities in the City of London of professors and students of the law residing each in its separate hostel, taking their meals in common, and governed by their Readers or Benchers as the colleges in Oxford and Cambridge were by their fellows. Did one of these Societies march westward and occupy the chambers left empty by the Knights Templars within the new City boundary? Or was this land, as some maintain, divided from the first between two already existing Societies of lawyers who had previously been occupying separate hospices? These questions we cannot answer positively, because we have not the deeds. In the year 1381 the followers of Wat Tyler went to the Temple, broke into the Church, seized all the books and papers, and all the reports of cases which were in the lockers of the apprentices of the law in the Temple, took them up to the high road, and burnt them there. The existing registers of the Middle Temple begin in 1501, those of the Inner Temple in 1505; both contain references to older records now unfortunately lost.

There is no doubt some reason to believe that while the Knights Templars occupied this land there were on it two halls. One, their refectory, stood where the Inner Temple Hall now stands—it was consecrated because the prior slept over it. The other hall stood on unconsecrated ground occupying a portion of the site on which at present stand Pump Court and Elm Court—in other words, in what is now the Middle Temple. But there is no reason why the same society may not own two halls; Lincoln's Inn does so at the present moment, and *ex hypothesi*, the Order of the Knights Templars did so before their exile. The presumed existence, therefore, of the two halls does nothing to settle the dispute.

[1] *Master Worsley's Book*, edition of 1910, p. 89.

More may perhaps be made of the undoubted existence of two rents. In the year 1331 William de Langford was Keeper of the New Temple under the Order of the Knights Hospitallers of St. John of Clerkenwell. He paid annually into the King's Exchequer for the Temple the sum of £24, namely £12:4:1 for the consecrated portion and £11:15:11 for the unconsecrated portion. But then a claim was made to the consecrated portion by Hugh le Despenser, who alleged that it had been sold to him by the Prior of the Order in the year 1324. The Prior, however, with the assistance of William de Langford, was able in 1336 to satisfy the King that this sale had been extorted from him by force by the said Hugh; so William de Langford remained in possession as tenant of the Prior. Two years afterwards, on 18th June 1338, the King, being in need of money for his foreign expedition, agreed for the sum of £100 to allow the Prior the residue or unconsecrated portion of the manor of the New Temple, together with the rent due therefrom of £7:5:2. It is explained in the *Calendar of Patent Rolls* of this date how the rent had become reduced from £11:15:11 to this figure; and it is stated that if this residue of the manor should be found by valuation to be worth more than £10 the Prior should pay the excess into the Exchequer. Thus it came about that the lawyers in occupation of this portion of the land paid the Prior only £10 a year rental; the Prior was not interested in obtaining more. But it was not until the year 1521 that a later prior agreed to reduce the rent of the consecrated portion to the same amount.[1] The Order of the Knights of St. John of Clerkenwell was dissolved in 1539 and their property all passed to the Crown. So from that time forward the Societies of the Inner and the Middle Temple each paid the King £10 a year, and these rents were retained by the Charter which King James I granted to the two Societies in 1609. It will be observed, however, that the two rents were originally one rent; and, again, there is no reason why two different rents may not be paid by the same society for two different properties if that society occupies them both.

We cannot, therefore, on the materials before us, definitely determine whether there were from the beginning two distinct

[1] For this detailed account of the two rents I am indebted to Mr. E. Williams, F.R.G.S., of the Prudential Assurance Company.

societies settled in the Temple. But this much is clear that within some fifty or sixty years after the first entry of the lawyers two separate societies were located there. The Prologue to the *Canterbury Tales* was written when Chaucer was on a journey in the year 1388, and it contains a well-known reference to a manciple, on which Dugdale[1] bases an argument: 'That they were here seated in King Edward the third's time, is out of all doubt, from what our famous old Poet Geffrey Chaucer expresseth in his Prologue to the Manciple, concerning them (he having also been a Student of this House, as the History of his life, printed in the front of his works,[2] sheweth).'

A Manciple there was of the Temple,
Of which all Catours might taken ensemple.

But Dugdale here is clearly quoting from an inferior version of the Prologue. In the best manuscript, the Ellesmere, the lines run thus:—

A Gentil Maunciple was ther of a temple,
Of which achatours mighte take exemple.

And the use of the phrase 'a temple' is some evidence that there was more than one temple known to Chaucer in the year 1388.

Next, we are indebted to Mr. W. C. Bolland of Lincoln's Inn for an interesting discovery.[3] He found an old will preserved at Somerset House which is dated St. Bartholomew's day, 24th August 1404. It was made by John Bownt of Bristol, and is written in Latin. It contains a bequest of two marks to Robert, the manciple of the Middle Temple (*Roberto mancipio medii Templi*). Can this be the very man who rode with Chaucer along the Pilgrim's Way to Canterbury? Again in the year 1440 in the Paston letters we find one of the Pastons writing to his son and bidding him 'quan your leysyr is, resorte ageyn on to your college, the Inner Temple.' So by this time there were two distinct 'colleges' or schools of law established on the lands formerly held by the Knights Templars within the boundary between the City of London and the county of Middlesex.

1 *Origines Juridiciales*, p. 145. The first edition of this book was published in 1666.

2 Dugdale is no doubt referring to Speght's edition, published in 1574.

3 See an article by him in the *Law Quarterly Review*, vol. xxiv., at p. 402.

The lands of the Knights Templars which lay outside that boundary came naturally to be known as the Outer Temple. The lawyers never got possession of any of this. The portion of this land which lay to the south of the Strand became the property first of the bishops of Exeter, then of Lord Paget, and later of the Earl of Leicester, and then of his stepson Robert Devereux, Earl of Essex. Upon it now stand Essex Hall, Essex Street, and Devereux Court. Much history lingers in the names of streets and houses. The portion north of the Strand formerly known as Fickett's Field was in the eighteenth century covered with a network of disreputable slums. These were later cleared away to make room for the stately pile of the Royal Courts of Justice, which were opened on 4th December 1882.

## THE LEGEND OF THAVY'S INN

But before proceeding farther northwards, we must pause to discuss a tradition mentioned by Dugdale connecting the Temple with Thavy's Inn. He tells us on p. 144 of his great work the *Origines Juridiciales* that

> by a Decree made in the great Councel at Vienna in anno 1324 (*sic*) (about the 19th year of the same King Edward the II reign) the lands of the Templars, being generally bestowed upon the Knights Hospitalers of St. John of Hierusalem, King Edward the 3d granted this Mansion unto the Knights of that Order here in England; who, soon after (as the tradition is) demised the same, for the Rent of $x^{l.}$ per annum, unto divers professors of the Common law, that came from Thavyes Inne in Holburne. Now that there is nothing but tradition left to us; for this cannot seem strange, considering what spoil Wat Tyler, with his fellow Rebells, made here, in 4 Ric. 2. by destroying and burning their Books and Records.

You will observe how guardedly Dugdale speaks of this 'tradition,' that the first Templars came from Thavy's Inn. Nevertheless a less learned and therefore a bolder writer makes the same statement in a manuscript still in the possession of the Society of the Inner Temple. His name is unknown, but he wrote at some date after the middle of the reign of Charles I, and he ventures to assign a precise date for the alleged migration. His statement is[1]

[1] *Calendar, Inner Temple*, i. p. xvii.

that the lawyers came from Thavie's Inn

> about the year 1347, ever since which time they and their successors, professors and students of the Common Law, have there resided, who in tract of time converted and regulated the same first into one Inne of Court and afterwards, viz., in the reign of King Henry VI, divided themselves into those two Societies or Inns of Court, viz., the Inner and the Middle Temple.

We shall see shortly[1] why the writer fixed on the year 1347; but his extraordinary looseness as to dates is shown by his startling statement that there was only one society of lawyers at the Temple till the reign of Henry VI! Indeed a few sentences later (p. xviii) he asserts that there was only one Hall in the Temple till the reign of Henry VI—

> then the lawyers were multiplied and grown into soe great a bulke as could not conveniently be regulated into one society, nor, indeed, was the old hall capable of containing so great a number, whereupon they were forced to divide themselves. A new hall was then erected, which is now the Junior Temple Hall, whereunto divers of those who before took their repast and diet in the old hall resorted, and in process of time became a distinct and divided society.

These are, I believe, the only 'authorities' for the suggestion that the first Templars came from Thavy's Inn; and neither of them carries any weight. As we shall shortly see, no Thavy's Inn existed in 1347. Moreover, at that date, in all probability, some lawyers had already entered the Temple.

But where was Thavy's Inn, and who was Thavy? Was he the same person as Tavy or Davy, who are also accredited by some with having founded Inns of Chancery in the fourteenth century?

There was in the reign of Edward III 'an honest citizen' called John Tavy who owned three shops on the south side of Holborn, and behind them a house or hostel in which apprentices were boarded. They lay to the east of Fetter Lane, pretty much on the site of the present Bartlett's Buildings; Tavy had purchased these in 1323. He was by trade an armourer, and a member of the Company of Armourers, and was one of the four members of that Company who were appointed in 1342 to supervise the new

[1] *Post*, p. 247.

regulations as to the making and selling of armour. He was also an armiger, which shows that he was a person of some little distinction in the City.

John Tavy made his will on 12th March 1348, and it was proved and enrolled in the Husting on 23rd November 1349. He directed his executors to sell a certain tenement which he had acquired from John Cok, and with the proceeds to pay his debts, etc. To Isabella, his daughter, he left a certain shop, and to his wife Alice all his other tenements in Holborn. After her decease 'the hostel in which the apprentices used to dwell' was to be sold and the proceeds devoted to the maintenance of a chantry.

On 16th January 1350–51, that is, fourteen months later, the executors, at Alice's request, sold the hostel and two shops and the reversion of the third shop held by Isabel, the testator's daughter, to Sir John de Houton, Baron of the Exchequer.[1] But this sale was only for the life of Alice. On the death of Alice, in 1366, the hostel was sold in fee to Roger de Barnburgh and Sir Ely de Sutton, clerks of the Chancery (St. Andrew's Church taking a rent). This was in accordance with the will of John Tavy, which directed that it should be sold after the death of Alice to provide a chaplain to pray for the souls of Alice and John.[2]

There was another and a very different man, John Davy, who in the year 1376 occupied the land which lay to the south of Holborn on the east side of John Tavy's land, stretching away towards St. Andrew's Church and Shoe Lane. He was a Chancery clerk, Receiver for the King for the counties of Carmarthen and Cardigan, and a man of great prominence in Holborn from 1350 to 1397, when he died. The land which he occupied is quite distinct from that which John Tavy owned in 1348. It extended from a tenement of John Tavy on the west to a tenement of John de Besville on the east, and stretched from the King's highway on the north to the tenements of John de Besville and John Tavy on the south, and is so described in a deed of 26th June 1346. And on this land there undoubtedly grew up, under the superintendence of Davy, a little school of law which was named

[1] The leading witness to this deed of sale was Thomas de Lincoln, serjeant-at-law, who at that time was the owner of the first 'Lyncolnesyn' in Holborn.

[2] For all these details as to the various properties in Holborn I am indebted to Mr. E. Williams, who holds the deeds.

after him Davy's Inn. It was sometimes called Thavy's Inn, but why we can only conjecture. Possibly Davy, the Receiver for the counties of Carmarthen and Cardigan, spelt his name with two 'D's,' for the Welsh are fond of double initials, and I am informed by a high authority that in Welsh 'dd' is pronounced like 'th' in 'this' or 'that.' Anyhow, both names seem to have been used indiscriminately for centuries. But 'Thavies Inn' eventually gained the mastery, and the place was called by that name till within living memory. The property is referred to as 'Davysynne' in an old Inquisition post-mortem in 1419, and in the minister's accounts of the Bishop of Ely in 1444. On 25th January 1550 Gregory Nicholas, citizen, quit-claimed to Edward Gryffith and others *gubernatoribus hospitii de Lyncolnsyn* a 'messuage with a garden adjoining commonly called Davyes Inne and of old time (*olim*) called Thavye's Inne with chambers, etc.,' in Holbourne.

It is clear from the title-deeds that John Tavy, the armourer, never owned any portion of what was called Davy's or Thavie's Inn. Yet legal writers soon jumped to the conclusion that this inn was called after the armourer. The confusion has, no doubt, been caused by the similarity between the names, but I think my Lord Coke was also to blame in the matter.

He stumbled one day in the Court of Husting upon John Tavy's will, and was struck by the fact that it contained the word *apprenticii*. It described the house behind the three shops as *hospitium in quo apprenticii habitare solebant*, and this collocation of the words *hospitium* and *apprenticii* made a great impression upon Lord Coke's mind. Remembering that John Tavy was an armourer, and a member of the Guild of Armourers, we should now naturally translate the Latin phrase as 'the house in which my apprentices used to dwell.' No doubt Tavy had a year before his death retired from business, and his apprentices had left him and set up for themselves. But in the fifteenth and sixteenth centuries the *apprenticii* had played a very important part in legal circles. There were the *apprenticii ad legem*—the men who lived in the Inns of Court, and who roughly corresponded to what we now call the 'junior Bar'—and the *apprenticii* attached to the various courts, who were in fact apprenticed to the clerks of those courts, and resided in the Inns of Chancery. With these looming large in his eye, Lord Coke jumped to the conclusion that apprentices of the law had lived in Tavy's house—though why students of law should reside with an armourer I cannot understand! And later came our friend who wrote the Inner Temple manuscript, from which I have copied on p. 244, and he said to himself: 'John Tavy's will was made in 1348, and in it he says that the apprentices *used* to dwell in his hostel (*habitare solebant*); so they must have left before he made his will. Ah, I see; they all moved in a body to the Temple in 1347!'

However this may be, Lord Coke refers to the matter on p. xxxvii of the Preface to the Reader in Part X of his *Reports*. After quoting the case of Thomas de Weylond (19 Edw. I) as to the antiquity of the Order of Serjeants, he adds:—

> And in 1 Edw. III 'there is mention made of an apprentice, and he is called an apprentice of the law . . . and is next in degree under a serjeant.' See also the ordinance of 20 Edw. I, rot. 5, addressed to Sir John de Metingham, etc.: 'And so is farther proved by a record inter communia placita tenta in Hustingo, London, die Lunæ in festo Sancti Clementis Papæ, anno regni Edw. III viz. die Jovis proxime ante festum Sancti Gregorii Papæ, anno domini 1348. Ego Johannes Tavie Armiger lego animam meam Deo, &c. Item lego omnia tenementa mea cum omnibus pertinentiis quæ habeo in parte australi in parochiâ Sancti Andreæ, &c. Aliciæ uxori meæ ad totum terminum vitæ suæ; et quod post decessum prædictæ Aliciæ, totum illud Hospitium in quo Apprenticii *legis* habitare solebant.'

This legend as to Davy's (*alias* Thavy's) Inn rapidly gained ground. Sir George Buc, who had himself been a student there, wrote an Account of the Schools of Learning in London, which he presented to Lord Coke, and which was published in 1631 as an appendix to Stow's *Chronicle of England*. And therein he speaks in glowing terms of his former inn.

> And I must and will begin with Thavis Inne, for besides that at my first comming to London, I was admitted for probation, into that good house, I take it to be the oldest Inne of Chancery, at the least in Holborne, and so may justly challenge precedence by Seigniority, and antiquitie: it was before the dwelling of an honest Citizen called John Thavie an armorer, and was rented of him in the time of King Edward the 3. by the chiefe professors then of the Law, viz. Apprentises, as it is yet extant in a record in the hustings, and whereof my Lord Coke, shewed to me the

transcript, but since that time it was purchased for the students and other professors of the Law of Chauncery by the Benchers of Lincolns Inne, about the Raigne of King Henry the seaventh, and retaineth the name of the olde Land-lord or owner, master Thavie.

There are two glaring misstatements in this passage. The apprentices certainly never were 'the chief professors then of the law.' They always took rank below the serjeants and readers. Again, the Society of Lincoln's Inn did not acquire Davy's Inn in the reign of King Henry VII, but in the year 1550, when his grandson, Edward VI, was King. Note also that what Lord Coke showed to Sir George Buc was not the original will in the Husting, but only a transcript of it.

Lastly, let us have Dugdale's version of this legend; it was written before the year 1666.[1]

In this Inne of Chancery were Students of the Law resident in King Edward the third's time, as may appear by these following words, taken out of the last Will and Testament of John Tavye, whose House it then was, and of whom it took this name; viz.—ego Johannes Tavie *Armiger*, &c. lego animam meam Deo, &c. Item lego omnia tenementa mea, cum omnibus suis pertinentiis, quæ habeo in parte Australi, in parochia S. Andreæ, &c. Aliciæ, uxori meæ, ad terminum vitæ suæ: Et quod post decessum prædictæ Aliciæ, totum illud Hospicium, in quo Apprenticii *ad Legem* habitare solebant, per Executores meos, si superstites fuerint, una cum Executoribus prædictæ Aliciæ, vendatur, et quod de pecunia inde precepta, unus Capellanus idoneus, pro anima mea, et anima prædictæ Aliciæ inveniatur, &c.

But in process of time, the inheritance thereof, coming to the hands of Gregory Nicholls, Citizen and Mercer of London; he, by his Deed, bearing date . . . Jan. 4, E. 6, granted it to the then Benchers of Lincolns Inne, and their successors for the use of Students of the Law: After which time, it was by them demised to the Principal and Fellows of this House, for the Rent iii$^{l}$. vi$^{s}$. viii$^{d}$. per annum; and hath had the like privilege, for admission of their Students into the Society of Lincolns Inne, as those of Furnivals Inne had, and still have.

When I compared the two versions cited above of the will of John Tavy, the armourer, I was struck by the difference of phraseology at the all-important point—Lord Coke writing *legis* and Dugdale writing *ad legem*. A suspicion entered my mind that these words must in each case be a gloss placed by the learned

[1] *Orig. Jur.* p. 271.

writer on the language of the original will; each felt sure in his own mind that the apprentices referred to must have been apprentices of law, and each of them put in a word or two to make this quite clear to others. I naturally endeavoured to obtain an unimproved transcript of the original will. I searched in vain in the *Calendar of Wills proved and enrolled in the Court of Husting, London*, under the name both of Tavy and Thavy. Then a friend suggested to me to look under the name of Tany, as an n and a v are often written much alike in old manuscripts. And so under the name of John Tany, on p. 619, I found the following:—

Tany (John), 'armurer.'—The tenement which he acquired from Master John Cok to be sold by his executors to pay his debts, and the residue to be devoted to pious uses. To Isabella his daughter a certain shop. All his tenements in the parish of S. Andrew (*sic*), with the exception of the aforesaid shop, he leaves to Alice his wife for life, after whose decease a hostel wherein *his* apprentices used to live is to be sold, and the proceeds devoted to the maintenance of a chantry, and his mansion house and shops to be given to the fabric of the church of S. Andrew in Holbourn. Dated in the parish of S. Andrew in Holbourn, Thursday next before the Feast of S. Gregory, Pope [12 March], A.D. 1348. Roll 77 (242).

It is clear then that neither the word *legis* nor the phrase *ad legem* occurs in the original will. Moreover, I am assured by my friend Mr. E. Williams, who holds the deed, that in the grant of 1366 by which the hostel was sold in fee to Roger de Barnburgh and Sir Ely de Sutton—only seventeen years after the death of Tavy—it is expressly described as 'a messuage or hospitium in which the apprentices of John Tavy used to dwell.'

I conclude therefore (*a*) that there is no evidence to show that any student of law ever dwelt on the land which John Tavy the armourer owned in 1348; (*b*) that a School of Law existed in 1376, and probably a few years prior to that date, on the land which John Davy occupied in that year; (*c*) that there is no evidence that this School of Law ever had anything to do with either Temple; it was no doubt from an early date intimately connected with the Society of Lincoln's Inn, which till 1412 or a few years later was located in its immediate neighbourhood.

## LINCOLN'S INN

As we have already seen, the ecclesiastics were the first to venture outside the City walls; take, for example, the Bishop of Ely who lived at Hatton Garden and the Bishop of Exeter who took up his abode in the Outer Temple. So it was that when Ralph Neville, the great Bishop of Chichester, needed a town house for himself and his successors in that See, his eye fell on the meadows to the immediate north and east of Fickett's Field just outside the new City boundary. And there he built himself a stately mansion in the year 1227, in which he died in 1244. This mansion must have occupied the site of the buildings which lie to the immediate south of Lincoln's Inn Old Hall. And behind his house was a garden, to the north of it a paddock, and on the west side of garden and paddock a coneygarth or warren for tame rabbits. This word was afterwards corrupted into coninger; for at a later date the spot is referred to as Coninger Field, and is now part of the gardens of Lincoln's Inn. It probably stretched as far north as the back gardens of the houses on the south side of Holborn.

Anyone can find out for himself exactly where the Bishop's mansion stood by walking up Chancery Lane from Fleet Street, crossing Carey Street (which did not then exist), and before he comes to the gateway of Lincoln's Inn he will find on his left hand two courts—Chichester Rents and then Bishop's Court. These names still commemorate the approach to the Bishop's house and identify its situation. And in this house successive Bishops of Chichester lived for nearly two hundred years. One of them, John de Langton, was Chancellor of England from 1292 to 1302, and again from 1307 to 1310. After him, it is said, the lane on the east side of his house was called Chancellor's Lane, which is now corrupted into Chancery Lane. The last Bishop who occupied this house died there in the year 1412; his successor preferred to live elsewhere.

What happened in the next ten years we do not know for certain; but by the year 1422 we find a fully constituted Society in occupation of the Bishop's property, which is henceforth known by the quaint name of the 'Inn of Lincoln's Inn.' The records, which are known as the Black Books, describe the life of the

Society in delightfully varied detail; but they tell us nothing of its origin. The first Black Book begins in the year 1422; it contains entries which show that at this time the Society was paying a rent of ten marks a year to the Bishop of Chichester for the occupation of all that portion of his premises that lay to the west of Chancery Lane. The exact date of the original demise is not known; it must have been between 1412 and 1422.

Ralph Neville, Bishop of Chichester, also held land on the other side of Chancery Lane prior to 1235.[1] He owned a garden there to the north of the land which the King had granted to the House for the support of the brethren converted from Judaism to the Catholic faith (afterwards part of the Liberty of the Rolls). This garden was bounded on the north by a ditch known in 1262 as 'Chaunceleresdich.' A portion of the land which lay to the north of this Chancellor's ditch—between it and Holborn—was occupied in the middle of the fourteenth century by Thomas de Lincoln, the King's serjeant, and certain students of the law. Their territory may be roughly defined as the site of Furnival Street, which we used to call Castle Street, and of the present Patent Office to the south of Staple Inn. It was acquired in the following way.

In 1334 the executors of Robert le Hende de Worcester granted a plot of land extending from the King's Street on the north to the tenement of the Bishop of Chichester on the south to Thomas de Lincoln of the Common Bench, the King's serjeant, who is described as the son of Thomas de Lincoln. In 1331 John de Totel de Lincoln had granted to Thomas de Lincoln some land to the east of this, and in 1332 Andrew Courtays had granted a garden to the south-east of this property to Thomas de Lincoln. He combined these three properties, and they formed the first home of the Society of 'Lyncolnesynne.' Mr. Paley Baildon has discovered that there was an enormous increase in the work of the law courts about 1340, and this would no doubt lead to an increase in the number of the students of the law and necessitate the erection of new hostels.

In 1348 Thomas de Bedic granted all his rights of lordship over this land to Thomas de Lincoln. By three deeds dated 1364, 1366, and 1369, the fee simple of the whole property was

[1] That is perhaps why we still find a court called Nevill's Court on the east side of Fetter Lane.

conveyed by Thomas de Lincoln to the Abbot and Convent of Malmesbury. In 1399 a 'Rental' of the property of the Convent of Malmesbury was drawn up which shows a payment to the Abbot of £8 *De Firmario novi hospicii apud Londoniam vocati Lyncolnesynne.* And in this Rental there is a later entry on the bottom margin of the same page; it is undated but it was probably written early in the fifteenth century. It is to the following effect:—*Hospicium Armigeri jam magnum hospitium quod est ruinosum reddit per annum* 40*s*. The rent had no doubt been reduced from £8 to 40s. because of the ruinous condition of the big mansion.[1]

Hence, early in the fifteenth century, we find the Society of Lincoln's Inn located in a mansion on the east side of Chancery Lane which had become ruinous. The landlord apparently did nothing towards the repair of the mansion. And so it seems clear that the Society moved across Chancery Lane and entered into occupation of the house and premises of the Bishop of Chichester,

[1] For the above details as to the title of these various properties I am indebted to Mr. E. Williams, who is in possession of the title-deeds. See also an article by Mr. G. J. Turner of Lincoln's Inn in the *Athenæum*, September 22, 1906, p. 335. It may be interesting to subjoin the text of the most important entries.

EXTRACT FROM THE RENTAL OF THE PROPERTY OF THE CONVENT OF MALMESBURY 1399

| | |
|---|---|
| 'De Firmario novi hospicii apud Londoniam vocati Lyncolnesynne ad iiiior terminos solvendo per annum . . | VIII li. pro missa Abbatis |
| De tenemento quondam Gaillardi Poet in Holbourne | XXs |
| De tenemento quondam Walter Bartone Allutarii . | XIIIs IIIId' |

Written in a different hand, with different coloured ink, at the bottom margin of the page, and certainly of a later date, the following remarks have been added:

| | | |
|---|---|---|
| 'London. | Hospicium Armigeri jam magnum hospitium quod est ruinosum reddit per annum . | XLs |
| Tenura tenencium | Celda proxima annexa hospicio reddit per annum . . . . . . . | IXs |
| infra silvam | Secunda celda reddit per annum . . | Xs |
| magni hospicii | Tertia celda reddit per annum . . | VIIIs |
| | Quarta celda que est . . .' | |

[Here the page is cut away]

The 'hospicium armigeri' of the marginal note is obviously the same building as the 'Lyncolnesynne' of the former entry. Serjeants were *ex officio* 'armigeri,' and, according to Foss, were often so designated in the fourteenth century.

which had lain empty since 1412. The exact date of this removal we cannot fix, but it must have been before 1422; for in that year commence the Black Books, the first volume of which is entitled *Liber Hospitii de Lincolnsin.* The earliest entries in this volume show that the persons then in possession of those premises formed a fully established society, possessing the constitution, powers, and privileges of an Inn of Court. And those persons retained their former title of the Society of Lincoln's Inn, and never called themselves Bishop's Inn or Chichester Inn, as would have been the case with a society newly created. That the Society of Lincoln's Inn existed before 1422 is clear from the fact that in the Corporation Letter Books one Thomas Broun is described as Maunciple of Lincoln's Inn, under date of 1417.

Lastly, we find in the Black Books another entry which seems to establish the continuity of the present Society with that formed on the other side of Chancery Lane by the King's serjeant. In 1466 the Society was paying 9s. yearly to the Prior of St. Giles' Hospital for Lepers for another part of its property; and no other rents, apparently, were being paid for any other part on the west side of Chancery Lane. But on p. 8 of vol. i of the Black Books of the present Society the following entry occurs:—

> In the vigil of the Apostles Peter and Paul 16 Henry VI (1438) John Row delivered to John Fortescue and others in the name of the Society to be paid to . . . Halssewylle for the farm of Lyncollysyn in arrear for the 15th year (Henry VI) in the time of Bartholomew Bolney then Pensioner in full payment 40s. out of money received by him.

That is to say, the Society of Lincoln's Inn, now settled in the Bishop of Chichester's mansion, was still paying the identical rent of 40s. which it paid at the commencement of the century for the ruinous hospitium of Lyncolnesynne.

## The Legend of the Earl of Lincoln

But, as time ran on, the King's serjeant was forgotten; no one remembered Thomas de Lincoln and his hospice to the north of the Chancellor's ditch. And men began to wonder why the Society was called 'Lincoln's Inn.' The name did not seem to have any connexion with the history of the Society's present abode; from what source then did it come? And some one must have recollected that there was an Earl of Lincoln who was a famous man in the reign of Edward I, and who resided somewhere in this locality; possibly he was the founder of the Society. And in that uncritical age the suggestion soon found favour.

Hence it is that we find in the *Origines Juridiciales* (at p. 231) the following remarkable passage:—

After this Ralph Nevill, Richard de Wihtz (commonly called Saint Richard) had also his residence here. But in the next age Henry Lacy, Earl of Lincolne became possest thereof, and resided in it; whereupon as many other great Houses, did in those dayes take denomination from their Owners, this had then accordingly the name of Lincolnes Inne, and hath ever since been so called.

Of this Henry, Earl of Lincolne, is the tradition still current amongst the Antients here; that he, about the beginning of King Edward the seconds time, being a person well affected to the knowledge of the Lawes, first brought in the professors of that honourable and necessary study, to settle in this place: but direct proof thereof from good Authority, I have not as yet seen any.

There was good ground for Dugdale's scepticism. No Earl of Lincoln ever owned or occupied any portion of the land which belonged in Dugdale's day to the Honourable Society of Lincoln's Inn. Every square inch of this land was the property of the See of Chichester from 1227, when it was granted to Bishop Neville, to 1537, when Bishop Sampson sold it to the Inn. And the only mansion on the land was, as we have seen, occupied by successive bishops from 1227 till 1412.

There was no doubt at the beginning of the fourteenth century a great man living in this neighbourhood, Henry De Lacy, Earl of Lincoln and Salisbury. He owned the whole manor of Holborn, having purchased it in 1286 for 550 marks from the Black Friars, who had occupied it from 1215. His mansion stood in Shoe Lane on the slope of Holborn Hill, to the south-east of St. Andrew's Church. He was a valiant knight and an able statesman; he was also a successful market-gardener. He made a considerable sum of money (for those days) by the sale of his fruit and vegetables. He was famous for the beauty of his gardens, which stretched down almost to Fleet Street. Think of him in his manor house on the slope of Holborn Hill looking across the Fleet brook at the little city still encircled by its Roman wall.

Forget six counties overhung with smoke,
Forget the snorting steam and piston stroke,
Forget the spreading of the hideous town ;
Think rather of the pack-horse on the down,
And dream of London, small, and white, and clean,
The clear Thames bordered by its gardens green.

And in this house Henry De Lacy, Earl of Lincoln, died in 1311 ; and his mansion and his manor passed to his son-in-law the Earl of Lancaster, Lord High Steward of England and cousin of the King, and was subsequently owned by other persons of high rank, whose title to them is well known. There is not the faintest evidence that any professors or students of the law ever occupied any portion of Earl De Lacy's house or grounds.

To get over this difficulty it has recently been suggested that what the Earl did was to establish the lawyers not in his residence, but in Thavie's Inn, which stood at a little distance from it on the other side of Shoe Lane. But this he would have had no right to do. The Earl never owned either the house which was later called Davy's or Thavie's Inn, nor that which twelve years after the Earl's death became the property of John Tavy, the armourer. The Earl would have had no possible right 'to bring in' professors of the law into either house.

And note that the tradition recorded by Dugdale does not assert either of these propositions. Still less does it assert that the Earl brought the lawyers into his house in Shoe Lane. It rests upon the assumption that in the reign of Edward II. he 'became possessed of, and resided in,' the mansion built by Ralph Neville, which we know to be untrue. The fact is that the name 'Lincoln's Inn' is in no way derived from or connected with Henry De Lacy, Earl of Lincoln. Yet the Society in 1518 placed his arms on the side of their gatehouse facing Chancery Lane, where they still remain. And in 1553 they placed them with other coats on the 'loover or lanthorn' over their Old Hall.[1]

## GRAY'S INN

Gray's Inn, like Lincoln's Inn, lies wholly without the City boundary ; for though it is in the parish of St. Andrew's, Holborn, none of it is within the ward of Farringdon. It is, in all prob-

[1] Dugdale, *Orig. Jurid.*, p. 232.

ability, as old or nearly as old as the other Inns of Court. Sir George Buc records a tradition currrent at the Bar in Elizabeth's reign that Gray's Inn had been an Inn of Court since the days of Edward III.[1] It lies within the Manor of Portpool; and this Manor undoubtedly belonged as early as 1298 to Reginald, Lord Grey de Wilton, Chief Justice of Chester. But there were no lawyers there during his lifetime. The precise date at which the students of the law ventured to come outside the City walls and settle in or near the ancient manor house of Lord Grey de Wilton cannot be precisely ascertained. They came no doubt from the Inns of Chancery on the south side of Holborn, and especially from Staple Inn and Barnard's Inn.

The earliest records which Gray's Inn now possesses are the Pension Books, which begin in the year 1569; there was an older volume, to which Dugdale had access, but which now is lost. The Inn also has preserved a list of its Benchers and Readers, prepared by its butler Segar in the time of Charles II, which makes the Inn date back to 1355; but this list is not trustworthy. In 1589 Yelverton, J., spoke of Gray's Inn as having been founded 'two hundred years ago at least,' but we cannot implicitly rely on a statement in round numbers such as this. One thing, however, is certain. I have already quoted the Paston Letters, and it is marvellous what valuable things we find in that collection of letters, discovered almost by an accident. In 1454 William Paston wrote to his father that when on a journey he had met Sir William Bylling, Chief Justice of the King's Bench, and this learned judge said to him: 'I was a felaw in Gray's Inn along with Ledam.' The word 'felaw' was applied in those days to any member of one of these Societies, and it would probably even then take a student forty years to attain to the dignity of a Chief Justice; so that there must have been a fully-constituted Inn, either of Court or of Chancery, on this spot at or soon after the accession of Henry V in 1413.

In 1505 the ninth Lord Grey de Wilton, by indenture of bargain and sale, assigned 'to Hugh Denys, Esquire, his heirs and assigns, the manor of Portpool, otherwise called Gray's Inn, including two messuages, four gardens, the site of a windmill, eight acres of land, ten shillings of free rent, and the advowson of the chantry of Port-

[1] *Stow's Chronicle*, p. 1073.

poole aforesaid.' Some eight years later, in 1513, the Prior and convent of Shene (that is Richmond, in Surrey) bought the manor from Denys' trustees. In 1516 a society consisting of two serjeants and four barristers took a lease of the Manor of Portpool from the Prior of Shene for 10s. a year and a fine of £6 : 13 : 4. On this manor still stood the ancient house of Lord Grey de Wilton, of which probably this society was already in occupation. The manor escheated to the Crown at the dissolution of the monasteries, but Henry VIII renewed the lease, and the Inn has long ago bought the freehold.

The beautiful Hall of Gray's Inn was finished in 1563—eight years before the Hall of the Middle Temple, which it much resembles. At this time houses had been built along Holborn, almost as far as Southampton Row; Warwick Court was already in existence, but there was no entrance into South Square from Holborn; that was made by Francis Bacon at a later date. Gray's Inn was approached by a gate leading into Gray's Inn Square, to the north of the chapel and the Hall; that is why the old gate of the Hall is on its northern side. And once more I would point out how history lingers in the names of streets. There is still a street called Portpool Lane, that runs in a line with Hatton Wall from Leather Lane to Gray's Inn, which it strikes to the north of the chapel and the Hall. This was no doubt a short cut from the bottom of Holborn Hill to the Manor of Portpool, and later to the northern gate of Gray's Inn.

## The Inns of Chancery

It is clear then that the Inner and Middle Temple, Lincoln's Inn, and Gray's Inn were all established as distinct societies by the end of the fourteenth century. They were by that time accepted as general schools of law, and had acquired recognized privileges as Inns of Court although they held no charter from the Crown. But, in addition to these four Inns of Court, there were—as we learn from Sir John Fortescue, who wrote in 1470—'ten lesser Inns, and sometimes more, which are called Inns of Chancery, in each of which there are an hundred students at the least.' In Lord Coke's time there were only eight.

There is much that might be said about the Inns of Chancery

if time permitted. In the Inns of Court dwelt those advocates who had not attained to the degree of serjeant-at-law, and also the more advanced students. In the Inns of Chancery resided the Clerks of the Chancery, who prepared the original writs for the King's Courts, and also the younger apprentices who copied these writs, and thus acquired some elementary knowledge of civil procedure. With the possible exception of Simond's Inn and Staple Inn, the Inns of Chancery differed in their constitutions in no essential particular from the Inns of Court. But the main distinction between these two classes of Inns was this—that the Inns of Court could call men to the Bar, and thus confer upon them the privilege of acting as advocates in the King's Courts. This no Inn of Chancery could do. How the Inns of Court acquired this privilege it seems now impossible definitely to ascertain. Nor is it clear why the Inns of Chancery did not possess it also; for some of these—Clifford's Inn, for instance—appear to be of as ancient a date as the present Inns of Court. But the four Inns of Court in some way acquired the mastery, while the Inns of Chancery fell into the second rank. They served as preparatory schools for the Inns of Court up to the end of the sixteenth century; each Inn of Court appears to have periodically sent to every Inn of Chancery attached to it a reader,[1] accompanied by two 'utter barristers,' who there discussed points of law and presided over 'moots.' This committee of three had the power of bringing over each term the two most promising students of the Inn of Chancery and passing them into the Inn of Court. Hence many students entered an Inn of Chancery in the first instance, and were thence transferred to an Inn of Court. Throughout the Tudor period this custom was generally observed, though by the time of Sir Matthew Hale it had become obsolete.

In the reigns of Queen Elizabeth and James I. Orders were passed by the four Inns forbidding 'common attorneys' and solicitors from joining an Inn of Court, and this exclusion was confirmed by further Orders passed by the judges and also by the Privy Council. But these new regulations were not strictly observed. Attorneys and solicitors were not wholly excluded from the Inns of Court until towards the close of the eighteenth

[1] Thus Mr. Thomas More of Lincoln's Inn went as reader to Furnival's Inn in the reign of Henry VIII, and Mr. Edward Coke of the Inner Temple was reader at Lyon's Inn in the reign of Elizabeth.

century. One consequence of this exclusion was that it now became impossible for attorneys and solicitors to be heard as advocates in the superior courts of law and equity. Another and a later result was the rule of our profession that a barrister can only plead in those courts when he has been instructed by an attorney or solicitor. But in the meantime the attorneys, being thus excluded from the Inns of Court, gradually obtained entire control of the Inns of Chancery.

The Inns of Chancery have now all ceased to exist as schools of law. Staple Inn, which Sir George Buc described as 'the fayrest Inne of Chancery in this University,' still stands intact; for this we have to thank the Prudential Assurance Company, its present owners. Barnard's Inn, close at hand, is now the property of the Mercers' Company. The boys of the Mercers' School have their lunch daily in its old hall, which the Company has carefully preserved. We have already traced the early history of Thavie's Inn; a small portion of one wall is all that is left standing; the rest is occupied by part of a modern street called St. Bride's Street. Furnival's Inn was pulled down in the reign of Charles I, but was rebuilt by Inigo Jones and lasted until 1820; it stood on the site now occupied by the offices of the Prudential Assurance Company. Passing south to Fleet Street we find Clifford's Inn still standing, close to St. Dunstan's Church. It was founded as a school of law by Lady Clifford in 1344. It was from the first connected with the Inner Temple, and many of its students have from time to time crossed Fleet Street to join that Inn of Court. But there is no evidence that there ever was a migration of any considerable body of students from one to the other. Clement's Inn, which adjoined St. Clement's Church and the Holy-well, is now a row of handsome offices. New Inn was demolished when Holywell Street and Wych Street were pulled down in order to widen the Strand. Lyon's Inn, which stood between Holywell Street and Wych Street, was pulled down in 1863 to make room for the Globe Theatre. Strand Inn, which stood on the south side of the Strand, opposite the Church of St. Mary-le-Strand, was demolished by Protector Somerset in the reign of Edward VI, in order to make room for his new palace, which we now know as Somerset House.

So the Inns of Chancery have one by one disappeared; none of them, at all events, are in use to-day as places of legal education.

But the Inns of Court still stand four-square—the Inns which were described by James I in his charter of August 13, 1608, as 'those four colleges, the most famous in all Europe.' Long may they flourish! To them has been entrusted the exclusive power of admitting students of law to the Bar of England; on them has been conferred the right and the duty of selecting those who shall enjoy the monopoly of audience in the superior courts of England. His call to the Bar confers great privileges and powers on the young advocate. He is given the right, the terrible right, of almost unfettered cross-examination. He has also the right in his discretion to attack the character of a party or a witness, and no action for slander can be brought against him. Such powers must be entrusted only to persons who will use them honourably and well. Should they pass into the hands of unfit and dishonourable men they will be taken away from the whole Bar. Those who confer the privilege of audience in the High Court of the Kingdom must therefore also have the power to take that privilege away.

The ancient Inns of Court, whose history I have been endeavouring to impart to you to-day, still retain, and rightly retain, the two high privileges of calling worthy men to the Bar, and of disbarring those who prove to be unworthy. And I may add, I think, that they exercise these powers to the general satisfaction of the English nation.

W. BLAKE ODGERS.

# XIII

# THE EARLY HISTORY OF ENGLISH EQUITY

ONE of the most striking features of the English system of justice prior to the Judicature Acts was the dual system of courts administering a dual system of justice—common law rules and remedies and equitable rules and remedies. This dual system of courts had not always existed; and the significance of the Judicature Acts lies in the fact that it brought back conditions that existed before the Chancery acquired its position as a court of equity. Even the Chancery exercised a common law as well as an equitable jurisdiction, and long before the establishment of the Chancery as a court of justice older tribunals had exercised a jurisdiction both at law and in equity. The beginnings of English equity are to be sought in the history of these older courts—the common law courts themselves, the local courts, the ecclesiastical courts, and Parliament and the Council acting in their judicial capacity. In the present paper I wish to draw attention to the equitable jurisdiction of the early common law courts, omitting all reference to the equity of local and ecclesiastical courts and of Parliament and the Council.

The Frankish king's court exercised what amounted to an equitable jurisdiction. Based, perhaps, partly upon this earlier practice in the land of our legal ancestors and partly upon the royal justice of Anglo-Saxon times, the English king's courts in the centuries immediately following the Norman Conquest not only developed the principles of the early common law, but also administered a softening and supplementing equity that was distinguished, both in the theory and in the practice of the times, from the rigour of the common law itself. As the king's courts were not yet greatly checked by legislation and by judicial precedent, but were possessed rather of very wide discretionary powers, the need of a separate and distinct equity court seems not to have been felt: the king's courts themselves could do whatever equity required. But this early equity of the common law courts —the King's Bench, Common Pleas, and Exchequer—was much more than a broad, vague, and mystical doing of justice; for these courts developed a rudimentary system of equitable principles and equitable remedies very like, in some respects, the more fully and elaborately developed system of the Chancery in a later age.[1] Procedure by bills in eyre, as we have so recently learned from Mr. Bolland, seems actually to have been the predecessor of the Chancery's procedure by bills in equity.[2] But what I am now desirous of showing is that even the common law system of original and judicial writs gave the common law courts an opportunity to administer equity. The oldest actions of the common law seem indeed to have been mostly actions brought not so much for 'damages,' the characteristic relief of the classical common law, as for what Chancery lawyers, at a later day, designated 'specific relief'; and in administering justice by writ process, the early justices not only gave judgments *in rem*, but also what we must designate 'decrees *in personam*,' decrees that under the influence of the subpoena became so marked a feature of the equity of the Chancellors.[3]

I propose in the present paper to give a short account of the following branches of this early equity of the common law courts: (1) Uses, (2) Gages, (3) Penalties, (4) Specific Performance, (5) Prohibitions, (6) Writs *Quia Timet*.

## I. Uses

The recent researches of Pollock, Maitland, and other legal historians prove that the practice of conveying land to uses began

[1] See the present writer's essay entitled 'Early History of Specific Performance of Contract in English Law' (*Festgabe für Kohler*, 68, 69).

[2] Y.B. Edward II, Eyre of Kent, 6 and 7 Edward II 1313–14 (Selden Soc.), vol. ii. (1912), xxi-xxx.

[3] See further the present writer's essay referred to in note 1 *supra*, and the literature therein cited; also Bigelow, *Hist. of Proced. in Eng.* chap. iv.

long before the interest of the *cestui que use* was protected by the subpoena of the Chancellor. It is the generally accepted view that in this earliest period of the history of the use of land the obligation of the feoffee to uses was purely moral, and was unenforced by judicial process in royal courts.[1]

In opposition to this view Mr. Justice Holmes maintains, in his essay on 'Early English Equity,'[2] that the enforcement of uses did not originate in the Chancery and was not based upon the personal obedience of the feoffee to the subpoena. According to Holmes the early feoffee to uses was but the salman or *treuhand* of early German law transplanted to English soil. This position is confirmed, in Holmes's view, by the fact that the executor of the Continent was simply the Germanic *treuhand* somewhat modified under the influence of Roman legal notions, and that the Continental executor and the English executor of Glanvill's time were undoubtedly identical. When we look at the protection accorded to the *cestui que use*, contends the learned justice, we find that both the common law and the ecclesiastical courts were prepared to give remedies. It was usual for feoffees to uses to enter into covenants in favour of their feoffors. In cases therefore where feoffors were themselves the *cestuis que usent*, they were protected as against their feoffees by the common law writ of covenant: and by this writ the feoffor might even recover the land itself. If the *cestui que use* was a third person and thus a stranger to the covenant, he was unable to invoke the protection of the common law courts on their doctrine of covenants, but he could and did reach the feoffee, in the ecclesiastical courts, for breach of faith. At a later time ecclesiastical Chancellors developed the use more fully than their predecessors of the church courts had been able to do.

Into the arguments that have been advanced against Mr. Justice Holmes's view I cannot now enter. I must be content to have drawn your attention to the fact that, at least in Holmes's view, the early common law courts were employing their writ of covenant for the enforcement of uses long before the Chancellor made use of a more comprehensive and effective remedy—the subpoena.

[1] See Pollock and Maitland, *History of English Law*, 2nd ed., 228-239; Ames, 'The Origin of Uses' (*Lectures on Legal History*, 1913, pp. 233-247).

[2] *Select Essays in Anglo-American Legal History*, vol. ii. 705-721.

It appears also that the early common law courts were enforcing uses or trusts of chattels and money by the writs of detinue and account. Ames, in his essays on the 'History of Parol Contracts Prior to Assumpsit'[1] and the 'Origin of Uses and Trusts,'[2] has dealt fully with this phase of the equity of the common law courts. He has shown that on the delivery of money by one man to another to the use of a third, this third person—the beneficiary—was permitted to bring the action of account against the one who had received the money to his use. In the same way the bailment of a chattel to the use of a third party was enforced by this third party—the beneficiary—in the action of detinue. It is Ames's view, to quote his own words, that 'a defendant's duty to account, whether as bailiff or receiver, arose from his receipt of property as a trustee, and that a plaintiff entitled to an account was strictly a *cestui que trust*. In other words, trusts for the payment of money were enforced at common law long before Chancery gave effect to trusts of land. . . . Account against a receiver was long ago superseded by the common count for money had and received by the defendant to the use of the plaintiff. But the words "to the use of" still bear witness to the trust relation.' 'It must have been all the easier for the Chancellor,' says Ames in another place, 'to allow the subpoena against the feoffee to uses because the common law gave a remedy against a fiduciary who had received chattels or money to be delivered to a third person, or, as it was often expressed, to the use of a third person, or to be redelivered to the person from whom he had received the chattels or the money.'

It is likewise contended by this distinguished historian of English law that 'as the Chancellor, in giving effect to uses declared upon a feoffment, followed the analogy of the common law bailment of chattels, or the delivery of money upon the common law trust, so in enforcing the use growing out of a bargain and sale, he followed another analogy of the common law, that of the sale of a chattel. The purchaser of a chattel, who had paid or become indebted for the purchase money, had an action of detinue against the seller. Similarly the buyer of land who had paid or become a debtor for the price of the land, was given the right of a *cestui que use* [by the Chancellor].'

1 *Select Essays in Anglo-American Legal History*, vol. iii. 304-319.

2 *Ibid.* vol. ii. 737-752.

Ames's doctrine as to the so-called common law trust of chattels and money has not gone unchallenged. Hening, for example, in his 'History of the Beneficiary's Action in Assumpsit,'[1] contends that the obligation of the bailee of a chattel and the receiver of money as regards the beneficiary cannot be ranged under the category of trusts, in the modern sense, because the conception of an 'equitable ownership' in the beneficiary was lacking in the early common law. Although we cannot pursue this inquiry further at the present time, we should note in passing that, whether or not we agree fully with Ames's view, certainly the early common law courts were enforcing by means of the writs of detinue and account obligations of at least a fiduciary character—the obligations of persons who received chattels and money to the use of others.

## II. Gages

A study of the law of securities on property in the time of Henry the Second throws much light upon the equitable nature of certain features of the procedure in the king's court.[2] The court enforced both the usufruct-gage and the property-gage of land. The property-gage assumed the form of a conveyance under condition precedent. If the parties include a clause of forfeiture in their contract, the gaged land, already in the creditor's possession, will at once become his absolute property, upon the principle of forfeiture, on the debtor's failure to pay at the fixed day. On the other hand, should the contract contain no clause of forfeiture, the creditor must go into court, and there must be certain legal proceedings before the law will view the gaged land as absolutely forfeited to the creditor for non-payment of the debt. These proceedings are essentially equitable in character, and show very clearly that the common law courts of the twelfth century had already arrived at a conception of what Chancery judges of later times will designate the 'equity of redemption' and the 'decree of foreclosure.' What are these equitable proceedings of the king's court?

[1] *Select Essays in Anglo-American Legal History*, vol. iii. 339-367.

[2] See the present writer's 'Gage of Land in Medieval England' (*Harvard Law Review*, xviii. 552 *seq.*; also *Select Essays in Anglo-American Legal History*, vol. iii. 646-672), and also his *Geschichte des englischen Pfandrechts*, 29, 198, 200, 213-232, 248 *seq.*

If the land be gaged for a term, and if the debtor fail to pay at the end of the term, the creditor must sue him. The debtor is then compelled to appear in court in answer to a writ ordering him to 'acquit' or redeem the gage. If then in court the debt and the gage be confessed by the debtor or otherwise proved by the creditor, the debtor is ordered by the court to redeem the gage within a 'reasonable' time by payment of the debt; and the court at the same time declares that, in case of default in payment at the end of this new period, the gaged land shall become the property of the gagee and thus forfeited for the debt.[1]

If, on the other hand, the gage be given indefinitely or without a term, the creditor may at any time demand the debt. To all seeming this means that the creditor can at any time go into court and get a judgment ordering the debtor to redeem within some fixed and reasonable period; and that the court will at the same time declare that, if the debtor fail thus to redeem, the creditor may do anything he pleases with the gaged land, as it has been forfeited by reason of the debtor's default.[2]

At a later time, when the dual system of Common Law and Equity, administered by two separate and distinct sets of tribunals, was fully developed, the equitable jurisdiction over gages of law belonged exclusively to the Court of Chancery. The property-gage of the time of Henry the Second had become obsolete, and the classical common law mortgage by conveyance under condition subsequent had taken its place. The common law courts rigidly enforced the forfeiture of the mortgaged land for non-payment of the debt at the very time fixed by the parties in their contract. It was the Chancery alone which gave relief. The equitable right of the debtor to redeem the mortgaged land, after absolute forfeiture at law, became known as the 'equity of redemption'; and the equitable right of the creditor to obtain a decree of Chancery ordering the debtor to pay or for all time to lose his mortgaged land by forfeiture, in equity as well as at law, became known as the 'right to a decree of foreclosure.' Now the interesting thing about the procedure of the earlier period—the time of Henry the Second—is that it was the procedure of the king's court, the court of the common law. This procedure is indeed a very enlightening illus-

[1] Glanvill, x. 6-8.

[2] Glanvill, x. 8; Pollock and Maitland, *op. cit.* ii. 120.

tration of the fact that, before the development of a system of equity administered by the Court of Chancery, the courts of the common law were accustomed, in the interests of justice and equity, to soften the harshness and rigour of the law by the exercise of what is known in later times as equitable jurisdiction. Even after non-payment of the debt on the day set by the parties in their contract of gage, the debtor was given a further opportunity of redeeming the land; and this second opportunity of the debtor essentially amounted to a rudimentary equity of redemption.[1] The patience of the creditor and of the court had its limits, however, and if the debtor failed to exercise his equitable right to redeem within the new period fixed by the court, the land then belonged, by decree of the court, finally, absolutely, and irrevocably to the creditor as a forfeiture for non-payment of the debt; and this final decree of the court essentially amounted to a rudimentary decree of foreclosure.

By the time of Edward the First the common law appears to have taken the position which it has ever since maintained; for Britton tells us that the equity (*equité*) of the common law will not assist the mortgagor who has allowed the set day to pass without payment of the debt.[2] After the early common law courts had thus ceased to give relief against forfeiture by means of the 'equity of redemption,' it was left to the Chancellors of later times to reintroduce it into the law of mortgages in the form in which it has ever since played a conspicuous rôle in the equity of Chancery. By failing thus to retain the equity of redemption as a working principle of their system of justice the common law courts lost for all subsequent ages jurisdiction over a highly important branch of English law.

## III. Penalties

The relief of the early justices in cases of gage of property was

[1] The spirit of the twelfth-century common law courts is expressed in the words of Glanvill, x. 8: 'It is, however, sometimes requisite that he [the debtor] should be present in court, before the thing in question be adjudged absolutely to the creditor; since, were he present, he might allege some reason why the thing should not irrevocably belong to the creditor.'

[2] Britton, Book III. chap. xv. 6 (Nichols' ed. ii. 128): 'Et si les pleintifs dient, qe equité les deit eyder pur la petitesce de la dette, ceo ne lour vaille rien . . .' See Holdsworth, *History of English Law*, vol. ii. 249.

relief against forfeiture. There is some evidence that the equity of the early common law courts also anticipated the equity of the Chancery in relieving against penalties.

Maitland, in his Introduction to the Selden Society's edition of the Year Books of 2 and 3 Edward II, drew attention[1] to the case of *Umfraville* v. *Lonstede*,[2] decided in the second year of Edward II (1308–9), which, in his view, 'seems to deserve the notice of every future historian of English equity.' In this case, to quote Maitland's words, 'a man has bound himself to pay a certain sum if he does not hand over a certain document on a certain day. Being sued upon his bond, he is unable to deny that he did not tender the document on the day fixed for the transfer; but he tenders it now, excuses himself by saying that he was beyond the sea, having left the document with his wife for delivery, and urges that the plaintiff has suffered no damage. The plaintiff relies upon the words of the bond, and we must confess to having thought that in and about the year 1309 judgment for the plaintiff would have followed as a matter of course. But, to our surprise, Bereford, C.J., after remarking that what is sought to be recovered is not, properly speaking, a debt (*purement dette*) but a penalty (*une peine*), exclaims, "What equity would it be to award you the debt when the document is tendered and you cannot show that you have been damaged by the detention?"[3] In the end the plaintiff is told that he will have to wait seven years for his judgment. Here certainly,' concludes Maitland, 'we seem to see "relief against penalties" and relief that is granted in the name of "equity," though it takes the clumsy form of an indefinite postponement of that judgment which is dictated by the rigour of the law.'[4]

I have not searched for other cases in which common law courts

[1] *Y.B.* 2 and 3 Edward II (Selden Soc.), p. xiii.

[2] *Y.B.* 2 and 3 Edward II (Selden Soc.), 58.

[3] Quel equité serra de agarder a vous le dette de pus qe l'escrit est prest, si vous ne porriez moustrer qe vous fustes endamagé par la de[tenue]? Par qei volez receivre l'escrit?

In another version Bereford's words are these:—D'autrepart, ceo n'est pas purement dette, mès une peyne, et veez par quele equité vous poez demander ceo peyne (Moreover, this is not, properly speaking, a debt; it is a penalty; and with what equity (look you!) can you demand this penalty?).

[4] In a footnote to the report of the case Maitland remarks: 'Observe that the court does not propose to give judgment against the plaintiff, who has the letter of the bond on his side.'

gave relief against penalties; but I do not believe that this remarkable case referred to by Maitland stands alone.

## IV. Specific Performance

We associate specific performance of contracts with the Chancery, but the history of this form of relief begins at least two hundred years before the earliest decree by the Chancellor; for the common law courts of Henry II and Henry III were giving, in their own way, much the same remedy,[1] and what the courts of the king were doing the courts of the fair and the manor and the church were doing also. The early common law courts, exercising very wide discretionary or equitable powers, and using their own judicial machinery, made indeed an honest and a fairly effectual effort to enforce the specific performance of contractual obligations. They thus enforced the covenant of the lessor, the covenant to convey, the obligations arising out of final concords, the agreements of lords to acquit their tenants from suit of court, the obligations of warrantors. Specific performance of these contractual obligations was compelled by the court in various ways. Sometimes the court ordered the defendant in general terms to keep his promise, i.e. to specifically perform; and sometimes the court ordered the defendant to perform his covenant by giving the plaintiff possession of the land or by executing a conveyance. On the defendant's failure to comply with the judicial order, performance was then enforced by the exaction of security from the defendant, by distraint, or even by the threatened loss of the promisor's land. We have here, in these cases, not judgments *in rem*, but what we must designate 'decrees *in personam*,' the characteristic relief of the equity of chancery in later times. The early common law courts seem, in fact, to have been striving as best they could to bring the contractual obligations of defendants home to their consciences. To that end the court directed the sheriff to command the defendant to specifically perform his agreement; and only on disobedience to this command was pressure exerted upon him. This common law method of enforcing specific performance seems to have served a highly useful purpose in the days before Chancery's advent as a

[1] See the present writer's 'Early History of Specific Performance of Contract in English Law' (*Festgabe für Kohler*, 67-87).

judicial tribunal. The weak point in the common law method lay, after all, in the inability of the court to do more than distrain the disobedient party. Chancery's procedure by subpoena, resulting as it might in the imprisonment of the party guilty of contempt of court by refusal to obey the court's decree, was undoubtedly a more effectual remedy, and naturally supplanted in time the older process of the common law.

## V. PROHIBITIONS

I pass now to the common law writs of prohibition. In Chancery the injunction was a judicial process, employed for various purposes, whereby a party was ordered to do a particular thing or to refrain from doing a particular thing; and injunctions, owing largely to the fact that they were judicial orders *in personam*, have generally been viewed as distinctively characteristic of Chancery as distinguished from common law procedure. Common lawyers have not been slow in drawing attention to the writ of prohibition as a common law process analogous to the injunction; but they have usually emphasized just that employment of this writ which has nothing to do with anything the Chancery lawyers call equitable; for, although common law courts made use of the prohibition to restrain ecclesiastical and other courts, Chancery never restrained common law or other courts by means of the injunction. What I wish now to point out is that, in the procedure of the early common law courts, writs of prohibition and of *estrepement* and judicial orders issued in proceedings begun by various other common law writs anticipated the Chancery injunction as a process *in personam* whereby parties, as well as courts, were commanded to do or to refrain from doing a particular thing.

Let us glance for a moment at the prohibition of waste.

Bracton, in his account of common law procedure in cases of waste by tenant in dower,[1] makes it quite clear that the first step to be taken was one of self-help. The law gave the one entitled to the inheritance in the land full permission, without injury to anyone, to stop the committing of waste. If these private efforts proved unavailing, recourse to the court was then necessary. A writ of prohibition of waste was issued to the sheriff, wherein he was enjoined that he do not permit the woman to cause waste;

[1] Bracton, ff. 315, 316.

and the sheriff was required to act promptly in carrying out this order of the court,[1] lest irreparable injury be done. If the dowress still persisted in committing waste contrary to the court's prohibition, the next step was for the heir, or other owner, to sue her in a common law writ of waste. She was attached to appear before the court to show cause why she committed waste contrary to the court's prohibition. On the woman's denial of waste, a view was taken of the property, and an inquest was held. On proof of the waste the woman was obliged to make amends (*emendetur vastum*) by payment of damages.

If the waste had been committed in a wood the court could, in exercise of its discretionary power (*de consilio curiae*), prohibit any further waste and issue a writ for the appointment of a forester[2] by the heir. The duty of the forester was to protect the wood and to see that the dowress took only her reasonable estovers and committed no further waste contrary to the prohibition. If the waste had been committed in houses, gardens, and pastures, the court could add a clause to the writ which empowered the heir to appoint one of his servants whose duty was to see that the dowress committed no further waste. The writ[3] was directed to the sheriff, who was enjoined not to impede in any way the appointment of forester and servant by the heir.[4]

It is carefully to be observed that we have here in this method of enforcing the court's order a procedure which is distinctly equitable in character and which, so far as we can see, had been developed by the common law courts since the time of Glanvill.[5] In certain respects it may be looked upon as an anticipation of the administrative side of the Chancery's activity.

Bracton's *Note-Book* contains two instructive cases upon prohibition of waste by dowress. In *John Sanford* v. *Cecilia Sanford*

1 Bracton, f. 315b.

2 Coke, *Second Institute*, 300, states that in the old books *forestarius* is equivalent to *custos boscorum*, a woodward. On woodwards see *Select Pleas of the Forest* (Selden Soc.), pp. xxiv-xxv, xlv, lxvii.

3 Bracton, f. 316.

4 See Bracton's *Note-Book*, pl. 27, 56, for a case of the year 1219 (referred to by Bracton, f. 316) in which the court ordered the appointment of a forester to prevent the dowress and her husband from committing waste by taking more from the wood than haybote and housebote. See also *ibid.* pl. 672.

5 See Twiss, Bracton (R.S.), vol. iv. pp. lxi, lxii; Pollock and Maitland, *op. cit.* ii. 596.

the defendant, a dowress, was sued for breach of a prohibition of waste. So far as one can see, this is a case where the court had prohibited not only voluntary waste but also permissive waste—permitting a fish-pond and mill to go dry (*molendinum omnino desiccatum est et fractum et vivarium similiter*).[1] In another case writ of waste was brought without prior prohibition. In rendering judgment the court required the defendant to pay damages and an amercement; and in addition it ordered the defendant not to commit further waste under penalty of loss of her land.[2]

On waste by a guardian he could be reached by the plaintiff with the common law writ of waste either before or after the issue of a writ of prohibition; although we may perhaps gather from Bracton's account that the usual course was first to issue the prohibition, and then, on breach of the prohibition, to bring the writ of waste. The writ of prohibition was directed to the sheriff, and in it he was enjoined not to permit the guardian to commit further waste. If breach of the prohibition necessitated the bringing of the writ of waste, and if the waste was proved, judgment was rendered that the guardian lose the guardianship, render damages to the plaintiff, and pay an amercement to the king. A distinction was thus drawn by the law between waste by a guardian and waste by a dowress, for the dowress did not, on committing waste, lose her dower, whereas the guardian, on the other hand, did lose his guardianship.[3]

This distinction between the penalties inflicted on dowress and guardian resulted, as will be observed, in an important difference between the judgment in the writ of waste against a guardian and the judgment in the writ of waste against a dowress. As the guardian lost his guardianship it was unnecessary for the court to include in its judgment a perpetual prohibition of waste. On the other hand, as the dowress did not lose her dower land, it was necessary for the court in its judgment to restrain waste for the future, and sometimes even to order the appointment of forester and servant to see that the prohibition was complied with by the defendant.

[1] Bracton's *Note-Book*, pl. 1617 (A.D. 1223); s.c. Fitz. *Wast*, pl. 141. Plowden, 322a, refers to this case. On this and other cases of waste in Brac. *N.-B.* see Kirchwey's valuable 'Liability for Waste' (*Columbia Law Review*, viii. 425-437). Modern equity courts do not restrain permissive waste.

[2] Bracton's *Note-Book*, pl. 540.

[3] Bracton, ff. 316, 317.

Attention should be drawn to two interesting cases in Bracton's *Note-Book*. In *Royesia de la Dene* a guardian in chivalry was sued for waste contrary to a prohibition. In its judgment the court ordered the defendant to restore a kitchen, which was burned during the tenancy, and two farm buildings, which had collapsed owing to non-repair, and also to repair all other buildings upon the land; while the court also prohibited her from causing any waste for the future.[1]

In another case[2] a guardian had given two houses and two trees to a dowress, who had taken them off the land. The guardian was amerced to the king. In addition he was ordered to build two other houses of the same value as those he had given away, and was required to find pledges that he would neither carry off trees nor commit any other waste, and that he would build the two houses as he had been ordered by the court.[3]

Bracton's *Note-Book* contains cases which show us that tenants for life and lessees for years were also prohibited by the king's courts from committing waste. In the case of *Nicholas Creusquer* v. *Peter Pejure* the defendant, who held lands *ad terminum*, was attached to answer the plaintiff for waste. The case was dismissed because the waste was of such slight value; but at the same time the court issued a prohibition, ordering the defendant to commit no further waste in the future.[4] *Ranulf de Gatesdena* v. *Matilda de Gatesdena* was a case in which the defendant, a tenant for life, was attached for waste. The inquest found that waste

[1] Bracton's *Note-Book*, pl. 1165 (A.D. 1235): consideratum est quod nullum fecit uastum, ita tamen quod tales etc. manuceperunt quod eadem Roeysia reparari faceret coquinam et grangias et ea que ceciderunt tempore quo eadem custodia exstitit in manu sua infra hunc annum, et quod de cetero sustentabit omnia alia edificia et quod nullum uastum faciet in situ mesuagii nec alibi ad exheredacionem predicti heredis.

This case is also fully given in Fitz. *Wast*, pl. 139, where the report concludes: et inuenit pleg. ad hec omnia etc.

[2] Bracton's *Note-Book*, pl. 1075 (A.D. 1225).

[3] Et idea pro paruitate uasti et modo uastandi consideratum est quod Godefridus faciet alias duas domos ad ualenciam predictarum domorum et sit in misericordia. Et invenit tales plegios quod amplius non faciet uastum nec arbores asportabit et quod faciet domos sicut predictum est etc.

[4] Bracton's *Note-Book*, pl. 607 (A.D. 1231): Consideratum est quod Petrus inde sine die, et prohibitum est ei quod de cetero nullum uastum faciat.

Bracton, f. 316b, refers to this case. See also Fitz. *Wast*, pl. 134.

had been committed. The judgment of the court was that the defendant be in mercy, pay the amount of the waste to the plaintiff, and find pledges; while in addition the prohibition of the court issued forbidding her to commit any further waste under penalty of the loss of her land.[1] In *Richard de Elmham* v. *Robert de Corneville* the plaintiff alleged that the defendant, a life tenant, had committed waste contrary to a prohibition. Both parties put themselves upon the country, and an inquest was ordered.[2]

Bracton's *Note-Book* contains twenty-six cases on waste. In twelve cases the writ of prohibition first issued; and then later, on breach of the prohibition, the aggrieved party brought the common law writ of waste.[3] In fourteen cases, on the other hand, the writ of waste appears to have been brought at once without a prior prohibition.[4] Proceedings upon the writ of waste ended, in six instances, in a prohibition of waste.[5]

Readers of the *Second Institute* will recall Coke's high praise of the writ of the prohibition of waste. I cannot forbear quoting his words, for they express very clearly the equitable character of this common law remedy in effecting the preventive justice that was later to be claimed by the Chancery as its own peculiar province. Coke draws attention to two common law remedies for waste, the

[1] Bracton's *Note-Book*, pl. 443 (A.D. 1230), 540 (A.D. 1231): Consideratum est quod ipsa sit in misericordia et satisfaciat eidem Ranulfo de predictis denariis et dictum est ei quod de cetero sub pena amissionis predicte terre non faciat uastum uel destruccionem et ipsa inuenit pleg'.

See Bracton, f. 316b; Fitz. *Wast*, pl. 132.

[2] Bracton's *Note-Book*, pl. 1304 (A.D. 1217), 1371 (A.D. 1220): Robertus de Corneuilla summonitus fuit ad respondendum Ricardo de Elmham de placito quare ipse fecit uastum contra prohibicionem Dom. Regis de bosco in Tolleslund'. . . . Et Robertus uenit et defendit contra eum et contra sectam suam quod nullum dampnum uel uastum fecit post prohibicionem ei factam sicut curia considerauerit, et inde ponit se super iuratam patrie. Et Ricardus similiter.

See Bracton, f. 316. The principal case will be found in Fitz. *Wast*, pl. 140.

On the writ of prohibition in cases of waste by ecclesiastics, see Cruise, *Digest of the Laws of England respecting Real Property*, 4th ed. vol. i. tit. iii. ch. ii. § 71.

[3] Bracton's *Note-Book*, pl. 27, 56, 388, 580, 632, 640, 718, 739, 880, 1075, 1371, 1617.

[4] Bracton's *Note-Book*, pl. 115, 443, 461, 485, 527, 540, 574, 607, 691, 717, 1131, 1165, 1304, 1743.

[5] Bracton's *Note-Book*, pl. 56, 540, 574, 607, 1075, 1165.

writ of prohibition and the action of waste. 'Now the remedy at the common law,' says Coke,[1] 'was in two degrees: first, if he that had the inheritance did feare (for example) that tenant in dower would doe waste, he that had the inheritance might before any waste done have a prohibition directed to the sheriffe, that he shall not permit her to do waste in this forme. *Rex vicecom' salutem. Praecipimus tibi quod non permittas quod talis mulier faciat vastum, vel venditionem, vel exilium de terris, hominibus, redditibus, domibus, boscis, vel gardinis, quae tenent in dotem de haereditate talis in tali villa, ad exhaeredationem ipsius talis ne amplius, etc.* And Bracton's advice hereupon is as followeth: *Et hoc faciat tempestive, ne per negligentiam damnum incurrat, quia melius est in tempore occurrere, quam post causam vulneratam remedium quaerere.* And the sheriffe having the warrant of this writ may, as in case of a writ of estrepement, take *posse comitatus*, and withstand the doing of any waste. And this was the remedy [by prohibition] that the law appointed before the waste done by the tenant in dower, tenant by the curtesie, or the gardien, to prevent the same, and this was an excellent law, for *praestat cautela quam medela*, and preventing justice excelleth punishing justice. And this remedy may be used at this day.'

Another striking illustration of the preventive justice administered by the early common law courts is furnished by the writs of *estrepement*,[2] writs that prohibited the commission of waste during the course of judicial process.

At common law the writ of *estrepement* could be brought *after* judgment in any real action and *before* execution of the judgment by delivery of possession on the part of the sheriff; and the object of the writ was to prevent the commission of waste by the one who, although in possession of the land, was not entitled to the land as his own by reason of the judgment against him in the real action.[3]

[1] *Second Institute*, 299.

[2] Blackstone, *Commentaries* (ed. 1768), iii. 225, says that *estrepement* is 'an old French word, signifying the same as waste or extirpation.'

Upon the writs of *estrepement* see Fitz. *Estrepement*; Brooke, *Estrepement*; Coke, *Second Institute*, 327-329; Fitzherbert, *Natura Brevium*, 9th ed., 60, 61; Blackstone, *Commentaries* (ed. 1768), iii. 225-227. For the writs themselves see *Registrum Brevium Originalium*, 76, 77; *Registrum Judiciale*, 33.

[3] Coke, *Second Institute*, 327, 328; Blackstone, *Commentaries* (ed. 1768), iii. 225-227.

So far as one can see, this common law writ of *estrepement* could not be brought at any stage in legal proceedings prior to judgment.[1] To remedy this defect in the common law system of preventive justice the Statute of Gloucester introduced, in the sixth year of the reign of Edward I, a new writ of *estrepement.* If a plaintiff justly feared that the tenant—perhaps fully knowing the weakness of his title—might commit waste while the legal proceedings were going on, he could bring this statutory writ of *estrepement* whereby the tenant would be prohibited from committing waste pending the suit.[2]

The writ of *estrepement*, if directed to the sheriff, ordered him firmly to prohibit the tenant from committing waste so long as the legal proceedings in regard to the land were in progress.[3] If the writ was addressed directly to the party himself, the tenant, he was likewise ordered by the court not to commit waste *pendente lite.*[4]

Suppose the defendant failed to observe the court's prohibition? If the writ was addressed to the sheriff, then he was obliged to see to it that the waste was stopped, and in fulfilment of his duty he could use necessary force, even to the extent of imprisonment or the raising of the *posse comitatus* to go to his assistance, 'so odious in law,' in Coke's words, 'is waste and destruction': the court itself would not imprison the waster, for the duty of preventing the waste rested solely upon the sheriff who had already received his orders in the writ addressed to him. On the other hand, if the writ was addressed directly to the waster himself, the aggrieved party could, on breach of the court's prohibition, sue the waster, recovering costs and damages, and get the court to imprison the defendant for his contempt of court in disobeying the prohibition.[5]

The interlocutory injunction of Chancery is an order of the court, issued before the final determination of the rights of the parties, and its object is the protection of the rights of the plaintiff pending trial and judgment. How like unto the interlocutory

[1] But see Coke, *Second Institute*, 327.

[2] Statute of Gloucester, 6 Ed. I, c. 13; Coke, *Second Institute*, 327, 329; Blackstone, *Commentaries*, iii. 225-227.

[3] *Registrum Brev. Orig.* 77; Blackstone, *Commentaries*, iii. 225-227.

[4] *Registrum Judiciale*, 21.

[5] Fitz. *N.B.* 60, 61; Coke, *Second Institute*, 329; Blackstone, *Commentaries*, iii. 225-227; *Playstow* v. *Bacheller*, Moore, 100; *Cumberland* v. *Dowager*, Hobart, 85; *Foliamb's Case*, Coke's Reports, v. f. 115a.

injunction was the old common law writ of *estrepement*! In its form it was an interlocutory order *in personam* and in its object it was a remedy of preventive justice. After the Chancery had fashioned its own interlocutory injunction, possibly in imitation of the writ of *estrepement*,[1] the Court of Common Pleas made an ineffectual effort to extend its own power to give preventive relief by a further development of the writ of *estrepement*; but in 1594 Lord Keeper Egerton made an order that no writ of *estrepement* should be issued by the cursitors unless it be in accordance with the ancient course of the law.[2] But for this order by the Lord Keeper the old writ of *estrepement* might well have held its own ground, at least for a time, as against the injunction. But Chancery's remedy gained the upper hand; and to-day, while the *estrepement* is obsolete and well-nigh forgotten, the interlocutory injunction is in almost daily use and in the minds of all who have to do with the administration of English justice.

In the long struggle of the common law courts with their rivals—in the Middle Ages, chiefly the ecclesiastical tribunals—the writ of prohibition proved itself a weapon of wonderful power. It was a writ which could be and was directed not only against parties, but also against tribunals. In cases involving subject matter claimed by the common law courts as falling within their own exclusive jurisdiction, not only were parties restrained by prohibition from suing in ecclesiastical courts, but those courts were themselves restrained by prohibition from entertaining such proceedings. It was thus largely by this writ that the courts of common law preserved and extended their jurisdiction, keeping other tribunals to their own peculiar province, and that they protected parties in their common law rights as opposed to rights good at ecclesiastical law. At a later day the Chancery, in its struggle with common law courts, employed the injunction to effect a similar purpose; but there was this important difference between the prohibition of common law courts and the injunction of Chancery, that

1 Ashburner, in his *Principles of Equity*, ed. 1902, p. 494, note (*d*), has suggested that it was the writ of *estrepement* 'which perhaps formed the model for the equitable remedy by injunction.'

2 Kerly, *History of Equity*, 150; Spence, *Equitable Jurisdiction of Chancery*, i. 672.

On the scope of the writ of *estrepement* see Fitz. *N.-B.* 60, 61; Blackstone, *Commentaries*, iii. 225-227.

the injunction restrained only parties, while the prohibition restrained both parties and courts.[1] Only, therefore, in its effect in restraining parties can we say that the prohibition anticipated the injunction.

Bracton is careful to explain why there should be two prohibitions—one to the ecclesiastical court and one to the party. At first sight, he says, it might seem that a prohibition to the judge alone or to the party alone should suffice, for if the judge, in obedience to the prohibition, refused to hear the case, the party's attempt to sue would be of no avail, and if the party, in obedience to the prohibition, did not proceed with his suit, the judge could give no judgment for lack of a plaintiff. But two prohibitions are nevertheless better than one, maintains Bracton, lest either the judge or the party might proceed in the matter with impunity. Apparently he means that two prohibitions, rather than one, will make assurance doubly sure by giving no loop-hole for either judge or party to assert that he has not been prohibited.[2] [3]

Not forgetting that the writ might serve either as an interlocutory or as a final prohibition,[4] and is thus directly analogous to the temporary and perpetual injunctions of the Chancery, we must now ask the question as to whether the writ of prohibition was addressed to the sheriff or directly to the ecclesiastical judge and the party. Glanvill's only form of the writ restraining a party from suing in the ecclesiastical court is addressed to the sheriff, and orders him not to permit the party to sue;[5] but his form of the

[1] See Glanvill, vi. 12-14, xii. 21, 22; Bracton, ff. 401-412; Spence, *op. cit.* i. 371, 673-676; Kerly, *op. cit.* 89, 109, 116, 293; Pollock and Maitland, *op. cit.* ii. 596; Holdsworth, *op. cit.* ii. 196, 197, 211, 251, 260, 395.

[2] Bracton, f. 405b.

[3] To enter into a consideration of the question as to when a prohibition could and could not be brought (see thereon, Bracton, ff. 401-412) would take us beyond the scope of the present paper, for my only concern is to indicate the procedural significance of the writ.

[4] Bracton, ff. 401-412, makes this quite clear.

[5] Glanvill, xii. 22: Rex vic' salutem. Prohibe R. ne sequatur placitum in curia christianitatis quod est inter N. et ipsum de laico feodo ipsius R. in villa ipsa unde ipse queritur quod prefatus N. inde eum traxit in placitum in curia Christianitatis coram iudicibus illis. Et si praefatus R. fecerit te securum de clamore suo prosequendo, tunc pone per vadium et salvos plegios predictum N. quod sit coram me vel Iustic' meis eo die, ostensurus quare traxit eum in placitum in curia Christianitatis de laico feodo suo in illa villa, de sicut illud placitum spectat ad coronam et dignitatem meam. T. etc.

Beames, *Translation of Glanville*, Beale's 1900 ed. p. 243, note 2: 'This writ stands in need of a transposition of the capitals to render it intelligible.'

writ restraining the court is addressed to the court directly.[1] By Bracton's time the writs appear always to be addressed directly to the court and directly to the party, without the interposition of the sheriff as an intermediary between the common law court and the party restrained;[2] and so far as we can see, from an examination of later sources, this continued to be the usual course of procedure.[3]

In studying the equitable procedure of the early common courts, this fact that the writs of prohibition in these cases are addressed in this direct and personal way to the ecclesiastical judge and the party is, it seems to me, of significance; for it shows us clearly that the courts of the common law were in this earlier period exercising a jurisdiction *in personam* by prohibition which anticipated Chancery jurisdiction *in personam* by injunction. Even writs of prohibition addressed to the sheriff, as the court's official, seem to have been essentially orders directed against the person of the defendant, as I shall hope to explain later on; but the point that the jurisdiction was *in personam* is brought out with even greater clearness by study of the writs addressed directly and personally to the parties themselves.

But even a royal prerogative writ of prohibition without the infliction of a penalty for its breach would be a weak thing indeed; and we need not be surprised to find that the common law courts of Bracton's time were possessed of powers to inflict severe penalties—even imprisonment—upon judge or party who dared disobey the king's order. The writs of prohibition, as given by Bracton, contain in themselves no hint as to penalty for breach of the court's order; but that the disobedient judge or party will actually suffer a penalty is made quite clear by Bracton, who

[1] Glanvill, xii. 21: Rex illis Iudicibus ecclesiasticis salutem. Prohibeo vobis ne teneatis placitum in curia christianitatis quod est inter N. et R. de laico feodo predicti R. unde ipse queritur quod N. eum trahit in placitum in curia christianitatis coram vobis, quia placitum illud spectat ad coronam et dignitatem meam. T. etc.

[2] All of the writs given by Bracton, ff. 401-412, are of this direct and personal character.

[3] See on writs of prohibition addressed directly to the party suing in the ecclesiastical court, *Y.B.* 1 and 2 Ed. II (Selden Soc.), pl. 5, 10; *Y.B.* 2 and 3 Ed. II (Selden Soc.), pl. 33; *Y.B.* 2 and 3 Ed. II (Selden Soc.), p. 203 (Appendix II.); *Y.B.* 3 Ed. II (Selden Soc.), pl. 45 (and see p. 135 for note from the record); *Registrum Brev. Orig.* ff. 33 *seq.* Cf. also Bracton's *Note-Book*, pl. 351.

gives a full account of the procedure on breach of prohibition.[1] If either judge or party has been guilty of a breach of prohibition the aggrieved party may sue him. In case the aggrieved party gives proper security for prosecuting his suit, a writ of attachment, directed to the sheriff, will issue. The sheriff must then place the offending judge or party under gage and pledge that he will appear before the royal justices to show cause why he has held the plea in the church court contrary to the prohibition, or why he has prosecuted the plea in the church court contrary to the prohibition. If either the judge or the party fail to appear on the set day, he is then attached by better pledges and distrained by all his lands to be present in court on another day, the order of attachment to be observed in other personal actions being followed. But if the defendant be a clerk, and if he be unwilling to find pledges, and have no lay fee by which he can be distrained, a mandate is then sent to the ordinaries and bishop that they shall cause the defendants to come before the royal court. When at last the parties and the offending judge are before the court, the plaintiff declares that the defendant, the party, has vexed and aggrieved him by suing in the ecclesiastical court in a temporal matter contrary to the prohibition. The plaintiff proceeds at once with his proof. Then the offending party and the judge are heard, several defences being open to them. If judgment be given against either the defendant party or the defendant judge, he must pay the plaintiff damages and may even be severely punished by a heavy amercement.[2] If the defendant be a layman he will also be imprisoned as a presumer against the royal dignity because he has disobeyed the prerogative writ of prohibition; he is treated as if he had committed the crime of high treason. If, however, the defendant be a clerk, he is sometimes dealt with more mildly by grace and out of reverence for the clerical order.

This method of enforcing the court's prohibition certainly seems rigorous and effective. Indeed, in certain of its features it is closely analogous to the method of the Chancellors—the writ of subpoena.

Before concluding this account of common law writs analogous to the injunction of Chancery, attention must be drawn to a remarkable case recorded on the De Banco Roll of Hilary,

[1] Bracton, ff. 401, 402, 409, 410.

[2] See Bracton, f. 402.

2 Edward II.[1] In this case, *Prior of Coventry* v. *William Graumpe of Coventry and others*,[2] the plaintiff complained that the defendants, men of Coventry, had been buying and selling outside his market upon market days. The Prior's right was denied by the defendants; but verdict was found against them for sixty pounds damages. The judgment reads: 'And therefore it is considered that the said Prior recover his said damages against them, and that the said William and the others henceforth on Fridays on which the said Prior has his said market do not expose for sale their vendible wares within the town of Coventry elsewhere than in the said market.'[3]

In commenting on this judgment Maitland says: 'If this is not an "injunction" and a "perpetual injunction," we hardly know what to call it. How could this "injunction," if such we may call it, have been enforced? It seems possible that if the defendants had repeated the tort, the plaintiff might have obtained a specially worded writ reciting the breach of the "injunction," and that in this new action the judgment would be that the defendants be taken and imprisoned, and not merely that they be amerced. It is to be remembered that the action known as *contra formam feoffamenti*[4] was based on the breach of a royal prohibition; and the same had been true of the action of waste.'[5]

[1] See Maitland's comments, *Y.B.* 2 and 3 Edward II (Selden Soc.), p. xiii.

[2] *Y.B.* 2 and 3 Edward II (Selden Soc.), 74.

[3] Et idea consideratum est quod predictus Prior recuperet versus eos dampna sua predicta, et quod predicti Willelmus et alii decetero mercimonia sua vendalia per dies Veneris quibus idem Prior habet mercatum suum predictum alibi in predicta villa de Coventre quam in predicto mercato suo non vendant seu vendicioni exponant, etc. Et predictus Willelmus et alii in misericordia etc.

In the *Y.B.* report of this same case Brabazon, J., says (see *Y.B.* 2 and 3 Edward II, 71; Selden Soc. ed.): 'Where the King grants a market to a man, he grants a market in such wise that no man may, in the same town in which the market is, sell any merchandise save in the market. So, since you have confessed that the Prior has a market in this town by the King's grant and that you are resident in the same town, common law will drive you to his market and prevent your marketing elsewhere in the same town (comune ley vous chacera de venir a son marché sans aillours marchander en mesme la ville).'

[4] Maitland here refers to cases in *Y.B.* 2 and 3 Edward II (Selden Soc.), 93, 95.

[5] In a footnote to the report of the case Maitland remarks: 'We can hardly say that the idea of an injunction was foreign to the common law.

Let me summarize what I desire to say in regard to prohibitions.

The early common-law jurisdiction *in personam* by means of prohibitions was not narrow. The orders of the court were not only issued in cases of waste,[1] nuisance,[2] and other torts,[3] but also in cases of contract[4] and property.[5] They not only effected, in a negative way, a restraint upon the doing of an act, but also effected, in a positive and mandatory way, the actual doing of an act; for parties were not only ordered not to commit waste,[6] not to commit nuisance,[7] not to sell land,[8] not to distrain the plaintiff to do suit of court,[9] not to destroy the wood in which the plaintiff has house-bote and hay-bote,[10] not to expose wares for sale elsewhere than in the plaintiff's market,[11] not to sue in the ecclesiastical courts;[12] but parties were ordered to repair walls and buildings,[13] to erect houses,[14] to place property in the same condition in which it had been,[15] and to remove existing nuisances.[16] The orders of the court were also not only temporary or interlocutory in character, but they were final or perpetual; for parties were not only ordered not to commit waste while legal proceedings were in progress, and not to sue in the ecclesiastical court till the rights of the parties at common law had been determined in the common law court, but they were also ordered never to commit waste, never to expose

But could this mandate have any other effect than that of estopping the defendants from raising the same question over again? As to this case see Mary Dormer Harris, *Life in an Old English Town* (1898), p. 64, where the history of the Prior's Half and the Earl's Half at Coventry is related.'

1 See the cases cited pp. 270-77, *supra*.

2 See Bracton's *Note-Book*, pl. 1081, 1162, 1253, 1284; Fitz. *N.-B.* 184, 185.

3 See *Y.B.* 2 and 3 Ed. II (Selden Soc.), p. xiii., 71, 74; *Y.B.* 18 Ed. III (R.S.), 236.

4 See Bracton's *Note-Book*, pl. 1920.

5 See *Y.B.* 30 and 31 Ed. I (R.S.), 324; *Y.B.* 2 and 3 Ed. II (Selden Soc.), pp. 93-96.

6 See pp. 270-77, *supra*.

7 See note 2, *supra*.

8 See Bracton's *Note-Book*, pl. 1920.

9 See *Y.B.* 2 and 3 Ed. II (Selden Soc.), pp. 93-96.

10 See *Y.B.* 30 and 31 Ed. I (R.S.), 324.

11 See *Y.B.* 2 and 3 Ed. II (Selden Soc.), p. xiii., 71, 74.

12 See pp. 277-80, *supra*.

13 See Bracton's *Note-Book*, pl. 1165; *Y.B.* 18 Ed. III (R.S.), 236; Fitz. *N.-B.* 184, 185.

14 See Bracton's *Note-Book*, pl. 1165.

15 Bracton's *Note-Book*, pl. 1081.

16 Fitz. *N.-B.* 184, 185.

wares for sale elsewhere than in the plaintiff's market, never to sue in the ecclesiastical court, and never to do other similar things.[1]

The order of the court was sometimes contained in the writ of prohibition itself; sometimes it was issued at the conclusion of proceedings, such as the common law writ of waste, brought upon breach of a prior prohibition; while sometimes it was issued at the conclusion of actions, such as trespass, brought independently of the breach of a prior prohibition.

I have stated that the jurisdiction of the common-law courts in cases of prohibition was a jurisdiction *in personam*, and such I believe it was. In all cases the prohibition was issued by the court itself. In some cases the writ was addressed to the sheriff, and it was through him, an officer of the court, that the court's order was conveyed to the party. In other cases the writ containing the prohibition of the court was addressed directly to the party without the employment of the sheriff as the court's instrument. In still other cases the court's prohibition was laid upon the party directly, especially at the close of legal proceedings, without the employment of writ or sheriff. As I have already indicated, I cannot think that in cases of the interposition of the sheriff the writ of prohibition is robbed of its character as the court's order *in personam*; for the sheriff acts merely as the court's officer in informing the party of the court's command. Even if this view of the writ addressed to the sheriff be not adopted, there is still evidence in plenty that the court frequently gave orders to the party directly, either by writ or by command issued to the party as he stood before the court in person.

Although the writs of prohibition contain no hint of the penalties attendant upon disobedience to the command of the royal court, it is nevertheless clear from our study of the sources that disobedience resulted in serious consequences. In some cases breach of the prohibition gave rise to self-help on the part of the aggrieved person, forceful measures by the sheriff, and even imprisonment of the disobedient party. So, too, breach of the prohibition might result in legal proceedings by the injured party, and in these proceedings the court might inflict severe penalties for past disobedience and might also take measures of severe character to ensure that no further breaches of prohibition take

[1] See pp. 270-82, *supra*.

place. Appearance of the offending parties could be compelled by one or more attachments by gage and pledge and even by distraint of all their lands; and if, on inquest, the breach of prohibition was proved, there might result payment of damages to the plaintiffs, heavy amercements to the King, loss of the defendants' lands, and even imprisonment for contempt of the King's prohibition. On the conclusion of the legal proceedings the court usually issued a further prohibition and ensured obedience to this new order by requiring the party to furnish sureties, by threat of loss of the party's land, or by appointment of persons, such as foresters and servants, whose duty it was to see that there should be no further breach of prohibition.

Surely the way of the disobedient party was not made easy by the early common law; and we may well believe that fear of the process of the courts acted, in the great majority of cases, as a wholesome restraint. The early common law tribunals had not the writ of subpoena at their command, but they did on occasion issue orders which closely resembled that writ, and they did have an effective machinery of punitive and preventive justice which operated both upon the person and the property of the one who did not comply with their prohibitions.

## VI.—Writs *Quia Timet*

I have dwelt upon the writs of prohibition because they illustrate so clearly the preventive justice of the early common law; but I cannot conclude this paper without a bare reference to certain other writs which are closely related to writs of prohibition. I refer to the writs *quia timet.* These writs anticipated the Chancery's bills *quia timet*, which are so called in analogy to the common law writs which they supplanted. Coke, in his commentary on Littleton, draws attention to the writs in these words: 'And note, that there be six writs in law, that may be maintained, *quia timit* (*sic*), before any molestation, distresse, or impleading: as 1. A man may have his writ of *mesne* (whereof Littleton here [§ 142] speaks) before he be distreyned. 2. A *warrantia cartae*, before he be impleaded. 3. A *monstraverunt*, before any distresse or vexation. 4. An *audita querela*, before any execution sued. 5. A *curia claudenda*, before any default of inclosure. 6. A *ne injustè vexes*, before any distresse or molestation. And these be called *brevia anticipantia*, writs of prevention.'[1] As explained by Story, in his *Equity Jurisprudence*, the bills in equity *quia timet* 'answer precisely to this latter description. They are in the nature of writs of prevention, to accomplish the ends of precautionary justice. They are, ordinarily, applied to prevent wrongs or anticipated mischiefs, and not merely to redress them when done. The party seeks the aid of a court of equity, because he fears (*quia timet*) some future probable injury to his rights or interests, and not because an injury has already occurred, which requires any compensation or other relief.'[2]

In the present paper I have not attempted to give an exhaustive account of the equity of the early common law courts. What I have said should be taken as merely suggestive of results that future detailed investigation may disclose; for there are evidences in plenty that in various ways other than those I have mentioned to-day the early justices were administering principles of equity. But enough has already been said, I hope, to indicate that not all the ideas which we associate with English Equity were either borrowed from the Roman system by the Chancellors or original with them. The advent of the Chancellor as a judicial officer of the Crown was at a time when the older tribunals, although expanding their own system to meet the needs of a growing society, were nevertheless fettered in their powers by statute and precedent as well as by the conservatism and technicality of the legal profession. The Chancellor's court, exercising very wide discretionary powers, gradually developed the elaborate and effective system of rules and principles which we of the twentieth century know as English Equity. But while fully recognizing the achievements of the Chancery, let us not forget that the new tribunal built partly upon the older practice of the common law and other courts whose equitable jurisdiction it supplanted. The new tribunal did not originate English Equity, for it simply carried on the work of the older courts by developing in greater fulness and with a different machinery the equity inherent in royal justice.

H. D. HAZELTINE.

[1] Co. Litt. 100a.

[2] Story, *Equity Jurisprudence*, 2nd Eng. ed., §§ 825, 826.

## XIV

# THE TRANSFORMATION OF EQUITY[1]

EQUITY, *aequitas*, ἐπιείκεια, and equivalents in modern Continental tongues, have for several centuries been current terms among jurists and publicists. In England, and in jurisdictions beyond seas which took their law from England, Equity has become, by a peculiar historical development, the name of a special body of judicial rules administered in the exercise of a special jurisdiction which in its origin was extraordinary. Historical students of legal ideas have to remember that this technical use of the word 'equity' is much less ancient than the jurisdiction itself. In the proceedings of the Court of Chancery before the sixteenth century the complainants appeal to the Chancellor most commonly in the name of conscience, pretty often in that of good faith, right, or reason, very seldom in that of equity.[2] Perhaps it is not too much to say that the term was only becoming current among English lawyers when St. German discussed it in his *Doctor and Student*, a discussion to which we shall presently return.[3] In the course of the sixteenth century the Greek word ἐπιείκεια was used by a few writers in an Anglicized form (see the *Oxford English Dictionary*, *s.v.* 'Epiky'), but the experiment was short-lived. Whatever words are used, the general notion underlying them is that of a doctrine or authority capable of preventing the hardship which otherwise would ensue either from the literal extension of positive rules to

[1] The present paper may be taken as in some measure supplementary to Professor Vinogradoff's on *Reason and Conscience in Sixteenth-Century Jurisprudence*, read at the Berlin Congress in 1908, and published in the *Law Quarterly Review*, xxiv. 373.

[2] See Baildon, *Select Cases in Chancery* (Selden Soc.), 1896, Introduction, p. xxix.

[3] St. German's immediate authority for the Aristotelian doctrine of equity was Gerson: *ib.* 374.

extreme cases or from the exclusion, also by a strictly literal construction, of cases that fall within the true intention of the rule.

Such being the purpose of equity stated in the widest terms, there are two quite distinct and almost opposite aspects under which it may be realized. In the first and more ancient of these we find equitable power exercised by some one, usually the king or a great officer of state, who can dispense with rules according to his discretion, conceived as a reasonable discretion but not defined beforehand. The other and modern form is the rational interpretation and qualification of the rules themselves by a dialectic and scientific process.

The first method works by occasional interference; the occasions may be frequent or not, but each interference is still an isolated act. The second method works, on the contrary, by continuous development. It is by this time almost a commonplace that the more archaic dispensing power, when it falls into a regular course of official administration, loses its arbitrary character and gradually assumes all the features of scientific law, becoming, as Blackstone said a century and a half ago, an artificial system. In the technical English terms, extraordinary jurisdiction ends by being ordinary. So gradual is the change that it is not altogether easy for the modern student to realize its extent or the discrepance of the original points of view.

Let us consider the nature of superior dispensing power apart from any particular forms. It appears to be called for and determined by the nature of archaic legal rules and archaic jurisdiction. Process of law was, in the beginning, a substitute for unrestrained private vengeance or self-help. For a long time there were no regular means at all, and for a much longer time no adequate means, of compelling parties to use it. Hence early legal formulas do not necessarily represent the general sense, at the date of their origin, of what is just and reasonable. They rather mark an outside limit beyond which vengeance or self-help will not be tolerated, and that limit has to be fixed with regard to the passions of ordinary men under provocation. The lawgiver does not advise taking an eye for an eye and a tooth for a tooth; he forbids taking the whole head. In like manner the harshness of archaic law towards debtors is capable of several explanations, and there may well be some truth in all of them. But this one,

I think, is fairly certain, that the law had to compromise with creditors on the least amount of power over the debtor which must be left to them if they were to renounce the use of lawless private force. At the date of the Twelve Tables that amount included, in the last resort, the power of life and death, although there is no reason to believe that the *partis secanto* clause was ever executed in historical times.[1] In matters of family law we know that early Indo-European custom hardly touched the despotic authority of the eldest ancestor. Accordingly the just man, in the estimation of archaic morality, is not he who stands on his right and expects others to stand on theirs, but he who knows how and when to forego the uttermost farthing: and, when once a competent executive authority has been established, the just ruler is he who gives effect to the moral sense of the commonwealth by relaxing penalties in cases of hardship and by putting forth his pre-eminent strength against enormous evil-doers. Such, indeed, is the prevailing sentiment in Eastern countries to this day. Great men and superior officials are conceived not as ministers of rule, but as wielders of a discretion transcending rule. Even educated Asiatics appear to have great difficulty in understanding that there can be such a thing as a rule not subject to a power of administrative dispensation in some one. A normal Eastern ruler would find nothing strange in one Pope treating Benvenuto Cellini as exempt from law and another subjecting him to rigorous imprisonment on mere suspicion, and would see nothing in the indignation roused by James II.'s prosecution of the seven bishops but one proof more that all Europeans are mad.

Not that it is an unknown thing in Western lands to sue for personal favour or indulgence unwarranted by rule, but the suitor, unless he is very ignorant, knows that he is begging for something irregular and hopes to persuade the man in authority, perhaps tries to persuade himself, that a small breach of duty will be venial. To find an European parallel to the normal Eastern attitude we must look outside the region of secular law to the popular and still half-pagan cult of the saints in the Mediterranean countries,

[1] 'Dissectum esse antiquitus neminem equidem legi neque audivi': A. Gellius, xx. I. 52: his guess as to the original intention of the extreme penalty, 'eo consilio tanta inmanitas poenae denuntiatast ne ad eam unquam perveniretur' is of course uncritical, but many modern antiquaries have made as bad guesses or worse.

where, as an ingenious French scholar has shown, the saints have taken up the heritage of the gods. There, to this day, patron and other saints are besought and expected, sometimes on pain of losing their worshipper's devotion, to perform a variety of good offices in the celestial court, often of a kind hardly in accordance with the doctrine or discipline of the Church. Among the more innocent of these favours is that of helping students to pass their examinations, for which it seems Ste. Radegonde of Poitiers has a special reputation. I know not whether the operation is in the nature of strengthening the candidate's brain (which the psychologist may regard as a not improbable effect of his faith) or of softening the examiner's heart. When it comes to invoking St. Antony of Padua to save a man harmless in a duel, in other words to protect him from the temporal inconvenience, and the still graver spiritual danger, of being killed in the commission of a wilful and deliberate mortal sin, the notion of dispensing power appears to be considerably strained. Such a votive tablet, however, I have seen, and I do not suppose they are hard to find in Italy. These archaic observances of imperfectly instructed Catholics may be regarded, it seems to me, as modern survivals from the prehistoric conception of executive authority in general.

To return to the ground of our own faculty, I took the *lex talionis* as a typical example of archaic positive ordinance, although it is strange to our own legal history: for the system of wergild and composition which, at the opening of that history, we find in force among all people of Germanic stock would not be appropriate for the same purpose. It seems to me to belong to a much later and more rational stage of ancient law, for it presupposes a long course of bargaining and settlement of feuds, not so much between individuals as between families and clans; and that again presupposes a more or less effectual desire for peace, not by way of submission to a ruler but by free consent of both parties. We know that such a process took place in the heroic age of Greece. The famous trial scene on the Homeric shield of Achilles exhibits this at the very moment when public opinion begins to enforce the acceptance of a wergild under proper conditions.

Homer omits to tell us what those conditions were. This is unlucky for our archaeology, but quite right for the artistic purpose, which is to describe not the cause in dispute or the scene itself, but the representation of it. According to the interpretation in which I agree with my friend Dr. Leaf, the question is precisely whether an aggrieved party who refuses the offer of a composition is not bound to accept it: there does not appear to be any difficulty about the amount. The choice on the other side, the manslayer's or offender's, to pay or to bear the feud, lasted into a comparatively recent period of Germanic antiquity, as is well known. On the Homeric development the curtain goes down abruptly, and when it next rises we are in a different order of civilization altogether, with very slight materials for guessing what has happened in the meantime. In any case, and even before acceptance or offer of a composition has become compulsory in form or in fact, the existence of an assessable value shows that something has been arrived at corresponding to what we call a market price or a reasonable price in the world of modern business. Thus the wergild presents itself not as the utmost that can be exacted by strict law but rather as an early form of equitable compromise; and the fixed scales of the early Germanic law-books are really codification of a fairly settled customary rule of *aequum et bonum*. It might be shown, I think, without much trouble, that such a scale of compensation was in its time and circumstances a much more sensible institution than it appears to us at first sight; but to pursue this would be somewhat too remote from the argument.

In England the archaic form of equity predominated in the king's administration of special remedial justice during the fourteenth and fifteenth centuries; the sixteenth was a period of transition; before the end of the seventeenth the Court of Chancery was not only a regular court of justice but had started on the road of technical and scientific elaboration.

We have only within the last year become acquainted with a form of this jurisdiction earlier than its exercise by the Chancellor or even by the Council, so early that all remembrance of it was long lost. Mr. Bolland, in the course of editing for the Selden Society the proceedings of Edward II's itinerant justices in Kent, found a course of practice of which no intermediate mention is known through very nearly six centuries.[1] Causes of action arising or continuing while the Eyre was in the county were brought

[1] 2 Eyre of Kent (Seld. Soc. 1912), Introd. p. xxi. As to bills on the Crown side, p. xxii.

before the justices by presenting a bill instead of suing out a writ in the appropriate form of action. Many of these bills are preserved, and they have a marked resemblance in their frame, and in many cases as to their contents also, to the earliest bills in Chancery. To understand the jurisdiction it must be remembered that the justices in eyre represented the king's authority in a special and eminent manner. If we may borrow a canonical term, they carried with them high legatine powers; they superseded all ordinary tribunals. Only the King's Bench, the Court held in contemplation of law before the king himself, could claim to rank above them. Thus the king's residual or extraordinary function of causing justice to be done where ordinary means failed lay in their hand, and they were not only entitled but bound to exercise it. Students of our legal history do not need to be reminded that this function had been recognized from the earliest times, and was treated as living much later. The witnesses for it extend from King Alfred's companion and biographer, the Welsh bishop Asser, to the Kentish antiquary Lambarde, one of Elizabeth's justices of peace. So the justices in eyre, being such exalted ministers of the king's power, were quite natural depositaries of this royal discretion when as yet the Court of Chancery was not.

Applications to the justices in eyre by way of bill were multifarious enough. Some of those which Mr. Bolland has published are founded on money claims for considerable sums, and the parties appear to be of good standing. But there is also a class of petitions by humble suitors for relief against oppression or extortion, alleging their poverty and inability to cope with their adversaries by regular process of law. This class anticipates, in almost every detail, the petitions to the Council and the Chancellor of which specimens were published in 1820 by the old Record Commission, and in 1896 by the Selden Society. We find here exactly the same characteristic mark that distinguishes those early Chancery proceedings, but in still greater prominence. In a large proportion of cases the complaint is such as, in the later settled practice, would have justified a demurrer 'for want of equity.' The justices are not called on to administer any special rules or to recognize rights outside the ordinary law. What the suitor asks them to dispense with is the formality of process; he claims a summary investigation, to use canonical language once more, *sine figura et strepitu iudicii.* Considering the predominant importance of procedure in medieval law,[1] this again is quite natural. Sometimes the petitions are so illiterate that the manner of the halting Anglo-French is almost more eloquent of the petitioner's distress than the matter. A specially illiterate one, which gave Mr. Bolland and myself a good deal of trouble before we arrived at the true rendering by the help of a French medievalist, relates the misfortunes of a man who had paid a sum down to secure board and lodging for the rest of his days. Obviously this crude makeshift for a life annuity[2] was at the mercy of the host's good faith; in this case avarice prevailed, and the host not only failed to make decent provision for his paying guest, but imprisoned him, tied him up, it seems, with a chain. This, of course, was a plain trespass at common law, supposing the fact to have been as stated. Perhaps the story gained something in the telling; at any rate the result was a settlement of some kind between the parties. We have said that there was no question, at this time, of applying any peculiar law to the suits initiated by bills in eyre; but it does appear that the justices, when once they had a case in their hands, could proceed in a summary manner and use a pretty free discretion. They could even interrogate the parties, a thing unknown to common-law process. On the other hand, a case begun in this way sometimes runs its later course to judgment as regularly as if it had started with a writ; and this may throw some light on singularities of early Chancery procedure to which Mr. Pike had called attention long before we knew that there was such a thing as a bill in eyre.

It is needless to say more here of Chancery suits in the fourteenth and fifteenth centuries, as the information is easily accessible in the Selden Society volume already referred to, and is summarized by Dr. Holdsworth. There is, however, one rather curious head of jurisdiction of which I have found no mention in text-books. It was not very uncommon to apply to the Chancellor for an injunction to restrain the defendant from

1 The 'lex terrae' of Magna Carta, for example, is rather due process of law than the substantive law defining offences.

2 Similar agreements were still in use in the latest years of the fifteenth century: Trice Martin in *Archaeologia*, lx. (1) at p. 378, where the complaint is of refusal 'to fynd or kepe' the plaintiff.

practising witchcraft against the plaintiff, or, it might be, from making false charges of witchcraft against him. This appears from a group of cases in which clergymen were concerned, printed in 1907 by Mr. Trice Martin in the *Archaeologia*,[1] as well as from the more generally known publications. If there was any usurpation of jurisdiction in matters of 'nygromancy' it was against the Court Christian.

There is no reason to believe that the jurisdiction of the mediaeval Chancellors was unpopular. Complaints began to be loud in the sixteenth century, and were heard of earlier.[2] But these were for the most part, if not altogether, made or instigated by practitioners of the common law who were aggrieved by the growing competition of the Chancery. If the competition had not met a public want it would not have been effective. What concerns us to note here is that the grievance was expressly founded on charges of arbitrary and uncertain interference with legal rights; the Chancellor and his officers went, it was said, by their 'conscience and discretion,' which might mean reasons borrowed from Roman law or anything else they chose. The only final and satisfying answer to such objections in a civilized country was to make it clear that the Court of Chancery was not a fountain of unlimited dispensations, but as regular a court of judicature as any other, a court whose existence precluded the king from setting up any new tribunals with like jurisdiction, or administering its remedies in any other way; and this was in fact the line taken by James I with Bacon's advice when the conflict became open and official.

Meanwhile Christopher St. German, a writer in advance of his contemporaries in many things, put an explanation of Equity in the mouth of his imaginary Doctor of Divinity,[3] and appropriately so, when it was still exceptional for the Chancellor to be a layman. The Doctor speaks, of course, from the canonical point of view, and does not profess to know Chancery practice. Equity is not yet a term of art among lawyers. The Student knows something, it appears later, about the cases in which the writ of *sub poena* does and does not lie, but does not care to go into details. Now the

1 Vol. lx. (or 2nd ser. 10) pt. 1, 353; cp. the same writer's miscellaneous specimens in vol. lix., pt. 1, 1 (1904).

2 Holdsworth, *H. E. L.* i. 246.

3 *Doct. and Stud.*, dial. 1, c. 16.

Doctor quite clearly takes the view that the fundamental principle of equity is not occasional and overriding interference, but enlightened scientific interpretation. I am putting St. German's thought into modern language, but I believe the words bear me out. 'Equity is a righteousness that considereth all the particular circumstances of the deed . . . and it is called also by some men *epieikeia*; the which is no other thing but an exception of the law of God, or of the law of reason, from the general rules of the law of man, when they by reason of their generality would in any particular case judge against the law of God or the law of reason —*the which exception is secretly understood in every general rule of general positive law*.' Of these last words it is hardly too much to say that they anticipate the reforming and constructive spirit of Mansfield. The conception of Equity as expounded by St. German was in itself nothing new. He was quite openly following the scholastic tradition which went back partly by direct and partly by indirect ways to Aristotle. But the treatment of it as practically applicable to English law shows a grasp and insight quite exceptional at the time. The Doctor goes on to suggest that there may be 'some like equities grounded on the general rules of the law of the realm' and elicits from the Student examples of equitable construction applied within the common law itself. In the next chapter the Student goes so far as to say that the only reason why the equitable relief granted upon bills in Chancery does not count as part of the common law is the absence of a formal record in the king's court. 'Forasmuch as no record remaineth in the king's court of no such bill, nor of the writ of *sub poena* or injunction that is used thereupon; therefore it is not set as for a special ground of the law, but as a thing that is suffered by the law.'

About a century later the Court of Chancery was solemnly recognized as a perfect and regular court of justice. Yet it was not till the end of the seventeenth century that James I's decisive action bore its due fruit. The causes of the check were not legal but political, and are to be found in the controversies between king and parliament, between prelates and Puritans, which led to the Civil War. The Chancellor was still eminently the king's minister; his jurisdiction was practically uncontrolled, for there was no appellate Court; and men saw in the Chancellor's discretion, as they had seen in the criminal equity of the Star Chamber, a power of being abused to political ends. Here, and not in any merely technical prejudice, is the explanation of Selden's famous gibe 'Equity is a roguish thing.' It is so because the measure of the Chancellor's foot may go too near to follow the measure of King Charles I.'s foot, peradventure even Archbishop Laud's: and so the fuller working out of equity on St. German's lines had to wait for the settlement of a free political constitution.

So far as England is concerned, the Puritan dislike of Chancery jurisdiction may be taken as belonging to the common knowledge of legal and other historians; and we know in a general way that it was carried across the Atlantic. The full extent of its working on the western continent has been disclosed to the learned world only by pretty recent publications of American scholars. While Story was setting forth the beauties of equity jurisprudence in his most elegant periods, the power of administering equitable remedies was still, in more than one State, altogether lacking or rudimentary. Traces of the old prejudice may be found even in much later American writers. We have to remember, however, that the Common Law itself found but little favour in the eyes of the Pilgrim Fathers and their successors. For a time it was in danger of being replaced by the Pentateuch, and its reception was precarious, even beyond the Puritan commonwealths of New England, down to the eighteenth century.[1] We have also to remember in extenuation that for some little time after the Restoration English Common Law judges themselves had not got clear of the old notions about equity, and wondered what it should have to do with precedents.

In our own time, it is almost needless to say, courts of equitable jurisdiction wholly disclaim any such roving powers of dispensation and administrative interference as were exercised by the medieval Chancellors. A judge of the Chancery Division can in plain terms deny that his Court is a Court of conscience.[2] It would be beyond my present scope, and beyond my competence, to look for any similar process of transformation in other systems of law; but the

[1] S. D. Wilson, 'Courts of Chancery in the American Colonies,' *Essays in Anglo-American Legal History*, ii. 779; Fisher, 'The Administration of Equity through Common Law Forms,' *ibid.* ii. 810; Reinsch, 'English Common Law in the Early American Colonies,' *ibid.* i. 369.

[2] Lord Justice (then Justice) Buckley [1903] 2 Ch. at p. 195.

case of *droit administratif* in France is so near at hand and so generally known that I may allow myself to mention it. The semi-political jurisdiction of the Conseil d'État, established under the First Empire in the interest of the government rather than of the citizen, has by this time acquired a perfectly judicial character, and it is said that the result is at times better for the suitor than what he could look for under the ordinary law.

During the last two centuries the scientific construction of equity jurisprudence in England has been in the hands of a highly specialized section of the Bench and Bar, concentrated in these very precincts of Lincoln's Inn where we are sitting. Practitioners of the common law regarded equity much as the lay people regarded all legal science, that is, as an inscrutable kind of magic, and rather black than white. Even since the jurisdiction of our present Supreme Court in all its branches has been made uniform this frame of mind has hardly become extinct, and there is still something esoteric about the doctrines of equity and conveyancing. The whole of the ground sacred to these mysteries would be included in a radius of five hundred yards, or for abundant caution let us say metres, drawn from this Old Hall of Lincoln's Inn, within or near whose walls the law of the Court of Chancery was discussed and settled by several generations of lawyers.

F. POLLOCK.

## XV

# THE INFLUENCE OF COKE ON THE DEVELOPMENT OF ENGLISH LAW[1]

THE age of Coke was a critical period in the history of our common law. During the sixteenth century the work of making England a territorial state of the modern type had been accomplished, partly by the legislature, partly by newly created or newly organized courts and councils, and partly by the common law courts. With the natural expansion of the jurisdiction of these courts and councils conflicts between them had become frequent; and they became more frequent and more bitter when the restraining influence of Elizabeth was removed. A settlement based upon an impartial consideration of the claims of these rival courts was eminently desirable. But it was never reached, because these disputes about jurisdiction soon became merged in that larger question of the whereabouts of the sovereign power in the State which underlay the various causes of conflict between the King and his Parliament. The newly created or newly organized courts naturally magnified the prerogative on which they leaned, and to which they owed their authority. They therefore gravitated to the royalist view that in the last resort the prerogative was the sovereign power in the State. On the other hand the common law was firmly based upon the

[1] This paper is printed in the form in which it was written for the International Historical Congress. It is a summary of a fuller account of Coke's career and influence which will appear in the succeeding volumes of the author's *History of English Law*. For this reason the author has thought it best not to overweight it by inserting the authorities for the statements contained in it. He has therefore only inserted explanatory references when these appeared to be necessary for the understanding of the text. The fuller account of Coke will, of course, contain detailed references to the authorities.

mediaeval idea that in the State the law was supreme, and that the prerogative was limited by it. The common lawyers therefore gravitated to the Parliamentary view that definite legal limits should be assigned to the prerogative, and that ministers who overstepped those limits should be made responsible to the law. Conversely the Parliamentary leaders naturally held that the law to which they were responsible was that common law in which alone they could find a legal justification for their political views.

But the additions made by the modern cases and statutes to the mediaeval principles on which the common law was founded made it often obscure and sometimes irrational. Was it capable, it might fairly be asked, of supplying the principles needed to guide the development of the public and private law of a modern state? The common lawyers maintained that it was all sufficient for this purpose; and though the growth of an independent system of equity, and the slow development of a reasonable system of commercial law, show that they to some extent exaggerated the capacity of their system, the history of English public law in the seventeenth century, and the growth of new branches of private law in the eighteenth and nineteenth centuries, have justified their faith. That the common law was given this chance of justifying the faith of those who believed in its capacity is largely due to the career and writings of Edward Coke.

The main facts of Coke's career are well known and a very brief recapitulation will suffice. He was born in 1551-2, and was called to the bar in 1578. He became Solicitor-General in 1592, and was Attorney-General from 1593 to 1606. It was during the latter part of this period that he published the first three volumes of his *Reports*, and gained the reputation of being the most learned lawyer in England. It was during this period also that he acquired that reverence for the common law which is the keynote of his whole career. In 1606 he became Chief Justice of the Common Pleas, and at once claimed for the common law the position of supremacy in the State to which he believed it to be entitled. This involved him in disputes with rival Courts, and, as James I claimed to be the arbiter of all these disputes about jurisdiction, with the king himself. These disputes merely confirmed Coke in his fixed belief as to the position of the common law in the State. Thus, when, in 1613, he was made Chief Justice of the King's Bench, the quarrel still continued; and at length, in 1618, he was dismissed from the Bench and ordered to revise his *Reports*. After a period of hesitancy he, in 1620, decisively threw in his lot with the Parliamentary opposition. Till 1628 he took a leading part in all the Parliaments of James I's and Charles I's reigns, except that of 1626. In the Parliament of 1628 he drafted and helped to carry the Petition of Right; and the stormy scenes which marked its passage were his last appearance in public life. His remaining six years were spent in retirement. Charles I, on his death in 1634, seized all his manuscripts, lest they should contain matter to the prejudice of the prerogative; for, as he said, 'he is held too great an oracle among the people, and they may be misled by anything that carries such an authority as all things do that he either speaks or writes.'

The fears of Charles are the best evidence of Coke's reputation. It was a reputation fairly earned by the manner in which he had devoted all his great powers to the single object of understanding, applying, explaining, and systematizing the common law. The large place which he fills in English history is no doubt due in a great degree to the character of the age. In quieter times he would simply have been a great common lawyer with conservative prejudices. But in the seventeenth century a great common lawyer, who was passionately convinced of the excellence of the common law and of its right to be the supreme law in the State, was necessarily drawn into politics in order to defend its claims. The fact that he was thus drawn into politics causes an apparent inconsistency in his career, and some real inconsistency in his statements of the doctrines of constitutional law. At first sight, there seems to be little in common between Elizabeth's zealous Attorney-General, and the man who framed and helped to carry the Petition of Right. But this inconsistency is, to a large extent, only apparent. He could be a zealous servant of the Crown under the balanced Tudor monarchy, which so skilfully and diplomatically shelved fundamental questions. Under James I he was driven to resist the attempts to substitute the supremacy of the Crown for the supremacy of the common law. In the later years of James I's reign, and under Charles I, he was driven into alliance with the Parliamentary opposition in order to uphold as against the Crown the laws which secured the rights and privileges of Parliament, and the liberties of the subject. He stood still. His outlook was always that of a statesman of the latter part of the Tudor period. It was the changing political scene which seemed to place him in constantly fresh positions, and necessarily led him to modify his views as to important doctrines of constitutional law.

The character of the man and of the age fully accounts for his vast influence upon the law and politics of the seventeenth century. But they do not fully account for the permanence of his influence upon the future development of English law. This permanence is due to the fact that his devotion to the common law led him to consider it to be his duty to employ the scanty leisure of a busy career in the work of restating in his writings all its principal doctrines. If, therefore, we would understand the reasons for the permanence of his influence, if we would estimate its nature and extent we must examine the character of these writings.

The two works which have had this great influence are the *Reports* and the *Institutes.*

The first part of the *Reports* was published in 1600, the next two shortly after, and the remaining eight at intervals between 1603 and 1615. The twelfth and thirteenth parts were published after Coke's death in 1655 and 1658. They were not prepared by him for the press; and are in fact simply rough notes of cases and other transactions in which he had taken part. They have never had the same authority as the other eleven parts, which he himself published as his considered views upon the matters therein contained.

When Coke wrote his *Reports* there was no agreement as to the proper style of making a law report. The *Year Book* reports are often very discursive narratives of the proceedings in Court. But it is clear that in Coke's day much more attention was being paid both to the actual discussion, and to the reasons on which it was based, than in the earlier period. The constant and frequent citation of cases in court, sometimes on the point and sometimes at a great distance from that point, is noted by Coke and contrasted with the earlier practice. But the report was still made primarily for the benefit of the reporter; and reporters adopted all styles from the short notes of Bendloe to the elaborate statements of record, argument, and judgment contained in Plowden. Coke did not adopt any one style. To a certain extent he was guided by the nature of the case which he was reporting. Occasionally he makes a case a mere peg for a disquisition on some branch of law.[1] Sometimes he groups together the reports of several cases on one topic, e.g. slander, by-laws, usury, copyhold;[2] and these reports are usually summary. When the case is important he often gives the pleadings at length, a summary of the argument on both sides, and the decision, together with the reasons for it. In these cases Coke no doubt intended to give the effect of what was said in Court. But it is probable that he added both explanations and disquisitions which his own reading, and his enthusiasm for what he regarded as sound doctrine, suggested to him. Bacon once said that in his *Reports* there was too much 'de proprio.'

The cases reported form a *corpus* of the common law in the sixteenth century. All parts of the law old and new are reviewed. The older learning where applicable is restated; the manner in which it had been modified by the statutes of the sixteenth and early seventeenth centuries is explained; and the statutes which introduced new branches of law are applied and interpreted. The new developments of the common law—such as the beginning of the struggle against perpetuities, the development of assumpsit, the practice of allowing actions on contracts made abroad—are noted and justified. Numerous cases, heard before courts other than the common law courts (e.g. the Court of Wards and the Court of Star Chamber), appear. The fact that the common law could appeal to some of these precedents was very useful to it when the results of the Great Rebellion gave it all and even more than all the jurisdiction which Coke had claimed for it.

The four books of the *Institutes* were designed to supply the student with a general introduction to the law. The older methods of legal education were hardly sufficient by themselves, now that the law was growing more complex. Coke set himself to write, for the benefit of the student, the earliest of our text-books on the modern common law. The *First Institute* contains his commentary on Littleton. The *Second* is a discursive commentary on some 39 statutes, of which 28 belonged to the mediaeval period. Many of them deal with matters of public law. The *Third* deals with the criminal law, and the *Fourth* with the jurisdiction of

1 Blackamore's Case, 8 Co. Rep. 156a—amendments of process; Beecher's Case 8 Co. Rep. 58a—amercements.

2 4 Co. Rep. 12b-21a (slander); 5 Co. Rep. 62b-64a (by-laws); *ibid.* 69a, 70b (usury); 4 Co. Rep. 21a-32a (copyhold).

courts. Throughout the *Second, Third,* and *Fourth Institutes* Coke insists on his views as to the supremacy of the common law courts which had cost him his seat on the bench. The *First Institute* was the only one which Coke published in his lifetime. The other three were published in 1641.

The *First Institute* is a book of a very different character to the other three. Littleton was one of the first books which a student read, and Coke had been collecting material for it all his life—from the time probably that he first read it as a student. Coke upon Littleton was meant to be Littleton up-to-date—bearing somewhat the same relation to Littleton as Justinian's *Institutes* bear to the *Institutes of Gaius*. But it is much more than this. The commentary is extraordinarily minute. It gives the most elementary pieces of information, and also disquisitions upon the most abstruse points of law. All parts of the law not dealt with in the other three books, and many that are, are introduced into this wonderful commentary. It could never have been a good students' text-book, and it is rather difficult to see how even its author could have supposed that it was suitable for this purpose. One reason may be found in the fact that he did not intend the student to read it all at once, and another in the fact that it was supplemented by the instruction given by the Inns of Court. Moreover, what is to our eyes one source of confusion, the grouping of a large number of miscellaneous legal topics round the land law, was the traditional historic order of the common law. Just as in Roman law many topics belonging to the general law of contract are grouped round the *stipulatio*, because it was the most general form of contract known to Roman law; so in English law, from the days of Bracton, many various topics had been grouped round the land law, because it was the most highly developed branch of the common law. The rapid development of the common law was fast making this grouping of topics obsolete—the law of contract and the law of personal property were fast becoming independent branches of law, and as important as the land law. But it was hardly to be expected that Coke, whose outlook was always to the past, should appreciate this. That was a point of view which came more naturally to a man like Bacon whose outlook was towards the future.

It is easy to see why Coke did not care to publish the last

three parts of the *Institutes* in his lifetime. The *First Institute* dealt with branches of the law very remote from any of the constitutional controversies of the day. But a large number of the topics treated of in the other three books touched them at many points. In 1628, when the *Second* and *Third Institutes* were finished, Coke's active career was over; and, when the *Fourth Institute* was finished, Parliament had been dissolved and the country was being governed by the Prerogative. We cannot blame Coke for not wishing to shorten his few remaining years by a close imprisonment in the Tower. He had recorded his opinions: their publication could well wait for a more favourable season.

When they were published in 1641 it was the hour of the victory of the common law and of the Parliament. Men did not stop to consider the accuracy or the validity of the arguments upon which Coke based his claim that the common law and the Parliament were supreme in the State. They simply accepted them and made them the basis, not only of our modern constitutional law, but also of the whole of that large part of our modern English law which is comprised under the general term 'common law.' It is not surprising therefore that, almost down to our own days, there have been many lawyers who would hardly admit of the existence of any serious shortcomings in Coke's work. But during the last century there has been a reaction. Coke has been attacked on opposite grounds by two very different schools of lawyers. In the first place he has been attacked by the historical school on the ground that he has sometimes carelessly and sometimes, it is even said, intentionally misrepresented historical facts. In the second place he has been attacked by lawyers of the school of Austin and Bentham on the ground that both the material and the form of his writings are obscure, illogical, and ill-arranged. Let us look at these two classes of criticism, and see to what extent they are justified.

### (1) The Exceptions taken by the Historians

Time has its revenges. Coke in his lifetime was at pains to advise and correct historians if they ventured into the domain of law. Now the historians have turned upon Coke and pointed out that his history is often inaccurate, and that his law is not the true mediaeval law that he represented it to be; and it must be admitted that there is a large amount of substantial truth in their criticisms. Coke was always the lawyer, always the advocate, and, in the latter part of his life, a keen politician. The lawyer, the advocate, and the politician must needs make excursions into the domain of the historian for their own special purposes. But history so produced will generally be, as history, worthless. If we remember that Coke's excursions into the domain of history are all made with a purpose, and that in addition he had no conception of history for its own sake, and no power of criticizing the historical sources which he used, we shall not be surprised that, as compared with the work of true historians like Selden or Bacon, his historical work is almost contemptible. If we glance at the various purposes for which Coke was obliged to trespass upon the domain of the historian, we shall be the better able to understand why, in this historical age, Coke's reputation has fallen to perhaps an unduly low ebb.

As a lawyer Coke was obliged to make a large use of history in order to explain his law. The continuity of the common law must make every sound common lawyer something of a historian. At the same time the peculiarities of our system of case law cause lawyers to exaggerate the amount of continuity which there is in the law. They talk as if the new decisions were merely developments of the old law; and this method of reasoning may easily deceive historians who are not lawyers. Moreover the present state of our knowledge of English legal history has led historians who are lawyers to join in condemning Coke. We know more about the legal doctrines of the twelfth and thirteenth centuries than about the legal doctrines of the fifteenth and sixteenth centuries. We see a doctrine in Bracton or the earlier *Year Books*. We see it in a somewhat different form in Coke, and we are apt to conclude that Coke has been perverting his sources. To take an illustration. Mr. Pike[1] has pointed out that when Coke, commenting on Littleton, states that an advowson lies in grant *but not in livery*, he is introducing a negative statement for which there is no warrant in Littleton. But Coke had authority. In 1490[2] Brian and Vavisor agreed that, because an advowson passed by grant, it could not pass by livery. Coke was not writing legal history. He was only using legal history to explain the law of

[1] *L.Q.R.* v. 36.

[2] *Y.B.* 6 Hy. VII, Pasch. pl. 5, p. 3.

his own day. Possibly many of his statements which seem at variance with the older authorities are based upon more recent authorities which he was bound to follow. A judge who at the present day followed seventeenth-century in preference to nineteenth-century decisions would find that his judgments were frequently reversed. I cannot, of course, say how many of Coke's departures from thirteenth-century law can be justified in this way—that would involve a knowledge to which I cannot pretend. But probably a good many can be so justified; and clearly for errors of this kind he cannot be censured. But this plea cannot be urged in defence of the errors into which he was led either from his habits of indiscreet advocacy or from his political bias.

A very cursory acquaintance with Coke's writings will show that he approached both law and history with the mind of a strenuous advocate. All through his life he never ceased to be an advocate of legal doctrines or political causes. Whether he is reporting a case, or arguing for the supremacy of the common law in the State, or upholding the rights and privileges of Parliament, he does it with all his strength; and the result is that he writes or talks himself into a decided view on the subject. I very much doubt whether in all Coke's writings a passage could be found in which he admits that he has left the law uncertain. On the other hand there are many passages in which he states that he has solved all doubts and reconciled all conflicting cases. No doubt he honestly thought he had done so. Now this defect in Coke's mind has led to two very grave shortcomings in his writings. (1) The various causes which he advocated during his long life were not always quite consistent. Thus the dicta in *Bonham's case*[1] as to the power of the common law to overrule Acts of Parliament are not quite consistent with the views which he elsewhere expresses as to the supremacy of Parliament. Some of the dicta in the case of *Non Obstante*[2] as to inseparable prerogatives of the Crown which no Act of Parliament can take away, are not quite consistent with his more considered statements that the prerogative is subject to the law. (2) This defect made him very uncritical in the use of his sources. He swallowed all the statements in the *Mirror of Justices* because they fitted in with his preconceived ideas as to the immemorial antiquity of the common law. Moreover, it led him to

[1] 8 Co. Rep 107. [2] 12 Co. Rep. 18.

read into his authorities meanings which they never possessed. I have elsewhere shown that he twice repeats a statement that one of the counts in an indictment of Wolsey contained an accusation that Wolsey had attempted to subvert the common law,—the facts being that the indictment cited is not of Wolsey at all, and that the passage as to subverting the common law was the common form of an indictment under the statute of Praemunire.[1] The similar errors into which he fell in connexion with his account of the Admiralty jurisdiction have been exposed by Prynne in the seventeenth century, and by Mr. Marsden in our own times. But this last illustration of Coke's use of his history to advocate his views is closely connected with the political uses to which he turned it.

We have seen that Coke in his later years had become a leader of the Parliamentary opposition. This naturally involved a reconsideration of some of his earlier opinions on such matters of public law as the right of the Crown to legislate by proclamation,[2] to levy impositions and exact loans,[3] to commit to prison without cause shown,[4] to get extra-judicial opinions from the judges.[5] In earlier days these recantations tended to make men believe in the infallibility of Coke. When men thought that the constitutional principles established in the seventeenth century were not merely beneficial to the State, but also incontestably sound law, the views of Coke on these matters in his published writings were taken to prove his legal infallibility on all matters. But in our own days they have had the opposite effect. We see now that the public law of the seventeenth century was very obscure; and that though the victory of constitutional principles was undoubtedly beneficial to the State, the legal principles upon which the leaders of the constitutional opposition relied were often very dubious. Hence we see in these recantations of Coke mere evidences of his political

[1] *L.Q.R.* xxviii. 135-6.

[2] Cp. Notes on the Prerogative in State Papers, Dom. (1598–1601), cclxxvi. 81, and the opinion given while Attorney-General, with the case of Proclamations (1611), 12 Co. Rep. 74.

[3] Spedding, *Life and Letters of Bacon*, v. 146; 12 Co. Rep. 119; Rushworth, Pt. i. 497; State Papers, Dom. (1634), cclxxviii. 35; *ibid.* (1603–1610), lv. 52.

[4] See his speech in the House of Commons, cited Foster, Elliot, ii. 26-28; and cp. his views in 1620–21, *Proceedings and Debates*, ii. 25, 109.

[5] Spedding, *Life and Letters of Bacon*, v. 114-18.

bias, and are apt to doubt whether in other branches of the law he is as infallible as our forefathers thought him. I do not think that either line of argument is quite legitimate. We must clearly separate Coke's views on matters which related to the political controversies of the day from matters which did not; and I think that on matters of law unconnected with these controversies a general charge of inaccuracy is not proved. No doubt dicta can be found which disparage his accuracy. But of some of these Mr. Wallace in his book on the *Reporters* has successfully disposed. No doubt later cases show that he was sometimes wrong. But they are small in number compared with the cases in which his ruling has been accepted. Neither Bacon nor Ellesmere found any serious faults with his *Reports*, except in cases of a political or semi-political character; and Bacon admitted that the *Reports*, 'though they may have errors, and some peremptory and extra-judicial resolutions more than are warranted, yet contain infinite good decisions and rulings over of cases.' Bacon and the lawyers who were the contemporaries or the immediate successors of Coke knew more of the older authorities at first hand than we do. I should therefore contend that the view that Coke is inaccurate in his statements of law on matters unconnected with the political controversies of the day is not proved.

Let us now turn to the criticisms made by the writers of another school.

(2) THE EXCEPTIONS TAKEN BY THE ANALYTICAL JURISTS

Though Coke's history is often unhistorical he was for all that a lawyer of the historical school. 'Out of the old fields must grow the new corn' was one of his favourite proverbs. And he had all the defects of the historical school in an exaggerated form. Thus he is ready with a defence for all the anomalies and anachronisms by which English law was disfigured. He could explain them; and between explanation and justification it never occurred to him that there could be any distinction. On the other hand he had the virtues of the historical school. The analytical lawyer usually bases his analysis mainly upon the ideas current in his own day. He is therefore inclined to reject as useless all that is not in accord with these current ideas. But the historical lawyer preserves the ideas of a past age; and these ideas often come into their own again in a future age. Coke's writings preserved for England the mediaeval idea of the supremacy of the law at a time when political speculation was tending in the direction of the supremacy of a sovereign body or person who was above the law; and the obscurity and indefinite character of some of the mediaeval rules of law which he states preserved for the common law a flexibility which is a condition precedent of natural development and expansion.

As Coke's writings thus possess the vices and the virtues of the historical school, they have naturally attracted the censure of those whose minds are cast in an analytical mould. Hobbes, the forefather of the school of analytical jurists, attacks Coke in his *Dialogue of the Common Law* with all the accustomed weapons of that school. Law should be defined as the command of the sovereign. Case law is no true law. Useless distinctions should be got rid of. Absurd rules should be altered. Law should be stated so plainly that the non-lawyer should be able to give a sound opinion upon its meaning. Hobbes's criticisms are approved by Sir James Stephen. But we should do well to remember that, though Stephen is the historian of our criminal law, he had the mind of an analytical jurist. And when we read his condemnation of Coke's disorderly mind, of his technical and pedantic divisions, of his puerile speculations, we might also recall the fact that, in Austin's opinion, Coke's mastery of the legal system as a whole was equalled only by that of the great Roman jurists. Hobbes and Stephen saw part of the truth, but not all.

That at the end of the sixteenth century a restatement of English law was needed was obvious to the leading lawyers and statesmen of the day. But what form should that restatement take? It was clear to Bacon that the construction of a logical code was impossible. 'I dare not,' he wrote, 'advise to cast the law into a new mould.' Instead, he had visions of doing for English law something of the same nature that Justinian had done for Roman law. There was to be a revision of the statute book, a revision of the reports, a book of institutes, and a book of legal history. But political causes rendered Bacon's scheme impossible of realization at the time when it was propounded; and the merits of Coke's writings rendered such a restatement at a later period less pressing.

His writings had, it seems to me, five very considerable merits.

(1) They cover the whole field of English law, and restate it from the point of view of the sixteenth century. In any age in which large political, social, and intellectual changes have taken place the law will need to be reconsidered and restated. And it is not one of the least of the advantages of our system of case law that it can thus be adapted to a new environment. What a succession of eminent lawyers have done for the common law in the nineteenth century, Coke did for the common law of his own day. Professor Maitland once said in a letter to me, 'Coke's books are the great dividing line, and we are hardly out of the Middle Ages till he has dogmatized its results.'

(2) He deduces from the scattered and inconsistent dicta in the Year Books positive rules of law. All through his writings Coke is reconciling Year Books. We could with considerable justice apply to his work the title applied to Gratian's work—*Concordia discordantium canonum.*

(3) His writings not only brought the Year Books into line with the modern reports, they brought the mediaeval literature of the common law into line with the modern literature. The great mediaeval books—Glanvil, Bracton, Britton, and Fleta—were made to explain and illustrate the law expounded by Perkins, Fitzherbert, Staundford, and Lambard.

(4) By the information which they gave as to the doings of other courts—notably the Star Chamber, the Chancery, and the Admiralty—they tended to familiarize the common lawyers with the new ideas which, in those courts, were giving rise to new legal developments. This made it easier for the common law to fill the great position which it acquired as a result of the constitutional conflicts of the seventeenth century.

(5) As a result, his writings ensured the continuity of the development of the common law amidst all the vast changes of this century of Renaissance, Reformation, and Reception. This signal merit of Coke's writings was fully recognized in his own day. 'Had it not been for Sir Edward Coke's *Reports*,' wrote Bacon, 'the law of this time had almost been like a ship without ballast; for that the cases of modern experience are fled from those that are adjudged and ruled in former times.'

Coke had thus adapted a thoroughly mediaeval body of law to the needs of the modern State, without any appreciable sacrifice of the mediaeval ideas contained in it. He had maintained that this body of law ought to be the supreme law in the State; and the results of the Great Rebellion had caused his views to prevail. Naturally the effect of his writings on the future development of English law has been enormous both for evil and for good.

It can hardly be denied that the victory of Coke's views has had unfortunate effects upon the form and the substance of English law. Rules and doctrines were retained which were already half obsolete in his day; and, as a result, it is hard to draw the line between obsolete and living law. Then, too, the appropriation by the common law of commercial causes made the growth of a reasonable system of commercial law very slow. Till the codifying statutes of the nineteenth century, English law could show no measures dealing with this topic comparable with the French ordonnances of two centuries earlier. And till the reforms of the same century our law of bankruptcy was a disgrace to a civilized community.

On the other hand we cannot doubt that the result of Coke's writings has been to make English law a very much more uniform system of law than it would otherwise have been. The result of the success of the Court of Chancery in its quarrel with the common law was to split our English law into two halves. If all the other rival courts had been equally successful, English law would have been split into many fragments. Coke's writings helped to save English law from this fate because they successfully asserted the supremacy of the common law.

And more was involved in the maintenance of the supremacy of the common law than the settlement of a mere legal quarrel about jurisdiction. If the common law had lost its supremacy, would Parliament, we may fairly ask, have gained the victory? And if it had gained the victory without the help of a common law which claimed to be the supreme law in the State, would our constitutional law be what it is to-day? This we may well doubt. In the past the common lawyers had helped to make the English Parliament an efficient representative assembly. In the seventeenth century the Parliament handsomely repaid the debt by helping Coke and his fellows to maintain the mediaeval conception of the rule of law, and to apply it to the government of a modern State. It was in Coke's writings that this, together with other mediaeval conceptions, were given their modern form; and therefore it is largely owing to the influence of his writings that these mediaeval conceptions have become part of our modern law. If their influence upon some parts of our modern law has not been wholly satisfactory, let us remember that they have preserved for England and the world the constitutional doctrine of the rule of law.

The effects of this doctrine were destined in the succeeding ages to be felt beyond the bounds of England, beyond the bounds even of English-speaking peoples—in all places and at all times wherever and whenever men have had the will and the power to establish constitutional government. We may surely claim that these large results of this part of Coke's work upon the civilized world of to-day entitle the most English of our English common lawyers to a place among the great jurists of the world.

W. S. HOLDSWORTH.

# XVI

## ÜBER DIE GESCHICHTE DES MAJORITÄTSPRINZIPS

Zu keiner Zeit vielleicht hat das Majoritätsprinzip eine so gewaltige Rolle gespielt wie in der Gegenwart. Bei staatlichen und kommunalen Wahlen, bei den Beschlussfassungen von Parlamenten und Gemeindevertretungen, in administrativen und richterlichen Kollegien, in allen öffentlichen und privaten Körperschaften, in Vereinen für wirtschaftliche wie für ideale Zwecke entscheidet Stimmenmehrheit. Überall gilt, was die Mehrheit will, als Ausdruck des Gemeinwillens. Durch ein Rechenexempel wird festgestellt, was alle Beteiligten als für sie bindend anerkennen müssen, mag es sich nun um 16 Millionen Stimmender, wie jüngst bei der amerikanischen Präsidentenwahl, oder mag es sich um die Abstimmung in einem Dreimännerkollegium handeln. Erst unterhalb der Dreizahl versagt dieses Allheilmittel für Meinungsverschiedenheiten. In der Gemeinschaft zu Zweien gibt es keine Majorität. Die innigste aller menschlichen Verbindungen, die Ehe, muss sich ohne Abstimmungen behelfen.

Infolge solcher allgemeinen Anerkennung nehmen wir heute das Majoritätsprinzip als etwas Selbstverständliches hin und zerbrechen uns nicht viel den Kopf darüber, warum denn hier überall der Teil so viel gilt wie das Ganze. Auch in juristischen, politischen und philosophischen Schriften begegnen nur selten eingehendere Versuche seiner Rechtfertigung.[1]

Dem war nicht immer so! Das Majoritätsprinzip hat keines-

[1] Eindringlich erörtert das Problem Simmel, *Soziologie*, 1908, S. 186-97 (Exkurs über Überstimmung). Eine Erklärung, die aber in den sinnlichen Vorstellungen primitiver Zeitalter stecken bleibt, versucht auch Bolze, *Der Begriff der juristischen Person*, 1879, S. 109 ff.

wegs von jeher in Kraft gestanden. Es hat sich erst in langem geschichtlichen Ringen durchgesetzt und dabei sehr verschiedene Entwicklungsstufen durchlaufen. Sein Geltungsgrund ist in mannigfach ungleicher Weise aufgefasst und formuliert worden. Ein Blick auf diesen Werdeprozess bietet um so grösseres historisches Interesse, als er sich in engem Zusammenhange mit dem Wandel der Grundanschauungen über das Wesen der menschlichen Verbände abgespielt hat. Zugleich aber mag er dazu dienen, ein tieferes Verständnis unseres heutigen Rechtszustandes zu fördern.

In diesem Sinne möchte ich es unternehmen, Ihre Aufmerksamkeit auf die Geschichte des Majoritätsprinzips zu lenken. Dabei beschränke ich mich aber auf die Darlegung der auf Grund des germanischen Rechts im Mittelalter und in der Neuzeit vollzogenen Entwicklung. Insbesondere gehe ich auf eine Untersuchung der Geschichte des Majoritätsprinzips in der antiken Kulturwelt nicht näher ein. Bei Griechen und Römern erfreut sich in den reifen Zeiten, von denen wir genauere Kenntnis haben, das Majoritätsprinzip bei allen Versammlungsbeschlüssen unbestrittener Herrschaft. Über Vorstadien, die es vermutlich gegeben hat, sind wir nicht sicher unterrichtet. Jedenfalls war man sich solcher nicht mehr bewusst, hegte vielmehr an der Berechtigung der Entscheidung durch Stimmenzählung keinerlei Zweifel. In der griechischen Staatslehre stossen wir überhaupt nicht auf Reflexionen über den Grund der Geltung des Stimmenmehrs. Erst die römischen Juristen suchen nach dem Geltungsgrunde. Sie begnügen sich aber mit einer sehr äusserlichen Rechtfertigung. *Refertur ad universos quod publice fit per majorem partem*, sagt Ulpian in l. 160 § 1 *D. de R. J.* Ähnlich meint Scaevola in l. 19 *D. ad municipalem* (56, 1): *Quod major pars curiae effecit pro eo habetur, ac si omnes egerint.* Diese Aussprüche, die später eine grosse Rolle gespielt haben, laufen auf eine juristische Fiktion hinaus, kraft deren die Mehrheit gelten soll, als seien es Alle. Wie sich zu dieser Fiktion der bekannte positive Rechtssatz verhält, der zur Gültigkeit eines Majoritätsbeschlusses der städtischen Kurie die Anwesenheit von zwei Dritteln fordert, lassen die römischen Juristen, die eine allgemeine Theorie der Korporationsbeschlüsse überhaupt nicht ausgebildet haben, unerörtert.

Dem germanischen Recht war auf der ungleich primitiveren Stufe, auf der es bei seinem Eintritt in das Licht der Geschichte stand, das Majoritätsprinzip fremd. Ihm deckte sich der Gesamtwille mit dem Versammlungswillen und der Versammlungswille mit dem Willen aller Versammelten. Für das durchaus sinnliche und konkrete Denken der alten Zeit waren Träger alles Verbandsrechtes sichtbare Versammlungen und sichtbare Herrscher. So wenig man bei dem Herrscher die Individualpersönlichkeit und die Stellung als Verbandshaupt unterschied, ebenso wenig unterschied man bei der Versammlung die Gesamteinheit von der Gesamtvielheit. Alles Gemeinschaftsrecht hatte daher die Versammlung der vollberechtigten Genossen in ihrer zugleich einheitlichen und vielköpfigen Erscheinung auszuüben. In dem kollektiven Wollen und Handeln Aller offenbarte sich das lebendige Ganze.

Grundsätzlich bedurfte es also zu jedem Volks- oder Gemeindebeschluss eines einhelligen Gesamtaktes. Im Falle der Meinungsverschiedenheit zu einem solchen zu gelangen, war das Ziel der Beratung. Wenn aber die Überzeugungskraft der Gründe oder das Ansehen und die Beredsamkeit der führenden Männer nicht zur Übereinstimmung führten, so setzte sich freilich in der Regel die Meinung der überwiegenden Mehrheit durch. Allein dies geschah ursprünglich keineswegs im Wege einer die Minderheit von Rechtswegen bindenden Abstimmung. Von Stimmabgabe und Stimmzählung war nicht die Rede. Vielmehr gab die versammelte Menge mit gesamter Hand und mit gemeinem Munde ihre Willensmeinung kund. Zusammenschlagen der Waffen mit Beifallsruf oder sonstige Billigung mit Hand und Mund galt als Annahme, lautes Murren oder missbilligender Zuruf als Verwerfung eines Vorschlags. So schildert uns Tacitus die Beschlussfassung in der altgermanischen Volksversammlung, und jüngere Quellen bestätigen es als gemeingermanische Übung.[1] Verhielten

[1] *Germ.* c. 11 : *sin placuit, frameas concutiunt; honoratissimum assensus genus est armis laudare.* Vgl. *Hist.* v. 17. Die Waffenrührung begegnet auch später bei den Franken als besonders feierliche Form des Volksbeschlusses: Zusammenschlagen der Schilde und Beifallsruf bei der Wahl Chlodwigs durch die ripuarischen Franken nach Gregor = Gregor Tur. ii. 40; *vocibusque simul et armorum plausu sententiam ducis firmaverunt* nach *Annales Mettenses* z. J. 690, MG. S.S. i. 318. Bei den nordischen Völkern als *vápnatak* bei Gesetzgebungsakten und Königsannahme. — Doch war, wie sich schon aus *Germ.*

sich Dissentierende schweigend, so hatte schliesslich doch die Versammlung mit gesamter Hand und gemeinem Munde ihren Willen erklärt. Und auch der Widerspruch des einen oder andern mochte, wenn er überhört oder übertönt wurde, die Verkündigung des Ergebnisses als eines einstimmigen Versammlungsbeschlusses nicht hindern.

Eine rechtliche Verpflichtung aber, sich dem Mehrheitsbeschlusse zu fügen, und ihn so zugleich als eigenen Beschluss anzuerkennen, gab es nicht. Wer seinen Widerspruch trotzig aufrecht hielt, war durch den Beschluss der andern Genossen, die nicht mehr Alle waren, nicht gebunden. Allein er löste sich damit von der in sich einigen Gesamtheit der Anderen, er trat ihr als Feind gegenüber und setzte sich ihrem gewaltsamen Zwange aus. War der Widerstand gegen solche Überwältigung wegen der Stärke der Mehrheit aussichtslos, so musste regelmässig schon die Erwägung der Folgen die Minderheit bewegen, den Widerspruch fallen zu lassen. Allein den Halsstarrigen konnte nur die tatsächliche Macht überwinden. Und wenn auch die Minderheit stark war und sich den Sieg zutraute, so trat an Stelle des einheitlichen Versammlungsbeschlusses die Spaltung in Teilgesamtheiten, zwischen denen dann äussersten Falles die Waffen entschieden.

Ein deutliches Bild der Fortdauer dieser ursprünglichen Anschauungen bieten bis tief in das Mittelalter hinein die deutschen Königswahlen. Sie forderten Einstimmigkeit, anfangs Einstimmigkeit der versammelten Stammeshäupter und der zustimmenden Volksmenge, sodann Einstimmigkeit der Fürsten [1] und dann noch, seitdem die Kurfürsten aus Vorwählern zu alleinigen Wählern geworden waren, Einstimmigkeit der Kurfürsten. Erst die goldene Bulle führte das Majoritätsprinzip als Grundsatz des Reichsrechtes ein.[2] Bis dahin musste eine Minderheit, die

---

c. 11 ergibt, der Waffenschlag nicht die einzige Form der Zustimmung. Es genügte die *acclamatio*. Bei den deutschen Königswahlen wird Emporheben der Hände neben dem Beifallsruf erwähnt; Widukind, *Res gest. Sax.* i. 26, ii. 1. Also, wie dies dem alten Rechtsformalismus entspricht, Billigung mit Hand und Mund.

[1] Noch der *Sachsensp.*, iii. 57 § 2, fordert Einigung aller Fürsten über die Wahl als Grundlage des formellen Kurspruchs: „sven die vorsten alle to koninge erwelt, den solen sie (die Kurfürsten) aller erst bi namen kiesen.“

[2] Für die kurfürstliche Genehmigung königlicher Veräusserungen hatte schon ein Reichsweistum von 1281 (MG. Const. iii. 290) das Mehrheits-

sich nicht freiwillig fügte, durch Waffengewalt zur Anerkennung des gewählten Königs gezwungen werden. Die zahlreichen Waffengänge zwischen Königen und Gegenkönigen bei zwiespältigen Wahlen sind aus der Geschichte bekannt.

Auch sonst erhielten sich vielfach mit Zähigkeit die alten Anschauungen. Im deutschen wie im fränkischen Reichstage war zunächst zur Beschlussfassung Einigung erforderlich und die Unterwerfung derer, die sich ausschlossen, vom Zwange der Übermacht abhängig. Frühestens seit dem Ende des dreizehnten Jahrhunderts wurden Mehrheitsbeschlüsse als bindend anerkannt, sehr viel später erst Stimmzählungen unter Fixierung des Stimmengewichts eingeführt, bis zuletzt in den drei Kollegien, in die er zerfiel, das Majoritätsprinzip durchdrang und nur Einstimmigkeit der Kollegien oder im Falle der *itio in partes* der beiden Religionskörper notwendig blieb. Langsam und anfänglich nur in beschränktem Umfange wurde in den landständischen Versammlungen und auch hier immer nur innerhalb der einzelnen ständischen Körper der Grundsatz der Einstimmigkeit durch die Mehrheitsentscheidung überwunden, langsamer noch in den foederativen Verbänden, wie in der deutschen Hanse und der schweizerischen Eidgenossenschaft. Ebenso musste überall in Europa das Majoritätsprinzip in den politischen Versammlungen die formale Geltung, die es endlich errang, sich erst mühsam erkämpfen. In manchen Ländern wurde sogar ihm gegenüber das Einstimmigkeitsprinzip zu formaler Geltung erhoben,[1] dem jedoch der endgültige Sieg nur im polnischen Reichstage mit dem berüchtigten *liberum veto* beschieden war.

Länger noch, als auf den Höhen des öffentlichen Lebens, behauptete sich in dessen Niederungen das alte Recht. Insbesondere wurden auf dem Lande in Markgenossenschaften und Bauerschaften die Beschlüsse stets von der versammelten Menge der Vollgenossen einmütig gefasst und einmündig erklärt. Dass Beschlüsse, die das Sonderrecht des einzelnen Genossen kränken, dessen Zustimmung forderten, ist begreiflich;

---

prinzip anerkannt. Bei der Königswahl wurde zuerst in der *Const. Lud. Licet juris* v. 6. Aug. 1338 die Beschlussfähigkeit einer Mehrheit von vier Kurfürsten festgesetzt, mit dem Erforderniss der Einhelligkeit der Versammelten aber noch nicht gebrochen.

[1] So bis 1292 in Arragonien.

zu diesen aber rechnete man unter dem Gesichtspunkte des alten Gesamteigentums an der Mark vielfach auch die Aufnahme neuer anteilsberechtigter Genossen und jede Verfügung über die Allmende oder deren Erträge zu Gunsten von Ungenossen, räumte daher in solchen Fällen jedem Genossen ein formales Widerspruchsrecht ein, das erst durch Verschweigung in Jahr und Tag erlosch.[1] Allein auch wo es sich lediglich um die Ausübung des Gesamtrechtes oder um das gemeine Beste handelte, wo Recht gewiesen oder Recht gesetzt, wo ein Vorsteher oder ein Beamter gewählt wurde, bedurfte es eines ungezweiten Versammlungsaktes. Hierbei machte sich nun freilich stets das Übergewicht der Mehrheit geltend. Und seit dem dreizehnten Jahrhundert wurde mehr und mehr auch in den Landgemeinden der Stimmenmehrheit ein rechtlicher Vorzug zugestanden.[2] Allein damit wurde, wie wir sehen werden, zunächst das Erfordernis der schliesslichen Übereinstimmung Aller keineswegs aufgegeben, sodass ausweislich unzähliger Weistümer und Urkunden fort und fort die Gemeindebeschlüsse als einstimmige Versammlungserklärungen verkündigt wurden.[3]

Nicht minder lebendig blieb die ererbte Denkweise bei dem Urteilsspruch in allen Gerichtsversammlungen. Das gefundene Urteil erlangte Rechtskraft nur durch die *vulbort*, die allgemeine Zustimmung der vollberechtigten Dingleute. Wo Schöffen oder andere Urtelsfinder ohne Umstand zu entscheiden

[1] Für die Aufnahme neuer Genossen vgl. mein *Genossenschaftsr.* ii. 232, Anm. 156, Maurer, *Einl.* 141 ff., *Markenv.* 112 ff., und dazu über das ursprüngliche Recht, wie es der richtig verstandene *Tit. leg. Sal. de migrantibus* bekundet, mein *Genossenschaftsr.* i. 76 ff. Für Verfügungen über die Allmende mein *Genossenschaftsr.* ii. 232, Anm. 153, 158-60, Lamprecht, *Deutsches Wirtschaftsleben im M.A.* i. 310, Anm. 6; insbesondere noch die Kundschaft von 1487, b. Grimm, *W.* i. 400. Für Gestattung der Rodung nach Zeugenaussage v. 1560, b. Landau, *Territorien*, S. 117, Anm. 1.—Dazu vgl. man Pollock and Maitland, i. 684.

[2] Ausdrücklich heisst es schon im *Sachsensp.* ii. 55: „Svat so die burmester schept des dorpes vromen mit wilkore der merren menie der bure, dat ne mach die minre deil nicht wederreden." Vgl. *Schwabensp.* (L.) 214 (mit dem Zusatz: „dass selbe recht sol man halden in den stetten"). *Rupr. Freis.* i. 142. Dazu zahlreiche Belege aus den Weistümern in meinem *Genossenschaftsr.* iii. 220 ff., 478 ff. Vgl. auch Maurer, *Markenv.* S. 359 ff., *Dorfv.* i. 220, ii. 86 ff.; Thudichum, *Gau. u. Markv.* S. 315.

[3] Vgl. mein *Genossenschaftsr.* iii. 483, 501 ff.

hatten, war mindestens ihre einhellige Billigung unerlässlich. Und dieser Grundsatz überdauerte wieder die Einführung des Majoritätsprinzips. Etwas anders verhielt es sich bei dem Wahrspruch der Geschworenen, der ja von Hause aus nicht Urteil sondern Zeugnis war.[1] Aber auch das Gesamtzeugnis forderte eine einhellige Gesamtaussage und scheiterte am Zwiespalt der Meinungen. Das blosse Nichtwissen des Einen oder Andern mochte der Kraft des gemeinen Wahrspruches nicht schaden, wie denn im normannischen Recht die feste Regel ausgebildet wurde, dass der einstimmige Wahrspruch von elf unter den zwölf Geschworenen genüge. Der ausdrückliche Widerspruch aber auch nur eines einzigen Geschworenen hinderte das Zustandekommen eines gültigen Spruchs.[2] Von hier aus konnte sich das starre Erfordernis der Einstimmigkeit in der englischen Jury entwickeln.[3] Es konnte aber auch das Majoritätsprinzip durchdringen, sei es nun, dass eine überwiegende Mehrheit erforderlich blieb, sei es, dass mit einfacher Mehrheit entschieden wurde, wie dies im normannischen Recht bei Besitzprozessen der Fall war[4] und in Deutschland bei der hier allein übrig gebliebenen Bekundung von Besitzverhältnissen durch die Umsassen galt.[5]

Die allgemeine Entwicklungstendenz war, wie wir gesehen haben, auf die fortschreitende Anerkennung des Majoritätsprinzips gerichtet, das in der zweiten Hälfte des Mittelalters auch in Deutschland unbestritten in ständischen Versammlungen, Gerichten, Landgemeinden, Städten, Gilden und Zünften galt und in den Rechtsbüchern, den Weistümern und zahlreichen anderen Rechtsquellen als generelle Regel ausgesprochen wird. Allein ich habe schon darauf hingewiesen, dass es zunächst keineswegs einen Bruch mit den alten Anschauungen bedeutete, sondern sich in deren Rahmen als ein juristisches Mittel zur Erzielung eines einheitlichen Versammlungsbeschlusses einfügte. Denn es empfängt die Fassung: „Die Minderheit soll der Mehrheit folgen,"

[1] Eingehend handelt von dem Stimmenverhältniss beim Wahrspruch Brunner, *Entstehung der Schwurgerichte*, S. 363-71.

[2] Brunner, a. a. O., S. 365.

[3] Pollock and Maitland, ii. 625 ff.

[4] Brunner, a. a. O., S. 367 ff.

[5] *Sachsensp.* iii. 21 § 1 a.l.: „Sve de merren mennie an'me getüge hevet, die behalt dat gut."

*minor pars sequatur majorem.*[1] Durch diese Wendung aber oder durch ähnliche gleichbedeutende Wendungen wird ausgedrückt, dass die Minderheit ihren Widerspruch aufgeben und der Mehrheit zustimmen soll, damit ein einhelliger Gemeinwille zu Stande komme: eine *sententia per approbationem et collaudationem communem, quae volga dicitur, ab omnibus et singulis stabilita,* wie ein Weistum von 1340 sagt.[2]

Hierin bekundet sich ein ausserordentlicher Fortschritt der Rechtsauffassung. Die Überwindung des Meinungszwiespaltes soll nicht mehr von tatsächlichem Übergewicht und gewaltsamem Zwange abhängen, sondern durch Erfüllung einer der Minderheit auferlegten Rechtspflicht herbeigeführt werden. Aus dem genossenschaftlichen Verhältnis entspringt für den Genossen die Pflicht, um der Einheit des Ganzen willen sich dem Ergebnis der Abstimmung zu fügen und durch seinen Beitritt den Mehrheitswillen zum Gesamtwillen zu erheben. Allein immer noch ist schliessliche Einstimmigkeit erforderlich, sodass der Beschluss nur Kraft erlangt, wenn wirklich die Minderheit der Mehrheit folgt. Verharrt sie bei ihrem Widerspruch, so begeht sie vielleicht ein strafbares Unrecht,[3] ein rechtsgültiger Gemeinbeschluss aber kommt dann nicht zu Stande. Ist eine Lösung des Konfliktes im Wege Rechtens unerlässlich, so kann sie nur durch höhere Entscheidung erfolgen.[4]

In besonders klarer Ausprägung treten diese Anschauungen im gerichtlichen Verfahren zu Tage.[5] Ist auf die richterliche Frage ein Urteil gefunden, so kann ihm jeder Schöffe oder Dingmann ein ihm besser dünkendes Urteil entgegen stellen. Damit beredet er die *vulbort*. Dann behält der, dem bei der Abstimmung die meisten folgen, sein Urteil. Dieses Urteil erhält dann dadurch, dass sich die Minderheit der Mehrheit anschliesst, die *vulbort* und steht nun als Rechtsspruch der Gesamtheit, als „gemeines",

[1] Zusammenstellung zahlreicher Belegstellen in meinem *Genossenschaftsr.* ii. 482-3.

[2] W. v. Treyse b. Grimm, i. 810.

[3] Bisweilen wird die Erfüllung der Folgepflicht im Voraus förmlich versprochen, ein solches Versprechen auch in den Schöffeneid aufgenommen; mein *Genossenschaftsr.* ii. 484, Anm. 25-26.

[4] Vgl. mein *Genossenschaftsr.* ii. 483, Anm. 23.

[5] Vor allem im *Sachsensp.* ii. a. 12, mit dem aber die anderen sächsischen und im Kern auch die süddeutschen Quellen übereinstimmen. Vgl. über die hier in Betracht kommenden Gesichtspunkte mein *Genossenschaftsr.* ii. 483 ff.

„gesamtes“, „einstimmiges“, „ungezweites“ Urteil unanfechtbar da. Allein der dissentierende Schöffe oder Dingmann kann, so lange die *vulbort* nicht erteilt ist, auch anders verfahren. Er kann das Urteil „schelten“ oder „verwerfen.“ Damit wirft er dem Urteilsvorschlage Rechtswidrigkeit vor und erklärt auf eigene Gefahr hin, dass er demselben niemals und auch nicht, wenn ihm die Mehrheit folgt, zustimmen werde. In diesem Falle kommt ein gemeines Urteil nicht zu Stande, es wird um *vulbort* überhaupt nicht gefragt und jede Möglichkeit rechtskräftiger Entscheidung durch das verhandelnde Gericht ist zerstört. Die Streiterledigung erfolgt durch Zug an ein anderes und womöglich höheres Gericht, vor dem in einem neuen Prozess über Gerechtigkeit oder Ungerechtigkeit des mit der Urteilsschelte erhobenen Vorwurfs entschieden wird. Wer unterliegt, verliert nicht nur sein Urteil, sondern wird auch bussfällig. Der *Sachsenspiegel* aber betont es als ein besonderes Vorrecht des Sachsen, dass er auch einen anderen Weg wählen kann, indem er das gescholtene Urteil an die rechte Hand zieht. Dann entscheidet gerichtlicher Zweikampf. Selbsiebent seiner Genossen muss er wider andere sieben fechten; auf welcher Seite die Mehrheit siegt, die behält das Urteil.[1] Hier ist also in eigenartiger Weise das Majoritätsprinzip in die altertümliche Waffenentscheidung, die in den Rechtsgang verlegt ist, hineingetragen: wo die Stimmenmehrheit versagt, dringt die Siegermehrheit durch.

Doch ist auch im Bereiche vorbehaltloser Geltung der Stimmenmehrheit mit dem Satze „Die Minderheit soll der Mehrheit folgen“ die alte sinnliche Vorstellung von den Verbandseinheiten noch nicht überwunden. Denn immer noch wird dabei die Gesamtheit als Einheit mit der Vielheit Aller identifiziert. Eine Änderung tritt erst ein, wenn der Mehrheitsbeschluss unmittelbar als Ausdruck des Gesamtwillens gilt. Diese Entwicklungsstufe musste erreicht werden, sobald der alte Genossenschaftsbegriff zum Körperschaftsbegriff gesteigert wurde, was am frühesten in den Städten geschah.[2] In der Tat lässt sich verfolgen, wie mit der korporativen Ausgestaltung der Verbände diese neue Auffassung des Majoritätsprinzips Hand in Hand geht

[1] *Sachsensp.* ii. 12 § 8 und i. 18 § 3 u. *Lehnr.* 69 § 3. Jeder Besiegte muss dem Richter Wette und dem Gegner Busse zahlen.

[2] Hiervon handelt mein *Genossenschaftsr.* ii. 573 ff., 829 ff.

und demgemäss die nachträgliche Zustimmung der Minderheit mehr und mehr als überflüssige Formalität in Wegfall kommt.

Vollzog das germanische Recht eine derartige Umbildung des Majoritätsprinzips aus sich heraus, so empfing sie doch ihre begriffliche Fassung durch die vom römischen und kanonischen Recht ausgehende mittelalterliche Jurisprudenz. Sie zuerst stellte eine bis in die feinsten Einzelheiten ausgearbeitete, für die ganze Folgezeit grundlegend gewordene Korporationstheorie auf, in der das Majoritätsprinzip eine zentrale Rolle spielte.

Die Legisten entnahmen dem *Corpus Juris Civilis* die grundsätzliche Geltung von Mehrheitsbeschlüssen und deren Rechtfertigung durch eine Fiktion, kraft deren die Mehrheit rechtlich so angesehen wird, als seien es Alle. Während aber die Glossatoren noch überwiegend in der Vorstellung befangen blieben, dass die Gesamtheit sich mit der Summe der Einzelnen deckt,[1] führten die Postglossatoren die Unterscheidung von *omnes ut universi* und *omnes ut singuli* ein, die schon bei Odofredus das Fundament der Lehre von den Korporationsbeschlüssen bildet und bei Bartolus ihre abschliessende Gestalt empfängt.[2] Nur wo das Gesetz eine Vielheit als *universitas* zusammenfasse, stelle es die Mehrheit Allen gleich, während überall, wo eine Vielheit nur als Summe von Einzelnen gelte, der Widerspruch eines Einzigen die Übereinstimmung aller Übrigen überwinde. Von hier aus erkannte man in dem Vorrang des Mehrheitswillens ein spezifisch korporatives Prinzip. Man leitete ihn aus dem Wesen der Korporation her, weil diese eben die Mitglieder zur *universitas* verbinde, und versagte umgekehrt, von singulären Ausnahmen abgesehen, dem Majoritätsprinzip die Anerkennung in der blossen Gesellschaft oder Gemeinschaft, weil diese nur ein Verhältnis von *plures ut singuli* sei. Weiter aber band man die Kraft des Mehrheitsbeschlusses an dessen Zustandekommen in einer gehörig berufenen und ordnungsmässig verhandelnden Versammlung, da nur in einer solchen die Gesamtheit sich rechtlich als Einheit darstelle, und baute die Lehre von den Erfordernissen eines jeglichen Korporationsbeschlusses im Einzelnen aus. Die Beschlussfähigkeit der Versammlung machte

1 Über die Lehre der Glossatoren vgl. mein *Genossenschaftsr.* iii. 220 ff. In der Gl. ord. zu l. 7 § 1 D. h.t.v. *non debetur* (ebend. Anm. 107) heisst es noch: *universitas nihil aliud est quam singuli homines qui ibi sunt.*

2 Mein *Genossenschaftsr.* iii. 391 ff.

man unter Verallgemeinerung des römischen Dekurionenrechtes von der Anwesenheit von zwei Dritteln der Mitglieder abhängig, sah aber abweichende Verfassungsbestimmungen als zulässig an. Endlich entwickelte man auf Grund der Unterscheidung von *omnes ut universi* und *omnes ut singuli* die Theorie von den für den Mehrheitsbeschluss unantastbaren *jura singulorum*,[1] die dann durch die Jahrhunderte hindurch sich behauptet hat, während die Abgrenzung der Sonderrechte bis heute das umstrittenste Problem des Körperschaftsrechtes geblieben ist. Konnte doch einerseits durch übermässige Ausdehnung des Begriffes der *jura singulorum* alle Kraft der Gemeinschaftsgewalt gebrochen werden, wie ja vielfach bei der ständischen Steuerbewilligung die Geltung des Stimmenmehrs unter dem Gesichtspunkt, dass die Verfügung über den Geldbeutel des Genossen sicherlich in dessen Sonderrecht eingreife, in Frage gestellt und später in Deutschland sogar die Reichsgewalt durch die Versteifung der *jura singulorum* lahmgelegt wurde. Auf der anderen Seite aber lag in der Festhaltung dieser Schranke ein unentbehrlicher Schutz gegen Majoritätstyrannei. Doch bildet der wechselvolle Kampf um die *jura singulorum* ein eigenes Kapitel der Rechtsgeschichte.

Mit der Lehre der Legisten berührte sich die Lehre des kanonischen Rechtes und der Kanonisten,[2] die mehr und mehr auch auf jene einen tiefgreifenden Einfluss gewann. Wenn in der Kirche das Majoritätsprinzip in Glaubenssachen stets ausgeschlossen blieb, so drang es doch bei Wahlen und bei allen kollegialen Beschlüssen über äussere Angelegenheiten, obschon auch hier Einstimmigkeit als das Erwünschtere galt, allgemein durch. Dabei wirkten im früheren Mittelalter auf die Ausgestaltung des Majoritätsprinzips germanische Anschauungen ein, sodass es nur als Mittel behandelt wurde, den Weg zum *communis consensus* zu ebnen.[3] Die ausgebildete kanonistische Theorie aber stimmte mit der romanistischen Theorie in der Gleichsetzung des Mehrheitswillens mit dem Gesamtwillen überein. Auch sie lehrte, dass im Gegensatz zu den *res communes pluribus ut singulis* bei allen *negotia universitatis* kraft gesetzlicher Fiktion *quod*

[1] Die Anfänge schon bei Azo und in der Glosse; a. a. O., S. 222, Anm. 108. Über die spätere Jurisprudenz S. 393, Anm. 163, S. 445 ff., S. 472 ff.

[2] A. a. O., S. 312 ff.

[3] A. a. O., S. 323 ff.

*major pars facit, totum facere videtur.* Sie suchte jedoch nach einem inneren Grunde dafür und fand ihn in der Wahrscheinlichkeit, dass Viele leichter als Wenige das Richtige treffen werden: *quia per plures melius veritas inquiritur.*[1]

Dies war der treibende Gedanke für die eigenartige Umprägung, die das Majoritätsprinzip durch die Einführung des Satzes erfuhr, dass wahre Mehrheit nur die *major et sanior pars* ist.[2] Die *pars numerosior* hat nur die Vermutung der besseren Einsicht für sich, kann aber nicht als der grössere Teil gelten, sobald diese Vermutung widerlegt wird. Von Theorie und Gesetzgebung seit dem 12ten Jahrhundert allmählich ausgebildet und im Jahre 1179 von Alexander III. auf dem dritten Lateranensischen Konzil bereits als allgemeingültig behandelt, errang sich das Dogma von der *major et sanior pars* alsbald die unbestrittene Herrschaft im kirchlichen Recht. Die Anschauung, dass die Stimmen nicht nur zu zählen, sondern zu wägen sind, war ja auch dem germanischen Recht nicht fremd und kam in dem Übergewicht der Stimmen der Angesehensten bei der Feststellung des Versammlungsbeschlusses zum Ausdruck. Das kanonische Recht aber goss sie in juristische Form und verinnerlichte den Massstab der Abwägung. Bei der Ermittlung, welcher Teil der „gesundere" ist, sollen neben dem Ansehen (*auctoritas*) der Stimmenden ihre geistigen und sittlichen Eigenschaften (*ratio et pietas*) und die Lauterkeit ihrer Motive (*bonus zelus et aequitas*) in Erwägung gezogen, zugleich aber soll die Vernünftigkeit des Ergebnisses (insbesondere bei Wahlen die Würdigkeit des Gewählten) geprüft werden. In den genauen Regeln über die Bewertung der einzelnen Momente offenbart sich in charakteristischer Weise der spiritualistische Zug des kanonischen Rechts. Gleichzeitig aber bedeutet das Erfordernis der *sanioritas* die Beugung des Majoritätsprinzips unter das hierarchische Autoritätsprinzip. Denn die Entscheidung liegt ausschliesslich in der Hand des kirchlichen Oberen. Vielfach wurde sogar die Ansicht verfochten, dass auch eine Minderzahl durch *sanioritas* zur *major pars* werde, womit im Grunde das Majoritätsprinzip überhaupt in die Luft gesprengt war. Doch siegte schliesslich die Meinung, dass zum gültigen Beschluss *major et sanior pars* unerlässlich sei, also Übergewicht der Zahl und des

[1] Ausspruch von Innocenz IV. ebd. S. 324, Anm. 246.

[2] Über Ursprung und Entfaltung dieser Lehne a. a. O., S. 324 ff., 475.

Wertes der Stimmen zusammentreffen müsse. Und mindestens bei Wahlen drang die Anschauung durch, dass bei einer Zweidrittelsmehrheit die Vermutung für *sanioritas* sich zur Gewissheit steigere. In dem einzigen Falle, in dem es an der Möglichkeit einer Prüfung der *sanioritas* durch einen kirchlichen Oberen fehlte, bei der Papstwahl, war gerade deshalb Zweidrittelsmehrheit erforderlich.

Wenn die Kanonisten anfänglich für ihre Forderung der *major et sanior pars* Allgemeingültigkeit beanspruchten und hier und da hiermit Beifall fanden,[1] so siegte schliesslich die Meinung, dass es sich um eine Besonderheit des kirchlichen Rechtes handle.[2] Nur vereinzelt begegnen Nachbildungen im weltlichen Recht.[3] Dagegen gewann die kanonistische Anschauung, dass ein starkes und zwar mindestens doppeltes Übergewicht der Zahl eine Gewähr für die Vernünftigkeit der Mehrheitsentscheidung biete, allgemeine Bedeutung. Auf sie geht das Erfordernis einer Zweidrittels- oder Dreiviertelsmehrheit zu besonders wichtigen Beschlüssen, insbesondere zu Verfassungsänderungen zurück, das schon im Mittelalter oft vorkommt[4] und heute zu den verbreitetsten Einschränkungen des Majoritätsprinzips gehört.

In vielen anderen Punkten führten die Kanonisten der Lehre von den Korporationsbeschlüssen bleibenden Gewinn zu. Nur auf zweierlei will ich hinweisen. Gegenüber der von den Legisten verfochtenen Regel, dass zur Beschlussfähigkeit einer Versammlung die Anwesenheit von zwei Dritteln erforderlich sei, setzten sie die Ansicht durch, dass an sich bei ordnungsmässiger Versammlung die Anwesenheit einer noch so geringen Zahl genüge, weil die Ausgebliebenen für dieses Mal sich selbst ausgeschlossen haben (*se alienos fecerunt*).[5] Alle Fälle, in denen die Beschlussfähigheit von der Anwesenheit einer bestimmten Zahl von Mit-

[1] Vgl. die Nachweise a. a. O., S. 394, Anm. 169, S. 475, Anm. 284.

[2] A. a. O., S. 475. Im kirchlichen Recht wurde das Prinzip der *major et sanior pars* niemals aufgegeben, allmählich aber zurückgedrängt. Mit der Zulassung geheimer Abstimmungen wurde es praktisch undurchführbar.

[3] Vgl. die Stellen aus Weistümern in meinem *Genossenschaftsr.* ii. 481, Anm. 14. Man denke auch an die Befugnis des Reichshofratspräsidenten, eine Entscheidung des Kollegiums, wenn sie nur eine geringe Mehrheit und nicht zugleich die offenbar besseren Gründe für sich hat, *ad votum Imperatoris* zu bringen.

[4] Mein *Genossenschaftsr.* ii. 481, Anm. 15.

[5] A. a. O. iii. 320 ff., 467 ff. Die Folge ist, dass *jus universitatis recidit in ceteros vel in unum.* Man sprach von einer „magna controversia“ zwischen Legisten und Kanonisten.

gliedern abhängt, erscheinen demgemäss, wie ja auch in heutigen Recht, als besonders begründete Ausnahmen. Sodann befruchteten die Kanonisten die Lehre von den Einzelrechten durch die erstmalige Unterscheidung zwischen den freien Individualrechten und den körperschaftlichen Sonderrechten, den *jura singulorum propria* und den *jura singulorum collegialia* oder *in universitate*.[1]

Fragen wir nach dem Verhältnis der romanistisch-kanonistischen Korporationstheorie zur Grundauffassung vom Wesen der Verbände, so leuchtet ein, dass sie mit der durchgängigen Unterscheidung der *omnes ut universi* und der *omnes ut singuli* die der älteren germanischen Vorstellung noch nicht geläufige Abstraktion der Gesamteinheit von der Gesamtvielheit vollzogen hatte. Allein in der Identifizierung der Körperschaft mit der Gesamtheit als einheitlichem Inbegriff blieb sie zunächst stecken. Die *universitas* deckt sich eben mit den *omnes ut universi*; darum wurde in stets wiederkehrenden Wendungen die wollende und handelnde Mitgliederversammlung als die Körperschaft selbst, die *universitas ipsa* bezeichnet.[2] Im Bereiche der Geltung des Majoritätsprinzips kommt in der *major pars* die *universitas ipsa* zur Erscheinung. Kraft einer neuen Fiktion werden Repräsentantenversammlungen, z.B. Stadträte, der *universitas ipsa* gleichgestellt.[3] Hier überall handelt die *universitas per se*. Dagegen liegt ein *agere per alium* vor, wenn Vorsteher und Beamte tätig werden. Sie sind blosse Vertreter der Gesamtheit und handeln nur da, wo die *universitas ipsa* nicht zu handeln vermag, kraft gesetzlicher oder rechtsgeschäftlicher Vollmacht an ihrer Stelle. Diese Unterscheidung zwischen dem eignen Handeln der Körperschaft und dem Handeln ihrer Vertreter war für den Aufbau der mittelalterlichen Korporationstheorie von fundamentaler Bedeutung und beherrschte namentlich die viel umstrittene Lehre von den Körperschaftsdelikten.[4]

Neben der kollektiven Verbandsauffassung aber brach sich eine ganz andere Auffassung Bahn, die von den Kanonisten und zwar in voller Schärfe zuerst von Innocenz IV. im Sinne des kirch-

[1] A. a. O., S. 297 ff., wo die wichtigsten Stellen aus Innocenz IV., Joh. Andreae, Antonius de Butrio und Panormitanus wiedergegeben sind; dazu S. 445 ff., 472.

[2] A. a. O., S. 219 ff., 390 ff., 461 ff., 477 ff.

[3] A. a. O., S. 222 ff., 394 ff., 478 ff.

[4] A. a. O., S. 234 ff., 402 ff., 491 ff.

lichen Anstaltsbegriffes entwickelt und dann auf alle korporativen Verbände erstreckt wurde. Sie findet die Verbandseinheit in einer der Mitgliedergesamtheit transzendenten Wesenheit, einer besonderen Verbandspersönlichkeit, die so gut von der Versammlung aller Mitglieder, wie von Vorstehern und Beamten nur repräsentiert wird. Das Mittel ihrer Konstruktion aber ist eine neue Fiktion. Es ist die im *Corpus Juris Civilis* erst angedeutete, nun jedoch scharf herausgemeisselte und in den Mittelpunkt gerückte fingierte Person, die *persona ficta*, *repraesentata*, *imaginaria*, das erdichtete künstliche Individuum! Bei folgerichtiger Durchführung dieser neuen Fiktion verschwindet die Gleichsetzung der Gesamtheit der Mitglieder mit der *universitas ipsa*. Die *universitas ipsa* ist allein das unsichtbare ideale Rechtssubjekt, das auch, wenn die Versammlung beschliesst, *per alium agit*. Damit wird die Theorie der Korporationsbeschlüsse auf eine höhere Stufe gehoben. Denn nunmehr kann die Wirksamkeit aller Versammlungsakte in Korporationsangelegenheiten in die Schranken einer der Versammlung selbst zugewiesenen verfassungsmässigen Zuständigkeit, innerhalb deren allein sie die fingierte Person repräsentiert, gebannt werden. Diese Zuständigkeit wird vor Allem durch den korporativen Lebensbereich, aber auch durch die Zuständigkeiten eines Vorstandes oder anderer Vertreter des künstlichen Rechtssubjektes begrenzt. Darüber hinaus vermag auch der einstimmige Versammlungsbeschluss nichts auszurichten, versagt daher erst recht das Majoritätsprinzip, das nur den Mehrheitswillen zum Versammlungswillen stempelt. Alle solche Fortschritte aber werden mit der Verdrängung der lebendigen Verbandseinheit durch das Gespenst der fingierten Persönlichkeit erkauft. Die neue Herrin der gemeinheitlichen Sphären ist ein willens- und handlungsunfähiges Begriffswesen. Sie gleicht dem Kinde oder vielmehr, da das Kind einmal mündig wird, dem unheilbar Wahnsinnigen. Die Verantwortlichkeit für unerlaubte Handlungen wird ihr abgenommen, sie wird aber zugleich in allem Handeln vormundschaftlicher Vertretung unterstellt. Der germanische Genossenschaftsgedanke wird ausgetilgt. Der Korporationsbegriff empfängt eine rein anstaltliche Färbung.[1]

[1] Über den kanonistischen Ursprung der Theorie der *persona ficta* und ihre Bedeutung für die Lehre vom körperschaftlichen Wollen und Handeln vgl. a. a. O., S. 277 ff., 308 ff., 342 ff.

Die Theorie der *persona ficta* wurde auch von den Zivilisten angenommen und beherrschte äusserlich die gesamte Jurisprudenz der folgenden Jahrhunderte. Sie leistete bei der Umbildung alles Verbandsrechtes im Geiste des obrigkeitlichen Staates wichtige Dienste. Allein selten wurde sie folgerichtig durchgeführt, ging vielmehr fast durchweg ein Kompromiss mit der zäh festgehaltenen kollektiven Auffassung ein. So setzte sich auch in der Lehre von den Korporationsbeschlüssen immer wieder die Behandlung des übereinstimmenden Willens aller Mitglieder als Willens der Körperschaft selbst durch. Fort und fort wurde daher, so weit die rechtliche Gleichsetzung der Majorität mit Allen reichte, der Mehrheitsbeschluss als Willenserklärung der *universitas ipsa* betrachtet und zwischen dem eigenen Handeln der Gemeinheit und ihrem Handeln durch Vertreter unterschieden.[1] Damit verwickelte man sich in zahlreiche Widersprüche, gewann aber die Möglichkeit, nach Benürfnis den fortlebenden Gebilden germanischer Herkunft gerecht zu werden und genossenschaftlichen Gedanken Raum zu geben. Erst im neunzehnten Jahrhundert machten Savigny und seine Schüler mit dem Begriffe der fingierten Person als eines der verbundenen Gesamtheit fremden künstlichen Individuums wieder Ernst und legten ihn ihrem Neubau der Lehre von den „juristischen Personen", wie man nun sagte, zu Grunde, in dem auch das Majoritätsprinzip wieder die entsprechende Fassung empfing.

Diese Restauration aber entsprang vor Allem dem Gegensatz gegen die naturrechtliche Gesellschaftslehre, die inzwischen zur Übermacht emporgediehen war und das positive Recht überschwemmt hatte. Denn das Naturrecht trieb die rein kollektive Auffassung aller menschlichen Verbände auf die Spitze. Es leitete alle Verbände bis aufwärts zum Staat aus der vertragsmässigen Vereinigung der von Hause aus freien und gleichen Individuen her und konstruierte alles Verbandsrecht als vergemeinschaftetes Individualrecht. Ihm war so gut der Staat wie die Ehe und jede Erwerbsgesellschaft eine vertragsmässig begründete *societas*. Der Sozietätsbegriff verschlang den Korporationsbegriff wie den Anstaltsbegriff. Nun fordert aber der Vertrag den Konsens aller

[1] A. a. O., S. 363 ff., 390 ff., 402 ff., 425 ff., 461 ff., 491 ff. Die Verneinung der Deliktsfähigkeit der Korporationen drang nicht einmal bei den Kanonisten durch; a. a. O., S. 343.

Kontrahenten. Darum bereitete gerade das Majoritätsprinzip den Naturrechtslehrern nicht geringe Schwierigkeiten. Sie halfen sich mit der Annahme, dass in den ursprünglichen Gesellschaftsverträgen einstimmig die künftige Geltung des Mehrheitswillens in Gesellschaftsangelegenheiten vereinbart sei. Die so errichtete Gesellschaft konnte dann durch Mehrheitsbeschlüsse sich eine Verfassung küren. Dabei konnte bestimmt werden, dass künftig die Gesamtheit durch eine engere Versammlung repräsentiert werde und in dieser wieder der Mehrheitswille entscheide. Weiter aber musste die als *societas aequalis* entstandene Gesamtheit, wenn die Innehaltung des Gesellschaftsvertrages gesichert werden sollte, sich einer Zwangsgewalt unterwerfen und so zur *societas inaequalis* werden. So erschien denn vor Allem der Staat erst als das Produkt eines zweiten Vertrages, durch den die bürgerliche Gesellschaft in irgend einer Weise die erforderliche *summa potestas* auf einen *imperans* übertragen hatte. In der Monarchie hatte sie sich einem Einzelherrscher, in der Republik einem Kollektivherrscher unterworfen. Und im letzteren Falle war es wieder eine Versammlungsmehrheit, der die Gewalt eingeräumt war, so dass man sogar nicht davor zurückscheute, in der Demokratie einen besonderen Unterwerfungsvertrag zwischen der mit Mehrheit beschliessenden ursprünglichen Gesamtheit und der jeweiligen künftigen Mehrheit Aller zu konstruieren. Aus einem solchen Netze von Verträgen liess man schliesslich einen einheitlichen gesellschaftlichen Körper hervorgehen. Allein dessen Einheit war das Werk künstlich geschaffner Kollektiv- und Repräsentationsverhältnisse. Wenn man daher auch den gesellschaftlichen Einheiten Persönlichkeit zuschrieb, so erhob man sich doch nicht zu dem Begriff einer selbständigen Persönlichkeit des Ganzen, sondern blieb in den Begriffen einer kollektiven Persönlichkeit der Gesamtheiten und einer repräsentativen Persönlichkeit der Herrscher stecken. Um das Verhältnis zwischen Volkspersönlichkeit und Herrscherpersönlichkeit drehte sich in der naturrechtlichen Staatslehre der grosse, weltbewegende Streit. Die lebendige Staatspersönlichkeit blieb unentdeckt. Ausgeschaltet aber wurde mehr und mehr die überindividuelle *persona ficta*. An ihre Stelle trat das, was die Naturrechtslehrer als *persona moralis* bezeichneten. Unter der moralischen Person aber verstanden sie nur eine kollektive Personeneinheit. Sie meinten, dass mehrere Menschen in ihrer gesellschaftlichen Verbundenheit die Rolle einer einzigen Person spielen, wie ja auch umgekehrt ein einzelner Mensch kraft repräsentativer Stellung mehrere Personenrollen spielen kann.

Verfolgen wir noch etwas näher die naturrechtliche Auffassung des Majoritätsprinzips, so findet sich zuerst bei Grotius eine eingehende Begründung des Satzes, dass die Geltung der Stimmenmehrheit auf einstimmiger Vereinbarung im ursprünglichen Gesellschaftsvertrage beruhe.[1] Seitdem wurde dieser Satz zum Axiom der naturrechtlichen Soziallehre. Hobbes und Locke, Ulrich Huber, Pufendorf, Thomasius, Christian Wolff, Nettelbladt und Achenwall tragen ihn übereinstimmend vor,[2] Rousseau legt ihn zu Grunde[3] und Kant erklärt ausdrücklich, dass die in grossen Staaten unentbehrlichen Einrichtungen der Mehrheitsentscheidung und der Repräsentation nur aus einer „mit allgemeiner Zustimmung, also durch einen Kontrakt," vollzogenen Annahme gerechtfertigt werden können.[4] Das Bedenken, dass doch jeder Einzelne zur Versagung seines Konsenses berechtigt gewesen sei, beseitigte man mit dem Hinweis darauf, dass er damit sich von der Gesellschaft ausgeschlossen haben und diese ohne ihn errichtet sein würde. Hobbes meint, dann hätten die zum Staate verbundenen Anderen ihm gegenüber das Kriegsrecht des Naturzustandes, der ja nach Hobbes ein *bellum omnium contra omnes* war, behalten. Die meisten Naturrechtslehrer aber bemühten sich gleichzeitig um eine rationelle Rechtfertigung des Majoritätsprinzips, aus der sie eine

[1] Grotius, *De j. b. et p.* ii. c. 5, § 17. In den früheren rechtsphilosophischen Erörterungen über den Staat und die anderen publizistischen Verbände wurde die Geltung des Majoritätsprinzips nebst den sonstigen Regeln über Korporationsbeschlüsse in Anlehnung an die romanistisch-kanonistische Theorie für jede einmal konstituierte *universitas* und somit auch für die Volksgesamtheit ohne Weiteres angenommen; vgl. mein *Genossenschaftsr.* iii. 599 ff., meine Schrift über Johannes Althusius, S. 85, Anm. 30, S. 138, Anm. 48, S. 215, Anm. 14.

[2] Hobbes, *De cive*, c. 6, § 1-2; Locke, ii. c. 8, § 96-99; U. Huber, *De jure civ.* i. 2, c. 3, § 27 ff., ii. 3, c. 1, § 21-22, c. 2, § 3-4; Pufendorf, *Elem.* i. d. 12, § 27, *Jus nat. et gent.* vii. c. 2, § 15-19, c. 5, § 6, *De officio civis*, ii. c. 6, § 12; Thomasius, *Inst. jur. div.* iii. c. 6, § 64; Wolff, *Inst.* § 841-845; Nettelbladt, *Syst.* § 388; Achenwall, *Jus nat.* ii. § 24-28. Besonders ausführlich Ickstatt, *De jure majorum in conclusis civitatis communibus formandis*, *Opusc.* ii. op. 1, insbes. c. 1, § 65-68. Vgl. auch Gundling, *Diss. de universitate delinquente*, § 6-8.

[3] Rousseau, *Contr. soc.* iv. c. 2. Vgl. auch Sieyès, i. 144 ff., 167, 207 ff.

[4] Kant, *Werke*, vi. 328 ff.

bis zum Nachweise abweichender Abreden durchgreifende Vermutung für dessen vertragsmässige Einführung bei jeder Gesellschaftsgründung herleiteten. Es sei anzunehmen, dass, wer eine Gesellschaft wolle, auch ihren Fortbestand und ihre Aktionsfähigkeit wolle. Zur Erreichung dieses Zieles aber sei die Anerkennung von Mehrheitsbeschlüssen das geeignetste Mittel. Grotius führt aus, dass, da es irgend eine vernünftige Art einheitlicher Geschäftserledigung geben müsse, das Verlangen aber der Unterwerfung der Minderheit unter die Mehrheit unbillig wäre, nichts übrig bleibe, als der Mehrheit das *jus integri* beizulegen. Hobbes, Pufendorf, Gundling und viele Andere betonen, dass jede zur Sozietät verbundene Gesamtheit im Stande sein müsse, einheitlich zu wollen, dass es aber hierfür kein besseres Auskunftsmittel gebe, als die Gleichsetzung des Mehrheitswillens mit dem Willen Aller. Locke geht von dem Begriffe des gesellschaftlichen Körpers aus, der gleich jedem Körper durch eine einzige Kraft in einheitlicher Weise bewegt werden müsse, und meint, dass hier die bewegende Kraft nur in der von der Mehrheit getragenen grösseren Kraft gefunden werden könne; darum entspreche es den Natur- und Vernunftgesetzen, den Mehrheitswillen als Willen des Ganzen gelten zu lassen. Auch sonst berief man sich öfter auf das Übergewicht der Mehrzahl an äusserer Stärke,[1] griff aber auch hier und da auf die germanische Vorstellung einer rechtlichen Folgepflicht der Minderheit zurück.[2] Rousseau suchte mit seiner berühmten Unterscheidung der *volonté générale* von der *volonté de tous* durch einen dialektischen Kunstgriff zu erweisen, dass der allgemeine Wille notwendig zugleich der vernünftige und gerechte Wille sei, weil er das Besondere und Zufällige der in ihm verschmolzenen Einzelwillen nicht in sich aufnehme; allein die Erklärung dafür, warum dieser allgemeine Wille sich mit dem Mehrheitswillen decke, blieb er schuldig, begnügte sich vielmehr mit der nichts erklärenden Fiktion der einstimmigen Vereinbarung im Urvertrage. Im Grunde hätte ihn

[1] So besonders Ickstatt, a. a. O., der ausführt, bei *motiva disparia* müssten die *motiva fortiora* entscheiden, der Massstab könne aber nur ein äusserer sein.

[2] Daries, *Inst. jurispr. univ.* § 750-762 (an sich ist Einstimmigkeit nötig, aber es besteht für die Minderheit eine *obligatio perfecta* zum Beitritt). So meint auch Pufendorf, wer aus blosser *pertinacia* sich seinen *consensus* vorbehalte, hindere den Versammlungsbeschluss nicht, dieser binde ihn vielmehr kraft der allgemeinen Vorschrift, *ut pars se conformet ad bonum totius*.

die Konsequenz der Gedanken, die ihn zur Ablehnung des Repräsentativprinzips führten, auch zur Verwerfung des Majoritätsprinzips bewegen müssen. Und zu dieser äussersten Konsequenz des Individualismus schritten dann auch einzelne Naturrechtslehrer vor. Sie behaupteten, dass aus dem Naturrecht allein die Forderung einstimmiger Beschlüsse zu begründen sei, dass daher in jeder Sozietät die Vermutung für das Einstimmigkeitsprinzip spreche und nur kraft besonders vereinbarter Ausnahmen das Majoritätsprinzip gelten könne. So z.B. die beiden Schlözer, Vater und Sohn.[1] Den Gipfel aber erklomm Fichte, indem er die rechtliche Geltung des Majoritätsprinzips schlankweg verneinte und höchstens in gewissen Fällen der Mehrheit das Recht zur Ausschliessung der Dissentierenden zugestand.[2]

In dem Masse, in dem im neunzehnten Jahrhundert die naturrechtliche Gesellschaftslehre überwunden wurde, verlor auch ihre individualistische Erklärung des Majoritätsprinzips an Ansehen. Bleibend aber behauptete sich die von ihr angebahnte Wiederbelebung des germanischen Genossenschaftsgedankens. Die genossenschaftliche Auffassung der menschlichen Verbände drang gegenüber der anstaltlichen Staats- und Korporationsauffassung wiederum siegreich vor. Darum war auch in Ansehung der Mehrheitsbeschlüsse der restaurierten romanistisch-kanonistischen Theorie kein endgültiger Erfolg beschieden. Vielmehr gewannen ihr neue Anschauungen, wie sie zuerst von der germanistischen Genossenschaftstheorie aus verjüngtem germanischem Recht entwickelt wurden, immer breiteren Boden ab.

Doch kann ich das bis heute nicht erledigte Ringen der gegensätzlichen Auffassungen und die mannigfachen Ausgleichsversuche hier nicht verfolgen. Nur das will ich kurz andeuten, welche Gesichtspunkte für die Wertung des Majoritätsprinzips bestimmend sein müssen, wenn die in allen Jahrhunderten lebendig gebliebene und im modernen Bewusstsein zur Vorherrschaft gelangte, der juristischen Konstruktion aber erst im Gefolge der Genossenschaftstheorie zu Grunde gelegte historisch-organische Verbandsauffassung durchgeführt wird.

[1] A. L. Schlözer, *Allg. Staatsr.*, S. 76 ff.; Chr. v. Schlözer, *De jure suffragii in societate aequali*, Gött., 1795, § 9-14.

[2] Fichte, *Naturrecht Einl.* Nr. III. i. 198, 217 ff., 225 ff. (*Werke*, iii. 16, 164, 178 ff., 184 ff.).

Sind die menschlichen Verbände soziale Organismen, bringen sie als selbständige Lebewesen über dem Einzeldasein das Gattungsdasein zur Entfaltung, so treten sie auch für das Recht den Einzelpersonen als Personen höherer Ordnung gegenüber. Sie lassen sich nicht im Sinne des Naturrechts als blosse Zusammenballungen von Individuen zu kollektiven Einheiten begreifen. Sie dürfen aber auch nicht im Sinne der Fiktionstheorieen als künstliche Individuen von den verbundenen Gesamtheiten losgerissen werden. Vielmehr sind sie reale Gesamtpersonen, selbständige Gemeinwesen mit immanenter Lebenseinheit, organische Ganze, die sich aus Einzelwesen aufbauen, aber keineswegs mit der Summe ihrer Teile decken. Darum ist nicht bloss das äussere, sondern auch das innere Leben der Verbandspersonen, das ja zugleich äusseres Leben der verbundenen Personen ist, Gegenstand der Rechtsordnung. Über Zusammensetzung und Gliederung des Verbandskörpers, über dessen Organisation zum einheitlichen Ganzen, über die Beziehungen der Teile zu einander und zum Ganzen entscheiden Rechtsnormen. So entsteht der Rechtsbegriff des verfassungsmässigen Organs. Organe sind die in einem bestimmten Tätigkeitsbereiche zur Darstellung der Verbandspersönlichkeit berufenen Glieder und Gliederkomplexe. Sie sind keine Vertreter im Sinne des Individualrechts, sondern sichtbare Werkzeuge der unsichtbaren Lebenseinheit des sozialen Körpers. Was das Organ innerhalb seiner Zuständigkeit will und tut, das will und tut im Rechtssinne die Verbandsperson selbst. Durch Organe und nur durch Organe tritt der Staat und jeder andere körperschaftliche Verband als wollendes und handelndes Gemeinwesen in die Erscheinung. So kann denn auch die Gesamtheit aller Mitglieder den einheitlichen Gemeinwillen nur insoweit zum Ausdruck bringen, als sie verfassungsmässig in ihrer rechtlich geordneten Versammlung oder in sonstigem kollektivem Zusammenwirken zum Willensorgan der Verbandsperson berufen ist. Das Gemeinwesen als solches ist etwas durchaus Anderes als die Summe der ihm jeweilig angehörigen Individuen, und keine Kunst vermag den übereinstimmenden Einzelwillen den einheitlichen Staats- oder Körperschaftswillen zu entlocken. Als Glieder des Verbandes aber können die einzelnen Menschen nur in ihrem organisierten Zusammenhange das lebendige Ganze in seiner rechtlichen Einheit zur Darstellung bringen. Jede Versammlung also ist nichts als Organ. Sie ist selbst dann, wenn sie alle jeweiligen Mitglieder umfasst und einstimmig beschliesst, nur Organ des Verbandes und daher nur im Bereiche ihrer verfassungsmässigen Zuständigkeit zur Bildung und Äusserung des Gemeinwillens befähigt. In gleicher Weise aber ist sie Organ, wenn sie kraft der Lebensordnung des Verbandes einen gültigen Mehrheitsbeschluss fasst. Zur Erklärung des Majoritätsprinzips ist also die Gleichsetzung der Mehrheit mit der Gesamtheit weder ausreichend noch erforderlich. Die Geltung des Mehrheitsbeschlusses als eines der verfassungsmässigen Mittel zur Beschaffung einer einheitlichen Versammlungsaktion ist lediglich ein Stück der rechtlich geordneten Organbildung. Sie ist ein Element der Organisation eines zusammengesetzten Organs.

Von diesem Standpunkte aus kommt nun freilich dem Majoritätsprinzip keine im Wesen der menschlichen Verbände begründete absolute Geltung, sondern nur ein historisch bedingter relativer Wert zu. Die Herrschaft des Stimmenmehrs allein vermag keinen Verband und am wenigsten den Staat zur lebendigen Verbandsperson zu stempeln. Immer bedarf es neben einer mit Mehrheit beschliessenden Mitgliederversammlung führender Organe, damit ein handlungsfähiges Gemeinwesen zu Stande komme. So weit durch eine monarchische Verfassung ein Verbandshaupt zum obersten Organ bestellt ist, versteht es sich von selbst, dass keine Versammlungsmehrheit für sich allein den einheitlichen Verbandswillen erzeugen kann. Aber auch wo kraft streng demokratischer Verfassung der mit Mehrheit beschliessende Inbegriff der Mitglieder als oberstes Organ fungiert, offenbart sich nur bei den ihm vorbehaltenen letzten Entscheidungen in dem Abstimmungsergebnis der Gemeinwille, während andere selbständige Organe in ihren Zuständigkeitsbereichen gleich unmittelbar die Persönlichkeit des Ganzen zur Erscheinung bringen. Irgendwie wird in jedem sozialen Organismus kraft der verfassungsmässigen Funktionenverteilung das Majoritätsprinzip durch das Autoritätsprinzip ergänzt. Darauf laufen auch die in grösseren Verbänden unentbehrlichen repräsentativen Einrichtungen hinaus, kraft deren anstatt der regelmässig auf den Vollzug von Wahlen beschränkten Gesamtheit der stimmberechtigten Mitglieder engere Versammlungen oder Kollegien, die nach organischer Auffassung keineswegs Vollmachtträger der Gesamtheit, sondern unmittelbare Willensorgane des Gemeinwesens sind, zur Bildung des Gemeinwillens berufen werden. Gilt für ihre Beschlussfassungen wiederum das Majoritätsprinzip, so kann es unmöglich mehr als ein Organisationsprinzip für einen Teil des Gesamtorganismus bedeuten. Soweit nun aber das Majoritätsprinzip kraft der geschichtlich entwickelten positiven Rechtsordnung gilt, hängt von dieser auch sowohl seine Ausgestaltung, wie seine Begrenzung ab. Hinsichtlich seiner Ausgestaltung sind mancherlei Einrichtungen darauf berechnet, die Überwindung der wahren Mehrheit durch eine bloss scheinbare Mehrheit zu verhindern. So die Anforderungen an die Beschlussfähigheit von Versammlungen, die Verhältniswahlen, die Abstimmungs- oder Wahlpflicht. Andere Einrichtungen aber zielen auf Ermässigung des Übergewichtes der grösseren Zahl ab. Dahin gehören alle Einschränkungen des Kreises der stimmberechtigten Mitglieder, alle Abstufungen des Stimmgewichts nach Fähigkeit, Bildung oder Besitz durch Klassenbildung oder Pluralstimmen, alle Gliederungen der Abstimmung nach Korporationen oder Berufsständen. Sie alle sind, wenn die Gleichsetzung des Gesamtwillens mit dem Mehrheitswillen durchgeführt wird, verwerfliche Fälschungen des Gesamtwillens. Dagegen kann die organische Verbandsauffassung dem mechanischen Kopfzahlprinzip keine Allgemeingültigkeit zusprechen. Eine Begrenzung des Majoritätsprinzips liegt in den Bestimmungen, nach denen es zu gewissen Beschlüssen einer verstärkten oder qualifizierten Mehrheit oder gar der Einstimmigkeit bedarf. Wird hierdurch oder durch andere Mittel eine Minderheit in den Stand gesetzt, einen Mehrheitsbeschluss zu verhindern, so neigt darüber hinaus gerade das neueste Recht auch zur Anerkennung positiver Minderheitsrechte, die eine Minderheit von bestimmter Stärke befähigen, in gewissen Fällen wirksam für das Ganze zu handeln und so als Organ der Verbandsperson zu funktionieren. Im Sinne der Herleitung des Majoritätsprinzips aus dem Wesen der Verbände sind solche Einrichtungen offenbar irrationell. Selbstverständlich wird endlich durchweg die Geltung des Majoritätsprinzips durch die Unantastbarkeit der Sonderrechte begrenzt. Hier aber handelt es sich um die Schranken, die im Sinne unserer Rechtsordnung aller Verbandsmacht überhaupt gezogen sind, weil jeder Verband die ihm eingegliederten Menschen nur hinsichtlich eines Teiles ihrer Wesenheit in sich schliesst und darüber hinaus ihre freie Einzelpersönlichkeit unberührt lässt. Die Sonderrechte aber fallen, auch wenn sie im Verbandsrechte wurzeln, in die den Mitgliedern vorbehaltenen Individualbereiche. Darum kann über sie nicht einmal ein einstimmiger Körperschaftsbeschluss verfügen. Vielmehr ist dazu die Mitwirkung eines individuellen Zustimmungsaktes erforderlich.

So ist in der Tat für die historisch-organische Betrachtungsweise das Majoritätsprinzip zwar ein bedeutungsvoller Faktor für den Aufbau der Verbände, aber für sich allein zur Gestaltung lebendiger sozialer Körper nicht befähigt. Sein Geltungsbereich kann nicht rationell, sondern nur geschichtlich begründet, sein Wert nicht absolut bestimmt, sondern nur nach seiner jeweiligen Wirkungsweise im organischen Leben der Gemeinwesen bemessen werden.

OTTO VON GIERKE.

# XVII

# UNE ANTITHÈSE DU PRINCIPE MAJORITAIRE EN DROIT POLONAIS[1]

QUICONQUE connaît tant soit peu l'histoire de Pologne, ou qui prétend seulement la connaître, devinera aisément que par « l'antithèse du principe majoritaire » nous entendons le trop fameux *liberum veto.* On sait bien en quoi consistait cette institution bizarre, unique, semble-t-il, dans son genre : elle donnait à chaque député le droit de rompre la diète et à chaque gentilhomme celui de rompre la diétine. Cependant, les connaissances de la littérature européenne ne vont guère au delà de cette définition. Le *veto* tenait parmi les institutions polonaises une place aussi centrale que le principe majoritaire dans la vie constitutionnelle des états modernes : il faisait, selon Montesquieu, « l'objet » même de la constitution de Pologne. Il entraîna la ruine de l'indépendance de la Pologne, mais non pas celle de sa nationalité, ni de sa civilisation distincte. Il plongea le pays dans une affreuse anarchie, mais lui-même n'était pas l'anarchie.

[1] Cet article résume d'une manière générale la deuxième partie d'un livre polonais qui va paraître en 1914 sous le titre : *Liberum veto.* La première partie sera consacrée à l'examen de l'origine et du développement du principe majoritaire, surtout en Angleterre, en France, en Allemagne, en Suisse et en Aragon. L'auteur conçoit parfaitement l'insuffisance des sources à portée d'un spécialiste isolé, ainsi que la nécessité du concours des savants de tous les pays, pour aprofondir ce problème obscur et compliqué. En communiquant cette esquisse au Congrès de Londres, nous avons tenté d'occasionner une discussion internationale sur la majorité et le *liberum veto*, sans laquelle les efforts des érudits isolés resteront dans ce domaine peu fructueux. Aussi nous osons nous adresser par l'intermédiaire de cette publication à tous ses lecteurs, pour les prier de nous faire envoyer leurs remarques supplémentaires ou critiques. En revanche de cette complaisance, nous espérons pouvoir offrir une version française de la première partie de notre livre à la disposition de tous nos collègues qui voudront bien nous fournir quelques contributions.

Au point de vue pratique c'était une folie, mais une de ces folies dont on peut dire avec le vieux Polonius :

Though this be madness, yet there is method in 't.

Et c'est justement grâce à sa propre « méthode » de développement, grâce à sa propre méthode d'application pratique et systématique, grâce à cette méthode de se combiner pendant 200 ans avec l'existence morale et politique d'une nation, que le *veto* mérite l'attention du monde savant de l'Europe. Il le mérite aussi pour une raison plus générale, bien qu'ici secondaire. Intéressante par elle-même, l'histoire du *veto* reflète à l'inverse l'influence de ces mêmes facteurs qui sur un autre terrain ont conduit au triomphe du principe du nombre. Jusqu'à un certain moment le développement du *liberum veto* est identique avec l'établissement du principe de l'unanimité, et jusqu'à cette date on se demande plutôt pourquoi le principe majoritaire ne s'est-il pas établi en Pologne, au lieu de se demander d'où provient le *liberum veto*.

Plus tard, l'étendue et la force de son fonctionnement s'élargissent d'une manière nouvelle et imprévue qui ne résulte point des causes qui ont agi contre le régime majoritaire. Ainsi d'une simple négation il se transforme en l'antithèse de la majorité. La première phase s'étend jusqu'à la moitié du XVIIe siècle, et correspond à la phase que le parlement anglais paraît avoir traversée à la fin du XIIIe siècle et à celle que les États Généraux de France avaient traversée sous les premiers Valois.

Dans l'espace de cette première période la procédure doit être essentiellement la même pour le terrain polonais, anglais ou espagnol. Il s'agit de découvrir quelles sont les influences qui permettent au plus grand nombre d'imposer ses décisions à la minorité et de constater si ces influences agissaient précisément en Pologne. L'induction et la déduction, le raisonnement par analogie et *a contrario*, concourent ici à découvrir des rapports de cause à effet, pour ne pas dire « des lois », d'après lesquels on peut, en observant toutes les précautions, reconstruire même des faits, à défaut de sources immédiates suffisantes. Nous croyons pouvoir nous dispenser d'exposer nos observations sur ce sujet à mesure qu'elles se sont présentées à notre esprit : il sera plus à propos d'exposer la thèse définitive en l'éclaircissant par des exemples.

Le point de départ de l'évolution assez homogène en Pologne et dans l'Europe occidentale est cet état primitif où il n'existe aucune règle pour former la volonté générale. La décision incontestable y provient de la concordance effective de toutes les volontés, lorsque personne ne proteste, ni au cours des délibérations, ni pendant l'exécution de ce qui a été résolu. Le point final du développement des institutions chez nous et en Occident n'est pas le même : en Pologne on aboutira à appliquer la règle d'unanimité à toutes les délibérations, pendant que le reste de l'Europe, excepté l'Aragon et la Catalogne, adoptera le régime majoritaire, à moins qu'il ne se soumette à la royauté établie.

Comment expliquer cette différence singulière ? Et, en général, comment se forme partout le principe majoritaire ?

Il ne fut octroyé nulle part, ni emprunté à des étrangers ; tout au moins l'imitation ne fut jamais assez puissante pour dominer les vieilles habitudes déréglées. Ce principe ne résulte nécessairement d'aucune théorie universellement reconnue ; il ne fut jamais l'objet d'une propagande suivie.

Seules la force normative de l'habitude et celle du fait accompli peuvent nous fournir une explication réelle. Tout ce qui se répète plusieurs fois s'appelle normal, et tout ce qui est normal fait une norme. Ceci paraît un sophisme ou un sorite mal construit, mais c'est par cette voie que le sentiment du droit se réconcilie avec la force ouverte de la foule. Voilà comment il faut entendre l'opinion qui prétend que le droit de la majorité repose sur la force : il repose sur une longue série d'antécédents.

Reste à savoir dans quelles conditions la supériorité du plus grand nombre devient constante et par conséquent normale. Il faut à cet effet un concours spécial de conjonctures favorables, dont aucune séparément ne suffirait pour expliquer la genèse du principe du plus grand nombre, mais dont les combinaisons semblent l'expliquer suffisamment.

1°. D'abord, le vote à la majorité des voix suppose un dénombrement des suffrages censés égaux en principe. Les groupements primitifs connaissent une coutume répandue de pondérer les suffrages : les volontés des éléments nombreux mais peu signifiants ont une moindre valeur que celles de quelques gens riches, braves et accrédités. Au fur et à mesure que les éléments les plus forts se concentrent en un collège spécial et que les plus faibles (quoique nombreux) se réduisent à un autre ou à plusieurs autres niveaux, on rencontre dans chaque collège à part la question du calcul des suffrages de première classe, de deuxième classe, etc. Dans l'histoire des élections allemandes la fixation du principe majoritaire coïncide avec l'établissement du collège des électeurs. Il est permis de supposer que dans les Chambres anglaises ce principe ne se serait pas établi aussi facilement sans la division de la noblesse en pairs et chevaliers de comtés.

Or, malgré toute la distance qui sépare la Pologne du XVIe et du XVIIe siècle de celle de l'état primitif, il ne faut pas oublier que les diètes et diétines polonaises étaient le rendez-vous de la petite noblesse ainsi que des grands seigneurs, puissants comme les princes de l'Empire, qui ne se sentaient point les égaux de la petite *szlachta*. Aussi le *liberum veto* devint en réalité, entre les mains des grands seigneurs, un instrument de lutte contre la majorité.

2°. Le nivellement des votants une fois accompli, il est indispensable qu'un certain ordre de délibérations s'établisse dans le groupe en question. Les précédents en faveur de la majorité ou contre elle ne pourront se produire sans que tout le monde ne voie bien que c'est précisément la majorité qui remporte la victoire et que ce n'est pas la minorité qui au cours des débats accède insensiblement à la majorité, reconstituant par là les apparences de l'unanimité.

En Pologne le règlement des diètes s'élabora dans la période où la victoire penchait du côté du principe de l'unanimité. En attendant il se forma une notion confuse des résolutions semi-obligatoires auxquelles les palatinats mécontents accédaient après coup.

3°. Rien n'inspire une telle solidarité et une telle discipline que le danger menaçant l'État entier ou au moins une de ses corporations ; c'est lui qui force à effacer les dissensions intestines et à ne tenir aucun compte de l'opposition vaincue.

La Pologne jouissait au XVIe siècle d'une tranquillité absolue du côté de l'Occident ; sa puissance tenait encore l'Orient en respect : la République put se permettre de ne pas user de violence à l'égard des opposants. Au surplus, la classe dominante, c'est-à-dire la noblesse, se vit hors de la concurrence avec les autres classes : elle n'avait plus contre qui manifester sa solidarité ou dissimuler son peu de discipline interne. Cela a puissamment poussé aux excès les mécontents tant au cours des diètes ou diétines qu'après leur séparation.

4°. Des crises révolutionnaires, grâce à leur caractère peu tolérant, attaquent vigoureusement l'indépendance des partis et des corporations. Elles soulèvent dans les partis prépondérants des passions qui leur font oublier tous les scrupules constitutionnels envers leurs adversaires. La Pologne a subi au XVIe siècle une crise religieuse; et ce fut justement alors, sous Sigismond Auguste, que la majorité protestante donna le branle à la chambre des nonces; quelquefois elle sembla être prête à faire ce coup de force salutaire, dont les suites eussent été incalculables pour l'avenir de la République. Malheureusement ce coup de force manqua—la vague protestante recula, et la crise se dissipa sans avoir guéri l'État de ses infirmités.

5°. Suivons ce même raisonnement. A l'époque de la réunion des premières diétines et diètes tous les mécontents pouvaient se transporter en Volhynie, en Podolie et ensuite en Ukraine. Il n'existait aucune catégorie de gens forcés à s'incliner devant les décisions de la majorité prépondérante, et pour celle-ci il n'existait aucun adversaire la tenant en éveil. Quand la possibilité de cette émigration cessa, le principe séduisant de l'unanimité était déjà bien enraciné.

6°. A cette contexture de circonstances imprévues s'en ajoutent d'autres qui furent plus ou moins durables mais qui paraissent comme fatalement assorties pour débiliter les éléments centralisateurs du parlementarisme polonais. Le vote électoral ou strictement législatif, de même que celui sur les questions internationales, contribue assez bien à accumuler des précédents favorables à la formation du régime majoritaire. Les affaires financières et militaires sont moins propres à atteindre ce résultat. En effet, la majorité peut aisément imposer son roi au pays ou son député à une circonscription électorale, car les opposants osent rarement élire un contre-roi ou même un contre-député. On peut facilement contraindre les mécontents à reconnaître soit une nouvelle magistrature, soit une nouvelle administration royale, soit un nouveau traité ratifié contre leur gré. Mais il est difficile de lever des impôts directs ou de convoquer un arrière-ban, si les opposants résistent activement, ou même passivement. En général, si l'exécution d'une décision commune se laisse émietter, ou si elle dépend du concours d'éléments réfractaires, on risque de créer un antécédent préjudiciable à la majorité. C'est justement ce qui arriva en Pologne sous Sigismond I$^{er}$ (1507–48) au moment où les destinées du parlementarisme subissaient une épreuve dangereuse : les diétines particulières rejetèrent coup sur coup les impôts, ainsi que la nouvelle organisation militaire qui avait été précédemment agréée à la dicte générale par la plupart des nonces, et le gouvernement dut plier devant cet obstacle.

7°. La résistance aux mesures financières des diètes n'aurait pas entraîné des conséquences préjudiciables au parlementarisme central si la majorité avait trouvé dans le pouvoir royal un ferme point d'appui et une garantie de l'exécution de ses décisions, comme cela eut lieu en Angleterre et en France. Ami ou ennemi, inspirateur ou adversaire des états, le pouvoir royal donnait partout et toujours de la consistance aux corps délibérants et les obligeait de renoncer au principe de l'unanimité. En Pologne cet appui salutaire fit défaut à la représentation nationale.

8°. Enfin, le dernier et peut-être le plus grand obstacle ne fut pas épargné aux diètes de Pologne. Nous voulons dire le mandat impératif, appelé chez nous « instruction de nonce ». Selon une opinion assez répandue, cette entrave aurait pu par elle-même faire fourvoyer la machine parlementaire et créer le *liberum veto*. On sait que la diète générale se forma grâce à la jonction des délégations des diétines en assemblées provinciales et de ces dernières en un seul corps. En principe les tendances particularistes terriennes devaient s'effacer au centre de la province pour disparaître entièrement dans la volonté de l'assemblée plénière des états. La réalité démentit ces espérances. Loin de rompre l'individualité des diétines, les assemblées provinciales leur servirent de bouclier contre l'autorité de la nation entière ; ayant sauvé l'indépendance des palatinats, elles disparurent, comme inutiles. Grâce à l'intervention de ces assemblées, les diétines tinrent tête à la diète pendant la crise déjà signalée sous les deux premiers rois Sigismonds. Leurs « instructions », appuyées par la menace d'une résistance à main armée des grands palatinats, montrèrent une vigueur infiniment plus énergique que celle dont portent témoignages les cahiers français, issus des petites circonscriptions électorales (bailliages ou sénéchaussées). La diète prit l'air plutôt d'un congrès de délégués avec un pouvoir limité que d'une assemblée nationale représentative et souveraine.

Sans doute, les mandats eux-mêmes n'auraient jamais empêché le régime majoritaire, comme ils ne l'ont pas empêché en France. Mais ce résultat fut inévitable faute de tendances permanentes centralisatrices au sein de la diète générale, et à défaut de tout autre facteur sur lequel la majorité aurait pu s'appuyer. Ainsi l'individu, couvert par le mandat impératif, commença à opposer son *veto* à l'accord du reste de l'assemblée, et cela même dans les cas qui n'étaient pas réglés d'avance par «l'instruction». L'unanimité des mandats impératifs se transforma peu à peu en unanimité de personnes.

Résumons nos remarques antérieures. Le concours de huit circonstances, à savoir :

1°, l'inégalité de fait des personnes participant aux diètes et aux diétines ;

2°, l'élaboration tardive et insuffisante d'un règlement pour les délibérations ;

3°, l'inexistence de toute pression du dehors ;

4°, la faiblesse des conflits intestins ;

5°, la possibilité d'émigration des mécontents en masse dans d'autres provinces de la République ;

6°, la nature divisible et susceptible d'empêchement des premières décisions des diètes ;

7°, la faiblesse du pouvoir exécutif séparé ;

8°, la puissance des diétines et l'importance de leurs mandats,—tout cela créa vers la fin de la dynastie des Jagellons une imposante série d'antécédents, après lesquels le parlementarisme polonais ne pouvait sortir de sa stagnation vers le régime majoritaire,—qu'au prix d'une révolution violente.

Les trois interrègnes après 1572 ne firent qu'aggraver l'incertitude des principes centripètes et centrifuges dans la constitution de la Pologne. Si les palatinats aspiraient à la souveraineté et prétendaient à gouverner la diète, on s'en pouvait tirer, en substituant à la forme quasi unitaire de l'État le fédéralisme pur à l'instar des Provinces-Unies. Une semblable décomposition aurait été une conséquence naturelle et saine des instructions impératives. Mais les interrègnes achevèrent de fermer cette issue. La nombreuse noblesse polonaise remportait de ces immenses assemblées électorales un sentiment raffermi de son unité. D'un autre côté, quiconque prenait une part personnelle (*viritim*) à l'élection, se considérait à juste titre comme titulaire immédiat et auteur de la souveraineté nationale : il contractait, conjointement avec ses pairs, les pactes fondamentaux avec le roi, donc il ne connaissait point d'instance intermédiaire entre lui et le chef d'État élu à l'unanimité. S'il a conservé l'intégrité de sa souveraineté personnelle sur le champ électoral, il la gardera d'autant plus facilement contre le plus grand nombre à la diétine. Aussi ce ne fut que depuis 1572 que le principe de l'unanimité commença à infecter les diétines.

Or, vers la fin du XVIe siècle trois principes fondamentaux se sont établis dans le droit public de la Pologne :

Personne ne peut devenir roi sans une élection libre et unanime par la noblesse ;

Aucun projet ne deviendra loi sans l'accord unanime du roi, du sénat et des nonces terriens donnant leurs votes selon la teneur des mandats ;

Aucune proposition ne pourra être adoptée par la diétine que du consentement de tous les gentilshommes qui y sont présents. Certainement, ce sont là des principes sans exemple dans l'Europe moderne, excepté dans le royaume d'Aragon et la principauté de Catalogne. Ils méconnaissent entièrement l'autorité du plus grand nombre ; ils sont généraux et absolus. Ils convergent dans l'idée d'un libre accord (*consensus*) embrassant toutes espèces de décisions collectives. Ils contrastent avec toute sorte de décret judiciaire (*decreta*) soumis à la majorité des suffrages. Ces principes agissent, en théorie, dans l'ordre normal sans restriction, quoique en pratique les exceptions n'aient pas été rares.

D'ailleurs, quelque nombreuses qu'aient été ces exceptions, il est étonnant que la nation ait pu vivre sous une telle constitution pendant deux siècles. On recourait, il est vrai, dans les cas extrêmes au lien d'une confédération, c'est-à-dire, à une convention qui suspendait l'exigence de l'unanimité et soumettait les matières les plus difficiles aux décisions majoritaires appelées *sancita*. Jean-Jacques Rousseau pouvait s'exprimer à ce propos que la Pologne vivait en règle dans l'état de nature, où il n'y avait qu'une « volonté de tous », et ne contractait le pacte social qu'en cas d'urgence, pour créer « la volonté générale ». Toutefois, même si l'on prend en ligne de compte les nombreux abus où les minorités étaient réduites au silence, on ne saurait méconnaître chez les Polonais au XVIe et au XVIIe siècle une flexibilité spéciale vers cet accord unanime dont le résultat fut les quatre grands *Volumina Legum*. Il est incontestable que cet idéal sublime d'une « union des esprits » (*unio animorum*) élevait les multitudes à une abnégation altruiste ; les générations successives apprenaient sous son influence à joindre la liberté et l'égalité à une fraternité inconnue ailleurs, et à retenir l'égoïsme dont les excès auraient flétri et compromis le principe même d'unanimité. Nier tout cela serait perdre de vue l'ensemble et le principal pour se restreindre au particulier.

Mais tout honneur accordé aux altruistes, il ne convient pas de fermer les yeux sur l'envers de la médaille. Nous avons mentionné les *Volumina Legum*. Ils sont vraiment volumineux, mais ils le seraient dix fois davantage si cette forme de décision difficile et presque impossible n'eût pas gêné l'initiative des nonces ou des diétines. Évidemment il n'y avait qu'une seule voie pour obtenir l'accord : c'était de heurter de front toute la chambre, de tenir ferme, de s'opposer à toute autre initiative, jusqu'à ce qu'on eut accédé aux propositions ainsi violemment soutenues. L'entêtement vaut mieux que toutes les raisons. Les instructions exigeaient souvent des choses incompatibles ou difficiles à concilier ; et même si elles ne le faisaient pas, elles en demandaient trop à la fois, et parfois plus qu'il n'était possible de faire aboutir pendant les six semaines prescrites par la loi. De là une obstruction réciproque ouverte ou insidieuse ; de là des tentatives de reléguer tout ce qu'il y avait de plus important à la fin des séances, afin de l'introduire par surprise ou contrebande ; de là vers la clôture des séances des abus multiples de la part de la majorité, abus sans lesquels l'État serait resté souvent sans défense ni ressources.

Peu à peu les contradicteurs trouvèrent un moyen efficace pour résister aux tentatives d'oppression ou de suppression : on n'avait qu'à demander acte de sa protestation, ou bien, d'après le terme courant en Pologne : à porter un manifeste au greffe. D'abord ce fut tout un parti mécontent qui fit signer sa protestation par une foule d'opposants, puis des individus commencèrent à suivre cet exemple. Enfin, même à l'époque de la pire anarchie, le *veto* par écrit, quoique signé par un seul nonce, resta l'organe des factions et non pas des individus. En vain le gouvernement chercha-t-il à refuser l'acte de protestation. Si le greffe à Varsovie ou à Grodno était fermé, il y en avait quantité d'autres à la portée des mécontents.

On vit de plus en plus souvent les diètes se dissoudre sans avoir obtenu aucun résultat. L'union des esprits demeurait l'idéal de la nation, mais en réalité on n'avait qu'à choisir entre la violation de ce qu'on appelait «la liberté dorée» ou le préjudice de l'État. La nation ne voulait pas se décider en faveur du fédéralisme pur et simple, et elle ne savait pas comment instituer la forme unitaire de la République. Strictement, l'infructuosité des diètes ne résultait pas encore d'une anarchie: c'était la négation suivie du principe majoritaire qui conduisait le plus régulièrement du monde à la paralysie de l'État. L'anarchie fut plutôt le fruit que la racine du *liberum veto*. Le public voyait assez bien les dangers du désordre, les écrivains politiques sonnaient le tocsin, mais toutes leurs exhortations ne pouvaient rien contre les tendances des deux forces sociales opposées à la réforme: les magnats et la petite noblesse. Les premiers, ennemis naturels de l'État, ne pouvaient que perdre leur influence sous le régime majoritaire; l'autre craignait en ce cas de perdre son repos et ses prérogatives au profit de l'État; elle se contentait de sa toute-puissance passive et apparente, sans aspirer à une liberté plus active, mais périlleuse.

Du haut de sa liberté absolue la noblesse polonaise regardait avec dédain ce qui s'appelait liberté publique en Europe, sans la prérogative du *veto*. Au cours du XVIIe siècle elle voyait avec inquiétude la lutte partout victorieuse de la royauté de droit divin contre les privilèges des classes sociales. Elle voyait la moindre faiblesse du côté du peuple encourager les monarques à des empiètements. Hongrois, Tchéques, Allemands, Danois, Suédois, sans parler des Espagnols et des Français, tous les peuples du continent européen qui s'étaient prêtés à la règle majoritaire tombèrent au cours de ce siècle sous le joug de la monarchie absolue. La Grande-Bretagne paraissait plongée dans des guerres civiles. En présence de telles expériences pouvait-on ne pas avoir l'illusion que l'unanimité et le *veto* constituaient l'unique garantie contre l'esclavage?

Mais le torrent de la vie ne s'arrête pas. Le développement qui tendait à élever l'individu au-dessus de l'État n'avait pas encore atteint son terme. Dans la sphère de la conquête des libertés, comme partout, le mieux reste l'ennemi du bien. Ayant réalisé la négation simple du principe majoritaire, le parlementarisme polonais se précipita dans son antithèse.

Car c'est ainsi qu'il faut qualifier logiquement la pratique qui s'introduit aux diètes de Pologne depuis la moitié du XVIIe siècle, ainsi que la théorie juridique qui devait l'exprimer. Pendant cette deuxième phase le *liberum veto* commence à décapiter des assemblées entières, et non pas seulement leurs projets. On commence à rompre les délibérations. Comment y est-on parvenu? Quelle a été ici la « méthode » de notre « folie » parlementaire? L'explication se trouve, d'un côté, dans le conflit des intérêts provinciaux dont nous avons parlé plus haut, de l'autre dans la structure originaire des diètes. On a prétendu que la première rupture de diète eut lieu en 1652. En vérité cette diète a fonctionné jusqu'à son terme légal, et ne fut dissoute qu'à cause d'une opposition légitime à la prolongation des séances. Ce n'est pas ce qu'on peut appeler une rupture. Mais ce fait arrivé en 1652 eut un retentissement dans tous les palatinats. Il démontra clairement que les États de la République étaient prêts à tout sacrifier pour l'amour des droits individuels. Alors on fit un pas de plus en avant. On se mit à protester et à quitter la salle des séances avant la fin de la diète. Les optimistes pouvaient attendre patiemment jusqu'au dernier jour ; les pessimistes qui prévoyaient que le contradicteur ne se laisserait pas fléchir rentraient chez eux désespérant du succès de la diète.

D'où venait ce désespoir? Pourquoi ne sanctionnait-on pas au moins cette partie des projets qui n'était contestée par personne? C'est qu'aucun projet ne pouvait passer loi avant la clôture solennelle des États. La diète polonaise ressemblait à un congrès où la noblesse obtenait la sanction de ses demandes en échange du consentement qu'elle donnait aux projets législatifs du roi, et surtout en échange des contributions publiques. Si une partie des contractants proteste et s'absente de l'acte de conclusion, tout le marché est nul et de nul effet : voilà pourquoi dans sa nouvelle phase le *liberum veto*, lancé contre telle ou telle proposition, a une force rétroactive contre tous les actes de la diète.

Bientôt tous les palatinats embrassèrent l'opinion que chaque particulier avait le droit de fermer la bouche à l'assemblée de ses égaux. La contagion devint générale, elle inonda tous les territoires, renversant toutes les digues. Le moindre gentilhomme s'arrogea le droit non seulement de paralyser les décisions, mais aussi d'empêcher de les mettre aux voix. Le *veto* envahit même les territoires qui avaient cru s'en garantir en admettant dans les élections, le vote majoritaire : inutilement alléguait-on cette loi locale, quand le contradicteur ne permettait pas même d'ouvrir les débats ! En 1688 la diète générale fut rompue pour la première fois avant l'élection du maréchal : on pourrait dire qu'alors « la libre voix du citoyen » eut plus de valeur que le règlement de la diète !

Le *veto* devint une puissance sans bornes, élémentaire, antérieure à toute constitution,—une idole, un tonnerre dans les mains de milliers d'insensés.

Et voilà l'antithèse du principe majoritaire à son apogée.

Baissons le rideau sur les conséquences destructives et ignominieuses de sa domination. Ce triste tableau n'est que trop bien connu ; on l'expose fréquemment et de parti pris, pour suggérer l'impression que la Pologne s'est tuée elle-même avant qu'on eût l'idée d'abréger son agonie. Jusqu'à quel point et jusqu'à quelle époque le *veto* domina-t-il la Pologne du consentement des Polonais, et d'autre part, depuis quand fut-il soutenu par la force étrangère, poussée jusqu'à la menace de la guerre ?—c'est une question qui n'appartient pas à l'examen juridique et historique de son origine ni de son application.

Mais nous nous sentirions coupable d'avoir confirmé une fausseté, si nous ne rappelions ici le fait notoire que malgré l'aveuglement de la société polonaise avant le partage, malgré les insinuations envenimées des voisins, on avait trouvé le chemin qui conduisait tout droit du labyrinthe de la « liberté dorée » vers la liberté publique moderne. On l'avait trouvé, ce chemin, à la lumière des flambeaux de la littérature éclairée du XVIII^e^ siècle ; on avait osé y marcher, encouragé par l'exemple de cette nation unique qui seule avec nous et avec les Hongrois, mais beaucoup mieux que nous autres, avait su conserver le trésor de ses libertés au milieu des royautés établies,—par l'exemple de la nation anglaise. Prenant pour modèle les lois de l'Angleterre, la Constitution du 3 mai 1791 a aboli définitivement le *veto* en dépit des garanties étrangères, mais au gré de tous les Polonais. Elle n'a pas sauvé l'indépendance de la République, mais elle est arrivée justement à temps pour sauver l'âme nationale et pour donner un démenti aux falsificateurs d'histoire qui nous imputent un suicide.

W. KONOPCZYNSKI.

# XVIII

# THE MODERN STUDY OF CANON LAW

AFTER Gratian, in the eleventh century, separated the study of Canon Law from that of practical theology, Canon Law formed, with Roman Law (*utrumque ius*), the foundation of legal studies in the universities of the Middle Ages.

The famous *Decretum* of Gratian, the *Concordia Discordantium Canonum*, a private work, which had obtained recognition in the whole Church, was the object of a series of commentaries (*Summae* or *Stromae*) by the 'Decretists,' who were followed by the 'Decretalists,' the commentators of the official collections of Decretals, which formed the second part of the *Corpus Iuris Canonici*.

This great scientific elaboration of Canon Law corresponded to its importance in mediaeval life. Canon Law covered at that time a much larger field than in later periods. It was international, it was Christian and therefore universal, and it was essentially conservative. For these reasons it exercised a very wide influence upon the development of legal theories in the Middle Ages all over the Western world.

The theory of sovereignty and of the relationship between Church and State, as well as the various political theories, were largely determined by the Canonists, as the Rev. A. J. Carlyle has demonstrated recently in his learned book, *The Political Theories of the Middle Ages*. But at the same time private law, the systems of land tenures, and especially the marriage law—this last considered by the Church as her exclusive and absolute domain—were under the direct influence of Canon Law. International law and the law of procedure took their fundamental ideas and principles from Canon Law; and for the reason that many crimes were subject to ecclesiastical jurisdiction on account of the element of 'sin' connected with them, the law of the Church had a decided influence on the development of penal law. The social action of the Church, the extension of her property, the monastic institutions and the philanthropic work connected with them, dominate the social and economic history of the Middle Ages, and carry into all branches of mediaeval life the influence of the legal elements of ecclesiastical ideas.

Perhaps in no other period of history have the doctrines of the Canonists influenced so deeply and directly the formation of the law of the Church as at this time, when Rolando Bandinelli, the eminent decretist, was elected Pope under the name of Alexander III., and Sinibaldo Fieschi, the famous decretalist, ascended the papal throne as Innocent IV.

At that time Canon Law emanated chiefly from the Papal authority. But when the occidental schism weakened the position of the Popes and created the necessity for an appeal from the contending Pontiffs to a higher authority, in order to re-establish the unity of the Church, the so-called reformatory Councils of Pisa (1409), Constance (1411–18), and Basel (1431) tried to substitute the authority of the Council for that of the Popes in ecclesiastical legislation, and to assert the position of the bishops against the supremacy of the Popes and of the Roman Court.

But if those Councils did not succeed in establishing an episcopal system against the Roman supremacy, their canons were partly accepted by the State in France and Germany. The Popes were obliged to make concessions to the sovereigns, under the form of privileges granted to them by the various Concordats of the end of the fifteenth century and the beginning of the sixteenth century.

Thus, at the end of the Middle Ages, the States took up an independent attitude towards the Church, and a radical change was brought about in their position as regards ecclesiastical matters by the Protestant Reformation.

The Reformed Churches accepted the supremacy of the State (*ius circa sacra*), granting to sovereigns a large *ius inspiciendi et cavendi* in their internal organizations. At the same time, owing to the fact that the State authorities were confronted by different denominations, the ecclesiastical legislation of the States developed on lines independent of the single denominations, and in consequence of that, there arose, besides the strictly denominational *canon law*, an *ecclesiastical law of the State*, which only gradually and with great difficulty applied the principles of religious liberty.

Thus a new field opened out to the scientific study of Canon Law. After the decline of the Commentators of the Decretals, whose last works show a lack of scientific individuality and an excessive predominance of casuistry and merely practical technicality, with the revival of humanistic studies France is the leading country in the study of Ecclesiastical Law, and the French school can boast of a series of great canonists, from Cujas to Thomassin, whose works are strictly connected with the special relationship of State and Church in France.

The defence of the *Libertates Ecclesiae Gallicanae*, which had in the *Assemblées dù Clergé* very effective means of safeguarding episcopal rights, led to the formation of a complete system of *Droit civil ecclésiastique*, which was only temporarily interrupted by the French Revolution.

The Council of Trent (1545–63), the greatest legislative work of the Catholic Church in modern times, marks a decided return to mediaeval theories of papal supremacy. The whole Council was presided over by Papal Delegates, all the proposals for its decisions came from Rome, and the canons of the Council were formally approved and promulgated by the Pope.

At the same time the new legislation of the Council of Trent, covering a very extensive field and regulating matters of vital importance for the State, as was the case with the marriage law, brought new life into the Canon Law and the studies connected with it.

Cardinal Bellarmino (1542–1621) and Franciscus Suarez (1548–1617) affirmed the papal supremacy in a new form, sustaining the *potestas indirecta* of the Popes in temporal matters; and the seventeenth century witnessed the completion of the *Annals* of Caesar Baronius (d. 1607) and of the *Italia Sacra* of Ferdinando Ughelli (d. 1670), while Antonio Augustino, with his great works, represents for Spain the humanistic revival of the study of Canon Law.

In the struggle between the Papacy and different States in the seventeenth and eighteenth centuries in France, in Spain, and in Italy, the defenders of the Erastian theories developed a whole system of *ius circa sacra* of the State towards the ecclesiastical institutions, and the episcopal theories found a vigorous support in the writings of Zeger van Espen (d. 1728), and in the famous *De statu ecclesiae*, which John Nikolaus von Hontheim (d. 1790) published in 1763 under the pseudonym of Febronius.

In Austria those Erastian theories were accepted by Eybel, Pehem, Riegger, and Rautenstrauch, and prepared the way for the great ecclesiastical reforms of Maria Theresa and Joseph II.

Besides the political writings on Canon Law, this period also produced the canonistic works of Prospero Lambertini (Benedict XIV), the researches of the Bishop of Oneglia, Stefano Berardi, and of the brothers Ballerini of Verona on the sources of Canon Law; also the *Prompta Bibliotheca* of Ferraris and the *Theatrum* of De Luca, the first encyclopaedic works covering the whole field of Canon Law.

The revival of the scientific study of Ecclesiastical Law in the nineteenth century is due to Germany, where Karl Friedrich Eichorn in his *Grundsätze des Kirchenrechts der katholischen und der evangelischen Religionspartei in Deutschland* (Göttingen, 1831) applied to Canon Law the principles of the historical school of Savigny, and gave a systematic exposition of Canon Law based on its natural structure, breaking the tradition of the division into *personae, res et actiones*, which, since Lancellotti, had dominated the treatment of Ecclesiastical Law.

Thus the merely dogmatic study of Canon Law was abandoned, and greater importance given to the historical development of ecclesiastical institutions.

The next phase of the study of Ecclesiastical Law in Germany is closely connected with the works of Friedrich von Schulte, Paul Hinschius, and Emil Friedberg, the most eminent canonists of the period of the so-called *Kulturkampf*.

Friedrich von Schulte, who later was one of the founders of the Old Catholic movement, edited a series of the *Summae* of the Decretists, and recorded in a monumental work (*Geschichte der Quellen und Literatur des kanonischen Rechtes von Gratian bis auf die Gegenwart*, Stuttgart, 1875 sq.) the works on Canon Law after Gratian.

To Paul Hinschius, the editor of the *Pseudoisidor*, canonistic science owes the largest and most exhaustive treatise on Church Law (*System des Kirchenrechts*, 6½ volumes, Berlin, 1868–96), which, although not completed, will remain for many years to come the basis for historical researches into ecclesiastical institutions.

Of the multifarious works of Friedberg special mention must be made of his great edition of the *Corpus Iuris Canonici*, after the first *Editio Lipsiensis* by Emil Ludwig Richter.

Thus the tradition of the study of Canon Law was kept in Germany, where, even in distinctly Protestant States, Canon Law was—as it still is—a subject of lectures and examinations not only in the theological, but also in the legal Faculties; and the German school of Canon Law had a direct influence on the revival of the canonistic studies in Italy.

In consequence of the theories of separation of Church and State expressed by Cavour in his famous formula *Libera Chiesa in libero Stato* ('A Free Church in a Free State'), and only partially applied in Italian ecclesiastical legislation, the Theological Faculties at the State Universities in the Kingdom of Italy were suppressed in 1873, and the teaching of Canon Law at the legal faculties, although not formally abolished, was practically abandoned for many years.

The revival of the study of Ecclesiastical Law in Italy was due to Francesco Scaduto, who wrote the first exhaustive treatise on modern Italian ecclesiastical law (*Manuale del diritto ecclesiastico*, 2 ed., Turin, 1894), and to Francesco Ruffini, whose work on *Religious Liberty* has recently been translated into English. They were, with their various writings, the pioneers of a flourishing school of Canon Law which has now been restored to the curriculum of all legal faculties in Italy.

In France researches into Canon Law were directed mainly to the study of the *droit civil ecclésiastique*. Canon Law was not taught at the legal faculties as an independent subject, but was included partly in the *histoire du droit* and in the *droit administratif*.

Among the most valuable contributions of French science to canonistic subjects in modern times we must record the work of Professor Esmein on 'Marriage' (*Le Mariage en droit canonique*, Paris, 1891 sq.), and the different works on canonistic subjects of the *École de hautes études*.

In Austria the old tradition of the study of Canon Law has been kept up at the theological and legal faculties of all the Universities. To the last generation of Austrian canonists belonged Maassen, the author of the great history of the sources of Canon Law in the earlier centuries of the Middle Ages (*Geschichte der Quellen und Literatur des kanonischen Rechtes im Abendlande bis zum Ausgang des Mittelalters*, vol. i., Graz, 1870), and I may point out that one of the most prominent canonists of Austria, Max von Hussareck, is at present Minister for Public Education in Vienna.

In Germany, after the period of the settlement of the *Kulturkampf*, the study of Canon Law, which had received such important assistance from the kindred studies of German law and ecclesiastical history (I need only recall the masterly chapters of Gierke's *Genossenschaftsrecht* dealing with ecclesiastical corporations, and Hauck's *Kirchengeschichte Deutschlands*), seemed for a moment to stagnate as an independent science. It was then that Ulrich Stutz with his *Geschichte des kirchlichen Benefizialwesens von seinen Aufängen bis auf Alexander III.* (Berlin, 1895) marked a new departure in the German studies of Canon Law. With a wider application of historical methods than had previously been made, and with great erudition, Stutz pointed out in a decisive way the importance of proprietary churches in the development of the ecclesiastical institutions of the Middle Ages, and in a series of various studies investigated the different aspects of the private property of churches. His work gave a new impetus to the historical researches on Canon Law.

For the historical study of ecclesiastical institutions Stutz founded in 1902 the collection of *Kirchenrechtliche Abhandlungen* (Stuttgart, Enke), in which have appeared up to the present time no fewer than eighty volumes by different authors, dealing with the most various branches of the historical development of ecclesiastical institutions in different countries, and mainly in Germany.

Those researches, in which scholars of different denominations have taken part, united by that impartiality of scientific investigation, which must be the base of any study of Canon Law worthy of the name of science, have brought into prominence the importance of local elements in Canon Law, and have contributed to the formation of the 'ecclesiastical legal history' advocated by Stutz. His foundation of the *Canonistische Abteilung* of the *Zeitschrift der Savigny-Stiftung* (1911), with contributions by canonists of different nationalities in their own language, has created an international medium of communication for the historical study of Canon Law.

Side by side with this historical investigation of Canon Law has proceeded the study of the strictly legal questions connected in the various countries with ecclesiastical institutions, and what may be called the 'comparative' study of ecclesiastical law, i.e. the study of the ecclesiastical legislation in different States, so that the field of canonistic research has been greatly enlarged in modern times. Besides, a series of historical publications threw new light on ecclesiastical institutions, and in this connexion may be quoted the new *Regesta Pontificum* by Kehr, the great collection of materials on the Council of Trent edited by the *Görresgesellschaft*, and the reports of the Papal Nuncii from different countries published during the last few years by various historical institutes.

At the conclusion of this brief survey of the development of the study of Canon Law, in which of course I have only been able to outline the main current of researches, without including all the individual contributions to the progress of our science, I should like to say a few words on the particular condition of the study of Canon Law in England.

Through the Middle Ages Canon Law had been one of the chief elements of the legal studies in the English Universities, and was the subject of scientific research. In England, as on the Continent, Canon Law was 'one of the great civilizing and humanizing influences of the Middle Ages.' When Henry VIII banished Canon Law from the academical studies of England he dealt a deadly blow to canonistic science in England. Although we can see in the *Ecclesiastical Polity* of Hooker an attempt to give a scientific basis to the legal institutions of the Church of England, Canon Law as an independent science was abandoned, and the legal side of ecclesiastical matters was dealt with mainly from a practical point of view.

And yet perhaps no other country presents so much interest for the study of Ecclesiastical Law as Great Britain, not only on account of the mediaeval elements which are still alive in her ecclesiastical institutions, but also for the variety and magnitude of ecclesiastical questions, so prominent in English public life. We only need to remind ourselves of the question, still *sub judice*, of Welsh Disestablishment and its connexion with innumerable questions of legal history, and we may recall that the 'Royal Commission on the Church of England and other Religious Bodies in Wales and Monmouthshire' of 1906 was obliged to declare the impossibility of proceeding to a legal-historical examination of the ecclesiastical foundations in Wales.

Some parts of Canon Law, in regard to England, have been dealt with in the histories of English Law (for example, by Pollock and Maitland, and Holdsworth), and many valuable contributions to legal history of ecclesiastical institutions in England are contained in local histories and in the historical records of bishoprics, chapters, parishes, etc. Also, among the English works of general interest for canonists, we must remember Phillimore's *Ecclesiastical Law*. Still, it would be most desirable that the study of the legal history of the English ecclesiastical institutions should be taken up in England on a wider, more comprehensive scale, and the results of those investigations would be most important, not only for the legal history of England, but for the history of the development of Canon Law in general.

The interest created by Maitland's book, *Roman Canon Law in England*, showed to a larger public the great importance of the study of Canon Law for England.

I should like, in conclusion, speaking in this old Hall of Lincoln's Inn, so full of ecclesiastical and legal memories, to express the hope that England, the country which has given to international science Lyndwood, Hooker, Stubbs, and Maitland, may revive her old canonistic traditions and take a vigorous share in the modern researches of Canon Law.

ANDREA GALANTE.

## BIBLIOGRAPHICAL NOTE

[Conf. Jacobson, 'Das kanonische und kirchenrechtliche Studium sonst und jetzt, in Italien, Frankreich, in den Niederlanden, Belgien und Deutschland' (*Zeitschrift für Kirchenrecht*, i., 1861); Schulte, 'Über die Bedeutung und Aufgabe des Kirchenrechts' (*Archiv für kathol. Kirchenrecht*, i.); Gross, *Zur Begriffsbestimmung und Würdigung des Kirchenrechts*, Graz, 1872; F. Ruffini, 'Lo Studio e il concetto odierno del diritto ecclesiastico' (*Rivista italiana per le scienze giuridiche*, 1892); Friedberg, *Das canonische Recht und das Kirchenrecht* (*Festrede*), Leipzig, 1896 (printed also in the *Deutsche Zeitschrift für Kirchenrecht*); Stutz, *Die kirchliche Rechtsgeschichte* (*Rede*), Stuttgart, 1905; Galante, 'Diritto ecclesiastico e storia locale' (in the *Reports of the International Historical Congress of Rome*, 1903).]

# XIX

# L'IDÉE DE L'ÉTAT ET SON ÉVOLUTION EN RUSSIE DEPUIS LES TROUBLES DU XVII$^{E}$ SIÈCLE JUSQU'AUX RÉFORMES DU XVIII$^{E}$

CONSIDÉRÉE dans son essence l'idée de l'État est une conception normative : c'est la notion de ce que doit être le rapport entre le souverain et les sujets, et non seulement la notion du pouvoir coercitif que l'État a sur les particuliers. C'est donc dans le sens normatif qu'on lui donnait jadis, d'après les principes d'une civilisation antérieure à la nôtre, que je traiterai de l'idée de l'État et de son évolution en Russie.

Cette évolution a pris une direction qu'il est facile de préciser : au commencement du XVI$^{e}$ siècle l'idée de l'État russe est plutôt religieuse que séculière ; au commencement du XVIII$^{e}$ elle devient plutôt séculière que religieuse. Tout en suivant ce développement dans ses grandes lignes, je ne prétends pas, du reste, en donner ici une exposition complète. Pour y parvenir il ne suffirait pas de noter les théories qui contribuèrent à cette métamorphose ; il faudrait s'arrêter plus longuement, que je n'ai pu le faire, aux institutions et aux évènements qui déterminèrent le cours réel de ces idées en Russie depuis les troubles du XVII siècle jusqu'aux réformes du XVIII$^{e}$.

La conception de la civilisation qu'on se faisait en Europe au moyen âge donnait une préeminence marquée à la religion, telle que l'entendait l'Église chrétienne ; mais pour systématiser les vérités divines concédées aux laïques et les imprégner de sa doctrine elle se servait de la scolastique. Quoique l'Église grecque se soit trouvée dans une position moins propice que l'Église latine pour jouer ce rôle, elle cultiva, pourtant, ces idées non sans succès et contribua à leur propagation dans des pays lointains.

La Russie, qui, sous le rapport clérical, dépendait au moyen âge du patriarche de Constantinople, a naturellement éprouvé cette influence ; mais elle n'en profita qu'avec un grand retard. La *Dialectique* de Jean Damascène, dans laquelle il tâchait d'adapter l'ancienne logique des écoles à la doctrine de l'Église, par exemple, a été traduite en « langue slave », et ses copies russes datent du XV^e^ siècle. L'un des admirateurs de Jean Damascène, déjà effleuré par la Renaissance, Maxime le Grec, préconisait aussi « la logique » en tant qu'elle servait à la gloire de Dieu et enflammait l'âme d'amour pour le Très-Haut, c'est-à-dire en tant qu'elle n'était pas contraire aux paroles divines et se conformait à elles.[1] En suivant ces règles, l'Église grecque pouvait mettre à profit même la scolastique latine : Maxime le Grec n'en était pas exempt ; les érudits de Kiev, tels que Stéfan Javorskij, par exemple, en usèrent largement dans leurs travaux.

Une doctrine analogue ne tarda pas à se former en Russie dans le domaine des idées morales et politiques, soumises, elles aussi, aux dogmes de l'Église : c'est du sein de l'Église grecque que sont sortis les premiers doctrinaires de l'État russe, et c'est du point de vue orthodoxe ou « pravoslave », et en conformité avec plusieurs idées byzantines, notamment avec celle du *basileus*, vicaire orthodoxe de Dieu et autocrate, régnant par le Christ qui l'inspire et le guide, qu'ils formulaient les principes de cet État.

L'idée religieuse de l'État formée à Byzance était déjà quelque peu connue en Russie à l'époque de Vladimir le Saint et de ses successeurs ; mais elle ne s'est développée qu'en Moscovie. Bien des circonstances contribuèrent à son développement, particulièrement celles qui, dans leur ensemble, produisirent la décadence de l'Empire byzantin et la formation de l'État moscovite,

[1] Іоаннъ Дамаскинъ, *Діалектика*, рус. пер., М. 1862, pp. 9, 10, 104, 106-107, 108 ; cf. А. Соболевскій, *Переводная литература Московской Руси*, 2 изд., СПБ., 1903, pp. 20, 281. Максимъ Грекъ, *Сочиненія*, Каз., 1859–1862, i. pp. 462-464.

de son unité et de son indépendance ; mais en considérant la portée subséquente de ces théories, c'est plutôt leurs principes que leur genèse qu'il importe de noter.

L'une d'elles, celle de Philophée du couvent d'Éléazar, développait une thèse que le métropolite Zocime avait déjà avancée en 1492. Philophée la formulait au point de vue religieux et providentiel, basé sur les Saintes Écritures : toutes ses épîtres sont imbues de l'idée de la Providence, grâce à laquelle tout ce qui arrive dans l'univers n'arrive que par la volonté de Dieu, Créateur de toutes choses, et pour le bien de l'humanité. C'est à ce point de vue, renforcé par les allégories de l'Apocalypse, que Philophée écrivit ses épîtres au grand duc Basile III et au tsar Jean IV : il y propose, de même que dans son épître au clerc Mounékhine, sa doctrine sur le déplacement providentiel du centre de la chrétienneté de Rome à Byzance, et de Byzance à Moscou, où il s'est fixé définitivement, et sur la mission providentielle de ce nouveau foyer du monde pravoslave. C'est de cette mission qu'il déduit le rôle historique désigné par Dieu à l'État moscovite, comme centre de réunion des divers royaumes de la chrétienneté pravoslave ; les prérogatives de l'élu de Dieu—du tsar, unique représentant du pouvoir, qui doit observer et maintenir les traditions pravoslaves dans l'Orient chrétien, ses devoirs et ses droits envers ses sujets, etc.[1]

La théorie de Philophée n'était pas dénuée de grandeur : au point de vue orthodoxe ou pravoslave on pouvait l'appliquer aux relations internationales et au régime intérieur ; mais elle ne développait pas les principes de gouvernement et de sujétion ; c'est dans des doctrines plus spéciales qu'on pouvait trouver ces développements.

Une théorie, basée sur l'orthodoxie la plus stricte et visiblement influencée par les idées byzantines—celle de Joseph Sanine—considérait, par exemple, le tsar comme l'élu de Dieu et le gardien suprême de l'orthodoxie, et en déduisait ses devoirs et ses droits, de même que sa responsabilité envers Dieu. L'abbé de Wolokolamsk comparait le pouvoir du tsar à celui de Dieu, et parlait de l'obéissance que lui devaient ses sujets comme de celle qui se pratique envers Dieu ou dans les cloîtres ; pour prouver ses thèses

[1] В. Малининъ, *Старецъ Елеазарова монастыря Филоѳей и его посланія*, Кіевъ, 1901 г., Прил., pp. 36-66.

il s'en rapportait, entre autres, à l'autorité des empereurs byzantins, notamment à celle de Constantin et de Justinien.[1]

Une théorie moins rigoureuse, développée par Maxime le Grec, introduisait les éléments de la justice ou de la *prawda* particulièrement dans le domaine de la juridiction. Comme St-Thomas d'Acquin, il distingue les vertus théologiques des vertus morales et place à leur tête la vertu de la justice (*justitia*) ou de la *prawda*. Quoique Maxime le Grec n'ait pas donné de définition du concept de la *prawda*, qu'il considère tantôt au point de vue religieux et métaphysique, tantôt au point de vue de la morale chrétienne, il en déduit les devoirs et les droits du souverain, particulièrement dans le domaine de la juridiction : le prince doit observer la *prawda* et la défendre dans ses cours de justice, ce qui mène à la «paix intérieure et à la force extérieure». Le prince qui plaide la cause de la *prawda* règne conjointement avec Dieu, «qui est Justice,» et ne gouverne que comme son intermédiaire ; cela donne à son pouvoir un éclat surnaturel et une puissance morale, et lui réserve le droit d'exiger la soumission absolue de ses sujets.[2]

Les doctrines de Philophée, de Joseph et de Maxime que ces derniers énoncaient, d'ailleurs, non sans réserves, ont joui d'une grande popularité parmi les lettrés moscovites : le tsar Jean IV lui-même en a largement profité ; elles ont certainement subi quelques développements et quelques modifications postérieures; mais elles n'ont pas été supplantées à cette époque par d'autres systèmes. Jean Péresvjétov, par exemple, avait certainement donné une conception différente de l'autorité «redoutable» du souverain envers ses sujets et avait indiqué, de même qu'Ostrorog, quelques problèmes que l'État moderne devait résoudre : il reconnaissait l'importance du principe «à chacune selon ses œuvres» et la nécessité des lois écrites; il proposait d'abolir les offices héréditaires et de rémunérer les fonctionnaires ; il insistait sur l'organisation des

[1] Іосифъ Волоцкій, *Просвѣтитель*, Каз. 1896, 3 éd., pp. 488, 544-551 ; pour les restrictions que Joseph Sanine faisait, en parlant des rois hérétiques, voir *ib.* pp. 286-288, et М. Дьяконовъ, *Власть Московскихъ Государей*, СПБ., 1899, pp. 26, 95, 103.

[2] Максимъ Грекъ, *Сочиненія*, v. i. pp. 142, 385, v. ii. pp. 152, 157-184, 209, 210, 286, 319-357, v. iii. p. 237, etc. D'ailleurs, quelques éléments de cette théorie se trouvent déjà dans *Le Discours sur la justice et l'injustice* de l'Ismaragde «de la 2^e rédaction» (xv. sc.); mais ils n'y sont pas développés systématiquement.

finances et de l'armée. Malgré la haute portée de ses idées, les projets de Péresvjétov ne reçurent pas la notoriété dont jouissaient les théories de Philophée et de ses émules : celles-ci ont prévalu au XVI^e siècle et ont été transmises au XVII^e.

Cependant ces doctrines «pravoslaves» sur l'État ne donnaient qu'une idée transcendante du rapport entre le souverain et les sujets ; elles s'exposaient, en outre, à quelques restrictions de la part des partisans zélés de l'Église, qui rehaussaient l'autorité spirituelle et réclamaient l'obéissance du monarque aux admonitions de ses représentants ; elles ne s'accordaient pas avec les serments que quelques-uns des tsars devaient prêter aux bojares à l'époque des troubles ; elles ne prévoyaient pas le rôle que devaient jouer les assemblées des états (*semskii ssobory*) au commencement du XVII^e siècle.

Il est vrai qu'au temps des troubles les Russes éprouvèrent le sentiment de la différence qu'il y a entre l'État et la forme du gouvernement ; mais ils avaient alors des raisons pour croire que l'État moscovite ne pouvait conserver son unité et sa force qu'en restant fidèle aux formes traditionnelles du gouvernement : le tsar Mihaïl Fédorovicz trouva un appui dans les états généraux pour rétablir l'ordre dans le pays, et les théories anciennes continuèrent à y circuler, même dans la seconde moitié du XVII^e siècle.

Le tsar Alexej Mihajlovicz, par exemple, usait volontiers de ces théories, sans y apporter, du reste, de changements essentiels ; néanmoins il accepta la disposition que le concile de 1667 avait prise et qui consistait à conserver au monarque son autorité suprême dans les affaires de l'État, tout en la réservant au patriarche dans les affaires de l'Église ; mais, après la déposition de Nicone, ce dédoublement du pouvoir ne pouvait durer : il portait atteinte à l'unité de l'État et fut définitivement aboli par Pierre le Grand.

Ce n'est qu'indirectement—par l'introduction de la scolastique, à laquelle le tsar Alexej Mihajlovicz avait accordé sa protection, que ces théories «pravoslaves» ont reçu leurs compléments dans les idées, sorties du sein des collèges des jésuites, dont le réseau couvrait déjà la plus grande partie de la Pologne.

Comme je l'ai remarqué plus haut, la religion orthodoxe grecque n'interdisait pas l'usage de la scolastique latine : et c'est justement pour défendre les droits de l'Église pravoslave qu'on en usa à Kiev ; mais la scolastique latine, qu'on transplantait des collèges des jésuites polonais à Kiev, et de Kiev à Moscou, contenait quelques principes de morale et de droit qui, de cette manière, pénétrèrent dans le milieu des lettrés moscovites.

Ces principes se reliaient, au fond, à la doctrine de St-Thomas d'Acquin, et, par son intermédiaire, à quelques idées d'Aristote ; ils caractérisaient en Moscovie l'époque de transition de l'idée religieuse à l'idée séculière de l'État.

L'un des lettrés moscovites de ce temps-là, Siméon Polotzkij, par exemple, s'en tenait à cette doctrine mixte. Il rattachait les origines de l'État et du pouvoir souverain non seulement à la volonté divine, mais à la tendance naturelle qu'ont les hommes à s'assembler en societé : les hommes, les cités et les royaumes dépendent réciproquement les uns des autres dans les choses matérielles et spirituelles ; ils éprouvent aussi le besoin de sécurité qui les pousse à se donner un chef, car une société sans chef tend à sa ruine. Il se représentait le souverain non seulement comme celui qui « mène ses sujets aux vertus divines», mais comme celui qui vaque à leur « bien commun » ; il présumait que le prince doit régner non seulement d'après les préceptes de la vertu, de la *prawda*, mais aussi d'après les principes de la justice distributive et commutative, qu'il distinguait, selon un schéma assez répandu dans les manuels de ce temps-là, de la justice vindicative. En développant ces principes Siméon Polotzkij donnait une espèce de *speculum principis christiani*, dans lequel on peut trouver quelques règles analogues à celles d'Agapithe le diacre dans son Ἔκθεσις κεφαλαίων παραινετικῶν et entrevoir, peut-être, quelque influence du traité *De regimine principum*, particulièrement dans les restrictions du pouvoir temporel en faveur du pouvoir spirituel que Siméon Polotzkij fait plutôt sous-entendre que formuler ouvertement.[1]

[1] Симеонъ Полоцкій, *Записки*, MS. de la Bibliothèque de la Typographie du Synode à Moscou, N° 1791, 4078, ff. 199 *sq.* ; *Вертоградъ Многоцвѣтный*, MS. conservé au département des manuscrits de la Bibliothèque de l'Académie Impériale des Sciences de St-Pétersbourg, N° 19, Préface, ff. 57v.-58v., 90v., 306v.-308v., 363v., 375-375v., 466v.-477. Le moine Siméon Polotzkij avait fait ses études à Kiev et au collège des jésuites de Wilno ; il s'établit à Moscou, probablement en 1663. Les notes qu'il avait prises au collège de Wilno, d'un cours de morale, c'est-à-dire de « monastique », « d'économique » et de « politique », qu'il y avait suivi, le recueil de pièces qu'il a intitulé *Le Jardin multiflore* (« Vertograd Mnogozwetnij ») et différents autres écrits prouvent qu'il s'était quelque peu familiarisé avec les doctrines de St-Thomas d'Acquin et d'Aristote. Cf., d'ailleurs, p. 359 note 1.

Ces théories ont été reprises par l'un des plus fervents élèves de Siméon Polotzkij, grand amateur de la scolastique et quelque peu connaisseur d'Aristote—par Silvestre Médvédjév; mais la doctrine de la justice n'a reçu des développements sensibles que dans les cours de théologie calqués sur la *Somme* de St-Thomas d'Acquin.

En effet, on distinguait, d'après la *Somme*, les vertus morales des vertus théologiques et on y comprenait la prudence, la justice, la vaillance et la tempérance; mais on considérait la prudence comme une vertu intermédiaire entre les vertus théologiques et morales, ce qui permettait de placer la justice à la tête des vertus morales; et on en traitait conjointement avec le droit.

C'est donc grâce aux cours de théologie, et particulièrement à leur partie intitulée *de jure et justitia*, que les notions juridiques commencèrent à s'infiltrer dans notre littérature.

L'un des représentants les plus caractéristiques de cette conception fut certainement un professeur de théologie à l'académie de Kiev, qui y lisait, en 1696–1697, un cours contenant un *tractatus theologicus de justitia.* L'auteur, selon toute apparence Stéfan Javorskij, donne dans son traité la définition de la justice autrefois formulée par Ulpien et reçue par St-Thomas d'Acquin, et tâche d'établir sur ce principe le rapport du souverain et des sujets.

Stéfan Javorskij délibère sur la justice commutative et distributive d'après Aristote, St-Thomas d'Acquin et quelques auteurs scolastiques plus récents; mais il admet, en outre, une distinction postérieure, quoique déjà inclue dans la *Somme*, de la justice légale et de la justice vindicative, notions qu'il pouvait puiser, par exemple, dans le traité de son confrère polonais Mlodzianowskij.

D'après cette théorie la justice commutative règle les rapports privés des hommes, les autres justices—les rapports réciproques du souverain et des sujets.

En effet, la justice distributive fixe les devoirs de la communauté (*communitas*) envers les personnes privées: elle établit ce à quoi chacune d'elles a droit, comme membre de la communauté. La justice légale fixe les devoirs des personnes privées envers la communauté—ce que chacune d'elles doit faire pour le bien commun de la communauté dont elle est membre; ce *nexus* légal est une sujétion formelle, si celui qui devient membre de la communauté exprime consciemment sa volonté d'en faire partie, ou reste traditionnel, s'il ne fait qu'admettre sa sujétion, dont l'acte a été accompli antérieurement par ceux qui ont été admis par la communauté et reconnu par elle. Donc, chaque sujet doit veiller au bien commun (*respicere bonum commune titulo nexus ad communitatem*). D'ailleurs, les devoirs de la communauté ou de ses membres deviennent respectivement des droits ; la communauté, par exemple, possède le pouvoir, fondé sur le *nexus* légal et sur la loi naturelle (*firmata lege naturali*), c'est-à-dire le droit d'exiger des citoyens le sacrifice de leur bien et même de leur vie pour la chose publique.

A l'instar de la justice distributive et de la justice légale, la justice vindicative a en vue l'intérêt de la communauté, mais elle le préserve, en en écartant le mal (*nocumentum*) par des peines qu'elle inflige à ceux qui les méritent ; elle les inflige « honnêtement » pour prévenir les dommages, ou pour punir ceux qui les ont occasionnés.

Comme on le voit, Stéfan Javorskij remonte aux principes de l'État, fondés sur la justice ; et c'est déjà en combinaison avec le droit naturel qu'il l'applique au régime des personnes et des biens ; il en traite non sans l'influence de St-Thomas d'Acquin et d'autres théologiens, par exemple, de Becanus. D'après cette théorie, les hommes, de par leur nature (*ex natura*), sont tous également libres : l'homme ne peut être [naturellement] l'esclave d'un autre homme ; mais il peut le devenir grâce au droit des gens, s'il est fait prisonnier dans une guerre juste ou en vertu de la loi positive (*lex positiva*) ; il peut aussi devenir esclave de son propre gré. De même la propriété n'est pas fondée sur le droit naturel, mais sur le droit des gens (*ius gentium*), c'est-à-dire sur le consentement des hommes, qui divisèrent les biens. Du reste, cette division correspondait aux exigences de la raison, et en ce sens au droit naturel : car l'homme a plus de soin de son propre bien que du bien commun, et dans l'état primitif chacun pouvait défendre aux autres d'user du bien commun, ce qui devenait une source de collisions perpétuelles, qu'on ne pouvait faire cesser que par la division des biens.

Il m'est impossible d'entrer dans les développements que donne Stéfan Javorskij de ces principes : il délibère, de même que Mlodzianowski, sur « l'objet » et le « sujet » de la justice ; il disserte, pareillement à Becanus, sur les applications des principes de la justice commutative et de la justice vindicative aux « cas juridiques », et traite, dans sa *Casuistique* des donations, des testaments et des contrats ; des devoirs du juge, de « l'accusateur », des témoins et du coupable ; des arrêts judiciaires, de la restitution des droits, etc.

J'espère tout de même que les remarques que j'ai faites suffisent pour conclure que Stéfan Javorskij donne dans son cours de théologie une espèce de traité systématique de jurisprudence générale, de provenance scolastique, mais d'une assez large portée : il commence à appliquer les principes du droit naturel du moyen âge dans le domaine du droit civil, mais ne s'en rapporte pas à ce droit dans celui du droit public et n'y remonte presque pas pour en déduire le rapport du souverain et des sujets.[1] Ce que je voudrais noter encore c'est que ces idées commençaient à s'infiltrer dans la pratique : la législation moscovite du temps du tsar Féodor Alexejévicz n'y était pas tout à fait étrangère. Le célèbre oukase de 1682 (janv. 12, v.s.) sur l'abolition des droits de rang et de préséance des familles nobles, c'est-à-dire du *mjestniczestvo*, en porte les traces. Dans l'allocution que le tsar avait adressée aux états assemblés, et qui a été inclue dans l'acte de l'abolition, il disait qu'il avait reçu son sceptre de la main de Dieu pour prendre soin de tout ce qui concerne le « bien commun » et d'écarter tout ce qui lui porte atteinte ; c'est de ce point de vue qu'il abolissait le *mjestniczestvo*, comme nuisible « au bien commun de l'État ».[2]

Comme on le voit, le tsar Féodor Alexejévicz avait déjà quelque notion théorique du « bien commun de l'État » ; il l'érigeait en principe de sa réforme, et lui donnait une valeur qu'il n'a acquise définitivement qu'aux temps de Pierre le Grand.

L'idée religieuse de l'État en Russie a donc subi une évolution, grâce à laquelle elle se reliait à l'idée séculière de l'État.

Plusieurs autres facteurs ont contribué à cette sécularisation ; je n'en relèverai ici que ceux qui ont influé plus ou moins directement sur l'évolution de nos idées politiques du XVIIe siècle.

D'abord, c'est le mouvement littéraire issu du milieu des judaïsants.

[1] *Tractatus theologici collegio Kiiowo-Mohileano traditi et explicati, Tractatus de iustitia*, MS. de la Kievo-Petcherskaja Lawra, N° vii. 40.

[2] *Собраніе госуд. грам. и дог.*, P. iv. N° 130 ; cf. *Пол. Собр. Зак.*, t. ii. N° 905, pp. 373-374.

Les judaïsants (*żidowstwoujouchczii*) ont joué en Russie au XVe-XVIe siècles un rôle analogue à celui des averroïstes du XIIIe : ils nous ont donné une logique et une politique, inclue dans le traité *Secreta secretorum.* Ce traité a été probablement connu en Russie dans une version juive (et non pas arabe ou latine), rédigée en Allemagne : c'est de là qu'elle a pu être importée dans la Russie de l'Ouest et se propager en Moscovie.

Les *Secreta secretorum*, faussement attribués à Aristote, ont, certes, un caractère médiéval fort prononcé : ils ne sont pas dénuées de superstitions, proposent toutes sortes de conseils sur l'utilité de l'astrologie, sur les propriétés miraculeuses ou salutaires des pierres précieuses et des plantes, etc.; mais ils contiennent aussi quelques principes plus rationnels que ceux qui avaient habituellement cours dans notre littérature du XVIe siècle. Les *Secreta secretorum* prônent, par exemple, les principes de la raison, grâce à laquelle les païens même ont pu connaître et établir quelques règles de justice et d'honnêteté utiles à l'ordre public. Les *Secreta secretorum* introduisent ces principes rationnels dans la politique : elle aussi doit être fondée sur la raison et sur la justice qui en découle ; c'est d'après ces principes que le prince doit gouverner ses sujets.

L'occultisme des *Secreta secretorum* présentait, probablement, beaucoup plus d'intérêt pour nos lecteurs que leur rationalisme, ce qui explique, probablement, leur propagation en Russie : nous n'en connaissons pas moins de dix copies, dont deux appartiennent même au XVIIIe siècle.[1]

D'ailleurs, outre ce mouvement collatéral, il est facile de constater que la Renaissance et la Réforme ont certainement influé sur l'évolution de l'idée séculière de l'État en Russie.

C'est grâce à l'influence de la Renaissance que la « philosophie pratique » s'est quelque peu différenciée de la religion et a commencé à servir de base plus indépendante aux théories politiques.

Du reste, les humanistes du XVIe siècle, tels que l'écrivain polonais Petricij, par exemple, se représentaient la philosophie

[1] *Aristotelis philosophorum maximi Secretum Secretorum ad Alexandrum de regum regimine, etc.*; j'avais à ma portée l'édition : Bononiae, 1516, de la Bibliothèque royale de Dresde ; l'ancienne traduction russe a été publiée par M. Spéranskij ; v. M. Сперанскiй, *Аристотелевы Врата*, *Пам. Древ. Письм. и Искус.*, N° clxxi. СПБ., 1908.

pratique dans un schéma qu'Aristote avait déjà admis dans ses ouvrages, et qui était depuis longtemps reçu dans la scolastique. Ils y distinguaient trois parties : la première traitait de la morale individuelle, en général (*monastica seu solitaria*) ; la seconde—des règles de la vie domestique (*economica seu domestica*) ; la troisième —des principes de la vie en commun, politique ou civile (*politica seu civilis*).

Ces diverses parties, qui survivent encore dans le système de Chr. Wolf, se retrouvent dans notre littérature du XVII^e^ siècle.

Il est vrai qu'elle n'est pas originale, et qu'elle ne fait que reproduire des traductions ou des ouvrages polonais, par exemple, le *Désidérius*, dialogue sur l'amour de Dieu, écrit par un catholique, mais dans un esprit mystique de morale individuelle ; l'*Économique* d'Aristote, interprétée par Petricij, les préceptes que Lorichius proposait aux princes et autres « chefs », etc.[1] Tous ces traités ont été traduits en russe d'une manière assez satisfaisante ; mais ces traductions ne sont pas toujours de fidèles reproductions des originaux. La traduction des *Loci communes* de Lorichius, par exemple, ne contient, pour la plupart, que des règles pratiques concernant l'éducation du « chef », et des « moyens secrets et astucieux » qu'il a à sa disposition pour gouverner ses sujets.

Je ne ferais qu'indiquer ici en passant que plusieurs idées sur les principes du gouvernement se trouvent encore dans des dissertations, d'ailleurs aussi peu originales, sur les causes de la décadence des empires, par exemple, dans une compilation de Ssadowskij, contenant quelques idées d'Aristote et d'autres auteurs sur la matière, notamment de Chokier, etc. Cette compilation a subi au moins deux rédactions, et fut assez prisée par nos lecteurs du XVII^e^ et du commencement du XVIII^e^ siècle.

Quoique la réforme n'ait pas eu le temps de s'affermir en Pologne et d'y jeter des racines plus ou moins profondes, elle a

[1] *Espejo de Religiosos*, Burgos, J. Junta, 1548 ; trad. latine de 1616 (*Desiderosus, dialogus . . de expedita ad Dei amorem vita*) ; trad. polonaise de G. Wilkowskij, 1589 (beaucoup de rééditions) ; trad. russe du moine Théophane du monastère du Miracle de l'archange Michel, faite en 1688 et imprimée à Moscou en 1785. S. Petrici, *Oekonomiki Aristotelesowej . . . księgi dwoje*, 2 éd. Krak., 1618 ; trad. russe au Musée public de Roumjanzev à Moscou, N° 627, R. Lorichius, *Loci communes de institutione principum*, Marburg, 1558 ; trad. polonaise, Crac., 1558 ; trad. russe, MS. appartenant au monastère « Florichtcheva Poustyń », N° 138/712.

eu quelque influence sur plusieurs hommes de lettres polonais, par exemple sur Frycz (Modrzevskij), auteur du fameux traité de la République.

Frycz a passé plusieurs années à étudier les lettres dans les centres protestants de la civilisation allemande, à Wittemberg et à Nuremberg, et est entré en relations personnelles avec Mélanchthon et ses collègues; cela a eu quelque influence sur son ouvrage. L'auteur du traité de la République reste, il est vrai, catholique, mais il veut profiter de quelques idées promues par la Réforme, pour réorganiser le monde catholique et l'État.

Grâce à cette largeur de vues Frycz a pu introduire dans sa politique non seulement les idées d'Aristote, mais les premiers éléments du droit naturel, élaboré principalement par les écrivains protestants, entre autres par Mélanchthon et ses émules. Frycz y raisonne sur l'égalité naturelle des hommes (du moins sous quelques rapports), et en déduit que l'exemption des nobles de la peine de mort appliquée aux classes rurales est injuste; il y démontre que les principes de cette justice doivent servir de fondement aux mœurs et aux lois; il y recherche les origines de l'État, et le relie (non sans quelques inconséquences) à l'acte de translation du pouvoir que les hommes ont remis (*deferebant*) à celui qu'ils estimaient le plus prudent et le plus juste, « se soumettant ainsi non pas à l'homme, mais à la raison, c'est-à-dire, à la loi naturelle . . . »; il y proclame, en conséquence de ces principes, que le pouvoir du roi est établi pour le bonheur de ses sujets, qu'il est soumis aux lois de même que ses sujets, que la loi doit être équitable pour tous, que (d'après une théorie chère à Cicéron) le gouvernement mixte est le meilleur, etc.

C'est dans l'édition polonaise de 1577 du traité de Frycz qu'on peut trouver le développement de toutes ces idées (excepté le livre sur l'Église); la traduction russe du traité, faite d'après cette édition et presque complète, est l'une des meilleures que nous possédons en ce genre; elle remonte probablement au XVII^e^ siècle; quoique elle ne soit connue que d'après une copie du XVIII^e^, et porte les traces d'un remaniement postérieur.[1]

[1] Andreae Fricii Modrevij *Commentariorum de Republica emendanda libri quinque*, 1 éd. (incomplète) Crac. Laz. 1551; je me suis servi de l'édition de Basileae, 1554; traduction polonaise, édition de 1577, *drukowano w Losku*, avec des additions; le MS. de la traduction russe, faite probablement du polonais, se trouve dans la collection de manuscrits du Comte Ouvaroff, N° 790. Le livre *De Ecclesia* est omis dans les traductions latine et russe.

Il est donc possible de conclure, que la Renaissance, et même la Réforme, ont eu quelque influence sur nos idées politiques par l'intermédiaire de la Pologne ; mais les idées essentielles de la Réforme, et la littérature postérieure qui se rapportait au droit naturel et à la jurisprudence pratique, nous sont parvenues grâce aux relations directes de la Russie avec l'Europe, et principalement avec l'Europe protestante.

C'est justement cette tendance qui a trouvé un adversaire décidé dans la personne de Crižanicz, émule de Possevin et partisan secret de l'Église grecque unie.

Crižanicz puise ses principes presque exclusivement dans la civilisation catholique : il n'est pas exempt des traditions scolastiques ; même dans ses thèses politiques il s'en rapporte plutôt à St-Thomas d'Acquin qu'à Aristote, aime mieux Bellarmin que Mariana, et préfère Juste Lipse à Paruta et Botero à Bodin. Crižanicz voulait inoculer cette culture aux peuples slaves, et particulièrement aux moscovites ; il pensait que la monarchie était la forme de gouvernement la plus propice à la propagande des idées qu'il s'était décidé à introduire en Russie.

Relativement à la fin religieuse, que Crižanicz se proposait d'atteindre, son traité politique n'était qu'un moyen, par lequel il croyait pouvoir gagner les bonnes grâces du tsar, en lui disant des choses « utiles et agréables ». C'est pourquoi il se gardait bien d'y toucher aux matières religieuses et cléricales, et donnait ainsi à son contenu un caractère séculier.

D'ailleurs, ce caractère se renforçait par la tendance nationaliste que Crižanicz recommandait aux peuples slaves et aux moscovites, en particulier dans leur politique séculière.

Quant au rapport entre le souverain et les sujets, Crižanicz préfère se le représenter sous la forme d'une monarchie absolue, qu'il reconnaît, de même que Juste Lipse, comme la meilleure forme de gouvernement—celle qui doit donner le plus de forces à la nation ; mais en distinguant la monarchie légitime, instituée par Dieu, de la tyrannie, il admet tout de même une espèce de pacte entre le monarque et ses sujets qui les garantit des excès de son pouvoir. A la manière de Faust d'Aschaffenburg, qui dissertait assez longuement sur le *iuramentum subiectionis*, Crižanicz parle des « serments » ou des « promesses », que le souverain et les sujets se prêtent ou se donnent mutuellement, mais sans leur attribuer la valeur supplémentaire d'obligations naturelles : ces serments consistent en ce que le monarque jure au peuple qu'il accomplira ses devoirs et prendra soin du bien commun, et que ses héritiers, à leur couronnement, en feront de même ; et que le peuple jure, à son tour, après le monarque, de lui être obéissant et fidèle. Tout en pensant que le pouvoir monarchique «légitime» avait été institué par Dieu, ne fusse que par l'intermédiaire du peuple, et que le monarque n'était responsable qu'à Dieu, les hommes n'ayant pas le droit de le juger et de le punir, Crižanicz ne croit pas pouvoir appliquer ces principes sans quelques restrictions : il les formule, probablement non sans l'influence des théories de quelques-uns de ses confrères sur la souveraineté du peuple dans les choses temporelles ; il trouve que cette sujétion a des bornes : elle peut être enfreinte, si le monarque, malgré ses promesses, devient un hérétique, ou livre son pays au pouvoir des étrangers, de même que s'il se transforme en tyran, que Dieu peut punir par l'intermédiaire du peuple ; elle ne subsiste plus envers l'étranger, qui s'est emparé du pouvoir. Dans ces cas-là le peuple peut se choisir un autre monarque, avec lequel il échange de nouvelles promesses ou de nouveaux serments.[1]

Du reste Crižanicz n'a pas réussi à obtenir la confiance et le crédit qu'il voulait acquérir auprès du tsar, et à entraver la propagation des idées nouvelles sur l'État, même en Moscovie. Une illustration assez curieuse de l'infiltration de ces idées, ou plutôt des écrits qui les contenaient, nous présente la bibliothèque d'un hollandais russifié—André Vinius.

Le djak moscovite André Vinius s'était établi à Moscou, mais il avait conservé des relations avec son pays natal, nommément avec Witsen, le docte bourguemestre d'Amsterdam.

Vinius était un grand amateur de livres : sa bibliothèque présentait un assortiment d'ouvrages assez variés, mais choisis non sans quelque discernement ; elle contenait, par exemple, des écrits sur la religion, la philosophie, les belles-lettres, le droit, etc. ; parmi les

[1] J. Crižanicz, *Razgowori ob wladátelstwu*, MS. de la Bibliothèque de la Typographie du Synode à Moscou, N° 1799/4307, ff. 338, 345, 744-745, 778, etc. ; texte publié par Bezssonov, v. i. pp. 276-278, 281, 310 *sq.*, 331, 334, 402 *sq.* ; v. ii. pp. 29 *sq.*, 49-80, 168-169, 239-240, etc. Voir aussi la notice de 1641, le rapport de Crižanicz à Levakovicz de 1646–1647 et quelques autres documents, publiés par M. Bjelokourov ; v. С. Бѣлокуровъ, *Изъ духовный жизни Московскаго Общества xvii. в.*, M. 1903, pp. 87-126, 144, 173-179, etc.

ouvrages sur la jurisprudence et la politique prédominaient ceux qui se rapportaient principalement à la littérature hollandaise et allemande du XVI^e-XVII^e siècles. On pouvait y trouver quelques traités concernant le droit naturel, par exemple, celui de Grotius *De jure belli ac pacis* et les *Annotata* de son antagoniste a Felde; les *Enarrationes* de Kling et le *Richterbüchelein* (Gerichtsbüchelein) de Vigel, tous deux ayant quelque rapport au droit naturel, et même le programme du cours sur la jurisprudence que Thomasius lisait en 1699 à Halle. On pouvait y rencontrer aussi quelques manuels relatifs à la jurisprudence allemande pratique, par exemple, le *Viridarium juridicum* de Gilhausen, la *Synopsis politicarum doctrinarum* de Besoldus, etc.[1]

La présence de ces ouvrages dans la bibliothèque du djak moscovite, qui devint l'un des collaborateurs de Pierre le Grand, peut servir d'indice des intérêts qui commençaient à poindre: dans ce temps-là l'idée séculière de l'État s'introduisait déjà en Moscovie; en somme, sa théorie se reliait au droit naturel, mais elle ne s'est affermie dans les esprits que grâce à la sécularisation ultérieure de l'idée de l'État, promue par la doctrine de l'intérêt de l'État et manifestée dans le *Polizeistaat.*

L'idée utilitaire de l'État a traversé, du reste, une période de transition avant d'acquérir le caractère foncièrement séculier et politique qui lui est propre.

En effet on peut indiquer, au XVII^e siècle et au commencement du XVIII^e, quelques doctrines mixtes, orthodoxes et utilitaires; par exemple, celles d'Ordine-Nachtchokine et de Possochkov.

Ordine-Nachtchokine, homme d'État éminent du temps d'Alexej Mihajlovicz, professait, par exemple, une doctrine dans laquelle les concepts de Moscou, comme centre du monde pravoslave et de la *prawda*, se combinaient avec le concept du profit du souverain (*gossoudarevo djelo*), qu'il identifiait avec le profit de l'État (*gossoudastwennyja djela*). C'est au point de vue utilitaire, et non seulement religieux qu'Ordine-Nachtchokine préfère, par exemple, la monarchie au régime républicain qui produit «toutes sortes d'erreurs et de perturbations»; c'est au même point de vue qu'il

[1] Catalogue de la bibliothèque d'André Vinius, MS. de la Bibliothèque Impériale des Sciences de St-Pétersbourg, N° xxi/a3; transcriptions russes dans «le Cabinet de Pierre le Grand», Archives de l'Etat, Вход. N° 42, ff. 37-70, et N° 92, ff. 321-357.

considère les rapports du souverain et des sujets, qu'il exige plus d'indépendance pour les pouvoirs intermédiaires et plus d'initiative dans le *self-government* des villes, qu'il recommande l'introduction de plusieurs institutions européennes, etc.

Ordine-Nachtchokine n'était pas le seul à émettre de ces idées : on pourrait trouver un mélange analogue dans les ouvrages de Possochkov.

La doctrine de l'intérêt de l'État commençait même en ce temps-là à se différencier des autres : Vinius, qui est probablement l'auteur d'un curieux projet sur les établissements de charité, y expose quelques-uns de ses éléments : au point de vue « du profit du souverain », qu'il entend principalement dans le sens mercantile, et du bien commun, il exige que les sujets s'instruisent et travaillent « pour ne pas manger en vain leur pain quotidien ». En lisant ce projet on dirait que c'est Pierre le Grand qui parle : en tout cas, il s'est très bien assimilé cette conception utilitaire de l'État, et a grandement contribué à son affermissement.[1]

Pierre le Grand ne pouvait, évidemment, rompre avec les anciennes traditions moscovites : dans ses ordonnances et autres écrits il cite les théories du tsar et de l'état pravoslaves, et mentionne le principe de la *prawda*, particulièrement dans ses applications à la justice ; mais c'est une idée séculière et utilitaire, celle de l'intérêt de l'État, qu'il prône le plus souvent.

C'est bien la conception de l'intérêt de l'État, intimement liée à celle de la « police », et non pas la notion étroite de la « raison d'État », que Pierre le Grand admet pour principe de sa politique.

Cette idée, effleurée par Seckendorff, précurseur des policéistes du XVIII$^{e}$ siècle, s'était déjà incorporée dans la « monarchie absolue » de Louis XIV et se pratiquait par Colbert ; elle se développait en Prusse dans le *Polizeistaat*, particulièrement depuis l'ordonnance du roi Frédéric Guillaume I$^{er}$ du 2 juin 1713 ; elle n'était pas tout à fait étrangère aux hommes d'État russes du XVII$^{e}$ siècle ; et c'est plutôt de la pratique que de la théorie, peu élaborée d'ailleurs, que Pierre le Grand a naturellement puisé l'idée utilitaire de l'État.

Pierre le Grand en a même fait le principe dominant de son système, et s'en rapportait à ce principe, conforme à sa nature active

[1] *Объ общественномъ призрѣніи въ Россіи*, изд. при Министерствѣ Юстиціи А. Стогомъ, СПБ., 1818 г., P. i. pp. 31-39.

et à son goût novateur, pour motiver la plupart de ses réformes. Le tsar ne distinguait pas le « profit (*polza*) du souverain » du « profit de l'État », et identifiait ces concepts avec ceux de l'intérêt de l'État ; le règlement général des collèges, par exemple, explique ce qu'il faut entendre par ce terme : « l'intêret » — c'est le « profit ou l'utilité » du souverain et de l'État.[1]

D'après ce principe le tsar et son gouvernement devait prendre soin du bien-être de la population, utile à l'État ; c'est en vue de « l'utilité commune » qu'il devait légiférer, gouverner, policer, protéger et juger ses sujets ; d'autre part, les sommations du pouvoir, dont il disposait envers ses sujets, devenaient d'autant plus irréfragables, qu'ils se proféraient au nom de ce principe ; les sujets lui devaient une obéissance incontestable.

Cependant, tout en renforçant les traditions du pouvoir autocratique qu'il avait la possibilité d'exercer sans contrainte, Pierre le Grand ne pouvait considérer l'intérêt de l'État comme un principe juridique de sa constitution ; en l'interprétant comme il l'entendait lui-même, il n'en faisait, au fond, qu'une règle de sa politique ; au nom de l'État, de son intérêt et du bien-être général qu'il lui subordonnait, le tsar établissait ses relations avec ses sujets même dans les détails de leur vie privée.

D'ailleurs, en prenant intérêt à la civilisation plutôt protestante que catholique, Pierre le Grand a favorisé lui-même la propagation de quelques notions du droit naturel, dans lequel on pouvait trouver les éléments d'une conception juridique de l'État : il a fait faire, par exemple, une traduction russe du petit traité de Pufendorff sur les devoirs de l'homme et du citoyen, et a contribué à l'expansion de quelques idées de Hobbes, conformes à ses fins politiques.

L'un des collaborateurs de Pierre le Grand — le gouverneur de Kiev, Golitzyne — organisa même toute une série de travaux, consistant à traduire les principaux ouvrages sur le droit naturel et la politique ; Théofane Prokopowicz y prenait part, avec quelques élèves de l'académie de Kiev. C'est grâce à cette organisation que les grands traités de Grotius, de Pufendorff, de Locke et de bien d'autres moralistes et politiques du XVII^e^ et du XVIII^e^ siècles ont paru dans des traductions russes. Ces traductions ne sont pas toujours complètes : elles présentent quelquefois des coupures ou des abréviations faites non sans quelque conformité avec le but

[1] *Пол. Собр. Зак.*, v. vi. N° 3534.

que les traducteurs se proposaient—de donner un aperçu général de telle ou telle doctrine.

Une notice préliminaire que je trouve à la tête de la traduction russe de l'essai de Locke sur le gouvernement présente quelque intérêt : cette notice donne une idée de ce qu'on entendait alors par le droit naturel, et est conçue ainsi qu'il suit. « Chacun doit connaître [les principes] d'après lesquels il doit vivre en société civile en conformité avec les lois naturelles. . . . Il est nécessaire de distinguer différents genres de relations civiles : celle du mari et de la femme ; celle des parents et des enfants ; celle des maîtres et des esclaves ; celle de plusieurs familles demeurant ensemble et subordonnées à une même loi. Bien des auteurs ont écrit sur ces matières, mais les modernes en ont traité avec plus de perfection que les anciens ; ils ont élucidé et affermi les principes de la morale et de la vie civile. Grotius et Pufendorff en sont les fondateurs ; plusieurs autres leur ont succédé, mais ne s'accordent pas entre eux. D'ailleurs, tous sont d'accord que la morale et la vie civile sont fondées sur les devoirs que chacun a envers soi-même et envers les autres. Les devoirs de chacun envers soi-même reposent sur le principe : connais-toi toi-même ; les devoirs de chacun envers les autres sur le principe : ne fais pas aux autres ce que tu ne voudrais pas qu'on te fasse. La divergence des opinions ne se fait jour que quand on commence à raisonner sur l'établissement de la société civile, sur les lois qui en ont été le fondement, et sur le pouvoir, auquel elle doit être subordonnée. En effet, les uns pensent que les hommes ont été obligés, pour se soustraire aux agressions et à la ruine, de se subjuguer au plus fort et de vivre sous les lois, qu'il voudrait bien leur donner. D'autres supposent que les hommes se sont spontanément rassemblés en société, ayant en vue leur intérêt et leur tranquillité, pour conserver leur liberté, leur propriété et leur vie de toute agression et violence ; que grâce à une entente commune ils se sont faits des lois et se sont choisis un gardien de ces lois, qui devait vivre selon elles et n'avait pas de pouvoir sur la liberté, la propriété et la vie des citoyens. D'aucuns pensent enfin que les hommes, rassemblés en vue de ces fins, ont donné les lois, qu'ils se sont faites, à garder non pas à un seul homme, mais à plusieurs, car un seul est plus apte à se tromper que plusieurs. »[1]

[1] MS. de la traduction russe de l'ouvrage de J. Locke sur « le gouvernement civil », à la Bibliothèque Impériale de St-Pétersbourg, F. ii. 41.

C'est dans ces conceptions différentes que le droit naturel a eu quelque propagation en Russie au commencement du XVIIIe siècle. Pierre le Grand et son collaborateur Théofane Prokopovicz ont particulièrement prisé la théorie de Hobbes, qu'il était facile d'adapter au pouvoir autocratique du tsar ; Golitzyne et Tatichczev ont préféré les idées de Grotius et de ses émules, et en ont profité, de façons différentes, dans leurs projets de 1730.

Pierre le Grand et Théofane Prokopovicz ont exposé leur doctrine principalement dans le traité intitulé *Prawda voli monarchej*, c'est-à-dire, « Du droit que le monarque a de se désigner un successeur ». Les principes de ce traité, hormis les Saintes Écritures, sont puisés en grande partie des ouvrages de Hobbes. On peut y remarquer surtout cette influence, par exemple, dans la dissertation sur l'origine du pouvoir absolu, dont le monarque est revêtu non seulement par la grâce de Dieu, mais aussi par « le peuple » qu'Il inspire ; « le peuple » s'est destitué de sa « volonté commune » et l'a donnée au monarque ; investi de ce pouvoir souverain, le monarque absolu n'est responsable qu'à Dieu ; il n'est pas subordonné aux lois qu'il donne à ses sujets ; il les exécute sans contrainte par son bon vouloir ; et même s'il les transgresse, il ne peut être jugé par ses sujets, s'il n'a pas été élu à condition d'observer certaines clauses restrictives, qu'il a expressément acceptées. Le monarque russe, dont le pouvoir n'a pas été limité par des clauses, est donc absolu, et la *Prawda voli monarchej* lui attribue la *summa potestas*, que Théofane Prokopovicz définit, d'après la formule de Grotius, comme « celle dont les actes sont indépendants de tout autre pouvoir supérieur, en sorte qu'ils ne peuvent être annullés par aucune autre volonté humaine ».[1]

Dans la formule de l'autocratisme que donnent les règlements de l'armée et de la marine de Pierre le Grand on retrouve ces éléments,

[1] H. Grotius, *De jure belli ac pacis*, lib. i. cap. 3, § 7. Правда воли монаршей, СПБ., 1726, ff. 11, 15, 16-16v., etc. Théophane Prokopovicz a probablement puisé ses idées non seulement dans les traités de Hobbes, Grotius, etc., mais aussi dans celui de T. F. Buddaeus intitulé : *Exercitatio juris naturalis de successoribus primogenitorum*, Halle, 1695 ; voyez ses *Selecta juris naturae et gentium*, 1717. Il est vrai que Théophane Prokopovicz introduit dans sa formule l'idée du « bien commun » : le peuple s'est destitué de sa volonté en faveur du monarque pour qu'il le gouverne « pour le bien commun » ; mais c'est plutôt comme motif ou comme fin, que comme clause, expressément acceptée par celui qu'on revêtait du pouvoir absolu.

exprimés, du reste, dans les termes de la décision du *rigsdag* suédois de 1693; mais la formule russe contient un mot, qui porte peut-être, si je ne me trompe pas, les traces de l'influence des idées de Hobbes ou de Pufendorff: d'après cette formule le souverain gouverne non seulement selon «sa volonté», mais comme il le trouve le plus «convenable» (*blagomnjenie*). Or, Hobbes admettait que le souverain peut user de son pouvoir, comme il le trouve le plus convenable (*expedient*) pour la conservation de la paix et de la sécurité commune; et Pufendorff exprimait aussi une idée analogue en disant que le monarque dispose du pouvoir absolu, grâce auquel il peut gouverner d'après son propre jugement . . . en tant que l'état présent des choses paraît l'exiger.[1]

Et c'est justement de cette manière que Pierre le Grand pouvait relier la théorie du pouvoir absolu du monarque à la doctrine de l'intérêt de l'État.

Il serait facile de déduire de ces propositions quelques conclusions concernant les prérogatives du monarque—la subordination de l'Église à l'État; la suppression des institutions qui pouvaient gêner le pouvoir autocratique, de la douma des bojares, des assemblées des états (*zemskii ssobory*), etc.; mais je n'ai pas la possibilité d'entrer dans ces développements.

D'ailleurs, les prérogatives du monarque, inclues dans la formule précitée, ne demandaient pas d'élucidations aussi étendues que ses devoirs. La *Prawda voli monarchej* les déduit des «lois inscrites par le Créateur dans le cœur des hommes», ce qui donnait la possibilité de les relier aux «lois naturelles»; les règlements et les ordonnances les rattachent plutôt à la doctrine utilitaire de l'État.

Quoiqu'il en soit, c'est en se basant sur la théologie naturelle, et particulièrement sur la politique utilitaire, qu'on pouvait se faire une idée du monarque comme du premier serviteur de l'État. Pierre le Grand a assez clairement exprimé cette pensée, en disant «qu'il n'épargnait pas sa personne pour l'utilité commune de l'État».

C'est d'après des principes analogues que Pierre le Grand concevait les droits et les devoirs de ses sujets: l'État leur concède des droits dont quelques-uns remontent même au droit naturel, mais la plupart se conforme aux services qu'ils lui rendent; car ils

[1] Th. Hobbes, *Leviathan*, Pt. ii. ch. 17 (*Works*, ed. W. Molesworth, v. iii. p. 158). S. Pufendorff, *De officio hominis et civis*, lib. ii. cap. ix. § 5. *Пол. Соб. Зак.* v. v. N° 3006 (ch. iii. § 20); v. vi. N° 3485 (liv. v. ch. i. § 2, glose).

doivent incontestablement servir au bien de l'État ; ils deviennent ses serviteurs, c'est-à-dire ceux du monarque, comme son représentant, et ils lui en sont responsables.

C'est un mélange analogue d'idées rationnelles et utilitaires qu'on retrouve dans plusieurs autres principes, assimilés par Pierre le Grand, par exemple, dans celui de légalité.

L'idée de « l'ordre rationnel » avait peut-être quelque peu influé sur le principe de légalité de Pierre le Grand, qu'il n'a pas réussi, d'ailleurs, à développer systématiquement dans un code des lois : il distinguait les lois « perpétuelles » des lois temporelles, le gouvernement de l'administration de la justice, les divers organes qui la pratiquaient, les uns des autres, etc. ; mais la doctrine de l'intérêt de l'État donnait encore plus de force à ces principes : « rien n'est plus indispensable au gouvernement de l'État, disait Pierre le Grand, que l'observation des lois » ; c'est en correspondance avec cette doctrine utilitaire qu'il proclamait, par exemple, la nécessité de son système de surveillance fiscale et de la justice administrative qu'il commençait à distinguer de celle qui administrait « les torts particuliers ».

Ce même principe de légalité réclamait évidemment l'observation obligatoire des lois par tous les particuliers, qui ne pouvaient s'en dédire par leur ignorance.

Du reste, Pierre le Grand n'était pas en état de donner à son principe de légalité des bases solides : comme monarque absolu il pouvait toujours s'immiscer dans toutes les affaires, et son régime bureaucratique tenait à sa merci les particuliers.

Ce n'est que dans le domaine de la justice que ce principe a reçu une valeur plus indépendante. Le *Tableau de la procédure civile*, composé sous l'influence du code de Saxe, se réfère même au droit naturel, qui en est « la base », car, d'après le droit naturel, « chacun a le droit de se conserver et de se défendre des attentats des autres » ; mais ce principe n'y est pas développé, par exemple, dans ses applications à la propriété. C'est plutôt la doctrine utilitaire du *Polizeistaat* qui réservait plus d'indépendance à la justice. Le tsar préférait donner des règles générales aux cours de justice que d'intervenir dans les cas particuliers qu'elles devaient juger d'après ces règles ; mais, en considérant « tout ce qui est nuisible à l'État » comme un crime, il donnait la possibilité d'appliquer ce point de vue utilitaire et politique à la procédure criminelle ; en définitive, il restait lui-même, pour bien des cas, l'instance suprême ou unique, par exemple, dans sa « chancellerie secrète », et pouvait toujours soumettre à son propre jugement tout ce que bon lui semblait, et rendre ses décisions conformément à ses fins politiques.

D'ailleurs, le principe de légalité dans l'administration de la justice garantissait l'inviolabilité des personnes et des biens et leur droit de se « défendre des attentats des autres », mais avec les réserves, impliquées dans le régime politique, que je viens d'indiquer.[1]

La doctrine de l'État, basée sur le droit naturel de Hobbes, recélait donc une grave lacune qu'elle ne réussissait pas à combler par les notions supplémentaires déduites de l'idée utilitaire de l'État : cette théorie n'établissait pas ce rapport juridique entre le souverain et les sujets, que Grotius présupposait déjà dans son *corpus voluntate contractum*, et que ses émules ont essayé d'élucider dans leurs traités.

Et c'est ce que quelques politiques russes ont su apprécier : Golitzyne et Tatichczev en profitèrent dans leurs projets de la constitution de 1730, quoique de manières différentes.

Golitzyne ne s'est mis à étudier le droit naturel qu'après un assez long stade préparatoire, que je n'ai pas le temps d'élucider ici : pendant son séjour en Italie il a pu connaître quelques idées de Machiavel, de Paruta et de Boccalini, qu'il pouvait lire dans les originaux, et quelques traditions du « Conseil des dix » de Venise ; mais c'est plutôt à Kiev, et peut-être non sans l'influence de Théofane Prokopovicz, qu'il s'intéressa aux traités de Grotius, de Pufendorff et de Locke, qu'il a fait traduire à l'académie de Kiev.

Il est vrai qu'au nombre de ces traductions Golitzyne en a fait faire plusieurs qui ne concernaient pas le droit naturel, comme celles, par exemple, des ouvrages de Furius, de Clapmaier, de Lange, de Richelieu, de Fredro, de Bessel et de Schroeder sur les règles de la politique ; que parmi les traités qui rentraient dans le domaine du droit naturel, il ne distinguait pas assez les classiques des ouvrages secondaires, tels que ceux de Vernulaeus ou de Cellarius, de Faust et de Felwinger ; mais, même dans ses ouvrages de seconde main, comme, par exemple, dans celui de Felwinger, qui s'en rapportait à Grotius, Golitzyne pouvait déjà puiser quelques idées sur la théorie contractuelle de l'État.[2]

[1] *Пол. Собр. Зак.*, v. v. N° 3006, P. i. ch. i. §§ i, 7 et 8.

[2] *Библ. Зап.*, 1861, v. iii. p. 320. *Матер. для исторiи Академiи Наукъ*, v. iv. pp. 135, 178-190. Кн. Н. Голицынъ, *Новыя данныя о библiотекѣ кн. Д. М. Голицына*, М. 1900.

D'ailleurs, Golitzyne connaissait probablement quelque peu les ouvrages classiques sur le droit naturel, qu'il pouvait étudier grâce aux traductions manuscrites de sa bibliothèque. La traduction du traité de Grotius, par exemple, du reste incomplète, porte peut-être les traces de son usage : elle a à ses marges quelques croix, faites à l'encre.[1] La traduction du traité de Pufendorff, peu original, mais systématique, en donne beaucoup plus de preuves : cette traduction, faite non sans quelques abréviations, du reste assez heureuses, est marquée de croix justement aux endroits qui pouvaient intéresser un homme et un politique tel que Golitzyne : les marges du livre vii., qui traite de l'origine et de la constitution des sociétés civiles et des États, des fondements de la souveraineté, des droits et des devoirs du souverain, des diverses formes de gouvernement et des diverses manières d'acquérir la souveraineté, par exemple, sont bariolées de croix. D'ailleurs, les textes relatifs à la théorie des deux conventions générales, grâce auxquelles la société civile se forme, présentent sous ce rapport une particularité curieuse : ce n'est pas le § 7, celui qui traite de l'engagement de chacun avec tous les autres, mais le § 8 (correspondant au § 7 de la traduction) qui est marqué de croix ; or, ce paragraphe traite de la seconde convention, c'est-à-dire de celle qui se fait après l'engagement de chacun avec tous les autres à se joindre ensemble pour toujours en un seul corps, et qui consiste en ce que, après avoir choisi une ou plusieurs personnes à qui l'on confère le pouvoir de gouverner la société, ceux qui sont revêtus de cette autorité suprême s'engagent à veiller avec soin au bien public, et les autres, en même temps, leur promettent une fidèle obéissance.[2]

Les théories de Pufendorff sur la distinction du pouvoir souverain et du pouvoir absolu, sur la monarchie limitée qu'il en déduisait, sur les promesses solennelles et « particulières » que les Princes font en acceptant cette autorité bornée, sur la clause « commissoire » d'après laquelle le roi est déclaré déchu de la couronne, s'il pèche contre ces lois, sur l'établissement d'un conseil sans le consentement duquel le roi ne puisse rien faire en matière des choses dont

[1] MS. de la Bibliothèque Impériale de St-Pétersbourg, F. ii. 36. Cette traduction, d'ailleurs incomplète, a été exécutée d'après l'édition d'Amsterdam de 1712, par les étudiants de l'académie de Kiev, Oronovskij et d'autres.

[2] S. Pufendorff, *De jure naturae et gentium*, lib. vii. cap. 2, §§ 7 et 8 ; cap. vi. §§ 9 et 10, etc. MS. de la traduction russe, à la Bibliothèque Impériale de St-Pétersbourg, F. ii. 26.

on ne veut pas le laisser absolument le maître, ou bien sur d'autres institutions analogues pouvaient évidemment intéresser Golitzyne : il était imbu d'idées aristocratiques ; il sympathisait probablement au rôle que les bojares et ses ancêtres en particulier avaient joué aux élections de Basile Schoujskij et de Mihaïl Romanov ; lui-même avide du pouvoir que les membres du conseil s'étaient arrogé quelquesfois, il était tout prêt à rédiger la convention qu'il voulait conclure entre Anna Ivanovna et le peuple, représenté par le conseil, et qu'il avait probablement pourvue dans sa rédaction définitive d'une «clause commissoire».

C'est donc une théorie fort analogue à celle de Pufendorff sur «la seconde convention», et non la doctrine de la souveraineté du peuple et du pouvoir législatif de Locke, dont le traité a été aussi traduit sous les auspices de Golitzyne, que nous retrouvons dans son projet de la constitution de 1730.[1]

Cette théorie était applicable non seulement à l'origine des sociétés, mais à un interrègne dans le genre de celui qui précéda l'élection d'Anna Ivanovna en 1730 : et Golitzyne voulait prouver aux membres du conseil, assemblés dans la nuit du 18 and 19 janvier, qu'on était en plein interrègne.

Dans ses projets Golitzyne ne parle point de la première convention : il n'avait pas l'intention de convoquer une assemblée générale pour régler la forme du gouvernement, et se bornait, probablement, à considérer le conseil des grands (*werhovniki*), à l'instar du conseil des électeurs de l'empire germanique, comme représentant «le peuple russe». En tout cas les clauses de 1730 ont été rédigées par le conseil (avec trois personnes qui n'y appartenaient pas), et les états supérieurs de l'empire n'ont été convoqués que pour décider la question s'il fallait «confier» le pouvoir à Anna Ivanovna.

D'ailleurs, Golitzyne concevait le rapport entre Anna Ivanovna et tous les états de l'empire comme une convention formelle : elle se réduisait à «la promesse» solennelle et particulière de la princesse d'observer les clauses qui limitaient son pouvoir monarchique, entre autres la clause commissoire, et à «la promesse» des états qui

[1] MS. de la Bibliothèque Impériale de St-Pétersbourg, F. ii. 41. La traduction russe du traité de Locke est, peut-être, la meilleure de celles qui ont été faites sous les auspices de Golitzyne ; Théofane Prokopovicz y a, peut-être, pris part. Golitzyne a pourvu son exemplaire de sa signature, ce qui donne lieu à supposer qu'il y attachait quelque prix.

s'engageaient à une fidèle obéissance envers elle. Ce pacte devait être validé par deux actes corrélatifs: les « conditions», signées par Anna Ivanovna et « le serment » (celui des 16 clauses), fait par ses sujets.

Les clauses de cette convention correspondaient en grande partie non seulement aux théories de Pufendorff et d'autres juristes, mais à la constitution suédoise, c'est-à-dire au « serment du roi » et à « la forme du gouvernement » de 1720. Cependant, je ne pense pas que Golitzyne y ait puisé tout le contenu de sa pensée intime: il mûrissait ses idées depuis une trentaine d'années sous diverses influences; dans les actes suédois de 1720, sur lesquels Fick a pu lui donner quelques renseignements opportuns, il trouva des formules tout prêtes, qu'il a pu utiliser à la hâte après la mort inattendue de Pierre II.[1]

C'est donc en se basant, du moins en partie, sur l'idée juridique ou contractuelle de l'État, que Golitzyne a élaboré la convention de 1730, qui devait servir à ses fins politiques.

Cependant, la théorie de Golitzyne prêtait le flanc à de sérieuses objections; il supposait que le conseil des grands représentait le peuple; mais c'est justement ce qu'il fallait prouver; et la noblesse (le *schljahetstwo*) assemblée à Moscou pour les fêtes qui devaient avoir lieu à l'occasion du mariage de feu l'empereur Pierre II, ne voulait pas y croire; elle craignait l'oligarchie des grands et ne pouvait avoir confiance en Golitzyne, malgré les quelques concessions qu'il a dû lui faire.

L'un de ses adversaires politiques les plus éclairés, Tatichczev,

[1] Д. Корсаковъ, *Воцареніе императрицы Анны Іоанновны*, Каз. 1880, pp. 179-188. D'ailleurs, la question sur l'origine et la signification du plan de Golitzyne, que je n'ai pas la possibilité d'analyser ici en détail, est encore sujette à controverse; voir les conceptions différentes de MM. H. Hjärne, « Ryska Konstitutions-project år 1730 eftêr svenska förebilder, » dans *Hist. Tidskrift*, 1884, pp. 189-272, et П. Милюковъ, « Верховники и шляхетство » dans *Изъ исторіи русской интеллигенціи*, СПБ., 1902, pp. 1-51; А. Алексѣевъ, *Легенда объ олигархическихъ тенденціяхъ верховнаго тайнаго совѣта*; *Сильныя персоны въ верховномъ тайномъ совѣтѣ*, etc., M. 1896, 1898; et W. Recke, « Die Verfassungspläne der russischen Oligarchen im Jahre 1730 und die Thronbesteigung der Kaiserin Anna Ivanovna, » dans *Zeitschrift für osteuropäische Geschichte*, Bd. ii. D'ailleurs, même ceux qui supposent, comme le font, par exemple, MM. Filipov et Recke, que les rapports qui s'étaient déjà établis entre le pouvoir souverain et le conseil après la disgrâce de Menchikov avaient beaucoup d'analogies avec les conditions de 1730, pensent que celles-ci donnaient au conseil *de jure* ce dont il disposait déjà *de facto*; mais c'est justement ce qu'il importe d'élucider; v. W. Recke, *op. cit.*, *ib.*, p. 39.

s'attacha à démontrer, en s'en rapportant à la raison et au droit naturel, que sa théorie péchait par la base.

Tatichczev avait étudié le droit naturel beaucoup plus systématiquement que Golitzyne : il connaissait les principes établis par Grotius et Pufendorff ; mais, en outre, il s'était assimilé quelques idées de Wolff et de Thomasius ; ceux de leurs traités qui étaient écrits en allemand lui étaient accessibles : tout en rattachant au Créateur des hommes la « loi naturelle » qui leur est « innée », il tire, par exemple, son principe « fondamental »—l'amour rationnel de soi-même et quelques-unes de ses applications—principalement de la doctrine de Thomasius, interprétée par Walch.

Tatichczev distingue le droit naturel de la loi civile, à laquelle il doit servir de fondement, et disserte sur la convention qui a eu lieu entre les hommes pour former une société civile ; d'ailleurs, il ne fait qu'effleurer « l'ordonnance » par laquelle les hommes, réunis en communauté, règlent « la forme du gouvernement », en parlant, par exemple, des changements que celui-ci subit au cours de l'histoire, des gouvernements réguliers et irréguliers, de même que des gouvernements mixtes ; mais dans son écrit de 1730 qu'il composait non sans se rappeler la « forme du gouvernement » de 1720, il se base, comme Golitzyne, particulièrement sur la théorie de la seconde convention, celle qui a lieu entre le souverain et les sujets ; d'ailleurs, en l'appliquant un peu plus strictement, il parvient tout de même à formuler des conclusions différentes.[1]

Dans son écrit sur « le gouvernement politique » Tatichczev raisonne comme il suit. Ce n'est qu'au monarque élu ou héréditaire que nous avons prêté serment de fidélité et d'obéissance, et que nous avons conféré le pouvoir législatif ; or, si le monarque meurt sans laisser de successeur, sa mort dispense les sujets de leur serment ; la souveraineté revient donc à la communauté qui dispose du pouvoir législatif : comme dans l'état naturel, les citoyens deviennent tous égaux les uns envers les autres. La mort du souverain met aussi fin aux pouvoirs intermédiaires, dont sont revêtues les institutions subalternes ; et tant que le nouveau souverain ne les confirme dans

[1] В. Татищевъ, *Разговоръ о пользѣ наукъ и училищъ*, изд. Н. Поповымъ, М. 1888, pp. 19-27, 54, 128-150. Tatichczev s'efforce de prouver que l'amour rationnel de soi-même est commun aux deux subdivisions de la « loi divine », c'est-à-dire aux « lois naturelles » et aux « lois traditionnelles et écrites », inclues dans les Saintes Écritures, tout en distinguant ces « lois » des lois que les hommes se donnent à eux-mêmes, c'est-à-dire des lois canoniques et civiles.

leurs pouvoirs ou n'en institue d'autres avec des pouvoirs correspondants, personne n'a de pouvoir sur les autres. Comme l'État, d'ailleurs, ne peut subsister sans gouvernement, même pendant un court espace de temps, la communauté concède à ses organes les pouvoirs dont chacun d'eux disposait d'après les lois précédentes ; mais sans la volonté de la communauté, expressément formulée, ces organes ne peuvent s'arroger de pouvoirs supérieurs ; il est donc évident qu'ils ne peuvent user du pouvoir législatif, que la communauté ne cède qu'au souverain, et que le conseil des grands n'avait pas le droit de légiférer sur la constitution de l'empire et de limiter la monarchie absolue par des clauses. Ce n'est donc que la communauté, représentée en partie directement par ses membres, en partie par des députés qui, selon la loi naturelle, se choisit le souverain, et non quatre ou cinq personnes, qui veulent le faire arbitrairement.

Du reste, Tatichczev n'objectait pas à l'élection d'Anna Ivanovna ; il pouvait même la concilier avec la résolution que les états supérieurs de l'empire avait prise, et que « personne ne contestait ». En effet, la doctrine du droit naturel admettait la possibilité d'un « consentement tacite » de la communauté, et c'est ce que Tatichczev avait précisément en vue en disant que « personne ne contestait » l'élection d'Anna Ivanovna. Mais en admettant cette élection, Tatichczev répliquait contre les « clauses » de Golitzyne et lui opposait son projet d'une assemblée constituante des représentants du *szljahetstwo.* D'ailleurs, il y préconisait « la monarchie » comme la forme de gouvernement « la plus utile » à la Russie, et se déclarait pour l'agrandissement presque exclusif des droits politiques de la noblesse, qui devait, du moins en partie et temporairement, prendre part au gouvernement suprême du pays, et recevoir un accroissement notable de ses privilèges.[1]

Ce projet, qui avait mérité, d'ailleurs, l'approbation de plusieurs de ses collègues, prouve que Tatichczev faisait, au fond, la faute qu'il imputait à Golitzyne : pour appliquer correctement la théorie de la convention il devait prouver que le *szljahetstwo* avait le droit de représenter toute la communauté et définir ses clauses avec moins d'indécision.

[1] В. Татищевъ, *Произвольное и согласное разсужденіе и мнѣніе собравшагося шляхетства русскаго о правленіи государственномъ*, dans le Recueil « Утро », M. 1859, pp. 369–379.

Les deux publicistes, comme on le voit, adaptaient, chacun à sa façon, le droit naturel à leurs fins politiques et s'efforçaient de les justifier par cette théorie : ils étaient presque étrangers à l'idée de la souveraineté nationale, et ne voulaient profiter de l'idée de la seconde convention que dans les limites circonscrites par les intérêts des classes dirigeantes ; mais tout de même ils avaient une idée juridique de l'État, et concevaient le rapport du souverain et des sujets, du moins en théorie, comme une convention immanente à l'État.

Il suffit de ce coup d'œil jetté sur l'histoire de l'idée de l'État en Russie pour apercevoir l'esprit nouveau qui commençait à la transformer.

Il est vrai que l'histoire de cette idée en Russie pendant cette période de transition n'avait pas encore acquis le caractère d'une évolution bien continue et progressive : les chaînons de cette chaîne ne rentraient presque pas l'un dans l'autre ; chacun d'eux dépendait plutôt du mouvement général et correspondant des idées européennes que du chaînon précédent, et ne déterminait que très faiblement le chaînon postérieur. C'était donc une évolution intermittente et même quelques fois assez accidentelle, sans caractère individuel bien prononcé ; mais c'était néanmoins une évolution et même un progrès.

En effet, l'idée du rapport entre le souverain et les sujets qu'on se faisait en Russie à l'époque des réformes avait subi quelques changements qui en témoignent : on commençait à se représenter ce rapport, qu'on croyait autrefois transcendant, comme immanent à l'État, et à puiser les éléments de ce concept du droit naturel ; on s'intéressait particulièrement à la théorie de la convention, et on pouvait déjà y apprécier l'idée de ce que devait être ce rapport, sa valeur formelle et juridique, et non seulement son contenu réel et sa fin utilitaire ; et, malgré le régime autocratique que précisaient les « règlements », on essayait même parfois de mettre cette idée en pratique, du reste, avec des restrictions et des inconséquences qui discréditaient la théorie et donnaient beau jeu à ses adversaires politiques.

A. LAPPO-DANILEVSKIJ.

# XX

# DER VERFASSUNGSENTWURF DER SIEBZEHN VERTRAUENSMÄNNER. EIN BEITRAG ZUR GESCHICHTE DES FRANKFURTER PARLAMENTS

## I

### Die Bedeutung des Entwurfs für die Verfassungsgeschichte des 19. Jahrhunderts

Ich möchte Ihre Aufmerksamkeit für wenige Augenblicke auf einen Abschnitt in der Verfassungsgeschichte des 19. Jahrhunderts lenken, einen Abschnitt in der Geschichte der lange Zeit hindurch vergeblichen Bestrebungen, Deutschland, das seit dem Untergange des alten heiligen römischen Reiches zu einem geographischen Begriff geworden war, von neuem staatlich zu einigen. Diese Bestrebungen fanden bekanntlich einen Höhepunkt in dem von der Frankfurter Nationalversammlung unternommenen Versuch einer Reichsgründung.

Auch dieser Versuch ist ja traurig gescheitert. Aber er spielt trotzdem nicht nur in der politischen und geistigen Entwicklungsgeschichte des deutschen Volkes eine ausserordentlich wichtige Rolle, sondern er darf auch die lebhafte Aufmerksamkeit desjenigen beanspruchen, der die allgemeine Verfassungsentwicklung der Neuzeit sich zu vergegenwärtigen sucht.

Denn wenn diese ohne Zweifel ihrem wesentlichen Inhalt nach sich als die schliesslich in allen zivilisierten Staaten vollzogene Rezeption der in England bodenständig erwachsenen Grundsätze des konstitutionellen Staatsrechts darstellt, so kommt auf diesem Gebiet moderner Geistesgeschichte — und die Entwicklung des

Rechts lässt sich letzten Endes nicht anders als Geistesgeschichte erfassen — jenem Versuch trotz seiner Ergebnislosigkeit eine nicht geringe Bedeutung zu.

Die Versammlung der Paulskirche hat zu einer so gründlichen Aussprache über die Probleme des konstitutionellen Staatsrechts geführt, sie hat Männer von so tief begründeter theoretischer Einsicht und doch vielfach auch so reicher praktischer Erfahrung zu Worte kommen lassen, dass ihre Verhandlungen als ein höchst vielseitiger, an Geist und Kenntnissen wenigstens in Deutschland nicht wieder erreichter parlamentarischer Ausdruck der damaligen Staatseinsicht angesehen werden können.

Die staatsrechtliche Tätigkeit der Frankfurter Nationalversammlung fand ihren Mittelpunkt in ihrem Verfassungsausschuss. Und dessen Arbeiten wiederum schlossen sich auf das engste an den Verfassungsentwurf an, den noch vor dem Zusammentritt der Nationalversammlung die siebzehn sogenannten Männer des allgemeinen Vertrauens ausgearbeitet hatten.

Diesen Entwurf möchte ich zum Gegenstand meiner Bemerkungen machen, unter anderem deshalb, weil mir für ihn einige bisher unbekannt gebliebene gleichzeitige Aufzeichnungen vorliegen, die wie ich glaube manche bezeichnende Lichter auf ihn fallen lassen.

Jene Männer wurden auf einen Beschluss des durch die Februarrevolution gewaltig aufgerüttelten Bundestags von den einzelnen deutschen Regierungen nach Frankfurt geschickt, damit sie dort der Bundesversammlung als Vertrauensmänner der in ihr vertretenen siebzehn Staatenstimmen bei der nun auch von ihr endlich beabsichtigten Revision der Bundesverfassung mit gutachtlichem Beirate an die Hand gingen. Allein die Siebzehn — denn diese Bezeichnung blieb ihnen, da bei der Abstimmung stets jene Stimmenzahl massgebend war, wenn auch die Versammlung selbst niemals genau aus siebzehn Mitgliedern bestand, denn Österreich und einige der zu Gesammtstimmen vereinigten kleinsten Staaten schickten mehrere Vertreter, während umgekehrt Baiern die längste Zeit hindurch unvertreten blieb — die Siebzehn setzten sich sofort über jenen beschränkten Auftrag hinweg und machten sich an die Ausarbeitung eines eigenen Entwurfs für die künftige Verfassung Deutschlands.

Dieser Entwurf, nach seinem einflussreichsten Miturheber wohl auch der Dahlmannsche Verfassungsentwurf genannt, ist die erste ausgeführte Skizze der heutigen Verfassung des deutschen Reiches. In den Verhandlungen der Siebzehn fand die erste und für die Zukunft, die nähere und die fernere, massgebend gebliebene Erörterung der schwierigen staatsrechtlichen Fragen statt, deren Lösung die Voraussetzung der schon damals als unbedingt notwendig erkannten, aber erst sehr viel später erreichten Umwandlung Deutschlands aus einem losen Staatenbund in einen festen Bundesstaat bildete. So heftet sich jenes allgemeine verfassungsgeschichtliche und staatsrechtliche Interesse, das überhaupt das Frankfurter Verfassungswerk erweckt, in ganz besonderem Masse an die Verhandlungen der Siebzehn und den von ihnen aufgestellten Verfassungsentwurf.

## II

### Die Quellen

Als unmittelbare Quellen, aus denen sich ein Einblick in die Tätigkeit der Vertrauensmänner gewinnen lässt, standen bisher als wichstigste die bekannt gewordenen offiziellen Berichte zur Verfügung, die einige der Siebzehn über die Tätigkeit der Versammlung an ihre Regierungen gerichtet haben. So der ausführliche des hannoverschen Vertreters, Professors Zachariae,[1] und der knappe aber sehr charakteristische von Ludwig Uhland,[2] dem württembergischen Vertrauensmann. Auch Dahlmann verdanken wir einige wichtige Bemerkungen über das Werk der Siebzehn und seinen Anteil daran.[3]

Von erheblichem Wert ist ferner die eingehende Erörterung, die Gervinus, der Vertreter der freien Städte, über den Entwurf un-

1 *Bericht über die Berathungen des Entwurfs des deutschen Reichsgrundgesetzes im Schoosse des Collegiums der 17 Beigeordneten zum deutschen Bundestage*, von Professor Zachariae; de dato Frankfurt, den 30. April 1848. Actenstücke zur neuesten Geschichte Deutschlands (mit besonderer Beziehung auf Hannover). Erstes Heft. Hannover, Helwingsche Hof-Buchhandlung, 1848, S. 122-46.

2 Veröffentlicht nach dem im Schiller-Museum zu Marbach befindlichen Original von Walther Reinöhl, *Uhland als Politiker* (Beiträge zur Parteigeschichte herausgegeben von Adalbert Wahl, 2). Tübingen, Mohr, 1911, S. 182-5.

3 Anton Springer, *Friedrich Christoph Dahlmann.* Zweiter Teil, Leipzig, Hirzel, 1872, S. 220-23.

mittelbar nach seiner Veröffentlichung in einer langen Reihe von Artikeln in der von ihm herausgegebenen *Deutschen Zeitung* erscheinen liess.[1] Diese Abhandlung verteidigte die Arbeit der Vertrauensmänner gegen die ausserordentlich zahlreichen Angriffe, die alsbald von fast allen Seiten gegen sie gerichtet wurden. Auch diese Kritiken wird man für die Würdigung des von den Siebzehn Geleisteten nicht übersehen dürfen, so unbefriedigend und unfruchtbar die grosse Mehrzahl von ihnen auch ist. Die in Gestalt von selbständigen Flugschriften erschienenen verzeichnet in irgend erreichbarer Vollständigkeit das wertvolle Sammelwerk von Wentzcke;[2] die bedeutendsten unter ihnen sind die von Otto Abel,[3] Schaumann,[4] Heinrich von Sybel,[5] dem Prinz-Gemahl Albert von England[6] und Bunsen.[7]

Bei weitem am unergiebigsten sind die dürftigen offiziellen Protokolle, die über die Sitzungen der Siebzehn damals veröffentlicht worden sind.[8] Dazu kommt, dass sie von den dreizehn Sitzungen, die der eigentlichen Verfassungsberatung gewidmet waren, elf vollkommen überspringen und nur die erste und letzte von ihnen zählen und bekannt machen.

Diese unerfreuliche Lücke können wir aber nunmehr aus dem

[1] *Deutsche Zeitung*, Nr. 121-30, 136, 137, 140-45. Heidelberg, 1. 24. Mai 1848.

[2] Paul Wentzcke, *Kritische Bibliographie der Flugschriften zur deutschen Verfassungsfrage* 1848–1851. Halle, Niemeyer, 1911.

[3] Otto Abel, *Das neue deutsche Reich und sein Kaiser.* Berlin, Hertz, 1848. Wentzcke, Nr. 199.

[4] A. F. H. Schaumann, *Kurze Randglossen zu dem Entwurf eines deutschen Reichs-Grundgesetzes* (Aus der *Minerva* besonders abgedruckt). Jena, Braun, 1848. Wentzcke, Nr. 221.

[5] Heinrich von Sybel, *Über das Reichsgrundgesetz der XVII Vertrauensmänner.* Marburg, Elwert, 1848. Wentzcke, Nr. 238.

[6] (Prinz-Gemahl Albert von England,) *Meinungsäusserung eines Prinzen über den Entwurf der Siebzehner.* Wentzcke, Nr. 240.

[7] Christian Karl Josias Bunsen, *Die deutsche Bundesverfassung und ihr eigenthümliches Verhältniss zu den Verfassungen Englands und der Vereinigten Staaten.* Zur Prüfung des Entwurfs der Siebzehn. Sendschreiben an die zum deutschen Parlament berufene Versammlung. Frankfurt a. M., Suchsland, 1848. Wentzcke, Nr. 247.

[8] Sie sind gleichlautend veröffentlicht worden in der Frankfurter *Oberpostamts-Zeitung*, Nr. 102-108, 124, 131. Frankfurt, 11.-17. April, 3., 10. Mai 1848 und in der zweiten Lieferung der von Jucho veranstalteten amtlichen Ausgabe der Verhandlungen des deutschen Parlaments; danach sind sie abgedruckt in Roth und Merck, *Quellensammlung zum deutschen öffentlichen Recht*: Erster Band, Erlangen, 1850.

Nachlasse eines der Vertrauensmänner in sehr erwünschter Weise ausfüllen. In den von dem Geschichtsschreiber Johann Gustav Droysen hinterlassenen Papieren hat sich nämlich einmal ein wie es scheint ganz vollständiges Exemplar des sogenannten „Separatprotokolls" gefunden, das der eine Stimmführer der sechszehnten Stimme, der in Nachfolge Uhlands zum Schriftführer bestellte Petri gerade besonders über jene mit der Verfassungsberatung ausgefüllten dreizehn Sitzungen geführt und beglaubigt hat und das in lithographischer Vervielfältigung an alle Vertrauensmänner verteilt worden zu sein scheint.

Droysen hat sich aber weiter, abgesehen von einem über den Anfang seiner Frankfurter Zeit geführten „Tagebuch", in dem an vielen Stellen auch die Tätigkeit der Siebzehn berührt wird, über deren Verhandlungen besondere protokollartige Aufzeichnungen gemacht, die sich gleichfalls, wie auch jenes „Tagebuch", in seinem Nachlass erhalten haben. Sie sind ganz ähnlich gehalten, wie die von ihm kurz darauf offiziell geführten und später in ihrem ersten Teil veröffentlichten Protokolle des Verfassungsausschusses der Nationalversammlung. Nur ist ihnen erklärlicherweise, da sie nur für den Privatgebrauch bestimmt waren, die für eine Veröffentlichung angebrachte Durchsicht und Glättung nicht zu Teil geworden. Sie behandeln die Verfassungsberatungen mit besonderer Ausführlichkeit und ergängen gerade durch ihre freiere Art die offiziellen Petrischen Protokolle auf das erfreulichste. Denn ohne Vollständigkeit zu beabsichtigen und erreichen zu können, folgen sie, offenbar unmittelbar während der Beratungen, oft in fliegender Eile, stets in kleinster und engster Schrift auf grosse Folioblätter niedergeschrieben, bei allen wichtigeren Gegenständen dem Gang der Verhandlung von Rede zu Rede und werden so zu unmittelbaren Zeugnissen des oft hitzigen Kampfes der Meinungen.[1]

[1] Ich beabsichtige demnächst die Protokolle Petris und die Aufzeichnungen Droysens als Anhang zu einer diesen Vortrag etwas näher ausführenden Studie über den Verfassungsentwurf der siebzehn Vertrauensmänner herauszugeben. Damit soll auch ein synoptischer Abdruck des Dahlmannschen Vorentwurfs und des fertigen Entwurfs verbunden werden, da die Texte, die C. Varrentrapp in den von ihm herausgegebenen *Kleinen Schriften F. C. Dahlmanns*, Stuttgart, 1886, S. 378-90, veröffentlicht hat, nicht ganz genau sind und es von Wert sein dürfte, das gesammte Material an einer Stelle zu vereinigen.

## III

### Der Gang der Verhandlungen

Werfen wir zunächst einen kurzen Blick auf den äusseren Gang der Verfassungsberatungen im Schoosse der Siebzehn,[1] so hatten bereits die offiziellen Protokolle ersehen lassen, dass gleich in der zweiten Sitzung (am 5. April) eine Kommission zur Ausarbeitung eines Verfassungsentwurfs niedergesetzt wurde, in die man vier Mitglieder unter Hinzuziehung des Vorsitzenden Max von Gagern wählte: es waren Dahlmann, der schon damals berühmte Geschichtsschreiber und Bonner Professor, der das Königreich Preussen vertrat; Albrecht, der Vertreter der 15. Stimme, Professor der Rechte in Leipzig, einer der bedeutendsten deutschen Rechtsgelehrten, mit Dahlmann in weiten Kreisen des Volkes wegen ihrer Beteiligung an dem mannhaften Auftreten der „Göttinger Sieben" verehrt und bewundert; dann Bassermann, der Abgesandte Badens, einer der im Vordergrund stehenden Wortführer der liberalen Patrioten. Wilhelm Jordan, der spätere geschätzte Dichter, der als viertes Kommissionsmitglied gewählt worden war, schied bald überhaupt aus dem Kreise der Siebzehn aus. Allein diese Viermännerkommission — auch das ist seit langem bekannt — überliess die Arbeit im wesentlichen ihren zwei am meisten dazu geeigneten Mitgliedern, Dahlmann und Albrecht. Bereits nach 9 Tagen (in der 9. Sitzung am 15. April) konnte der Kommissionsentwurf der Versammlung der Vertrauensmänner vorgelegt werden. Welchen Gang die Verhandlungen nun des weiteren nahmen, zeigen deutlich die Petrischen und Droysenschen Aufzeichnungen. Der Vorentwurf wurde zunächst einer ersten Lesung unterzogen, die sich meist, wenn auch nicht ohne Ausnahmen, der Reihenfolge seiner Artikel und Paragraphen anschloss, nicht selten aber streitige Sätze vorläufig zurückstellte oder auch an die Kommission zurückverweis, damit sie auf Grund des stattgehabten Meinungsaustausches eine neue Fassung ausarbeite. Einmal, bei Beratung über den vom Reichsgericht handelnden

[1] Eine Tabelle über die Daten sämmtlicher Sitzungen und den Abdruck der über sie geführten Protokolle soll der S. 388 Anm. 1 in Aussicht gestellten Studie beigefügt werden, wie auch dort ein Verzeichnis der Vertrauensmänner gegeben werden wird.

Abschnitt, wurde eine neue Kommission aus den Juristen Albrecht, Bassermann und Zachariae zur weiteren Vorbereitung des Gegenstandes gebildet. Todt, der Vertreter des Königreichs Sachsen, wurde mit der Ausarbeitung der auf das Reichsfinanzwesen bezüglichen Bestimmungen betraut; doch fanden seine ins Einzelne gehenden Vorschläge schliesslich keine Aufnahme in den Entwurf.

Die Debatten verliefen sich wohl gelegentlich — wenigstens nach dem Urteil Droysens — ins Kleinliche. Aber im allgemeinen — das lassen Droysens Niederschriften deutlich erkennen, wie es sich ja auch bei der geistigen Bedeutung vieler der Siebzehn von selbst versteht — sind sie offenbar würdige Vorläufer der glänzendsten Tage der Paulskirche gewesen. Bei manchen Gelegenheiten steigerten sie sich zu lebhaften dramatischen Szenen, so vor allem — auch darin die Redekämpfe der Nationalversammlung vorausnehmend — bei der Beratung über das Reichsoberhaupt. Auch ganz am Schluss, als der endgültig redigierte Gesammttext in letzter Lesung angenommen worden war, kam die erregte Stimmung noch einmal zum Ausdruck: Uhland verlangte, dass die nur durch Mehrheitsbeschluss erfolgte Annahme des Entwurfs ausdrücklich bei der Veröffentlichung bekannt gegeben werde. Nach offenbar scharfen Erörterungen entsprach man diesem Verlangen und zwar in der Weise, dass Dahlmann beauftragt wurde, eine entsprechende Bemerkung in das Vorwort aufzunehmen, das er auf Wunsch der Versammlung, wenn auch erst nach einigem Sträuben verfasste, und mit dem dann der Entwurf gedruckt worden ist.

## IV

## Die verfassungsrechtlichen Probleme und der Versuch ihrer Lösung

Nicht nur über den äusseren Gang der Verhandlungen, sondern — was wichtiger ist — auch über die Beweggründe, von denen sich die Siebzehn bei ihrem Werke leiten liessen, geben uns die neuen Materialien, besonders die Droysenschen Niederschriften, näheren Aufschluss.

Freilich zeigt ja schon der fertige Verfassungsentwurf an sich, welcher Geist in der Versammlung herrschte. Aber wir sehen doch jetzt erst deutlich, wie schon hier der vielfältige Meinungsgegensatz zu Tage trat, der nur allzu bald das versuchte Einigungswerk als aussichtslos erscheinen liess.

Im allgemeinen freilich hatten unter den Siebzehn durchaus diejenigen Anschauungen das Übergewicht, die später während der Nationalversammlung in der Partei des sogenannten rechten Zentrums oder der erbkaiserlichen Partei ihre Vertretung fanden. Das kann nicht überraschen, da nicht weniger als acht der Vertrauensmänner später zu den Mitgliedern dieser Partei gehörten (Bassermann, Dahlmann, Droysen, M. v. Gagern, Gervinus, Schmerling, Wippermann, Zachariae); einige freilich nur vorübergehend, andere aber als massgebende Leiter (Bassermann, Dahlmann, Droysen). Von denjenigen Vertrauensmännern, die nicht in das Parlament eintraten, gehörten Albrecht und wohl auch Gabelentz, Jaup und Petri der gleichen Richtung an. Demgegenüber fand der demokratisch-liberale Standpunkt eigentlich nur in Ludwig Uhland eine allerdings sehr ausgesprochene und hartnäckige Vertretung. Er verband sich bei Uhland zugleich mit einer eifersüchtig partikularistischen Gesinnung; bei anderen war umgekehrt diese Gesinnung in immerhin verschieden starker Ausprägung das Ergebnis konservativer, selbst reaktionärer Anschauungen, so bei dem Sachsen Todt, dem Hannoveraner Zachariae, dem Mecklenburger Stever. Die radikale, eine deutsche Republik erstrebende Zeitströmung kam in der Siebzehnerversammlung nicht zu Wort, auch Uhlands Anschauungen gingen nicht so weit nach links.

Aber schon die vertretenen Gegensätze genügten, um wiederholt und vor allem in der grossen Debatte über das Reichsoberhaupt zu einem heftigen Zusammenstoss zu führen. Zwar war die Versammlung in dem Wunsche nach einer monarchischen Spitze des Reichs einig. Aber der demokratische und der konservative Partikularismus, auch hier durch Uhland und Zachariae vertreten, wollte nur einen Wahlkaiser zugestehen. Der Erbkaiser konnte in der ersten Lesung nur mit acht gegen fünf Stimmen,[1] in der ganz für den Schluss aufgesparten zweiten Lesung, an der alle Stimmen mit einziger Ausnahme der bairischen teilnahmen, nur mit neun gegen sechs durchgesetzt werden; die 16. Stimme (Hohen-

[1] Nach der in Droysens lithographiertes Exemplar des Entwurfs der Vorkommission (es scheint zweifelhaft, ob von ihm selbst) eingetragenen Bleistiftangabe ergibt sich für die erste am 17. April in der elften Sitzung

zollern, Liechtenstein, Reuss, Schaumburg-Lippe, Lippe und Waldeck) war bei der ersten und offenbar auch bei der zweiten Lesung gespalten. Selbst Bassermann wurde erst in letzter Stunde gewonnen.

Die Frage des Oberhauptes war derjenige Punkt, an dem sich die Gefährlichkeit der Klippen, zwischen denen es hindurchzusteuern galt, am schärfsten offenbarte. Deutschland sollte, das war damals der Wunsch des ganzen Volkes, ein einheitliches Staatswesen werden, denn der Staatenbund, die Negation eines solchen, hatte seine Unzulänglichkeit zur Genüge und zum Überdruss erwiesen. Einen Bundesstaat also musste man errichten. Aber wie sollte und konnte man mehr als dreissig Monarchien, darunter zwei europäische Grossmächte, einer zentralen Bundesgewalt unterstellen, da doch nach heiliger Überlieferung des Bundesrechts nichts unverletzlicher war, als die Souveränität der Einzelstaaten? Das war eine Aufgabe, wie sie die Weltgeschichte noch niemals gestellt hatte. Die in ihr liegenden Schwierigkeiten überstiegen selbst diejenigen, die bei der Begründung des grossen amerikanischen Bundesstaates, der Vereinigten Staaten, zu überwinden gewesen waren.

Dahlmann und seine Gesinnungsgenossen stellten es schon in dem Siebzehnerentwurf klar hin und sprachen es schon in den ihm geltenden Beratungen scharf aus, dass an die Spitze Deutschlands nicht nur ein erblicher, sondern auch ein mächtiger Kaiser treten müsse. Daher gaben sie dem Reiche eine weite Kompetenz, in

---

vorgenommene Abstimmung über die Erblichkeit folgendes Stimmenverhältnis:

Es stimmten

| gegen die Erblichkeit | für die Erblichkeit |
|---|---|
| Zachariae | Gagern |
| Todt | Gervinus |
| Langen | Droysen |
| Willmar | Stever |
| Uhland | Gabelentz |
| Jaup für die halbe 16. Stimme | Schmerling |
| —— | Albrecht |
| 5½* | Dahlmann |
| | Petri für die halbe 16. Stimme |
| | —— |
| | 8½ |

* Irrtümlicherweise wird in dieser Spalte auch Bergk angeführt; er fehlte bei der Abstimmung. Auch Bassermann fehlte. Ebenso war Baiern auch hier unvertreten.

allen wesentlichen Stücken die gleiche, die heut unserem Reiche zusteht: das Verzeichnis der dem Reich überwiesenen Angelegenheiten, das unsere Reichsverfassung enthält, lässt deutlich die Herkunft aus dem entsprechenden Verzeichnis des Dahlmannschen Entwurfs erkennen.

Und wenn die Siebzehn in einer damals gebräuchlichen Redewendung ihre Verfassung erklären liessen, dass „die Fülle der Reichsgewalt in dem Reichsoberhaupte und dem Reichstage vereinigt" sei (§ 4), so gaben sie — anders wie die heutige Reichsverfassung — dem Kaiser die volle Stellung eines konstitutionellen Monarchen mit allen einem solchen zustehenden Befugnissen. Sie gaben ihm — was auf anderem Wege auch im heutigen Reich verwirklicht worden ist — vor allem die volle Verfügung über die militärische Macht: hier war es besonders dem energischen Eingreifen Droysens zu verdanken, dass dem Kaiser das Ernennungsrecht nicht blos (wie Dahlmanns Vorentwurf gewollt hatte) hinsichtlich der höheren, sondern schlechthin aller Offiziere übertragen wurde.

Und ferner machte der Entwurf den Kaiser — wesentlich abweichend von der heutigen Regelung — zu einem neben dem Reichstag gleichberechtigten Faktor der Gesetzgebung. Erst durch seine Verkündigung, so wurde festgesetzt, sollten die Beschlüsse des Reichstags verbindliche Kraft erhalten. Man nannte das damals ungenau das Vetorecht. „Der Monarch", so schreibt Droysen, offenbar das Ergebnis der hierauf gerichteten Beratungen zusammenfassend, „erhalte diese grosse Befugnis; hoffen wir, dass wir es üben mit derselben Diskretion wie Englands Könige."

Die Selbständigkeit der Reichsgewalt, ihre den Einzelstaaten übergeordnete Souveränität fand auch darin Ausdruck, dass der Entwurf, an die amerikanische Lehre von der überragenden Kraft der Verfassung anknüpfend, alle mit dem Reichsgrundgesetz in Widerspruch stehenden Rechtsquellen des deutschen Bundes und der deutschen Einzelstaaten ausser Kraft setzte und damit mittelbar auch den künftigen Erlass solcher Bestimmungen unmöglich machen wollte. Wenn damit auch noch nicht der unbedingte Vorrang der Reichsgesetze vor den Landesgesetzen ausgesprochen war — wie dies in unserer Reichsverfassung geschehen ist, — so konnte doch Bassermann nicht ohne Grund schon jene Aufhebung einen „Staatsstreich" nennen; denn sie traf die bisher für unantastbar gehaltene Souveränität der Einzelstaaten an ihrer Wurzel.

Wenn Dahlmann und die Seinen kein Bedenken trugen, die Einzelstaaten in dieser Weise zu Gunsten des Reichs zu beschränken, so waren die meisten von ihnen hierzu nur in der festen Zuversicht entschlossen, dass Preussens König der Kaiser des neuen Deutschlands werden und dass damit Preussen das, was es als Einzelstaat aufzugeben habe, als deutsche Vormacht reichlich ersetzt erhalten werde. Immerhin gab doch auch in dieser Versammlung ein so glühender preussischer Patriot wie Droysen seiner auch schon anderwärts geäusserten Befriedigung darüber Ausdruck, dass Preussen noch nicht durch eine Verfassung in zentraler Weise konstituiert worden sei, denn ein solches einheitliches Preussen würde Deutschland unmöglich machen.[1]

Lagen bei der Kompetenzverteilung zwischen Reich und Einzelstaaten und ebenso beim Oberhaupt wenigstens die verschiedenen gangbaren Wege von vornherein klar vor Augen, so dass man nur zu entscheiden hatte, welchen die Mehrheit einzuschlagen wünschte, so tappte man bei der Gestaltung des Reichstags völlig im Dunkeln. Man war zwar einig, dass nach englischem Vorbild das Zweikammersystem anzunehmen und also ein Oberhaus und ein Unterhaus zu schaffen sei. Auch für die Bildung des Unterhauses standen die leitenden Gesichtspunkte ohne weiteres fest. Aber wie und woraus sollte das Oberhaus eingerichtet werden? Das war hier wie überall, wo man die aus Englands eigenartigen geschichtlichen Zuständen erwachsene Einrichtung nachahmen wollte, eine verzweifelte Frage. Die verschiedensten Vorschläge wurden gemacht; die Debatten zogen sich in schleppende Länge. Was schliesslich beschlossen wurde, nämlich ein Oberhaus, in das die regierenden Fürsten und die Vertreter der vier freien Städte, sowie „aus dem Kreise der bewährten Verdienste des Vaterlands" auf Zeit gewählte Reichs-

[1] Vgl. G. Droysen, *Johann Gustav Droysen*, Erster Teil, Leipzig und Berlin, 1910, S. 347 ff. Friedrich Meinecke, *Weltbürgertum und Nationalstaat. Studien zur Genesis des deutschen Nationalstaates.* Zweite durchgesehene Auflage, München und Berlin, 1911, S. 352 ff. Durch die im Text berührte Stelle in Droysens Niederschrift erledigt sich die von Meinecke a. a. O. S. 356 aufgeworfene Frage, ob Droysen auch im Siebzehnerausschuss seine Gedanken über das Aufgehen Preussens vertreten hat, wohl zweifellos in bejahendem Sinne.

räte eintreten sollten, konnte kaum befriedigen; mit Recht hat Dahlmann selbst später die betreffenden Bestimmungen des Entwurfs als eine unglückliche Kombination bezeichnet, die der Verbesserung unumgänglich bedürfe.[1] Hier hat erst Bismarcks Genialität in der Einrichtung des Bundesrats den einzig möglichen Ausweg gefunden.

Glücklicher sind die eigenartigen Bestimmungen des Siebzehnerentwurfs über das Reichsgericht, das freilich eine ganz andere Stellung erhalten sollte, als sie der gegenwärtige höchste deutsche Gerichtshof in Leipzig einnimmt. Es sollte einerseits eine Fortsetzung der alten sogenannten Bundesausträgalinstanz bilden und als solche Streitigkeiten zwischen den Einzelstaaten und auch sonstige öffentlichrechtliche Streitigkeiten entscheiden, andrerseits gewisse schwerste Kriminalfälle aburteilen und schliesslich auch als politischer Gerichtshof für die Verhandlung von Ministeranklagen dienen. Hier waren offensichtlich Einrichtungen der alten Reichs- und Bundeszeit mit Gedanken des englisch-amerikanischen Verfassungsrechts verbunden.

Ein näheres Eingehen hierauf würde zu weit führen, wie denn auch über die im ganzen knappen Bestimmungen über die „Grundrechte des deutschen Volkes“, die der Entwurf der Zeitströmung folgend verzeichnete, nur das bemerkt werden soll, dass auch hier vor allem der Gedanke an die herzustellende Einheit, Einheit auch in rechtlicher Beziehung, im Vordergrund stand. Deshalb wurde ausdrücklich ausgesprochen, dass diese Grundrechte auch zugleich der Verfassung jedes einzelnen deutschen Staates zur Norm dienen sollten.

Einer künftigen deutschen Verfassungsgeschichte, die wir zumal für die neueren Zeiten noch schmerzlich entbehren, oder einer Geschichte des Frankfurter Parlaments, die gleichfalls leider noch ungeschrieben ist, muss es vorbehalten bleiben, dem Verfassungsentwurf der siebzehn Vertrauensmänner seine Stellung in der allgemeinen Entwicklung der staatsrechtlichen Anschauungen zuzuweisen und die Rolle des näheren zu schildern, die er in der Geschichte der deutschen Einheitsbestrebungen und Verfassungskämpfe gespielt hat.

Hier sollte nur ein kurzer Hinweis auf die neuen demnächst

[1] Springer, a. a. O. S. 225.

bekannt zu machenden Materialien gegeben werden, die demjenigen, der jene Aufgabe in Angriff nehmen wird, wenigstens nach manchen Richtungen hin von Wert sein dürften.

Ich freue mich, dass es mir vergönnt war, den Siebzehnerentwurf gerade bei dieser Gelegenheit und an dieser Stelle zu besprechen. Führt doch die Entwicklung des modernen Staatsrechts in letzter Linie stets in dieses Land und in diese Stadt!

R. Hübner.

*Printed by* R. & R. Clark, Limited, *Edinburgh.*